London

Steve Fallon
Pat Yale

D0067761

LONELY PLANET PUBLICATIONS
Melbourne • Oakland • London • Paris

London
2nd edition – January 2000
First published – March 1998

Published by
Lonely Planet Publications Pty Ltd ABN 36 005 607 983
90 Maribyrnong St, Footscray, Victoria 3011, Australia

Lonely Planet Offices
Australia Locked Bag 1, Footscray, Victoria 3011
USA 150 Linden St, Oakland, CA 94607
UK 10a Spring Place, London NW5 3BH
France 1 rue du Dahomey, 75011 Paris

Photographs
Many of the images in this guide are available for licensing from
Lonely Planet Images.
email: lpi@lonelyplanet.com.au

Front cover photograph
London's calling (Charlotte Hindle)

ISBN 0 86442 793 X

text & maps © Lonely Planet 2000
photos © photographers as indicated 2000

Printed by Colorcraft Ltd, Hong Kong

Contents – Text

2 Contents – Text

The Authors

Steve Fallon

Born in Boston, Massachusetts, Steve can't remember a time when he was not obsessed with travel, other cultures and languages. As a teenager he worked in an assortment of jobs to finance trips to Europe and South America, and he graduated from Georgetown University with a Bachelor of Science in modern languages. The following year he taught English at the University of Silesia near Katowice, Poland. After he had worked for several years for a Gannett newspaper and obtained a master's degree in journalism, his fascination with the 'new' Asia took him to Hong Kong, where he lived and worked for 13 years for a variety of publications and was editor of Business Traveller magazine. In 1987 he put journalism on hold when he opened Wanderlust Books, Asia's only travel bookshop. Steve lived in Budapest for 2½ years from where he wrote Lonely Planet's *Hungary* and *Slovenia* guides before moving to London in 1994. He has written or contributed to a number of other Lonely Planet titles.

Pat Yale

Pat was born and brought up in Ealing, west London. As a student she supplemented her grant through stints of photographing students for ID cards at Southall College, issuing rail tickets to MPs in the House of Commons travel office, numbering pieces of old clay pipe at Gunnersbury Park Museum and weeding out the files at the Council for Places of Worship in All Hallows, London Wall. These days she's retreated to Bristol and has worked on Lonely Planet's *Britain*, *Ireland*, *Dublin* and *Turkey* guides.

FROM THE AUTHOR

Steve Fallon It may seem a very long time ago to many people but, well, *plus ça change* ... This book is dedicated to the more than 30,000 people killed in the defence of London during WWII and about whom we thought a lot as we walked the streets of their beloved city. It is largely due to these grannies and brothers and daughters and lovers of decent, ordinary people that we can enjoy London past, present and future. They shall never be forgotten.

A number of people helped in the updating of London and I would like to thank the staff at the Lonely Planet London office for their tips, leads, suggestions and, above all, their great enthusiasm for their city. Stars all. In particular, 'ta' to Jolyon Attwooll, Neal Bedford, Jennifer Cox, Tom Hall, Michelle Hawkins and Charlotte Hindle. It was a pleasure working with editor Tim Ryder and cartographer/designer Gadi Farfour; computer supremo

David Green got me out of a mess on more than one occasion. Others who helped enormously in researching and fact-checking this edition include: Caroline Birch, Bryony Darnell, Pascale De Lacoudraye-Harter, Imogen Franks and Gesa Giesing. Yura Brengauz vetted parts of the manuscript and made useful corrections and suggestions. Special thanks to ace photographer Juliet Coombe for smearing the Vaseline on the lens before taking my photo.

As always, I'd like to state my admiration, gratitude and great love for my partner, Michael Rothschild.

This Book

Pat Yale wrote the first edition of *London*. This edition was revised and updated by Steve Fallon.

From the Publisher

This second edition of *London* was edited in Lonely Planet's London office by Tim Ryder, with the assistance of Anna Jacomb-Hood. It was proofread by Anna, with help from Tim. Gadi Farfour was responsible for design, layout and mapping. David Wenk assisted with the mapping. Gadi designed the cover and Jim Miller drew the back-cover map. The index was produced by Paul Bloomfield and Tim. Ed Hillyer supplied the illustrations. Thanks to all the staff in Lonely Planet's London office who contributed ideas for this book.

Thanks

Many thanks to the following travellers who used the last edition and wrote to us with helpful hints, useful advice and interesting anecdotes:

Paul Alkon, Jim Anderson, Kerry Barker, Linda Berg, Helen Bissland, Yura Brengauz, Miachelle Brideau, Philip Brough, Julie Burnett, Simon L Carr, Lucia Chambers, Robin Chan, E Richard Churchill, SE Collins, Angelo de Silva, Mari DeWees, Natalie Doherty, Revital Dor-Vilc, Cate Dowling, Bert Flower, Joseph Y Garrison, Eva Golle, Chris Gossip, Michael Grace, John Graydon, Shannon Grosse, Ben Haines, Dean Harrington, C Hatch, Deborah & Barry Hurwitz, Loretta Jakubiec, Derek Jewson, Jens Kappey, Martin Laderman, Sarah Lang, Lucie Laplante, Thomas Lim, Y Lowe, John T Mabon, Paul Mansfield, John Mason, Daniel Meijer, Amy Minden, Reeves Novak, Walace M Olson, P Pearson, David Peck, Jane Perry, Stuart Pritchard, Hilton Purvis, Jackie Rabb, Tim Reilly, Ana Ringwelski, Alessandro Risso, Robert, Kathleen Robson, Mark Roddick, Nicky Rose, Marcin Sadurski, Con Schroders, Doris Shearman, Morrie Shepard, Tia Short, Dave Skiles, Maryanne Snyder, Otfried Staudigel, Geoff Stephens, John WP Storck, Omri Tal, Mohit Tandon, Lisa Tapert, Kirsty Taylor, Mordechai Tennenhaus, Keith M Warwick, Derek Wee, Sandra L Wehrley, Andrew Williams, OK Williams, C Wilson, Kim Wilson, Hilary Wunsch, Adele Wyers.

Foreword

ABOUT LONELY PLANET GUIDEBOOKS

The story begins with a classic travel adventure: Tony and Maureen Wheeler's 1972 journey across Europe and Asia to Australia. Useful information about the overland trail did not exist at that time, so Tony and Maureen published the first Lonely Planet guidebook to meet a growing need.

From a kitchen table, then from a tiny office in Melbourne (Australia), Lonely Planet has become the largest independent travel publisher in the world, an international company with offices in Melbourne, Oakland (USA), London (UK) and Paris (France).

Today Lonely Planet guidebooks cover the globe. There is an ever-growing list of books and there's information in a variety of forms and media. Some things haven't changed. The main aim is still to help make it possible for adventurous travellers to get out there – to explore and better understand the world.

At Lonely Planet we believe travellers can make a positive contribution to the countries they visit – if they respect their host communities and spend their money wisely. Since 1986 a percentage of the income from each book has been donated to aid projects and human rights campaigns.

Updates Lonely Planet thoroughly updates each guidebook as often as possible. This usually means there are around two years between editions, although for more unusual or more stable destinations the gap can be longer. Check the imprint page (following the colour map at the beginning of the book) for publication dates.

Between editions up-to-date information is available in two free newsletters – the paper *Planet Talk* and email *Comet* (to subscribe, contact any Lonely Planet office) – and on our Web site at www.lonelyplanet.com. The *Upgrades* section of the Web site covers a number of important and volatile destinations and is regularly updated by Lonely Planet authors. *Scoop* covers news and current affairs relevant to travellers. And, lastly, the *Thorn Tree* bulletin board and *Postcards* section of the site carry unverified, but fascinating, reports from travellers.

Correspondence The process of creating new editions begins with the letters, postcards and emails received from travellers. This correspondence often includes suggestions, criticisms and comments about the current editions. Interesting excerpts are immediately passed on via newsletters and the Web site, and everything goes to our authors to be verified when they're researching on the road. We're keen to get more feedback from organisations or individuals who represent communities visited by travellers.

Lonely Planet gathers information for everyone who's curious about the planet – and especially for those who explore it first-hand. Through guidebooks, phrasebooks, activity guides, maps, literature, newsletters, image library, TV series and Web site we act as an information exchange for a worldwide community of travellers.

Research Authors aim to gather sufficient practical information to enable travellers to make informed choices and to make the mechanics of a journey run smoothly. They also research historical and cultural background to help enrich the travel experience and allow travellers to understand and respond appropriately to cultural and environmental issues.

Authors don't stay in every hotel because that would mean spending a couple of months in each medium-sized city and, no, they don't eat at every restaurant because that would mean stretching belts beyond capacity. They do visit hotels and restaurants to check standards and prices, but feedback based on readers' direct experiences can be very helpful.

Many of our authors work undercover, others aren't so secretive. None of them accept freebies in exchange for positive write-ups. And none of our guidebooks contain any advertising.

Production Authors submit their raw manuscripts and maps to offices in Australia, USA, UK or France. Editors and cartographers – all experienced travellers themselves – then begin the process of assembling the pieces. When the book finally hits the shops some things are already out of date, we start getting feedback from readers, and the process begins again ...

WARNING & REQUEST

Things change – prices go up, schedules change, good places go bad and bad places go bankrupt – nothing stays the same. So, if you find things better or worse, recently opened or long since closed, please tell us and help make the next edition even more accurate and useful. We genuinely value all the feedback we receive. Julie Young coordinates a well-travelled team that reads and acknowledges every letter, postcard and email and ensures that every morsel of information finds its way to the appropriate authors, editors and cartographers for verification.

Everyone who writes to us will find their name in the next edition of the appropriate guidebook. They will also receive the latest issue of *Planet Talk*, our quarterly printed newsletter, or *Comet*, our monthly email newsletter. Subscriptions to both newsletters are free. The very best contributions will be rewarded with a free guidebook.

Excerpts from your correspondence may appear in new editions of Lonely Planet guidebooks, the Lonely Planet Web site, *Planet Talk* or *Comet*, so please let us know if you *don't* want your letter published or your name acknowledged.

Send all correspondence to the Lonely Planet office closest to you:

Australia: Locked Bag 1, Footscray, Victoria 3011
UK: 10A Spring Place, London NW5 3BH
USA: 150 Linden St, Oakland CA 94607
France: 1 rue du Dahomey, Paris 75011

Or email us at: talk2us@lonelyplanet.com.au

For news, views and updates see our Web site: www.lonelyplanet.com

HOW TO USE A LONELY PLANET GUIDEBOOK

The best way to use a Lonely Planet guidebook is any way you choose. At Lonely Planet we believe the most memorable travel experiences are often those that are unexpected, and the finest discoveries are those you make yourself. Guidebooks are not intended to be used as if they provide a detailed set of infallible instructions!

Contents All Lonely Planet guidebooks follow roughly the same format. The Facts about the Destination chapter or section gives background information ranging from history to weather. Facts for the Visitor gives practical information on issues like visas and health. Getting There & Away gives a brief starting point for researching travel to and from the destination. Getting Around gives an overview of the transport options when you arrive.

The peculiar demands of each destination determine how subsequent chapters are broken up, but some things remain constant. We always start with background, then proceed to sights, places to stay, places to eat, entertainment, getting there and away, and getting around information – in that order.

Heading Hierarchy Lonely Planet headings are used in a strict hierarchical structure that can be visualised as a set of Russian dolls. Each heading (and its following text) is encompassed by any preceding heading that is higher on the hierarchical ladder.

Entry Points We do not assume guidebooks will be read from beginning to end, but that people will dip into them. The traditional entry points are the list of contents and the index. In addition, however, some books have a complete list of maps and an index map illustrating map coverage.

There may also be a colour map that shows highlights. These highlights are dealt with in greater detail in the Facts for the Visitor chapter, along with planning questions and suggested itineraries. Each chapter covering a geographical region usually begins with a .ocator map and another list of highlights. Once you find something of interest in a list of highlights, turn to the index.

Maps Maps play a crucial role in Lonely Planet guidebooks and include a huge amount of information. A legend is printed on the back page. We seek to have complete consistency between maps and text, and to have every important place in the text captured on a map. Map key numbers usually start in the top left corner.

Although inclusion in a guidebook usually implies a recommendation we cannot list every good place. Exclusion does not necessarily imply criticism. In fact there are a number of reasons why we might exclude a place – sometimes it is simply inappropriate to encourage an influx of travellers.

Introduction

What can be said about London that hasn't been said so many times before? That the weighty resonance of its very name suggests history and might? That it is the premier city in Europe in terms of size, population and per-capita wealth? That its opportunities for entertainment by day and by night go on and on and on?

London is all these things and much, much more. Not only is it home to such familiar landmarks as Big Ben, the Eros statue, Tower Bridge, the murky River Thames and now the Millennium Dome, it also boasts some of the greatest museums and art galleries anywhere and more lush parkland than any other world capital. It is an amazingly tolerant place for its size, its people pretty much unshockable. As long as you don't scare the horses, mate, you'll be all right here.

It's not all sweetness and light, of course

– never is (especially the latter). Mid-week afternoons in London seem to stretch on from early November to sometime in March, with the cold, drizzly perma-darkness weighing down even more heavily as the months wear on. A yobbo in a white van cuts you off while driving, and when you protest he dissolves into road rage as only the Londoner knows it. And let's face facts: a city where the pubs and restaurants close at a time when the rest of Europe is choosing its first course simply cannot be the 'coolest city' in the world.

But then April – 'with his shoures', as Chaucer wrote – brings spring, turning the city's glorious open spaces into an Impressionist tapestry of indigo, green and gold. Shortly after White Van Man threatens to 'punch your lights out' (ie do untold damage to you), your fellow passengers on the

Old man river: the murky Thames has been London's lifeline since time immemorial.

Underground apologise to *you* for stepping on *their* toes or a shopkeeper abandons the till and leads you out to the pavement to give you more precise directions. And once you find one of the many clubs with extended licences, you'll party like you've never partied before. Clubbing is not just a form of entertainment here but a career at which Londoners work very, very hard.

Perhaps more than anything else London is the link that unites all of us who were rocked in the soft cradle of the English language or slept on its comfortable cushions for the first time at a later age. Our common language is the tie that binds an Irishman from Boston with an ethnic Slovene Sydneysider and a Chinese Vancouverite with a Jew from Johannesburg, and this is both our tongue's birthplace and its epicentre.

London is where Portia first told Shylock that 'The quality of mercy is not strained/It droppeth as the gentle rain from heaven' in *The Merchant of Venice*; where Dickens penned the poignant words 'It's a far, far better thing that I do, than I have ever done' for Sydney Carton as he faced the guillotine in *A Tale of Two Cities*; where the women in TS Eliot's *The Love Song of J Alfred Prufrock* did first 'come and go, talking of Michelangelo'. For many of us a visit to London is something of a homecoming. And as the Internet and further developments in communications technology send English even further afield, we'll be welcoming an increasing number of people 'home'.

Visitors are often surprised to find how multicultural the British capital is, with a quarter of all Londoners belonging to one of almost three dozen ethnic minorities, most of whom get along fairly well together. It is no exaggeration to say that visitors will encounter more mixed-race couples on the streets of central London in a single day than they will in a year in New York.

But this is London – cool, hot or plain lukewarm – and it belongs as much to them as it belongs to you and me. Having survived the long-anticipated (and much hyped) turn into the third millennium, this world-class city belongs to all of us.

'London; a nation, not a city'
Benjamin Disraeli (*Lothair*, 1870)

Facts about London

HISTORY

London has been continuously inhabited at least since Roman times. As a result, archaeologists and other seekers of clues from the past have had to wait for redevelopment to make excavation sites available. The 1980s building boom revealed an astonishing number of finds, especially in the City of London. More recently, archaeologists from the Museum of London digging near today's Spitalfields Market unearthed a priceless stone and lead coffin containing the remains of a well-to-do 4th-century AD Roman woman and personal effects. The tales she will tell us about London's earliest history will be epic.

The Celts & the Romans

Areas along the River Thames were already occupied by the Iron Age. The misleadingly named Caesar's Camp, an earthwork fort on Wimbledon Common, was probably constructed in the 3rd century BC by the Celts, who had arrived from Europe about 500 years before. A beautiful shield found in the Thames near Battersea Bridge (and now in the British Museum) also dates from that time.

The Celts settled round a ford in the river, which – being twice as wide as it is today – probably served as a frontier between tribal groups. Under the Celts London failed to develop into a major centre like Colchester (Camulodunum in Latin); for that London had to wait for the arrival of the Romans.

Armies of Romanised Gauls under Caesar's lead made short reconnaissance trips to the British Isles in 55 and 54 BC and presumably traded with the Celts, judging from Roman artefacts found in Iron Age burial sites. But the Romans did not arrive in large numbers until almost a century later.

In 43 AD, an invasion force led by Claudius established the port of Londinium, the first real settlement at what is now London, and used it as a springboard to capture the tribal centre of Camulodunum. They constructed a wooden bridge across the Thames near today's London Bridge, and this became the focal point for a network of roads fanning out around the region.

In about 60 AD members of the Iceni tribe from what is now East Anglia were outraged when Roman soldiers, trying to expropriate their property, flogged their queen, Boudicca (or Boadicea), and raped her daughters. The Iceni overran what had now become the capital of Roman Britannia at Camulodunum and then turned south-west to Londinium, massacring its inhabitants and burning the settlement to the ground. If you dig deep enough, they say, you'll find a layer of rubble and soft red ash dating from the conflagration.

Because of the Thames' deep anchorage for their fleet and the area's relatively good defensibility, the Romans rebuilt Londinium around Cornhill, the highest elevation north of the bridge, between 80 and 90 AD and wrapped a defensive wall 2.7m thick and 6m high around it about one hundred years later. Towers were then added to strengthen it. Excavations in the City have revealed that Londinium, a centre for business and trade but not a fully fledged *colonia* (settlement), was an imposing city whose massive buildings included a basilica, an amphitheatre, a forum and the governor's palace.

By the middle of the 3rd century Londinium was almost as multicultural as modern London, with some 30,000 people of various ethnic groups (but of course Roman citizens all) and temples dedicated to a wide range of cults. When Constantine converted to Christianity in 312, the fledgling religion became the empire's – and London's – official cult, seeing off its rival Mithraism (see the boxed text 'Mithras & the Great Sacrifice'). In 314 a bishop from Londinium attended the Council of Arles in France; in the following years, the Mithras temple was attacked and vandalised.

Mithras & the Great Sacrifice

Mithraism, the worship of the god Mithras, originated in Persia. As Roman rule extended into Asia, the religion became extremely popular with traders, imperial slaves and mercenaries of the Roman army and spread rapidly throughout the empire in the 2nd and 3rd centuries AD. It was the principal rival of Christianity until Constantine came to the throne in the 4th century.

Mithraism was a mysterious religion with devotees sworn to secrecy. What little is known of Mithras, the god of the sun, justice and social contract, has been deduced from reliefs and icons found in sanctuaries and temples, such as the temple in Queen Victoria St in the City of London. Most of these portray Mithras clad in a Persian-style cap and tunic, sacrificing a white bull. From the bull's blood and semen sprout grain, grapes and living creatures. The bull is then transformed into the god Soma, the moon, and time is born.

Mithraism and Christianity were competitors partly because of the striking similarity in many of their rituals. Both involve the birth of a deity on 25 December, shepherds, death and resurrection, and a form of baptism. Devotees knelt when they worshipped and a common meal – a 'communion' of bread and water – was a regular feature of both liturgies.

The Saxons & the Danes

In the 4th century, the Roman Empire in Britain began to decline, with attacks by the Picts and Scots in the north and Saxons in the south-east. In 410, when the embattled Emperor Honorius refused them military aid, the Romans abandoned Britain, and Londinium was reduced to a sparsely populated backwater. Little firm evidence from this period survives – there's no record whatsoever of the town from 457 to 604 – although it is clear that Saxon settlers established farmsteads and small villages in the area during this time.

In the late 6th century, Ethelbert, king of the East Saxons (who exercised control over what was left of London), converted to Christianity. In the following years London received a new bishop from Rome and the first church on the site of St Paul's Cathedral was built in 604. Saxon settlement appears to have clustered outside the city walls to the west, towards what is now Aldwych and as far as Charing Cross. This new community, called Lundenwic, seems to have bartered with Frisia, France and the Rhineland, but as it grew in importance it attracted the attention of the marauding Vikings from Denmark, who attacked in 842 and again nine years later, burning the settlement to the ground.

Under the leadership of King Alfred of Wessex (Alfred the Great), the Saxon population fought back and the Danes were driven out. Alfred resettled the old Roman city, known as Lundunburg or Lunduntown, farther east towards the River Lea, with a trading wharf at Billingsgate, and south of the Thames to Southwark (*sud werke* or 'south work').

Saxon London grew into a prosperous and well organised town divided into 20 wards, each with its own alderman, and resident colonies of German merchants and French vintners. But attacks by the Danes continued apace and the Saxon leadership was weakening; in 1016 Londoners were forced to accept the Danish leader Canute (Cnut) as king of England. With the death of Canute's son Harold in 1042, the throne passed to the Saxon Edward the Confessor, who went on to found an abbey and palace at Westminster on what was then an island at the mouth of the River Tyburn (see the boxed text 'London's Rivers Styx' under Geography later in this chapter). When Edward moved his court to Westminster, the process began whereby the port would become the trading and mercantile centre of London, with Westminster its seat of justice and administration.

The Normans

By the turn of the first millennium the Vikings, who were also known as the Norsemen or Normans, were in control of the north and west of today's France. In 1066 they mounted a successful invasion – the so-called Norman Conquest – of England under the leadership of William, the duke of Normandy.

After the watershed Battle of Hastings, London at first held out against William, but when all of south-east England had capitulated, London followed suit and William (dubbed 'the Conqueror') was crowned king on Christmas Day in Westminster Abbey, which had been consecrated less than a year before.

William found himself in control of a city that was by far the largest, richest and most powerful in the kingdom. He distrusted the 'vast and fierce populace' of London and built several strongholds, including the White Tower, the core of the Tower of London, but he also confirmed the city's independence and right to self-government.

Medieval London

In 1154 Stephen, the last of the Norman kings, died and the throne passed to Henry II of the powerful House of Plantagenet, which would rule England for the next two and a half centuries. According to an account written by the monk William Fitz Stephen, the London of the time was a 'flourishing city a prey to frequent fires' (in 1087 fire had consumed the third St Paul's).

Always short of a penny or two, Henry's successors were happy to let the City keep its independence so long as its merchants continued to finance their wars or building projects. When Richard I (known as 'the Lionheart') needed money to go crusading, he recognised the City as a self-governing commune in return for cash; the city's first mayor, Henry Fitz Aylwin, was elected sometime around 1190. In 1215, Richard's successor, John (nicknamed 'John Lackland' because he'd lost Normandy and almost all the other English possessions in France), was forced to cede some say in

government to the powerful barons he had alienated and to cease making excessive demands for money without their consent. Among those pressing him to seal (he did not *sign*) the Magna Carta at Runnymede was the powerful mayor of the City of London, the privileges of which were also guaranteed.

Old London Bridge and the fourth St Paul's were built in stone towards the end of the 12th century. The descendants of the Runnymede barons built themselves sturdy houses with riverside gardens along what is now the Strand linking Westminster to the City. The area flourished on trading wine, furs, cloth and other goods with Europe. The population at the time was 40,000.

By this time the Palace of Westminster was firmly established as the centre of royal power. In 1295 a model parliament with representatives of the barons, clergy and knights and burgesses had met for the first time in Westminster Hall, but by

RICHARD I'ANSON

The Tower of London has stood guard over the City for more than 900 years.

the 14th century the embryonic House of Lords was meeting in the Palace of Westminster and the House of Commons in the Westminster Abbey Chapter House. To raise more revenue the crown levied taxes on City merchants and moneylenders, notably the Jews, in exchange for its 'protection'. When the kingdom's entire Jewish population was expelled in 1290, the king turned to the Italian bankers who had followed them and based themselves on and around today's Lombard St in the City.

Though fire was a constant threat in the cramped and narrow houses and lanes of 14th-century London, disease – exacerbated by unsanitary living conditions and the impurity of drinking water brought up from the Thames – posed an even greater risk. In 1348, rats carrying the bubonic plague unleashed a 'Black Death' on London that left between a third and a half of the total population (around 100,000 at the time) dead within a year.

Along with fire and disease there was the danger of violence, with tradesmen fighting competitors or each other over turf or wages. In 1381, when the king tried to impose a poll tax on every individual in the realm, the soldier Wat Tyler and priest Jack Straw led a horde of some 60,000 peasants from Essex and Kent to London. Several ministers were murdered and many buildings, including John of Gaunt's grand Savoy Palace, were razed before the so-called Peasants' Revolt ended. Tyler himself was stabbed to death by the mayor; Straw was beheaded at Smithfield.

London continued to rise in wealth and stature in the 15th century, which saw an increase in the power of the craft guilds known as livery companies (see the boxed text 'The City's Livery Companies' in the City section of the Things to See & Do chapter), the tenure of the munificent mayor Dick Whittington (see the boxed text 'A Boy, a Puss & City Hall') and the arrival of the first printing press in England, set up by William Caxton at Westminster in 1476 (and moved to Fleet St after his death 15 years later). It was also a time of much political intrigue.

A Boy, a Puss & City Hall

London's new mayor is going to have to work hard to earn the same respect and affection Londoners had (and still have) for 15th-century mayor Dick Whittington.

Legend tells us that Dick was a country lad who came to the city to seek his fortune with his faithful feline in tow. Soon disillusioned, he was about to turn back when he heard the bells of St Mary-le-Bow ringing out the message 'Turn again, Whittington, thrice mayor of London'. Dick did just that and went on to find fame and fortune. A 19th-century stone on Highgate Hill, at the point where he is said to have heard the bells, features a bronze cat and makes reference to the 'thrice' mayor 'Sir' Richard Whittington.

It's a nice story but almost entirely inaccurate or just plain untrue. Dick Whittington was the third son of an affluent Gloucestershire family who arrived in London in a 'cat' as coastal boats were then called. He may indeed have heard those bells but they told lies too: he was mayor *four* times between 1397 and 1419. Oh, and Dick was never knighted.

In 1483 12-year-old Edward V of the House of York reigned for only two months before vanishing with his younger brother into the Tower of London, never to be seen or heard from again. Whether or not Richard III, their uncle and the next king, had them murdered has been the subject of much conjecture over the centuries. (In 1674 workers found a chest containing the skeletons of two children near the White Tower, which were assumed to be the princes' remains and were reburied in Innocents' Corner in Westminster Abbey.) Few tears were shed, however, when Richard himself was deposed from the throne by Henry Tudor, first of the Tudor dynasty, originally from Wales, towards the end of the century.

Tudor London

By the time Henry Tudor was crowned Henry VII in 1485, London was the largest and wealthiest town in England. During Henry's reign commerce continued to flourish (the trade in wool was a mainstay) and the population started to rise again, reaching 75,000. Most manufacturing industry was concentrated south of the river in Southwark and Bermondsey.

Between 1536 and 1540, Henry's successor and son, Henry VIII, dissolved the many monasteries and priories during his quarrel with the pope over his right to divorce his queen, Catherine of Aragon, and marry Anne Boleyn, although this move had as much to do with getting his hands on the church's tax-free property (church revenue at the time went directly to Rome). Some 50 London churches and monastic buildings were shut – some became warehouses, hospitals or private houses, others were demolished. Church plate was expropriated by the king – and most of it melted down and refashioned – and church land was requisitioned as royal hunting ground.

The peripatetic Henry VIII lived in dozens of palaces during his 38-year reign but spent much of his time at Richmond, Whitehall, Greenwich and Nonsuch palaces – the last a castle 'without compare' (it was originally called 'Nonesuch') near today's Cheam in Surrey, south-west of central London. When his lord chancellor, Cardinal Thomas Wolsey, had the temerity to build himself a grand palace at Hampton Court that caught Henry's eye, he was forced to make a gift of it to the king, which didn't prevent Henry from charging Wolsey with high treason in 1529 because of his opposition to Henry's divorce. (Wolsey died the following year, before the trial could commence.) Keen on public display, Henry brought skilled craftsmen from Europe to decorate his palaces; Leeds Castle in Kent and parts of Hampton Court Palace are superb examples that survive to this day.

Because of his predilection to settling differences with the axe (two of his six wives – Anne Boleyn and Catherine Howard – and Thomas More, Wolsey's replacement as lord chancellor, were all beheaded) and his persecution of both Catholics and his fellow Protestants (who maintained his changes had not gone far enough), Henry VIII gets a very bad press. But he was responsible for building most of today's St Bartholomew's Hospital and the docks at Woolwich and Deptford, and for establishing the Royal Navy. He remained a popular monarch until his death in 1547.

The reign of Mary I, Henry's daughter by Catherine of Aragon, saw an attempt to return England to the Catholic fold, although London seems to have been particularly unsympathetic to renewed Catholicism. Some 200 Protestants were burned at the stake at Smithfield. Though naturally humane, Mary sanctioned the persecutions and was therefore nicknamed 'Bloody Mary'.

By the time Elizabeth I, Henry VIII's daughter by Anne Boleyn, began a reign that would last some 45 years, the Catholic cause was effectively lost and their persecution resumed, with hundreds carted off to the gallows at Tyburn. London began to expand physically (in the half-century up to 1600 the population doubled to 200,000) and economically, establishing itself as the premier world trade market with the opening of the Royal Exchange in 1572.

It was also a time of literary renaissance, especially in theatre, with the works of William Shakespeare, Christopher Marlowe and Ben Jonson staged at new playhouses like the Rose (1587) and the Globe (1599). These two were built in Southwark, which was outside the jurisdiction of the City and notorious for its brothels, bear-baiting and prisons. The first recorded map of London was published in 1558, and John Stow produced the first history of the city (*A Survey of London*) in 1598.

Early Stuart London & the Civil War

When Elizabeth died without an heir in 1603, she was succeeded by her second cousin, James VI of Scotland, who was crowned James I of England. James was the son of the Catholic Mary Queen of Scots, but when he was slow to improve conditions for England's Catholics, Guy Fawkes and his co-conspirators concocted an unsuccessful plot to blow up the Houses of Parliament on 5 November 1605 – an event still marked annually throughout Britain with bonfires and fireworks. Public outrage saw to it that London remained firmly in the Protestant camp.

James was succeeded by Charles I in 1625, and a period of great animosity began between the Crown and Parliament. After Charles had recalled the dissolved Parliament following a hiatus of 11 years, he attempted to arrest five antagonistic Members of Parliament (MPs) who fled to the City. The Puritans, extremist Protestants who wanted to rid the Church of England of any vestiges of Roman Catholic ritual, and the City's expanding merchant class (who had everything to gain) threw their support behind Oliver Cromwell and the Parliamentarians (the so-called Roundheads) in the ensuing Civil War. Charles surrendered in 1646 and was beheaded outside the Banqueting Hall in Whitehall three years later.

After Charles' execution, the Commonwealth held sway for a brief period (1649-60), during which time the Puritans closed down the theatres and rampaged through the churches, smashing stained glass and destroying anything they regarded as idolatrous. As Lord Protector, Cromwell took up residence in Whitehall but his popularity was short-lived. In 1660 Parliament invited Charles I's son to return as king, and Charles II was reinstated at the Royal Exchange.

Plague & Fire

In mid-17th-century London, the shout 'garde loo' alerted passers-by that a chamberpot was about to be emptied into the street from an upstairs window. Crowded, filthy London had suffered from recurrent outbreaks of bubonic plague since the 14th century, but nothing had prepared it for the Great Plague of 1665, in which around 100,000 people died.

The beginning of the end of the plague in London was spurred by another disaster that proved to be a watershed in the city's physical development. On 2 September 1666 a fire broke out at a bakery in Pudding Lane in the City. At first it was regarded as a local fire and the lord mayor himself dismissed it as 'something a woman might pisse out' before going back to bed. But the hot, dry conditions that summer and rising winds fanned the flames and it raged out of control. Samuel Pepys, who watched the blaze from the steeple of All Hallows-by-the-Tower, provided a wonderful eyewitness account of the catastrophe in his diary. It was, he

CHARLOTTE HINDLE

All Hallows-by-the-Tower was heavily rebuilt after being devastated in the Blitz.

proclaimed, 'the saddest sight of desolation' though he was 'afeared to stay there long'.

By the time the fire was finally brought under control four days later, 80% of London had burned to the ground. But though damage to property was great – 88 churches, including St Paul's, the halls of 44 livery companies and 13,000 houses had been destroyed – only eight people died in the fire.

The fire removed almost all traces of medieval, Tudor and Jacobean London in a stroke, but it did have two long-lasting benefits. First, it at long last cleansed the city of plague; and second, it gave architects like Sir Christopher Wren the chance to redesign a modern city. Wren had his plans for a new London ready within a week of the fire, but with no powers of compulsory purchase it proved impossible to force reluctant landowners to give city planners leeway.

A special Fire Court composed of 22 judges was established to settle disputes over property, and by 1671 9000 houses – around 70% of those destroyed – had been rebuilt, this time of stone and brick instead of combustible wood and pitch. Wider streets were given pavements for the first time, and new squares ensured that it would be harder for any future fire to gain such purchase. The fire also accelerated the movement of the wealthy away from the City and into what is now the West End. In 1710 the present St Paul's Cathedral, Wren's masterpiece, opened as the culmination of the 'Great Rebuilding'.

Restoration London

With the work almost completed, including a great column topped with a golden blaze of flames commemorating the conflagration raised in 1677 – the so-called Monument – London again turned to trade and manufacturing, which began attracting much-needed workers from other parts of the British Isles and abroad. In 1685, after Louis XIV of France revoked the Edict of Nantes, which had granted freedom of worship to French Protestants for almost a century, some 1500 Huguenot refugees arrived in London, most

Wren's Churches

After the Great Fire of 1666 had destroyed 88 of London's churches, Sir Christopher Wren was commissioned to rebuild 51 of them, as well as to create a new St Paul's Cathedral. The money for the work was raised by putting a tax on all the coal imported through the Port of London. Perhaps the most striking features of Wren's new designs were the graceful Renaissance steeples that were to take the place of the solid square towers of the medieval churches.

Wren later built another three churches in London, but some 19 of his churches have been destroyed since 1781. For a partial list of some of the surviving churches and their locations, see Maps 6 & 8.

of them quickly turning their hand to the manufacture of luxury goods – including clocks and watches, silks and silverware – in and around Spitalfields. Italian artisans flocked to the area around Clerkenwell.

In 1688 the Glorious – ie bloodless – Revolution brought the Dutch king William of Orange to the English throne with his wife Mary, daughter of the same James II the couple had deposed. When William's asthma was badly affected by the proximity of Whitehall Palace to the Thames, they moved into a house in Kensington Gardens and had it converted into a new palace. In 1694 William's need to raise loans to wage war with France led to the creation of the Bank of England, backed by the security of the state and an institution London merchants had long been clamouring for.

By 1700 London was Europe's largest city, with some 600,000 inhabitants. The influx of foreign workers led to expansion to the east and the south while the more affluent headed for the north and the west to escape the pollution, disease and violence of inner-city life. These divisions remain more or less in place in today's London.

Georgian London

William and Mary had no heir and were consequently succeeded by Mary's sister Anne. Although she had 17 pregnancies only one of Anne's children survived and then not to adulthood. Since the 1701 Act of Settlement forbade a Roman Catholic to ascend the throne, the hunt was on for any crownable Protestant relative when Anne died in 1714. Eventually the search produced one George of Hanover, who arrived in London speaking no English.

London was increasingly becoming a financial rather than a commercial centre, with all the gains and losses that implies. Sure enough, it had its first major financial disaster in 1720, an incident known as the South Sea Bubble, when an orgy of speculation in a company set up to trade with South America ended with its collapse and the ruin of thousands. It was only through the intervention of Robert Walpole, George I's prime minister and the first resident of 10 Downing St, that the government was saved.

At the same time London was becoming ever more segregated and lawless; indeed, contemporary newspapers suggest it was the most crime-ridden city in Europe, and even George II was mugged in the gardens of Kensington Palace by a robber who, 'with a manner of much deference, deprived the King of his purse, watch and buckles'.

This was the London of the artist William Hogarth (see the boxed text 'Of Rakes & Harlots: Hogarth's World' under Painting & Sculpture in the Arts section later in this chapter), in which the wealthy built fine new houses in attractive squares while the poor huddled together in appalling slums, downing a per-capita average of two pints of gin a week. Dram shops enticed them with signs like 'Drunk for a penny, dead drunk for twopence', while the wealthy sipped the curious new drink from Turkey at coffeehouses like the Jamaica in St Michael's Alley (now a wine bar). The advent of street lighting helped reduce crime but, more importantly, in 1751 two magistrates at Bow formed a private police force of a half-dozen 'thief-takers'. The 'Bow Street Runners' would become the capital's first effective police force (though the metropolitan police force didn't come into existence until 1829).

Until Westminster Bridge opened in 1750, the horse ferry between Lambeth and Millbank was the only crossing on the Thames apart from London Bridge, not counting the water 'taxis' whose rowers would attract customers with the shout 'Oars? Oars?' (according to contemporary accounts, some visitors from the countryside mistook this for an offer of more carnal services). But as the population grew, so did the pressure to make it easier to move around. The bulging, higgledy-piggledy shops and houses on the old London Bridge, which severely restricted the movement of traffic from one bank to the other, were torn down, as were much of the medieval city wall and the gates that led into it; these days the latter survive only in place names like Bishopsgate, Aldgate and Ludgate.

In 1780 Parliament proposed lifting the law that prevented Catholics from buying or inheriting property, but one MP, the demented Lord George Gordon, led a 'No Popery' demonstration that turned into what became known as the Gordon Riots when a furious mob of at least 30,000 burned Newgate and Clink prisons, foreign chapels – the 'Papishe dens' – and several of the courts. Between 300 and 850 people died during the riots, including at least 20 who drank themselves to death after breaking into a distillery in Holborn.

As George III descended into dementia towards the end of the century, his son, the Prince Regent, set up an alternative and considerably more fashionable court at Carlton House in Pall Mall. When George III died in 1820, his son attempted to divorce his wife Caroline on the grounds of adultery, only to have her attempt to force her way into his coronation at Westminster Abbey. The public generally sided with the queen, but she died shortly afterwards and her funeral sparked street riots.

Georgian London saw a great surge in creativity in music, art and architecture. Court composer Handel wrote his *Water*

Music (1717) and *The Messiah* (1742) while living in London, and in 1755 Dr Johnson produced the first dictionary of the English language. Hogarth, Gainsborough and Reynolds were producing some of their finest engravings and paintings, and many of London's most elegant buildings, streets and squares were being erected or laid out by the likes of John Soane, his pupil Robert Smirke and the incomparable John Nash.

Victorian London

In 1837 the 18-year-old Victoria ascended the throne. During her long reign London would become the nerve centre of the largest and richest empire the world had ever known, covering a quarter of the world's surface area and ruling over 500 million people. New docks were built to meet the needs of the booming trade with the colonies and, as congestion in the capital worsened, railways began to fan out from London, linking it with all the major cities by 1850. The world's first underground railway, from Paddington to Farringdon Rd, opened in 1863 and was such a success that other lines followed in quick succession.

The development of London infrastructure continued apace; the year 1843 saw the opening of the first tunnel under the Thames, from Shadwell to Rotherhithe. And while his name may not be instantly recognisable, London owes more than it realises to Joseph Bazalgette, who supervised the installation of 2100km of tunnels and pumps to deal with the sewage outflow responsible for recurrent cholera outbreaks. He also oversaw the reclamation of 15 hectares of foreshore mud and the construction of almost 6km of the Victoria, Albert and Chelsea embankments to protect the capital's streets from flooding, and drew up the plans for the Albert, Battersea and Hammersmith bridges. Many of London's recognisable landmarks were also built at this time: the Clock Tower at the Houses of Parliament known as Big Ben (1859), the Royal Albert Hall (1871) and Tower Bridge (1894).

As a result of the Industrial Revolution and rapidly expanding trade and commerce, the population of London jumped from just under one million in 1801 (the year of the first national census) to 6.5 million a century later. The result was the steady growth of both sprawling inner-city slums for the poor and leafy suburbs for the affluent.

Though the Victorian age is chiefly seen as one of great imperial power founded on industry, trade and commerce, intellectual achievement in the arts and sciences was

Prince Albert & the Great Exhibition

In 1851 Victoria's beloved consort, the German-born Prince Albert, organised a huge celebration of new technology from around the world in Hyde Park. The so-called Great Exhibition was held in a 7.5-hectare iron and glass hothouse, a 'Crystal Palace' designed by gardener and architect Joseph Paxton. Some two million people flocked from throughout the country and abroad to marvel at the more than 100,000 exhibits. So successful was this first world fair that Albert arranged for the profits to be ploughed into building two permanent exhibitions, which eventually became the Science Museum and the Victoria & Albert Museum. The revolutionary structure itself was moved to Sydenham, where it burned down in 1936, but the area in south-east London – and its First Division football club – retain the name. Exactly 10 years after the exhibition the 42-year-old prince died of typhoid and the queen was so prostrate with grief that she wore mourning clothes until her death in 1901.

MARK HONAN

The Albert Memorial in Hyde Park.

enormous. The greatest chronicler of Victorian London was Charles Dickens, whose *Oliver Twist* (1837) and other works took as their themes the poverty, hopelessness and squalor of working-class London. In 1859 Charles Darwin published his seminal and immensely controversial *On the Origin of Species*.

Some of the UK's most capable prime ministers served during the course of Victoria's 64-year-long reign, including William Gladstone (four terms between 1868 and 1894) and Benjamin Disraeli (who served in 1868 and from 1874 to 1880). Monuments to them and others can be seen in Westminster Abbey.

Queen Victoria – she of 'We are not amused' fame – is often seen as a dour, humourless old curmudgeon but was in fact a highly intelligent, progressive and passionate woman. She lived to celebrate her Diamond Jubilee in 1897, but died four years later at the age of 81 and was buried in Windsor. In retrospect, the reign and achievements of this remarkable woman can be seen as the climax of British world supremacy.

Edwardian London & WWI

Victoria's dissolute son Edward, the Prince of Wales, was 60 when he was crowned Edward VII. By now change was occurring at an ever-increasing pace. With the creation of the London County Council (LCC) in 1889, London had its first ever directly elected government. The first motor buses went into service in 1904 and within seven years they had replaced the horse-drawn omnibuses introduced in 1829. Edwardian London saw a surfeit of new luxury hotels (such as the Ritz, 1906) and department stores (such as Selfridges, 1909) open their doors. In 1918 women over the age of 30 won the right to vote (lowered to 21 – the age for men – a decade later).

What became known as the Great War broke out in August 1914 and the first Zeppelin bombs fell near the Guildhall a year later, killing 39 people. Planes were soon dropping bombs on the capital, killing in all some 650 people (half the national total). Tragic as these deaths were, however, they

were but a drop in the ocean compared with the carnage that would follow a generation later during the Blitz of WWII.

The Interwar Period

After the war ended in 1918, London's population started to rise again, reaching nearly 7.5 million in 1921. The LCC started clearing the slums and creating new housing estates, while the suburbs spread ever deeper into the countryside. Unemployment was rising steadily, and May 1926 saw a wage dispute in the coal industry erupt into a nine-day General Strike in which so many workers downed tools that London virtually ground to a halt and the army was called in to keep the buses and Underground running and to maintain order. This heavy-handed action set the stage for the labour unrest that would plague the UK for the next 50 years.

The 1920s were the heyday of the so-called Bloomsbury Group, among them the writers Virginia Woolf and Lytton Strachey and the economist John Maynard Keynes, but in the following decade the centre of London's intellectual life shifted westwards to Fitzrovia, where George Orwell, Dylan Thomas, Thornton Wilder and Cyril Connolly lived and/or clinked glasses at the Fitzroy Tavern in Charlotte St. This was the great age of cinema and radio; the British Broadcasting Corporation (BBC), which had been established in 1922, broadcast the first television programme from Alexandra Park 14 years later.

The world economic slump of the late 1920s ushered in a decade of misery and political upheaval. Even the royal family took a knock when Edward VIII abdicated in 1936 to marry a woman who was not only twice divorced but – egad! – an American. The less-than-charismatic George VI succeeded his brother Edward. The scandal hinted at the prolonged trial by media that the royal family would undergo some 50 years later.

In the same year Oswald Mosley attempted to lead the British Union of Fascists on an anti-Jewish march of Blackshirts from the Tower of London through the East End. In Cable St he was repulsed by a mob of around half a million. By 1938 the German threat looked sufficiently alarming for children to be evacuated to areas north and west of London.

WWII & the Blitz
In September 1939 WWII broke out when Germany invaded Poland, to which the UK was allied. The first year was one of anxious waiting; although more than 600,000 women and children had been evacuated from London and 1600 members of Clerkenwell's Italian community had been interned as aliens, no bombs fell to disturb the blackout. But on 7 September 1940 this 'Phoney War' came to a swift and brutal end when German planes dropped hundreds of bombs on the East End, killing 430 people and injuring more than three times that number.

This *Blitzkrieg* (German for 'lightning war'), or 'Blitz', continued for 57 nights, and the Underground was turned into a giant bomb-shelter. For six months after that bombs continued to rain down, if less frequently. Westminster Abbey, Buckingham Palace, St Paul's Cathedral, the Guildhall, Broadcasting House and innumerable City churches were all hit, some of them destroyed forever. The air raids finally stopped in May 1941, only to start up again in 1944 when pilotless V-1s – popularly known as 'doodlebugs' – began to fly overhead, slyly dropping their bombs when their humming engines stopped. London then became the target of some 500 V-2s, the first long-range ballistic missiles.

When Nazi Germany sued for peace in May 1945, up to a third of the East End and the City had been flattened, including a 16-hectare site where the Barbican complex now stands. In all, almost 32,000 Londoners had been killed and another 50,000 seriously wounded. It was during these appalling times that Queen Elizabeth (now the Queen Mother) ventured out of the partially bombed Buckingham Palace to inspect the ravaged streets, earning the enduring admiration of Londoners when she said: 'I'm glad we've been bombed – now I can look the East End directly in the face.'

CHARLOTTE HINDLE

The cruiser HMS *Belfast*, now moored on the Thames, saw extensive action during WWII.

Winston Churchill succeeded Neville Chamberlain as prime minister in 1940. He orchestrated much of the nation's war strategy from the Cabinet War Rooms deep beneath Whitehall and it was from here that he made such stirring wartime speeches as the one later that year (at the height of the Battle of Britain) that concluded: 'Never in the field of human conflict was so much owed by so many to so few.' Indeed, Winny, indeed.

Postwar London

After the war, ugly housing and low-cost developments were thrown up on bomb sites in Pimlico, the East End and Roehampton, and the character of the city began to change as immigrants from the West Indies and the Indian subcontinent arrived in London. Notting Hill, Ladbroke Grove and Brixton acquired a Caribbean feel, Southall became markedly Sikh and the old Jewish East End vanished as Jews moved north to Golders Green and were replaced by Bengalis. Finsbury saw an influx of Cypriots; Hong Kong Chinese settled in Soho.

The Festival of Britain took place in London in 1951 both to recall the Great Exhibition 100 years before and to boost postwar morale. Its only permanent legacy is the ugly concrete arts buildings of the South Bank. Rationing of most goods ended in 1953, the year of Elizabeth II's coronation. The first civil flight left Heathrow airport in 1946 and the first red Routemaster bus appeared on the streets in 1956.

During the 1960s, the time that was truly 'Swinging London' (as opposed to the 'Cool Britannia' media hype of the late 1990s), the capital was very much the place to be, with flamboyantly dressed young people flocking to Carnaby St and the King's Rd, bringing colour and vitality to the streets, the Beatles recording in Abbey Rd in north London and the Rolling Stones playing for free before 500,000 fans in Hyde Park. In 1965 London's local government was reformed as the Greater London Council (GLC), whose jurisdiction covered a much wider area than the LCC's.

Even during the harsher 1970s and early 1980s London was spared much of the economic hardship experienced by northern England and Scotland, although the docks never recovered from the loss of empire, the changing needs of modern container ships and poor labour relations, and disappeared between 1968 and 1981. Shipping moved 42km east to Tilbury, and the Docklands declined to a point of dereliction, only to be rediscovered by developers in the 1980s.

The 1970s was a nondescript decade squeezed in between the rampant optimism of the 1960s and the disastrous recession of the early 1980s. In 1973 a bomb went off at the Old Bailey (the Central Criminal Court), signalling the arrival on English soil of the IRA's campaign for a united Ireland. But the mid-70s were at least brightened up by the spike-haired punks, pogoing their way to fame at clubs like the Marquee on Charing Cross Rd.

The Thatcher Years

In 1979 the Conservative (Tory) leader Margaret Thatcher became the UK's first female prime minister. Her monetarist policy soon sent unemployment rocketing upward; an inquiry following the Brixton riots of 1981 found that an astonishing 55% of men aged under 19 in that part of London were jobless. Riots flared in Tottenham in 1985, and again unemployment and heavy-handed policing were seen as contributing factors.

Meanwhile, the GLC, under the leadership of Ken Livingstone, fought a spirited campaign to bring down the price of public transport in London. Thatcher responded by abolishing the GLC in 1986 (but see the Government & Politics section later in this chapter for information on London's new mayor and council).

While poorer Londoners suffered under Thatcher's assault on socialism, things had rarely looked better for the business community. Riding on a wave of confidence partly engendered by the deregulation of the Stock Exchange in 1986 (the so-called Big Bang), London underwent explosive economic growth in the latter part of the decade.

The new property developers proved to be only marginally more discriminating than the Luftwaffe during WWII, though some outstanding modern structures, including the Lloyd's of London building (see the special section 'London's Contemporary Architecture' at the end of this chapter), went up amid all the other rubbish.

Like previous booms, the one of the late 1980s proved unsustainable. As unemployment started to rise again and people found themselves living in houses worth much less than what they had paid for them, Thatcher introduced a flat-rate poll tax. Protests all round the country culminated in a march on Trafalgar Square, ending in a full-blooded riot in 1990. Shortly afterwards Canary Wharf, the flagship of the much hyped Docklands redevelopment scheme, went into receivership. Thatcher was sent packing and John Major was named prime minister.

The 1990s
In 1992 the Conservatives were elected for a fourth successive term in government. Unfortunately for them, the economy went into a tailspin shortly thereafter, and the UK was forced to withdraw from the European Exchange Rate Mechanism (ERM), a humiliation from which it was impossible for the government to recover. To add to the government's troubles, the IRA exploded two huge bombs, one in the City in 1992 and another in the Docklands four years later, killing several people and damaging millions of pounds' worth of property.

The May 1997 general election returned a Labour government to power for the first time in 18 years, but it was a much changed 'New Labour' party, one that had shed most of its socialist credo and supported a market economy, privatisation and integration with Europe. Although Tony Blair and his government came under much criticism in the media soon after coming to power for what was seen as their 'third way revisionism' and their failure to deliver on election promises, the capital's booming economy and low unemployment, a feeble and divided opposition and the charisma

and statesmanship (particularly on the world stage) of the youthful prime minister himself have kept Labour high in the popularity polls among Londoners. At the start of the third millennium London is without a doubt headier and more confident than it has been at any time since the 1960s.

GEOGRAPHY
The 1580 sq km of Greater London that are enclosed by the M25 ring road lie in the south-east of England on the River Thames, which rises in the Cotswolds and flows eastwards through Oxford, Maidenhead and Windsor before reaching London. It is a clay and gravel-lined tidal river with its estuary some 80km to the east on the North Sea.

London's Rivers Styx

You would be forgiven for being unaware that the Thames is not London's only river: many have been culverted over the centuries and now course underground – the city's own Rivers Styx. Some survive only in place names: the Fleet, Hole Bourne, Wells, Tyburn, Walbrook and Westbourne, which was dammed up in 1730 to form the Serpentine in Hyde Park. The most famous of all, the Fleet, rises in Hampstead and Kenwood ponds and flows south through Camden Town, King's Cross, Farringdon Rd and New Bridge St, where it empties into the Thames at Blackfriars Bridge. It had been used as an open sewer and as a dumping area for entrails by butchers for centuries; the Elizabethan playwright Ben Jonson describes a voyage on the Fleet on a hot summer's night in which every stroke of the oars 'belch'd forth an ayre as hot as the muster of all your night-tubs discharging their merd-urinous load'. After the Great Fire Wren oversaw the deepening and widening of the Fleet into a canal, but this was covered over in 1733 and the rest of the river three decades later.

London is currently divided into 33 widely differing boroughs (13 of them in central London), which are run by local councils with significant autonomy. Two traditional 'cities', Westminster and the City of London, technically make up London. The 'one square mile' (about 2.7 sq km) of the City of London at the heart of the conurbation is known simply as 'the City'. Boroughs are subdivided into districts, which generally tally with the first group of letters and numbers of the postcode (see the boxed text 'London's Bewildering Postcodes' under Post & Communications in the Facts for the Visitor chapter).

Districts and postcodes often appear on street signs and are quoted when giving directions; this is vital since names are frequently duplicated (there are 48 Station Rds alone and just as many Park Rds) or cross through a number of different districts. To further confuse visitors, many streets change name (Holland Park Ave becomes Notting Hill Gate, which turns into Bayswater Rd before becoming Oxford St) or duck and weave like the country lanes they once were. Street numbering can also be bewildering: in big streets the numbers on opposite sides can be way out of kilter – 315 might be opposite 520 – or go up one side and down the other.

At the same time some London suburbs well within the M25 don't even give London as a part of their addresses and don't use London postcodes. Instead they're considered part of a county; perhaps Surrey, which still exists, or Middlesex, which was absorbed into Greater London in 1965.

GEOLOGY

The chalk basin upon which London is built is filled with the famous London clay, a stiff, grey-blue muck reaching up to 130m in depth that supports most of the city's tunnels and deeper foundations. Topping the subsoil are rock and pebbles, gravel and brick earth, a mixture of clay and sand that is often excavated for building material. The legacy of centuries of continuous human habitation can be seen in deposits averaging 5.5 to 6.5m in the oldest parts of the City and Westminster.

CLIMATE

The old adage that 'London doesn't have a climate, it has weather' refers first and foremost to the fickleness of the atmospheric conditions in this part of the world. Plan a picnic in a park in the morning and it will be raining by noon; go to a film to escape a wet and dreary afternoon, and you'll emerge to bright sunshine in a cloudless sky. You just never know.

But London does have a climate – in fact, among the mildest in England – known as temperate maritime, with mild and damp winters and moderate summers. It's wise to expect cloudy weather and rain even in high summer.

In July and August temperatures average around 18°C but can occasionally soar to 30°C or more. You'll wish they hadn't as the tube turns into the Black Hole of Calcutta and the heat concentrates the traffic fumes in the streets. Also many public buildings and venues – from offices to cinemas and restaurants – are not air-conditioned, even though average annual temperatures rise year by year. But during most summers you'll be lucky if the mercury tops the lower 20s.

In spring and autumn temperatures drop to between 11 and 15°C. In winter they hover just below 6°C; it very rarely freezes in London these days. That may seem mild, but the dampness can often make it feel twice or three times as cold. Fortunately most of the capital's main attractions are safely undercover, with heating systems geared to keeping the cold at bay.

For the Greater London weather forecast ring Weathercall on ☎ 0891 500401.

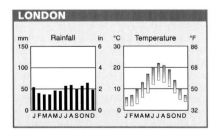

Not-So-Dirty Old Man River

JULIET COOMBE

The cleanliness of the River Thames has improved greatly in recent years – things could hardly be worse than in 1858, when during the 'Great Stink' the stench was so bad that the windows of the House of Commons had to be covered in sheets soaked in lime chloride. As species after species of fish died out during Victorian times, the banks of the river became a purple-pink mass of writhing, uneaten tube worms; by 1962 the combined impact of untreated sewage and industrial pollution had killed off virtually every sign of life in the river. But since 1974 a cleanup has brought back almost 120 species of fish, including salmon – last seen in the Thames in 1833 – for which special ladders over the weirs have been built. With them have come the herons and cormorants who feed on them; even otters have been spotted on the river's upper reaches. Much of the murkiness of the river in London is because it is the brackish centre of two tidal zones: a freshwater one and a marine zone.

ECOLOGY & ENVIRONMENT

London's most serious environmental problems will be apparent to visitors on even the shortest of stays. With some 143,000 commuters driving into the centre of London every day to join the cars, taxis and lorries already there, traffic moves at an average 20km/h – about what it did when horses and coaches clogged the city's narrow streets in the 19th century.

The traffic congestion is also largely responsible for the other obvious problem: poor air quality. Eight of the 10 most polluted streets in the UK are in London, and many cyclists wear masks to protect themselves from breathing in the toxic fumes. The areas of London with the highest levels of nitrogen dioxide pollution are Mayfair, Knightsbridge, Kensington and Hyde Park.

Smog, a word coined by the Victorians to describe the poisonous combination of smoke from coal-fuelled furnaces and London's ubiquitous fog, is a thing of the past, thanks to the Clean Air Act promulgated in 1956 after around 4000 Londoners died from the effects of the notorious winter smog of 1952-53. However, these days anyone with asthma or other respiratory problems should take note of the air quality forecasts attached to weather bulletins.

To look at the Thames' murky waters you'd assume it was another pollution black spot, but in fact things are improving remarkably on that front (see the boxed text 'Not-So-Dirty Old Man River' above).

FLORA & FAUNA

London boasts more parks and open spaces than any city of its size in the world – from the neatly manicured (Holland Park, St James's Park) to the semi-wild (Richmond Park, Bushy Park). Between them they provide suitable habitats for a wide range of animals and birds.

Flora

Plant-lovers won't want to miss Kew Gardens in west London (see the Kew section in the Things to See & Do chapter), but if you're more interested in less exotic plants London's parks boast a wide range of common or garden trees, shrubs and flowers. Many Londoners also take pride in their private gardens, which range from pocket-handkerchief-sized back yards to sprawling mini-estates, some of which open for a few days each year (generally from May to September) through the National Gardens Scheme (NGS) for an admission fee of £1 or £2, which goes to charity. For a pamphlet listing dates and participants (*London Gardens*; 50p) contact the NGS (☎ 01483-211535) at Hatchlands Park, East Clandon, Guildford GU4 7RT.

Fauna

The mammal you're most likely to spot in London is the grey squirrel, a North American import that has colonised every big park and decimated the indigenous red squirrel population. Foxes and hedgehogs also live here, though their nocturnal habits make them difficult to spot except in the very wee hours. Badgers lurk amid the bracken of Richmond Park, which, along with Bushy Park, boasts herds of red and fallow deer.

Old MacDonald's London Farms

To demonstrate to urban Londoners that cows' udders are not shaped like milk bottles or cartons, farms have been set up all over the city in the last decade with real, live bovines (as well as ovines and porcines) on display, chewing and mooing and doing what barnyard animals are supposed to do. The farms are more popular with local people than visitors so they also offer a way of getting off the beaten track.

Coram's Fields
(Map 4; ☎ 7837 6138)
93 Guildford St WC1
(⊖ Russell Square).
Open daily from 9 am to
7 pm (4.30 pm in winter).

Crystal Palace Farmyard
(☎ 8778 7148)
Crystal Palace Park,
Thicket Rd SE20
(Crystal Palace station).
Open daily from 7.30 am
to 30 minutes after dusk.

Freightliners Farm
(Map 2; ☎ 7609 0467)
Sheringham Rd N7
(⊖ Highbury & Islington).
Open Tuesday to Sunday
from 9 am to 1 pm and
2 to 5 pm.

Hackney City Farm
(Map 2; ☎ 7729 6381)
1A Goldsmith's Row E2
(⊖ Bethnal Green).
Open Tuesday to Sunday
from 10 am to 4.30 pm.

Kentish Town City Farm
(Map 11; ☎ 7916 5420)
Cressfield Close,
Grafton Rd NW5
(⊖ Kentish Town).
Open Tuesday to Sunday
from 9.30 am to 5.30 pm.

Mudchute Park Farm
(Map 12; ☎ 7515 5901)
Pier St E14
(DLR Mudchute).
Open daily from 9 am to
5 pm (from 10 am to
4 pm in winter).

Spitalfields Farm
(Map 4; ☎ 7247 8762)
Weaver St E1
(⊖ Shoreditch).
Open Tuesday to Sunday
from 10 am to 5.30 pm.

Stepping Stones Farm
(Map 2; ☎ 7790 8204)
Stepney Way E1
(⊖ Stepney Green).
Open Tuesday to Sunday
from 9.30 am to 6 pm.

Surrey Docks Farm
(Map 12; ☎ 7231 1010)
South Wharf,
Rotherhithe St SE16
(⊖ Rotherhithe).
Open Tuesday to Sunday
from 10 am to 5 pm.

A Regal Bird

How many times have we stood by St James's Park Lake, looking out at those long-necked, cantankerous hissers that look so pretty on a placid pond, only to hear a mum or dad tell their kid: 'Did you know all the swans in England belong to the Queen?' But why does Liz covet swans and not bustards or titmice or pigeons?

Swans *(Cygnus olor)* have always had royal associations and they feature in mythologies as far back as ancient Greece. In the early Middle Ages they were also regarded as a delicacy; a roasted swan, often stuffed with smaller birds, was a key item on many medieval menus. Ownership of 'game' swans became a mark of noble privilege and prestige, conferred by the Crown, which also retained ownership of all swans on open and common waters.

In the 17th century two city livery companies (see the boxed text 'The City's Livery Companies' in the City section of the Things to See & Do chapter), the Dyers' and the Vintners', were given the concession to keep swans and today, along with the monarch, they are the only ones allowed to keep swans on the Thames 'from the towne of Graveshende to Cicester'. In July the Queen's Keeper of the Swans presides over the ceremony of Swan Upping in which the beaks of all young swans and cygnets between Sudbury and Abingdon are marked – one nick for the Dyers, two for the Vintners and none for the Queen – and their particulars entered on a swan roll. They then all sit down for a banquet of swan meat.

Birdwatchers, especially those keen on waterfowl, will have a field day in London. There are ducks, pelicans and the Queen's swans (see the boxed text 'A Regal Bird') in St James's Park, and more ducks and beautiful, chestnut-headed great crested grebes in Hyde Park's Serpentine. Herons can often be seen feeding in the Thames, which also attracts cormorants, especially as you head east into the Docklands.

Garden birds, like blue and great tits, robins and blackbirds, roost in all the parks, but some parks attract more interesting migrants. In Holland Park in spring, for example, you might be lucky enough to glimpse flocks of tiny goldcrests. Kestrels also nest around the Tower of London. Other birds can be seen at the reservoirs, particularly Staines Reservoir on Stanwell Moor Road, west of central London and accessible from Hampton train station. The open stretches of the commons in Barnes and Wimbledon also harbour a rich assortment of birds and mammals.

The London Wildlife Trust (LWT) maintains more than 50 nature reserves in the city, which offer the chance to see a range of birds and occasionally small mammals. Battersea Park Nature Reserve has several nature trails for visitors, while the Trent Country Park (✚ Cockfosters) even boasts a Braille trail through the woodlands. Parts of Hampstead Heath have been designated a Site of Special Scientific Interest for their wealth of natural history. Other important LWT reserves easily accessible from central London are Camley St Natural Park (✚ King's Cross); Chase Nature Reserve, Romford (✚ Dagenham East); Crane Park Island, Whitton (Whitton station); Gunnersbury Triangle (✚ Chiswick Park); and Sydenham Hill (or Dulwich) Wood (Sydenham Hill station).

For more information on nature reserves and wildlife habitats contact the LWT (☎ 7261 0447) at Harling House, 47-51 Great Suffolk St, London SE1 0BS.

GOVERNMENT & POLITICS
National Government

The UK is a constitutional monarchy with no written constitution and parliamentary government that is not entirely elected by the people. As the capital city, London is home to almost all the national offices of state except those that fall under the jurisdiction of the new Scottish Parliament in Edinburgh and the Welsh National Assembly in Cardiff.

Parliament has three separate elements: the monarch, who is head of state but in effect a figurehead who takes advice from ministers and Parliament; the House of Commons, a national assembly of 659 constituencies (seats) that is directly elected every four to five years; and the House of Lords, which consists of the Lords Spiritual (two archbishops and two dozen bishops of the Church of England), more than 1100 Lords Temporal (hereditary peers and those appointed for life) and nine Lords of Appeal (or Law Lords). No member of the House of Lords is chosen by general suffrage.

In practice, the supreme parliamentary body is the House of Commons and the prime minister is the leader of the majority party sitting there. The 20-odd ministers responsible for government departments – from foreign affairs to agriculture and transport – are appointed by the prime minister and make up the Cabinet.

The antiquated House of Lords has a certain amount of power but it is tempered by democratic processes. If, for example, the House of Lords vetoes a bill but it is passed twice by the Commons, it is sent to the Queen for her automatic assent, and the bill becomes law. The Labour government announced its intention early on to remove some or all of the hereditary peers from the House of Lords (but not to do away with the peerage itself). A White Paper published in early 1999 recommended that the Lords be replaced with a 'modern, fit and effective second chamber' and outlined steps to achieve this.

Local Government

History records that when the 12th-century king Richard the Lionheart sold London the right to self-government for a little travelling money (see Medieval London in the earlier History section), supporters of the move cried 'Londoners shall have no king but their mayor'. That pronouncement seems to have fallen on deaf ears for well over a decade, however: among the many superlatives concerning London is the fact that it is at present the only capital city in the world without a self-governing authority and mayor (or equivalent).

But that's about to change. In a May 1998 referendum, Londoners voted to re-install a city-wide council and directly elected mayor, and elections were scheduled for May 2000. The new mayor will preside over an assembly of 25 to 30 members that will have a say on transport, economic development, strategic planning, the environment, the police, fire brigades, civil defence and cultural matters.

The City of London has its own government in the form of the Corporation of London, headed by the Lord Mayor and an assortment of oddly named (and even more oddly dressed) aldermen, beadles and sheriffs; it sits at the Guildhall. These men – and they usually are male – are elected by the City of London's freemen and liverymen (see the boxed text 'The City's Livery Companies' in the City section of the Things to See & Do chapter). Though its government may appear out of time and obsolete in the third millennium, the Corporation of London still owns roughly a third of the supremely wealthy 'square mile' and has a good record for patronage of the arts in the City.

Different areas (boroughs) of London also have democratically elected local councils (as does the rest of the UK), which deal with education and less absorbing matters like road sweeping and rubbish collecting.

ECONOMY

London and the south-east of England continue to be the driving force behind the national economy, but you'll see few signs of heavy industry here. Instead, London is one of the world's major financial centres, with a flourishing service sector (more than 50% of all Londoners are employed in it) in

RICHARD I'ANSON

The Palace of Westminster seen from the Thames: one of the world's finest neogothic buildings.

which tourism is one of the three most successful industries. Overall unemployment is low and falling (7.8% at the time of writing) in London and inflation (1.3%) is the lowest it's been in almost a quarter of a century.

London is now Europe's richest city. The city's wealth might not be obvious as you pass endless blocks of high-rise housing on a crawling bus or travel along in a dirty Underground carriage, but London comes ahead of, for example, Hamburg and Vienna in terms of per-capita wealth.

If you like statistics, central London's gross domestic product (GDP) per capita – that's the total output of all goods and services for every man, woman and child – is £22,214, double that of Paris. Admittedly the £60 billion GDP total calculated by the statistical office of the European Union only includes innermost London, with some 2.7 million residents, but that's still a decent-sized population and encompasses some poorer boroughs. The GDP for all of London is more than double that figure, and accounts for some 15% of the national total.

The boom in banking and insurance has a lot to do with London's wealth, especially as fat bonuses are paid to an increasing number of workers in the City and the rehabilitated Docklands. But more than anything else, London's switch to a service-oriented economy is responsible for the relatively high standard of living.

Despite Europe's attempts to unify its economies by introducing a single currency, the euro, many multinational companies both on the Continent and in the USA continue to use London as their regional base. They're drawn by a common language and not a common currency; the UK has decided not to join the 11 nations that banded together to establish the euro, at least for now.

Some of London's biggest employers are its airports. Heathrow, the world's busiest commercial airport, Gatwick and Stansted together provide some 35,000 jobs. Heathrow, in particular, has grown as a hub for tourists and businesspeople flying to and from Europe, North and South America and Asia.

Pockets of industry and manufacturing can still be found around London, though shipping – the city's mainstay for centuries – was dead as a doornail as long ago as 1981. To the east of London Ford has a sprawling assembly plant that seems to grow larger by the day. Greenwich residents might be overpowered from time to time by the less-than-sweet smells coming from the 120-year-old Tate & Lyle sugar refinery across the river, but at least it still provides jobs.

Sweatshops in east London continue to churn out cheap garments – you can still find locally made bargains at Petticoat Lane Market and in the streets leading off Brick Lane and Commercial Rd in the East End. Now they're more likely to be staffed by Bengali workers than the Jews and Cockneys employed until the 1960s.

Trendy pub microbreweries like the Orange Brewery in Pimlico have replaced traditional ones like the massive Truman Brewery in up-and-coming Spitalfields, while the printing shops of Clerkenwell have been converted to lofts and are now London's most expensive pieces of property.

If anything, London's high cost of living could drive jobs out of the city. The pound remains especially strong – as most Australasian and American visitors will realise upon arrival – increasing the cost of imports. Interest rates are higher than in the USA or continental Europe, adding more to the cost of taking out mortgages and bank loans.

This could change if the UK finally elects to join European Monetary Union (EMU) and drop the pound sterling in favour of the euro, bringing interest rates into line with those in the rest of Europe. But it is a fair bet that sterling will continue to rule Britannia and her finances for some time to come.

POPULATION & PEOPLE

Roughly 12 million people live in Greater London, just over seven million of them (ie one in every eight Britons) in central London. Another 26 million people visit London every year.

While most residents are white and of Anglo-Saxon stock, the capital becomes more multicultural by the year. Ever since the

ED HILLYER

You meet all kinds of people on the Underground, from any one of dozens of ethnic groups.

from a number of African countries. Both immigrant and refugee groups have tended to settle in specific areas together: Cypriots, Turks and Kurds in Stoke Newington, Sikhs in Southall, Bengalis in Spitalfields and Shoreditch, Chinese in Soho, West Indians in Brixton, Africans in Hackney and Dalston, Irish in Kilburn, Vietnamese in Hackney and Jews in Golders Green, Hendon and Finchley. Many refugees and other victims of conflict and persecution – from Kurds and Somalis to Bosnians and Kosovans – settled here in the 1980s and 90s.

Just under 25% of all Londoners are from ethnic minorities, according to a survey conducted by the London Research Centre (LRC) in 1999. London has a total of 33 ethnic communities of more than 10,000 people who were born outside England. These range from the largest groups like the Irish, with some 214,000 people born in Ireland now living in London, and Indians (151,000) to smaller ones like those from Trinidad & Tobago (just over 10,000). The LRC counted some 300 different languages regularly spoken in the capital.

EDUCATION

Schooling is compulsory in the UK up to the age of 16 and free up to 18. A growing number of young people are staying on at school (or a sixth-form or further-education college) until they're 18 years old, but by US standards, for example, the drop-out rate is astonishingly high. The number of young people going on to university is also on the increase, putting such pressure on funding that the government now expects students to pay part of their own tuition fees and living costs by taking out loans.

In London, primary and secondary education is currently the responsibility of the city's 33 boroughs. Some 90% of all children attend state schools, with the remainder at fee-paying private schools (such schools providing secondary education are called 'public schools' in the UK), the oldest and most prestigious of which include Westminster, St Paul's, Highgate and the City of London, as well as Dulwich College.

Industrial Revolution, it has been attracting (if not always welcoming) people from all round the British Isles. Since the late 17th century there have also been significant numbers of refugees from abroad. Huguenots arrived from France after 1685 to avoid religious persecution. Around the same time, Jews were welcomed back from France, Flanders and the Rhineland by the restored Stuarts (after having been booted out *in toto* in 1290) and some 20,000 fled the pogroms of Russia and Poland in the late 19th century. Immigrant Italians began to cluster in Clerkenwell and Holborn, Chinese at Limehouse in the Docklands and Irish in Wapping and Camden in the early 20th century.

Since the 1950s there has also been significant immigration from many of the nation's former colonies, especially Africa, the West Indies, Pakistan and India. Ethnic Indians arrived here in large numbers in the 1960s and 70s, after having been expelled

The most famous of Greater London's numerous universities are the 42 institutions and colleges of the University of London (founded 1826), which includes the London School of Economics and Political Science, King's College, University College and the Imperial College of Science, Technology and Medicine, whose research excellence places it second only to the University of Cambridge, according to recent national newspaper surveys.

SCIENCE & PHILOSOPHY

The contributions made by Londoners – or those with a strong London link – to diverse fields of science and technology have been innumerable. Isaac Newton (1642-1727), who legend tells us promulgated the law of gravity after an apple conked him on the noggin, moved from Cambridge to London in 1701 and was president of the Royal Society of London from 1703. He lies in Westminster Abbey. Edmund Halley (1656-1742), the scientist who first observed the comet that bears his name, and James Bradley (1693-1762), who provided direct evidence for the revolution of the earth around the sun, were the second and third Astronomers Royal at Greenwich between 1720 and 1762.

The evolutionary theorist Charles Darwin (1809-82) lived for more than four decades at Down House in south-east London. Here he wrote *On the Origin of Species* (1859), in which he used his experiences during a five-year voyage to South America and the Galapagos Islands to develop the theory of evolution by natural selection. The chemist and physicist Michael Faraday (1791-1867), a pioneer in electromagnetism and inventor of the electric battery (1812), spent much of his adult life in Islington and is buried in Highgate Cemetery.

In this century, London residents who have made a great impact on science have included the Scot Alexander Fleming (1881-1955), who discovered penicillin more or less by mistake while working as a research immunologist at St Mary's Hospital in Paddington; and John Logie Baird (1888-1946), who invented television and

gave the first public demonstration of the newfangled medium in a room above a Greek St restaurant in Soho in 1925.

In the field of philosophy, London can claim a link to Thomas Hobbes (1588-1679), author of *The Leviathan* and the first thinker since Aristotle to develop a comprehensive theory of nature including human behaviour. He was tutor to the exiled Prince Charles and a great favourite at court when the latter assumed the throne as Charles II in 1660. Karl Marx (1818-83), Friedrich Engels (1820-95), George Bernard Shaw (1856-1950) and Mahatma Gandhi (1869-1948) all studied, thought and wrote in the British Museum Reading Room. The influential thinker and pacifist Bertrand Russell (1872-1970) was a lecturer at the London School of Economics and Political Science at the end of the 19th century and was elected to the Royal Society of London in 1908. He was awarded the Nobel Prize for Literature in 1950.

ARTS

London has a flourishing cultural life. It doesn't matter whether you're talking about art as it is found in the National Gallery, the Tate Britain, the Victoria & Albert Museum and the British Museum or present-day works by the likes of Damien Hirst, Tracey Emin and Rachel Whiteread – London still manages to cream off the best.

Dance

John Playford (1623-86) thoroughly democratised dance with the publication of *The English Dancing Master* (1651), in which he outlined 900 choral dances of rustic origins that could be enjoyed by everyone, with no discrimination by social class. As suggested by such names as the 'Hide Park' and 'Mayden Lane', many of these 'country dances' were directed at urban dwellers. The morris dance, England's most popular folk dance, is believed to have been introduced to England by John of Gaunt after a visit to Spain in the 14th century. It apparently takes its name from the blackened ('Moorish') faces of some of the original dancers.

FACTS ABOUT LONDON

BILL COOPER/COURTESY OF ROYAL OPERA HOUSE

Sugar-Plum Fairies: the Royal Ballet performing Tchaikovsky's *The Nutcracker*.

Ballet originated in Italy and was first imported to France in the late 16th century by Catherine de Médecis. But classical ballet as we know it today only emerged in the 18th century, followed by romantic ballet in the 19th century. London embraced the latter more than most and 1845 saw the *Pas de Quatre*, in which French choreographer Jules Perrot brought to the English capital four of the greatest ballerinas of the time.

Today London is home to five major dance companies and a host of small and experimental ones. The most celebrated corps de ballet is the Royal Ballet, created in 1956 from Ninette de Valois' Vic-Wells Ballet (1931) and based at the rebuilt Royal Opera House in Covent Garden. Two acclaimed modern dance troupes are the Richard Alston Dance Company, based at The Place, and the London Contemporary Dance Theatre at Sadler's Wells (see Ballet & Dance in the Entertainment chapter).

Music

Classical Music Although the UK in general is not known for its great composers, London is passionate about classical music and has five symphony orchestras, various smaller groups, a brilliant array of venues, reasonable prices and high standards of performance.

Handel moved to London in 1712 and became a naturalised citizen in 1727, dying here in 1753; many of his operas and oratorios (such as *Samson*, 1743) were written in the capital. JS Bach's youngest son, Johann Christian, also worked in London from 1762 until his death 20 years later, which earned him the sobriquet 'the English Bach'. Haydn, too, visited London on two occasions (1791-2 and 1794-5), composing his last 12 symphonies here; his *Symphony No 104 in D* is also called the 'London Symphony'. The young Mozart visited London for 15 months in the mid-1760s with his parents and it was here that he composed his first symphonies (three of which survive).

When it comes to home-grown composers, however, the ones worth mentioning are few: Henry Purcell (1659-95); Thomas Augustus Arne (1710-78); Edward Elgar (1857-1934), whose mustachioed mug can be seen on the new £20 note; and Ralph Vaughan Williams (1872-1958), who composed his own London Symphony. Other virtuosos from the 20th century include Benjamin Britten (1913-76), who wrote the opera *Peter Grimes* (1945) and the orchestral work *Young Person's Guide to the Orchestra* a year later, and William Walton (1902-83), who also composed for the ballet and opera.

Gilbert & Sullivan They're neither classical nor pop but the comic operas produced by WS Gilbert, who wrote the words, and Arthur Sullivan, who wrote the scores, between 1871 and 1896 deserve a mention since their authors were Londoners; from 1882 onwards all their works were produced at the Savoy Theatre. The *Yeoman of the Guard* (1888) is the only musical as yet to be set inside the Tower of London. If you get a chance to see it, don't think twice; you'll be humming all the way home.

Popular Music After Elvis Presley, the UK quickly snatched the musical lead from the USA. The swinging 60s produced the Beatles, the Rolling Stones, the Who and the Kinks. The late 60s and the glam years of the early 70s brought stardust-speckled heroes like David Bowie, Marc Bolan and Bryan Ferry, and bands like Fleetwood Mac, Pink Floyd, Deep Purple, Led Zeppelin and Genesis. Then came punk and its best-known spokesmen, the Sex Pistols, the Clash and the Jam.

The turbulent, ever-changing music scene of the 1980s brought the new romantics and left-wing 'agit-pop'; a frenetic club and rave scene featuring house and techno music also developed. New bands that made it big included the Police, the Eurythmics, Wham!, Duran Duran, Dire Straits, UB40 and the Smiths. And who will ever forget forever beau/belle Bexley-born Boy

George, band leader of Culture Club? Thanks for the memories, Boy.

The Americans snatched back the cutting edge with Seattle grunge at the start of the 1990s but recent years have seen a renaissance of the quintessentially English indie pop band: Suede, Pulp, Blur, Elastica and Oasis. As for the London-based Spice Girls ... well, enough said.

Literature
The history of English literature is peppered with writers for whom London provided the greatest inspiration – and not all were native to the city or even British. Literally thousands of books take London as their setting; we can only highlight a selection. For a much more detailed listing, consult *Waterstone's Guide to London Writing* (£3.99), available at Waterstone's bookshops everywhere.

The first literary reference to London comes in Chaucer's *Canterbury Tales* (1387-1400), where the pilgrims gather for their trip to Canterbury at the Tabard Inn in Southwark. While William Shakespeare lived much of his adult life in London, acted in several Southwark theatres and probably wrote his greatest tragedies – *Hamlet*, *Othello*, *Macbeth* and *King Lear* – for the original Globe, only *Henry IV: Part II* includes a London setting: a tavern called the Boar's Head in Eastcheap. Daniel Defoe's *Journal of the Plague Years* is a celebrated account of the Black Death in London during the summer and autumn of 1665.

Two 18th-century poets found inspiration in London. Keats wrote his *Ode to a Nightingale* while living near Hampstead Heath and his *Ode on a Grecian Urn* after inspecting the Portland Vase in the British Museum. Wordsworth visited London in 1802, which inspired him to write the poem *On Westminster Bridge*.

Perhaps no writer is more closely associated with London than Charles Dickens (1812-70). Although Dickens had been born into a middle-class family, his father eventually wound up in the Marshalsea, a debtors' prison in Southwark; only the young Charles and one of his sisters managed to avoid joining the rest of the family there. His novels most closely associated with the city are

RICHARD I'ANSON

London has countless places for stocking up on every kind of literary tome.

DENNIS JOHNSON

Cashing in on London's literary connections: The Old Curiosity Shop in Holborn.

Oliver Twist, with its story of a gang of boy thieves organised by Fagin in Clerkenwell; *Little Dorrit*, whose heroine was born in the Marshalsea and married in nearby St George the Martyr on Borough High St (there's a road called Little Dorrit Court almost opposite the church); and *The Old Curiosity Shop*. An Old Curiosity Shop still exists just off Lincoln's Inn Fields in Portsmouth St, but it has nothing to do with Dickens' story.

Forever associated with 221b Baker St is Arthur Conan Doyle's unflappable detective Sherlock Holmes and his sidekick Dr Watson. Indeed, some 20 letters a week still arrive there addressed to our hero.

Towards the end of the 19th century Jerome K Jerome inserted a memorably witty description of visiting the maze at Hampton Court Palace into his *Three Men in a Boat*. At the turn of the century Joseph Conrad chose Greenwich as the setting for *The Secret Agent*; HG Wells' *War of the Worlds* has wonderful descriptions of the London of that epoch. Somerset Maugham's first novel, *Liza of Lambeth*, was based on his experiences as

an internee in the slums of south London; his *Of Human Bondage* provides a truer portrait of late Victorian London than any other work.

Of the Americans writing about London at the end of the 19th century, Henry James, who settled and died here, stands supreme with, for example, *Daisy Miller* and *The Europeans. The People of the Abyss* by the American socialist writer Jack London is a sensitive portrait of the poverty and despair of life in the East End. And who could forget Mark Twain's *Innocents Abroad* in which the inimitable humorist skewers both the Old and the New Worlds?

For a taste of Chelsea between the wars read *The Naked Civil Servant* by the indefatigable Quentin Crisp. Graham Greene's wartime *The End of the Affair* takes place in and around Clapham Common; Colin MacInnes described the bohemian, multicultural world of 1950s Notting Hill in *City of Spades* and *Absolute Beginners*. Doris Lessing painted a picture of 1960s London in *The Four-Gated City*, part of her *Children of Violence* series.

Some of the funniest and most vicious portrayals of 1990s Britain come in Lessing's *London Observed*, a collection of stories set in the capital. *London Fields* by the insufferable Martin Amis uses the capital as a backdrop but is pretty heavy going. His more acclaimed *Money* takes place in Notting Hill. In *Metroland*, Julian Barnes wrote of growing up in the suburbs connected to London by the Metropolitan line. Nick Hornby immortalised Arsenal football club in the virtually unreadable – for non-football fans anyway – *Fever Pitch*. His *High Fidelity*, about a fanatical indie-music lover, is a much easier read.

Other modern writers look at London from the perspective of its ethnic minorities. Hanif Kureishi writes about the lives of London's young Pakistanis in *The Black Album*, and his *The Buddha of Suburbia* is set in Bromley. Caryl Phillips describes the Caribbean immigrants' experience in *The Final Passage* while Timothy Mo's *Sour Sweet* has Soho's Chinatown of the 1960s as its backdrop. David Leavitt's *While England Sleeps*, set in the London of the 1930s and loosely based on the life of the poet Stephen Spender, tells the story of an upper-class young writer who falls in love with a self-educated Underground train conductor.

An excellent sampler of contemporary writing on London is *Granta 65: London – The Lives of the City*, edited by Ian Jack. If, for some unknown reason, you fancy reading a novel set in the London Underground, read Tobias Hill's thriller *Underground* or *The Dying Light* by Alison Joseph, which deals with – God save us – the Jubilee Line extension.

Architecture

London retains plenty of architectural reminders from every part of its long history, but they are often hidden: a Roman wall in the shadow of a utilitarian building from the 1970s, for example, or a perfect galleried coaching inn dating from the Restoration tucked away in a courtyard off a high street. This is a city for explorers. Remember that and you'll be surprised at every turn.

Few traces of Londinium – Roman London – survive outside museums, although you can see the relocated Temple of Mithras built in 240 AD (see the boxed text 'Mithras & the Great Sacrifice' under History earlier in this chapter) at the eastern end of Queen Victoria St in the City. Stretches of the Roman wall also survive, as foundations to a medieval wall outside Tower Hill Underground station and below Bastion Highwalk, just south of London Wall and the Museum of London.

Excavations carried out by archaeologists from the Museum of London at the Royal Opera House have uncovered extensive traces of the Saxon settlement of Lundenwic, including wattle and daub housing. But the best place to see what the Saxons left behind *in situ* is the church of All Hallows-by-the-Tower, north-west of the Tower of London, which boasts an important archway and the walls of a 7th-century Saxon church.

Complete Norman buildings are also rare. The finest survivor from the period is arguably the sturdy White Tower, the Norman keep at the heart of the Tower of London. The church of St Bartholomew-the-Great at Smithfield also has Norman arches and columns marching down its nave; the west door and elaborately moulded porch at the Temple Church in Inner Temple is a very fine example of Norman architecture.

Although the Great Fire of 1666 obliterated many of the city's medieval churches, Westminster Abbey is a splendid reminder of what the master masons of the Middle Ages were capable of. Temple Church as a whole illustrates the transition between the round-arched, solid, Norman Romanesque style and the pointed-arched delicateness of Early English Gothic, but most surviving medieval churches in London reflect centuries of rebuilding and additions. What you see before you now is a hotchpotch of different Gothic styles from Early English to perpendicular. Perhaps the finest surviving medieval church in the City of London is the 13th-century St Ethelburga-the-Virgin in Bishopsgate, which fell victim to the powerful IRA bombs of 1992 and

1993 but has since been wondrously restored. The 15th-century church of St Olave in Hart St, north-west of Tower Hill, is one of the City's few remaining Gothic parish churches, while the crypt at the largely restored St Etheldreda church in Ely Place, north of Holborn Circus, dates from 1251.

Traces of the medieval city's secular buildings are even more scarce, although the ragstone Jewel Tower opposite the Houses of Parliament dates from 1365, and most of the Tower of London goes back to the Middle Ages. Staple Inn in Holborn dates back to 1378, but the half-timbered façade is mostly Elizabethan and comprises London's only remaining domestic architecture of the 16th century.

The finest London architect of the first half of the 17th century was Inigo Jones (1573-1652), whose *chefs-d'oeuvre* include the Banqueting Hall in Whitehall and the Queen's House at Greenwich. Often overlooked is the much plainer church of St Paul's in Covent Garden, which he designed to go with the new piazza and described as 'the handsomest barn in England'.

But the greatest architect ever to leave his mark on London – thus far – was Sir Christopher Wren (1632-1723), who was responsible not just for St Paul's Cathedral but also for many of central London's finest churches (see the boxed text 'Wren's Churches' in the History section of this chapter) and for the Royal Hospital in Chelsea and the Old Royal Naval College at Greenwich. His neoclassical buildings are taller, lighter and generally more graceful than their medieval predecessors, which is immediately apparent at his masterpiece and monument, St Paul's.

Nicholas Hawksmoor (1661-1736) was a pupil of Wren who worked with him on several of his churches before going on to design his own masterpieces: the newly restored Christ Church at Spitalfields, St George's Bloomsbury, St Anne's Limehouse, St George in the East at Wapping, St Alfege at Greenwich and the City's St Mary Woolnoth.

A few pre-18th-century domestic buildings

RICHARD l'ANSON

The view south-west from St Paul's Cathedral, one of London's finest vantage points.

still survive, among them the half-timbered Prince Henry's Room and several old pubs on Fleet St and along the Strand. But the Great Fire effectively wiped out most of the old cityscape and many more secular buildings survive from the 18th century, when some of London's finest squares were laid out.

The Georgian period saw the revival of classicism. John Nash (1752-1835), whose contribution to London's architecture compares to that of Sir Christopher Wren, was responsible for the layout of Regent's Park and the surrounding elegant crescents. He also planned Trafalgar Square and Regent St, although his façades there have long since been replaced. His hand is also visible in some of the more attractive rooms of Buckingham Palace.

John Soane (1753-1837) was architect to the Bank of England (though much of his work was lost during the rebuilding by Herbert Baker from 1921 to 1939) and the Dulwich Picture Gallery. His pupil, Robert Smirke (1780-1867), designed the British Museum, one of the finest expressions of the Greek Revivalist style.

Other 18th-century architects who made their mark on the city were Robert Adam (1728-92), whose work can be seen at Syon, Kenwood and Osterley houses; George Dance (1741-1825), who designed Mansion House; James Gibbs (1682-1754), who designed the church of St Mary-le-Strand; William Kent (1695-1748), who worked on both Kensington Palace and Chiswick House; and William Chambers (1723-96), whose works include Somerset House and the Japanese-style Pagoda in Kew Gardens.

In the next century a reaction set in as the highly decorative neogothic style got into its stride. Champions of this style were George Gilbert Scott (1811-78), Augustus Pugin (1812-52), Alfred Waterhouse (1830-1905) and Charles Barry (1795-1860). Scott was responsible for the elaborate Albert Memorial, Waterhouse designed the flamboyant Natural History Museum, and Pugin and Barry worked together on the Houses of Parliament.

The Arts & Crafts movement of the late 19th century – 'British Art Nouveau', for want of a better term – was founded by William Morris (1834-96), incorporated both design and architecture and stressed the importance of manual processes over machines. The fire station (1902) at the corner of Euston Rd and Eversholt St, opposite St Pancras New Church, is a wonderful example of Arts & Crafts architecture.

The Edwardian baroque styles of the early 20th century are best exemplified by the works of Aston Webb (1849-1930), who designed the Queen Victoria Memorial and Admiralty Arch and worked on the front of Buckingham Palace. Edwin Lutyens (1869-1944), whose work is classified as British Art Deco, designed the Cenotaph on Whitehall, the Reuters building on Fleet St and Britannic House (formerly Lutyens House)

at Moorgate and Finsbury Square. The elegant and humorous Penguin Pool at London Zoo, designed by the Russian-born architect Berthold Lubetkin in 1934, is one of London's earliest modernist structures.

Some unfortunate rebuilding took place immediately after WWII, partly in the rush to make good the bomb damage as quickly and cheaply as possible. But one person's muck is another's jewel; the Royal Festival Hall, designed for the Festival of Britain (1951) by Robert Matthew and J Leslie Martin, attracts as many accolades as brickbats, although hardly anyone seems to have a good word for Denys Ladun's bunker-like Royal National Theatre (1967-77), a stone's throw away.

The 1960s saw the ascendancy of the workaday glass and concrete high-rises exemplified by the unspeakable Centre Point (1967) on New Oxford St, above Tottenham Court Road tube station. Fortunately, the 1980s and 1990s have witnessed the erection of some outstanding new buildings (see the special section 'London's Contemporary Architecture' at the end of this chapter).

Painting & Sculpture

Although London is home to numerous astounding art collections, British artists have never dominated any particular epoch or style in the way that Italian, French and Dutch artists have. It's not unfair to say that the romantic landscape painter JMW Turner (1775-1851) is the only British artist who can consistently and universally be counted among the all-time greats.

There are a few medieval gems around, notably the 14th-century Wilton Diptych in the National Gallery, which depicts Richard II with three saints receiving the blessing of Mary and the Christ Child. But art in London only really got into its stride under the Tudors. The German artist Hans Holbein (1497-1543) lived in London on two occasions and was court painter to Henry VIII; one of his finest works, *The Ambassadors* (1533), can be seen in the National Gallery. The English miniaturist Nicholas Hilliard (1547-1619) had similar access to the court of Elizabeth I and did the portraits of Sir Francis Drake and Sir Walter Raleigh.

The 17th century saw a batch of great portrait artists working at court. Best known is probably Anthony Van Dyck (1599-1641), a Belgian artist who spent the last nine years of his life in London and painted some hauntingly beautiful portraits of Charles I, including *Charles I on Horseback* (1638), now in the National Gallery.

Charles I was himself a great art lover; it was during his reign that many great paintings, including the Raphael Cartoons now in the Victoria & Albert Museum, came to London. Van Dyck was succeeded as court artist by Peter Lely (1618-80), a Dutchman who moved to London in 1641 and was a prolific painter of baroque portraits, many of them on display in Hampton Court Palace. He was succeeded as court artist by German-born Godfrey Kneller (1646-1723), whose portraits of the Stuart kings can be seen in the National Portrait Gallery.

The 18th century saw art move away from court portraits painted by imported talent, and local artists began to emerge. Thomas Gainsborough (1727-88) still went for portraits in a big way, but at least some were of the gentry rather than the real aristocrats; his landscapes were the first realistic ones painted by a Briton. William Hogarth (1697-1764), in contrast, is famous for his moralising serial prints of London lowlife, especially *The Rake's Progress* and *The Harlot's Progress* (see the boxed text on this page). Thomas Rowlandson (1756-1827) went for gentler cartooning that nonetheless packed a punch; some of his works are on display in the Courtauld Gallery.

Perhaps the diffused (some might say washed-out) quality of the light helps, but England has a fine tradition of watercolourists, beginning with the poet and engraver William Blake (1757-1827), whose romantic pictures and illustrations (he illustrated Milton's *Paradise Lost*) hang in the Tate Britain. In contrast, John Constable (1776-1837) did landscapes on Hampstead Heath as well as the countryside around the Essex-Suffolk border. He worked for years in a studio on Charlotte St in Fitzrovia and influenced a whole generation of French Impressionists. Turner was equally at home

Of Rakes & Harlots: Hogarth's World

William Hogarth (1697-1764) was an artist and engraver who specialised in satire and what these days might be considered heavy-handed moralising on the wages of sin. His plates were so popular in his day that they were actually pirated, leading Parliament to pass the Hogarth Act of 1735 to protect copyright. They provide us with an invaluable look at life (particularly among the lowly) in Georgian London.

The *Marriage à la Mode* series satirises the wantonness and marriage customs of the upper classes, while *Gin Lane* was produced as part of a campaign to have gin distillation made a crime (as it became under the Gin Act of 1751). It shows drunkards lolling about in the parish of St Giles, with the church of St George's Bloomsbury clearly visible in the background. His eight-plate series *The Harlot's Progress* traces the life of a country lass from her arrival in London to imprisoned whore; some of the plates are set in Drury Lane. In *The Rake's Progress*, the debauched protagonist is seen at one stage being entertained in a Russell St tavern by a bevy of prostitutes, one of whom strokes his chest while the other relieves him of his pocket watch. The women's faces are covered with up to a half-dozen beauty marks, which were all the rage at the time.

Hogarth's works can be seen in the Tate Britain, the National Gallery, Sir John Soane's Museum in Holborn and Hogarth's House in Chiswick.

with oils, and he increasingly subordinated detail to the effects of light and colour. By the 1830s, with paintings such as *Snow Storm: Steam-boat off a Harbour's Mouth* and the later *Rain, Steam, Speed* (1844), his compositions seemed entirely abstract and were widely vilified.

Members of the Pre-Raphaelite Brotherhood of the mid-19th century – painters Holman Hunt, John Everett Millais, Dante Gabriel Rossetti and Edward Coley Burne-Jones – threw aside pastel-coloured rusticity in favour of big, bright, detailed invocations of medieval legends and biblical stories that go hand-in-hand with the gilded neogothic architecture of men like Pugin.

In the 20th century the monumental sculptures of Henry Moore (1898-1986), the contorted, almost surreal, paintings of Francis Bacon (1909-92) and Lucien Freud, and David Hockney's stylish, pop-art realism and flat, shadowless paintings of friends, swimming pools in California and dachshunds, have ensured the place of British art in the international arena.

Londoner Richard Hamilton's photomontage of pin-ups lounging in a suburban living room, *Just what is it that makes today's homes so different, so appealing?* (1956), launched the pop-art movement in the UK. Recently, attention has been focused on artists like Damien Hirst, the late Helen Chadwick, the mysterious duo Gilbert & George and the Chapman brothers, all of whom seem as interested in shocking – cows sawn in half and preserved in formaldehyde (Hirst), flowers sculpted from urine streams (Chadwick), self-portraits of the artists (G&G) defecating – as in pleasing. Other names to watch out for include Rachel Whiteread, who turned a whole East End house into a sculpture only to see it knocked down, and Tracey Emin, who erected a tent with the names of everyone she'd ever slept with sewn into it.

Cinema

Surprisingly for its size and stature, London is not as familiar as, say, New York, Los Angeles or San Francisco to cinema-goers,

though the number of films that have been based and shot here is legion. For a much more detailed listing than we can provide, see Colin Sorensen's *London on Film: 100 Years of Filmmaking in London*, published by the Museum of London and on sale there.

The first sighting of London on film was a jerky, primitive glimpse of Trafalgar Square shot by Wordsworth Donisthorpe in 1889. A few pre-talkie films of the 1920s were set in London, but it was a London of the back lot rather than actual locations. For films using real London sets you have to jump forward a few decades and even then there can be deceptions, as in *My Fair Lady* (1964) with Audrey Hepburn and Rex Harrison, shot in a mock-up of Covent Garden in California.

Leytonstone-born Alfred Hitchcock shot several of his films in London, including *The Lodger, Sabotage, The Man Who Knew Too Much, The Lady Vanishes* and *Stagefright* – mostly at Gainsborough Studios, on the border of Islington and Hackney, which is about to get a facelift – and the much later *Frenzy* (1972), his return to Covent Garden. The villain in Hitchcock's *Blackmail* (1929), his first talking picture, came crashing through the massive glass dome of the British Museum Reading Room in the film's climax.

Absolute Beginners (1986), a dreadful film based on the book by Colin MacInnes, was set in 1950s Soho and Notting Hill, but more films have celebrated the 'Swinging London' of the 1960s. Foremost among these is Nicholas Roeg's *Performance* (1969) with Mick Jagger and James Fox, but Michelangelo Antonioni's *Blow-Up* (1966), starring David Hemmings as the photographer, is a much better film; the dead body scenes were filmed in Maryon Park in Charlton. *Alfie* with Michael Caine, *Georgy Girl* with Lynn Redgrave and *To Sir with Love* with newcomer Lulu (all 1966) homed in on the social changes that were taking place on a more workaday level.

Many film-makers have used London as a backdrop for crime and horror stories. One of the earliest was *The Ladykillers* (1955), starring Alec Guinness, which focused on a rather less dodgy-looking

Leicester Square in the West End, the setting for many British film premieres.

DOUG McKINLAY

romance was the one portrayed in Stephen Frears' *My Beautiful Laundrette* (1985), in which an ex-member of the National Front (Daniel Day Lewis) helps his young Asian friend (Gordon Warnecke) create his commercial dream, a glittering laundrette, and falls in love with him in the process. It's an immensely funny and touching film, and a grand indictment of Thatcher's London.

The Docklands has provided a setting for all sorts of films, including *The Long Good Friday* (1979) with Bob Hoskins as an East End hood, which preceded the redevelopment; *A Fish Called Wanda* (1988), with the most attractive riverside flat we've ever seen; and the touching black-and-white *Elephant Man* (1980), about a deformed man (John Hurt) who was exhibited as a fairground freak in Victorian London; much of it was filmed in Shad Thames opposite the Tower of London.

Royalty, especially the Tudors and Stuarts, crop up time and again in films that feature the best-known London landmarks, including *A Man for All Seasons* (1966), the story of Thomas More; *Lady Jane* (1985), in which Dover Castle stood in for the Tower of London at the time of Bloody Mary; and *Cromwell* (1970), in which Alec Guinness played the doomed Charles I to Richard Harris' loud Cromwell. Scenes at Kew Gardens and Syon House crop up in *The Madness of King George* (1994).

Not surprisingly several of Dickens novels have wound up on celluloid; the lengthy, two-part version of *Little Dorrit*, filmed in 1987, is regarded as the best of the genre, although David Lean's *Oliver Twist* (1948) does an excellent job at recreating the horrors of Victorian slum life. Shakespeare, too, has found his way onto film, although not always in the way one might expect. In *Richard III* (1995) the action has shifted to prewar London, with sets including Bankside Power Station (now the Tate Modern) and St Pancras train station.

Some films include vignettes of a London long since lost. The old police epic *The Blue Lamp* (1949), for example, preserves footage of the area around Paddington

King's Cross than *Mona Lisa* (1986), which starred Cathy Tyson as a high-class lesbian call girl who runs rings around her would-be suitor Bob Hoskins. In *Dance with a Stranger* (1984), Miranda Richardson plays Ruth Ellis, the last woman to be hanged in the UK, and Rupert Everett is her faithless lover whom she finally kills. John Landis' campy comic horror film *An American Werewolf in London* (1981) ends with a fabulous chase scene in Piccadilly Circus.

Other film-makers have taken a look at London's 'villages' and neighbourhoods. Harold Pinter's *The Pumpkin Eater* (1964), with Anne Bancroft, focused on St John's Wood and London Zoo, while Mike Leigh (*Life is Sweet*, *Naked* and *Secrets and Lies*) has preferred to concentrate on the more down-at-heel corners. A more modern

Green that was levelled to make space for the Westway elevated motorway. Others present a futuristic look at the city, as in Stanley Kubrick's notoriously violent *A Clockwork Orange* (1971), which was shot in and around the grim Thamesmead housing estate in south-east London. *1984*, released in the year of its title and Richard Burton's last film, is full of monochromatic shots of how Orwell imagined London would look in the mid-1980s when he wrote his book in 1948, including a looming, sinister-looking Battersea Power Station.

Some children's films with London settings include *Mary Poppins* (1964), in which our heroine floats across the city borne by her umbrella and hooks up with a virtually unintelligible 'Cockney' chimney sweep, Dick Van Dyke, and the original *101 Dalmatians* (1960), with scenes of Scotland Yard. The 1996 remake has Glenn Close as the evil Cruella de Vil, with the base of her world empire at the postmodern Gothic monstrosity Minster Court on Mark Lane in the City.

Should you get a chance to see it, Patrick Keillor's art-house semi-documentary *London* (1994) is set around events in 1992. It's a wonderful one-off, full of details you'd never otherwise notice in places like Twickenham and Stoke Newington, with Paul Schofield as the smooth-voiced, sardonic narrator.

More recent films portray London in its many, many guises. Hettie MacDonald's *Beautiful Thing* (1996) is a feel-good film about two working-class teenage boys living in Thamesmead who happen to fall in love; the soundtrack featuring the late Mama Cass was a stroke of genius. *Sliding Doors* (1997) has a pre-*Shakespeare in Love* Gwyneth Paltrow doing her best to get that London accent just 'roight'. The highly recommended *Shakespeare in Love* (1998) is an excellent evocation of Elizabethan London (see the boxed text 'William's the Bard, the Lad's Willy' in the Excursions chapter) and includes great shots of Bankside. *Lock, Stock and Two Smoking Barrels* (1998), starring ex-Wimbledon footballer Vinnie Jones, has Battersea Bridge as the setting for its cliffhanger climax. In *Notting Hill* (1999),

Richard Curtis' lightweight comedy about an improbable romance between Hugh Grant and the delectable Julia Roberts, you get to see Portobello Rd, the Ritz hotel and the Strand – but that's about all.

Theatre

London has been the centre of English drama ever since James Burbage built its first theatre – called the Theatre, appropriately enough – in Shoreditch in 1576.

Little is known about drama before then, when rowdy theatres were banned from the City and exiled to the east (eg the Theatre, the Curtain on Curtain Rd and the Fortune on Fortune St) and to Southwark on the southern side of the Thames. The Globe was just one of a cluster of theatres there, including the Swan, the Hope and the Rose; recently remains of the Rose, where *Titus Andronicus* and *Henry VI* were first performed, were excavated and there is now a sound-and-light show displaying them (see the Bankside section in the Things to See & Do chapter).

Other playwrights working in Southwark included the duo Francis Beaumont and John Fletcher, Thomas Middleton (*A Chaste Maid in Cheapside*), Philip Massinger, Ben Jonson (*Eastward Hoe*, *Bartholomew Fair*) and Christopher Marlowe (*Dr Faustus*, *Edward II*), who was killed in a tavern brawl in Deptford in 1593. Southwark Cathedral was the parish church for these theatres and contains a memorial to Shakespeare as well as the tombs of his actor-brother, Edmond, and the dramatists Fletcher and Massinger.

The Puritans closed the theatres as dens of iniquity, but with the return of the Stuarts came a revival with a spate of Restoration comedies. Among the new writers were William Congreve (1670-1729), whose masterpiece, *The Way of the World*, is still staged occasionally, the outstanding John Dryden (1631-1700) and John Vanbrugh (1664-1726), who wrote *The Provoked Wife*.

By the 18th century the theatre was well established in London and largely respectable. These were the years when John Gay wrote his *Beggar's Opera* (1728), a sort of early *Les Misérables* set in Newgate Prison

All the world's a stage, and nowhere more so than on Shaftesbury Avenue, the heart of London's Theatreland.

and the basis for Bertold Brecht's *Three-penny Opera*. In 1773 Oliver Goldsmith's uproarious farce *She Stoops to Conquer* was first staged, followed in 1775 by Richard Sheridan's *The Rivals* and, two years later, his *The School for Scandal*.

The 19th century saw the great comedies of Oscar Wilde (1854-1900) hit the stage, including his *chef-d'oeuvre*, *The Import-ance of Being Earnest*, and *An Ideal Husband*, now a wonderful film starring Rupert Everett, although his popularity was soon eclipsed by scandal, persecution and a jail sentence for homosexuality. George Bernard Shaw (1856-1950) produced such evergreen plays as *Pygmalion*, *Major Bar-bara*, *Androcles and the Lion* and *Saint Joan*. Shaw and Wilde were both Irish by origin but moved to London for much of their working lives, as had Goldsmith (1731-74) before them.

Of the playwrights working in the first half of the 20th century who have remained popular, first and foremost is Noël Coward (1899-1973), *bon vivant* author of *Private Lives*, *Blithe Spirit* and *Brief Encounter*, which are witty, brittle and sophisticated comedies that are still given regular airings in the capital. *An Inspector Calls* by JB Priestley (1894-1984) is rarely off the stage for long.

Despite the tendency to err on the side of conservatism and guaranteed success at the box office, London's theatres (especially the subsidised ones) still stage a wide range of plays by modern writers. Harold Pinter is known for his obscure language and story lines; *The Caretaker* and *The Homecoming*, the latter set in north London, are two of his best-known works. Plays by David Hare *(Plenty, The Judas Kiss)* and the late John Osborne *(Look Back in Anger, A Patriot for Me)* will be more accessible for those who don't go to the theatre regularly.

Alan Ayckbourn and Michael Frayn con-tinue to turn out genuinely entertaining farces; *Absurd Person Singular* and *The Norman Conquests* are two of Ayckbourn's finest, *Noises Off* and *Donkey's Years* among Frayn's best. The new Mafia of young London-based Irish playwrights – a kind of Paddy Brat Pack – whose works are regularly staged in London include the immensely talented Martin McDonagh *(The Cripple of Inishmaan, The Beauty Queen of Leenane)* and Conor McPherson *(The Weir)*; if any of these are on, beg, borrow or steal a ticket.

Musicals The signs were already in place in the 1960s when *Hair* and *Jesus Christ Superstar* achieved phenomenal success on the London stage. Then, during the cash-strapped 1980s, London theatres started to fill up with blockbuster musicals, proven favourites with audiences (especially tourists) and a safe bet for paying the bills. It sometimes seems as if they're all by Andrew Lloyd-Webber *(Cats, Starlight Express, The Phantom of the Opera)* but there have also been musicals by Lionel Bart *(Oliver!)*, Boublil and Schonberg *(Miss Saigon, Martin Guerre* and *Les Misérables)*, Willy Russell *(Blood Brothers)*, Jonathan Larson *(Rent)* and Bob Fosse *(Chicago)*. Among the most popular at the time of writing were *Beauty and the Beast* (Menken, Ashman and Rice) and *Mamma Mia!* by the two male members of Abba.

SOCIETY & CONDUCT

It's difficult to generalise about a city of 12 million people, but we're going to give it a go. The most common preconceptions about Londoners – reserved, inhibited and stiflingly polite – are not far off the mark, and visitors are often amazed at the silence on the tube and trains, where the general approach is to get in, grab a seat, open a newspaper or book (studiously avoiding catching anyone's eye) and keep your mouth shut. But London is among the planet's most crowded places, and such behaviour is partly a protective veneer, essential for coping with the constant crush of people.

Londoners rise to the fore in a crisis or emergency; older people still reminisce about the 'good old days' during WWII when no one had anything and people helped each other with accommodation, rationing and/or mourning loved ones killed by German bombs. Fall down or have your wallet pinched and the crowds will descend, offering advice, solace and calling the police or an ambulance. But don't try to be their friend; they're too absorbed in their own world of workmates, school friends and family to ask anything 'personal', like where you're from, whether you're married or even how you are. We hasten to add, however, that when you do *really* befriend a Londoner, you'll have made one of the most loyal, supportive and understanding friends of your life.

Londoners are a tolerant bunch, unfazed by outrageous dress or even behaviour (we know – we've been there), and seem to take pride in ignoring anyone who appears to be trying to draw attention to themselves – it just ain't on to show any interest. On the whole, this tolerance means relatively low levels of chauvinism, racism, sexism or any other 'ism' you can think of. The annual Mardi Gras Festival is a vast celebration of homosexual culture that passes off without incident, and London has a long history of absorbing wave after wave of new immigrants and refugees.

Of course the picture can never be completely rosy. There are pockets of bigotry all over the capital, and the south-east, in particular, has been the scene of unprovoked, vicious racist attacks, even murders. Nor are the police – London's celebrated 'bobbies' – always as colour-blind as people would like to believe.

Dos & Don'ts

It's not especially easy to cause offence in London – unless you're trying to. Having said that, it's worth remembering that most Londoners would no more speak to a stranger in the street than fly to the moon. If you're obviously a tourist in need of directions, there's no problem. But try starting a general conversation at a bus stop or on a tube platform and you'll find people reacting as if you were mad. It's OK to eye people up, but don't stare, particularly on the tube. Some people take offence and react accordingly.

Queuing The British have always been notoriously addicted to queuing, and many comedy sketches depend on the audience accepting that people might actually join a queue without knowing what it's for. The order of the queue at banks, post offices, newsagents and so on is sacrosanct – few things are more calculated to spark an outburst of noises of disapproval than an attempt to 'push in' to a queue. Sadly, however, queues at bus stops in central London appear to be going the way of the dodo.

The Underground Given the vital role it plays, it's hardly surprising that the tube has its own relatively rigid etiquette that starts as soon as you pass through the turnstile. Where there's an escalator you absolutely *must* stand on the right so that people in a hurry or keen to get in some exercise can rush up or down on the left. This is an extremely important rule – we kid you not – and should you break it, you risk getting pushed aside or verbally abused. Once on the platform you should move along, away from the entrance (this is vital for safety as crowds blocking doorways could cause someone to fall onto the rails). When the train pulls in you should stand aside until everybody inside has got off.

Once in the carriage, it's acceptable to rush for a seat. In theory you're supposed to surrender it to anyone in greater need than you (such as the elderly, the disabled and pregnant women), but as the years go by Londoners get steadily worse at doing this. Putting your feet (or your bags) on the seats is antisocial but happens all the time. And if you see an unattended parcel or bag you should wait until you've reached the next station and *then* pull the communication cord to alert a guard.

Dress In some countries what you wear or don't wear in churches can get you into trouble. In general, London is as free and easy about this as it is about how you dress in the streets. Bear in mind, however, that if you go into any of the city's mosques or temples you may be expected to take off your shoes and cover your arms, legs and/or head. Men should take care to uncover their heads when visiting Christian churches; one of the authors' hats was snatched off the last time we visited Westminster Abbey.

A few classy restaurants and many clubs operate strict dress-codes. In the restaurants that usually means a jacket and tie for men and no jeans or trainers (runners) for anyone; in clubs it means whatever the management and their bouncers choose it to mean and can vary from night to night.

RELIGION
The Church of England, a Christian church that split from Rome in the 16th century, is the largest, wealthiest and most influential in the land. It's an 'established' church, meaning it's the official church of the country, and it has a close relationship with the state: the monarch appoints archbishops and bishops on the prime minister's advice.

CHARLOTTE HINDLE

Going Underground: it's difficult to imagine getting around London without it.

It's difficult to generalise about the form of worship, which varies from High Church – full of pomp and ceremony and sometimes almost indistinguishable from Roman Catholicism – to Low Church, which is less traditional and austere and has been more influenced by Protestantism. In 1994, the first women were ordained as priests after many years of debate. Now the spotlight is on whether the church will accept practising homosexuals as priests.

Both the Anglican and Roman Catholic hierarchies administer their flocks through cathedrals north and south of the river. The Anglicans have St Paul's to the north and Southwark to the south. The Catholics have Westminster Cathedral to the north and St George's Southwark to the south.

Other significant Protestant churches include the Methodists, the Baptists, the United Reformed Church and the Salvation Army. Evangelical and charismatic churches are the only Christian movements that still appear to be gaining converts, though the proselytising Mormons, Jehovah's Witnesses and Scientologists are having some success.

At various times since the 16th century Roman Catholics have been terribly persecuted. They didn't gain political rights until 1829 or a formal structure until 1850, but today about 10% of all Britons call themselves Catholics. An estimated 225,000 Jews make London their home but by no means all of them claim to be religious. They too have not always been treated fairly; they were expelled en masse from England in 1290 by Edward I and not allowed to return for almost four centuries.

Recent estimates suggest that there are now well over a million Muslims, as well as significant congregations of Sikhs and Hindus. Nowadays more non-Christians worship regularly than Christians.

LANGUAGE

The English language is by far England's greatest contribution to the modern world. It is astonishingly rich, containing an estimated 600,000 uninflected words (compared with, for example, Indonesian's or Malay's 60,000), and particularly abundant in descriptive words like nouns and adjectives, as any thesaurus will quickly (swiftly, speedily, rapidly, promptly) prove. These days, however, you'll encounter a veritable Babel of languages – an estimated 300, in fact – being spoken in London, and there are pockets of the capital where English is very much in the minority (eg Shoreditch in the East End, Soho's Chinatown, Dalston and Stoke Newington). You might even bump into residents who can't understand English at all – though this is usually only the case among older people and housewives of the more conservative communities, who depend on their children or grandchildren as translators.

LONDON'S
CONTEMPORARY

ARCHITECTURE

NEIL SETCHFIELD

CHARLOTTE HINDLE

The 'shock of the new' has always knocked the UK (and by extension London) sideways. This is the capital of a country where things old – from buildings and newscasters to pub names – are venerated, regardless of their aesthetic value, talent or current usefulness. On the other hand, everything new is immediately suspect.

Of course everything old had to be new once and Londoners have generally reacted in a predictable fashion. John Nash was harpooned – literally – in the press by the graceful spire of his All Souls Church in Langham Place (Map 6) when it was completed in 1824, and the landmark Eros statue in Piccadilly Circus (1892; Map 7) was so ridiculed that its designer, Alfred Gilbert, went into self-imposed exile for the next 30 years. Recently the graceful British Library (Colin St John Wilson, 1998; Map 3), with its warm red-brick exterior and Asianesque touches and its wonderfully bright interior, has met with a very hostile reception (even though the original design was almost 25 years old by the time the building was completed), as has the innovative Millennium Dome (Richard Rogers, 1998; Map 1), the world's largest such structure.

Unlike, say, Paris, Washington or Budapest, very little of London has ever been planned; instead it has developed in an 'organic' (for which read haphazard) fashion. There has always been an aversion to the set piece here, and only rarely are buildings used as parts of a larger town or district plan.

The 1970s saw very little building in London (apart from roads), and the recession of the late 1980s and early 1990s brought much of the development and speculation in the Docklands and the City of London to a standstill. In 1990 the publication of *A Vision of Britain*, a reactionary tract by Prince Charles, in which the self-proclaimed architecture expert argued for a synthetic 'English tradition', helped polarise traditionalists and modernists. For these and other reasons the London skyline has nothing to compare to that of Hong Kong, Tokyo or New York.

ELLIOT DANIEL

Top left: Paolozzi's statue of Sir Isaac Newton outside the British Library.

Left: Over £750 million worth of controversy: the Millennium Dome.

ELLIOT DANIEL

ANTHONY BATTLE

The problem has not been a lack of talent. The UK has produced some of the world's finest architects since WWII and one only has to go to Hong Kong and the Hongkong Shanghai Bank building (1985) or to Nîmes and the Carrée d'Art (1993) to see the remarkable talents of Norman Foster or to Paris and the Pompidou Centre (1977) for the work of Richard Rogers. In recent years the construction boom across the capital, thanks to large-scale private sector investment and proceeds from the National Lottery Fund, has brought the work of this modern-day Wren and Hawksmoor and that of equally talented (though perhaps less well-known internationally) British architects closer to home.

Top left: Canary Wharf – the tallest building in the UK – can be seen from all over London.

Top right & title page: City innovation: Richard Rogers' uncompromising Lloyd's of London building.

London's contemporary architecture was born in the Docklands and the City some 10 to 15 years ago. Taking pride of place in the Docklands (Map 12) was Cesar Pelli's 500m-high One Canada Square (1991), commonly known as Canary Wharf and easily visible from central London. The residential Cascades building (CZWG Architects) and the former Financial Times Print Works by Nicholas Grimshaw (both 1988) were just two other examples of innovative (and controversial) architecture.

The architectural centrepiece in the City (Map 8) was Lloyd's of London (1986), Rogers' 'inside-out' masterpiece of ducts, pipes, glass and stainless steel. Two other City buildings (both by GMW Partnership) breaking new ground included Minster Court (1991), a postmodern Gothic structure that Cruella de Vil used as her headquarters in the film *101 Dalmatians*, and 54 Lombard St (1993), a monolith that somehow manages to remain sensitive to (and reflective of) its neighbouring buildings.

Not everything new and different was restricted to the Docklands and the City, of course. Embankment Place (Terry Farrell, 1990; Map 7) took advantage of its invaluable position atop Charing Cross station to offer 32,000 sq metres of new office space. The symmetrical Vauxhall Cross (Farrell, 1993; Map 2), better known as the MI6 Building, was erected south of the river in Vauxhall, an area not celebrated for its cutting-edge architecture at the time. Far-flung Hammersmith was chosen as the site for Ralph Erskine's boat-like London Ark (1991; Map 2). The independent television station Channel 4 was considered very bold indeed when it moved from the media ghetto of Soho to its new horseshoe-shaped, glass-clad and very asymmetrical headquarters (Rogers, 1994; Map 10) in Victoria.

JULIET COOMBE

Left: The eco-friendly London Ark unfortunately finds itself next to the roaring traffic of the A4.

DOUG McKINLAY

ELLIOT DANIEL

NEIL SETCHFIELD

Top left: Gateway to Europe: Waterloo International Terminal.

Top right: Alternative TV: the cutting-edge Channel 4 building.

Bottom left: Richard Seifert's unimaginative but unmistakeable NatWest Tower (1980) on Bishopsgate dominates the City skyline.

If modern architecture in London was not restricted by area, it was also not limited by use; there is plenty of innovative architecture to be seen away from the mammoth office blocks and media centres. The Mound Stand at Lord's cricket ground (Michael Hopkins, 1987; Map 3) is a tent-like structure of stretched PVC-coated fabric built for spectators; as it is only used during the warmer months, it is open on all sides and recalls a ship at sea. The NatWest Media Centre at Lord's (Future Systems, 1999), an aluminium and glass pod on stilts, is reminiscent of a 1960s vision of the future – a gigantic alien 'eye' peering down on the field. For such a conservative organisation as the Marylebone Cricket Club, these structures standing side by side with older buildings are highly adventurous.

Other interesting buildings with nonstandard uses include Waterloo International Terminal (Grimshaw, 1993; Map 6), a glass and steel arch over a concrete viaduct supporting 800-tonne trains and a brilliant solution for a site 400m long and only 30 to 50m wide; the Sainsbury's supermarket (Grimshaw, 1988; Map 3) in Camden Town; the wholesale Billingsgate fish market (Rogers; Map 12); the unique Buckingham Palace Ticket Office (Hopkins, 1994; Map 6) on the edge of Green Park, with its bizarre flyaway roof; and the award-winning public lavatory

LONDON'S CONTEMPORARY ARCHITECTURE

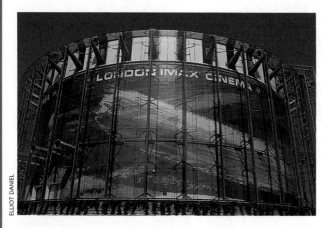

ELLIOT DANIEL

with its cantilevered Art Deco-ish glass roof (CZWG Architects, 1993; Map 5) on the corner of Westbourne Grove and Colville Rd. The new London IMAX Cinema building (Brian Avery, 1999; Map 6) in Waterloo is impressive: it's shaped like a drum, sits on 'springs' to reduce vibrations and traffic noise, and the exterior changes colour at night.

DOUG McKINLAY

Given the propensity for hanging on to every reminder of the past, it's not surprising to find that many interesting architectural developments of recent years have been adaptations of existing buildings for new uses. Fine examples are the old Michelin factory built in 1911 on Fulham Rd, which now houses the Bibendum restaurant (Conran Roche, 1987; Map 9); the Oxo Tower building, an erstwhile meat warehouse on the South Bank, converted into a mixture of restaurants, shops and flats by Lifschutz Davidson in 1996 (Map 6); the Cochrane Theatre (Map 6) in Bloomsbury, transformed by Nigerian-born Abiodun Odedina in 1991 from a faceless 1960s playhouse; the old Bankside Power Station, which now houses the new Tate Modern (Herzog & de Meuron, 1999; Map 8); and the Imagination Building (Herron Associates, 1989;

Top: The London IMAX Cinema, housing the biggest screen in Europe.

Left: Art Deco by night: the Oxo Tower.

Map 6) in Bloomsbury, whose unassuming façade (an Edwardian school) hides a dazzling, multipurpose interior.

Buildings and other structures to keep an eye out for in the near or distant future include the Millennium Bridge (Map 8) – Norman Foster's magnificent 'blade of light' – and his London Assembly building (Map 8) south of the river near Potter's Fields, a striking circular glass and steel structure that will house the new Greater London Authority and its mayor and has been compared to a car headlight, a fencing helmet and a glass ashtray. The 11 new stations (1998-99) of the Jubilee Line extension have each been designed by a different architect, but especially notable are Southwark station (Map 6), with its luminous glass walls, arches and silver tubes, by Richard MacCormac; the elegant, curving canopy of Chris Wilkinson's Stratford station; and Will Alsop's North Greenwich station (Map 1), whose blue tiles and hull-shaped interior recall Greenwich's maritime past.

One that we can't wait to see is Daniel Libeskind's zigzag-shaped extension of the Victoria & Albert Museum (Map 9) called the Spiral and due to open in 2004. No doubt this innovative and striking modern structure will do for London what American architect Frank O Gehry's Guggenheim Museum did for Bilbao in Spain.

Right: Elegance and functionality: Norman Foster's striking Millennium Bridge.

Facts for the Visitor

WHEN TO GO

London is a year-round tourist centre, with few of its attractions closing or significantly reducing their opening hours in winter. Your best chance of good weather is, of course, at the height of summer in July and August, but there's certainly no guarantee of sun even in those months and that is when you can expect the biggest crowds and highest prices.

April/May and September/October are good times to visit London: there's a better than average chance of good weather and the queues for popular attractions are a lot shorter. Choosing these off-peak times will also reduce the cost of getting to London by plane or ferry and may mean cheaper room rates in some hotels. If you don't mind braving the winter winds and aren't particularly partial to light, the cheapest air and boat fares and hotel prices are in force from November to March.

You may want to schedule your visit for a certain event – the London Open House

Spoilt for choice: in central London there are world-famous attractions everywhere you turn.

days in September, say, when more than 400 buildings and other sites not normally accessible to visitors open their doors, Trooping of the Colour in mid-June or the Chelsea Flower Show in late May. See the Public Holidays & Special Events section later in this chapter for details.

ORIENTATION

'Goodness me, but isn't London big?' exclaims Bill Bryson in his *Notes from a Small Island*. Bill's right: London does sprawl over an enormous area, but at least it has a helpful defining element.

The city's main geographical feature is the Thames, a sufficiently deep (for anchorage) and narrow (for bridging) tidal river that enabled the Romans to build a port that was easily defended from the dangers of the North Sea. Running from west to east, it divides the city into its northern and southern halves. But because it flows in wide bends, creating peninsulas in its wake, it is not always clear on what side of the river you are – especially in the far west and east.

Despite London's great size, the Underground system (the 'tube') makes most of it easily accessible, and the official and ubiquitous – though geographically misleading – Underground map is easy to use. Most

Telephone Code Change

On 22 April 2000, the area code for all of London will change to 020, and numbers will gain an extra digit at the front: either 7 for 0171 numbers or 8 for 0181 numbers. Thus what was until recently 0171-123 4567 will become 7123 4567 while the former 0181-765 4321 will now be 8765 4321. The changes are reflected in all the telephone and fax numbers quoted in this book.

If you want to use the new eight-digit numbers as they appear in this book before 22 April 2000, you must dial 020 first – even *within* London. After that date the code is only necessary when calling from *outside* the city.

important sights, theatres, restaurants and even affordable places to stay lie within a reasonably compact rectangle formed by the tube's Circle Line (colour-coded yellow), which encircles central London just north of the river.

In this chapter, the nearest tube or train station has been given for each address; Map 2 shows the location of tube stations and the areas covered by the detailed district maps. The boxed text 'London's Bewildering Postcodes' and accompanying map under Post & Communications later in this chapter will also be helpful, especially for locating outlying suburbs.

Most of London's airports lie some distance from the centre, but transport is easy (if not cheap). See the Getting Around chapter for details of how to get to and from them.

MAPS

A good map is vital for getting around London. The maps in this book will help, but you should also arm yourself with a single-sheet one so you can see all of central London at a glance. The Lonely Planet *London City Map* (£3.99) has three separate maps at different scales as well as an inset map of Theatreland and a street index. The two versions of *Benson's London Map & Guide* (both £1.99), one of which has sightseeing walks, are good, basic choices. More detailed single-sheet maps are the *AA London Street Map* (£3.99) and the *Collins London Street Plan* (£2.99).

For a longer stay you might want to invest in either the *A-Z Map of London* or the *A-Z Visitor's Atlas & Guide* (both £2.95). The foldout map has an advantage in that the

FACTS FOR THE VISITOR

What's in a Name?

Do you know the muffin man, the muffin man, the muffin man?
Do you know the muffin man who lives on Drury Lane?

That ditty was sung to one of us on our mother's bouncing knee sometime in the early Dark Ages in a far-off English-speaking outpost in New England. We were Irish, without a drop of 'Limey' blood coursing through our veins, but thanks to nursery rhymes like this one, the film *Mary Poppins* and the Beatles, London place-names – from Trafalgar and Berkeley squares to Carnaby St and Piccadilly Circus – were as familiar to us as those in Boston. But what's behind those names? Many City street names still recall the goods that were traded there (eg Poultry, Cornhill, Fish St Hill, Sea Coal Lane and Milk St). Other meanings are not so immediately apparent.

The '-wich' or '-wych' of names like Greenwich, Aldwych, Dulwich and Lundenwic (London's original name) comes from the Saxon word *wic*, meaning 'settlement'. *Ea* is the old word for 'island'; thus Chelsea (island of shingle), Bermondsey (Bermond's Island), Battersea (Peter's Island) and Hackney (Hakon's Island). In Old English *ceap* meant 'business', 'trade', 'purchase' or 'market'; hence Eastcheap is where the plebs shopped in medieval times, while Westcheap (now Cheapside, but often still called this by taxi drivers) was reserved for the royal household. 'Borough' comes from *burg*, Old English for 'fort' or 'town'. And the odd names East Ham and West Ham came from the Old English *hamm* or 'hem' – they were just bigger enclosed ('hemmed-in') settlements than the more standard hamlets.

And Drury Lane? It has a rather pedestrian etymology; it was named after one Thomas Drury, who built a house here in Elizabethan times. And the muffin man? He vanished without a trace, but since Drury Lane was notorious for its prostitutes in the 18th century (Hogarth set one of the plates of *The Harlot's Progress* here), our man the muffin man may have been selling more than something tasty you eat at teatime.

ED HILLYER

A London bobby warily eyes a circling pack of tourists.

place you want is never on the join between two pages, but the map books are easier to consult. If you're staying longer in London invest in a *Mini A-Z* (£3.75) or the *A-Z London Street Atlas*, which comes in variously sized editions costing from £3.25 to £7.50. They show the city down to its smallest side street.

Two other maps are important for taking public transport. The first is the map of the Underground reproduced in this book (Map 15); it's a design classic (see the boxed text 'Mapping the Underground' in the Getting Around chapter) and shows not just where the stations are in relation to one another but which zone they lie in, something you need to know in order to buy the right ticket. Some people prefer the newfangled Underground geographical map (reproduced in this book as Map 14), which shows the tube lines and stations in relation to streets, train stations and other features above ground.

To identify all of London's bus routes you'd need to cart around 36 separate map sheets. Luckily the whole of central London is covered on sheet No 1, the all-London bus map, which is available free from London Regional Transport information centres (see the Getting Around chapter for locations). If

you need one of the three-dozen local bus maps, ring ☎ 7371 0247 to have one sent or write to London Transport Buses, Freepost Lon7503, London SE16 4BR.

RESPONSIBLE TOURISM

London is a very (sometimes intolerably) crowded city, even before the peak season brings yet more millions to the streets. Anything you can do to minimise your impact as a tourist is a good thing.

Traffic congestion on the road – and its polluting effects – is a major problem (85% of all Londoners say they are dissatisfied with traffic levels), and visitors will do themselves and residents a favour if they forgo driving and use public transport. See the Ecology & Environment section in the Facts about London chapter for more information.

Some 'fragile' attractions are strained to capacity and have had to institute a timed-ticket system, with tickets sold only on the day of your visit or for a day selected in advance at the ticket office. Unless you are really keen on the subject matter, opt for something else.

If you'd like to know more about the problems caused by tourism, contact Tourism Concern (☎ 7753 3330) at Stapleton House, 277-281 Holloway Rd, London N7 8HN (⊖ Holloway Road). It has a library of press cuttings and other source materials.

TOURIST OFFICES

London is a major travel centre, so along with information on London tourist offices can help with England, Scotland, Wales, Ireland and most countries worldwide.

Local Tourist Offices

Britain Visitor Centre The Britain Visitor Centre (Map 7), 1 Regent St SW1 (⊖ Piccadilly Circus), is a comprehensive information and booking centre, with the tourist boards of Wales, Scotland, Northern Ireland, the Irish Republic and Jersey as well as a map and guidebook shop on the ground floor. On the mezzanine level are a Thomas Cook outlet where you can arrange accommodation and tours as well as train, air and car travel, a theatre ticket agency, a *bureau de change*, international telephones and computer terminals for accessing tourist information on the Internet. It can get *very* busy but opens daily: Monday to Friday from 9 am to 6.30 pm, Saturday and Sunday from 10 am to 4 pm (Saturday from 9 am to 5 pm from late June to September). The centre deals with direct queries and walk-in customers only; there are no telephone inquiries. If you're not in the area and need information about Britain or Ireland ring British Tourist Authority (BTA) general inquiries on ☎ 8846 9000 or consult the BTA Web site at www.visitbritain.com.

Tourist Information Centres As well as providing information, London's main tourist information centre (TIC), on the forecourt of Victoria train station (Map 10; ⊖ Victoria), handles accommodation bookings. It's open Monday to Saturday from 8 am to 8 pm and to 6 pm on Sunday, April to October (from 8 am to 6 pm Monday to Saturday and from 9 am to 4 pm on Sunday the rest of the year). It too can get positively mobbed in the peak season.

There's also a TIC in the arrivals hall at Waterloo International Terminal (Map 6; ⊖ Waterloo), open daily from 8.30 am to 10.30 pm, and one in Liverpool Street station (Map 8; ⊖ Liverpool Street), open weekdays from 8 am to 6 pm and at weekends from 8.45 am to 5.30 pm. There are TICs at Heathrow Terminal 3 (arrivals concourse), open daily from 6 am to 11 pm, and in the Heathrow Terminals 1, 2, 3 Underground station, open from 8 am to 6 pm. Gatwick, Stansted, Luton and London City airports, Paddington train station and Victoria Coach Station also all have information desks.

Like the Britain Visitor Centre, the main TICs handle walk-ins only. Otherwise, phone London Tourist Board (LTB) general inquiries on ☎ 7932 2000 or make use of the Visitorcall system described below. Written inquiries should be sent to the London Tourist Board & Convention Bureau, Glen House, Stag Place, London SW1E 5LT (or fax 7932 0222).

The Corporation of London also maintains an information centre (Map 8; ☎ 7332 1456) in St Paul's Churchyard EC4, opposite St Paul's Cathedral (⊖ St Paul's). It's open daily from 9.30 am to 5 pm, April to September. During the rest of the year, the weekday hours are 9.30 am to 5 pm (to 12.30 pm on Saturday).

Other, possibly less overstretched, TICs include the following:

Greenwich
  (☎ 8858 6376, fax 8853 4607)
  46 Greenwich Church St, London SE10 9BL
Islington
  (☎ 7278 8787, fax 7833 2193)
  11 Duncan St, London N1 8BW
Richmond
  (☎ 8940 9125, fax 8940 6899)
  Old Town Hall, Whittaker Ave, Richmond, Surrey TW9 1TP
Southwark
  (☎ 7403 8299)
  London Bridge, 6 Tooley St, London SE1 2SY
Tower Hamlets
  (☎ 7375 2549, fax 7375 2539)
  18 Lamb St, London E1 6EA

Given how busy the tourist offices can get, you may want to make use of their Visitorcall system. You simply dial ☎ 09064 123 and then add another three digits, depending on what information you're looking for. Bear in mind that these are premium-rate calls costing 49p a minute. The numbers can only be dialled within the UK:

What's on this week	400
Event of the month	410
What's on for the next three months	401
Sunday in London	407
Summer in the parks	406
Christmas & Easter events	418
Changing the Guard	411
Current exhibitions	403
Rock & pop concerts	422
State Opening of Parliament, Trooping of the Colour & Lord Mayor's Show	413
Getting to/from the airports	433
Getting around London	430
River trips/Boat hire	432
Guided tours & walks	431
Booking a guide	420

Tourist Offices Abroad

The BTA stocks masses of information about London and the rest of Britain, much of it free. Be sure to contact the BTA *before* you leave home; some discounts are only available to people who book before arriving in Britain. Travellers with special needs (such as those with a disability or dietary restrictions) should also contact their nearest BTA office. Overseas offices include:

Australia
(☎ 02-9377 4400, fax 9377 4499)
Level 16, The Gateway, 1 Macquarie Place, Sydney, NSW 2000
Canada
(☎ 905-405 1840, fax 405 1835, toll-free ☎ 1-888 VISIT UK)
Suite 120, 5915 Airport Rd, Mississauga, Ontario L4V 1T1
France
(☎ 01 44 51 56 20, fax 01 44 51 56 21)
Maison de la Grand Bretagne, 19 rue des Mathurins, 75009 Paris
Germany
(☎ 069-97 112 3, fax 97 112 444)
Westendstrasse 16-22, 60325 Frankfurt-am-Main
Ireland
(☎ 01-670 8000)
18-19 College Green, Dublin 2
Netherlands
(☎ 020-685 50 51, fax 618 68 68)
Aurora Gebouw (5e), Stadhouderskade 2, 1054 ES Amsterdam
New Zealand
(☎ 09-303 1446, fax 377 6965)
3rd floor, Dilworth Building, corner Queen & Customs Sts, Auckland 1

South Africa
(☎ 011-325 0343, 325 0344)
Lancaster Gate, Hyde Park Lane, Hyde Park, Sandton 2196
USA
(toll-free ☎ 1-800 GO 2 BRITAIN)
Suite 1510, 625 North Michigan Ave, Chicago, IL 60611 (personal callers only)
(☎ 212-986 2200)
Suite 701, 551 5th Ave, New York, NY 10176-0799

DOCUMENTS

Unlike many other European countries, people in the UK are not required by law to carry identification but it's always a good idea to have your passport or some other sort of photo ID on your person. Also, with very few exceptions, London is an excellent place to gather information about and visas for other countries worldwide.

Visas

At present, citizens of Australia, Canada, New Zealand, South Africa and the USA are given 'leave to enter' the UK at their point of arrival for up to six months but are prohibited from working. If you're a citizen of the European Union (EU), you don't need a visa to enter the country and may live and work here freely.

Visa regulations are always subject to change, so it's essential to check with your local British embassy, high commission or consulate before leaving home.

The immigration authorities in the UK are tough; dress neatly and be able to prove that you have sufficient funds to support yourself. A credit card and/or an onward ticket will help.

Several travel companies provide quick foreign visa services for a fee. Trailfinders (Map 5; ☎ 7938 3848), 194 Kensington High St W8 (⊖ High Street Kensington), handles visas for more than a dozen countries. Top Deck Travel (Map 9; ☎ 7373 3026), 131 Earl's Court Rd SW5 (⊖ Earl's Court), has a Rapid Visa & Travel Service. Global Visas (Map 7; ☎ 7734 5900), 181 Oxford St W1 (⊖ Oxford Circus), claims it can obtain visas for more than 150 countries.

Visa Extensions Tourist visas can only be extended in clear emergencies (eg an accident). Otherwise you'll have to leave the UK (perhaps going to Ireland or France) and apply for a fresh one, although this tactic will arouse suspicion after the second or third visa. To extend (or attempt to extend) your stay in the UK, contact the Home Office's Immigration & Nationality Department (☎ 8686 0688), Lunar House, 40 Wellesley Rd, Croydon CR2 2BY (East Croydon station), *before* your existing visa expires. It's open Monday to Friday from 10 am to noon and 2 to 4 pm. You can also ring the Visa & Passport Information Line on 08706-067766.

Student Visas Nationals of EU countries can enter the country to study without formalities. Otherwise you need to be enrolled on a full-time course of at least 15 hours a week of weekday, daytime study at a single educational institution to be allowed to remain as a student. For more details, consult the British embassy, high commission or consulate in your own country.

Work Permits EU nationals don't need a work permit to work in London, but everyone else does. If the *main* purpose of your visit is to work, you have to be sponsored by a British company.

However, if you're a citizen of a Commonwealth country aged between 17 and 27 inclusive, you may apply for a Working Holiday Entry Certificate, which allows you to spend up to two years in the UK and take work that is 'incidental' to a holiday. You're not allowed to engage in business, pursue a career or provide services as a professional sportsperson or entertainer.

You must apply to the nearest UK mission overseas – Working Holiday Entry Certificates are *not* granted on arrival in Britain. It's not possible to switch from being a visitor to a working holiday-maker, nor is it possible to claim back any time spent out of the UK during the two-year period. When you apply, you must satisfy the authorities that you have the means to pay for a return or onward journey and that you will be able to maintain yourself without recourse to public funds.

If you're a Commonwealth citizen and have a parent born in the UK, you may be eligible for a Certificate of Entitlement to the Right of Abode, which means you can live and work in Britain free of immigration control.

If you're a Commonwealth citizen with a grandparent born in the UK, or if the grandparent was born before 31 March 1922 in what is now the Republic of Ireland, you may qualify for a UK Ancestry Employment Certificate, which means you can work full time for up to four years in the UK.

Visiting students from the USA who are at least 18 years old and studying full time at a college or university can get a permit allowing them to work for six months. It costs US$200 and is available through the Council on International Educational Exchange (☎ 212-661 1414), 205 East 42nd St, New York, NY 10017, which has a Web site at www.ciee.org. The British Universities North America Club (BUNAC; ☎ 7251 3472, fax 7251 0215, email enquiries@ bunac.org.uk), 16 Bowling Green Lane, London EC1R 0QH, can also help you organise a permit and find employment; its Web site is at www.bunac.org.

If you have any queries once you're in the UK, contact the Home Office's Immigration & Nationality Department (see the earlier Visa Extensions section).

Travel Insurance

Whichever way you're travelling, make sure you take out a comprehensive travel insurance policy that covers you for medical expenses and luggage theft or loss, and for cancellation of or delays in your travel arrangements. Ticket loss should also be included, but make sure you have a separate record of all the details – or better still, a photocopy of the ticket. There are all sorts of policies, but the international student travel policies handled by STA Travel and other student travel organisations are usually good value. Some policies offer lower and higher medical expense options – unless you're eligible for free NHS treatment (see the Health section later in this chapter), go for as much as you can afford. Other policies are cheaper if you forgo cover for lost baggage.

Buy insurance as early as possible. Otherwise you may find that you're not covered for delays to your flight caused by strikes or other industrial action. Always read the small print carefully for loopholes.

Paying for your ticket with a credit card often provides limited travel accident insurance, and you may be able to reclaim the payment if the operator doesn't deliver. In the UK, credit card providers are required by law to reimburse consumers if a company goes into liquidation and the amount in contention is more than £100.

Driving Licence & Permits

Your normal driving licence is legal for 12 months from the date you last entered the UK; you can then apply for a British licence at post offices. It's still a good idea to carry an International Driving Permit (IDP) as well. This should be obtainable from your local motoring association for a small fee.

Hostel Cards

To stay in one of London's seven Youth Hostels Association/Hostelling International (YHA/HI) hostels you must be a member of the organisation. If not you'll be charged a £1.70 surcharge for the first six nights, which will add up to the joining fee. For membership details, see the YHA/HI Hostels section in the Places to Stay chapter.

Student & Youth Cards

Most useful of these is the International Student Identity Card (ISIC), a plastic ID-style card with your photograph that costs £5 in the UK and provides cheap or free admission to museums and sights, inexpensive meals in some student restaurants and discounts on many forms of transport.

There's a worldwide industry in fake student cards, and many places now stipulate a maximum age for student discounts or simply substitute a 'youth discount' for a

'student' one. If you're aged under 26 but not a student, you can apply for a GO25 card issued by the Federation of International Youth Travel Organisations (FIYTO) or a Euro<26 Card, which give much the same discounts for the same fee as the ISIC.

All these cards are issued by student unions, hostelling organisations and student travel agencies.

Seniors' Cards

Many attractions reduce their admission price for people aged over 60 or 65 (sometimes as low as 55 for women); it's always worth asking even if you can't see a discount listed.

Museum Discount Cards

If you plan to do a lot of sightseeing the GoSee Card (☎ 7923 0807) offers admission to 16 museums and galleries for three days for £16 or seven days for £26. Family cards, offering admission for up to two adults and four children aged 16 years or under, cost £32/50 for three/seven days.

Tickets are available from TICs – including those at Waterloo International Terminal, Victoria train station, Liverpool Street station and Heathrow – and London Regional Transport information centres. They're also available at the museums and other attractions participating in the scheme: Apsley House (Wellington Museum), Barbican Art Gallery, BBC Experience, Design Museum, Hayward Gallery, Imperial War Museum, London Transport Museum, Museum of London, National Maritime Museum (with Greenwich Royal Observatory), Natural History Museum, Royal Academy of Arts, Science Museum, Theatre Museum, Tower Bridge Experience and the Victoria & Albert Museum. More information is available on the Web at www.london-gosee.com.

There's also a South Kensington Museum Pass costing £24/£13 for adults/seniors & students (family £45), which is valid for a year and allows unlimited entry to the Victoria & Albert, Natural History and Science museums (available at all three museums).

Photocopies

Copy your passport, air tickets, insurance policy and serial numbers of your camera and travellers cheques before you leave home. Take one set of copies with you (keeping them separate from the original documents) and leave a second set with someone you can rely on back home.

It's also a good idea to store details of your vital travel documents in Lonely Planet's free online Travel Vault in case you lose the photocopies or can't be bothered with them. Your password-protected Travel Vault is accessible on-line anywhere in the world – create it at www.ekno.lonely planet.com.

EMBASSIES & CONSULATES
British Embassies, High Commissions & Consulates

British missions overseas include those listed below. If you need the details of others, consult the Foreign & Commonwealth Office Web site at www.fco.gov.uk.

Australia
    High Commission:
    (☎ 02-6270 6666, fax 6270 6653)
    Commonwealth Ave, Yarralumla, Canberra, ACT 2600
    Consulate:
    (☎ 02-9247 7521, 9251 6201)
    Level 16, The Gateway, 1 Macquarie Place, Sydney, NSW 2000
Canada
    High Commission:
    (☎ 613-237 1530, fax 232 2533)
    80 Elgin St, Ottawa, Ontario K1P 5K7
    Consulate:
    (☎ 416-593 1290, fax 593 1229)
    Suite 2800, 777 Bay St, College Park, Toronto, Ontario M5G 2G2
France
    Embassy:
    (☎ 01 44 51 31 00, fax 01 44 51 31 28)
    35 rue du Faubourg Saint Honoré, 75008 Paris
Germany
    Embassies:
    (☎ 0228-916 70, fax 916 7200)
    Friedrich-Ebert-Allee 77, 53113 Bonn
    (☎ 030-201 840, fax 201 84158)
    Unter den Linden 32/34, 10117 Berlin

Ireland
    Embassy:
    (☎ 01-205 3822, fax 205 3890)
    29 Merrion Rd, Ballsbridge, Dublin 4
Netherlands
    Embassy:
    (☎ 070-427 0427, fax 427 0345)
    Lange Voorhout 10, 2514 ED The Hague
    Consulate:
    (☎ 020-676 43 43, fax 676 10 69)
    Konigslaan 44, 1075 AE Amsterdam
New Zealand
    High Commission:
    (☎ 04-472 6049, fax 471 1974)
    44 Hill St, Wellington 1
    Consulate:
    (☎ 09-303 2973, fax 303 1836)
    17th floor, Fay Richwhite Building, 151 Queen St, Auckland 1
South Africa
    High Commission:
    (☎ 021-461 7220, fax 461 0017)
    91 Parliament St, Cape Town 8001
    Consulate:
    (☎ 011-327 0015, fax 327 0152)
    Dunkeld Corner, 275 Jan Smuts Ave, Dunkeld West, Johannesburg 2196
USA
    Embassy:
    (☎ 202-588 6500, fax 588 7850)
    3100 Massachusetts Ave, NW, Washington, DC 20008
    Consulate:
    (☎ 212-745 0444, fax 745 9292)
    27th floor, One Dag Hammarskjold Plaza, 885 2nd Ave, New York, NY 10017

Embassies, High Commissions & Consulates in London

It's important to realise what your own embassy – the embassy of the country of which you are a citizen – can and can't do to help you if you get into trouble.

Generally, it won't be much help if the trouble you're in is remotely your own fault. Remember that while in London you are bound by English law. Your embassy will not be sympathetic if you end up in prison after committing a crime locally, even if such actions are legal in your own country.

In genuine emergencies you might get some assistance, but only if other channels have been exhausted. For example, if you need to get home urgently, a free ticket home

Australia House, one of the grandest buildings on the Strand, topped by Bertram Mackennal's *The Horses of the Sun.*

is exceedingly unlikely – the embassy would expect you to have insurance. If you have all your money and documents stolen, it might assist with getting a new passport, but a loan for onward travel is out of the question.

Some foreign missions in London are:

Australia
  High Commission:
  (Map 6; ☎ 7379 4334, fax 7240 5333)
  Australia House, Strand WC2 (⊖ Temple)
Belgium
  Consulate:
  (Map 10; ☎ 7470 3700, fax 7259 6213)
  103 Eaton Square SW1 (⊖ Victoria)
Canada
  High Commission:
  (Map 6; ☎ 7258 6600, fax 7258 6506)
  1 Grosvenor Square W1 (⊖ Bond Street)
France
  Consulate:
  (Map 9; ☎ 7838 2050, fax 7838 2046)
  6A Cromwell Place SW7 (⊖ South Kensington)

Germany
  Embassy:
  (Map 10; ☎ 7824 1300, fax 7824 1435)
  23 Belgrave Square SW1 (⊖ Hyde Park Corner)
Ireland
  Embassy:
  (Map 6; ☎ 7235 2171, fax 7245 6961)
  17 Grosvenor Place SW1 (⊖ Hyde Park Corner)
Netherlands
  Embassy:
  (Map 5; ☎ 7590 3200, fax 7590 3334)
  38 Hyde Park Gate SW7 (⊖ High Street Kensington)
New Zealand
  High Commission:
  (Map 7; ☎ 7930 8422, fax 7839 4580)
  New Zealand House, 80 Haymarket SW1 (⊖ Piccadilly Circus)
South Africa
  High Commission:
  (Map 7; ☎ 7451 7299, fax 7451 7284)
  South Africa House, Trafalgar Square WC2 (⊖ Trafalgar Square)

Spain
    Consulate:
    (Map 9; ☎ 7589 8989)
    2 Draycott Place SW3 (⊖ Sloane Square)
USA
    Embassy:
    (Map 6; ☎ 7499 9000, fax 7495 5012)
    5 Upper Grosvenor St W1 (⊖ Bond
    Street)

CUSTOMS

Like other EU nations, the UK has a two-tier customs system: one for goods bought duty-free and one for goods bought in another EU country where taxes and duties have already been paid.

Duty Free

Duty-free sales to those travelling from one EU country to another were abolished from July 1999. For goods purchased at airports or on ferries *outside* the EU, you are allowed to import 200 cigarettes or 250g of tobacco, 2L of still wine plus 1L of spirits over 22% or another 2L of wine (sparkling or otherwise), 50g of perfume, 250cc of toilet water, and other duty-free goods (including cider and beer) to the value of £136.

Tax & Duty Paid

Although you can no longer bring in duty-free goods from another EU country, you *can* bring in goods from another EU country, where certain goods might be cheaper, if taxes have been paid on them. The items are supposed to be for individual consumption but a thriving business has developed, with many Londoners making day trips to France to load up their cars with cheap grog and cigarettes, which they often sell back in the UK. The savings can more than pay for the trip.

If you purchase from a normal retail outlet, customs uses the following maximum quantities as a guideline to distinguish personal imports from those on a commercial scale: 800 cigarettes, 200 cigars, 1kg of tobacco, 10L of spirits, 20L of fortified wine, 90L of wine (of which not more than 60L are sparkling) and 110L of beer.

MONEY
Currency

The British currency is the pound sterling (£), which is divided into 100 pence (p). Coins of 1p and 2p are copper; 5p, 10p, 20p and 50p coins are silver; and the bulky £1 coin is gold-coloured. The £2 coin introduced in 1998 is gold-coloured on the edge with a silver centre.

Notes come in £5, £10, £20 and £50 denominations and vary in colour and size. The £50 notes can be difficult to change – avoid them.

Exchange Rates

Exchange rates at the time of going to print were:

country	unit		pounds
Australia	A$1	=	£0.40
Canada	C$1	=	£0.42
euro	€1	=	£0.66
France	1FF	=	£0.10
Germany	DM1	=	£0.34
Ireland	IR£1	=	£0.84
Japan	¥100	=	£0.56
Netherlands	f1	=	£0.30
New Zealand	NZ$1	=	£0.33
USA	US$1	=	£0.62

Exchanging Money

By 2002, most of the EU will have a single currency called the euro. Until then francs, Deutschmarks, pesetas and so on will remain in place or share equal status with the euro. The pound will continue to be the unit of currency in the UK as the British government has decided not to adopt the euro for the time being.

Cash Nothing beats cash for convenience – or risk. It's still a good idea, however, to travel with some cash in pounds sterling, if only to tide you over until you get to an exchange facility. There's no problem if you arrive at any of London's five airports; all have good-value exchange counters open for incoming flights (see Money-changers later in this section).

Travellers Cheques & Eurocheques
Travellers cheques offer protection from
theft. Ideally your cheques should be in
pounds and preferably issued by American
Express (Amex) or Thomas Cook, which
are widely recognised, well represented
and don't charge for cashing their own
cheques (though they often offer inferior
exchange rates). Both have offices and
bureaux de change all over London; see
Moneychangers later in this section or look
in the phone book for the nearest branch.

Bring most cheques in large denominations. It's only towards the end of a stay that
you may want to change a small cheque to
make sure you don't get left with too much
local currency. Travellers cheques are rarely
accepted outside banks or used for everyday
transactions in London so you need to cash
them in advance.

Eurocheques, available if you have a
European bank account, are guaranteed up
to a certain amount. When cashing them,
you will be asked to show your Eurocheque
card bearing your signature and registration
number as well as your passport or ID card.
Eurocheques are not as commonly used in
the UK as they are in continental Europe,
and many places refuse to accept them.
Some people may have never even seen
them before.

Buying Travellers Cheques The cost of
buying travellers cheques varies considerably, depending on the seller. Amex is often
the cheapest, charging 1% commission with
no minimum charge. Main post offices also
offer very competitive rates. The banks are
usually more expensive and often want
advance warning: NatWest charges 1%
commission for sterling travellers cheques,
with a £4 minimum charge; Lloyds TSB,
HSBC and Barclays all charge 1.5% commission, with a minimum charge of £3.

Lost or Stolen Travellers Cheques Keep
a record of the numbers of your cheques
and which cheques you have cashed, then if
they're lost or stolen you will be able to tell
the issuing agency exactly which cheques

are gone. Keep this list separate from the
cheques themselves.

As soon as you realise any cheques are
missing, you should contact the issuing
office or the nearest branch of the issuing agency. Amex (☎ 029-2066 6111) and
Thomas Cook (☎ 01733-318950), both of
which operate 24 hours a day, seven days
a week, can often arrange replacement
cheques within 24 hours.

ATMs Plastic cards make the perfect travelling companions – they're ideal for major
purchases and let you withdraw cash
from selected banks and automatic telling
machines (ATMs), God's greatest gift to
the travelling world since the backpack
was invented. ATMs are usually linked up
to international money systems like Cir-
rus, Maestro or Plus, so you can enter your
card, punch in your personal identification
number (PIN) and get instant cash. But
ATMs aren't fail-safe, especially if the card
was issued outside Europe, and it's safer
to go to a human teller. It can be a major
headache if an ATM swallows your card.

Debit cards, which you use to withdraw
money directly from your bank or savings
account, are widely linked internationally –
ask your bank at home for advice. Credit
cards, on the other hand, may not be hooked
up to ATM networks unless you specifically
ask your bank to do this for you and request
a PIN. You might also ask which UK banks'
ATMs will accept your particular card, and
whether you pay a fee to use them.

Credit Cards Visa, MasterCard, Amex
and Diners Club cards are widely accepted
in London, although small businesses like
B&Bs prefer cash. Businesses sometimes
make a charge for accepting payment by
credit card so this isn't always the most
economical way to go. You can get cash
advances using your Visa card at HSBC
and Barclays banks, or on your MasterCard
at NatWest, Lloyds TSB and Barclays. If
you have an Amex card, you can cash up
to £500 worth of personal cheques at Amex
offices in any seven-day period.

If you plan to use a credit card make sure you have a high-enough credit limit to cover major expenses like car hire or airline tickets. Alternatively, leave your card in credit when you start your travels.

If you're going to rely on plastic, go for two different cards – an Amex or Diners Club with a Visa or MasterCard. Better still, combine cards and travellers cheques so you have something to fall back on if an ATM swallows your card or the bank won't accept it.

Lost or Stolen Cards If a card is lost or stolen you must inform the police and the issuing company as soon as possible – otherwise you may have to pay for the purchases that the unspeakable thief has made using your card. Here are some numbers for cancelling your cards:

Amex	☎ 01273-689955
Diners Club	☎ 01252-516261
MasterCard	☎ 01702-362988
Visa	☎ 0800 895082

International Transfers If you instruct your bank back home to send you a draft, be sure you specify the bank and the branch to which you want your money directed, or ask your home bank to tell you where a suitable one is. The whole procedure will be easier if you've authorised someone back home to access your account.

Money sent to you by telegraphic transfer should reach you within a week; by mail, allow at least two weeks. When it arrives, it will most likely be converted into local currency – you can then take it as is or buy travellers cheques. The charge for this service is usually around £20.

You can also transfer money using Amex or Thomas Cook or by post office Money-Gram. Americans can also use Western Union (☎ 0800 833833), although it has fewer offices in London from which to collect and charges 10% plus commission.

Other Methods Personal cheques are still widely used in the UK – a group of diners will often write separate cheques to pay for their share of a meal – and are validated by a cheque guarantee card. Increasingly, retail outlets are linked to the Switch and Delta networks, which allow customers to use a debit card (deductions are made directly from your UK current account).

If you plan to stay a while in London, you may want to open a bank account, but it's no simple matter. Building societies tend to be more welcoming than banks and often have better interest rates. You'll need a permanent address in the UK, and it will smooth the way if you have a reference or introductory letter from your bank manager at home, *plus* bank statements for the previous year. Owning credit/charge cards also helps.

Make sure you look for a current account that pays interest (however tiny), gives you a cheque book and a cheque guarantee/debit card, and gives access to ATMs.

Moneychangers Changing your money is never a problem in London, with banks, *bureaux de change* and travel agencies all competing for your business. Just make sure you're getting the best deal possible. Be particularly careful using *bureaux de change*; they may seem to offer good exchange rates but frequently levy outrageous commissions (branches of Chequepoint charge up to 8% to cash a sterling travellers cheque) and fees. Check the exchange rate, the percentage commission and any minimum charge very carefully.

The exchange desks at the international airports charge less than most high-street banks and cash sterling travellers cheques for free; for other currencies they charge about 1.5% with a £3 minimum. They can also sell you up to £500 worth of most major currencies on the spot.

There are 24-hour exchange bureaus in Heathrow Terminals 1, 3 and 4. The one in Terminal 2 is open daily from 6 am to 11 pm. Thomas Cook has branches at Terminals 1, 3 and 4. There are 24-hour exchange desks in Gatwick's South and North Terminals and at Stansted; at Luton and the City airport *bureaux de change* open for arrivals and departures.

The main Amex office (Map 7; ☎ 7930 4411), 6 Haymarket SW1 (✚ Piccadilly Circus), is open for currency exchange Monday to Friday from 9 am to 5.30 pm (till 6 pm in July and August), on Saturday from 9 am to 4 pm (till 6 pm from June to September), and on Sunday and holidays from 10 am to 1 pm and 2 to 4 pm (till 5 pm June to September). Other services are available weekdays from 9 am to 5 or 5.30 pm and on Saturday from 9 am to noon (to pick up mail) and to 4 pm (for card services). Amex has offices scattered throughout London. The one at 96 Victoria St SW1, near Victoria train station, is open weekdays from 9 am to 5.30 pm and on Saturday to 4 pm.

The main Thomas Cook office (Map 6; ☎ 7853 6400), 30 St James's St SW1 (✚ Green Park), opens Monday to Friday from 9 am (10 am on Wednesday) to 5.30 pm, and on Saturday from 10 am to 4 pm. There are branches throughout central London. The one on the 1st floor of the Victoria Place shopping centre at Victoria station opens Monday to Saturday from 7.30 am to 8 pm and on Sunday from 8 am to 6 pm.

Security

Whichever way you decide to carry your funds, it makes sense to keep most of it out of easy reach of thieves in a money belt or something similar. It always makes sense to keep something like £50 apart from the rest of your cash for use in an emergency.

Take particular care in crowded places like the Underground and never leave wallets sticking out of trouser pockets or day-packs. Also watch out on buses and around popular attractions like the Tower of London and the big museums. Be warned that pickpocketing is a growing problem at Heathrow.

Costs

London may not be the world's most expensive city, but it certainly feels that way most of the time. Prices can be horrific, especially for anyone trying to stick to a tight budget. Indeed, as the writer William Shenstone remarked more than two centuries ago: 'Nothing is certain in London but expense'.

You will need to budget between £25 and £35 a day for bare survival in London. Dormitory accommodation alone will cost a minimum of £10 to £20 a night, a one-day Travelcard is £3.80, and drinks and the most basic sustenance will cost you at least £8 to £10, with any sightseeing or nightlife on top. There's not much point visiting if you can't enjoy some of the city's life, so if possible add another £15 a day.

Costs will be even higher if you choose to stay in a central B&B or hotel and eat restaurant meals. B&B rates start at around £25 per person and a very cheap restaurant meal costs £10. Add a couple of pints of beer (£4.50) and entry fees to a tourist attraction or club and you could easily spend £55 a day without being extravagant.

For advice on the best of London's free sightseeing, see the boxed text 'London's Top 10 Free Sights' at the end of the Things to See & Do chapter.

Tipping & Bargaining

Many restaurants now add a 'discretionary' service charge to your bill, but in places that don't you are expected to leave a 10 to 15% tip unless the service was unsatisfactory. Waiting staff are often paid derisory wages on the assumption that the money will be supplemented by tips. It's legal for restaurants to include a service charge in the bill, but this should be clearly advertised. You needn't add a further tip. And you never tip to have your pint pulled in a pub.

You can tip taxi drivers up to 10%, but most people round up to the nearest 50p or pound. It's less usual to tip minicab drivers as you have (or should have) already established the fare. If you take a boat trip on the Thames you'll find the guides and/or drivers importuning for a tip in return for their commentary. Whether you pay is up to you.

Bargaining is virtually unheard of in London, even at markets (though haggling is often in order at the Bermondsey antique market on Friday). It's fine to ask if there are discounts for students, young people or hostel members, and some 'negotiation' is also OK if you're buying a vehicle.

Discount ticket agencies can help keep theatre costs down – but beware of hidden commissions.

Discounts

Virtually all attractions offer discounts to some of the following groups:

- children aged under 12, 14 or 16
- people aged under 25 or 26 with youth cards
- students with ISIC cards (age limits may apply)
- people aged over 60 or 65
- disabled visitors
- family groups

Sometimes the discounts form an impressive list by the ticket office, at other times there may just be a separate price for 'concessions', in which case you'll need to ask if you're eligible. Throughout this book, where two prices are given (eg £7/3.50), the first is the regular adult price, the second is the usual concession (unless we're more specific – eg £7/3.50/2 for adults/seniors & students/children). Family tickets, allowing entry for two adults and usually two or three children, are also common.

Taxes & Refunds

Value-added tax (VAT) is a 17.5% sales tax levied on most goods and services except food and books. Restaurants must by law include VAT in their menu prices.

It's sometimes possible for visitors to claim a refund of VAT paid on goods – a considerable saving. You're eligible if you've spent fewer than 365 days out of the two years prior to making the purchase living in the UK, and if you're leaving the EU within three months of making the purchase.

Not all shops participate in the VAT refund scheme, called the Retail Export Scheme or Tax-Free Shopping, and different shops will have different minimum purchase conditions (normally around £75 in one shop). On request, participating shops will give you a special form (VAT 407). This form must be presented with the goods and receipts to customs when you depart (VAT-free goods can't be posted or shipped home). After customs has certified the form, it should be returned to the shop for a refund (minus an administration/handling fee), which takes eight to 10 weeks to come through.

Several companies offer a centralised refunding service to shops and participating shops carry a sign in their window (eg Tax-Free Shopping). You can avoid bank charges for cashing a sterling cheque by using a credit card for purchases and asking that the VAT refund be credited to your account. Cash refunds are sometimes available at major airports.

POST & COMMUNICATIONS
Post
If Londoners start to feel dispirited about the way that many things work (or rather don't work) in a city that often feels like it's held together with paste, string and tape, they need only think about the national postal service to get all cheered up. It's a cracker, with nine out of 10 letters with a 1st class stamp posted before noon delivered the following morning *anywhere* in the country! Try to get a letter across town in, say, New York and we'll see you in a week, pal.

For general postal inquiries ring ☎ 0845 722 3344.

Postal Rates Domestic 1st class mail is quicker and more expensive (26p per letter up to 60g or postcard) than 2nd class (19p).

Postcards and letters up to 20g cost a uniform 30p to anywhere in Europe; to the Americas and Australasia it's 44p up to 10g, 64p up to 20g. Packets and parcels must be taken to the post office for weighing.

Air-mail letters to the USA or Canada generally take three to five days; to Australia or New Zealand, allow five days to a week.

Poste Restante Unless you (or the person writing to you) specify otherwise, poste restante mail sent to London ends up at the Trafalgar Square post office (Map 7), 24-28 William IV St, London WC2N 4DL (⊖ Charing Cross). It's open weekdays from 8 am to 8 pm and on Saturday from

9 am to 8 pm. Mail will be held for four weeks; ID is required.

Amex offices will also hold clients' mail for free (see Moneychangers in the earlier Money section for addresses and opening hours) as will Drifters in Bayswater (see Australasian Clubs in the Useful Organisations section of this chapter).

Telephone
British Telecom's famous red phone-boxes survive in conservation areas only (notably Westminster) while some private phone companies have painted theirs black and installed them around Piccadilly and Charing Cross. More common these days are the glass cubicles with phones that accept coins, prepaid phonecards and/or credit cards.

All phones come with reasonably clear instructions. BT offers phonecards for £2, £5, £10 and £20 that are widely available from all sorts of retailers, including post offices and newsagents. A digital display on the telephone indicates how much credit is left on the card.

Some special phone codes worth knowing are:

☎ 0500 & 0800
    toll-free
☎ 0845
    local call rates apply
☎ 0870
    national call rate applies
☎ 0891 & 09064
    premium rates apply (49p per minute)

Calling London London's area code is 020 followed by an eight-digit number starting with 7 or 8. The old system, in which you had to dial 0171 or 0181 before a seven-digit number if you were outside the area concerned, remains in operation jointly with the new system only until 22 April 2000. To call London from abroad, dial your country's international access code, then 44 (the UK's country code), then 20 (dropping the initial 0) followed by the eight-digit phone number. If you're dialling London from elsewhere in the UK, dial 020 then the eight-digit number.

London's Bewildering Postcodes

And they say the French make life difficult for themselves ... Just take a look at the 20 *arrondissements* in Paris that spiral clockwise from the centre in such a lovely – and logical – fashion. If you've got a letter for someone in the 5th, you simply write 75005. And then take a look at London's codes on the map below. How on earth can SE23 border SE6? If there's a north (N), a west (W) and an east (E) why isn't there a south (S)? And what happened to the north-east (NE)?

When they were introduced in 1858, the postcodes were fairly clear, with all the compass points represented as well as an east and west central (EC & WC). But not long afterwards NE and S were merged with E, SE and SW and the problems began. The real convolution came during WWI when a numbering system was introduced for inexperienced sorters (regular employees were off fighting in 'the war to end all wars'). No 1 was the centre of each zone, but other numbers related to the alphabetical order of the postal districts' names. Thus anything starting with a letter near the beginning of the alphabet, like Chingford, would get a low number (E4), even though it was miles from the centre at Whitechapel, while Poplar, which borders Whitechapel, is E14.

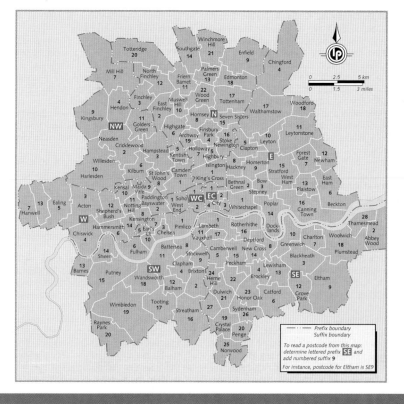

DOUG McKINLAY

Old-fashioned phone-boxes can still be seen in London, though not always in gangs of four.

Local & National Calls & Rates Local calls are charged by time alone; national calls are charged by both time and distance. Daytime rates apply from 8 am to 6 pm, Monday to Friday; the cheap rate applies from 6 pm to 8 am, Monday to Friday; and the cheap weekend rate applies from midnight Friday to midnight Sunday. The latter two rates offer substantial savings.

For directory inquiries/information call ☎ 192. These calls are free from public phones but cost 25p if you call from a private one. To get the operator call ☎ 100.

International Calls & Rates To call someone outside the UK dial 00, then the country code, the area code (you usually drop the initial zero if there is one) and the number. International direct dialling (IDD) calls to almost anywhere in the world can be made from almost all public telephones.

To make a reverse-charge (collect) call, dial ☎ 155 for the international operator. Direct dialling is cheaper. For international directory inquiries dial ☎ 153 (50p from private phones).

For most countries (including Europe, the USA and Canada) it's cheaper to phone overseas between 8 pm and 8 am Monday to Friday and at weekends; for Australia and New Zealand, however, it's cheapest from 2.30 to 7.30 pm and from midnight to 7 am every day. The savings are considerable.

The private company CallShop offers cheaper international calls than BT. You can find them open from 9 am to 12.30 am at 181a Earl's Court Rd SW5 (Map 9; ☎ 7390 4549; ⊖ Earl's Court) and till midnight at 189 Edgware Rd W2 (Map 5; ☎ 7390 4075; ⊖ Edgware Road). In CallShops you phone from a metered booth and then pay the bill.

Lonely Planet's eKno Communication Card is aimed specifically at travellers and provides cheap international calls, a range of messaging services and free email – you're usually better off with a local card for local calls. To join visit www.ekno.lonelyplanet.com on the Web or call ☎ 0800 376 1704 from London. Once you've joined, dial ☎ 0800 376 1705 to use eKno from the UK.

It's also possible to undercut BT international call rates by buying a special card (usually denominated £5, £10 or £20) with a PIN that you use from any phone, even a home phone, by dialling a special access number. There are dozens of cards available – with sci-fi names like Alpha, Omega, Phone Com, Climax, Swiftlink and America First – available from newsagents and grocers. To decide which is best you really have to compare the rate each offers for the particular country you want – posters with the rates of the various companies are often displayed in shop doors or windows.

Emergencies In an emergency phone ☎ 999 (toll-free) for the fire service, the police or an ambulance.

Fax & Telemessage
CallShop (see International Calls & Rates on this page) is the best place for sending or receiving faxes. It charges for the connection and time plus 99p to send a fax and 25p a page to receive one. You can also send and receive faxes at many cybercafés, including Cyberg@te and Global Talk (see the Email & Internet Access section on the next page).

If you need to get a message somewhere in the UK or overseas urgently, call ☎ 0800 190190 to send a telemessage. It costs £8.99 for up to 50 words in the UK, delivered by post the following day.

FACTS FOR THE VISITOR

Email & Internet Access

Most hotels and even some pubs are geared up for Internet access. Among the hostels that have terminals for the use of their guests are the Museum Inn and the Generator in Bloomsbury and the Hyde Park in Bayswater (see Budget in the Places to Stay chapter).

If you can't access the Internet from where you're staying, London is chock-a-block with cybercafés. EasyEverything, a division of the no-frills airline easyJet, has opened the first of what it says will be many 'Internet shops' across London just opposite Victoria train station at 12-14 Wilton Rd SW1 (Map 10; ☎ 7233 8456; ✪ Victoria). It is open 24 hours and access costs just £1 per hour.

Here are some independent cybercafés:

Buzz Bar
(Map 5; ☎ 7460 4906, email buzzbar@ hotmail.com) 95 Portobello Rd W11 (✪ Notting Hill Gate). Upstairs from the Portobello Gold Hotel (see B&Bs, Guesthouses & Hotels in the Places to Stay chapter), Buzz Bar has six terminals available (£6 per hour) Monday to Saturday from 10 am to 7 pm. Web site: www .buzzbar.co.uk.
Cyberg@te
(Map 4; ☎ 7387 3810, email cybergate@ c-gate.com) 3 Leigh St WC1 (✪ Russell Square). Computer access costs £1.50/1.20 per 15 minutes for adults/students. It's open Monday to Saturday from 9 am to 9 pm and on Sunday noon to 5 pm. Web site: www.c-gate .com.
Cyberia
(Map 6; ☎ 7681 4224, email cyberia@ easynet.co.uk) 39 Whitfield St W1 (✪ Goodge Street). The first Internet café in London, Cyberia has full Internet access with 15 terminals in the café (£3 per 30 minutes) and 12 in the training room. Weekday training costs £30 for two hours. It's open weekdays from 10 am to 8 pm and at weekends from 11 am to 7 pm (6 pm on Sunday). Web site: www.cyberiacafe .net.
Global Talk
(Map 9; ☎ 7584 1277) 42-44 Thurloe St 3W7 (✪ South Kensington). Internet access costs £3 per hour. It's open weekdays from 8.30 am to 11.30 pm and at weekends from 9.30 am.

Vibe Bar
(Map 8; ☎ 7247 3479) Truman Brewery, 91 Brick Lane E1 (✪ Shoreditch or Aldgate East). Four terminals are available at no charge to customers. It's open Monday to Saturday from 11 am to 11 pm and on Sunday from noon. Web site: www.vibe-bar.co.uk.
Webshack
(Map 7; ☎ 7439 8000, email webmaster@ webshack-cafe.com) 15 Dean St W1 (✪ Tottenham Court Road). This is the most central of the Internet cafés with 20 terminals (£3/5 per 30/60 minutes). It's open Monday to Saturday from 10.30 am to midnight and on Sunday from 1 to 8 pm. Web site: www .webshack-cafe.com.

INTERNET RESOURCES

Britain is second only to the USA in its number of Web sites, and there are lots of sites of interest to travellers. An increasing number of attractions, hotels and transport companies have their own sites, and we have listed them in this book when they would be of use to travellers.

Big Brother is listening to you: the British Telecom Tower looming over Fitzrovia.

FACTS FOR THE VISITOR

JULIET COOMBE

There's no better place to start your Web explorations than the Lonely Planet Web site at www.lonelyplanet.com. Here you'll find summaries on travelling to most places on earth, postcards from other travellers and the Thorn Tree bulletin board, where you can ask questions before you go or dispense advice when you get back. You can also find travel news and updates to many of our most popular guidebooks, and the sub-WWWay section links you to the most useful travel resources elsewhere on the Web.

Although accurate at the time of going to press, the Web site addresses given in this book may change. Either use the Lonely Planet site for hyperlinks or a good search engine to check the latest details. Lycos is at www.lycos.com and Yahoo at www.yahoo.com.

BOOKS

London has innumerable good book and map shops (see Books in the Shopping chapter). In addition, the YHA Adventure Shop (Map 7; ☎ 7836 8541), 14 Southampton St WC2 (☻ Covent Garden), the Britain Visitor Centre and the TIC at Victoria train station (see Tourist Offices earlier in this chapter) all stock a wide range of titles.

Most books are published in different editions by different publishers in different countries. As a result, a book might be a rarity in one country while it's readily available in another. Fortunately, bookshops and libraries search by title or author, so your local bookshop or library is best placed to advise you on the availability of the following recommendations.

Lonely Planet

Lonely Planet also publishes *Britain*, *Walking in Britain*, *Scotland* and *Edinburgh*, which provide information for those planning to travel around the rest of the island. *Cycling Britain* is the perfect companion for those wanting to see the island by bike. Lonely Planet's *Ireland* guide covers Northern Ireland as well as the Irish Republic. Those who want to get to grips with British English – Cockney in particular – should

get hold of the Lonely Planet *British phrasebook*. *Out to Eat – London* describes an enormous selection of London's best eateries, while the *London City Guide* video provides a visual complement to this book.

Guidebooks

Guides to London cover every aspect and specialist interest; we can provide just a brief sampling.

Culture vultures who want to find out more about the city's art and architecture should look for the *Blue Guide London* by Ylva French or Malcolm Rogers' *Blue Guide Museums & Galleries of London*. *A Guide to the Architecture of London* by Edward Jones & Christopher Woodward is a seminal, complete work with fine illustrations, but using the computer-manual-style index is frustrating. If you want to get to know London better than most Londoners, you might browse through a copy of *The London Encyclopaedia* by Ben Wienreb & Christopher Hibbert. But don't even *think* of taking a copy along with you; it's got 1072 pages and weighs more than your average infant.

For hidden corners of the capital and a host of interesting trivia, look for anything by Geoffrey Fletcher (eg *The London Nobody Knows*), whose books often come with pleasing sketches of the sights. Sadly, many of Fletcher's other works are now out of print. Visitors from Canada and the USA should look out for *American Walks in London* by the prolific Richard Tames, which describes 10 itineraries covering places with links to North America.

London for Free by Brian Butler is the cheapskate's bible though *Harden's London for Free* gives Butler a run for his, ah, money. *Cheap Eats in London* by Sandra Gustafson lists more than 170 budget pubs, restaurants, wine bars and tea rooms.

People travelling with children can turn to a number of titles, including *In and Around London for Kids* by Judith Milling and *Help! I've Got Kids – London Edition* by Sheila Harries & Pauline Dale. To keep the kids amused, *I-Spy London* (I-Spy Books) comes with boxes to tick off the sights.

Gay London by Will McLoughlin takes up where the simple (and often confusing) listings of the *Spartacus International Gay Guide* leave off.

For noncarnivores, there's Alex Bourke's *Vegetarian London* from Cruelty Free Living, as political as it is useful. Travellers who keep kosher should get a hold of a copy of *The Real Jewish Food Guide* published by the London Beth Din Kashrut Division.

Travel

London doesn't seem to have inspired too many modern-day travel writers to set pen to paper though they were pretty thick on the ground in the last century with the likes of Mark Twain and others (see Literature under Arts in the Facts about London chapter). Bill Bryson's exploits in the capital are as witty and quirky as those elsewhere in Britain in his wonderful best seller, *Notes from a Small Island*.

London, England is an irreverent tour of 'cool London' by Derek Hammond, journalist and ex-punk musician. It paints an excellent portrait of the capital on the cusp of the new millennium. Iain Sinclair's *Lights Out for the Territory*, subtitled 'Nine Excursions in the Secret History of London', is another kettle of fish: dark, brooding and as difficult to put down once you've got going as it is to get into in the first place.

History & Politics

A *Traveller's History of London* by Richard Tames is an excellent and highly readable introduction to London's history – from Roman Londinium to the Millennium Dome. Christopher Hibbert's *London: The Biography of a City* is a longer social history of the British capital with excellent illustrations and colour plates. To get to grips with London's complicated history in potboiler fictional form, look out for *London* by Edward Rutherford.

It's a bit of a paperweight, but anyone interested in 17th-century London (eg the Great Fire and all the bawdy goings-on) should try battling through *Samuel Pepys' Diary*. Written in shorthand between 1660 and 1669, it contains enough references to women other than his wife to confirm that London was lewder and less inhibited during the Restoration than it is even today. It comes in several chunky volumes; you might be more successful wading through *The Concise Pepys* (Wordsworth Editions), though this still comes in at 800 pages. *Restoration London* by Liza Picard, a social history of the same decade, covers a lot more ground – from cooking, shopping and laundry to medicine, crime and sex.

Longitude by Dava Sobel tells the riveting story of John Harrison, an 18th-century clockmaker who established longitude and thus helped to keep sailors on course. It may sound something of a niche subject but, hey, it all happened in Greenwich.

To discover how London turned out to be the cultural melting pot that it is today, look out for *The Peopling of London* by Nick Merriman, which describes 15,000 years of settlement from overseas. It's published by the Museum of London.

For a readable account of where Britain is economically, try *The State We're In*, *Observer* editor Will Hutton's analysis of Britain's position at the close of the 20th century, or its sequel *The State to Come*.

NEWSPAPERS & MAGAZINES
Newspapers

'I read the news today, oh boy ...' Most major newspapers in the UK are national though many are published outside London. The only daily that is well and truly a Londoner is the *Evening Standard*, a widely read afternoon tabloid that can vacillate from being right-wing to radical (usually when matters directly affecting London are concerned) from page to page and week to week. Its restaurant reviews (particularly those by the incomparable Fay Maschler) are worth reading and its entertainment supplement *Hot Tickets*, published on Thursday, can often be a better and more eclectic source of information than *Time Out*. There is also a précis of the *Evening Standard* called *Metro*, which is handed out at tube station entrances; it's surprisingly good for a freebie.

At the very bottom end of the newspaper market in terms of content – though tops in circulation – are the *Sun*, *Mirror*, *Daily Star* and *Sport* tabloids. The middle-level *Daily Mail* and *Daily Express* tabloids are Conservative bastions.

Of the broadsheets, the *Telegraph* far outsells its rivals. It's sometimes thought of as an old-fogeyish, Tory paper but it nonetheless features excellent writing and world coverage. The *Times* is still conservative and influential and has good travel pages. The *Independent* tries to live up to its name but is struggling to stay afloat. It is drier than an old bone in the Sahara and too politically correct for words. The mildly left-wing *Guardian* is read by the so-called chattering classes (the liberal middle class, the 'champagne socialists' etc). Its review of the world media called *The Editor*, which comes out as a supplement every Friday, is required reading for anyone who wants to know what's happening outside Blighty. The *Guide* entertainment supplement with Saturday's *Guardian* is also worthwhile. The business-oriented *Financial Times* has a great travel section in its weekend edition.

Read all about it: both the *Evening Standard* and the *Big Issue* are hard to avoid in London.

ED HILLYER

The Sunday papers are an institution in the UK, but they are often so full of trashy gossip, fashion supplements and mean-spirited diatribes directed at government officials, foreigners (especially the French) and anyone who's 'made it' as to rankle the least flappable of readers. The *Sunday Times* must destroy at least one rainforest per issue, but most of it can be tossed in the recycling bin on purchase. The Sunday-only *Observer* is similar in tone and style to the *Guardian*, which owns it. In fact, almost every daily has a Sunday stablemate, which usually – but not always – shares its political views.

You can also buy the Paris-based *International Herald Tribune*, arguably the best brief source of international news available, and many foreign-language papers in central London. For a particularly good selection, try the newspaper stands in the Victoria Place shopping centre at Victoria train station, along Charing Cross Rd, in Old Compton St and along Queensway.

Magazines

Time Out (£1.80), the London events magazine published every Wednesday (though available Tuesday) and covering a week of events to the following Wednesday, is a very complete listing of what's on and where. The same company publishes the *Time Out Eating & Drinking Guide* (£9), which lists almost 2000 restaurants, cafés and gastropubs, and the *Time Out Pubs & Bars Guide* (£5.99), with more than 1000 listings plus commentary. They're all sold in bookshops as well as from newspaper kiosks.

London sells an astonishing range of magazines. Good places to stock up are the kiosks in the main-line stations where *Time* and *Newsweek* are also available.

The weekly freebies *TNT Magazine*, *Traveller*, *Southern Cross* and *SA Times* have Australasian and South African news and sports results, but are invaluable for any budget traveller, with entertainment listings, excellent travel sections and useful classifieds covering jobs, cheap tickets, shipping services and accommodation. They can be picked up outside tube stations, especially in Earl's Court, Notting Hill and Bayswater. *TNT Magazine* is the glossiest and most comprehensive; ring ☎ 7373 3377 for the nearest distribution point to you.

Loot (£1.30), which appears five times a week, is a paper made up of classified ads that are placed free by sellers. You can find everything from kitchen sinks to cars, as well as an extensive selection of flat and house-share ads. Also worth considering, if you're planning to do some *serious* shopping, is the comprehensive *Time Out Guide to Shopping & Services* (£7).

RADIO & TV
Radio
London's radio stations include Capital FM (95.8kHz FM), the commercial equivalent of the BBC's Radio 1 and the most popular pop station in the city, and Capital Gold (1548kHz AM), which plays oldies from the 60s, 70s and early 80s. BBC GLR (94.9kHz FM) is a talk station with a London bias. Xfm on 104.9kHz FM bills itself as an alternative radio station and plays indie music.

There are many other commercial radio stations, sometimes offering local news and chat alongside the music. Virgin (105.8kHz FM) is a pop station while Choice FM (96.9kHz FM) and Kiss FM (100kHz FM) are the soul and dance stations respectively. Classic FM (100.9kHz FM) does classical music with commercials, and the excellent Jazzfm (102.2kHz FM) caters for jazz and blues aficionados. The much hyped Talk Radio (1053kHz AM) brings tabloid news values to the radio dial; LBC (1152kHz AM) is a less sensationalist talk channel. Magic Fm (105.4kHz FM) is as middle-of-the-road as you'll ever hear. News Direct (97.3kHz FM) is an all-news station with full reports every 20 minutes.

While in London you'll be able to pick up all the national BBC services. Radio 1 (98.8kHz FM), the main public pop/indie music station, has undergone a revival after some years in the doldrums. At the same time, Radio 2 (89.1kHz FM) has broadened its outlook and now plays gooey 60s, 70s and 80s stuff alongside even older tracks.

Four-ward thinking: Channel 4 prides itself on its innovative programme-making.

JULIET COOMBE

Radio 3 (91.3kHz FM) sticks with classical music and plays, while Radio 4 (720kHz AM, 93.5kHz FM) offers a mixture of drama, news, current affairs and talk; its *Today* programme (Monday to Friday from 6 to 9 am, on Saturday from 7 am) is particularly popular. Radio 5 Live (693kHz AM), sometimes known as 'Radio Bloke', provides a mix of sport and current affairs.

The BBC World Service (648kHz AM) offers brilliant news coverage and quirky bits and pieces from around the globe.

TV
Britain still turns out some of the world's best TV, padding out the decent home-grown output with American imports, Australian soaps, and inept sitcoms and trashy chat and game shows of its own. There are five regular TV channels. BBC1 and BBC2 are publicly funded by a TV licensing system and don't carry advertising; ITV, Channel 4 and Channel 5 are commercial channels and do. These are now competing with the satellite channels of Rupert Murdoch's BSkyB – which offers a variety of channels but mostly churns out rubbish – and assorted cable channels.

VIDEO SYSTEMS

The UK, like most of Europe, uses the PAL system, which is incompatible with the American and Japanese NTSC system. Since many tourist attractions sell both PAL and NTSC videos as souvenirs, make sure you select the right one.

PHOTOGRAPHY & VIDEO
Film & Equipment

Although print film is widely available, slide film can be more elusive; if there's no specialist photographic shop around, Boots, the chemist (drugstore) chain, is likely to have what you want. At Jessop Photo Centres, which offer a discount if you buy 10 rolls of film at once, a roll of 36-exposure print film costs just £2.69 for ISO 100 to £3.49 for ISO 400. With slide film it's usually cheapest to go for process-inclusive versions; at Jessop 36-exposure slide film costs from £5.79 for ISO 100 to £6.59 for ISO 400. The most central Jessop branch is at 63-69 New Oxford St WC1 (Map 7; ☎ 7240 6077; ⊖ Tottenham Court Road).

Technical Tips

With dull, overcast conditions common in London, high-speed film (ISO 200 or 400) is the way to go. In summer, the best times of day for photography are usually early in the morning and late in the afternoon when the sun's glare has passed.

Restrictions

Many tourist attractions either charge for taking photos or prohibit it altogether. Use of a flash is frequently banned to protect light-sensitive paintings and fabrics. Video cameras are sometimes forbidden because of the inconvenience they can cause to other visitors.

Airport Security

You will have to put your camera and film through the X-ray machine at all airports in the UK. The machines are supposed to be film-safe, but you may feel happier putting exposed films in a protective lead-lined bag.

TIME

A century ago the sun never set on the British Empire, so the British could be forgiven for thinking that London (or more precisely Greenwich) was the centre of the universe. Greenwich is still the location for the prime meridian, which divides the world into eastern and western hemispheres.

Wherever you are in the world, the time on your watch is measured in relation to the time at Greenwich – Greenwich Mean Time (GMT) – although strictly speaking GMT is used only in air and sea navigation and is otherwise referred to as universal time coordinated (UTC).

British Summer Time, the UK's form of daylight-saving time, muddies the water so that even London is ahead of GMT from late March to late October. To give you an idea, San Francisco is usually eight hours and New York five hours behind GMT, while Sydney is 10 hours ahead of GMT. Phone the international operator on ☎ 155 to find out the exact difference.

ELECTRICITY

The standard voltage throughout Britain is 230/240V AC, 50Hz. Plugs have three square pins and adapters to fit European-style plugs are widely available.

WEIGHTS & MEASURES

In theory, the UK has now embraced the metric system although nonmetric imperial equivalents are likely to be used by much of the population for some time to come. Distances continue to be given in miles, yards, feet and inches though most liquids – apart from milk and beer (which come in half-pints and pints) – are now sold in litres. In this book we use the metric system but give distances in both kilometres and miles to make reading local maps and signposts easier. For conversion tables, see the inside back cover.

LAUNDRY

'Time weighs heavily in a laundrette', as the saying goes, but you're going to have to face washing your gear at some stage. Many

At the Royal Observatory in Greenwich you can stand with one foot either side of the meridian.

hostels and some hotels have self-service washing machines and dryers, and virtually every high street has its own laundrette – with rare exceptions, a disheartening place to spend much time. The average cost for a single load is £1.60 for washing and from 60p to £1 for drying. Hours vary but are usually daily from 7 or 8 am to 8 or 9 pm.

The following is a selected list of laundrettes that may be within striking distance of your hotel or hostel:

Bloomsbury
    Red & White Laundrette, 78 Marchmont St WC1 (Map 4)
    Red & White Laundrette, 88 Cleveland St WC1 (Map 6)
Chelsea, South Kensington & Earl's Court (Map 9)
    Bendix, 395 King's Rd SW3
    Bubbles, 113 Earl's Court Rd SW5
    Wash & Dry, 34 Harrington Rd SW7

Kensington (Map 5)
    Laundrette Centre, 116 Gloucester Rd W8
Bayswater & Notting Hill (Map 5)
    Laundrette Centre, 5 Porchester Rd W2
    Notting Hill Laundrette, 12 Notting Hill Gate W11
    Sandwich Bar Laundrette, 28 Craven Terrace W2
Camden (Map 3)
    Forco, 60 Parkway NW1
Hampstead (Map 11)
    Hampstead Laundrette, South End Rd NW3

TOILETS

Although many toilets in central London are still pretty grim, those at main train stations, bus terminals and attractions are generally good and usually have facilities for disabled people and those with young children. At the train and bus stations you usually have to pay 20p to use the facilities, which is not much but irksome when you consider how much rail fares cost. You also have to pay to use the self-cleaning concrete pods in places like Leicester Square (and, yes, they do open automatically after a set amount of time, so no hanky-panky – or make it snappy).

In theory it's an offence to urinate in the streets (and men could be arrested for indecent exposure). However, as everywhere, those who've passed the evening in the pub happily make use of alleyways, thereby rendering them unpleasant for others.

Many disabled toilets can only be opened with a special key obtainable from the tourist offices or by sending a cheque or postal order for £2.50 to RADAR (see the Disabled Travellers section later in this chapter), together with a brief statement of your disability.

LEFT LUGGAGE

All the train stations and Victoria Coach Station (see the Getting There & Away chapter) have left-luggage offices or lockers, as do the airports (see Getting Around). They cost between £2 and £6 a day, depending on the size of the bag or locker. For some time the left-luggage facilities at the main bus and train stations were closed for security reasons, but at the time of writing they were all operating normally. Be advised that the situation can change at short notice.

HEALTH

Aside from the threats posed by the wild nightlife and widely available liquids, herbs and chemical substances, London presents no major health risks. Care about what you eat and drink and good personal hygiene should see you through. Serious problems are unlikely, but mild stomach upsets as a result of a change in diet are not unknown.

Tap water is always safe (though with a very high lime content) so there's no need to pay the high prices restaurants ask for bottled water. No jabs are needed to visit Britain. Whether you eat British beef after the bovine spongiform encephalopathy (BSE or 'mad cow disease') scare is up to you, but you can read all about it in Jennifer Cooke's award-winning *Cannibals, Cows & the CJD Catastrophe*.

Medical Services

Reciprocal arrangements with the UK allow residents of Australia, New Zealand and several other countries to receive free emergency medical treatment and subsidised dental care through the National Health Service (NHS); they can use hospital emergency departments, GPs and dentists (check the Yellow Pages phone directory). Long-term visitors with the proper documentation will receive care under the NHS by registering with a specific practice near where they live. Again check the phone book for one close to you. EU nationals can obtain free emergency treatment on presentation of an E111 form, validated in their home country.

Travel insurance, however, is advisable as it offers greater flexibility over where and how you're treated and covers expenses for an ambulance and repatriation that won't be picked up by the NHS (see the Travel Insurance section under Documents earlier in this chapter). Regardless of nationality, anyone will receive free emergency treatment if it's a simple matter like bandaging a cut.

For the address of a local doctor or hospital, look in the phone book or phone ☎ 100 (toll-free). The following hospitals have 24-hour accident and emergency departments:

Charing Cross Hospital
(Map 2; ☎ 8383 0000) Fulham Palace Rd W6
(⊖ Hammersmith)
Guy's Hospital
(Map 8; ☎ 7955 5000) St Thomas St SE1
(⊖ London Bridge)
Homerton Hospital
(Map 2; ☎ 8919 5555) Homerton Row E9
(Homerton station)
Royal Free Hospital
(Map 11; ☎ 7794 0500) Pond St NW3
(⊖ Belsize Park)
Royal London Hospital
(Map 8; ☎ 7377 7000) Whitechapel Rd E1
(⊖ Whitechapel)
University College Hospital
(Map 3; ☎ 7387 9300) Grafton Way WC1
(⊖ Euston Square)

Dental Services

To find an emergency dentist phone the Dental Emergency Care Service on ☎ 7955

2186 weekdays between 8.45 am and 3.30 pm or call into Eastman Dental Hospital (Map 4; ☎ 7915 1000), 256 Gray's Inn Rd WC1 (⊖ King's Cross).

Chemists (Pharmacies)

Chemists can advise on minor ailments such as sore throats, coughs and earache. There's always one local chemist that's open 24 hours; other chemists should display details in their window or doorway, or look in a local newspaper. Since all medication is readily available either over the counter or on prescription there's no need to stock up.

Immunisation Services

Several travel agencies offer immunisation services but at very different prices. Trailfinders (☎ 7938 3999) has a clinic at 194 Kensington High St W8 with a full range of travel vaccines available. The International Medical Centre (☎ 7259 2180) has an immunisation clinic at Top Deck Travel (see Visas in the Documents section) while Nomad (☎ 8889 7014), 3-4 Wellington Terrace, Turnpike Lane N8 (⊖ Turnpike Lane), sells travel equipment and medical kits and gives immunisations on Thursday and Saturday evenings. They'll jab you during the week at their immunisation centre at STA Travel at 40 Bernard St WC1.

HIV/AIDS Organisations

Help and support are available from the National AIDS Helpline (☎ 0800 567123). The Terrence Higgins Trust (Map 6; ☎ 7831 0330), 52-54 Gray's Inn Rd WC1 (⊖ Chancery Lane), is another useful source of advice. Body Positive (☎ 0800 616212) offers support to people who are HIV-positive.

WOMEN TRAVELLERS

In general, London is a fairly laid-back place, and you're unlikely to have too many problems provided you take the usual big-city precautions.

Attitudes Towards Women

The occasional wolf-whistle and unwelcome body contact on the tube aside, women will find the city reasonably enlightened. There's nothing to stop women going into pubs alone, although this is unlikely to be a comfortable experience even in central London.

Safety Precautions

Solo women travellers should have few problems, although common-sense caution should be observed, especially at night. It's particularly unwise to get into an Underground carriage with no one else in it or with just one or two men, and there are a few tube stations, especially on the far reaches of the Northern Line, where you won't feel comfortable late at night. (The government has proposed special women-only carriages on the Underground and main-line trains.) The same goes for some of the main-line stations in the south (such as Lambeth) and south-east (like Bromley), which may well be unstaffed and look pretty grim. In such cases you should hang the expense and take a black taxi.

Condoms are now often sold in women's toilets as well as men's. Otherwise, all chemists and many service stations stock them. The contraceptive pill is only available on prescription in the UK, as is the 'morning-after' pill (actually effective for up to 72 hours after unprotected sex).

Information & Organisations

The Well Women Centre (Map 6; ☎ 7388 0662), Marie Stopes House, 108 Whitfield St W1 (⊖ Warren Street), is the place to go for advice on contraception and pregnancy. It's open Monday to Saturday from 9 am to 5 pm (till 8 pm on Tuesday and Wednesday).

The London Rape Crisis Centre phone line (☎ 7837 1600) is open daily from 6 to 10 pm (at weekends from 10 am).

GAY & LESBIAN TRAVELLERS

London has a flourishing gay and lesbian scene. Certainly it's possible for people to acknowledge their homosexuality in a way that would have been unimaginable two decades ago; the current government has several openly gay MPs, and in a bid to attract more 'pink pound' tourists the BTA recently launched a massive advertising campaign overseas under the slogan 'You don't know the half of it'.

Having said that, pockets of out-and-out hostility remain – you only need read the scurrilous tabloids to realise the limits of toleration – and overt displays of affection are not necessarily wise away from acknowledged gay venues and areas like Soho (and Old Compton St in particular).

The battle by the Labour government to lower the homosexual age of consent from 18 to 16, in line with that for heterosexuals, continued throughout 1999, with the House of Lords vetoing the measure twice. At the time of writing, the government was about to introduce the bill for the third time. When it passes it will automatically go to the Queen for her assent.

For more information on the homosexual scene in London, see Gay & Lesbian London in the Entertainment chapter.

Information & Organisations

To find out what's going on in London pick up a free listings magazine like the *Pink Paper* or *Boyz*, or the *Gay Times* (£2.50), which also has listings. *Diva* (£2) is for lesbians. They're all available at Gay's The Word bookshop (Map 4; ☎ 7278 7654), 66 Marchmont St WC1 (✪ Russell Square), and the freebies at most gay bars, clubs and saunas.

Another useful source of information is the 24-hour Lesbian & Gay Switchboard (☎ 7837 7324), which can help with most inquiries, general and specific. London Lesbian Line (☎ 7251 6911) offers similar help but only on Monday and Friday from 2 to 10 pm and Tuesday to Thursday from 7 to 10 pm.

DISABLED TRAVELLERS

For many disabled travellers, London is an odd mix of user-friendliness and downright disinterest. These days new hotels and modern tourist attractions are usually accessible by wheelchair, but many B&Bs and guesthouses are in hard-to-adapt older buildings. This means that travellers who have mobility problems may end up having to pay more for accommodation than those who don't.

It's a similar story with public transport. Some newer trains and buses have steps that lower for easier access (eg the Stationlink buses that follow a similar route to that of the Circle Line and are described in the Getting Around chapter), but it's always wise to check before setting out. London Transport's Unit for Disabled Passengers (☎ 7918 3312) can give you detailed advice and it publishes *Access to the Underground*, which indicates which stations have ramps and lifts (all DLR stations do). To receive a copy ahead of your visit write to the London Transport Unit for Disabled Passengers, 172 Buckingham Palace Rd, London SW1 9TN.

Many ticket offices, banks and so on are fitted with hearing loops to assist the hearing-impaired; look for the ear symbol.

The LTB publishes a newsletter called *London for All*; see Tourist Information Centres under Tourist Offices for the address to write to or pick up a copy at any TIC. *Access in London* by Gordon Couch, William Forrester & Justin Irwin (Quiller Press; £7.95) is a comprehensive guide for disabled people in London and is required reading for visitors. General information on wheelchair access to theatres, cinemas and other cultural venues is also available from Artsline (☎ 7388 2227) weekdays between 9.30 am and 5.30 pm.

Information & Organisations

The Royal Association for Disability and Rehabilitation (RADAR) stocks *Access in London* (see the previous paragraph). Contact RADAR (☎ 7250 3222) at Unit 12, City Forum, 250 City Rd, London EC1V 8AF.

The Holiday Care Service (☎ 01293-774535), 2nd floor, Imperial Buildings, Victoria Rd, Horley, Surrey RH6 7PZ, publishes *A Guide to Accessible Accommodation and Travel* for Britain (£5.95) and can offer general advice.

A Disabled Person's Railcard (£14) is available, providing discounts on fares of 34%, but it isn't easy to get hold of. First you must fill out a form published in a booklet available from the Railcards Office, TRMC CP 328, 3rd floor, The Podium, 1 Eversholt St, London NW1 1DN. You then post it to the Disabled Person's Railcard Office, PO Box 1YT, Newcastle-upon-Tyne NE99 1YT. It can take up to three weeks to process so apply well in advance.

SENIOR TRAVELLERS

Senior citizens are entitled to discounts on things like public transport and museum admission fees, provided they show proof of their age. Sometimes they need a special pass. The minimum qualifying age is generally 60 to 65 for men, 55 to 65 for women. It's always worth asking even if you can't see a discount listed.

In your home country, there may be a lower age entitling you to special travel packages and discounts (on car hire, for instance) through organisations and travel agencies that cater for senior travellers. Start hunting at your local senior citizens advice bureau.

LONDON FOR CHILDREN

Although London's crowds, traffic and pollution might be off-putting to some parents, the city is jam-packed with things to entertain the young 'uns. The following attractions are particularly recommended for children:

- Battersea Park Children's Zoo
- Bethnal Green Museum of Childhood
- Brass Rubbing Centre, Church of St Martin-in-the-Fields
- *Cutty Sark* clipper ship
- HMS *Belfast* cruiser
- Horniman Museum
- Imperial War Museum
- London Aquarium
- London Dungeon (not for very young children)
- London IMAX Cinema
- London Zoo
- Madame Tussaud's & Planetarium
- National Maritime Museum (especially the All Hands exhibit)
- Natural History Museum (especially the Earthquake exhibit and the dinosaur galleries)
- Pepsi Trocadero & Segaworld
- Pollock's Toy Museum
- Science Museum (Garden and Things galleries for those aged three to 11)
- Tower of London (for older children)

Attack of the Stuffed Octopus – but don't worry, he likes kids.

For details, prices and opening hours, see the Things to See & Do chapter. *Time Out* issues a bimonthly supplement, *Kids Out* (£2), with all sorts of information for parents in search of something to entertain their kids. It's available at newsstands throughout London.

London has several theatres specially aimed at children:

Little Angel Theatre
(Map 4; ☎ 7226 1787) 14 Dagmar Passage N1 (⊖ Angel)
Polka Theatre for Children
(☎ 8543 4888) 240 The Broadway SW19 (⊖ South Wimbledon or Wimbledon)
Unicorn Theatre for Children
(Map 2; ☎ 7609 1800) Pleasance Theatre, Carpenter's Mews, North Rd N7 (⊖ Caledonian Road)

To see some farm animals doing their stuff see the boxed text 'Old MacDonald's London Farms' in the Flora & Fauna section of the Facts about London chapter.

FACTS FOR THE VISITOR

CHARLOTTE HINDLE

USEFUL ORGANISATIONS

Membership of English Heritage (EH) and the National Trust (NT) are worth considering if you plan to travel a lot around the UK and are interested in stately homes and other historical buildings. Both are nonprofit organisations dedicated to the preservation of the environment, and both care for hundreds of spectacular sites. If you're just sticking to London, however, they're of limited use.

National Trust
  (☎ 8315 1111) Most NT properties cost nonmembers up to £5.50 to enter. Membership for those aged over/under 26 is £29/14.50; membership for a couple is £50 and for a family £56. It provides free entry to all the NT's English, Welsh and Northern Irish properties as well as an excellent guidebook and map. You can join at most major sites. There are reciprocal arrangements with the National Trust organisations in Scotland, Australia, New Zealand and Canada and the Royal Oak Foundation in the USA. Web site: www.nationaltrust.org.uk.
English Heritage
  (☎ 7973 3434) EH properties cost nonmembers between £1.50 and £6 to visit. Adult membership is £26, a couple pays £42.50 and family membership is £45.50. Those aged under 16 pay £11; it's £16 for those aged 16 to 20. Membership gives free entry to all EH properties, half-price entry to Historic Scotland and CADW (Wales) properties during the first year (free with membership thereafter), and an excellent guidebook and map. Web site: www.english-heritage.org.uk.
Great British Heritage Pass
  This pass gives you access to almost 600 NT, EH and expensive private properties. A seven-day pass costs £30, 15 days is £42, one month is £56. It's available overseas (ask your travel agent or contact the nearest Thomas Cook office) or at the Britain Visitor Centre in London.
Australasian Clubs
  Deckers London Club (Map 9; ☎ 7244 8641), 35 Earl's Court Rd SW5 (⊖ Earl's Court), and Drifters (Map 5; ☎ 7262 1292), 22a Craven Terrace W2 (⊖ Lancaster Gate), offer back-up services like mail holding, local information, freight forwarding and equipment purchase, and cheap tours. They're mainly aimed at Aussies and Kiwis, but anyone is welcome. Membership is from £10 to £15. These clubs are associated with tour companies.

Globetrotters Club
  If you'd like to meet other travellers it's worth going along to Globetrotters, which holds meetings on the second Saturday of every month at the Friends Meeting House (Map 7; ☎ 7836 7204), 52 St Martin's Lane WC2, at 3.30 pm. Admission is under £3.

LIBRARIES

London's most important library is the British Library, which has finally moved into its new home in St Pancras. This is the UK's main copyright library and receives one copy of every British publication. The new library has 11 reading rooms accommodating more than 1200 people. However, access is limited to those with specific research needs, and there is a stringent application procedure; for details contact the Reader Admissions Office, British Library (Map 3; ☎ 7412 7677, email reader-admissions@bl.uk), 96 Euston Rd NW1 (⊖ King's Cross). The library's Web site is at www.bl.uk, and its catalogue can be accessed on the Web at opac97.bl.uk.

A scholar's paradise by the roaring traffic of Euston Rd: the £500 million British Library.

You're free to use any local library for newspapers, books and magazines provided you don't want to take them away; consult the local phone book for the nearest branch. The Westminster Central Reference Library (Map 7; ☎ 7641 4634), 35 St Martin's St WC2 (⊖ Charing Cross), is a public reference library with all sorts of publications, including newspapers and telephone directories on three floors.

The Chamber of Commerce & Industry Reference Library (Map 8; ☎ 7248 4444), 33 Queen St EC4 (⊖ Mansion House), stocks all manner of commercial materials and information.

UNIVERSITIES

For general information about London's universities, see Education in the Facts about London chapter. The University of Westminster and many colleges of the University of London, including the London School of Economics and Political Science and the Imperial College of Science, Technology and Medicine, let their residence halls to nonstudents during the holidays, which usually run from the end of June to mid-September. See Student Accommodation in the Places to Stay chapter for details.

DANGERS & ANNOYANCES
Crime

Considering its size and the disparities in wealth, London is remarkably safe; most visitors will spend their two weeks in the capital without anything worse happening than being overcharged for an ice-cream cone. That said, you should take the usual precautionary measures against pickpockets, who operate in crowded public places like the Underground and major tourist attractions. Always carry your day-pack or other bag in front of you and don't put it down without keeping an eye on it, especially in a crowded pub or outside at a café. Never put a wallet in a back pocket – the thieves will be laughing all the way to the shops.

Take particular care at night. When travelling by tube, choose a carriage with other

CHARLOTTE HINDLE

The 'Old Bill', your first port of call if you're unlucky enough to be the victim of theft.

people in it and avoid some of the deserted suburban stations; a bus or a taxi is a safer choice.

The most important things to guard are your passport, papers, tickets and money – in that order. It's always best to carry these next to your skin or in a sturdy leather pouch on your belt. Use your own padlock for hostel lockers. Be careful even in hotels; don't leave valuables lying around in your room. Never leave valuables in a car, and remove all luggage overnight. Report thefts to the police and ask for a statement, or your travel insurance won't pay out.

Traffic

Remember that as cars drive on the left in the UK you need to look to the right at pedestrian crossings. Couriers on motorcycles, scooters or bicycles who belt down London's roads at full tilt, weaving in and out of the traffic at death-defying speeds, can be even more of a menace than pickpockets. Keep your wits about you while crossing the road.

Terrorism

While the horrific memories of bombings by the IRA began to fade in early 1999, Londoners were jolted out of their false sense of security when three nail bombs exploded – in crowded areas of Brixton,

Brick Lane in the East End and Old Compton St in Soho – that had been quite clearly directed at blacks, Asians and gays respectively. Three people were killed instantly and more than 100 injured, many of them very seriously. As a result, it's just as well to restate the ground rules.

Never leave your bag unattended in case you trigger a security alert. If you see an unattended package, keep calm and alert those in authority and anyone nearby as quickly as possible; do *not* touch it.

There is a much higher sense of security here than in, say, Sydney or even New York, and precautions are taken regularly – and seriously. If asked to open your bag for inspection in museums or other public places, do so willingly – it's for your own safety ultimately.

Petty inconveniences due to terrorism include transport delays while suspicious packages are inspected, the 'ring of steel' around 75% of the City with police checking cars and other vehicles as they enter or leave, and, at times, the sealing of left-luggage lockers at bus and train stations.

Lost Property

Every year thousands of items are lost by their owners in London: mobile phones, keys, bags of money, jewellery – even sets of false teeth. Eventually most items found on buses and Underground trains find their way to London Regional Transport's Lost Property Office (Map 5; fax 7918 1028), 200 Baker St, NW1 5RZ (⊖ Baker Street), where you can call in person to collect them from Monday to Friday between 9.30 am and 2 pm. A charge of £3 per item is made; it's £2 if you retrieve it from the bus garage where it was found instead.

Items left on main-line trains usually end up back at the main terminals. If you leave something in a black taxi, phone Taxi Lost Property on ☎ 7833 0996.

Touts & Scams

Hotel and hostel touts descend on backpackers at tube and main-line stations such as Earl's Court, Liverpool Street and Victoria. Treat their claims with scepticism and don't accept any offers of free lifts unless you know exactly where you're going.

Every year foreign men are lured into Soho strip clubs and hostess bars and are efficiently separated from huge amounts of money; refuse to pay and things may rapidly turn nasty. Do yourself a favour and give them a wide berth.

Cardsharping, where tourists are lured into playing a game that seems to be going all one way until they join in (whereupon the luck changes sides), seems to be on the wane, but in its place have come the mock auctions that operate primarily along Oxford St. At advertised venues you'll see attractive goods on display, but you're usually asked to bid for goods in black plastic bags or cartons that you can't remove until the auction is over. When you do look inside, you'll find your wonderful bargain has turned into fool's gold. Buyer beware.

Beggars

These days London has a depressing number of beggars, and it's difficult to know how best to deal with them. All the arguments against giving to beggars in developing countries apply in London too; it's probably better to donate something to a recognised charity than give directly. Shelter (☎ 7505 2000), 88 Old St EC1, is a charity that helps the homeless and gratefully accepts donations. Also consider buying the *Big Issue* (£1), a weekly magazine available from homeless street sellers who benefit directly from sales.

Racism

London is not without racial problems, particularly in some of the more deprived areas of the East End, but tolerance generally prevails. Visitors are unlikely to have problems because of their skin colour, but please let us know if you find otherwise.

Smoking

Virtually every cinema and all theatres have banned smoking, and only the most obdurate restaurateurs refuse to provide no-smoking sections. Pubs remain one of the last strongholds of the smoker, though the Wetherspoon chain of pubs and bars now sets aside corners for nonsmokers. See Pubs & Bars in the Entertainment chapter for more information.

Litter

Many first-time visitors are shocked at how dirty the capital is, with rubbish strewn everywhere. The excuse would be to say that litter bins have been removed in large parts of central London in response to the threat of bombs. In reality, however, Londoners seem to be a bunch of litterbugs. Dog owners are particularly irresponsible here.

LEGAL MATTERS
Drugs

Illegal drugs of every type are widely available, especially in clubs. Nonetheless, all the usual dangers associated with drugs apply and there have been several high-profile deaths associated with ecstasy, the purity of which is often dubious. Possession of small quantities of cannabis usually attracts a small fine (still a criminal conviction) or a warning; other drugs are treated more seriously.

Driving Offences

The laws against drink-driving have got tougher and are treated more seriously than they used to be. Currently you're allowed to have a blood-alcohol level of 35mg/100mL but there's talk of reducing the limit. The safest approach is not to drink anything at all if you're planning to drive. For information about current speed limits and parking violations, see Car & Motorcycle in the Getting Around chapter.

Fines

In general you rarely have to cough up on the spot for an offence. The two main exceptions are trains (including those on the Underground) and buses where people who can't produce a valid ticket for the journey when asked to by an inspector can be fined there and then; £5 on the buses, £10 on the trains, no excuses accepted.

BUSINESS HOURS

Offices are usually open Monday to Friday from 9 am to 5 or 5.30 pm, with shops opening on Saturday as well and often staying open much later. A growing number of shops and department stores also open on Sunday, typically from 10 am to 4 pm or noon to 6 pm. Late-night shopping in the West End is on Thursday.

Post office hours vary slightly, but most open Monday to Friday from 8.30 or 9 am to 5 or 5.30 pm, with main ones open on Saturday to noon or 1 pm. The post office on Trafalgar Square, where poste restante is usually sent, is open weekdays from 8 am to 8 pm and on Saturday from 9 am to 8 pm.

Bank hours vary considerably, but you'll be safe if you visit from Monday to Friday between 9.30 am and 3.30 pm (Friday afternoon gets very busy). Some banks also open on Saturday, generally from 9.30 am till noon.

PUBLIC HOLIDAYS & SPECIAL EVENTS
Public Holidays

Most banks and businesses are closed on the following public holidays: New Year's Day (1 January), Good Friday and Easter Monday (late March/April), May Day Bank Holiday (first Monday in May), Spring Bank Holiday (last Monday in May), Summer Bank Holiday (last Monday in August), Christmas Day and Boxing Day (25 & 26 December).

Museums and other attractions may well observe the Christmas Day and Boxing Day holidays, but they generally stay open for the other ones. Exceptions are those that normally close on Sunday; they're quite likely to close on bank holidays too. Some smaller museums close on Monday and/or Tuesday, and several places, including the British Museum, close on Sunday morning.

Special Events

Countless festivals and events are held in and around London. Look out for the LTB's bimonthly *Events in London* or its *Annual Events* pamphlet. Don't forget its Visitorcall service; see Tourist Information Centres under Tourist Offices earlier in this chapter.

MARK HONAN

What a racquet: strawberries and sky-high prices every June at Wimbledon.

Throughout 2000 and into 2001, more than 50 institutions (many normally closed to the public) within a 10-minute walk of the Thames will take part in the London Spring of Pearls Millennium Festival in a bid to bring the river 'back to the people'. For details ring ☎ 7665 1540 or check out their Web site at www.stringofpearls.org.uk.

New Year (1 January)
London Parade – the Mayor of Westminster leading a parade of 10,000 musicians and street performers, as well as floats and carriages, from Parliament Square to Berkeley Square.
Early to mid-January
International Boat Show – Earl's Court Exhibition Centre.
Last Sunday in January
Commemoration of Charles I – outside Banqueting House, Whitehall.
Late January/early February
Chinese New Year – with lion dances etc in Soho.
Clowns' Service – clowns gather at Holy Trinity Church, Beechwood Rd, Dalston E8, to commemorate clown of clowns Joey Grimaldi (1778-1837), who lived in Clerkenwell's Exmouth Market.

Late February/March
Shrove Tuesday Pancake Day Races – Lincoln's Inn Fields, Covent Garden and Spitalfields.

Last week in March
Oxford vs Cambridge University Boat Race – the traditional rowing race on the Thames, from Putney to Mortlake.

Head of the River Race – a less well-known race from Putney to Mortlake, with 400-odd teams.
London International Book Fair – Olympia.
Late March/April
Easter Fair – Battersea Park.

Early May
London Marathon – a 42km (26-mile) race from Greenwich Park to the Mall via the Isle of Dogs and Victoria Embankment.
Mid-May
FA Cup Final – the final of England's premier football tournament, usually played at Wembley Stadium, but at various other venues from 2000 to 2002.
Royal Windsor Horse Show – showjumping event.
Last week in May
Chelsea Flower Show – Royal Hospital, Chelsea.
Oak Apple Day – Chelsea Pensioners decorate a statue of Charles II with oak leaves.

June
Spitalfields Festival – three-week celebration at Spitalfields Market with music, theatre, talks and walks.
Greenwich Festival, Islington International Festival and *Stoke Newington Festival* – all offer similar fun and games during the same month.
First week in June
Beating of the Retreat – military bands and marching in Horse Guards Parade, Whitehall.
Second Saturday in June
Trooping of the Colour – celebrates the Queen's official birthday with parades and pageantry in Horse Guards Parade, Whitehall.
Late June
Wimbledon Lawn Tennis Championships – runs for two weeks.
Late June to early July
City of London Festival – top-notch (this is big-bucks territory) performances of music, dance, theatre and so on in City churches and squares.

July
Hampton Court Palace International Flower Show – flowers galore in one of London's finest gardens.
Doggett's Coat & Badge Race – a rowing race from London Bridge to Albert Bridge.
Early July
London Mardi Gras – gay and lesbian march and festival, Finsbury Park.
Mid-July
Clerkenwell Festival – fun and games around Farringdon.
Vintners' Company Procession – vintners in traditional costume parading from Upper Thames St to St James's Garlickhythe church.

From mid-July to mid-September
Promenade Concerts (or 'Proms') – Royal Albert Hall.

Last Sunday & Monday in August
Notting Hill Carnival – Europe's biggest outdoor festival, a vast Caribbean carnival in Notting Hill, held over the Summer Bank Holiday weekend.

Third weekend in September
London Open House – the public is admitted to some 500 buildings and other sites normally closed.

Great River Race – barges, dragon boats and longships racing 36km (22 miles) from Ham House in Richmond to Island Gardens on the Isle of Dogs.

Late September
Horseman's Sunday – a vicar on horseback blesses more than 100 horses outside the Church of St John & St Michael, Hyde Park Crescent W2, followed by horse jumping in Kensington Gardens.

October/early November
Dance Umbrella – British and international companies perform at venues across London for five weeks.

Early October
Punch & Judy Festival – a gathering of puppet fanatics in Covent Garden piazza.

Pearly Harvest Festival Service – over 100 Pearly Kings and Queens attend a service in St Martin-in-the-Fields church.

Late October
Trafalgar Day Parade – marching bands descend on Trafalgar Square to lay wreaths commemorating Nelson's victory over Napoleon in 1805.

Late October/early November
State Opening of Parliament – the Queen visits Parliament by state coach amid gun salutes.

November
London Film Festival – at the National Film Theatre, South Bank.

London to Brighton Veteran Car Run – pre-1905 vintage cars line up in Serpentine Rd, Hyde Park, to race to Brighton.

November 5
Guy Fawkes Night – commemorates an attempted Catholic coup with bonfires and fireworks around town but especially in Battersea Park, Primrose Hill, Blackheath, Clapham Common and Crystal Palace Park.

Second Saturday in November
Lord Mayor's Show – his and her honour travel in a state coach from the Guildhall to the Royal Courts of Justice, amid floats, bands and fireworks.

Second Sunday in November
Remembrance Sunday – the Queen, members of the government and other notables lay wreaths at the Cenotaph to remember the dead of the two world wars.

Mid-November
World Travel Market – the world's largest travel show, at Earl's Court Exhibition Centre.

December
Lighting of the Christmas Tree – Trafalgar Square.

FACTS FOR THE VISITOR

PAUL DCYLE

Dancing in the streets: camping it up for the Notting Hill Carnival in August.

DOING BUSINESS

Roughly five million people a year come to do business in London, one of the world's major commercial centres and home to almost a quarter of the head offices of Europe's 500 largest companies. As a result most of London's biggest hotels depend on business travellers for their livelihood and come equipped with business centres with faxes, ISDN lines, Internet access, secretarial services and so on. More countries can be dialled direct from London than from anywhere else in Europe and international call rates are cheaper here too. In any given week there are flights to more than 250 different destinations worldwide, and more than 70 million people a year use Heathrow, the world's busiest commercial airport.

The main source of general information for businesspeople in London is the staid, pink-tinged *Financial Times*, published Monday to Saturday, while the *Economist* is a more detailed weekly magazine. Other useful sources of information include:

Bank of England
(Map 8; ☎ 7601 4846, fax 7601 4356, email library@bankofengland.co.uk)
Threadneedle St, London EC2R 8AH
Board of British Trade International
(Map 10; ☎ 7215 4936, fax 7215 4653, email sarah.barrow@lond04.bti.gov.uk)
Department of Trade & Industry, Kingsgate House, 66 Victoria St, London SW1E 6SW
Board of Inland Revenue
(Map 6; ☎ 7438 6622)
Somerset House, Strand, London WC2R 1LB
Confederation of British Industry
(Map 7; ☎ 7379 7400, fax 7240 0988)
Centre Point, 103 New Oxford St, London WC1A 1DU
Department of Trade & Industry
(Map 6; ☎ 7215 5000, fax 7222 0612, email dti.enquiries@imsv.dti.gov.uk)
1 Victoria St, London SW1H 0ET
London Chamber of Commerce & Industry
(Map 8; ☎ 7248 4444, fax 7489 0391, email lc@londonchamber.co.uk)
33 Queen St, London EC4R 1AP
Office of the European Commission
(☎ 7973 1992, fax 7973 1900)
8 Storey's Gate, London SW1P 3AT

For word processing or secretarial services go to Typing Overload (Map 6; ☎ 7404 5464), 1st floor, 67 Chancery Lane WC2 (✜ Chancery Lane). It has a branch at 170 Sloane St SW1 (☎ 7235 6855; ✜ Sloane Square). For photocopying, computer services like scanning, computer rentals and video-conferencing, try Kinko's (Map 6; ☎ 7539 2900), a reliable Virgin company at 326-328 High Holborn WC1 (✜ Chancery Lane), with another branch at 29-35 Mortimer St W1 (☎ 7643 1900; ✜ Goodge Street).

WORK

If you're prepared to work at menial jobs and long hours for relatively low pay, you'll almost certainly find work in London. The trouble is that without skills, it's difficult to find a job that pays well enough to save money. You should be able to break even, but will probably be better off saving in your home country.

Traditionally, unskilled visitors have worked in pubs and restaurants and as nannies. Both jobs often provide live-in accommodation, but the hours are long, the work exhausting and the pay not so good (and then there are all those pissheads to deal with). A minimum wage of £3.60 per hour (£3 for those aged 18 to 21) was introduced in April 1999 but if you're working under the table no one's obliged to pay you even that. Before you accept a job, make sure you're clear about the terms and conditions, especially how many (and which) hours you will be expected to work.

Accountants, health professionals, journalists, computer programmers, lawyers, teachers and clerical workers with computer experience stand a better chance of finding well paid work. Even so, you'll probably need some money to tide you over while you search. Don't forget copies of your qualifications, references (which will probably be checked) and a CV (résumé).

Teachers should contact the individual London borough councils, which have separate education departments, although some schools recruit directly. To work as a trained nurse you have to register (£56) with the United Kingdom Central Council for Nursing, a process that can take up to three months; write to the Overseas Registration Department, UKCCN, 23 Portland Place, London W1N 4JT, or call ☎ 7333 9333 or fax 7636 6935. If you aren't registered you can still work as an auxiliary nurse.

The free *TNT Magazine* is a good starting point for jobs and agencies aimed at travellers. For au pair and nanny work buy the quaintly titled *The Lady*. Also check the *Evening Standard*, national newspapers and the government-operated Jobcentres, which are scattered throughout London and listed under Employment Services in the Yellow Pages. Whatever your skills, it's worth registering with several temporary agencies.

For details on all aspects of short-term work consult the excellent *Work Your Way Around the World* by Susan Griffith. Another good source is *Working Holidays*, published by the London-based Central Bureau for Education Visits & Exchanges.

If you play a musical instrument or have other artistic talents, you could try working the streets. As every Peruvian pipe-player (and his fifth cousin once removed) knows, busking is fairly common in London. It has traditionally been banned in the Underground (£20 fine), though that has hardly stopped many musicians and there is now talk of LRT licensing buskers to play in certain stations after they have auditioned. The borough councils are also moving to license buskers at top tourist attractions and popular areas like Covent Garden and Leicester Square. You will still be able to play elsewhere, but those areas will be off-limits to anyone without a permit.

Tax

As an official employee, you'll find income tax and National Insurance automatically deducted from your weekly pay-packet. However, the deductions will be calculated on the assumption that you're working for the entire financial year (which runs from 6 April to 5 April). If you don't work as long as that, you may be eligible for a refund. Contact the Board of Inland Revenue (see the previous Doing Business section) or use one of the agencies that advertise in *TNT Magazine* (but check their fee or percentage charge first).

Getting There & Away

London is one of the world's busiest air transport hubs and with intense competition between airlines there are always plenty of opportunities for finding cheap flights. In addition, there is a range of bus, rail and ferry services between Europe and the UK, including those using the Channel Tunnel.

The national weekend newspapers and the *Evening Standard* carry ads for cheap fares. Also look out for *TNT Magazine*; you can often pick it up free outside main train and tube stations. For recommended travel agencies, see Travel Agencies later in this chapter.

AIR

Greater London has five main airports: Heathrow is the largest, followed by Gatwick, Stansted, Luton and London City. For information on getting to and from all five airports, see The Airports in the Getting Around chapter.

Departure Tax

All domestic flights and those to destinations within the EU from London carry a £10 departure tax. For flights to other cities abroad you pay £20. This is usually built into the price of your ticket.

Other Parts of the UK

Almost all regional centres in the UK are linked to London. However, unless you're travelling from the outer reaches of Britain, and in particular northern Scotland, planes are only marginally quicker than trains if you include the time it takes to get to and from the airports.

The main operators are British Airways (BA; ☎ 0845 722 2111), British Midland (☎ 0870 607 0555) and KLM uk (☎ 0870 507 4074); their Web sites are www.british-airways.com, www.iflybritishmidland.com and www.klmuk.com respectively. There are several other smaller companies, including easyJet (☎ 0870 529 2929) and

BA's no-frills offshoot, Go (☎ 0845 605 4321); visit their Web sites at www.easyjet.com and www.go-fly.com respectively. Most airlines offer a range of tickets, including full-fare (very expensive but flexible), Apex (for which you must book at least 14 days in advance) and, on some services, special offers (BA calls these Seat Sale fares and also has occasional World Offer fares that may be even cheaper). There are also youth fares (usually for under-26s), but Apex and special-offer fares are usually cheaper.

Prices vary enormously. For example, at the time of writing a return ticket from Edinburgh, Glasgow or Aberdeen to London on BA costs £225 full fare, but just £68 Apex or £47 with a World Offer fare. British Midland charges £264 full fare from Edinburgh or Glasgow, but this can drop to as low as £47 if you book in advance and stay over on Saturday night. KLM uk has Saver fares from Edinburgh, Glasgow or Aberdeen to London for £68. The no-frills airline easyJet has one-way flights between Edinburgh, Glasgow or Aberdeen and Luton from £19 to £99; easyJet tickets are only sold direct, by phone or via their Web site. Tickets are sold on a first-come, first-served basis; when the £19 fares are gone the price jumps up to the next level and so on up to £99. Most cheap fares carry restrictions that a travel agency or the airline will explain; staying over on Saturday night or travelling midweek are two of the most common.

Examples of other BA return fares from Scotland to London include from Kirkwall (Orkney) for £508, or £211 with advance booking, and from Lerwick (Shetland) for £536/233. BA also offers regular connections between Belfast and Heathrow; fares range from £45 to £260. Jersey European Airways (☎ 0870 567 6676) have fares from Belfast to Gatwick or Stansted in the range £78 to £243.

Other Countries

Ireland Dublin is linked to all the major London airports. BA fares from Dublin to Gatwick range from around IR£82 to IR£475, British Midland fares to Heathrow from around IR£59 to IR£395. With the advent of price-cutting Ryanair (☎ 0870 156 9569), single tickets are sometimes available for as little as IR£19, including tax. Ryanair's Web site is www.ryanair.ie.

Continental Europe Typical discount return fares to London include from Amsterdam f250, Frankfurt-am-Main DM400, Madrid 30,000 pta, Paris 450FF and Rome L260,000. EasyJet offers one-way fares from Barcelona to Luton in the range 19,000 pta to 24,000 pta and from Nice in the range 370FF to 920FF, while Go has nonflexible return fares from Madrid to Stansted in the range 17,250 pta to 34,700 pta and from Venice for L14,200. Standard tickets with carriers like BA can cost a great deal more.

You might also try Last Minute at www.lastminute.com, a UK Web site selling late deals. Other sites for cheap tickets include www.flightbookers.com, www.travelocity.com and www.bargainholidays.com.

USA & Canada Council Travel and STA have offices throughout the USA. Their Web sites are www.counciltravel.com and www.statravel.com respectively. You should be able to fly New York-London return for around US$400 to US$500 in the low season and US$500 to US$700 in the high. Equivalent fares from the West Coast are US$100 to US$300 higher.

Priceline is a 'name your price' service on the Web, at www.priceline.com. You enter your destination, dates of travel and the price you'll pay for a ticket and if one of the participating airlines has an empty seat for which it would rather get something than nothing, it'll email you back within an hour. Airhitch (☎ 212-864 2000) is worth contacting for one-way tickets and can get you to London for around US$175/225/255 from the East Coast/Midwest/West Coast; its Web site is www.airhitch.org.

Another option is a courier flight, where you accompany a parcel or freight to be picked up at the other end. A New York-London return can be had for around US$300 in the low season. You can also fly one way. The drawbacks are that your stay in Europe may be limited to one or two weeks, your luggage is usually restricted to hand luggage (the parcel or freight you carry comes out of your luggage allowance), and you may have to be a resident and apply for an interview before they'll take you on.

You can find out more about courier flights from the International Association of Air Travel Couriers (☎ 561-582 8320, fax 582 1581), Now Voyager Travel (☎ 212-431 1616, fax 334 5243) or As You Like It Travel (☎ 212-779 1771, fax 779 9674); their Web sites are www.courier.org, www.nowvoyagertravel.com and www.asulikeit.com respectively.

Travel CUTS (☎ 888-838 CUTS) has offices in all major cities in Canada; its Web site is www.travelcuts.com. Airhitch has stand-by fares to/from Toronto, Montreal and Vancouver. Typical discount return fares to London include C$600 from Montreal or Toronto and C$800 from Vancouver.

Australia & New Zealand STA Travel and Flight Centres International are major dealers in cheap air fares. Discounted return fares on mainstream airlines through STA cost between A$1800 (low season) and A$2350 (high season). Flights to/from Perth are a couple of hundred dollars cheaper. A Britannia charter service also operates between Britain and Australia/New Zealand. Between November and April, prices can drop as low as A$1300 return from Sydney to London. Contact UK Flight Shop (☎ 02-9247 4833) at 7 Macquarie Place in Sydney or, in the UK, Austravel (☎ 7838 1011), 152 Brompton Rd SW3.

STA and Flight Centres International are popular travel agencies in New Zealand as well. The cheapest fares to Europe are usually routed through the USA, but a round-the-world (RTW) ticket may be cheaper than a return.

GETTING THERE & AWAY

Air Travel Glossary

Baggage Allowance This will be written on your ticket and usually includes one 20kg item to go in the hold, plus one item of hand luggage.

Bucket Shops These are unbonded travel agencies specialising in discounted airline tickets.

Bumped Just because you have a confirmed seat doesn't mean you're going to get on the plane (see Overbooking).

Cancellation Penalties If you have to cancel or change a discounted ticket, there are often heavy penalties involved; insurance can sometimes be taken out against these penalties. Some airlines impose penalties on regular tickets as well, particularly against 'no-show' passengers.

Check-In Airlines ask you to check in a certain time ahead of the flight departure (usually one to two hours on international flights). If you fail to check in on time and the flight is overbooked, the airline can cancel your booking and give your seat to somebody else.

Confirmation Having a ticket written out with the flight and date you want doesn't mean you have a seat until the agent has checked with the airline that your status is 'OK' or confirmed. Meanwhile you could just be 'on request'.

Courier Fares Businesses often need to send urgent documents or freight securely and quickly. Courier companies hire people to accompany the package through customs and, in return, offer a discount ticket that is sometimes a phenomenal bargain. In effect, what the companies do is ship their freight as your luggage on regular commercial flights. This is a legitimate operation, but there are two shortcomings – the short turnaround time of the ticket (usually not longer than a month) and the limitation on your luggage allowance. You may have to surrender all your allowance and take only carry-on luggage.

Full Fares Airlines traditionally offer 1st class (coded F), business class (coded J) and economy class (coded Y) tickets. These days there are so many promotional and discounted fares available that few passengers pay full economy fare.

ITX An ITX, or 'independent inclusive tour excursion', is often available on tickets to popular holiday destinations. Officially it's a package deal combined with hotel accommodation, but many agents will sell you one of these for the flight only and give you phoney hotel vouchers in the unlikely event that you're challenged at the airport.

Lost Tickets If you lose your airline ticket an airline will usually treat it like a travellers cheque and, after inquiries, issue you with another one. Legally, however, an airline is entitled to treat it like cash and if you lose it then it's gone forever. Take good care of your tickets.

MCO An MCO, or 'miscellaneous charge order', is a voucher that looks like an airline ticket but carries no destination or date. It can be exchanged through any International Association of Travel Agents (IATA) airline for a ticket on a specific flight. It's a useful alternative to an onward ticket in those countries that demand one, and is more flexible than an ordinary ticket if you're unsure of your route.

No-Shows No-shows are passengers who fail to show up for their flight. Full-fare passengers who fail to turn up are sometimes entitled to travel on a later flight. The rest are penalised (see Cancellation Penalties).

On Request This is an unconfirmed booking for a flight.

Onward Tickets An entry requirement for many countries is that you have a ticket out of the country. If you're unsure of your next move, the easiest solution is to buy the cheapest onward ticket to a neighbouring country or a ticket from a reliable airline that can later be refunded if you do not use it.

Open Jaw Tickets These are return tickets where you fly out to one place but return from another. If available, this can save you backtracking to your arrival point.

Overbooking Airlines hate to fly empty seats and since every flight has some passengers who fail to show up, airlines often book more passengers than they have seats. Usually excess passengers make up for the no-shows, but occasionally somebody gets 'bumped' onto the next available flight. Guess who it is most likely to be? The passengers who check in late.

Point-to-Point Tickets These are discount tickets that can be bought on some routes in return for passengers waiving their rights to a stopover.

Promotional Fares These are officially discounted fares, available from travel agencies or direct from the airline.

Reconfirmation If you don't reconfirm your flight at least 72 hours prior to departure, the airline may delete your name from the passenger list. Ring to find out if your airline requires reconfirmation.

Restrictions Discounted tickets often have various restrictions on them – such as needing to be paid for in advance and incurring a penalty to be altered. Others are restrictions on the minimum and maximum period you must be away, such as a minimum of 14 days or a maximum of one year.

Round-the-World Tickets RTW tickets give you a limited period (usually a year) in which to circumnavigate the globe. You can go anywhere the carrying airlines go, as long as you don't backtrack. The number of stopovers or total number of separate flights is decided before you set off and they usually cost a bit more than a basic return flight.

Stand-by This is a discounted ticket where you only fly if there is a seat free at the last moment. Stand-by fares are usually available only on domestic routes.

Transferred Tickets Airline tickets cannot be transferred from one person to another. Travellers sometimes try to sell the return half of their ticket, but officials can ask you to prove that you are the person named on the ticket. This is less likely to happen on domestic flights, but on an international flight tickets are compared with passports.

Travel Agencies Travel agencies vary widely and you should choose one that suits your needs. Some simply handle tours, while full-service agencies handle everything from tours and tickets to car rental and hotel bookings. If all you want is a ticket at the lowest possible price, then go to an agency specialising in discounted fares.

Travel Periods Ticket prices vary with the time of year. There is a low (off-peak) season and a high (peak) season, and often a low-shoulder season and a high-shoulder season as well. Usually the fare depends on your outward flight – if you depart in the high season and return in the low season, you pay the high-season fare.

Africa Nairobi and Johannesburg are probably the best places in Africa to buy tickets to London. A typical one-way/return fare to London is about US$700/900. If you're travelling to London from Cairo, it's often cheaper to fly to Athens and take a low-cost bus or train from there.

Student Travel Centre (☎ 011-716 3945) in Johannesburg and the Africa Travel Centre (☎ 021-235555) in Cape Town are worth trying for cheap tickets.

Asia Hong Kong, Bangkok and Singapore are all discount air-fare centres. Shop around and ask the advice of other travellers before buying a ticket. Many of the cheapest fares from South-East Asia to Europe are with Eastern European carriers. STA has branches/affiliates in Hong Kong (Sincerity Travel), Tokyo, Singapore, Bangkok, Jakarta and Kuala Lumpur.

From India, the cheapest flights also tend to be with Eastern European carriers like LOT Polish Airlines and the Russian flag-carrier Aeroflot, or with Middle Eastern airlines such as Syrian Arab Airlines and Iran Air. Bombay is the air transport hub, with many transit options to/from South-East Asia, but tickets may be slightly cheaper around Delhi's Connaught Place.

Airline Offices

All major airlines have ticket offices in London. The following are the ones you're most likely to want, but others can be found in the business telephone directory.

Aer Lingus	☎ 0845 973 7747
Aeroflot	☎ 7355 2233
Air Canada	☎ 0870 524 7226
Air France	☎ 8742 6600
Air New Zealand	☎ 8741 2299
Alitalia	☎ 7602 7111
American Airlines	☎ 0845 778 9789
British Airways	☎ 0845 722 2111
British Midland	☎ 0845 755 4554
Canadian Airlines International	☎ 0845 761 6767
Cathay Pacific Airways	☎ 7747 8888

Continental Airlines	☎ 0800 776464
Delta Air Lines	☎ 0800 414767
El Al Israel Airlines	☎ 7957 4100
Iberia	☎ 7830 0011
KLM-Royal Dutch Airlines	☎ 0870 507 4074
KLM uk	☎ 0870 507 4074
Lufthansa Airlines	☎ 0845 773 7747
Olympic Airways	☎ 7409 2400
Qantas Airways	☎ 0845 774 7767
Ryanair	☎ 0870 156 9569
Sabena	☎ 8780 1444
Scandinavian Airlines (SAS)	☎ 0845 701 0789
Singapore Airlines	☎ 8747 0007
South African Airways	☎ 7312 5000
TAP Air Portugal	☎ 7828 0262
Thai Airways International (THAI)	☎ 7499 9113
Turkish Airlines	☎ 7766 9300
United Airlines	☎ 0845 844 4777
Virgin Atlantic	☎ 01293-747747

BUS

Most long-distance express buses (usually referred to as coaches in the UK) leave London from Victoria Coach Station (Map 10; ☎ 7730 3466 for information), an attractive 1930s-style building at 164 Buckingham Palace Rd SW1 (⊖ Victoria, about 10 minutes' walk south of Victoria train and tube stations. The arrivals terminal is in a separate building across Elizabeth St from the main coach station.

There are information desks in the main entrance (open daily from 7.45 am to 8.30 pm) and near Gate 11 (open daily except Tuesday from 10 am to 6 pm). The ticket hall, behind Gate 11, is open from 6 am to 11.30 pm. To avoid queuing, you can book tickets up to two hours before departure by phone on ☎ 7730 3499 (open Monday to Saturday from 9 am to 7 pm). You must pick up the tickets at least 30 minutes before the coach is due to depart. The left-luggage office, behind Gate 6 (open daily from 7 am to 11 pm), charges £1 for deposits of less than two hours and £2 to £2.50 for periods of between two and 24 hours, depending on baggage size.

Other Parts of the UK

Buses in the UK are almost entirely privately owned and run. National Express (☎ 0870 580 8080) runs the largest network – it completely dominates the market and is a sister company to Eurolines (see the later Other Countries section); its Web site is www.nationalexpress.co.uk. However, there are often smaller competitors as well on the main routes.

Generally speaking, if you want to travel by coach it's cheaper to do so midweek. Booking a week ahead can also result in a discount. Oddly, there are some routes where it can be several pounds cheaper to buy two singles than a return.

National Express Discount Coachcards (£8 per year, £19 for three years), which allow 30% off the standard adult fare, can be bought from all National Express agencies and are available to full-time students and those aged between 16 and 25 or over 50. A passport photo is required; ISIC cards are accepted as proof of student status and passports for date of birth.

Other Countries

Even without using the Channel Tunnel, you can still get from/to Europe by bus with a short ferry/hovercraft ride as part of the deal. Eurolines (Map 10; ☎ 0870 514 3219), 52 Grosvenor Gardens SW1 (⊖ Victoria), an association of companies that together form Europe's largest international bus network, connects an enormous number of European destinations – from Ireland and Morocco to Finland and Greece. Eurolines' Web site at www.eurolines.com has links to the sites of all the national operators. Buses are slower and less comfortable than trains, but they are cheaper, especially if you qualify for the 10 to 20% discount available to people aged 13 to 25 or over 60, or take advantage of the discount fares on offer from time to time.

You can book Eurolines tickets through any National Express office, including Victoria Coach Station, and at many travel agencies. Eurolines offices and affiliated companies can be found across Europe,

Suburban trains are an essential part of London's transport network.

including Amsterdam (☎ 020-560 87 87), Barcelona (☎ 93 490 4000), Berlin (☎ 030-86 0960), Brussels (☎ 02-203 0707) and Madrid (☎ 91 528 1105).

The following single/return adult fares and journey times are representative: Amsterdam f85/140 (nine hours); Barcelona 14,000/25,000 pta (22 to 24 hours); Berlin DM170/300 (22½ hours); Brussels f1700/2600 (seven hours). At peak times in summer (when you should add between 5 and 10% to the above fares), you should make reservations a few days in advance.

TRAIN

The former British Rail has been privatised into 25 separate train-operating companies (TOCs), with another company, Railtrack, responsible for the track and stations. In this book, when you should use a train to get to or from somewhere, we differentiate this from the tube by using the word 'station'.

Each company is able to set whatever fare it chooses. Thus on routes served by more than one operator, passengers can buy a cheaper ticket for a more circuitous journey or pay more for a faster or more direct service.

Other Parts of the UK

The main routes are served by excellent InterCity trains that travel at speeds of up to 225km/h and can whisk you from London to Edinburgh, say, in just over four hours.

Main-Line Terminals London has 10 main-line terminals, each serving a different geographical area of the UK:

Charing Cross
    South-east England
Euston
    North and north-west England, Scotland
King's Cross
    North London, Hertfordshire, Cambridgeshire, north and north-east England, Scotland
Liverpool Street
    East and north-east London, Stansted airport, East Anglia
London Bridge
    South-east England
Marylebone
    North-west London, the Chilterns
Paddington
    South Wales, west and south-west England, south Midlands, Heathrow airport
St Pancras
    East Midlands, south Yorkshire
Victoria
    South and south-east England, Gatwick airport, Channel ferry ports

Waterloo
    South-west London, south and south-west England

In recent years a lot of work has been done to make the terminals more attractive and efficient. Liverpool Street station has been restored to its Victorian splendour, while Brunel's Paddington station is getting a much needed overhaul.

Most stations now have left-luggage facilities and lockers, toilets (20p) with showers (around £3), newsstands and bookshops, and a range of eating and drinking outlets. Victoria and Liverpool Street stations have shopping centres attached.

Rail Classes There are two classes of rail travel: 1st class and what is now officially referred to as standard class (though everyone still calls it 2nd class). You'll pay 30 to 50% more in 1st class than in 2nd, and it's not really worth the extra money except on very crowded trains.

A neogothic masterpiece: Sir George Gilbert Scott's magnificent St Pancras station.

On some overnight trains there are sleeping compartments. The additional costs for these berths are £35/25 for 1st/2nd class between Exeter, Plymouth and Penzance and London and £39/29 on the routes from Scotland. You must book these in advance.

Tickets Since privatisation the complexity of the ticketing system has significantly increased, so finding the best ticket for your journey isn't easy. The best thing to do is to keep asking; you'll soon discover that everyone does that in London.

Children aged under five travel free; aged between five and 15 they pay half-price for most tickets, and full fare for Apex tickets.

If you're planning a long journey, the cheapest tickets on offer must be bought at least one week in advance. Buying an Apex ticket includes a reserved seat. Phone the 24-hour National Rail Enquiries (☎ 0845 748 4950) for timetables, fares and the numbers to ring for telephone bookings, as they differ according to the train operator. For shorter journeys, it's not really necessary to purchase tickets or make seat reservations in advance; just buy them at the station before you embark.

You can also check domestic timetables and frequencies on the Internet. Enter your departure and arrival stations on the www .rail.co.uk/ukrail Web site, and it will provide you with the best route and departure times – though not fares.

Other Countries

Since the advent of the Channel Tunnel (see the boxed text), London's main terminus for trains from Europe has been Waterloo International (though there are plans to transfer it to King's Cross by 2003).

Two separate services operate through the tunnel: a high-speed shuttle train known as Eurotunnel for cars, motorcycles, bicycles, coaches and freight from Coquelles (5km south-west of Calais) to Folkestone, and a high-speed passenger service, known as Eurostar, between Paris, Brussels and London, connecting London with cities all over Europe.

The Channel Tunnel

The Channel Tunnel, inaugurated in 1994 after massive cost overruns, is the first dry-land link between England and France since the last Ice Age. The three parallel, concrete-lined tunnels – two rail tunnels and one for servicing both – were bored between Folkestone and Calais through a layer of impermeable chalk marl 25 to 45m (27 to 49 yards) below the floor of the English Channel and completed in seven years. The tunnels are 50km (31 miles) long, with about 38km (24 miles) directly under the Channel. Just under US$15 billion in private capital was invested in the project, the fourth real attempt at linking the two countries underground – efforts in 1880, 1922 and 1974 were eventually abandoned.

Rail/ferry links generally arrive at Victoria, Liverpool Street and King's Cross train stations, depending on the European departure point. There are information centres at all the main stations. For inquiries about European trains contact Rail Europe/ Rail International on ☎ 0870 584 8848 or visit the Web – for example, the international Deutsche Bahn site at www.bahn.de.

Eurotunnel Specially designed Eurotunnel (☎ 0870 535 3535, 0891 555566 in the UK; ☎ 03 21 00 61 00 in France) trains run 24 hours a day, every day of the year, with up to four departures an hour during peak periods (once an hour from 10 pm to 6 am).

Eurotunnel terminals are clearly signposted and linked to motorway networks. Customs and immigration formalities are carried out before you drive on to the train. Total travel time from motorway to motorway, including loading and unloading, is estimated at one hour; the train journey itself takes 35 minutes.

Regular one-way fares for a passenger car, including all its passengers, range from

1000FF to 1600FF depending on the time of year, time of day and type of vehicle. Same-day returns range from 1100FF to 1600FF, five-day returns from 1400FF to 2100FF. Incredibly cheap excursion fares valid for one to five days are sometimes available. The fee for a bicycle, including its rider, is 150FF; advance booking is mandatory.

You can make an advance reservation by phone or simply pay by cash or credit card when you arrive at the toll booth. Eurotunnel's Web site is www.eurotunnel.com.

Eurostar The highly civilised passenger trains of Eurostar (☎ 0870 518 6186, 01233-617575 in the UK; ☎ 01 49 70 01 75 in France) run around 15 times a day between Paris' Gare du Nord and London. There are around 13 a day (11 on Sunday) between Brussels and London. In London, trains

A Eurostar train revs up at Waterloo International.

CHARLOTTE HINDLE

arrive at and depart from Waterloo International Terminal. Some trains stop at Ashford International station in Kent, and at Fréthun (near Calais) or Lille in France. Immigration formalities are usually completed on the train, but British customs is at Waterloo.

The Paris-London journey takes three hours (which will drop to just 2½ hours when the high-speed track through Kent is *finally* completed). The journey from Brussels to London takes two hours and 40 minutes; this will be reduced to two hours and 10 minutes.

You can buy tickets from travel agencies, major train stations, the Eurostar Ticket Shop at 102-104 Victoria St SW1 (Ⓞ Victoria), or by phoning Eurostar directly. The Eurostar Web site is www.eurostar.com. The normal single/return fare from Paris is a whopping 1400/2300FF, but special offers and advance-purchase tickets can reduce the return fare to around 700FF. The normal single/return fare from Brussels is f6200/13,400, falling to around f3300 return with discounts and special deals. There are also discount fares for children and those aged 12 to 25 or over 60.

Bicycles are only allowed on the Eurostar if they're collapsible; otherwise you can use the Esprit Parcel Service (☎ 01 55 31 58 31), which will take your bike for around 200FF.

Rail/Ferry Eurostar has eclipsed many of the long-established rail/ferry links, but they still provide the cheapest cross-channel travel.

There are train-boat-train services in association with Hoverspeed (☎ 0870 524 0241) and others to Charing Cross station from Paris' Gare du Nord via Dover that take between seven and eight hours and cost 200FF one way and from 200FF return. These are obviously cheaper than Eurostar but take a lot longer, and you've got to mess around transferring by bus between the train station and the ferry terminal on both sides. Hoverspeed's Web site is at www.hoverspeed.co.uk.

From Belgium you arrive at Ramsgate in Kent, from Germany at Harwich in Essex.

Direct services from the Netherlands will bring you to Liverpool Street station via Harwich, and Scandinavian Seaways ships from Hamburg, Esbjerg (Denmark) and Gothenburg (Sweden) also arrive in Harwich. A final option is for travellers from Norway; the Color Line ferry from Bergen, Haugesund and Stavanger arrives in Newcastle-upon-Tyne, three hours by train from King's Cross station.

At the time of writing, train/ferry one-way/return fares to London with Stena (☎ 017-431 58 11 in the Netherlands; ☎ 01-204 7777 in Ireland) and one of five TOCs include: from any Dutch station f140/250; from Dublin IR£77/78 (Saver fare IR£67/68). See the Boat section on this page for further details of ferry services.

CAR & MOTORCYCLE

Getting to London by car or motorcycle couldn't be easier, but do you really want to add to the traffic in this overly congested city? From France or Belgium you can use Eurotunnel or the ferries, from the other countries detailed in the Boat section just the ferries. See the preceding Train section for information on services through the tunnel. The Getting Around chapter has information about buying a car or camper van as well as road rules.

Once in the UK there are good road connections from all the ports to London, which is ringed by the M25, useful for getting close to the area you want before trying to deal with normal city streets. If you are thinking of driving in or out of London, it might be worth buying the *A-Z M25/London* road map (£4.25), which highlights the arterial red routes where no stopping is allowed.

BICYCLE

Bringing a bicycle to London is pretty straightforward. Trains, boats and planes all transport them but usually for a fee (eg 150FF on Eurotunnel). Folding bikes usually go free, though. You need to contact the carrier directly to check what arrangements you are required to make.

Cycling along the South Bank: bringing a bike is a good way to take in some of the sights.

DALE BUCKTON

HITCHING

Hitching is never entirely safe, and we can't recommend it as a way of getting to London. Having said that, if you're determined to risk it, you can minimise the likelihood of problems by hitching with someone else and making sure someone knows where you're going and when you expect to arrive.

Both ferry and Eurotunnel fares rarely cost any extra to carry additional passengers. This should make it easier to persuade a driver to give you a lift.

BOAT

There is a bewildering choice of ferries and other seagoing vessels between Britain and Ireland and mainland Europe. This section outlines the main options, but it doesn't give a complete listing. The bible for sea travel is the *OAG Cruise & Ferry Guide*, published by the Reed Travel Group (☎ 01582-600111), Church St, Dunstable, Bedfordshire LU5 4HB. Most travel agencies will have a copy.

Competing companies operate on the main routes, and the resulting range of services is comprehensive but complicated. The same ferry company can have a host of different prices for the same route, depending on the time of day or year, the validity of the ticket or the size of vehicle. Five day returns are generally among the cheapest options. Return tickets may be much cheaper than two single fares, and vehicle

GETTING THERE & AWAY

tickets may also cover a driver and passenger (or passengers). Very cheap day-return tickets are also available, but they're strictly policed so if you don't plan on coming back the same day (or at all), hide your backpack or luggage.

It's worth planning (and booking) ahead where possible as there are sometimes special reductions on off-peak crossings. The ferries and hovercrafts all carry cars, motorcycles and bicycles.

Ireland

There are many ferry services from Ireland to Britain using modern car ferries. Figures quoted are one-way fares; there are often special deals, return fares and other money-savers worth investigating.

There are services from eight ports in the Irish Republic and Northern Ireland to 12 ports in England, Scotland and Wales. Details of the most popular routes with travellers to and from London are given here; for details of the others see Lonely Planet's *Ireland*, *Britain* and *Scotland* guides.

You can get from Rosslare in Ireland to Fishguard or Pembroke in Wales. These popular short crossings take 3½ hours to Fishguard with Stena Line (☎ 01-204 7777) or 4½ hours to Pembroke with Irish Ferries (☎ 01-638 3333). Foot passengers to Fishguard pay IR£20/40 one way/return (50% discount with an ISIC card), while a car with up to five passengers costs from IR£129 to IR£138 return; five-day returns are cheapest. The 99-minute Stena Lynx catamaran to Fishguard costs IR£30/60 one way/return for foot passengers and IR£159 to IR£208 return for a car with passengers. There are five-day return specials on offer.

Foot passengers on the Irish Ferries Rosslare to Pembroke service pay £20/40 single/return, while taking a car with passengers costs from £129 to £138 return. Foot passengers on Irish Ferries' 3½-hour crossing from Dublin to Holyhead pay the same fare as for Rosslare to Pembroke, while taking a car with passengers on this route costs from £139 to £198 return,

depending on the date. Again, there are five-day return specials on offer.

The fastest run is the Stena Line service between Dun Laoghaire, south of Dublin, and Holyhead, which takes an hour and 40 minutes and costs IR£30/60 single/return for foot passengers and from IR£184 to IR£218 return for a car with four passengers. Again five-day returns are cheapest.

France

The shortest ferry links between France and Britain are Calais or Boulogne to Dover or Folkestone. Dover is the most convenient port for those going on to London by bus or train. P&O Stena Line (☎ 03 21 46 04 40 in France) and Hoverspeed (☎ 0800 901777 in the UK) operate between Calais and Dover every one or two hours. It's worth checking prices for both.

Fares are extremely volatile, but at the time of writing P&O Stena was charging foot passengers from Calais to Dover 241FF one way and from 245FF return; and cars and drivers with up to nine passengers from 1238FF to 2115FF, depending on the number of days away, time of day and day of the week; five-day returns are again cheapest. These fares are for their fast 45-minute catamaran service and the 90-minute ferry.

The hovercraft operated by Hoverspeed takes only 35 minutes to cross the Channel. The fare is 242FF one way or return for foot passengers, and from 1100FF to 1300FF for a five-day return by car.

Other routes across the Channel include the recently resurrected Dieppe to Newhaven run; Cherbourg to Poole; Cherbourg, Ouistreham (Caen) or Le Havre in Normandy or St Malo in Brittany to Portsmouth; Roscoff to Plymouth; and St Malo to Weymouth.

Belgium & the Netherlands

Stena Line (☎ 017-431 58 11 in the Netherlands) has two ferries a day between the Hook of Holland in the Netherlands and Harwich. Hoverspeed operates ferries between Ostende and Dover.

GETTING THERE & AWAY

Not everyone arriving in Dover gets there by ferry ...

JULIET COOMBE

Scandinavia & Germany

Scandinavian Seaways (☎ 79 17 79 17 in Denmark; ☎ 031-65 06 00 in Sweden; ☎ 040-3 89 03 71 in Germany) operates a number of ferry services to Britain. The ferry between Esbjerg (Denmark) and Harwich runs every two days in summer and every three days in winter; the Hamburg-Harwich service runs every three days in summer, every two days in winter. The service from Gothenburg (Sweden) to Newcastle operates every other day throughout the year. You can visit the company's Web site at www.scansea.com.

Spain

Brittany Ferries (☎ 942 36 06 11) operates a car ferry twice a week from Santander on the northern coast of Spain to Plymouth. The journey takes 24 hours; a foot passenger pays 15,900 pta one way and from 16,000 pta return. A vehicle costs from 50,000 pta to 75,000 pta one way, depending on the passenger numbers, or 54,000/

80,000 pta for a five/10-day return. P&O European Ferries (☎ 944 23 44 77) operates a twice-weekly service between Bilbao and Portsmouth (35 hours). Foot passengers pay 25,000 pta one way and from 33,000 pta return. Cars cost 89,000 pta one way and from 100,000 pta return.

WALKING

Although Dick Whittington (see the boxed text 'A Boy, a Puss & City Hall' in the Facts about London chapter) supposedly had no problem with it, walking to London would not have seemed a very bright idea until recently. But now that the Thames Path National Trail has been established there's nothing to stop you hiking all the way from its source near Kemble in the Cotswolds to the Thames Barrier, a distance of 278km (172 miles; for the less intrepid, the 26km – 16-mile – section from Battersea to the barrier takes about 6½ hours). Full details can be found in Lonely Planet's *Walking in Britain*.

Warning

The information in this chapter is particularly vulnerable to change: prices for international travel are volatile, routes are introduced and cancelled, schedules change, special deals come and go, and rules and visa requirements are amended. Airlines and governments seem to take a perverse pleasure in making price structures and regulations as complicated as possible. You should check directly with the airline or a travel agency to make sure you understand how a fare (and any ticket you may buy) works. In addition, the travel industry is highly competitive, and there are many lurks and perks.

The upshot of this is that you should get opinions, quotes and advice from as many airlines and travel agencies as possible before you part with your cash. The details given in this chapter should be regarded as pointers and are not a substitute for your own careful, up-to-date research.

Alternatively you could walk Britain's first National Waterway Walk, which follows the Grand Union Canal from Gas St Basin in Birmingham to Little Venice in London, a distance of 232km (144 miles). Contact British Waterways (☎ 01923-201120) for a leaflet outlining the route; its Web site is www.british-waterways.co.uk.

TRAVEL AGENCIES

London has countless travel agencies, some of dubious reliability. Among the best are Trailfinders, STA Travel and Usit Campus, whose staff understand what a budget is and offer competitive, reliable fares. You don't have to be a student to use their services.

Council Travel
    (Map 7; ☎ 7437 7767) 28A Poland St W1 (☉ Oxford Circus). Open weekdays from 9.30 am to 6 pm, on Saturday from 10 am to 5 pm. Web site: www.counciltravel.com.

STA Travel
    (☎ 7361 6161 for European inquiries, ☎ 7361 6262 for worldwide inquiries, ☎ 7361 6160 for tours, accommodation, car hire or insurance) 86 Old Brompton Rd SW7 (Map 9; ☉ South Kensington). Open weekdays from 10 am to 6 pm, on Saturday 11 am to 5 pm; 117 Euston Rd NW1 (Map 3; ☉ Euston); 38 Store St WC1 (Map 6; ☉ Goodge Street); and 11 Goodge St W1 (Map 6; ☉ Goodge Street). Web site: www.statravel.co.uk.

Trailfinders
    (Map 5; ☎ 7938 3939 for long-haul travel, ☎ 7938 3444 for 1st and business class flights) 194 Kensington High St W8 (☉ High Street Kensington). Open Monday to Saturday from 9 am to 6 pm (Thursday to 7 pm), from 10 am on Sunday; 215 Kensington High St W8 (☎ 7937 5400 for transatlantic and European travel); 42-50 Earl's Court Rd W8 (☎ 7938 3366 for long-haul travel; ☉ Earl's Court). There's also a visa and passport service (☎ 7938 3848), immunisation centre (☎ 7938 3999), foreign exchange (☎ 7938 3836) and information centre (☎ 7938 3303) at the 194 Kensington High St branch. Web site: www.trailfinders.com.

Travelbag
    (Map 7; ☎ 7287 5558), 52 Regent St W1 (☉ Piccadilly Circus); 373-375 Strand, London WC2 (☎ 7497 0515, ☉ Temple). Has excellent-value long-haul scheduled flights.

Usit Campus
    (Map 10; ☎ 7730 3402 for European travel, ☎ 7730 8111 for worldwide inquiries) 52 Grosvenor Gardens SW1 (☉ Victoria). Open weekdays from 9 am to 6 pm, on Saturday from 10 am to 5 pm, on Sunday from 11 am to 3 pm. Branches at the YHA Adventure Shops at 174 Kensington High St W8 (Map 5; ☎ 7938 2948; ☉ High Street Kensington) and 14 Southampton St WC2 (Map 7; ☎ 7836 8541; ☉ Covent Garden). Web site: www .usitcampus.co.uk.

Plenty of other agencies advertise in the travel sections of the weekend newspapers, *Time Out* and *TNT Magazine*. All agencies should be covered by an Air Travel Organiser's Licence (ATOL). This scheme, operated by the Civil Aviation Authority (CAA), means that if either the agency or airline goes bust you are guaranteed a full refund or, if you are already abroad, to be flown back more or less on schedule. It's worth noting that, under existing consumer-protection legislation, the only way you can lose out is if you book direct from an airline; using an agency – even a 'bucket shop' – gives you more protection. But to be covered by the scheme, you must be given either the ticket or an official ATOL receipt showing the agency's number when you hand over the cash.

ORGANISED TOURS

Companies with trips pitched at a young crowd include the following: Top Deck Travel (Map 9; ☎ 7370 4555, 7244 8641), 131 Earl's Court Rd SW5 (✆ Earl's Court); Drifters (Map 5; ☎ 7262 1292), 22a Craven Terrace W2 (✆ Lancaster Gate); and Contiki (☎ 7637 0802), Russell Square WC1 (Map 6; ✆ Russell Square).

If you don't fit into this category, try Shearings Holidays (☎ 01942-824824), Miry Lane, Wigan, Lancashire WN3 4AG, which has a wide range of four to 12-day coach tours covering the whole country. They also offer Club 55 holidays for more mature holiday-makers.

For the over-60s, Saga Holidays (☎ 0800 300500, 0800 300456 for a brochure), Saga Building, Middleburg Square, Folkestone, Kent CT20 1AZ, offers holidays ranging from cheap coach-tours and resort holidays to luxury cruises around the UK and abroad. Saga also operates in the USA as Saga International Holidays (☎ 800-343 0273, 617-262 2262) at 222 Berkeley St, Boston MA 02116, and in Australia as Saga Holidays Australasia (☎ 02-9957 4266) at Level 1, 110 Pacific Highway, North Sydney 2060.

GETTING THERE & AWAY

Getting Around

THE AIRPORTS
Heathrow

Heathrow (airport code LHR), 24km (15 miles) west of central London, is the world's busiest commercial airport, handling upwards of 60 million passengers a year. It now has four terminals, with a fifth one planned. Two Piccadilly Line tube stations serve the airport: one serving Terminals 1, 2 and 3, the other at Terminal 4. Make sure you know which terminal your flight is departing from when leaving London (see the boxed text).

Heathrow can appear chaotic and overcrowded, though there are the requisite pubs and bars, restaurants and duty-free outlets (for those flying to non-EU countries). Each terminal has competitive currency-exchange facilities, information counters and accommodation desks.

There are several large international hotels – none particularly cheap or noteworthy – at or near Heathrow, should you be leaving or arriving at a peculiarly early or late hour. To reach them you must take the Heathrow Hotel Hoppa bus (☎ 01293-507099) costing £2. The buses run between 6 am and 11 pm, with a service every 10 minutes at peak times, every 15 minutes otherwise, for the first three terminals. Services from Terminal 4 run every 30 minutes.

There are left-luggage facilities at Terminal 1 (☎ 8745 5301), open daily from 6 am to 11 pm; Terminal 2 (☎ 8745 4599), open from 6 am to 10.30 pm; Terminal 3 (☎ 8759 3344), open from 5.30 am to 10.30 pm; and Terminal 4 (☎ 8745 7460), open from 5.30 am to 11 pm. The charge is £3 per item for the first 12 hours and £3.50 per item for up to 24 hours. All can forward baggage.

For general inquiries and flight information (except for British Airways; BA) phone ☎ 8759 4321. For BA ring ☎ 0870 544 4000. Other useful numbers are Car Park Information (☎ 0845 740 5000) and the Hotel Reservation Service (☎ 8564 8808).

Heathrow's Terminals

The two tube stations at Heathrow serve the following airlines:

Terminal 4
  Air Lanka
  Air Malta
  Atlantic Island Air
  British Airways intercontinental flights
  British Airways flights to Amsterdam, Paris, Moscow and Athens
  British Mediterranean
  Canadian Airlines International
  KLM (Cityhopper & Royal Dutch Airlines)
  Kenya Airways
  TAT
  Qantas Airways
Terminals 1, 2, 3
  All British Airways domestic and other European flights
  All other flights

To/From Heathrow The fastest way to get to central London is via the new Heathrow Express (☎ 0845 600 1515), an ultra-modern train that whisks passengers from Heathrow Central station (serving Terminals 1 to 3) and Terminal 4 station to Paddington station (Map 5; ⊖ Paddington) in 15 minutes. It's a pricey way to go, though: £12/22 single/return in express class (£20/40 in 1st class) for everyone over the age of 15. Trains leave Paddington every 15 minutes from platform No 6 or 7 behind the ticket office. The first train departs at 5.10 am, the last at 11.40 pm. From the airport, the first train of the day leaves Terminal 4 station at 5.02 am (5.07 am from Heathrow Central); the last one at 11.47 pm (11.52 pm). The service's Web site is at www.heathrowexpress.co.uk. Many airlines, including American Airlines and BA, now have full check-in facilities at Paddington.

The Underground remains the cheapest way of getting to Heathrow (£3.40/1.40 for adults/under-16s) and runs between 5.30 am and 11.30 pm every day. To use a Travelcard (see Fares in the later London Underground section), it must be valid for all six zones. Be advised that you can buy tickets for the tube from machines in the baggage reclaim areas of the Heathrow terminals so you don't have to queue up in the station itself. The journey to/from central London takes about an hour.

The services of the Airbus Heathrow Shuttle are being extensively reorganised and you should call ☎ 7222 1234 or visit www.airbus.co.uk on the Web for the latest information. At the time of writing it ran along Notting Hill Gate and Bayswater Rd to Russell Square and King's Cross. Buses go every 30 minutes and cost £6/10 single/return (£3/6 for students & children aged five to 15). The trip takes about 1¼ hours.

The first bus leaves from the southern side of Russell Square at 5.18 am (and at 6.40 am from the Great Northern Hotel at King's Cross), the last at 8.58 pm (8.50 pm from King's Cross). The first bus bound for London leaves Terminal 4 at 5.40 am via Terminals 3, 2 and 1. The last departure from Terminal 4 is at 9.30 pm.

A minicab to/from central London will cost from around £20, and a metered black cab around £35.

Gatwick

Gatwick (airport code LGW), some 48km (30 miles) south of central London, is smaller and better organised than Heathrow. The North and South terminals are linked by an efficient monorail service.

For information phone the central Gatwick directory on ☎ 01293-535353. This will also connect you to Thomas Cook, which deals with hotel reservations. For BA ring ☎ 0870 544 4000, for information on parking your car call ☎ 0845 740 5000.

The left-luggage office at the North Terminal (☎ 01293-502013) is open daily from 6 am to 10 pm, the one in the South Terminal (☎ 01293-502014) round the clock.

To/From Gatwick The Gatwick Express (☎ 0870 530 1530) trains link the station near the South Terminal to platform Nos 13 and 14 at Victoria station (Map 10; ⊖ Victoria) every 15 minutes from about 5 am to just before midnight; they then run every 30 minutes until about 1.30 am when they go hourly (though there are plans to increase the frequency to every 15 minutes round the clock). Singles are £9.50/4.75 for adults/under-15s, and the journey takes about 30 minutes. BA and American Airlines passengers can check in at Victoria. The service's Web site is www.gatwickexpress.co.uk.

The Connex South Central service from Victoria, which runs every 15 to 30 minutes (once an hour in the wee hours), takes a little longer but costs only £8.20/4.10 one way. There's also a Thameslink service from King's Cross, Farringdon and London Bridge costing £9.50/4.75. For rail inquiries, call ☎ 0845 748 4950.

Flightline buses (☎ 0870 574 7777) run from central London to Gatwick every hour from 7.15 am to 11.35 pm (between 5 am to 8.10 pm from the airport to town). A single/return valid for three months costs £7.50/11. Go to the Flightline Web site at www.speedlink.co.uk for more details.

A minicab to/from central London will cost £35, a black taxi around £50.

Stansted

Some 56km (35 miles) north-east of central London, Stansted (airport code STN), London's third international gateway, is its most ambitious – with plans to double the annual number of passengers it handles (currently seven million) – and attractive; the futuristic terminal building was designed by Norman Foster. There's a single number (☎ 01279-680500) for general inquiries, hotel reservations and rail information.

To/From Stansted The direct Stansted Skytrain to Liverpool Street station (Map 8; ⊖ Liverpool Street) takes about 40 minutes and costs £10.50, departing every 30 minutes. If you need to connect with the tube from the airport, change at Tottenham Hale for the Victoria Line or stay on to Liverpool Street station for the Central Line. The first train leaves Liverpool Street station at 5 am, the last at 11 pm. From the airport, the first train goes at 6 am (8 am on Sunday), the last just before midnight. For rail inquiries, call ☎ 0845 748 4950.

Flightline buses (☎ 0870 574 74777) link central London with Stansted every hour from 6 am to 9.30 pm. From the airport buses leave once an hour between 8 am and 10.15 pm. A single/return valid for three months from Victoria costs £9/13. The Flightline Web site is at www.speedlink .co.uk.

Minicabs to/from central London will cost about £35, a black cab around £75.

London City

London City airport (airport code LCY; ☎ 7646 0088, 07000 CITYAIRPORT), 10km (six miles) east of central London, is in the Docklands by the Thames. Seen as a businessperson's airport and under-utilised until recently, London City now has flights to 17 continental European destinations as well four cities in the British Isles (Dublin, Edinburgh, Glasgow and Manchester). A fully equipped business and conference centre is also available (☎ 7646 0900, email info@londoncityairport.com). You can get further information by visiting the airport's Web site at www.londoncityairport.com.

To/From London City The airport is to the east of the Blackwall Tunnel and the Thames Barrier. A shuttle bus connects the airport with Liverpool Street train station (£5) via Canary Wharf (£2) between 6.50 am (11 am on Sunday) and 9.20 pm (1.10 pm on Saturday) daily. The first bus leaves Liverpool Street station (bus stop A) at 6.30 am (10.30 am on Sunday); the last departs at 9.08 pm weekdays (12.40 pm on Saturday and 8.50 pm on Sunday). Services are every 10 minutes, and the journey takes 25 minutes from Liverpool Street and eight minutes from Canary Wharf.

You can also use the North London/ Silverlink line (see the Underground map

for connections to this line); get off at Silvertown & London City Airport station, which is a few minutes' walk south-west of the terminal. Alternatively, take the Docklands Light Railway (DLR) to the Prince Regent stop and then bus No 473.

A black taxi costs about £15 to/from central London.

Luton

By London standards a small, remote airport some 56km (35 miles) to the north, Luton (airport code LTN; ☎ 01582-405100 for general inquiries, hotel reservations and car-park information) caters mainly for cheap charter-flights, though the discount airline easyJet (☎ 01582-445354) operates scheduled services (you can visit its Web site at www.easyjet.com to get further details).

To/From Luton Green Line bus No 757 (☎ 8668 7261, 0845 778 8788) from Victoria Coach Station serves Luton (£7.20/ 11.80 single/return). Buses leave hourly from 6.25 am (6.30 am at weekends) to 11 pm. The first departs from Luton at 5.18 am (5.15 am at weekends), the last at 9.30 pm. The company's Web site is at www.greenline.co.uk.

Alternatively catch the airport shuttle bus outside the arrivals hall for the eight-minute trip to Luton station, then take the Thameslink train into central London (35 to 45 minutes; £10.20). Trains depart every 20 minutes or so throughout the day and most of the night.

LONDON UNDERGROUND

The London Underground, or 'tube', first opened in 1863 (it was then essentially a roofed-in trench) and sometimes it feels like not a whole lot has changed since then; it is slow, unreliable, and, as the ageing system has suffered from decades of underfunding, breakdowns are common. Sometimes entire sections of the tube are closed and there's the constant threat of strikes by operators and other staff opposed to the government's proposed privatisation.

Worst of all, it's terribly expensive: compare the cheapest full single fare in central London of £1.40 with those charged on the Paris Métro (8FF/88p) and the New York Subway (US$1.50/90p). And in Paris and New York you can travel on the entire system for the flat fare; in London £1.40 gets you around central London (Zone 1) only.

Still, the tube is normally the quickest and easiest way of getting round London and extends as far afield as Amersham in Buckinghamshire to the north-west, Epping in Essex to the north-east, Heathrow airport in the south-west and, via the DLR, Beckton to the south-east. An estimated 2.5 million tube journeys are made every day.

The Tube: Fun Facts to Know & Tell

The tube is the world's oldest (1863), most extensive (408km of track) and busiest (785 million journeys a year) underground transport system. With breakdowns every 16 minutes on average, it is also the most unreliable, and for the journey between Covent Garden and Leicester Square (£1.40 for 250m), the per-kilometre price makes taking the tube more expensive than flying Concorde. But those aren't the tube's only superlatives and oddities:

- The longest line is the Central Line (74km), with the Piccadilly Line running a close second at 71.3km; the shortest is the Waterloo & City Line (2.2km), known as 'the Drain' that links Bank with Waterloo.
- With its 16km extension now completed, the Jubilee Line is the only one in the entire system to connect with all the other lines as well as the Docklands Light Railway.
- The longest journey possible *without* changing trains is from West Ruislip to Epping on the Central Line (54.9km).
- The longest distance between stations is from Chesham to Chalfont & Latimer on the Metropolitan Line (6.3km); the shortest is between Leicester Square and Covent Garden (250m).
- The deepest station is Hampstead on the Northern Line (58.5m).
- The District Line has the most stations with 60, followed by the Piccadilly (52) and Central (49) lines; the Waterloo & City has a mere two.
- The busiest stations are Victoria (86 million passengers a year), Oxford Circus (85 million), King's Cross (69 million), Liverpool Street (44 million) and Baker Street (43 million).
- The stations with the most platforms are Moorgate and Baker Street; each has 10.
- There are 303 escalators on the Underground. Bank has the most (15, not including its two moving walkways) while the one at Angel on the Northern Line is the longest (60m, up a vertical rise of 27.5m).
- There are some 40 'ghost' (disused) stations on the Underground, including British Museum on the Central Line (closed in the 1930s); Down Street near Hyde Park Corner on the Piccadilly Line, used by Churchill and his family during WWII; Marlborough Street on the Metropolitan Line near Lord's, now a Chinese restaurant; South Kentish Town near Camden on the Northern Line, which closed during a power cut and never reopened; and poor Hounslow Town on the District Line, which functioned from 1883 to 1886 and then again from 1903 to 1909, when it closed permanently through lack of use.
- You will never hear 'Mind the gap' on the Jubilee Line extension as all platforms have 'platform-edge doors' to cut out draughts and bridge gaps; the gappiest gaps – caused by curvatures in the platform – are at Embankment and Bank.
- Unproven but assumed: everyone has complained about the tube at some stage in their life.

Shopping by Tube and bus

Printing commissioned by London Transport from Christopher Corr
This poster is available from
the London Transport Museum, Covent Garden Piazza.
Supported by
TDI

Shoppers – as well as commuters, tourists and buskers – keep LRT very busy indeed.

Information

London Regional Transport (LRT) is responsible for the tube and its information centres sell tickets and provide free maps. There are centres at all four Heathrow terminals, and at Victoria, Piccadilly Circus, Oxford Circus, St James's Park, Liverpool

---

What Kind of Train?

Throughout this book the nearest Underground station is indicated by the ⊖ symbol. If you must use a suburban train or the DLR to get there this is indicated by the word 'station' or 'DLR'.

Street, Euston and King's Cross tube and main-line train stations. There are also information offices at Hammersmith and West Croydon stations. For general information on the tube, buses, the DLR or trains within London ring ☎ 7222 1234 or visit the LRT Web site at www.londontransport .co.uk. For news of how services are running, call Travelcheck on ☎ 7222 1200.

Network

Greater London is served by 12 tube lines, along with the independent (though linked) and privately owned DLR and an interconnected railway network (see the later DLR & Train section). The first tube train is at around 5.30 am Monday to Saturday and around 7 am on Sunday; the last train leaves between 11.30 pm to 12.30 am depending on the day, the station and the line.

Remember that any train heading from left to right on the map is designated as eastbound, any train heading from top to bottom is southbound. If your two stations are not on the same line, you need to note the nearest station where the two lines intersect, where you must change trains (transfer).

Tube lines vary in their reliability and the Circle Line, which links most of the main-line stations and is therefore much used by tourists, has one of the worst track records. Other lines low in the league tables are the Northern Line (though improving), the Central Line (despite the millions of pounds spent on its new signalling system) and the Hammersmith & City (often referred to as the 'Hammersmith & Shitty'). The Piccadilly Line to/from Heathrow is generally pretty good.

There have been quite a few changes on the tube in recent years. Mornington Crescent on the Northern Line, almost a 'ghost station' it was closed for so long, reopened in 1998, as did the East London Line, useful for the flagship YHA hostel in Rotherhithe. But the biggest news in decades was the completion of the 16km Jubilee Line extension in 1999, east to Canary Wharf and North Greenwich and north to Stratford.

The 11 new Jubilee Line stations were all designed by different architects, and many are ultramodern works of art in themselves.

If you're caught on the Underground without a valid ticket (and that includes crossing into a zone that your ticket doesn't cover) you're liable for an on-the-spot £10 fine. If you do get nabbed, do us all a favour: shut up and pay up. The inspectors – and your fellow passengers – hear the same stories every day of the year.

The seriously organised may want to pick up a copy of *The Clever Tube Hopper* (published by the Clever Map Company), a pocket-sized booklet that tells you which carriage to get on in order to arrive level with your station's exit or the correct interchange point.

Fares

LRT divides London into six concentric zones. The basic fare for adults/children under 16 years for Zone 1 is £1.40/60p, for Zones 1 & 2 £1.70/80p, for three zones £2.10/1, for four zones £2.60/1.20, for five zones £3.10/1.30 and for all six zones (eg to/from Heathrow) £3.40/1.40. But if you're travelling through a couple of zones or several times in one day, consider a travel pass or some other discounted fare.

Travel Passes & Discount Fares A Travelcard valid all day offers the cheapest way of getting about in London and can be used after 9.30 am on weekdays and all day at weekends on all forms of transport in London: the tube, suburban trains, the DLR and buses (but *not* night buses). Most visitors will find that a Zones 1 & 2 card (£3.80) will be sufficient, but a card for Zones 1, 2, 3 & 4 costs £4 and one for Zones 2, 3, 4, 5 & 6 £3.30. A card to cover all six zones costs £4.50, just £1.10 more than a one-journey all-zone ticket – and you get to use it all day. A one-day Travelcard for children aged five to 15 costs £1.90 regardless of how many zones it covers but those aged 14 and 15 need a Child Rate Photocard to travel on this fare. You can buy Travelcards several days ahead but not on buses.

Mapping the Underground

The London Underground map is so familiar that it's often used as a symbol for the city itself. Millions of people refer to it every year without giving a thought to Harry Beck (1902-74), the engineering draughtsman responsible for designing the map in 1931.

It was Beck who realised that the entire network could be fitted into a realistic amount of space and still be perfectly usable – even if strict geography was ignored. After all, once you're underground you don't really need to know exactly where places are, just so long as you understand where they lie in relation to each other in the network.

Beck expanded the space devoted to the central London stations, redrew all the lines until they were horizontal, vertical or at 45 degrees to each other, and devised the colour-coding system for the different lines. For his efforts he was paid the grand sum of five guineas (about £5.25), but every London Underground map still carried his name until 1960. Even now the map is basically unchanged, except for the addition of new lines and stations.

On the prowl for fare-dodgers: London Underground's feline ticket inspectors at Barbican tube station.

GETTING AROUND

JULIET COOMBE

If you plan to start moving before 9.30 am on a weekday, you can buy a Zones 1 & 2 LT Card for £4.80/2.40 (£6/2.90 for Zones 1, 2, 3 & 4, and £7.50/3.20 for all six zones), valid on the tube, the DLR and buses (but *not* suburban trains) for one day with no time restrictions.

Weekly Travelcards are also available but require an identification card with a passport-sized photo. A Zone 1 card for adults/children aged five to 15 costs £14.30/5.50; Zones 1 & 2 £17.60/6.50; Zones 1, 2 & 3 £21.50/9; Zones 1, 2, 3 & 4 £26.70/11.50; Zones 1, 2, 3, 4 & 5 £32/12.50; all six zones £34.90/13.50. These allow you to travel at any time of day and on night buses as well, but before buying one decide whether you're really likely to travel much early in the morning or at night; five one-day Travelcards for all zones plus a weekend card (see the following) for a total of £28.20 is cheaper than a weekly pass. Monthly and annual Travelcards can also be purchased for between one and six zones (between £55 and £134.10 for a month, between £572 and £1396 for a year).

At £5.70/2.80 for adults/children in Zones 1 & 2, Weekend Travelcards valid on Saturday and Sunday are 25% cheaper than two separate one-day cards. Family Travelcards are also available for one or two adults and up to four children aged under 16 (who need not be related to them); they start at £3 per adult and 60p per child for Zones 1 & 2 up to £3.60/60p for all six zones.

If you will be making a lot of journeys within Zone 1 *only*, you can buy a carnet of 10 tickets for £10, a saving of £4. But do remember that if you cross over into Zone 2 (eg from King's Cross to Camden Town for the weekend market) you'll be travelling on an invalid ticket and liable for a penalty fare.

BUS

If you're not in much of a hurry, travelling round London by double-decker bus can be more enjoyable than using the tube. Even though they were privatised in 1994, London's 5500 buses are still regulated by LRT. An estimated 3.8 million people travel on them every day.

Information

The All London bus map (No 1), available free from most LRT information centres, is for general use but there are also 36 separate (and free) ones available to areas as far-flung as Harrow, Romford and Hounslow. Most visitors, however, will find map No 1 sufficient. If you can't get to an LRT information centre, ring ☎ 7371 0247 to have one sent or write to London Transport Buses, Freepost Lon7503, London SE16 4BR. For general information on London buses call ☎ 7222 1234 (24 hours). For news of how services are running, phone Travelcheck on ☎ 7222 1200.

Network & Useful Routes

One of the best ways to explore London is to buy a Travelcard and jump on a bus (especially the double-decker Routemaster ones with a conductor and an access platform at the rear, which makes the jumping on and off so easy).

From north to south (or vice versa) the No 24 is especially good. Beginning at South End Green in Hampstead Heath, it travels through Camden and along Gower St to Tottenham Court Rd. From there it goes down Charing Cross Rd, past Leicester Square to Trafalgar Square, then along Whitehall, past the Palace of Westminster, Westminster Abbey and Westminster Cathedral. It reaches Victoria station and then carries on to Pimlico, which is handy for the Tate Gallery at Millbank.

Another north-south route worth trying is the No 19, which departs from Finsbury Park tube station, travels down Upper St in Islington, through Clerkenwell, Holborn and Bloomsbury, then along New Oxford St and down Charing Cross Rd. It then travels down Shaftesbury Ave and Piccadilly, along the northern edge of Green Park and Hyde Park Corner, before carrying on down Sloane St and along King's Rd. If you get off at the southern end of Battersea Bridge, you'll be well placed for Battersea Park.

From east to west, or the reverse, try the No 8. This is a Routemaster bus and comes from Bow in east London. It goes along

DENNIS JOHNSON

Many bus routes are excellent for sightseeing on the cheap.

Bethnal Green Rd and passes the markets at Spitalfields and Petticoat Lane, Liverpool Street station, the City, the Guildhall and the Old Bailey. It then crosses Holborn and enters Oxford St, travelling past Oxford Circus, Bond St, Selfridges and the flagship Marks & Spencer store at Marble Arch before terminating at Victoria.

Other good tour buses are Nos 9 and 10, which leave from Hammersmith and go through Kensington and Knightsbridge, passing the Albert Memorial, Royal Albert Hall and Harrods before reaching Hyde Park Corner. The No 9 then goes along Piccadilly to Piccadilly Circus and Trafalgar Square before carrying on down the Strand to Aldwych (good for Covent Garden), where it terminates. The No 10 heads north from Hyde Park Corner to Marble Arch and heads down Oxford St and then up Tottenham Court Rd to Euston, King's Cross and eventually Archway tube station.

The wheelchair-accessible Stationlink buses (☎ 7918 3305), which have a ramp operated by the driver, follow a similar route to that of the Underground Circle Line, joining up all the main-line stations – from Liverpool Street, Waterloo and Victoria to Paddington, Euston, St Pancras and King's Cross. People with mobility problems and those with heavy luggage may find this easier to use than the tube, although it only operates once an hour. From Paddington there are services clockwise (designated the SL1) from 8.15 am to 7.15 pm, and anticlockwise (the SL2) from 8.40 am to 6.40 pm. To find out how the services are running ring ☎ 7918 3312.

GETTING AROUND

Night Buses Trafalgar Square is the focus for all but six of LRT's network of 50 night buses (prefixed with the letter 'N'). They run from about midnight to 7 am but services can be infrequent and only stop on request, meaning you must signal clearly to the driver to stop. LRT publishes a free credit-card-sized timetable that lists all the routes. Only Travelcards valid for a week or longer are valid on night buses; everyone else pays.

Fares

Single-journey bus tickets sold on the bus (drivers and conductors can give you change) cost anywhere from 60p to £1.20, depending on whether you're travelling within one zone or crossing several (a £1 all-in adult fare is being seriously considered and may be in effect by the time you read this). Children aged five to 15 pay a uniform 40p. The Travelcards described earlier in the London Underground section are valid on buses.

Stationlink buses cost £1/50p for adults/children aged five to 15 though Travelcards, including single Zone 1 ones, are also valid. Night buses cost from £1 to £1.50 from midnight to 4.30 am at which point normal daytime fares are charged.

Travel Passes If you plan to use only buses, you can buy a one-day bus pass valid throughout London for £2.80/1 for adults/children. Unlike the one-day Travelcards, these are valid before 9.30 am. Weekly passes are also available for £12.50/4, as are monthly and annual ones.

DLR & TRAIN

The independent, driverless Docklands Light Railway links the City at Bank and Tower Gateway at Tower Hill with Stratford, Beckton and Island Gardens at the southern end of the Isle of Dogs. A DLR extension under the Thames as far as Lewisham, with stations at Cutty Sark, Greenwich, Deptford Bridge and Elverson Rd, opened at the end of 1999. The DLR runs from 5.30 am to 12.30 am weekdays,

from 6 am to 12.30 am on Saturday and from 7.30 am to 11.30 pm on Sunday. Fares are the same as those on the tube though there are a range of daily, weekly, monthly and annual passes valid on the DLR only. The one-day Sail & Rail ticket (£7.80/4.10), for example, allows unlimited travel on the DLR and a single river-boat trip in either direction between Westminster and Greenwich piers. For general information on the DLR phone ☎ 7918 4000 (24 hours). For news of how services are running, call Travelcheck on ☎ 7222 1200 or DLR Customer Services on ☎ 7363 9700.

Several rail companies also operate passenger trains in London, including the North London/Silverlink line – which links Richmond in the south-west with North Woolwich in the south-east – and the crowded Thameslink 'sardine line', which goes from Elephant & Castle and London Bridge in the south through the City to King's Cross and as far north as Luton. Most lines connect with the tube and Travelcards can be used on them.

If you're staying in south-east London where suburban trains are usually much more useful than the tube, it may be worth buying a one-year Network Railcard, which offers a third off most rail fares in south-east England and on one-day Travelcards for all six zones. Travel is permitted only after 10 am on weekdays and at any time at weekends. The card costs £20 and is available from any staffed station.

CAR & MOTORCYCLE

By all means, avoid bringing a car into London. The roads are horribly clogged, drivers are aggressive in the extreme, road rage is a common occurrence (75% of all London drivers have experienced it to some degree, according to a 1999 survey) and parking space is at a premium. Traffic wardens and wheel clampers operate with extreme efficiency, and if your vehicle is towed away you won't see much change from £100 to get it back. If you do get clamped, ring the 24-hour Clamping & Vehicle Section hotline on ☎ 7747 4747.

Road Rules

Vehicles drive on the left-hand side of the road. Wearing seat belts in the front is compulsory, and if they are fitted in the back passengers there must wear them as well. You give way to your right at roundabouts (traffic already on the roundabout has the right of way). Motorcyclists must wear helmets at all times.

The current speed limits are 30 miles per hour (48km/h) in built-up areas, 60mph (97km/h) on single carriageways and 70mph (113km/h) on motorways and dual carriageways. Other speed limits will be indicated by signs. Many side streets now come complete with speed humps ('sleeping policemen'), aimed at reducing the traffic flow to a crawl.

If you do plan to drive in London you should get hold of the *Highway Code* (99p), which is available at outlets of the AA and RAC (see Motoring Organisations below) as well as some bookshops and tourist information centres. A foreign driving licence is valid in Britain for up to 12 months from the time of your last entry into the country. If you're bringing a car from Europe make sure you're adequately insured.

See Legal Matters in the Facts for the Visitor chapter for information on drink-driving rules.

Motoring Organisations

The two largest in the UK, both of which offer 24-hour breakdown assistance, are the Automobile Association (AA; ☎ 0800 919595) and the Royal Automobile Club (RAC; ☎ 0870 572 2722). One year's membership starts at £43 for the AA and £39 for the RAC, and both can also extend their cover to include continental Europe. Your motoring organisation at home may have a reciprocal arrangement with the AA or RAC.

Petrol

At around 72p per litre, petrol is extremely expensive; compare this with the 19p per litre paid in the USA! About 86% of the price of a litre of petrol in the UK is government tax.

Parking

Avoid driving at peak hours (ie from 7.30 to 9.30 am, and from 4.30 to 7 pm) and plan ahead if you need to park in the centre.

Look out for yellow lines along the roadside. A single line indicates that parking restrictions are in force; you need to find the nearby sign that spells out exactly what they are. A double line means no parking at all; a broken line means more limited restrictions. Single red lines on main routes in and out of central London indicate a ban on stopping, loading or parking from 7 am to 7 pm, while a double red line means no stopping, loading or parking at all.

There are 'short-stay' and 'long-stay' car parks. Prices will often be the same for stays of up to two or three hours, but for lengthier ones the short-stay car parks rapidly become much more expensive. The long-stay car parks may be slightly less convenient, but they're much cheaper. Phone National Car Parks (NCP; ☎ 7404 3777) for car park addresses in London.

The City of London Information Centre (☎ 7332 1456) can supply a leaflet on parking in the City for people with disabilities.

Rental

Car hire rates are very expensive in the UK; often you'll be better off making arrangements in your home country for some sort of package deal. The big international rental companies charge £150 to £200 a week for their smallest cars (such as a Ford Fiesta).

Among the main players are Avis (☎ 0870 590 0500), British Car Rental (☎ 7278 2802), Budget (☎ 0800 181181), Eurodollar (☎ 0870 536 5365), Europcar (☎ 0845 722 2525), Hertz (☎ 0845 755 5888) and Thrifty Car Rental (☎ 7403 3458).

Holiday Autos (☎ 0870 530 0400) operates through a number of rental companies and generally offers excellent deals, starting at £135 a week. For other cheap operators check the ads in *TNT Magazine*.

If you'd prefer a motorbike to a car, try Scootabout (☎ 7833 4607), 1-3 Leeke St WC1 (⊖ King's Cross St Pancras), which has a wide range of bikes available.

GETTING AROUND

Purchase

If you're planning to tour around when you leave London you may want to buy a vehicle. It's possible to get something reasonable for around £1000. Check *Loot* (five times a week) or *Autotrader* (every Thursday) for ads. The monthly *Motorists' Guide* lists models and their average prices.

All cars require a Ministry of Transport (MOT) safety certificate valid for one year and issued by a licensed garage; full third-party insurance – shop around but expect to pay at least £300; a registration form signed by the buyer and seller, with a section to be sent to the MOT; and a licence disc proving you've paid your Vehicle Excise Duty (VED), a tax of £82.25/155 for six months/one year (£55/100 for a vehicle with an engine of 1100cc or less). The discs are sold at post offices on presentation of a valid MOT certificate, registration document and proof of insurance.

You're strongly advised to buy a vehicle with a valid MOT certificate and a VED disc; both remain with the car through a change of ownership. Third-party insurance goes with the driver rather than the car, so you'll still have to arrange this (and beware of letting others drive the car unless they are listed on the policy). For further information contact a post office or a Vehicle Registration Office for leaflet V100.

Camper Van Camper vans provide a popular method of touring around the UK and the rest of Europe, particularly for shoestring travellers. Often three or four people will band together to buy or rent a van. Look at the adverts in *TNT Magazine* if you wish to form or join a group.

Both *Autotrader* and *Loot* carry ads for vans. The Van Market in Market Rd N7 (⊖ Caledonian Road) is a long-running institution where private sellers congregate on a daily basis. Some second-hand dealers offer a 'buy-back' scheme for when you return, but buying and reselling privately is better if you have the time.

Vans usually feature a fixed high-top or elevating roof and from two to five bunk beds. Apart from the essential camping gas cooker, professional conversions may include a sink, a fridge and built-in cupboards. You will need to spend a minimum of £1000 to £2000 for something reliable enough to get you around.

TAXI

The black London taxi cab is as much a feature of the cityscape as the red double-decker bus, although these days it comes in a variety of colours, bespattered with advertising, and a new, more streamlined black version has also been introduced.

Taking a taxi can be worthwhile for a group of three or four people and can avoid the sometimes long waits for trains and buses. They also come into their own at

The Knowledge Is with Them

When you climb into one of London's 23,000 black cabs you can rest assured you'll get where you want to go – by the quickest possible route – because all drivers must complete a rigorous learning and testing process known as 'The Knowledge' before they can hit the streets. For an All London licence, this means buying or renting a moped, getting hold of a good map and spending up to two years studying and memorising 25,000 streets within a 10km-radius of Charing Cross.

But it's not just about learning how to get from street A to street B. Drivers are expected to know the locations of hospitals, clubs, hotels, theatres, train stations, places of worship – the list is endless. All this culminates in a series of 15-minute interviews and tests that may take months to pass. It takes a lot of time, money and patience – which, according to the Public Carriage Office, means only committed cabbies will join the 'noble trade'. But this is not a perfect world and in the event that you get a less than noble driver you can phone the Public Carriage Office on ☎ 7230 1631.

JULIET COOME

'Where d'you wanna go, mate?' Black cabs lie in wait at every main-line train station.

night, although prices are higher. Cabs are available for hire when the yellow sign above the windscreen is lit; just stick your arm out to signal one. Fares are metered, with flag fall at £1.40, and increments of 20p for each 219m (after the first 438m). Additional charges include 40p for each additional passenger, 10p for any baggage stored in the front seat next to the driver, 60p for journeys made between 8 pm and midnight and 90p for those between midnight and 6 am. You can tip up to 10% but most people just round up to the nearest pound.

To order a cab by phone (£1.20) try Radio Taxis on ☎ 7272 0272. Do not expect to hail down a taxi in popular nightlife areas of London like Soho late in the evening (and especially after pub closing time). But if you do find yourself in any of those areas, signal even taxis with their lights off and try to look sober. A lot of drivers are very choosy about their fares at this time of night.

Minicabs are cheaper, freelance competitors of the black cabs, but they are driven by untrained individuals who are usually not insured. Minicabs cannot legally be hailed on the street but must be hired by phone or directly from one of the minicab offices (every high street has one). You'll probably be approached by minicab drivers seeking fares in Soho and around Leicester Square and Tottenham Court Rd at night.

Some minicab drivers have a *very* limited idea of how to get around efficiently (and safely) – you may find yourself being pressed to map read. They don't have meters, so it's essential to fix a price before you start. Bargain hard – most drivers will start at about 25% higher than the fare they're prepared to accept. Minicabs can carry up to four people.

Ask a local for the name of a reputable minicab company, or phone one of the large 24-hour operators (☎ 7387 8888, 7272 2612, 7383 3333, 8340 2450 or 8567 1111). You can also order one on the Web by visiting www.proteus.demon.co.uk/taxi .html. Women travelling by themselves at night can choose Lady Cabs (☎ 7254 3501), which has women drivers. Gays and lesbians can choose Freedom Cars (☎ 7734 1313).

GETTING AROUND

BICYCLE

Cycling around London is one way of cutting transport costs, but it can be a grim business, with heavy traffic and fumes detracting from the pleasure of getting a little exercise. The London Cycling Campaign (☎ 7928 7220) is working towards improving conditions, not least by campaigning to establish the London Cycle Network, which is up and running on the South Bank and in Bankside and hopes to see almost 2000km of cycle routes throughout the capital in the next few years. A pack they produce called *On Your Bike* (£4.95) includes a map showing both established and suggested cycle routes, and a pamphlet with all sorts of information on such issues as maintenance and security. It's advisable to wear a helmet and increasingly Londoners wear face-masks to filter out pollution.

If you want to buy a bike it might be worth heading for the auction (☎ 8870 3909) at 63 Garratt Lane SW18 (Wandsworth Town station), where the police off-load lost or stolen bikes every Monday at 11 am. Second-hand bikes are also advertised in *Cycling Weekly*, *Loot* and *Exchange & Mart*.

If you prefer to hire, all the places listed below offer mountain or hybrid bikes in mint condition. Each demands deposits of £100 to £200 (credit-card slips are accepted), however long the rental period.

Bikepark
   (Map 7; ☎ 7430 0083) 11 Macklin St WC2 (⊖ Holborn). The minimum charge is £10 for the first day, £5 for the second day and £3 for subsequent days.
Dial-a-Bike
   (Map 10; ☎ 7828 4040) 18 Gillingham St SW1 (⊖ Victoria). Rentals cost from £6.99 per day and £29.90 per week.
London Bicycle Tour Company
   (Map 6; ☎ 7928 6838) 1a Gabriel's Wharf, 56 Upper Ground SE1 (⊖ Blackfriars). Rentals cost £9.95 for the first day, £5 for subsequent ones, £29.95 for the first week and £25 for the second. It also offers daily three-hour bike tours of London at 2 pm for £11.95, including bike.

There's a central bike-park (Map 7; ☎ 7430 0083) at 11 Macklin St WC2 (⊖ Holborn).

It's open weekdays between 7.30 am and 8.30 pm and at weekends from 8.30 am to 6.30 pm. To park costs 50p an hour up to £2 a day, £7.50 a week and £20 a month. There's a Chelsea branch (Map 9; ☎ 7565 0777) near the Chelsea Farmers Market at 250 King's Rd SW3 (⊖ Sloane Square).

Bikes can be taken only on the District, Circle, Hammersmith & City and Metropolitan tube lines outside the rush hours (ie from 10 am to 4 pm and after 7 pm on weekdays). Folding bikes, however, can be brought on any line. Bicycles can also travel on the above-ground sections of some other tube lines, but not on the deeper lines. Bikes are banned on the DLR.

Restrictions on taking a bike on suburban and main-line trains vary from company to company so you need to check with the relevant one before setting out. For information, call ☎ 0845 748 4950.

WALKING

Many of the sights you'll want to visit are relatively close together in the centre. Get hold of a good map or street atlas (see Maps in the Facts for the Visitor chapter) and you'll be on your way.

You can also buy several booklets detailing self-guided walks. A good one to look out for is *The London Wall Walk* (Museum of London; £1.95), which takes in 21 landmarks on a 3km walk along the old Roman and medieval city wall. The Britain Visitor Centre sells a map (£1.50) showing the route of the 20km Silver Jubilee Walkway, which starts in Leicester Square and runs through the City, along the South Bank and round Westminster, with silver boards describing the sights along the way. The free *Explore London's Canals*, available from British Waterways (see Walking in the Getting There & Away chapter), details six walks along London's canal towpaths.

You'll find other ideas for self-paced walks in the Things to See & Do chapter. For guided walking see the Organised Tours section later in this chapter. A good Web site for walks around lesser known areas of London is www.londonwalking.com.

Blue Plaques

The system of placing 'Blue Plaques' on the houses (or sites of houses in this forever developing city) of distinguished people originated in 1867, and you can even buy a guidebook – *The London Blue Plaque Guide* by Nick Rennison (Sutton Publishing; £9.99) – identifying some 700 of them now in place. The candidate must have been dead for at least two decades or have been born 100 years before and be known to the 'well-informed passer-by'. Guess we're not as smart as we thought we were; we never recognise the vast majority of the names, many of which must surely belong to people occupying the footnotes of history.

BOAT
River Shuttle

City Cruises (☎ 7237 5134) operates a Pool of London jump-on, jump-off ferry service from April to October, travelling from Tower Pier to London Bridge City Pier, HMS *Belfast*, Butlers Wharf and St Katharine's Pier in a continuous loop every 30 minutes from 11 am to 5 pm daily. Tickets cost £2/1 for adults/seniors & children aged under 16 and are valid all day. It runs at weekends only from November to March.

Circular Cruises (☎ 7936 2033) offers a similar service from Westminster Pier every 30 to 40 minutes between 11 am and as late as 7 pm, depending on the time of year. Vessels call at London Bridge City Pier, St Katharine's Pier and, in the summer season, Festival Pier on the South Bank at weekends. Tickets cost £5.60/4.60/2.80 for adults/seniors/children aged under 16 and £15 for a family. Fares are cheaper between just two stages (eg Westminster Pier to/from London Bridge City Pier for £4/3/2).

A Thames circular cruise with Catamaran Cruisers (☎ 7987 1185), leaving from Embankment Pier hourly from 11 am to 5 pm and 6.30 to 10.30 pm, costs £6.70/4.70.

City Cruises also runs services between Tower and Westminster piers with a stop at Bankside and the Globe daily from 10.20 am to 5 pm (as late as 8.30 pm from June to August). Single/return fares are £4.60/5.80 for adults and £2.30/2.90 for seniors and children aged under 16. The single/return fares for the trip between Tower or Westminster piers and the Globe at Bankside (every 30 minutes from 10.30 am to just before 6 pm, depending on which way you're headed) are £2.70/5.20 for adults and £1.35/2.60 for seniors and children aged under 16.

There's also City Cruises' Millennium Express river-boat service every 30 minutes from Festival Pier at South Bank to the Millennium Dome. The trip takes about 45 minutes. The first boat sails at 9 am (one hour before the dome opens) and the last one leaves Millennium Pier at 7 pm or midnight, depending on whether there are one or two sessions scheduled at the Dome (see Around Greenwich in the Things to See & Do chapter).

Canal Trips

London has 65km (40 miles) of inner-city canals, most of them constructed in the early 19th century to transport goods from the industrial Midlands to the Port of London. After a long period of neglect, these canals are being given a new lease of life as a leisure resource for boaters, walkers, anglers and cyclists. For information, contact British Waterways (Map 5; ☎ 7286 6101) at the Toll House, Delamere Terrace W2 (⊖ Warwick Avenue); its Web site is at www.british-waterways.co.uk.

Regent's Canal loops round north London for about 4km (2½ miles) from Little Venice in Maida Vale to Camden Lock, passing London Zoo and Regent's Park on the way. The London Waterbus Company (☎ 7482 2550) runs 90-minute trips on an enclosed waterbus between Camden Lock (⊖ Camden Town) and Little Venice (⊖ Warwick Avenue). From April to October boats leave from the locks at Camden and Little Venice every hour between 10 am and 5 pm and every 30 minutes at weekends; the last

GETTING AROUND

return trip departs at 3 pm, the last one-way trip at 3.45 pm. From November to March boats go only at weekends, hourly from 11 am to 4 pm. One-way tickets are £3.80/2.40 for adults/children, return tickets £5/3.

If you want to go to the zoo, a return ticket from Little Venice, including admission for one hour, costs £10.30/6.60 (£2.70/1.80 extra if you want to come back later) or £8.50/6 if you want to be ferried from Camden Lock. If you'd like to leave the zoo by boat, a one-way ticket to Camden Lock is £1.50/1.10, while to Little Venice it's £2.70/1.80. Boats from the zoo to Camden Lock leave at 10.35 am, then hourly until 5.35 pm (till 3.35 pm in winter); to Little Venice they leave at 10.15 am, then hourly to 5.15 pm (between 11.15 am and 4.15 pm in winter). From June to September there are services every 30 minutes on Sunday.

Alternatively you can travel the same route on an open-sided canal cruiser with Jason's Canal Trips (☎ 7286 3428). Boats leave Little Venice at 10.30 am, 12.30 and 2.30 pm from April to October, with an extra 4.30 pm departure in June, July and August but no 10.30 am departure in October. Tickets cost £4.95/3.75 for adults/under-15s one way, £5.95/4.95 return. Check its Web site at www.jasons.co.uk.

Jason's Canal Trips boats leave from opposite 60 Blomfield Rd W9 in Little Venice, while the London Waterbus Company ones leave from a little farther east across the Westbourne Terrace bridge.

Jenny Wren (Map 3; ☎ 7485 4433) offers a similar service from Camden Lock. You can also book a dinner (£29.95) or Sunday lunch (£16.95) cruise aboard the *My Fair Lady* through Jenny Wren. The dinner cruise departs from the Garden Jetty next to the

London Bridges Up & Down

London now counts 15 bridges between the neogothic Tower Bridge and Battersea Bridge. The one with the longest and most interesting history – going back to Roman times – is London Bridge, which spans the Thames between Southwark and the City. The newest (and some might say the most beautiful) is the Millennium Bridge, linking Bankside and the City.

The *Anglo-Saxon Chronicle* tells us that a convicted witch was thrown off London Bridge (Map 8) in the 10th century, and the words of that grating children's ditty – 'London Bridge Is Falling Down' – refer to an attack on it by King Olaf of Norway in support of King Ethelred the Unready in 1015. In 1176 Peter of Colechurch began work on what is believed to have been the first post-Roman stone bridge in Europe; the work wasn't completed until 1209. The new bridge stood on 19 piers but was only just wide enough for two carts to pass each other. Nevertheless, by 1358 there were already 139 shops clinging to its sides. Until 1749, when Westminster Bridge was built, this was the sole crossing point on the Thames, and less than a decade later the old shops were pulled down to ease traffic congestion. In 1823 work began on a new bridge designed by Sir John Rennie and worked on by his son. In 1973 this bridge was, in turn, replaced with another, this time a flattened concrete number with three arches, designed by Harold Knox King. Rennie's old bridge was carefully dismantled and shipped to the USA where it now forms the centrepiece of the park at Lake Havusu in Arizona.

The Millennium Bridge (Map 8) was designed by Norman Foster and Anthony Caro; it is the first bridge to be built over the Thames in central London (not counting replacements) since Tower Bridge was completed in 1894. Half of its £14 million cost came from a National Lottery grant. It is 370m long and 4m wide, hovers 9.5m above the water, weighs some 360 tonnes and takes five minutes to cross on foot. It is estimated there will be four million crossings a year.

Waterside Café, 250 Camden High St NW1, at 8 pm Tuesday to Saturday, returning at 11 pm. Sunday lunch cruises leave from the same place at 1 pm, returning 2½ hours later.

Along the River Lea in east London, river and canal cruises are available weekdays on the *Pride of Lea* from 9 am to 5 pm from the Lock Office (☎ 7515 8558), Gillender St E3 (⊖ Bromley-by-Bow). They include trips to Waltham Abbey (£18/16 including lunch); to the London Canal Museum (£16/14 including entry); and a four-hour East Ring Cruise (£11/8 or £14.50/12.30 including lunch).

ORGANISED TOURS

If you're short of time and you prefer to travel in a group, there are plenty of companies offering organised sightseeing tours, many of them of the hop-on, hop-off variety and often in open-top buses. For organised tours to sights on London's periphery and beyond see the Excursions chapter.

Air

The London Balloon (☎ 0845 702 3842) at Spring Gardens, Kennington Lane SE11 (⊖ Vauxhall) will take you 170m off the ground and provide fabulous views of London and the Thames, but don't expect to get very far; the helium-filled balloon remains firmly tethered to the ground. Rides are available daily from 10 am to dusk (midnight from Friday to Sunday). It costs £12/7.50 for adults/children (family £35).

Bus

The Original London Sightseeing Tour (☎ 8877 1722), which has a Web site at www.theoriginaltour.com, the Big Bus Company (☎ 8944 7810) and London Pride Sightseeing (☎ 01708-631122) all offer tours around the main sights in double-decker buses that allow you to go straight round without getting off or to hop on and off at the sights along the way and reboard the next bus. They're all around £12/6 for adults/children aged under 16. The Big Bus Company now runs tours round the clock for those with jet lag or insomnia.

CHARLOTTE HINDLE

Richard Branson-wannabes can emulate their hero for a few minutes in the London Balloon.

Convenient starting points are in Trafalgar Square in front of the church of St Martin-in-the-Fields, in front of Baker Street tube station near Madame Tussaud's in Marylebone, on Haymarket south-east of Piccadilly Circus and in Grosvenor Gardens opposite Victoria train station.

Boat

The main starting points for cruises along the Thames are Westminster Pier and Embankment Pier (also called Charing Cross Pier). Westminster Pleasure Cruises (☎ 7930 2062) has 45-minute evening cruises from Westminster Pier to the Tower of London on Friday at 7.20 and 8.20 pm for £5/2.50 and cruises lasting 1¾ hours to the Millennium Dome on Tuesday, Thursday and Saturday for £8/5.

GETTING AROUND

RICHARD I'ANSON

Take me to the river: the most novel way of getting around in London is on the Thames.

East along the Thames Cruise boats run by Westminster Passenger Services Association (WPSA; ☎ 7930 4097 for information on boat services eastward) leave Westminster Pier for Greenwich every 30 minutes from 10 am to 4 or 5 pm, passing the Globe Theatre, stopping at the Tower of London and continuing under Tower Bridge and past many of the famous docks. The last boats return from Greenwich at about 5.30 pm in summer and 4.15 pm in winter, depending on demand. Singles cost £6/4.80/3.20 for adults/seniors/children, returns are £7.30/6/3.70. There's also a family single/return ticket for £16.20/19.20.

City Cruises (☎ 7237 5134) links Tower and Embankment piers with Greenwich daily from April to October between about 10.30 am and 5.15 pm. The single/return fares are around £6.45/7.50 for adults and £3.70/4.10 for children to/from Embankment Pier and £5.40/6.65 and £3.10/3.60 to/from Tower Pier.

West along the Thames WPSA riverboats also head west (☎ 7930 4721 for information) from Westminster Pier, an enjoyable excursion although it takes much longer and is not, perhaps, as interesting as the trip east. The two main destinations are Kew Gardens and Hampton Court Palace. It's also possible to get off the boats at Richmond in July and August. There are no boats running in this direction from the end of October until the end of March.

Boats to the Royal Botanic Gardens at Kew sail from Westminster Pier via Putney up to eight times a day from 10.30 am to 2.30 pm from late March to September with limited services in October. They take about 1½ hours and a single/return costs £6/10 for adults, £5/8 for seniors and £3/5 for children.

Boats to Hampton Court Palace leave from Westminster Pier from April to September/October at 10.30 and 11.15 am and noon. The journey takes 3½ hours and costs £8/12 for adults, £7/10 for seniors and £4/7 for children.

You can also get to Hampton Court from St Helena Pier in Water Lane in Richmond. From May to late September, Turk Launches (☎ 8546 2434) has boats at 11 am, 2.15 and 4.15 pm Tuesday to Sunday. The journey takes 1¾ hours and single/return fares are £5.40/6.80 for adults and £4.40/5.80 for children (and seniors on weekdays).

Walking

Several companies offer themed guided walking tours; popular ones include London at the time of certain writers – be they Shakespeare, Dickens or Pepys – and other such themes as legal London, Jewish London and, inevitably, Princess Diana's London. There are also various ghost walks and the most popular one of all: Jack the Ripper tours of Whitechapel.

Walks take place throughout the year but the choice is greater between April and

October. They usually last around two hours, cost around £4.50/3.50 for adults/ seniors & students and leave from outside tube stations. Check the Around Town/ Visitors section of *Time Out* for details of what's on offer for the week ahead.

Companies that offer guided walks include:

Capital Walks (☎ 8650 7640)
Cityguide Walks (☎ 01895-675389)
Historical Tours (☎ 8668 4019)
Original London Walks (☎ 7624 3978; Web site www.walks.com)
Mystery Walks of London (☎ 8558 9446)
Ripping Yarns (☎ 7488 2414)
Stepping Out (☎ 8881 2933)

Among the most fascinating tours available are those run by Architectural Dialogue (☎ 8341 1371), which examine London's architecture in all its many forms – from Georgian and contemporary to the regeneration of the Docklands. Half-day tours (£17.50/11 for adults/seniors & students) leave from outside the Royal Academy, Burlington House, Piccadilly W1 (✪ Green Park), on Saturday at 10.15 am and last three hours. Full-day tours (£20 to £39) are also scheduled from time to time.

Clerkenwell & Islington Guides (☎ 7622 3278) offers regular walks round Clerkenwell, leaving from outside Farringdon tube at 11 am on Wednesday, 6.30 pm on Thursday and 2 pm on Sunday. They also have a Smithfield Trail walk, leaving from outside Barbican tube station at 2 pm on Saturday, an Angel Trail leaving from the Angel tube ticket-barrier at 2 pm on Sunday and

a Canonbury Trail leaving from Highbury & Islington tube at 11 am on certain Sundays (call for exact dates). All these walks cost £4.50/3.50.

The Society of Voluntary Guides offers walks round Richmond, Twickenham and Kew from June to October. Tours of historic Richmond and/or Richmond Hill leave the Old Town Hall daily at 11 am. Tickets (£2/1) are available from the Richmond tourist information centre (see Tourist Offices in the Facts for the Visitor chapter). Kew walks leave St Anne's Church on Kew Green at 11 am on Saturday, and Twickenham walks leave St Mary's Church, Church St, York House End, Twickenham, on Sunday at 2.15 pm. Tickets (£2/1) can be bought from the guides.

For information about guided walking tours in Greenwich, see Greenwich in the Things to See & Do chapter.

La crème de la crème are the 900 knowledgeable guides of the Association of Professional Tourist Guides (APTG), who study for two years and sit both written and practical examinations before being awarded their coveted 'Blue Badge'. You can decide where you want to go and for how long or take advice from them. They're not cheap (eg £81/121 for a half/full day of guiding in English), but it can work out rather cheaply if there's a number of you. For information contact the APTG (☎ 7171 4064, email aptg@touristguides.org.uk), 50 Southwark St, London SE1 1UN, visit its Web site at www.touristguides.org.uk or ask the London Tourist Board for a copy of their pamphlet *Registered Guides*.

GETTING AROUND

Things to See & Do

Highlights

- British Museum
- St Paul's Cathedral
- National Portrait Gallery
- Victoria & Albert Museum
- Boat trip to the Millennium Dome
- London's parks, especially St James's
- The Globe Theatre and its excellent productions
- Eltham Palace
- Greenwich, especially the National Maritime Museum
- Hampton Court Palace

Lowlights

- 11 pm pub closing
- The Circle Line on the Underground
- Buckingham Palace
- Leicester Square
- Rock Circus
- Sealed letter-boxes and the lack of rubbish bins in the City
- London Dungeon
- Bad signposting on many streets
- Very bad value for money in restaurants
- Heathrow airport

SUGGESTED ITINERARIES

Depending on much time you have in London, there will be some hard choices to make about what to see and do. The following is a suggested itinerary for a first-time visitor with a week to spend in this fair city:

First Day
  Visit Westminster Abbey and view the Houses of Parliament and Big Ben. Walk up Whitehall, passing Downing St, the Cenotaph and Horse Guards Parade. Cross Trafalgar Square to visit the National Gallery. Walk to Piccadilly Circus to see the statue of Eros.
Second Day
  Visit the British Museum and walk/shop along Oxford St.
Third Day
  Visit the Natural History, Science or Victoria & Albert museums in South Kensington, then take a bus to Harrods. Have a look at Buckingham Palace and St James's Park.
Fourth Day
  Visit St Paul's Cathedral and the Museum of London.
Fifth Day
  Visit the Tower of London and Tower Bridge. Take the Docklands Light Railway (DLR) to the Isle of Dogs.
Sixth Day
  Cross the Thames to visit the new Globe Theatre. Walk along the South Bank.
Seventh Day
  Use the new Jubilee Line extension or take a boat to the Millennium Dome in north Greenwich. Spend the afternoon in Greenwich proper, visiting the National Maritime Museum and the *Cutty Sark*.

With another week you could explore some of the markets, go to London Zoo and Camden Lock, and visit some of the smaller museums like the unique Sir John Soane's Museum in Lincoln's Inn Fields, Leighton House in Holland Park and the Old Operating Theatre near London Bridge. You could also head north to Hampstead to explore the heath and Freud's and Keats' houses or take a boat west to Hampton Court Palace.

A third week would let you explore some of the outer suburbs like Chiswick and Richmond, perhaps taking in Ham House and Osterley House. You could also take one or two day trips to any of the places outside London listed in the Excursions chapter.

Please note that all the hours listed in this chapter are literally the opening and closing times. Last entry at most museums and attractions is 30 minutes or even an hour before closing time.

Central London

TRAFALGAR SQUARE (Map 7)

Trafalgar Square WC2 (⊖ Charing Cross) is the heart of visitors' London. This is where many great marches and rallies take place, and where the new year is seen in by thousands of drunken revellers. It's also where you'll fight for space with flocks of pigeons – those dirty flying rats.

The square was designed by John Nash in the early 19th century on the site of the King's Mews and executed by Charles Barry, who was also partly responsible for the Houses of Parliament. The 43.5m-high **Nelson's Column**, which incorporates granite from Cornwall to the Scottish Highlands, was completed in 1843 and commemorates Admiral Nelson's victory over Napoleon off Cape Trafalgar in Spain in 1805. The four bronze lions at its base were designed by Edwin Landseer and added in 1867. If you glance up at the statue of the good admiral, you'll see that he is facing to the south-west, surveying his fleet, some say, of ships atop the lampposts lining The Mall.

Trafalgar Square is flanked by many imposing buildings and important thoroughfares fan out from it. To the north is the **National Gallery** and behind it the **National Portrait Gallery**; Pall Mall, which derives its name from a croquet-like Italian game called *palla a maglio* (ball to mallet), played here by Charles II and his court, runs south-west from the north-western corner. The church of **St Martin-in-the-Fields** is to the north-east, and directly to the east stands **South Africa House** (1933), where the stone heads of African wildlife once gazed down on anti-apartheid protesters. To the south, the square opens out and you catch glimpses down Whitehall through the traffic. To the south-west stands **Admiralty Arch**, erected in honour of Queen Victoria in 1910, with The Mall leading to Buckingham Palace beyond it. To the west is **Canada House** (1827), designed by Robert Smirke.

RICHARD I'ANSON

Relaxing by the pool on Trafalgar Square (gangs of marauding pigeons not shown).

The traffic swirling past makes it difficult to appreciate Trafalgar Square. Westminster City Council is now considering plans drawn up by architect Norman Foster to pedestrianise much of the square. The road to the north (Pall Mall East) would be closed to traffic along with the square itself, linking it with the National Gallery and National Portrait Gallery for the first time ever.

National Gallery

The National Gallery's porticoed façade (☎ 7839 3321, 7747 2885 for a recording) extends along the square's northern side. With some 2100 western paintings on display, it's one of the world's largest – and finest – art galleries. The lovely Sainsbury Wing on the west side was added only after considerable controversy; Prince Charles, not known for a cutting-edge design sense in architecture, dismissed one proposal as 'a carbuncle on the face of a much loved friend'. Oh dear. Outside the gallery – rather incongruously in this, the heart of London – is a statue of the man who 'robbed' England of its colonies in the New World, the heroic General George Washington, presented to London by Virginia in 1921.

The paintings in the National Gallery are hung in a continuous time-line; by starting in the Sainsbury Wing and progressing eastwards you can take in a collection of pictures painted between the mid-13th and early 20th centuries in chronological order. If you're keen on the real oldies (1260-1510), head for the Sainsbury Wing; for the Renaissance (1510-1600), go to the West Wing in the museum's main building. Rubens, Rembrandt and Murillo are in the North Wing (1600-1700); if you're after Gainsborough, Constable, Turner, Hogarth and the Impressionists visit the East Wing (1700-1900). For a larger collection of paintings by British artists you should visit the Tate Britain (see the following Westminster & Pimlico section).

The highlights listed in the boxed text will give you an idea of the *crème de la crème* at the gallery, but if you want to know a lot more, borrow an audioguide

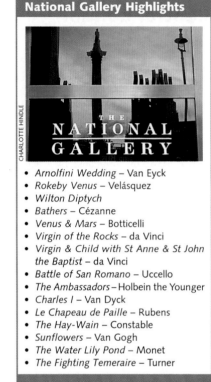

National Gallery Highlights

CHARLOTTE HINDLE

- *Arnolfini Wedding* – Van Eyck
- *Rokeby Venus* – Velásquez
- *Wilton Diptych*
- *Bathers* – Cézanne
- *Venus & Mars* – Botticelli
- *Virgin of the Rocks* – da Vinci
- *Virgin & Child with St Anne & St John the Baptist* – da Vinci
- *Battle of San Romano* – Uccello
- *The Ambassadors* – Holbein the Younger
- *Charles I* – Van Dyck
- *Le Chapeau de Paille* – Rubens
- *The Hay-Wain* – Constable
- *Sunflowers* – Van Gogh
- *The Water Lily Pond* – Monet
- *The Fighting Temeraire* – Turner

(contribution suggested) from the central hall. Each painting is numbered; punch this into the machine and it will skip to the appropriate place on the CD-ROM. There are also highlights audioguide tours (featuring 30 paintings) and activity sheets for kids (50p). Free one-hour guided tours, which introduce you to a manageable half-dozen paintings at a time, leave at 11.30 am and 2.30 pm on weekdays and at 2 and 3.30 pm on Saturday (additional tour at 6.30 pm on Wednesday). There's a branch of the Pret à Manger café chain in the main building's basement; the museum's popular Brasserie is on the 1st floor of the Sainsbury Wing.

The National Gallery (free) is open daily

from 10 am to 6 pm (on Wednesday to 9 pm). For further information you can visit its Web site at www.nationalgallery.org.uk.

National Portrait Gallery

A visit to the National Portrait Gallery (☎ 7306 0055, 7312 2463 for a recording), St Martin's Place WC2, is not so much about art as history – to put faces to the famous and infamous names in British history from the Middle Ages to the present day. The gallery, founded in 1856, houses a primary collection of some 9000 works on five floors, and there is no restriction on media; there are oil paintings, watercolours, drawings, miniatures, sculptures, caricatures, silhouettes, photographs and even electronic art. Being the subject of one of the 40-odd annual acquisitions is said to be more prestigious than the making the Queen's Honours List.

The pictures are displayed in chronological order, starting with the early Tudors on the top floor landing and descending to the late 20th century on the ground floor. The portraits of Elizabeth I from 1575 in all her finery and of Byron in romantic oriental garb (1813) by Thomas Phillips are as wonderful as the more recent works: Elizabeth II as seen by Andy Warhol; Prince Charles posing under a banana tree; photographs of Oscar Wilde, Virginia Woolf and the late Diana, Princess of Wales.

Audioguides (£3 donation suggested) highlighting some 200 portraits let you listen to the voices of some of the people portrayed. A redesign of 12 of the top-floor galleries will expand the display from the 16th century to the Regency period. At present the Portrait Café and bookshop are in the basement.

The National Portrait Gallery (free) is open Monday to Saturday, from 10 am to 6 pm (on Sunday from noon). Its Web site is at www.npg.org.uk.

Edith Cavell Memorial

On a traffic island outside the entrance to the National Portrait Gallery is a statue of Edith Cavell (1865-1915), a British nurse who helped Allied soldiers escape from Brussels during WWI and was executed by the Germans. The statue is the work of George Frampton, who also designed the Peter Pan statue in Hyde Park.

St Martin-in-the-Fields

An influential masterpiece by James Gibbs (1682-1754), the 'royal parish church' of St Martin-in-the-Fields (☎ 7930 0089), Trafalgar Square WC2, occupies a prime site at the north-eastern corner of the square. The wedding-cake spire (wonderfully floodlit at night) is offset by the splendid visual harmony of the white stone used for both St Martin's and the National Gallery.

St Martin's has a tradition of tending to the poor and homeless that goes back to WWI. There's an adjoining craft market, and in the crypt you'll find a brass-rubbing centre (☎ 7930 9306), bookshop and popular café (see the Trafalgar Square section in the Places to Eat chapter). For details of concerts, see Churches under Classical Music in the Entertainment chapter.

The church is open daily from 8 am to 6.30 pm, the brass-rubbing centre from 10 am (noon on Sunday) to 6 pm.

Cockney Royalty

The Cockney monarchs are the Pearly Kings and Queens, who used to be appointed by hawkers to represent them in brushes with the law. In the 19th century an orphan roadsweeper, Henry Croft, dreamed of creating a charity army to help the poor and sewed pearly white buttons onto his clothes to attract attention. The coster kings were duly impressed, and soon they too were decking themselves out in pearls to go fund-raising. The Pearly Harvest Festival Service in early October, when over a hundred Pearly Kings and Queens attend a service in St Martin-in-the-Fields church, is a sight you'll never forget. Each suit is made of around 30,000 buttons sewn into mystic symbols like the sun, moon and stars. The most elaborate one has 90,000 buttons.

WESTMINSTER & PIMLICO (Maps 6 & 10)

While the City of London (known simply as 'the City') has always concerned itself with trade and commerce, Westminster is the centre of political power and most of its places of interest are linked with the monarchy, Parliament or the Church of England.

Pimlico (Map 10), to the south and southwest, has never been as smart as, say, Belgravia, but contains some wonderful early 19th-century houses and the incomparable Tate Britain.

Whitehall

Whitehall SW1 (Map 6; ☻ Charing Cross or Westminster) and its extension Parliament St is the wide avenue that links Trafalgar Square with Parliament Square. It is lined with so many government buildings, statues, monuments and other historical sights that the best way to take it all in is to follow the short walk described in the Whitehall walking tour. Those interested in only the most important sights – including Westminster Abbey and the Houses of Parliament – can read on.

Westminster Abbey

Westminster Abbey (Map 6; ☎ 7222 5152), Dean's Yard SW1 (☻ Westminster), is one of the most visited churches in Christendom. It has played a pivotal role in the history of both England and the Anglican church and, with the exception of Edward V and Edward VIII, every sovereign has been crowned here since William the Conqueror in 1066. All the monarchs from Henry III (died 1272) to George II (1760) were buried here as well, but since the death of George III in 1820 they have been laid to rest in St George's Chapel in Windsor.

In September 1997, millions of people around the world got to see the inside of Westminster Abbey when TV cameras were allowed in for the funeral service of Diana, Princess of Wales (she was laid to rest at the Spencer family estate at Althorp in Northamptonshire). Since then the number of visitors to the abbey has increased by an estimated 300% and the visit is now more restricted, with certain areas cordoned off to protect the floors and the north transept now serving as the main entrance.

The abbey, though a mixture of various architectural styles, is the finest example of Early English Gothic (1180-1280) still standing. The original church was built by the 11th-century King (later St) Edward the Confessor, who is buried in the chapel behind the main altar. Henry III (reigned 1216-72) began work on the new building but didn't complete it; the French Gothic nave was finished in 1388. Henry VII's huge and magnificent chapel was added in 1519.

Unlike St Paul's, Westminster Abbey has never been a cathedral but is a 'royal peculiar', administered directly by the Crown.

Orientation The main entrance is through the north door. Immediately past the barrier you come to the **Statesmen's Aisle**, where politicians and eminent public figures are commemorated, mostly by staggeringly large marble statues. The Whig and Tory prime ministers who dominated late Victorian politics, Gladstone (who is buried here) and Disraeli (who is not) have their monuments uncomfortably close together. Nearby is a monument to Robert Peel who, as home secretary in 1829, created the metropolitan police force. They became known as 'Bobby's boys' and later simply 'bobbies'. Above them is a rose window, designed by James Thornhill and depicting 11 of the Apostles (Judas is omitted).

On your left as you turn and walk eastward are several small chapels with fine 16th-century monuments, including a lovely Madonna and Child in alabaster in Crewe Chapel. Opposite the Islip Chapel in the north ambulatory are three wonderful medieval tombs, including that of Edmund Crouchback, youngest son of Henry III and founder of the House of Lancaster. Farther on are the tombs of Edward I and Henry III.

At the eastern end of the sanctuary, opposite the entrance to the Henry VII Chapel, is the rather ordinary-looking **Coronation Chair**, upon which almost every monarch is said to have been crowned since 1066. In fact, the oaken chair dates from the late 13th century – it must have been another chair before. Below it used to lie the Stone of Scone (pronounced skoon) – the Scottish coronation stone pilfered in 1297 by Edward I. It was finally returned to Scotland in 1996, though the Scots have to lend it back for future coronations.

Up the steps in front of you and to your left is the narrow **Queen Elizabeth Chapel** (although technically it's not a chapel at all, as it doesn't have its own altar, but the northern aisle of the Henry VII Chapel). Here Elizabeth I, who gave the abbey its charter, and her half-sister 'Bloody Mary' share an elaborate tomb. In front of the altar are memorials to James I's daughters who died in childhood; the effigy of Princess Sophia, a baby in her cradle, is reflected in a mirror.

In the easternmost part of the abbey

you'll find the **Henry VII Chapel**, an outstanding example of late perpendicular architecture (a variation of English Gothic) with spectacular circular vaulting on the ceiling. The magnificently carved wooden choir-stalls, reserved for the Knights of the Order of the Bath, feature colourful headpieces bearing their owners' chosen symbols: dragons, roosters etc.

Behind the chapel's altar, with a 15th-century *Madonna and Child* by Vivarini, is the elaborate sarcophagus of Henry VII and his queen, Elizabeth of York, designed by the Florentine sculptor Pietro Torrigiano. Beyond this is the **Royal Air Force Chapel** and the Battle of Britain stained-glass window. Next to it a plaque marks the spot where Oliver Cromwell's body lay until the Restoration, when it was disinterred, hanged at Tyburn and beheaded.

The chapel's south aisle contains the

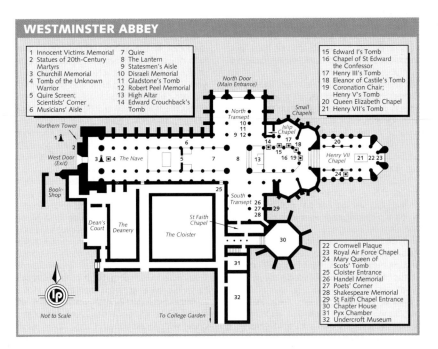

WESTMINSTER ABBEY

1 Innocent Victims Memorial
2 Statues of 20th-Century Martyrs
3 Churchill Memorial
4 Tomb of the Unknown Warrior
5 Quire Screen; Scientists' Corner
6 Musicians' Aisle
7 Quire
8 The Lantern
9 Statesmen's Aisle
10 Disraeli Memorial
11 Gladstone's Tomb
12 Robert Peel Memorial
13 High Altar
14 Edward Crouchback's Tomb
15 Edward I's Tomb
16 Chapel of St Edward the Confessor
17 Henry III's Tomb
18 Eleanor of Castile's Tomb
19 Coronation Chair; Henry V's Tomb
20 Queen Elizabeth Chapel
21 Henry VII's Tomb
22 Cromwell Plaque
23 Royal Air Force Chapel
24 Mary Queen of Scots' Tomb
25 Cloister Entrance
26 Handel Memorial
27 Poets' Corner
28 Shakespeare Memorial
29 St Faith Chapel Entrance
30 Chapter House
31 Pyx Chamber
32 Undercroft Museum

North Door (Main Entrance)
North Transept
Small Chapels
Islip Chapel
Northern Tower
West Door (Exit)
The Nave
Henry VII Chapel
Book-Shop
Dean's Court
The Deanery
St Faith Chapel
The Cloister
South Transept
Chapter House
To College Garden
Not to Scale

tomb of **Mary Queen of Scots** (beheaded on the orders of her cousin Elizabeth and with the acquiescence of her son, the future James I) and the stunning tomb of Lady Margaret Beaufort, mother of Henry VII. Also buried here are Charles II, William and Mary, and Queen Anne.

The **Chapel of St Edward the Confessor**, the most sacred spot in the abbey, lies just east of the sanctuary and behind the high altar; access may still be restricted to protect the 13th-century floor. St Edward was the founder of the abbey and the original building was consecrated a few weeks before his death. His tomb was slightly altered after the original was destroyed during the Reformation. On the casket that lies below the green wooden canopy there are still some of the original mosaics and the niches in which pilgrims would pray for a cure and leave votives.

Some of the surrounding tombs in the chapel – those of Henry III, Edward I, Edward III, Richard II, Henry V and four queens – are visible from the north and south ambulatory. **Eleanor of Castile**, the wife of Edward I, lies in one of the oldest and most beautiful bronze tombs, designed by the goldsmith William Torel in 1291. The abbey's south transept contains **Poets' Corner**, where many of England's finest writers are buried, a precedent established with Geoffrey Chaucer (although he was actually buried here because he had been clerk of works to the Palace of Westminster, not because of his literary efforts; the practice actually began in earnest in 1700).

In front of medieval wall-paintings of the doubting apostle St Thomas and St Christopher on the eastern wall stands the **William Shakespeare memorial** (although like Byron, Tennyson, William Blake, TS Eliot and various other luminaries, he wasn't actually buried here). Here, too, you'll find memorials to Handel (holding a score of the *Messiah*), Edmund Spenser, Tennyson and Robert Browning, as well as the graves of (or memorials to) Charles Dickens, Lewis Carroll, Rudyard Kipling and Henry James. St Faith's Chapel (entrance to the east) is reserved for private prayer.

ELLIOT DANIEL

Westminster Abbey: inveterate tourist magnet and resting place of the great and the good.

Just north of Poet's Corner is the **Lantern**, the heart of the abbey, where coronations take place. If you face east while standing in the centre, the **sanctuary** is in front of you. The ornate **high altar** was designed by George Gilbert Scott in 1897. Behind you (ie to the west) Edward Blore's mid-19th-century **quire** (or chancel) is a breathtaking structure of gold, blue and red Victorian Gothic. Where monks once worshipped, 20 boys from the Choir School and 12 lay vicars now sing the daily services.

The entrance to the **Cloister** dates from the 13th century, the rest of it from the 14th. East down a passageway off the Cloister, the octagonal **Chapter House** has one of Europe's best-preserved medieval tile floors and retains traces of religious murals. It was used as a chamber by the king's council, and as a meeting place by the House of Commons in the second half of the 14th century. The state still runs the Chapter House and the adjacent **Pyx Chamber**, once the Royal Treasury and containing the pyx, a chest with standard gold and silver pieces for testing coinage weights. It now contains the abbey's treasures and liturgical objects as well as the oldest altar in the abbey.

The **Undercroft Museum** (or the Abbey Museum) exhibits the death masks of generations of royalty, and there are wax effigies representing Charles II and William III (who is on a stool to make him as tall as his wife Mary) as well as armour and stained glass.

To reach the 900-year-old **College Garden**, the oldest in England, enter Dean's Yard (Map 6) and the **Little Cloisters** off Great College St. There are free lunch-time concerts in the College Garden on Thursday in July and August.

A walk around the Cloister brings you to the western end of the nave. Set in the floor is the **Tomb of the Unknown Warrior**, surrounded by poppies in remembrance of those who died on the WWI battlefields. Just before it is a stone commemorating **Winston Churchill**, prime minister during WWII.

Straight up the aisle is a screen separating the nave from the quire; built in 1834, it is the fourth one to be placed here. Against this stand monuments to Isaac Newton, Darwin, Lord Stanhope, Michael Faraday and four Nobel laureates, including Lord Kelvin and Ernest Rutherford – a veritable **Scientists' Corner**. Above the screen is a magnificent organ dating from 1730. Look up at the beautiful stone vaulted ceiling in the nave and at the fan-vaulted aisles.

The north aisle of the nave is known as the **Musicians' Aisle**, with memorials to music-makers who served the abbey. Look out for memorials to the composer Henry Purcell, who served as an organist at the abbey, and to Vaughan Williams, Edward Elgar and Benjamin Britten.

The two towers above the west door, through which you exit, were designed by Nicholas Hawksmoor and completed in 1745. Just above the door, perched in 15th-century niches, are the latest sacred addition to the abbey: 10 stone statues of the **20th-century martyrs**, which were unveiled in 1998. They include US civil rights leader Martin Luther King; the Polish priest Maximilian Kolbe, who was murdered by the Nazis at Auschwitz; and Elizabeth of Hesse-Darmstadt, who founded an order of charitable nuns in Moscow in the early 20th century and was shot by the Bolsheviks in 1918. Protestant or Catholic, they were all Christians.

To the right as you exit is a memorial to victims of oppression, violence and war around the world. 'All you who pass by, is it nothing to you?' it asks poignantly.

Hours & Tickets The abbey is open weekdays from 9 am to 4.45 pm (and on Wednesday also from 6 to 7.45 pm) and on Saturday from 9 am to 2.45 pm. Sunday is for services only. The Chapter House is open from 9.30 am to 5.30 pm April to September (to 5 pm in October) and from 10 am to 4 pm November to March. The Pyx Chamber and Undercroft Museum are open daily from 10 am to 4 pm. The College Garden is open on Tuesday and Thursday from 10 am to 6 pm, April to September (to 4 pm on the same days the rest of the year).

Admission to Westminster Abbey costs £5/3/2 for adults/seniors & students/those aged 11 to 18 (family £10). Entry to just the Chapter House, Pyx Chamber and Undercroft Museum (accessible via Dean's Yard and the Cloister) costs £2.50/1.90/1.30 (£1 with an abbey ticket, free for English Heritage (EH) members and those renting an abbey audioguide). Tickets to the abbey are half-price during the evening session on Wednesday, which is the only time photographs may be taken in the abbey.

One of the best ways to visit the abbey is to attend a service, particularly evensong (5 pm weekdays, 3 pm at weekends). Sunday Eucharist is at 11 am.

For further information on the abbey visit its Web site at www.westminster-abbey.org.

Guided Tours Guided tours (☎ 7222 7110) of the abbey last about 1½ hours (£3) and depart between three and six times a day, Monday to Saturday, from April to October; they leave three or four times a day the rest of the year (call for exact times). There's also a portable audioguide (£2) available but it's not very good.

WHITEHALL

What was once the administrative heart of the British Empire remains the focal point for British government. Start your walk at the southern end of Trafalgar Square as it leads into Whitehall. On the small traffic island is an equestrian **statue of Charles I (1)**, which was cast in 1633, buried in a garden during the Commonwealth and not erected until after the Restoration. As you walk south you'll see **Admiralty Arch (2)** (1910) and the **Old Admiralty (3)** on the right and farther along on the left the **Ministry of Defence (4)**.

distance: about 2km

start: Trafalgar Square
⊖ Charing Cross

finish: Broad Sanctuary
⊖ Westminster

Just in front of the latter is **Banqueting House (5)** (☎ 7930 4179), the only surviving part of the Tudor Whitehall Palace, which once stretched most of the way along Whitehall but burned down in 1698. Designed by Inigo Jones in 1622, it was England's first purely Renaissance building. Its claim to fame is that it was on a scaffold built against a 1st floor window that Charles I, accused of treason by Cromwell, was executed on 30 January 1649. After Whitehall Palace burned down, Banqueting House became the Chapel Royal. It's still occasionally used for state banquets, concerts and other events, and is open to the public. Inside there's a video account of the house's history and on the 1st floor a huge, virtually unfurnished hall whose ceiling displays nine panels painted by Rubens in 1634. It is open Monday to Saturday from 10 am to 5 pm. Admission costs £3.60/2.80/2.30 for adults/seniors & students/children.

Opposite Banqueting House is **Horse Guards Parade (6)**, where the mounted troopers of the Household Cavalry are changed Monday to Saturday at 11 am and on Sunday at 10 am, offering a more accessible version of the ceremony than the one outside Buckingham Palace. Ring the Visitorcall service on ☎ 09064 123411 or call ☎ 0891 505452 for the latest information.

South of Horse Guards Parade is **Downing St**, site of the British prime minister's official residence since 1732, when George II gave **No 10 (7)** to Robert Walpole. Tony Blair and his family actually now live in the larger apartments at No 11 while Chancellor of the Exchequer Gordon Brown, the country's senior economic and financial minister, lives at No 10. The other two houses are used as government offices. During Margaret Thatcher's time in office the gates were erected and the street closed off to the public for fear of IRA terrorist attacks.

A short distance farther on in the middle of Whitehall is the **Cenotaph (8)** (Greek for 'empty tomb'), a memorial to Commonwealth citizens who were killed during the two world wars. The Queen and other public figures lay poppies at its base on 11 November.

To the west of the Cenotaph is the restored **Foreign & Commonwealth Office (9)** (FCO; 1872) by Sir George Gilbert Scott and Matthew Digby Wyatt. In a bid to rid itself of its reputation as a highly secretive ministry, the FCO has now opened a visitor centre (☎ 7270 1500), with an information-technology centre, an exhibition gallery and a cinema explaining how the FCO projects Britain through its diplomatic posts around the world. It's free and open weekdays from 10 am to 5 pm.

If you walk west along King Charles St, you'll reach the **Cabinet War Rooms (10)** (☎ 7930 6961), where the British government took refuge underground during WWII, conducting its business from beneath 3m of solid concrete. It was from here that Winston Churchill made some of his most stirring speeches. Particularly interesting are the actual room where the Cabinet held more than 100 meetings during the war; the Map Room with charts showing the movements of troops and ships around the globe; and the Telegraph Room, its door marked with a borrowed 'vacant/engaged' sign to suggest it was Churchill's private lavatory. It's open daily from 9.30 am to 5.15 pm (from 10 am October to March), and admission costs £4.80/3.50 for adults/seniors & students (under-16s free).

Whitehall ends at **Parliament Square**, where swirling traffic makes it hard to appreciate the statues of past prime ministers, such as **Winston Churchill (11)**, and other worthies, including **Abraham Lincoln (12)**. To the north-east along Bridge St is the new ultramodern **Parliament Building (13)**. Farther east along this same street is **Big Ben (14)** and, by Westminster Bridge, a **statue of Queen Boudicca (15)** and her daughters in a chariot, who gave the Romans a run for their money in 60 AD.

To the south and south-east of the square are **Westminster Abbey (16)** and the **Houses of Parliament (17)**. Just in front of the former is tiny **St Margaret's, Westminster (18)**, consecrated in 1523. It is the House of Commons' church and famous for society weddings. Notice the small **bust of Charles I (19)** in a niche of the outside wall facing the Houses of Parliament and (more appropriately) the statue of **Cromwell (20)** (1899), his nemesis. To the west stands the elaborately decorated neogothic **Middlesex Guildhall (21)** (1913), which now houses Middlesex Crown Court.

An interesting building often overlooked to the south-west on Storey's Gate is **Westminster Central Hall (22)**, built in 1911 in 'ornate French style' and the seat of the Methodist church. It hosted the first assembly of the United Nations in 1946 and is used for concerts, meetings and religious services. Guided tours (☎ 7222 8010) of the hall take place on Tuesday and Thursday between 11 am and 3.30 pm. The Central Café in the basement is a good place for lunch.

Under Churchill's gaze: some of the illustrious figures you'll find milling about around Parliament Square.

ED HILLYER

Houses of Parliament

The Houses of Parliament (comprising the House of Commons and the House of Lords) are in the Palace of Westminster (Map 6; ☎ 7219 4272), Parliament Square SW1 (⊖ Westminster). It was built by Charles Barry and Augustus Pugin in 1840 when the neogothic style was all the rage, and a thorough cleaning has revealed the soft golden brilliance of the original structure. The most famous feature *outside* the palace is the Clock Tower, commonly known as **Big Ben** (the real Ben, a bell named after Benjamin Hall, who was commissioner of works when the tower was completed in 1858, hangs inside). Big Ben has rung in the new year ever since 1924 and, of course, announced the new millennium to London (and, via the BBC, the world). The best view of the whole complex is from the eastern side of Lambeth Bridge.

At the opposite end of the building is **Victoria Tower**, completed in 1860; the medieval-looking little structure with the colourful tile roof in triangular Victoria Tower Gardens to the south is a **monument to the emancipation of slaves** in the British Empire erected in 1834.

The **House of Commons** is where Members of Parliament (MPs) meet to propose and discuss new legislation and to question the prime minister and other ministers. The layout of the Commons Chamber is based on that of St Stephen's Chapel in the original Palace of Westminster. The current chamber, designed by Giles Gilbert Scott, replaced the earlier one destroyed by a 1941 bomb. Although the Commons is a national assembly of 659 MPs, the chamber has seating for only 437 of them. Government members sit to the right of the Speaker and Opposition members to the left. The Speaker presides over business from a chair given by Australia while ministers speak from a despatch box donated by New Zealand.

Visitors are admitted to the **Strangers' Gallery** (free) of the House of Commons via St Stephen's Entrance from Monday to Thursday after 4.15 pm and on Friday from 10 am; expect to queue for at least an hour. Parliamentary recesses (holidays) last for three months over the summer and another few weeks over Easter and Christmas, so it's best to ring in advance to check whether Parliament is in session. To find out what's being debated on a particular day, check the notice board posted beside the entrance or look in the *Daily Telegraph* or the freebie *Metro* newspaper under 'Today in Parliament'. Handbags and cameras must be checked at a cloakroom before you enter the gallery, and no large suitcases or backpacks are allowed through the airport-style security gate.

RICHARD I'ANSON

The Palace of Westminster: for thirsty or peckish MPs, it comes with eight bars and six restaurants.

As you're waiting for your bags to go through the X-ray machines, take a look to the left at the stunning roof of **Westminster Hall**, originally built in 1099 and today the oldest surviving part of the Palace of Westminster, the seat of the English monarchy from the 11th to the early 16th centuries. Added between 1394 and 1401, the roof is the earliest known example of a hammerbeam roof and has been described as 'the greatest surviving achievement of medieval English carpentry'. Along with being used for coronation banquets in medieval times, Westminster Hall also served as a courthouse until the 19th century. The trials of William Wallace (1305), Thomas More (1535), Guy Fawkes (1606) and Charles I (1649) all took place here. In the 20th century monarchs and Winston Churchill have lain in state here.

It is possible to visit parts of the **Palace of Westminster** when the houses are not sitting, although arrangements must be made in advance through the Public Information Office, 1 Derby Gate, London SW1A 2DG. Visit permits are free, but guides charge around £25 for a group of 16.

Jewel Tower

Once part of the Palace of Westminster, the Jewel Tower (☎ 7973 3479, 7222 2219), opposite the Houses of Parliament and beside Westminster Abbey, was built in 1365 to house Edward III's treasury. Originally it was surrounded by a moat but this was filled in 1664. Later the tower served as an office for clerks of the House of Lords. Now it houses exhibitions describing the history of Parliament and showing how it works. There's also a 25-minute explanatory video in which you can see some of the present-day MPs in action. It's well worth visiting before attending a Commons debate so you'll understand more of what you're seeing.

The Jewel Tower is open from 10 am to 6 pm April to September, closing at 5 pm in October. From November to March the daily hours are 10 am to 4 pm. Admission costs £1.50/1.10/80p for adults/students & seniors/children (free for EH members).

RICHARD I'ANSON

On the hour: the Clock Tower (aka Big Ben).

Westminster Cathedral

Completed in 1903, Westminster Cathedral (☎ 7798 9064), Victoria St SW1 (Map 10; ⊖ Victoria), is the headquarters of the Roman Catholic Church in Britain and is the only good example of neo-Byzantine architecture in London. Its distinctive candy-striped red-brick and white-stone tower features prominently on the west London skyline, although remarkably few people think to look inside.

The interior is part splendid marble and mosaic and part bare brick; the money ran out and the cathedral was never completed. The highly regarded stone carvings of the 14 Stations of the Cross (1918) by Eric Gill and the marvellously sombre atmosphere, especially in early evening when the mosaics glitter in the candlelight, make this a welcome haven from the traffic outside.

The cathedral is open daily from 7 am to 7 pm. Eight Masses are said daily from Monday to Friday, six on Saturday and seven on Sunday. For £2 you can take a lift up the tower for panoramic views of London. The tower is open daily from 9 am to 5 pm April to October, and Thursday to Sunday only at the same times the rest of the year.

Tate Britain

The Tate Britain (Map 2; ☎ 7887 8000, 7887 8008 for a recording), Millbank SW1 (✆ Pimlico), serves as the historical archive of British art from the early 16th century to the present. Its sister gallery, the Tate Modern, is at Bankside (see the Bankside section later in this chapter).

The Tate Britain, built in 1897 and now with a new entrance on Atterbury St, is expanding and there will soon be six new Sainsbury Galleries for temporary exhibitions and nine new or refurbished ones for the permanent collection. With all the moving about it is impossible to say what will be on display (and where) but likely highlights include the mystical paintings by William Blake in Room 7, the Hogarths in Room 3 and the Constables in Room 5, along-side works by Reynolds and Gainsborough (Room 4), Rossetti, Whistler, Bacon, Spencer and those stuffy paintings of thoroughbred racehorses by the pre-Victorian artist George Stubbs.

Adjoining the main building is the quirky **Clore Gallery**, James Stirling's stab at acceptable, postmodern architecture, where the bulk of JMW Turner's paintings can be found.

The Tate Britain (free) is open daily from 10 am to 5.50 pm. Major special exhibitions have an admission fee of up to £7/5 for adults/concessions (family £20). Guided tours of the museum are available weekdays at 11.30 am and 2.30 and 3.30 pm, on Saturday at 3 pm. An audioguide to the collection called Tate Inform is available for £3/2. The basement restaurant (☎ 7887 8877), with a splendid mural by Rex Whistler, is enormously popular. It's open daily for lunch only from noon to 3 pm (4 pm on Sunday). The Tate's Web site is at www.tate.org.uk.

ST JAMES'S & MAYFAIR (Map 6)

St James's is a mixture of exclusive clubs (17 at last count, including the Army & Navy, Reform and Carlton clubs), historic shops and elegant buildings; indeed, there are some 150 historically noteworthy buildings within its 36 hectares. It has largely escaped the redevelopment that has taken place in much of London.

Mayfair is the area bordered by Oxford St to the north, Piccadilly to the south, Park Lane and Hyde Park to the west and Regent St to the east. Regent St owes its original design to John Nash (see Architecture under Arts in the Facts about London chapter), who tried to separate refined Mayfair from teeming, working-class Soho. Nash's architectural blueprint, the closest London has ever come to a grand plan, was for Regent St to reach all the way from The Mall to Regent's Park. He was unable to continue with his plan north of Oxford St due to the intractability of property owners, but his immaculate stuccoed terraces around the perimeter of Regent's Park survive.

Institute for Contemporary Arts

The Institute for Contemporary Arts (ICA; ☎ 7930 3647), The Mall SW1 (✆ Charing Cross), has a reputation for being at the cutting edge of all kinds of arts. In any given week this is the place to come for obscure films, dance, photography, art, theatre, music, lectures, multimedia works and book readings. You can visit its Web site at www.ica.org.uk.

The complex includes a bookshop, gallery, cinema, bar, theatre and licensed café-restaurant (see Trafalgar Square in the Places to Eat chapter). The ICA is open Monday to Saturday from noon to 1 am and on Sunday to 10.30 pm. A day pass costs £1.50.

Up the steps beside the ICA into Waterloo Place you'll see the **Duke of York Column**, commemorating the grand old duke, a son of George III. It was erected in 1834 but never quite caught the public imagination like Nelson's Column in Trafalgar Square, though it's just 6m shorter.

MARK HONAN

Gazing into the serene waters of St James's Park Lake.

St James's Park & St James's Palace

St James's Park, The Mall SW1 (✆ St James's Park or Charing Cross), is the neatest and most royal of London's royal parks and has the best vistas, including Westminster, Buckingham Palace, St James's Palace, Carlton Terrace and Horse Guards Parade. In summer, the flower beds are sumptuous and colourful, some of them newly replanted to mimic John Nash's original 'floriferous' beds that mixed shrubs, flowers and trees. But what makes St James's so particularly special is its large lake and the waterfowl that inhabit it, including a group of pelicans. Pelicans have lived here since the reign of James I, when the Russian ambassador presented some of the large-beaked birds as a gift to him. This lot, though, comes from Florida and can be vicious. Come in the early evening (open daily from 5 am to midnight) and you'll see Londoners whose lives revolve around the birds, summoning them with imitation tweeting and whistling. The Cake House café by the lake is open daily from 10 am.

The striking Tudor gatehouse of **St James's Palace**, the only surviving part of a building initiated by the palace-mad Henry VIII in 1530, is best approached from St James's St to the north of the park. It is the residence of Prince Charles and his sons, the princes William and Harry, and is never open to the public. Princess Diana, who detested the place, did time here until her divorce from Charles and her move to Kensington Palace in 1996. Ironically the powers that be thought St James's the most suitable place for her body to lie in state after her tragic death in 1997. Foreign ambassadors to the UK are still accredited to 'the Court of St James'. Next door is **Clarence House** (1828), the residence of the Queen Mother.

Spencer House Just outside the park, Spencer House (✆ 7499 8620), 27 St James's Place SW1 (✆ Green Park), was built for the first Earl Spencer, an ancestor of the late Diana, Princess of Wales, in the Palladian style between 1756 and 1766. The Spencers moved out in 1927 and eventually their grand house became an office, but a recent £18 million restoration by Lord Rothschild has returned it to its former glory. The house can be visited on a guided tour only on Sunday from 11.45 am to 4.45 pm year-round except in January and August. Admission costs £6/5 for adults/under-16s.

Buckingham Palace

Buckingham Palace (☎ 7839 1377, 7799 2331 for a recording; ✆ St James's Park or Victoria) is at the end of The Mall, where St James's Park and Green Park meet at a large roundabout. In the centre is the **Queen Victoria Memorial**, close to where Marble Arch stood until it was moved to its present location in 1851. The memorial (1911), by Thomas Brock, is almost 25m high and portrays the seated Regina, carved from a single block of white marble, surrounded by a number of allegorical figures representing everything from Charity, Truth and Justice (near the plinth) to Progress, Painting, Shipbuilding and so on farther out.

Buckingham Palace was built in 1803 for the Duke of Buckingham and has been the royal family's London home since 1837 when St James's Palace was judged too old-fashioned and insufficiently impressive. A total of 18 rooms (out of 661) are open to visitors for a brief period each year, but don't expect to see the Queen's bedroom. She and the Duke of Edinburgh share a suite of 12 rooms in the north wing overlooking Green Park; this is a tour of the state apartments only. Many people find the visit overpriced and disappointing.

The tour begins in the **Guard Room**, which is way too small for the Ceremonial Guard, who are deployed in adjoining rooms, and includes a peek at the **State Dining Room** (all red damask and Regency furnishings, with a portrait of George III looking rather fetching in fur); **Queen Victoria's Picture Gallery** (a full 76.5m long, with works by Rembrandt, Van Dyck, Canaletto, Poussin and Vermeer); the **Blue Drawing Room**, with a gorgeous fluted ceiling by John Nash; the **White Drawing Room** (where the monarch receives foreign ambassadors); and other rooms. But most visitors will get the biggest kick out of seeing the **Throne Room**, with his-and-hers pink chairs initialled 'ER' and 'P' sitting smugly under what looks like a theatre arch.

The palace is open daily from 9.30 am to 4.30 pm from early August to early October, and admission costs £10/7.50/5 for adults/seniors/under-17s (family £30). Tickets are sold from a futuristic kiosk (open daily from 9 am to 4 pm) in Green Park to the north, but you can also book by credit card on ☎ 7321 2233. You can get more information from the palace's Web site at www.royal.gov.uk.

We are not amused: Queen Victoria looks down on the tourist kerfuffle.

Changing of the Guard This is a London 'must see' – though you'll probably go away wondering what all the fuss was about. The old guard (Foot Guards of the Household Regiment) comes off duty to be replaced by the new guard on the forecourt of Buckingham Palace, which gives tourists a chance to gape at the bright red uniforms, bearskin hats (synthetic alternatives are being looked at), shouting and marching. If you arrive early, grab a prime spot by the railings; more likely, however, you'll be 10 rows back. The ceremony takes place daily at 11.30 am from April to June and on odd dates (eg 1, 3, 5 July and so on) at the same time during the rest of the year. This can change so ring the Visitorcall service on ☎ 09064 123411 or ☎ 0891 505 452 for up-to-the-minute information. For the schedule of the changing of the Horse Guard in Whitehall, see the Whitehall walking tour in the Westminster & Pimlico section.

Queen's Gallery The Queen's Gallery (☎ 7839 1377, 7799 2331 for a recording), in the south wing of Buckingham Palace (enter from Buckingham Gate), is where works from the extensive Royal Collection of paintings, drawings, cartoons, miniatures and engravings usually go on display in regularly changing exhibitions. Designed by Nash as a conservatory and converted into a chapel for Victoria in 1843, it was destroyed in a 1940 air raid and reopened as a gallery in 1962. The present gallery is relatively small and is currently undergoing a £10 million transformation that will enlarge the small entrance hall, add a Greek Doric portico and expand the exhibition space. The gallery will reopen in 2002 in time for Elizabeth II's Golden Jubilee.

Royal Mews South of the palace, the Royal Mews (☎ 7839 1377, 7799 2331 for a recording), Buckingham Palace Rd SW1 (⊖ Victoria), started life as a falconry but now houses the flashy vehicles the royals use for getting around on ceremonial occasions, including the stunning Gold State Coach of 1762, used for every coronation

CHRIS MELLOR

On parade: 'A bit hot this morning, Stan ...'
'Bleedin' roasting, Reg.'

since that of George III, and the Glass Coach of 1910, which is used for royal weddings. Don't forget to look at the stables designed by John Nash in the 1820s.

The Royal Mews is currently open Monday to Thursday from noon to 4 pm, but it may return to its original schedule early in the new millennium: Monday to Thursday from 10.30 am to 4.30 pm in August and September, and on Tuesday, Wednesday and Thursday from noon to 4 pm during the rest of the year. Admission costs £4.20/3.20/2.10 for adults/seniors/under-17s (family £10.50).

Green Park
Green Park adjoins St James's to the northwest across The Mall, and is a less fussy, more naturally rolling park, with trees and open space, sunshine and shade. Once a duelling ground and, like Hyde Park, a vegetable field during WWII, Green Park tends to be quieter than its illustrious

neighbour. If you need to get to Hyde Park Corner from, say, Buckingham Palace a stroll through the park is much more enjoyable than taking the tube or a bus.

Mayfair

Mayfair is one of London's most exclusive neighbourhoods – as everyone who's ever played the British version of Monopoly will know. At the heart of the district is **Grosvenor Square**, dominated by the US embassy on the western side and with a **memorial to Franklin D Roosevelt** in the centre. The statue, showing FDR cloaked and leaning on a stick to hide his disability resulting from polio, was unveiled by Eleanor Roosevelt in 1948. It was paid for by 200,000 British subscribers, whose contributions were limited to five shillings (25p) each. Such was the popularity of America's 32nd president after WWII that the sum was raised within 24 hours.

The other famous Mayfair landmark is **Berkeley Square**, where nightingales might conceivably still sing amid the plane trees, although you'd never hear them for the traffic. The house at No 44 still retains its fine old iron railings, complete with snuffers for extinguishing the torches carried by footmen.

THE WEST END: PICCADILLY, SOHO & CHINATOWN (Maps 6 & 7)

No two Londoners ever agree on the exact borders of the West End but let's just say it takes in Piccadilly Circus and Trafalgar Square to the south, Oxford St and Tottenham Court Rd to the north, Regent St to the West and Covent Garden and the Strand to the east. A heady mixture of consumerism and culture, the West End is where outstanding museums and galleries rub shoulders with tacky tourist traps, and world-famous buildings and monuments share the streets with some of the capital's most popular shopping and entertainment venues. This is the London of both postcard and T-shirt stands and folk memory.

CHRIS MELLOR

Piccadilly Circus, London's most famous advertising hoarding.

Piccadilly Circus

Piccadilly Circus (Map 7) is home to the statue of the *Angel of Christian Charity*, commonly known as **Eros** and dedicated to Lord Ashley, the Victorian Earl of Shaftesbury, who championed social and industrial reform. It was London's first memorial built of aluminium and was despised when it was unveiled in 1893. We may sound like Philistines but we prefer the statue outside what was until recently the Sogo department store on the corner of Piccadilly and Haymarket: the **Horses of Helios fountain**, with their flaring nostrils and all that rushing water. It's a great meeting place.

Piccadilly Circus used to be the hub of London, where flower girls flogged their wares and people arranged to meet or simply bumped into each other. Nowadays it's fume-choked and pretty uninteresting, overlooked by Rock Circus and Tower Records.

The streets fanning out from Piccadilly Circus are another story. Running northeast is **Shaftesbury Ave**, named after the eponymous earl and the heart of London's theatreland. To the east Coventry St heads past Planet Hollywood to Leicester Square and Covent Garden. To the south, Regent St passes the Britain Visitor Centre, and Haymarket the main American Express (Amex) office, before they both join up with Pall Mall. To the west Piccadilly itself leads past Fortnum & Mason, the Royal Academy and Green Park to end at Hyde Park Corner. From the north-western corner of the circus Regent St doglegs north towards Oxford Circus and is lined on both sides with elegant arcades of shops.

Rock Circus The completely revamped Rock Circus (Map 7; ☎ 7734 7203), London Pavilion, Piccadilly Circus W1 (⊖ Piccadilly Circus), is one of the capital's most popular attractions, despite the fact that many of those immortalised in wax would be unknown to those aged under 40. You're whipped back to rock's cotton-picking origins so fast you barely have time to take in what's happening, after which you're treated to a succession of animated

ANTHONY BATTLE

All you need is love: Eros does the business.

models who lip-sync to their music while jerking their limbs around like puppets. It's hardly cutting edge.

Rock Circus is open daily from 10 am (from 11 am on Tuesday) to 10 pm from late June to early September. During the rest of the year it's open on Monday, Wednesday, Thursday and Sunday from 10 am to 8 pm; on Tuesday from 11 am to 8 pm; and on Friday and Saturday from 10 am to 9 pm. Admission costs £8.25/7.25/6.25 for adults/seniors & students/children.

Pepsi Trocadero & Segaworld The Pepsi Trocadero (Map 7; ☎ 7434 0030), 1 Piccadilly Circus W1 (⊖ Piccadilly Circus), is a huge indoor entertainment complex on six levels with several high-tech attractions, anchored by the Segaworld indoor theme-park (☎ 7734 2777, 0870 550 5040). It's a good

DOUG McKINLAY

Bright lights, big city: neon thrills and spills inside the Pepsi Trocadero.

place to take youngsters who can't be sold on London's more cultural attractions, but don't expect a peaceful – or cheap – night or day out. There's no admission charge to Sega-world, but you must pay £3 for each of the eight rides (or save by buying a four/eight-ride ticket for £7.90/14.90). Also inside the Trocadero you can scare yourself half to death on the **Pepsi Max Drop Ride** (£3) or visit the **Pepsi IMAX Theatre** (£6.75/5.50; family £19.98) for one of three movies in 3-D or with other special effects. In addition, **Funland** has upwards of 400 video games to keep even the most hyperactive active. The centre is open daily from 10 am until midnight (on Friday and Saturday to 1 am).

Piccadilly

Piccadilly (Map 7), the road running west from Piccadilly Circus, is said to take its curious name from 'picadils', stiff collars or ruffs popular at court in the 17th century and made by a tailor who built himself a house here. As you leave Piccadilly Circus look on the left for **St James's Piccadilly**, designed by

Sir Christopher Wren after the Great Fire of 1666. It's another of those sociable London churches, with both lunch-time and evening concerts and a small antiques market Wednesday to Saturday from 10 am to 6 pm.

On the right you'll come to the **Royal Academy of Arts** (☎ 7300 8000), Burlington House, Piccadilly W1 (✆ Green Park), which has traditionally played poor relation to the Hayward Gallery. But in recent years exhibitions here have broken all records; its *Monet in the 20th Century* in early 1999 saw 800,000 visits over three months and forced the academy to open its doors nonstop for the last 36 hours of the show. Each summer, the academy holds its traditional Summer Exhibition, an open show that anyone can enter. The quality can be mixed, but in the glorious setting of one of London's few remaining 18th-century mansions it never seems to matter much. It's open daily from 10 am to 6 pm (on Friday often to 8.30 pm). Admission prices depend on what's on, but expect to pay around £6/5/4 for adults/seniors & students/children aged under 12.

A little farther along on the right you'll come to the **Burlington Arcade**, which was built in 1819 and recalls a bygone age – selling the kinds of things that only the very rich are likely to want. Watch out for the Burlington Berties, the uniformed guards who patrol the arcade, with a brief to prevent high spirits, whistling and the inelegant popping of bubble gum. At the far end turn right on to Burlington Gardens and you'll see an imposing 19th-century Italianate building that was, until recently, home to the Museum of Mankind. The ethnography collection it contained is now being returned to the British Museum.

Head west along Burlington Gardens and you'll come to Old Bond St, where many of London's commercial art galleries can be found. The **Royal Arcade**, a covered thoroughfare lined with extremely expensive shops selling such English wares as hunting jackets, pipe tobacco, cashmere jumpers and golfing knickerbockers, runs off Old Bond St. Built in 1879, it reflects that era's love affair with the neogothic style.

Keep on going and on the left you'll see **The Ritz** (Map 6), perhaps the most glitzy of London's upmarket hotels. This was one of London's first steel-framed buildings, but that's unlikely to interest you much if you're coming here for tea (see the boxed text 'Tea for Two or More' in the Places to Eat chapter). Immediately west of the Ritz is **Green Park**. Keep going and you'll come out at **Hyde Park Corner**.

Regent St

Regent St (Map 7), originally designed by John Nash as a ceremonial route linking Carlton House, the Prince Regent's now-demolished city dwelling, with the 'wilds' of Regent Park, later became a buffer between workaday Soho and affluent, residential Mayfair. The street is lined with elegant shop-fronts but they date back only to 1925. Here you'll find Hamley's, London's premier toy and game store, and the upmarket department store Liberty (see the Shopping chapter). Go east along Great Marlborough St and you'll reach the northern end of **Carnaby St**, which runs parallel to Regent St. It was the street for fashion in the 'swinging London' of the 1960s, and this lives on in the Union Jack-emblazoned gewgaws it off-loads to tourists.

All Souls, Langham Place Nash's solution for the curving, northern sweep of Regent St was this delightful church (Map 6; ☎ 7580 3522), Langham Place W1 (⊖ Oxford Circus), with its circular columned porch and distinctive needle-like spire, reminiscent of an ancient Greek temple. The church was very unpopular when completed in 1824; a contemporary cartoon by George Cruikshank shows Nash rather painfully impaled on the spire through the bottom with the words 'Nashional Taste!!!' below it.

The BBC Experience A short distance north of All Souls is **Broadcasting House** (Map 6), from which the BBC began broadcasting in 1932. The basement now houses the BBC Experience (☎ 0870 603 0304)

where, on a semi-guided tour lasting about 1½ hours, you can watch clips of popular BBC programmes and see the Marconi Collection of early wireless equipment. Interactive displays let you try your hand at presenting a weather report or a sporting event, handling a television camera or directing an episode of the evergreen BBC1 soap opera *EastEnders*.

The BBC Experience is open daily from 10 am (on Monday from 11 am) to 5.30 pm. Admission costs £6.95/5.95/4.95 for adults/ seniors & students/children (family £19.95). There's a shop stocking any number of videos, tapes and books relating to BBC programmes.

Oxford St

Once London's finest shopping street, Oxford St (Maps 6 & 7) is a big disappointment for most visitors, especially if

ELLIOT DANIB

Shops (and their signs) on Oxford St range from the high class to the positively tacky.

you emerge from Oxford Circus tube and head east towards Tottenham Court Rd and the flagship HMV and Virgin record stores. It sometimes feels as if you're running the gauntlet of permanent 'closing down' sales and slimy shop-front salespeople who draw people in by offering dubious bargains, usually on electrical goods (see Touts & Scams under Dangers & Annoyances in the Facts for the Visitor chapter). Things are much better if you head west towards Marble Arch; this is where you'll find the famous department stores, including John Lewis, Selfridges and Marks & Spencer (see the Shopping chapter).

Soho

East of Regent St and south of Oxford St, with Shaftesbury Ave and Charing Cross Rd to the south and the east, is Soho (Map 7), one of the liveliest corners of London

CHARLOTTE HINDLE

You can stock up on kinky undies and sex toys at any number of Soho boutiques.

and the place to come for fun and games after dark. Hard though it is to believe, this area was once a hunting ground; 'So-ho!' was a rallying cry, something like a 'tally-ho', hence the name. A decade ago Soho was an extremely sleazy neighbourhood filled with strip clubs and peepshows where unwary males were easily separated from large sums of cash. The strip joints are still there, of course, but these days they rub shoulders with some of London's trendiest clubs, bars and restaurants (see the Places to Eat and Entertainment chapters for more details). There's also a move by Westminster City Council to buy up premises now housing unlicensed sex shops and hostess bars and redevelop the properties.

Leicester Square

Despite efforts to smarten it up and the presence of four huge cinemas, various nightclubs, pubs and restaurants, pedestrians-only Leicester (**les**-ter) Square (Map 7) still feels more like a transit point between Covent Garden and Piccadilly Circus than its own world. You're bound to pass through at some point, but it's hard to imagine a time when artists Joshua Reynolds and William Hogarth actually chose to live here.

The patch of green in the middle of the square is a barely acceptable picnic spot if you haven't got the energy to press on to St James's Park. The fountain in the centre commemorates Shakespeare and there's a small statue of Charlie Chaplin to one side. Plaques in the ground also list the distances from central London to the capitals of various Commonwealth countries. More plaques in the pavement outside incorporate the hand-prints of various Hollywood stars; the cinemas here are where many British film premieres take place.

The **Silver Jubilee Walkway**, 20km (12 miles) in length, starts in Leicester Square and loops round Lambeth Bridge to the south and Tower Bridge in the east. A map shows the entire route (see Walking in the Getting Around chapter for more details).

RICHARD I'ANSON

Stir-fry heaven: sights, sounds and smells to awaken even the sleepiest appetite in Chinatown.

Chinatown

Immediately north of Leicester Square are Lisle and Gerrard Sts, the heart of London's Chinatown (Map 7), where street signs are in both English and Chinese, and red lanterns and dragon-adorned moon gates are commonplace. This is the place to come for an after-hours Chinese meal; at least one place is open round the clock (see The West End: Piccadilly, Soho & Chinatown in the Places to Eat chapter). But to see it at its over-the-top best, time your visit for the Chinese New Year in late January/early February, when the streets explode with lion dances and firecrackers.

Covent Garden

In the 1630s Inigo Jones converted something that had started life as a vegetable field belonging to Westminster Abbey into the elegant square – or piazza – at Covent Garden. In time it became the haunt of writers like Pepys, Fielding and Boswell in search of stimulating nightlife, but by Victorian times a fruit and vegetable market had been set up (immortalised in *My Fair Lady*, the 1964 screen adaptation of George Bernard Shaw's play *Pygmalion*). When the market was moved out to Nine Elms in Battersea in the 1980s, the old market was transformed into one of central London's liveliest hubs, with shops built into the old arcades. Where stallholders once flogged fresh produce, they now sell antiques, clothes and overpriced bric-a-brac.

Covent Garden (Map 7; ✪ Covent Garden) gets horribly overcrowded in summer but remains one of the few bits of London where pedestrians rule, and there's always a corner of relative peace where you can listen to the licensed buskers.

Tucked away in the basement of the central market hall is the **Cabaret Mechanical Theatre** (☎ 7379 7961), a treasure trove of automata with buttons to push and handles to turn, guaranteed to bring out the child in all of us. It's open weekdays from 10 am to 6.30 pm (on Saturday to 7 pm and on

Sunday from 11 am to 6.30 pm) and costs £1.95/1.20 (family £4.95).

Overlooking the piazza to the south-west is **St Paul's Church**, long associated with the theatre and actors. Designed by Inigo Jones in the 1630s, it's little more than a stone rectangle with a pitched roof; 'the handsomest barn in England', he called it. In the square in front, where Samuel Pepys watched England's first Punch and Judy show in 1662, you can still see buskers perform.

To the south-east of the piazza stand Jubilee and Floral halls. Excavations carried out by the Museum of London in the area have uncovered extensive traces of the Saxon settlement of Lundenwic, including wattle-and-daub housing.

Beyond the piazza are lively streets of clothes shops and bars, restaurants and designer gift shops. To the north, Floral St is where swanky designers like Paul Smith, Jigsaw, Jones and Agnès B have their outlets. Another block north and you're in Long Acre, which boasts Emporio Armani, Woodhouse, Gap and Flip (a true charity shop selling 50s American clothing). Here too you'll find bookshops (including Stanford's for guidebooks and maps) and St Martin's College of Fashion & Design. Neal St, a narrow lane leading from Long Acre to Shaftesbury Ave, is particularly worth exploring for both shopping and eating (see Covent Garden & The Strand in the Places to Eat chapter for details of Neal's Yard).

London Transport Museum Tucked into the corner of Covent Garden between the Jubilee Hall and Tutton's restaurant, the London Transport Museum (Map 7; ☎ 7379 6344) tells how London made the transition from streets choked with horse-drawn carriages to the arrival of the DLR and the ultramodern Jubilee Line extension – a more interesting story than you might suspect. It's a great favourite with kids, with lots of hands-on exhibits and activities.

Café life in Covent Garden: taking a break from the buskers and boutiques.

The museum is open daily from 10 am to 6 pm (on Friday from 11 am) and entry costs £4.95/2.95 for adults/seniors, students & children over five years (family £12.85). There's an excellent shop and an Aroma coffee-shop. For details of talks on varied aspects of transport, phone ☎ 7836 8557.

Theatre Museum A branch of the Victoria & Albert Museum, the Theatre Museum (Map 7; ☎ 7836 7891), Russell St WC2 (⊖ Covent Garden), displays costumes and artefacts relating to the history of the theatre, including memorabilia of great actors and actresses like David Garrick, Edmund Kean, Henry Irving and Ellen Terry. Exhibits highlight how stage make-up is used, and you can hear recordings from the National Video Archive of Stage Performance before you return along a corridor where famous performers have left their hand-prints in paint.

The museum is open Tuesday to Sunday from 11 am to 7 pm. Admission costs £4.50/2.50.

The Strand

At the end of the 12th century nobles built sturdy houses of stone with gardens along the 'beach' of the Thames. The Strand (Maps 6 & 7) linked Westminster, the seat of political power, with the City, London's centre of industry and trade, and became one of the most prestigious places in London to live; in the 19th century Disraeli pronounced it the finest street in Europe. Today this 1.2km thoroughfare is a hotchpotch of shops, fine hotels, theatres and offices, in whose doorways the homeless lay out their sleeping bags for the night. For things to see along the Strand, see the Fleet St & the Strand walking tour in the City section of this chapter.

Somerset House This splendid Palladian masterpiece (Map 6; ⊖ Temple), designed by William Chambers in 1775, contains two fabulous museums: the Courtauld Gallery and the new Gilbert Collection of decorative arts. There are plans to convert the central Great Court, long used as a car park for civil servants, into a concert hall.

Quality rather than quantity: the Courtauld Gallery has a small but exceptional collection.

CHARLOTTE HINDLE

Courtauld Gallery Housed in the North Wing (or Strand Block), the Courtauld Gallery (☎ 7848 2526) displays some of the Courtauld Institute's marvellous collection of paintings in grand surroundings following a £25 million architectural refurbishment. Exhibits include works by Rubens, Bellini, Velásquez and Botticelli. However, for many visitors the most memorable display is of Impressionist and postimpressionist art by Van Gogh, Cézanne, Rousseau, Gauguin, Toulouse-Lautrec, Manet, Pissarro, Sisley, Renoir, Degas and Monet.

The gallery also has a small exhibition of paintings by the 20th-century Bloomsbury artists Duncan Grant, Vanessa Bell and Roger Fry, together with colourful furniture produced by the Omega Workshops (also in Bloomsbury) and influenced by what were then newly discovered African masks and other ethnographical items.

The gallery is open Monday to Saturday from 10 am to 6 pm, on Sunday from noon. Admission costs £4/2 for adults/seniors, but is free for under-18s, students and, on Monday between 10 am and 2 pm, everyone. A joint ticket allowing entry to the Courtauld Gallery and the Gilbert Collection costs £7/5.

Gilbert Collection The Gilbert Collection (☎ 7240 5782), a valuable collection including such treasures as European silver, gold snuffboxes and Italian mosaics bequeathed to the nation by London-born

American businessman Arthur Gilbert, is housed in the vaults beneath the South Terrace, which boasts one of the finest views of the Thames. Opening hours are the same as for the Courtauld Gallery; admission is £4/3/2 for adults/seniors/disabled visitors, £3 for part-time and foreign students, and free for under-18s, UK students and, on Monday from 10 am to 2 pm, everyone.

Royal Courts of Justice At the eastern end of the Strand, where it joins Fleet St and opposite No 217, you'll see the entrance to the Royal Courts of Justice (Map 6; ☎ 7936 6000), a gargantuan mélange of Gothic

In the steps of Virginia Woolf et al: literary ghosts linger on in Bloomsbury.

spires and pinnacles and burnished Portland stone, designed by GE Street in 1874. This is where civil cases (eg libel) are tried and where many famous appeals against conviction have wound up. Criminal cases (murders, bank robberies etc) are heard at the Old Bailey, near St Paul's (see Central Criminal Court in the City section of this chapter).

Visitors are welcome to come in and watch cases in progress (unless they're closed proceedings) on weekdays from 9.30 am to 4.30 pm. Expect airport-like security checks and note cameras are banned.

BLOOMSBURY (Maps 3, 4 & 6)

East of Tottenham Court Rd and north of High Holborn, south of Euston Rd and to the west of Gray's Inn Rd, Bloomsbury is a peculiar mix of the University of London, the British Museum, beautiful Georgian squares and architecture, literary history, traffic, office workers, students and tourists. **Russell Square** (Map 6), the very heart of Bloomsbury, is London's largest square. It was laid out in 1800. At night it becomes a very busy gay cruising area.

Between the world wars these pleasant streets were colonised by a group of artists and intellectuals who became known collectively as the Bloomsbury Group. The novelists Virginia Woolf and EM Forster and the economist John Maynard Keynes are perhaps the best-known members.

The centre of literary Bloomsbury was **Gordon Square** (Map 3) where, at various times, Bertrand Russell lived at No 57, Lytton Strachey at No 51 and Vanessa and Clive Bell, Maynard Keynes and the Woolf family at No 46. Strachey, Dora Carrington and Lydia Lopokova (later the wife of Maynard Keynes) all took turns living at No 41. Not all the buildings, many of which now belong to the university, are marked with blue plaques.

Until recently, lovely **Bedford Square** (Map 6), the only completely Georgian square still surviving in Bloomsbury, was home to many London publishing houses now swallowed up by multinational conglomerates and moved out to west London.

They included Jonathan Cape, Chatto and the Bodley Head (set up by Woolf and her husband Leonard). These publishers were part-conspirators in creating and sustaining the Bloomsbury Group legend, churning out seemingly endless collections of letters, memoirs and biographies.

British Museum

The British Museum (Map 6; ☎ 7636 1555, 7580 1788 for a recording), Great Russell St WC1 (✪ Tottenham Court Road or Russell Square), is Britain's largest museum and one of the oldest in the world. It's also the most visited tourist attraction in London with more than six million annual visitors.

Like so many other sights in London, the British Museum has been undergoing major renovation in time for the millennium. Most importantly, the museum's inner courtyard, hidden from the public for almost a century and a half, has now been turned into the **Great Court**, covered with a spectacular glass and steel roof designed by Norman Foster. As a result of all this work some collections may have been moved around or closed temporarily. If you can't find a particular item, ask a custodian to direct you.

The collection is vast, diverse and amazing – so much so that it can seem pretty daunting. To make the most of the museum don't plan on seeing too much in one day; the fact that admission is still free means you can come back several times and appreciate the museum's exhibits at your leisure.

The museum building is, in itself, striking. It was designed by Robert Smirke in 1823 and completed in 1847 (though the central Reading Room with its large copper dome didn't open until 1857). The collections inside originated with the curiosities collected by Sir Hans Sloane (of Sloane Square fame), which the physician sold to the nation in 1753, and were augmented not long afterwards with manuscripts and books from two other major collections.

The British Museum has two entrances: the imposing Smirke-designed porticoed main entrance off Great Russell St, and a back entrance off Montague Place, which

British Museum Highlights

- Benin Bronzes
- Elgin Marbles
- Egyptian mummies
- Rosetta Stone
- Sutton Hoo Treasure
- Lewis chess-set
- Mildenhall Treasure
- Battersea shield & Waterloo helmet
- Lindow Man
- Oxus Treasure
- Portland Vase

tends to be less congested. If you come in through the front entrance, head straight for the information desk at the back of the main hall and ask for a list of the free Eye Opener tours (see Guided Tours later in this section). If you don't want to be shown around by someone else, use the plan of the museum to find your way around. The most obvious strategy is to home straight in on the highlights, but bear in mind that most people will do the same thing.

From the main hall you can choose to go left or upstairs. The following quick tour of the museum assumes you start by turning left and bypass the crowded bookshop to arrive in the galleries housing the ancient Assyrian finds from Nimrud, Nineveh and Khorsabad (rooms 16 to 21 and 26). Most striking are the vast human-headed winged bulls that used to guard the temple of Ashurnarsipal II, but the carved reliefs dating from the 7th century BC are almost as fascinating. To the east in room 25 are Egyptian sculptures and the **Rosetta Stone**, written in two forms of ancient Egyptian (hieroglyphics and demotic) and in Ancient Greek and discovered in 1799. The Rosetta Stone was the key to deciphering Egyptian hieroglyphics, which had stymied scholars up to that time. The famous mummies have been moved to the new Mummies Gallery on the 2nd floor, accessible via the eastern staircase.

Avoiding Museum Fatigue

Warm-up exercises, half-hour breathers, a portable seat, bottled water and an energy-giving snack ... It might sound as if you're preparing for a mountain trek, but these are some of the recommendations for tackling London's museums offered by the experts.

The British Museum alone has more than 4km of corridors, over seven million exhibits and almost that many visitors, all elbowing each other to see what they want to see in a limited amount of time. It's hardly surprising that many people feel worn out almost before they've crossed the threshold.

To avoid museum fatigue wear comfortable shoes and make use of the free cloakrooms. Be aware that standing still and walking slowly promote fatigue; whenever possible, sit down. Reflecting on the material and forming associations with it causes information to move from your short to long-term memory; your experiences will thus amount to more than a series of visual sound-bites.

Tracking and timing studies suggest that museum-goers spend no more than 10 seconds viewing an exhibit and another 10 seconds reading the label as they try to take in as much as they can before succumbing to fatigue. Your best bet in a large museum is to choose a particular period or section and pretend that the rest is somewhere across town. You can get some useful sneak previews and make your decisions in advance by checking out the 24 Hour Museum Web site at www.24hourmuseum.org.uk; it is linked to more than 200 museums in London, with virtual-reality tours and details of great paintings and other works of art.

There are other ways to avoid museum fatigue. You could join a guided tour of the highlights. Many of these are free, though the British Museum charges £5/3 for its daily 60-minute tour. Remember too that you can buy tickets to many attractions in London (including admission-charging museums) from ticket agencies and hotel concierges, which means you don't have to queue. Every tube station now sells tickets to the Tower of London, which can boast the mother of all queues in summer.

West of these rooms you'll come to the galleries housing finds from the classical Greek, Roman and Hellenistic empires (rooms 1 to 15). Best known of the exhibits here are the **Elgin Marbles**, pilfered from the walls of the Parthenon on the Acropolis in Athens by Lord Elgin from 1801 to 1806. The marbles used to provide parts of the frieze round the top of the temple; they are thought to show the great procession to the temple that took place during the Panathenaic Festival but have been pretty battered and beaten over the centuries. Other fine monuments on display here include the reconstructed façade of the **Nereid Monument** from Xanthos in Turkey.

In room 6 you can see one of the caryatids (female figures) from the portico of the Erechtheion in Athens, while room 12 has sculptures from the Mausoleum of Halicarnassus and from the Temple of Artemis at Ephesus, two of the Seven Wonders of the Ancient World (both in modern-day Turkey).

Tucked away at the foot of the eastern staircase is the Mexican Gallery, with the fine **Mask of Tzcatlipoca**, with a turquoise mosaic laid over a real skull on display. Beyond that is the collection of Indian goddesses, dancing Shivas and serene cross-legged Buddhas in copper and stone.

If you climb the eastern staircase and turn left you'll enter more galleries devoted to western Asia (rooms 51 and 52). Here you'll find the stunning **Oxus Treasure**, a collection of 7th to 4th-century BC pieces of Persian gold rescued from bandits in a Rawalpindi bazaar. It's believed that they originally hailed from the ancient Persian capital at Persepolis. Here, too, you'll discover the **Ur finds** of the Chaldees, including a beautiful model of a goat on its hind legs peering through gold leaves. These artefacts are believed to date back to the third millennium BC, placing them among the oldest exhibits in the museum.

Rooms 49 and 50 contain artefacts from Roman Britain and from Bronze Age and Celtic Europe (approximately 900 to 100 BC). This is where you'll see the stunning **Mildenhall Treasure**, a 28-piece silver dinner service dating from the 4th century, and the Celtic **Snettisham Treasure**, a hoard of gold and silver torques (necklaces). Also here are the **Battersea shield** and **Waterloo helmet** dredged from the Thames near the bridges whose names they bear. The Battersea shield dates from around 350 to 150 BC, the horned helmet, the only one of its kind ever found, from around 150 to 50 BC.

This is also where you'll find **Lindow Man**, an Iron Age unfortunate who seems to have been struck on the head with a narrow axe (there are holes in the skull) and then garrotted. His throat was probably slit open to bleed him as part of a ritualistic sacrifice. A Cheshire peat-bog preserved his gruesome, leathery remains until 1984 when he was sliced in half by a peat-cutting machine and uncovered. Poor old sod.

Eventually you'll arrive in rooms 41 to 43, which display medieval European art. Particularly interesting for the visitor to London are the fragmentary **murals from St Stephen's Chapel** in the Palace of Westminster, now the Houses of Parliament. The chapel burned down in 1834 – but not before these scenes from the Book of Job were rescued. The two panels from the ceiling of the King's State Bedchamber, known as the Painted Chamber because of its 14th-century murals, were rediscovered in Bristol in 1993. They show a seraph and a prophet.

Here, too, you'll see the finds from **Sutton Hoo**, an Anglo-Saxon ship-burial site in Suffolk that was excavated in 1939. Inside the remains of the wooden ship wonderful

gold and garnet cloisonné shoulder clasps and purse decorations were found. Perhaps the most evocative sight is the helmet of the presumed king.

Also worth seeking out are the 67-piece **walrus ivory chess-set** (or sets) found in the sandbanks on the Isle of Lewis in 1831 and dating from the mid-12th century, and the tiny **Dunstable Swan Jewel**, a 15th-century gold masterpiece with its feathers picked out in white enamel.

The *objets d'art* in rooms 44 to 48 would seem more at home in the Victoria & Albert Museum, but it's worth inspecting the late 16th-century Bohemian **ship-clock** – you'll be hard pressed to spot the clock-face tucked away at the foot of the main mast of a miniature ship. The **Hull-Grundy jewellery collection**, which includes pieces by Tiffany, Boucheron and other masters, should also not be missed.

On the landing leading up from the main stairs you'll see the stunning 4th-century **Roman mosaic** from Hinton St Mary, which incorporates the Christian chi-rho symbol. Look down into the stairwell and on the wall you'll see the 17th-century **Benin Bronzes**, plaques depicting soldiers, musicians and other scenes from everyday life that were stolen from the king and his chiefs in 1897 when a British company seized Benin City and overthrew the ruler.

Across the corridor you'll see more finds from the Greek and Roman empires in southern Italy and Cyprus (rooms 69 to 73), including the blue and white **Portland Vase**, one of the first objects made of glass but perhaps most famous for having been smashed into 200 pieces by a visitor in 1845 and then painstakingly put back together again. More antiquities from Egypt and from western Asia line the corridor between the eastern and western staircases. Room 66 covers Coptic Egypt, and beyond that and up some stairs lies a temporary exhibition gallery (room 90) that often has fine free displays from the prints and drawings collection. Beyond that is a gallery devoted to Korean art. Continue upstairs and you'll come to the lovely Japanese Galleries (rooms 92 to 94).

At the heart of the museum, the **Reading Room** in the centre of the covered Great Court is a grand structure where George Bernard Shaw and Mahatma Gandhi studied and Friedrich Engels and Karl Marx wrote *The Communist Manifesto*. The northern end of the courtyard's lower level is to house the museum's African collections and will be linked with new galleries for the American, Asian, Middle Eastern, European and Pacific ethnographical collections on the ground floor of the main hall.

Hours & Tickets The British Museum (free, £2 donation suggested) is open Monday to Saturday from 10 am to 5 pm and on Sunday from noon to 6 pm. Information for visitors with disabilities is available on ☎ 7637 7384. The museum's Web site is at www.british-museum.ac.uk.

Guided Tours The museum offers visitors free Eye Opener tours of individual galleries (eg World of Asia and Treasures of Islam). These last an hour and generally take place Monday to Saturday between 11 am and 3 pm and on Sunday between 1.30 and 4.30 pm. There are also 90-minute Collections tours, but these cost £7/4 for adults/students & under-16s and get booked up quickly. They depart Monday to Saturday at 10.30 am and 1 pm and on Sunday four times between 1 and 4 pm. A daily 60-minute Highlights tour (£5/3) leaves Monday to Saturday at 3.15 pm.

St George's Bloomsbury

A short distance south of the British Museum is St George's (Map 7; ☎ 7405 3044), Bloomsbury Way WC1 (✆ Holborn or Tottenham Court Road), another of Nicholas Hawksmoor's creations and finished in 1731. It's notable not just for its portico of Corinthian capitals but for its steeple, which was inspired by the Mausoleum of Halicarnassus and is topped with a statue of George I in Roman dress. This steeple can just be made out in the background of Hogarth's influential print of the goings-on in *Gin Lane* in the area known as the Rookery (now Clerkenwell). The church is open weekdays from 9.30 am to 5.30 pm.

Dickens' House

Charles Dickens' House (Map 4; ☎ 7405 2127), 49 Doughty St WC1 (✆ Russell Square), is the only surviving residence of the many the great Victorian novelist occupied before moving to Kent. While living here, from 1837 to 1839, he wrote *The Pickwick Papers*, *Nicholas Nickleby* and *Oliver Twist*, between bouts of worry over debts, deaths and the burden of an ever-growing family.

In Dickens' day, Doughty St was an exclusive neighbourhood with porters in gold-laced livery guarding gates at each end. The house itself has 11 reasonably interesting rooms, including a complete Victorian kitchen and lots of memorabilia. Two desks illustrate Dickens' own rags-to-riches story: the rough-hewn wooden table where he worked as a 15-year-old Gray's Inn lawyer's clerk for a pittance and the velvet-topped desk he later used on reading tours of England and America. Keep an eye out on the stairwell for a goldsmith's shop sign of an arm and hammer that once graced Manette St in Soho and is mentioned in *A Tale of Two Cities*.

Dickens' House is open Monday to Friday from 9.45 am to 5.30 pm and on Saturday from 10 am to 5 pm. Admission costs £3.50/2.50/1.50 for adults/students/children (family £7).

HOLBORN & CLERKENWELL (Maps 4 & 6)

Holborn (**hoe**-bun; Map 6), the area north of the Strand and Fleet St and wedged between the City to the east, Covent Garden to the west and High Holborn to the north, includes several of the Inns of Court, the defunct Inns of Chancery and the wonderful Sir John Soane's Museum. It is the smallest of London's former metropolitan boroughs and takes its name from a tributary of the River Fleet (see the boxed text 'London's Rivers Styx' in the Facts about London chapter).

Immediately north-west of the City, Clerkenwell (**clarken**-well; Maps 4 & 6) gets

JULIET COOMBE

**Down on the farm: traces of London's rural
past in Clerkenwell Green.**

its name from Clerk's Well in Farringdon Lane (below house Nos 14 to 16) where, according to a contemporary account by the monk William Fitz Stephen in 1174, the Parish Clerks of London performed miracle plays. Known in Victorian times for its appalling slums – the so-called Rookery – and street crime, Clerkenwell was settled by Italians whose mark can still just be made out in some of the surviving cafés. The Italian revolutionary Mazzini settled here and Garibaldi dropped by in 1836. The great tenor Caruso also performed on the steps of St Peter's Church and Lenin edited the influential *Iskra* (The Spark) from 37a Clerkenwell Green (now the Karl Marx Memorial Library; see Other Attractions later in this chapter), where he lived from 1902 to 1903.

Recently Clerkenwell has become a very trendy corner of the capital, with the usual batch of pricey restaurants and expensive property. The area around Clerkenwell Green is very attractive, with St James's Church looming over the houses, and the Clerkenwell Conference Centre housed in the 18th-century Sessions House, supposedly haunted by a woman whose lover had been transported.

Inns of Court

There are four Inns of Court, clustered around Holborn and to the south of Fleet St (Map 6): **Lincoln's Inn** (☎ 7405 1393), Lincoln's Inn Fields WC2 (◒ Holborn); **Gray's Inn** (☎ 7405 8164), Gray's Inn Rd

WC1 (◒ Holborn or Chancery Lane); **Inner Temple** (☎ 7797 8250), King's Bench Walk EC4 (◒ Temple); and **Middle Temple** (☎ 7427 4800), Middle Temple Lane EC4 (◒ Temple). The last two are part of the Temple complex between Fleet St and Victoria Embankment; for information on Temple Church, see the City section later in this chapter.

All London barristers work from within one of the Inns, which boast a roll call of former members ranging from Oliver Cromwell and Charles Dickens to Mahatma Gandhi and Margaret Thatcher. It would take a lifetime spent working here to grasp all the intricacies and subtleties of the arcane protocols of the Inns – they're a lot like the Freemasons (both organisations date from the 13th century) and a lot of barristers are Masons as well.

Both Gray's Inn and the much prettier Lincoln's Inn have chapels and quadrangles as well as peaceful, picturesque gardens with lawns and plane trees that offer the chance for a stroll, especially early on weekday mornings before the hordes of barristers in wigs and gowns have started to rush around.

All four Inns were badly damaged during the war. Lincoln's Inn is relatively intact, with original 15th-century buildings, including the Tudor Lincoln's Inn Gatehouse on Chancery Lane (although the archway leading from the adjoining park, Lincoln's Inn Fields, is a replacement). Inigo Jones helped plan the chapel at Lincoln's Inn, which was built in 1623 and remains pretty well preserved. The Gray's Inn chapel, which dates from 1689, was destroyed during WWII and rebuilt and expanded.

The Lincoln's Inn grounds are open Monday to Friday from 9 am to 6 pm; the Lincoln's Inn chapel is open Monday to Friday from 12.30 to 2.30 pm; Gray's Inn is open Monday to Friday from 10 am to 4 pm; the Gray's Inn chapel is open weekdays from 10 am to 6 pm; Inner Temple is open Monday to Friday from 10 am to 4 pm; Middle Temple is open weekdays from 10 to 11.30 am and 3 to 4 pm.

Staple Inn

Just opposite the start of Gray's Inn Rd on Holborn stands Staple Inn (1589; Map 6), one of the eight Inns of Chancery, whose functions were superseded by the Inns of Court by the 18th century. Much of the original structure still stands, including the 16th-century shop-front façade, which was completely restored in the 1950s after wartime bombing. The building is now occupied by the Institute of Actuaries and private offices. On the same side of Holborn but closer to Fetter Lane stood **Barnard's Inn**, redeveloped in 1991. Pip lived here with Herbert Pocket in Dickens' *Great Expectations*.

Sir John Soane's Museum

Sir John Soane's Museum (Map 7; ☎ 7405 2107), 13 Lincoln's Inn Fields WC2 (⊖ Holborn), is partly a beautiful – if quirky – house and partly a small museum representing one man's personal taste. Some visitors consider it their favourite 'small' sight in London.

John Soane (1753-1837) was a leading architect who also designed the Bank of England, Dulwich Picture Gallery and Pitshanger Manor, drawing on ideas he'd picked up while on a grand tour of Italy. He married into money, which he poured into customising two houses in Lincoln's Inn Fields close to the Inns of Court. The building itself is a curiosity, with a glass dome bringing light to the basement, a lantern room filled with statuary, and a picture gallery where each painting folds away if pressed to reveal another one behind.

Soane's collection of Egyptiana predated the Victorian passion for such things and includes a sarcophagus of Seti I. It also includes the original *Rake's Progress*, William Hogarth's set of cartoon caricatures of late 18th-century London lowlife (see the boxed text 'Of Rakes & Harlots: Hogarth's World' under Arts in the Facts about London chapter).

The museum (free) is open Tuesday to Saturday from 10 am to 5 pm and again on the first Tuesday of every month from 6 to 9 pm. There's also an hour-long lecture tour (£3) on Saturday at 2.30 pm.

St Andrew Holborn

This church (Map 6) on the south-eastern corner of Holborn Circus, first mentioned at the end of the 10th century, was rebuilt by Wren in 1686 and was the largest of his parish churches. The interior suffered severe damage during the bombings of 1941; much of what you see inside is original but brought from other churches.

Holborn Viaduct

This fine iron bridge (Map 6) with its four bronze statues was built in 1869 to link Holborn and Newgate St above what had been a valley created by the River Fleet and part of St Andrew Holborn's churchyard. The four statues represent Commerce and Agriculture (on the north) and Science and Fine Arts (on the south).

St John's Gate & Museum

What looks like a toy-town medieval gate cutting across St John's Lane (Map 6; ⊖ Farringdon) turns out to be the real thing, albeit restored in the 19th century. During the crusades the Knights of St John of Jerusalem were soldiers who took on a nursing role. In Clerkenwell they established a priory that originally covered around four hectares. Their church, St John's Clerkenwell in St John's Square, had a round nave like Temple Church and you can still see some of the outline picked out in brick outside.

St John's Gate was built as a grand entrance to the church in 1504. Although most of the buildings were demolished when Henry VIII dissolved the priory along with all the others in the country between 1536 and 1540, the gate lived on to have a very varied afterlife, not least as a Latin-speaking coffee house run, without much success, by William Hogarth's father during Queen Anne's reign. The restoration dates from the period when it housed the Old Jerusalem Tavern in the 19th century.

Inside is a small and fairly pedestrian

museum (☎ 7253 6644) recounting the history of the knights and their properties around the world, and of the modern British Order of St John, which has taken the knights' place. There's also a mock-up of the coffee house.

The museum (free) is open weekdays from 9 am to 5 pm and on Saturday from 10 am to 4 pm. To get the most out of a visit try to time it for 11 am or 2.30 pm on Tuesday, Friday or Saturday when you'll be given a guided tour (£4) of the restored church remains, including the fine Romanesque crypt with a sturdy alabaster monument commemorating a Castilian knight (1575), a battered monument showing the last prior William Weston as a skeleton in a shroud, and stained-glass windows showing the main figures in the story. You'll also be shown the Chapter Hall where the Chapter General of the Order meets every three months.

House of Detention

From 1616 to 1890, when it was demolished to make way for a school, a prison stood in what is now Clerkenwell Close. Visitors to the House of Detention (Map 4; ☎ 7253 9494) can descend into a murky, damp-smelling basement to inspect the old kitchen and laundry and some refitted cells with details of a tide of criminality to make you think twice before complaining about modern pickpockets. Here you'll learn how it was once thought wise to keep prisoners in darkened, solitary cells, wearing masks whenever they were let out. It's well done (better than the Clink Exhibition, for example), and you'll probably be very glad to escape to the outside again.

The museum is open daily from 10 am to 6 pm. Admission costs £4/3/2.50. To get here from Clerkenwell Green (Map 4), the notorious spot where Fagin introduced young Oliver Twist to the fine art of stealing silk handkerchiefs, walk north-west along Clerkenwell Close and follow it as it veers to the right. The museum is on the right just as Clerkenwell Close crosses Sans Walk.

THE CITY (Maps 6 & 8)

The City of London is 'the square mile' (about 2.6 sq km) on the north bank of the Thames where the Romans first built a walled community 2000 years ago. The boundaries of today's City haven't changed much, and you can always tell when you're within them because the Corporation of London's coat of arms appears on the street signs, and the small statue of a griffin emblazoned with the motto *Domine Dirige Nos* (God Direct Us) marks the City's borders. This is the business heart of London where you'll find not only the Bank of England, but also the headquarters of many British and overseas banks, insurance companies and other financial institutions. Only 5500 people actually live in the City but around 300,000 commute there to work every day.

St Paul's Cathedral and the Tower of London are both in the City. Here too you'll find the headquarters of many of London's livery companies and many of the churches

Greetings from a griffin as you enter the square mile.

JULIET COOMBE

THINGS TO SEE & DO

The City's Livery Companies

In the Middle Ages most craft-workers belonged to guilds that organised apprenticeships and were the prototypes of today's trade unions. The wealthier guilds built themselves magnificent halls, and their leaders wore suitably fine costumes, or liveries. These same leaders were eligible to stand for the series of offices that culminated in Lord Mayor of the City of London.

While the old craft guilds may be no more, more than one hundred livery companies live on, and their leading lights still stand for office at the Court of Common Council, which runs the Corporation – and thus the City – of London. Although most of the original halls were razed by the Great Fire or the Blitz, some have since been rebuilt and they're impressive, if largely inaccessible, places. One of the oldest and most interesting is the Merchant Taylors' Hall in Threadneedle St, which still retains its 15th-century kitchen. The wealthy Vintners' Company now occupies a new neoclassical building on the waterside beside Southwark Bridge.

If you'd like to visit one of the halls you'll have to inquire at the City of London Tourist Information Centre (Map 8; ☎ 7332 1456) in St Paul's Churchyard EC4, opposite St Paul's Cathedral (⊖ St Paul's), weeks ahead of your visit. They receive stocks of tickets for the Goldsmiths', Fishmongers', Ironmongers', Tallow Chandlers', Haberdashers' and Skinners' halls in February each year but they're snapped up pretty quickly. Otherwise, you can visit the Guildhall, where the liverymen meet to choose two sheriffs in June and again in September to elect the Lord Mayor.

built by Sir Christopher Wren after the Great Fire of 1666. There's been a feverish construction boom in the City over the past few years with dozens of blocks and towers either being planned or under way.

A quiet weekend stroll when the banks and offices are closed offers a unique chance to appreciate the architectural richness of its many famous buildings and the atmospheric little alleyways that now separate futuristic office towers. Bear in mind, though, that some of the sights close on Saturday and Sunday, as do the shops in Leadenhall Market.

Barbican

Tucked into a corner of the City of London where there was once a watchtower (or 'barbican'), the Barbican (Map 8; ☎ 7638 4141), Silk St EC2 (⊖ Barbican or Moorgate), is a vast urban development built on a large bomb site from WWII.

The original ambitious plan was to create a terribly smart, modern complex for offices, housing and the arts. Perhaps inevitably, the result was a forbidding series of wind tunnels with a dearth of shops, plenty of expensive high-rise apartments and an enormous cultural centre lost in the middle. Here you'll find the London home of the Royal Shakespeare Company (RSC), the London Symphony Orchestra and the London Classical Orchestra. There are also two cinemas, smaller theatrical auditoriums, the Museum of London and the wonderful **Barbican Art Gallery** (☎ 7588 9023) on Level 3, with among the best photographic exhibits in London (open Monday and Thursday to Saturday from 10 am to 6.45 pm, on Tuesday to 5.45 pm, on Wednesday to 7.45 pm and on Sunday from noon to 6.45 pm). But be warned – even Londoners get here early to make sure of finding their way to the right spot at the right time.

For details of the theatres, cinemas and concert halls, see the Entertainment chapter. For details of the highly regarded Searcy's brasserie, see the City section in the Places to Eat chapter. You can also check out the Barbican's Web site at www.barbican.org.uk.

Museum of London Despite it's unprepossessing setting amid the concrete walkways of the Barbican (look for gate 7), the

Museum of London (Map 8; ☎ 7600 3699, 7600 0807 for a recording), London Wall EC2 (⊖ Barbican), is one of the city's finest museums, showing how the city has evolved from the Ice Age to the Internet. It is also the world's largest urban-history museum, with more than one million objects on display and in its archives. The museum's Web site is at www.museumoflondon.org.uk.

The museum is divided into sections: the Department of Early London History (from the prehistoric period to 1700), including the Archaeological Archive, housing material from archaeological excavations in London; and the Department of Later London History, with material relating to London from 1700 to the present day.

The sections on Roman Britain and Roman Londinium make use of the nearby ruins of a Roman fort discovered during road construction and examine such finds as the spectacular 4th-century lead coffin and stone sarcophagus containing the remains of a well-to-do young Roman woman that were discovered at a development site at Spitalfields in early 1999. Otherwise, the displays work steadily through the centuries, using audiovisual materials to show such events as the Great Fire of London.

There are items such as one of the two shirts Charles I wore on the morning of his execution in 1649 'lest my shivering be taken as a sign of fear', but the focus is on ordinary people as much as on the buildings and streets; Dickens' London – a city of mass prostitution and sweatshop labour – makes for particularly poignant stories. The London Now gallery brings the story up to date.

The Museum of London also has ace special exhibitions; recent ones have covered such diverse topics as Bethlehem Royal Hospital, shoes in London from the 1st to the 20th centuries, long-forgotten favourite toys and Cromwell. Part of the museum's collection dealing with London's port and the Thames will be transferred to a new museum in the Docklands when it opens in 2001.

The museum is open Monday to Saturday from 10 am to 5.50 pm and on Sunday from noon. Admission costs £5/3/12 for adults/seniors & students/families; it's free for under-16s and for everyone after 4.30 pm. Tickets are valid for a year. The pleasant Museum Café opposite the entrance serves light meals from 10 am (11 am on Sunday) to 5 pm. The fine shop has a wide selection of fictional and factual accounts of London.

Smithfield Market

Smithfield, West Smithfield EC1 (Map 6; ⊖ Farringdon), is central London's last surviving produce market. For details see the special section 'The Markets of London' after the Shopping chapter.

St Bartholomew-the-Great

One of London's oldest churches, adjoining one of London's oldest hospitals, St Bartholomew-the-Great (Map 6; ☎ 7606 5171), West Smithfield EC1 (⊖ Barbican), is a stone's throw from the Barbican and worth more than a fleeting visit. The authentic Norman arches and details lend this holy space

JULIET COOMBE

St Bartholomew – inspiration behind a number of City churches and London's oldest hospital.

an ancient calm; approaching from nearby Smithfield Market through the restored 13th-century archway is like walking back in time.

The church is open Monday to Friday from 8.30 am to 5 pm, on Saturday from 10.30 am to 1.30 pm and on Sunday from 8 am to 8 pm.

Central Criminal Court (Old Bailey)

All Britain's major gangsters and serial killers eventually find themselves at the Central Criminal Court, better known as the Old Bailey (Map 6) after the street on which it stands. Look up at the great copper dome and you'll see the figure of justice holding a sword and scales in her hands; oddly she is *not* blindfolded, which has sparked many a sarcastic comment from those being brought in here.

The old Newgate Prison, site of innumerable hangings, once stood here. Like most London prisons it was burned down during the Gordon Riots of 1780, only to rise again from the ashes to incarcerate yet more prisoners until 1902.

The court's public gallery (☎ 7248 3277) on Newgate St is open weekdays from 10.30 am to 1 pm and 2 to 4 pm.

St Paul's Cathedral

St Paul's Cathedral (Map 8; ☎ 7236 4128; ✆ St Paul's) was built, amid much controversy, by Sir Christopher Wren between 1675 and 1710. It stands on the site of four previous cathedrals, the first of which dated from 604.

St Paul's was one of the 50 commissions that Wren was given after the Great Fire of London. Plans for alterations had already been made, but the fire presented him with the opportunity to build from scratch. Several plans were spurned before the authorities accepted the current design.

The dome still dominates the City and the only church dome that exceeds it in size is that of St Peter's in Rome. Pictures of the cathedral miraculously surviving the devastation of WWII bombing can be seen in a glass case in the south choir aisle; fortunately, the dome survived virtually unharmed, although other parts of the cathedral were not entirely unscathed. The windows were blown out (hence the large quantity of clear glass) and various other parts were also damaged.

A **statue of Queen Anne** stands in front of the west door, which is the main entrance. But before you enter, take a moment to walk around to the north of the cathedral (that's to the left as you face the large stairway). A long overdue **monument to the people of London** – not all those warmongers, sabre-rattlers and heroes at rest in the crypt – has been unveiled in the small garden just outside the north transept in St Paul's Churchyard. Simple, elegant, it honours the 32,000 civilians killed (and another 50,000 seriously injured) in the defence of the city and the cathedral during WWII. It is largely due to them that you can still stand and admire the gem that is St Paul's now. Enjoy, but never forget these brave souls. As the inscription says: 'Remember before God, the people of London 1939-1945'.

From the main entrance, proceed up the north aisle, past the **Chapel of St Dunstan**, dedicated to the 10th-century archbishop of Canterbury, and the grandiose **Duke of Wellington Memorial** (1875), until you reach the central pavement area under the dome. It is decorated in a compass design and bears Wren's epitaph in Latin: *Lector, si monumentum requiris, circumspice* (Reader, if you seek his monument, look around you). Some 30m above the paved area is the first of three domes – actually a dome, inside a cone, inside a dome – supported by eight massive columns. The walkway around its base is called the **Whispering Gallery**, because if you talk close to the wall it carries your words around to the opposite side 32m away.

In the north transept chapel is Holman Hunt's celebrated painting *The Light of the World*, which depicts Christ knocking at an overgrown door that, symbolically, can only be opened from the inside. Beyond are the **quire** (or chancel), whose ceilings and arches dazzle with green, blue, red and gold

RICHARD I'ANSON

The only way is down: a view from the top of St Paul's Cathedral.

mosaics, and the high altar. The ornately carved **choir stalls** by Grinling Gibbons are worth a look as are the **ornamental wrought-iron gates** separating the aisles from the altar by Jean Tijou (both men also worked on Hampton Court Palace). Walk around the altar, with its massive gilded oak canopy, to the **American Chapel**, a memorial to the 28,000 Americans based in Britain who lost their lives during WWII.

As you walk round the southern side of the ambulatory look for the **memorial to John Donne** (1573-1631), once dean of St Paul's, standing upright in his shroud in a niche. For whomever the bell tolled, it most decidedly tolled for him. Almost opposite is a glass case with photographs of **St Paul's during WWII**.

On the eastern side of the south transept, close to a memorial to the painter JMW Turner, a staircase leads down to the Crypt,

RICHARD I'ANSON

Looking up at the Golden Gallery: it's a long way up but the views are truly breathtaking.

Treasury and OBE Chapel, where services (weddings, funerals etc) reserved for members of the Order of the British Empire are held. The **Crypt** has memorials to up to 300 military demigods, including Wellington, Kitchener and Nelson, who is below the dome in a black sarcophagus (originally made for Cardinal Wolsey); on the surrounding walls are plaques in memory of those from the Commonwealth who died in various wars and conflicts in the 20th century: from Gallipoli (1915) through the world wars and Korea to the Falklands (1982) and Kuwait (1991). There are also effigies rescued from the previous cathedral that look rather the worse for wear; a few were saved from the Great Fire but most were damaged by Cromwell's men. A niche exhibits Wren's controversial plans and his 'great' model.

The most poignant memorial of all is to Sir Christopher himself. It is south of the **OBE Chapel** and is just a simple slab with his name, the year of his death (1723) and his age ('XCI'). An amusing memorial is that to the sculptor George Frampton (1860-1933), who did the statue of Peter Pan in Hyde Park. It shows a very young child with Peter perched on his outstretched hand. The ashes of the architect Edwin Lutyens (1869-1944) rest in a nearby niche. The **Treasury** displays some of the cathedral's plate, along with some spectacular needlework including Beryl Dean's Jubilee cope (bishop's cloak) of 1977 showing spires of 73 London churches and its matching mitre. There is also a café and a shop in the crypt open Monday to Saturday from 9 am to 5 pm (on Sunday from 10.30 am).

Back upstairs in the nave, the Whispering Gallery as well as the **Stone Gallery** and the **Golden Gallery** can be reached by a staircase on the western side of the south transept. All in all there are 259 steps to the first gallery, another 116 to the Stone Gallery and 155 more steps to the top gallery; that's a total of 530 steps to climb up and down. But even if you can't make it right up to the Golden Gallery, it's worth struggling as far as the Stone Gallery for one of the best views of London.

ST PAUL'S CATHEDRAL

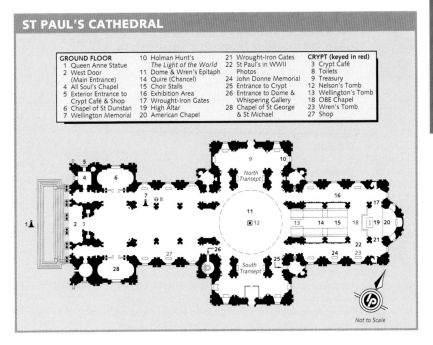

GROUND FLOOR	10 Holman Hunt's	21 Wrought-Iron Gates	CRYPT (keyed in red)
1 Queen Anne Statue	*The Light of the World*	22 St Paul's in WWII	3 Crypt Café
2 West Door	11 Dome & Wren's Epitaph	Photos	8 Toilets
(Main Entrance)	14 Quire (Chancel)	24 John Donne Memorial	9 Treasury
4 All Soul's Chapel	15 Choir Stalls	25 Entrance to Crypt	12 Nelson's Tomb
5 Exterior Entrance to	16 Exhibition Area	26 Entrance to Dome &	13 Wellington's Tomb
Crypt Café & Shop	17 Wrought-Iron Gates	Whispering Gallery	18 OBE Chapel
6 Chapel of St Dunstan	19 High Altar	28 Chapel of St George	23 Wren's Tomb
7 Wellington Memorial	20 American Chapel	& St Michael	27 Shop

Not to Scale

The cathedral is open Monday to Saturday from 8.30 am to 4 pm. Admission costs £3.50/3/1.50 for adults/seniors & students/ children or £6.50/5.50/4 if you wish to visit the dome galleries as well (family £9/ 16.50). Audioguide tours lasting 45 minutes are available for £3/2.50 for adults/ concessions (family £7), and guided 90-minute tours (£2.50/2) leave the tour desk at 11 and 11.30 am, and 1.30 and 2 pm. There are organ concerts at St Paul's most Sundays at 5 pm. Evensong takes place most weekdays at 5 pm and on Sunday at 3.15 pm.

For further information on the cathedral visit its Web site at www.stpauls.london .anglican.org.

Fleet St

Ever since Wynkyn de Worde moved Caxton's printing press from Westminster to a shop beside St Bride's Church in 1500,

Fleet St (Map 6; ⊖ Blackfriars) has been ink-splattered. In this century it earned the nickname of 'London's Street of Shame', where printing presses stoked by gossip and lies churned out their scurrilous product: the UK's tabloid newspapers. But then the mid-1980s brought Rupert Murdoch, new technology and the Docklands redevelopment. Now that the action has moved east only ghosts linger on, such as El Vino's, the journos' No 1 watering hole, and the glamorous former Daily Telegraph building (1928), now occupied by assorted banks.

Like Whitehall in Westminster, Fleet St and its surroundings are so full of so many interesting sights that the best way to take it all in is to follow the Fleet St & the Strand walking tour in this section. Those interested in only the most important sights – St Bride's church, Dr Johnson's House and Prince Henry's Room – should read on.

WALKING TOUR

FLEET ST & THE STRAND

This walk takes you along Fleet St to the Strand, the thoroughfares that have linked London's two opposing worlds for centuries: the City of London and Westminster.

Begin the tour at Ludgate Circus (⊖ Blackfriars) and walk west along Fleet St. Almost immediately on the left is a gateway leading to **St Bride's Church (1)**, designed by Sir Christopher Wren. On the northern side of Fleet St at No 135 is the **former Daily Telegraph building (2)** (1928), designed by Elcock and Sutcliffe in 1928 and variously described as 'jazz modern' and 'neo-Greek'. It now houses bank offices.

Farther along on the same side you'll see a narrow alleyway called Wine Office Court (where the excise office stood until 1665), which leads to a famous London pub, **Ye Olde Cheshire Cheese (3)** (see The City in the Places to Eat chapter and Pubs & Bars in the Entertainment chapter). Several Georgian buildings line the alleyway.

Walk back to Fleet St and continue west along the same side. At No 154 you pass **Bouverie House (4)**, once home to the *Sun* newspaper. Turn right at narrow Johnson's Court, which leads to Gough Square and **Dr Johnson's House (5)**. The wooden chair on which he used to sit while drinking at **Ye Olde Cock Tavern (6)** is preserved on the 1st floor landing. The tavern, the oldest on Fleet St, is a short distance to the west on the other side of the street at No 22 and was a favourite of the poet TS Eliot. The colourful cockerel on its pub sign is said to have been designed by Grinling Gibbons, whose work adorns many London churches, including St Paul's Cathedral. Pepys, Dr Johnson, Goldsmith and Dickens all drank here – when they weren't knocking them back at Ye Olde Cheshire Cheese.

Across from Ye Olde Cock stands the octagonal **St Dunstan-in-the-West (7)**, which was built by John Shaw in 1832 and boasts a spectacular lantern tower. On the façade look out for Elizabeth I, the only such outdoor statue of the Virgin Queen, which stood on Ludgate until it was demolished in 1760. You can't miss the Gog and Magog on the clock outside (see the boxed text under Guildhall later in this chapter); they swing round and club the bells beside them on the hour.

Farther west at No 17 is the entrance to **Prince Henry's Room (8)** and just beyond that an archway leading to **Temple Church (9)** in the Inner Temple, one of the Inns of Court.

In the centre of Fleet St a statue of a griffin bestriding an elaborately carved plinth marks the site of the original **Temple Bar (10)**, where the City of Westminster becomes the City of London. The plinth is decorated with statues of Queen Victoria and her husband, Prince Albert, together with symbols of Art and Science, and War and Peace.

The **Wig & Pen Club (11)** at Nos 229 to 230 on the Strand dates from 1625 and is the only Strand building to have survived the Great Fire of 1666; it's now a restaurant. Have a look at the symbolic wigs and pens in the external plasterwork.

As you proceed west look up to appreciate the fine architecture. A

distance: about 2.5km

start: Ludgate Circus
⊖ Blackfriars

finish: Lancaster Place
⊖ Covent Garden

few doors west of the Wig & Pen the Law Courts branch of **Lloyd's Bank (12)** has carved fish twined around its circular windows and elaborate tiles adorning the recess now housing its cash machines. Just beyond on the same side at No 216 is **Twinings (13)**, a teashop opened by Thomas Twining in 1706 and believed to be the oldest company in London still trading on the same site and owned by the same family. The colourful sign above the door incorporates two Chinese and a lion (the original shop was called the Golden Lyon). On the northern side of the Strand is the extraordinary neogothic confection of the **Royal Courts of Justice (14)**.

The church in the centre of the road is **St Clement Danes (15)**. The original church was designed by Sir Christopher Wren in 1682, with the steeple added to the tower by James Gibbs in 1719; only the walls and steeple survived the bombings of 1941. In 1958 the church was rebuilt for the Royal Air Force; 800-plus slate badges of different squadrons and units of the RAF are set into the nave pavement. At 9 am, noon, and 3 and 6 pm the church bells chime out the old nursery rhyme 'Oranges and Lemons' (see the boxed text 'A Church for All Chimes' under Bank later in this chapter).

Continue west along the Strand with **Australia House (16)**, designed by Marshall Mackenzie between 1912 and 1918, and **Bush House (17)**, built in 1920, on your right. Part of the latter houses the offices of the BBC World Service. The pile that is **India House (18)** dates from 1930.

In the centre of the road is **St Mary-le-Strand (19)**, designed by James Gibbs between 1715 and 1724.

The elegant building to the south is **Somerset House (20)**, designed by Sir William Chambers in 1774 and finally completed in 1835. It now houses assorted government offices as well as the **Courtauld Gallery (21)** and the new **Gilbert Collection (22)**.

All manner of city types – from judges to journalists – hang out at Ye Olde Cock Tavern.

ED HILLYER

RICHARD I'ANSON

Looking down Fleet St towards the Strand and the Royal Courts of Justice.

St Bride's, Fleet St St Bride's (Map 6; ☎ 7353 1301), Fleet St EC4, is a small, perfect church and the eighth on this site. The present structure was designed by Sir Christopher Wren in 1671 and was his tallest (and most expensive) church after St Paul's. The add-on spire (1703) is said to have inspired the design of the tiered wedding cake. The church was hit by bombs in 1940, and the interior layout is wood-panelled, modern and not particularly attractive.

St Bride's is still referred to as 'the journalists' church' or 'the printers' cathedral' and a chapel in the north aisle honours journalists who have died or been injured in the course of their work. Be sure to descend to the crypt, which contains a small museum of the printing trade amid the foundations of previous churches and Roman remains found during postwar renovations, including traces of a Roman house and the skeleton of a woman. On display, too, is the party dress of Susannah Pritchard, wife of William Rich (1755-1811), the pastry cook credited with modelling his wedding cakes on the steeple.

The church is open Monday to Friday from 8 am to 4.45 pm, on Saturday from 9 am to 4.45 pm, and on Sunday from 9.30 am to 12.30 pm and 5.30 to 7.30 pm.

Dr Johnson's House Dr Johnson's House (Map 6; ☎ 7353 3745), 17 Gough Square EC4, is the well preserved Georgian town house where Johnson lived from 1748 to 1759. Johnson was a lexicographer who, along with six full-time assistants working in the attic upstairs, compiled the first English dictionary.

Johnson is also famous for his witty, scathing aphorisms, all written down by his amanuensis and fellow Scot, James Boswell. (A modern office building nearby – Boswell House – carries on the latter's memory.) It was Johnson who claimed: 'When a man is tired of London he is tired of life; for there is in London all that life can afford'.

The house is full of pictures of friends and intimates of Johnson, including his black manservant Francis Barber to whom he was very generous in his will, a copy of which is also on display. A video provides background information on Johnson and Boswell, and the 18th-century antiburglar devices fitted to the front door are interesting. Out in the little square fronting the house is a modern statue of Johnson's cat, Hodge, haughtily eyeing oysters.

Dr Johnson's House is open Monday to Saturday from 11 am to 5.30 pm, May to September (to 5 pm the rest of the year). Admission costs £3/2/1 for adults/seniors & students/children aged over 10.

Prince Henry's Room Prince Henry's Room (Map 6; ☎ 7294 1158), 17 Fleet St EC4, which is just before the archway leading to Temple Church, dates from the 16th century but was extensively remodelled as a tavern with an overhanging half-timbered façade in 1611. Since the overhanging rooms were known as the Prince's Arms, the feathers of the prince of Wales appear in the external woodwork. The 1st floor room, with items related to the life and writings of Samuel Pepys, boasts the best Jacobean plaster ceiling surviving in London, some original oak panelling and stained glass.

Prince Henry's Room (free) is open Monday to Saturday from 11 am to 2 pm.

Temple Church

Temple Church (Map 6; ☎ 7353 1736), Inner Temple, King's Bench Walk EC4 (⊖ Temple or, on Sunday, Blackfriars), is just off Fleet St under the archway beyond Prince Henry's Room at No 17. Duck under it and you'll find yourself in the Inner Temple, one of the Inns of Court. Temple Church was originally planned and built by the secretive Knights Templar between 1161 and 1185. They modelled it on the Church of the Holy Sepulchre in Jerusalem, using Purbeck marble for the pillars, and the core of the building is the only round church left in London. In 1240 a more conventional, if elongated, Early English chancel was added on.

Although the Knights Templar were eventually suppressed for being too powerful and their lands leased to the lawyers who set up the Inns of Court, stone effigies of 13th-century knights still adorn the floors of the circular nave; some of them are cross-legged but contrary to popular belief this doesn't necessarily mean they were crusaders. Look out, too, for the grotesque faces peeping down from the circular wall just above eye level. In a couple of instances ears are being nibbled by monsters.

Externally the most interesting feature is the Norman west door with its elaborately moulded porch. It's set into a dip that shows how far the ground level has risen over the centuries. The church was badly damaged during WWII but has since been sensitively restored to serve as the private chapel of Middle and Inner temples.

Temple Church is open Wednesday to Saturday from 10 am to 4 pm. Westminster Abbey and St Paul's Cathedral aside, this is possibly London's most interesting and architecturally important church. Don't miss it.

Guildhall

The Guildhall (Map 8; ☎ 7606 3030), off Gresham St EC2 (⊖ Bank), which sits exactly in the centre of the square mile, has been the City's seat of government for nearly 800 years. The present building dates from the early 15th century and the walls have survived both the Great Fire of 1666 and the Blitz of 1940, although the surrounding development makes it hard to appreciate them from the outside.

Visitors can see the **Great Hall** where the mayor and sheriffs are still elected, a vast empty space with church-style monuments and the shields and banners of the 12 principal livery companies of London (see the boxed text earlier in this section) lining the walls. The impressive wooden roof is a postwar reconstruction by Giles Gilbert Scott. The minstrels' gallery at the western end carries statues of Gog and Magog (see the boxed text), modern replacements of the 18th-century figures destroyed in the Blitz. Among the monuments to look for are those to Winston Churchill, Admiral Nelson, the Duke of Wellington and the two prime ministers Pitt the Elder and Younger.

Gog & Magog

According to the 12th-century *Historia Regum Britanniae* (History of the Kings of Britain) by Geoffrey of Monmouth, Britain was once inhabited by giants who were conquered by Brutus the Trojan and his compatriot, Corineus. Brutus founded Troia Nova (New Troy), or London, while Corineus established Cornwall after hurling the last of the great giants, the 3.5m-tall chieftain, Gogmagog, into the sea.

By the 18th century Gog and Magog were thought to have been the last two surviving giants, forced to work for Brutus in his palace on the site of today's Guildhall. The effigies of the giants there are the third since the reign of Henry V.

The Guildhall's stained glass was blown out during the Blitz, but a modern window in the south-western corner depicts the City's history; look out for Dick Whittington and his cat, old and new St Paul's, and modern landmarks such as the Lloyd's of London building. Set into two nearby windowsills you can also see standard measures for feet, yards and metres.

Meetings are still held in the hall every third Thursday of each month (except August) at 1 pm, and the Guildhall hosts an annual flower show and various ceremonial banquets, including the one for the Booker Prize, the leading British literary prize.

Beneath the Great Hall is London's largest surviving medieval crypt with 19 stained-glass windows showing the coats of arms of the livery companies.

The new **Guildhall Art Gallery** to the south-east in Guildhall Yard brings together the Corporation's art collection for the first time since WWII. The **Guildhall Clock Museum** (☎ 7332 1868), around the corner on Aldermanbury in a room next to the Guildhall Library, has more than 700 clocks and watches dating back some 500 years.

The Guildhall (including its art gallery; £2.50/1) is open daily from 10 am to 5 pm (on Sunday to 4 pm) and is closed on Sunday from October to April. The clock museum (free) is open weekdays from 9.30 am to 4.45 pm but sometimes closes for an hour or two on Monday to wind the clocks.

Church of St Lawrence Jewry Along the south-western side of Guildhall Yard stands St Lawrence Jewry (Map 8; ☎ 7600 9478), Gresham St EC2 (⊖ Bank), the church of the Corporation of London, which explains its excellent condition. It was originally built by Sir Christopher Wren in 1677 but almost completely rebuilt after WWII. The arms of the City of London adorn the organ case at the western end. In the northern **Commonwealth Chapel**, bedecked with the flags of member-nations, a modern (and bad) painting of the Madonna and Child incorporates images of the sins of the modern world: financial greed, use of drugs and

pornography, and a preoccupation with living standards. The church is open weekdays from 7.30 am to 2 pm.

As the name of the church suggests, this was once part of the Jewish quarter, the centre being Old Jewry to the south-east. The district was ransacked and some 500 Jews were killed in 1262 when a Christian claimed he had been charged too much interest by a Jewish moneylender. Edward I expelled the entire community from London to Flanders in 1290. They did not return until the late 17th century.

Bank

One of the best tube stations for exploring the heart of the City is Bank (Map 8), which brings you out at the point where seven bank-filled streets converge. Take Prince's St north-west to get to the Guildhall or head north-east along Threadneedle St for the Bank of England Museum.

Squeezed in between Threadneedle St and Cornhill to the east is the **Royal Exchange**, the third building on a site originally chosen in 1564 by Thomas Gresham, whose grasshopper emblem appears on the weather vane. Until 1992 you could go inside to watch the London International Financial Futures Exchange in hectic action. Now, however, it has moved to newer concrete-and-glass premises at the **Stock Exchange** farther along Threadneedle St and this is closed to the public. The steps of the Royal Exchange provide a great vantage point for observing the citadel that is the Bank of England to the north.

Lombard St, named after the Italian bankers who ran London's money markets between the 13th and 16th centuries after the Jews had been expelled, heads off to the south-east. Notice the large banking signs, some with the year of the bank's founding: a grasshopper (1563), a running mare (1677), a cat and a fiddle. Such signs were commonplace everywhere in London until they started falling in high winds and killing people. They were banned here until 1901 when they were first hung out again to mark Edward VII's coronation.

In the angle between Lombard St and King William St to the south you'll see the twin towers of Hawksmoor's **St Mary Woolnoth** (1717), the huge Corinthian columns of its interior a foretaste of his even more splendid Christ Church in Spitalfields.

Between King William St and Walbrook stands the grand, porticoed **Mansion House**, the mid-18th-century work of George Dance the Elder built as the official residence of the Lord Mayor of London. It's not open to the public though group tours are sometimes available. Ring ☎ 7626 2500 for information.

Walbrook, which heads off to the south, is named after one of London's lost rivers (see the boxed text 'London's Rivers Styx'

in the Facts about London chapter). Here you'll find **St Stephen Walbrook** (1679), which many would regard as the finest of Wren's City churches; it's certainly the one where he experimented with a dome before embarking on St Paul's Cathedral. Some 16 pillars with Corinthian capitals rise up to support the dome and ceiling, parting in the middle to provide a central open space now filled with a large creamy-grey boulder, actually an altar by Henry Moore and referred to as 'the Camembert' by early critics who were less than impressed.

Queen Victoria St cuts south-west from Bank. A short way along it on the left and in front of the Temple Court building at No 11 you'll find all that remains of the Roman

A Church for All Chimes

St Anne, Soho.

Oranges & lemons, say the bells of St Clements
Bulls eyes & targets, say the bells of St Margarets
Pokers & tongs, say the bells of St Johns
Pancakes & fritters, say the bells of St Peters
Two sticks & an apple, say the bells at Whitechapel
Old Father Baldpate, say the bells at Aldgate
Maids in white aprons, say the bells of St Catherines
Brickbats & tiles, say the bells of St Giles
Kettles & pans, say the bells at St Annes
You owe me five farthings, say the bells of St Martins
When will you pay me, say the bells of Old Bailey
When I grow rich, say the bells of Shoreditch
Pray, when will that be, say the bells of Stepney
I'm sure I don't know, says the great bell at Bow
Here comes a candle to light you to bed
Here comes a chopper to chop off your head.

CHARLOTTE HINDLE

'Oranges & Lemons', the nursery rhyme that incorporates the names of many churches and landmarks in the City and east London, first surfaced in 1744. It's generally agreed that St Clements was St Clement Danes and St Martins was St Martin-in-the-Fields, while the bells of Old Bailey belonged to St Sepulchre, Holborn, the bells of Shoreditch to St Leonards, and the bells of Stepney to St Dunstan, Stepney. The great bell at Bow belonged to St Mary-le-Bow and was the one whose range decided who was and wasn't technically a Cockney. The rest is just guesswork and it has been suggested that the writer just plucked out of the air the names of saints that happened to rhyme (sort of) with the chosen phrase. That theory is given more credence by the fact that the names of the churches are not always the same. In some surviving versions of the rhyme, for example, Shoreditch is Fleet Ditch and Bow has become Paul.

JULIET COOMBE

Time for some wheeling and dealing: the Royal Exchange's elegant clock.

Temple of Mithras, excavated from 5.5m below ground in 1954 and moved here from a short distance away. Mithras was a Persian god of justice and social contract whose cult travelled round the Roman Empire with its legionaries (see the boxed text 'Mithras & the Great Sacrifice' under History in the Facts about London chapter). The finds from the temple – such as sculptures and silver incense-boxes – can be seen in the Museum of London.

Due west of Bank is Poultry, which runs into Cheapside, site of a great medieval market (see the boxed text 'What's in a Name?' under Orientation in the Facts for the Visitor chapter). On the left you'll see another of Wren's great churches, **St Mary-le-Bow** (☎ 7248 5139), built in 1673 and famous as the church whose bells dictate who is – and is not – a Cockney (see the boxed text 'A Church for All Chimes'). Its delicate steeple is one of Wren's finest works and the

modern stained glass is striking. There's a good basement café called The Place Below (see The City in the Places to Eat chapter).

Bank of England Museum The Bank of England (Map 8; ☎ 7601 5545), Bartholomew Lane EC2 (⊖ Bank), is in charge of maintaining the integrity and value of sterling and of the British financial system. It was originally set up in 1694 when the government needed to raise money to finance a war with France. At first it was housed in the Mercers' and Grocers' halls, but in 1734 it moved to a new home on the present site. From 1788 to 1833 John Soane, whose statue graces the Lothbury side of 'the old lady of Threadneedle St', was architect to the Bank of England, and although much of his work was destroyed during the rebuilding after WWI, some of it was recently reconstructed.

The first room of the museum you come to is a reconstruction of Soane's 18th-century banking hall, the Bank Stock Office, complete with mannequin clerks and customers. A statue of William III, who was king when the Bank was founded, stands to one side. You can also inspect the caryatids that supported Soane's original rotunda in Herbert Baker's later replacement.

The museum's various rooms trace the history of the bank and of bank notes. Highlights include a pair of Roman gold ingots in the rotunda and a diorama showing an attack on the bank during the Gordon Riots of 1780. Finally, if you ever fancied a career as a foreign-exchange dealer, an interactive video lets you try your hand.

The museum (free) is open Monday to Friday from 10 am to 5 pm.

The Monument

At the south-eastern end of King William St, near London Bridge, stands the Monument (Map 8; ☎ 7626 2717; ⊖ Monument), designed by Sir Christopher Wren to commemorate the Great Fire of 1666, which started in a bakery on Pudding Lane east of the Monument. The height of the monument, which was completed in 1677, is

60.6m (202 feet), the exact distance to the bakery. It is topped off with a gilded bronze urn of flames that looks, to some, like a big gold pincushion. If you're up to it, 311 tight steps lead to a balcony beneath the urn offering panoramic views over the City.

It's open daily from 10 am to 6 pm. Admission costs £1.50/50p.

Leadenhall Market

There's been a market on this site in Whittington Ave off Gracechurch St (Map 8; ✆ Bank) since Roman times when it served as a forum. In the late 14th century, out-of-towners were allowed to sell their goods here and in 1445 the City Corporation made it an official food-market. For details of the market in more recent times, see the special section 'The Markets of London' after the Shopping chapter.

Lloyd's of London

Although it is the most famous house of insurance brokers in the world, where everything from ships, ships' cargoes and planes to film stars' faces and dancers' legs are insured by underwriters known as 'Names', Lloyd's of London, 1 Lime St EC3 (Map 8; ✆ Aldgate or Bank), wouldn't be much of a tourist destination were it not for the building that houses it.

In 1986, Richard Rogers, one of the architects of the Pompidou Centre in Paris, created a stunning new building in a part of London not then known for avant-garde architecture. Lloyd's, with its external pipes and ducts of stainless steel, was a triumphant exception, especially at night with its spectacular illuminated framework of yellow and electric blue. Part of the façade of the old Lloyd's building dating from 1925 was retained; you can see it on Leadenhall St.

Access to the equally excellent interior is restricted to professional groups, who must book in advance. Ring ✆ 7623 7100 for information.

Tower of London

One of London's three World Heritage Sites (the others are Westminster Abbey and its surrounding buildings and Maritime Greenwich), the Tower of London (Map 8; ✆ 7709 0765), Tower Hill EC3 (✆ Tower Hill), has dominated the south-eastern corner of the City of London since 1078 when William the Conqueror laid the first stone of

The Tower of London, the finest medieval fortress in Britain.

RICHARD I'ANSON

Bye-bye Blackbird

Make my bed and light the light, I'll be home late tonight
Blackbird, bye-bye

Ray Henderson & Mort Dixon, 1926

The problem is, should blackbird say bye-bye and fly the coop forever, we – that's both a royal and a plebeian 'we' – will all be in deepest do-do. Ravens, scavengers on the lookout for scraps chucked from the Tower's windows (and feasting on the corpses of beheaded traitors that were displayed as a deterrent), have been here for centuries; the first reported sighting was made by no less than Thomas à Becket in the early 13th century. By the 17th century, however, the numbers had become so great that it was proposed to kill them all, until someone remembered the old legend: should the ravens leave it, the White Tower would crumble and a great disaster would befall England. The newly restored Charles II was sufficiently superstitious to take note of this and a compromise was reached. Now there are never fewer than six ravens in residence, all with their wings clipped so that they can't fly away. One precocious bird named Thor has actually begun speaking recently, saying things like 'Come on then' and 'Where's mine?' It is hoped that he'll limit his vocabulary to such words lest he offend the royals' sensibilities should they drop by to check out the family jewels.

While at the Tower you're also bound to come across a more recently introduced species with far more colourful plumage: the Yeoman Warders, better known as the Beefeaters, who sport dark-blue (almost black) and red Tudor costumes for everyday wear, and more elaborate gold and red Victorian ones for ceremonial occasions that cost £12,000 a go.

The more than three dozen Beefeaters have all spent at least 22 years in the Army, Royal Marines or Royal Air Force and reached the rank of sergeant major. They can stay in the job until they're 60 and live within the Tower precincts. The Beefeaters conduct engaging tours of the Tower and also enact the age-old Ceremony of the Keys each evening, in which the Tower gates are locked and the keys ceremoniously locked away in the Queen's House.

The Beefeaters received a daily ration of beef and beer and since beef was a luxury beyond the reach of the poor, this generated much jealousy and the envious nickname back in the 17th century.

the White Tower to replace the earth and timber castle he'd already built on the site.

William II completed his father's work on the White Tower and between 1190 and 1285 two walls with towers and a moat were built around it. A riverside wharf was later added and since then the medieval defences have barely been altered.

Until the reign of Henry III (1216-72), the kings had been content to live within the White Tower itself, but, as well as strengthening the Tower's defences, Henry had a palace constructed between the White Tower and the river. He also started the Royal Menagerie, London's first zoo, after Louis IX of France presented him with an elephant in 1255. The menagerie was moved to Regent's Park in the 19th century and became London Zoo.

In the early Middle Ages, the Tower of London acted not just as a royal residence but also as a treasury, a mint, an arsenal and a prison. After Henry VIII moved to Whitehall Palace in 1529, the Tower's role as a prison became increasingly important, with Thomas More, queens Anne Boleyn and Catherine Howard, Archbishop Cranmer, Lady Jane Grey, Princess (later Queen) Elizabeth and Robert Devereux, earl of Essex, just some of the most famous Tudor prisoners.

After the monarchy was restored in 1660, a large garrison was stationed in the Tower and the arsenal was expanded. For the first time the public was admitted to see the coronation regalia and the armoury.

When the Duke of Wellington became constable of the Tower in 1826 he was worried that revolution might spread across the Channel from France and so set about reinforcing its military strength. The Royal Menagerie was closed and the public records moved out. A new barracks quickly replaced the Grand Storehouse when it burned down in 1841.

Queen Victoria's husband, Prince Albert, saw things very differently and oversaw the demolition of some of the newer buildings and the repair or reconstruction of the medieval towers. From then on the Tower's gruesome and sometimes ferocious history became little more than a tourist attraction although prisoners were still occasionally housed here right up to WWII, most notably Rudolf Hess in 1941.

These days the Tower is visited by more than two million people a year, with impressive crowds even on cold winter afternoons. The queues move quickly and you won't wait longer than 20 minutes or so to see the Crown Jewels even in summer, but you can buy tickets in advance from any tube station.

Orientation You enter the tower via the West Gate and proceed across the walkway over the moat between the **Middle Tower** and **Byward Tower**.

Walking along Water Lane between the walls you come to **St Thomas's Tower** on the right. Built by Edward I between 1275 and 1279, it stands immediately above **Traitors' Gate**, the gateway through which prisoners being brought by river entered the Tower. Rooms inside the tower show what the king's hall might once have looked like and also how archaeologists peel back the layers of newer buildings to find out what were before.

Immediately opposite St Thomas's Tower is the **Wakefield Tower**, built by Henry III between 1220 and 1240. The ground floor was once a guardhouse and shows its original stonework. In sharp contrast the upper floor has been furnished with a replica throne and a huge candelabra to give an impression of how it might have looked in Edward I's day. It is believed that Henry VI was murdered in the tower's chapel in 1471.

Passing under Henry III's Watergate you come to the **Cradle Tower**, the **Well Tower** and the **Develin Tower** on the southern side. On the left is the **Lanthorn Tower**, a Victorian copy of the original, which burned down in 1774. Passing through to the inner ward and turning right you'll come to the **Salt Tower**, built around 1238 and perhaps used to store saltpetre for gunpowder. Some Beefeaters believe the Salt Tower to be haunted. On the 1st floor you can see graffiti carved into the wall by Tudor prisoners.

The Salt Tower gives access to the **Wall Walk** along 13th-century ramparts. Beside

GLENN BEANLAND

Another brick in the wall: imposing fortifications within the Tower of London.

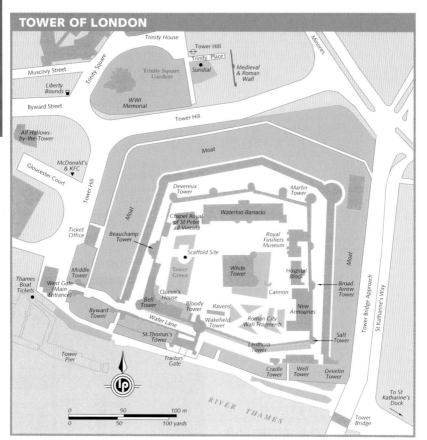

TOWER OF LONDON

the Salt Tower stands the massive **New Armouries** built in 1664. These display an assortment of exhibits, including old prints of the Tower, pictures of the Royal Menagerie, the elaborately carved pediment of the Grand Storehouse, which survived the 1841 fire, and a list of the Tower's most famous prisoners, from Ranulf Flambard, bishop of Durham, in 1100 to Josef Jakobs, a German spy who was executed by firing squad in 1941. On the lawn opposite are fragments of the **Roman city wall** and a bit farther

north a magnificent **Flemish cannon** built in 1607 and brought from Malta in 1800. It bears the arms of the Order of St John of Jerusalem and of Grand Master Alof de Wignacourt, together with a pewter plaque showing St Paul shipwrecked off Malta.

Passing the **Hospital Block** completed in 1700 as houses for officials of the Board of Ordnance, you'll see the **Royal Fusiliers Museum** for which a separate nominal charge is made. It covers the history of the Royal Fusiliers dating back to 1685, and has models of several battles. A 10-minute video gives details of the modern regiment.

The Wall Walk ends at the **Martin Tower**, which houses an exhibition about the original coronation regalia. Here you can see some of the older crowns designed so that the jewels in them could be removed. The oldest surviving crown is that of George I, which is topped with the ball and cross from James II's crown. The crown of George IV (1821) was originally set with some 12,314 cut diamonds. It was from the Martin Tower that Colonel Thomas Blood attempted to steal the Crown Jewels in 1671 while disguised as a clergyman. The **Broad Arrow Tower**, built in 1238, has been furnished as the bedchamber of Simon Burley, tutor to the young Richard II.

The most striking building in the Tower is undoubtedly the huge **White Tower**, in the centre of the courtyard, with its solid Romanesque architecture and four turrets. It was whitewashed during the reign of Henry III and thus got its name. After extensive renovations lasting eight years, it now houses a collection from the Royal Armouries in nine galleries, including a child's suit of armour designed for James I's young son Henry. Another exhibit deals with gruesome implements of torture and punishment, including the Block and Axe used to execute the 80-year-old Scottish Jacobite Simon Fraser, the 11th Lord Lovat, in 1747. You can also see the restored Line of Kings, a set of models of monarchs on horses, dating from 1660. On the 2nd floor is the **Chapel of St John the Evangelist**, which dates from 1080 and is therefore the oldest church in London.

Facing the White Tower to the north is the **Waterloo Barracks**, a neogothic structure built while the Duke of Wellington was constable of the Tower to house some 1000 soldiers. It now contains the Crown Jewels: orbs, sceptres and the centrepiece, the Imperial State Crown, set with diamonds (2868 of them to be exact), sapphires, emeralds, rubies and pearls. It's quite a bonnet – and insured for US$1 billion. Topping the Sceptre with the Cross is the First Star of Africa diamond weighing in at 530 carats. It's quite a walking stick.

Beside the Waterloo Barracks stands the **Chapel Royal of St Peter ad Vincula** (St Peter in Chains), which can only be visited on a group tour or after 4.30 pm; if you aren't already part of a group you can hang around until one shows up and then tag on, or attend a service. This is the third church on the site and a rare example of ecclesiastical Tudor architecture, but it's most interesting as the burial place of those beheaded on the scaffold outside or at nearby Tower Hill. Buried without much care at the time, these bodies were disinterred and reburied with proper memorials in Victorian times. Sunday services take place at 9.15 and 11 am.

What looks quite a peaceful, picturesque corner of the Tower is in fact one of its most tragic. On the small green in front of the church stood the **scaffold**, set up during Henry VIII's reign and where seven people were beheaded. On it were executed his two allegedly adulterous wives, Anne Boleyn and Catherine Howard, together with Jane Rochford, lady-in-waiting to Catherine Howard. Also executed here was Margaret Pole, countess of Salisbury. The fact that she was 70 and guilty of no particular offence except being descended from the House of York couldn't protect her from Henry's ire.

Lady Jane Grey, on the other hand, was only 16 when she was executed here during the reign of Henry's daughter, Mary I. Proclaimed queen on the death of Edward VI to ensure that a Catholic wouldn't recover the crown, Jane came to the Tower to await her coronation but lasted only nine days before Mary's supporters rose against her. From her room overlooking Tower Green, Jane watched her husband being taken away for execution on Tower Hill before she too was dragged to her fate.

These five women were executed within the Tower precincts largely to spare the monarch the embarrassment of their public execution. The two men executed here were William, Lord Hastings, in 1483, and Robert Devereux, the earl of Essex, once a favourite of Elizabeth I. Although he had betrayed her it was believed to be a mark of her continued affection that he was spared public execution. The authorities may also have feared a popular uprising in his support.

To the west of the scaffold site is the **Beauchamp Tower**, built in about 1281 and taking its name from Thomas Beauchamp, earl of Warwick, who was imprisoned here from 1397 to 1399. The walls, especially of the upper chamber, are densely carved with graffiti. A numbered list is available to help you pick out the most interesting scribbles.

Set around Tower Green are attractive half-timbered Tudor houses that are now home to Tower personnel. The **Queen's House**, where Anne Boleyn is believed to have been imprisoned and etched her signature into the wall of her cell, is now home to the Resident Governor; when Prince Charles or his son, Prince William, succeeds the Queen, its name will change to the King's House.

Beside the Wakefield Tower stands the **Bloody Tower**, probably the best-known part of the complex. On the 1st floor you can see the windlass that controlled the portcullis, the grating that could be dropped down to guard the gateway, with a 17th-century wooden screen separating it from a room furnished with artefacts dating from 1520 to 1620. It was here that Sir Walter Raleigh was imprisoned and where he wrote his *History of the World* (a copy is on display). The upstairs room is similarly equipped with 16th-century bedchamber furnishings, including a fine oak four-poster bed.

Once called the Garden Tower, the Bloody Tower acquired its unsavoury nickname from the story that the 'princes in the Tower', Edward V and his younger brother, were murdered here. The blame is usually laid at the door of their uncle Richard III, but there are those who prefer to finger Henry VII for the crime.

Don't leave the Tower without taking a look at the stretch of green between the Wakefield and White towers where the Great Hall once stood. Here you'll find the Tower's famous ravens (see the boxed text 'Bye-bye Blackbird').

Hours & Tickets The Tower is open Monday to Saturday from 9 am to 6 pm and on Sunday from 10 am, March to October; and Tuesday to Saturday from 9 am to 5 pm and on Sunday and Monday from 10 am, November to February. Last admission is an hour before. Entry costs £10.50/7.90/6.90 for adults/seniors/children aged five to 15 (family £31).

Further information on the Tower can be found on its Web site at www.hrp.org.uk.

Guided Tours Hugely entertaining, hourlong tours led by the Yeoman Warders (see the boxed text 'Bye-bye Blackbird') leave from the Middle Tower every 30 minutes daily from 9 am (on Sunday from 10 am) to 3.30 pm. The Warders also conduct about eight different short talks (35 minutes) and tours (45 minutes) on specific themes. The first is at 9.30 am Monday to Saturday (10.15 am on Sunday), the last at 5.15 pm. A self-paced audioguide is available in five languages for £1.50 from the information point on Water Lane.

Around the Tower

Despite the Tower's World Heritage Site status, the area immediately to the north is thoroughly disappointing. Just outside Tower Hill tube station, a giant bronze **sundial** depicts the history of London from 43 to 1982. It stands on a platform offering a view of the neighbouring **Trinity Square Gardens**, once the site of the Tower Hill scaffold and now home to Lutyens' **WWI memorial** to the marines and merchant sailors who lost their lives. A grassy area off the steps leading to a subway under the main road lets you inspect a stretch of the **medieval wall** built on Roman foundations, with a modern statue of Emperor Trajan (ruled 98 to 117 AD) standing in front of it. At the other end of the tunnel is a postern (or gate) dating from the 13th century.

All Hallows-by-the-Tower A church by this name (meaning 'all saints') has stood on this site since 675. Despite its proximity to the spot where the Great Fire of 1666 started (Samuel Pepys watched the blaze from the brick tower), All Hallows-by-the-Tower (Map 6; ☎ 7481 2928), Byward St EC3 (⊖ Tower Hill), survived virtually unscathed, only to be all but flattened by German bombs in 1940.

All that remains of the pre-fire building is the brick tower, the church's outer walls and an important Saxon archway. The copper spire was added in 1957 to make the church stand out more in an area devastated by bombs. Notice the pulpit taken from a Wren church on Cannon St destroyed in the war, the beautiful 17th-century font cover decorated with three cherubs and a dove by the master woodcarver Grinling Gibbons, and the memorial brasses dating from the 14th to 17th centuries. Several people executed at the Tower or on Tower Hill were buried here – at least for a while – including Thomas More and Archbishop William Laud. William Penn, founder of Pennsylvania, was baptised here in 1644, and John Quincy Adams, sixth president of the USA, was married here in 1797.

The church is open weekdays from 9 am to 6 pm, on Saturday from 10 am to 5 pm and on Sunday from 12.30 to 5 pm. A small museum in the crypt reveals a pavement of reused Roman tiles and walls of the 7th-century Saxon church. It's open from 10 am (on Sunday from 1 pm) to 4.30 pm. An audioguide tour of the church costs £2, of the church and crypt £2.50. The brass-rubbing centre is open from 11 am to 4 pm; rubbings cost from 75p to £5.45.

Tower Bridge

Tower Bridge (Map 8; ☎ 7378 1928; ⊖ Tower Hill) was built in 1894 when London was still a thriving port. Until then London Bridge had been the easternmost crossing point, and congestion was so bad that shipowners were forced to agree to a new bridge equipped with an ingenious bascule (seesaw) mechanism that could clear the way to oncoming ships in three minutes. The 25m-high twin towers were given a steel frame and then faced with stone.

The bridge's walkways afford excellent

RICHARD I'ANSON

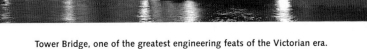

Tower Bridge, one of the greatest engineering feats of the Victorian era.

views across the City and Docklands. For the Tower Bridge Experience a lift takes you up from the modern visitors' facility in the north tower where the story of its building is recounted. Afterwards, the basement engine room and engineers' gallery are well worth visiting, although the re-enactment of the royal opening of the bridge can be skipped if time is tight.

The Tower Bridge Experience is open daily from 10 am to 6.30 pm April to October, from 9.30 am to 6 pm November to March. Entry costs £5.95/3.95 for adults/concessions, including an audioguide.

Although London's port days are over, the bridge still does its stuff, lifting some 500 times a year and as many as 10 times a day in summer. For information on the next lifting ring ☎ 7378 7700. You can also visit the bridge's Web site at www.towerbridge.org.uk.

SOUTH OF THE THAMES: BERMONDSEY TO BATTERSEA

As recently as 10 years ago, the southern part of central London was the city's forgotten underside – run-down, neglected and offering little for foreign visitors once they'd visited the South Bank arts venues. Recently, however, all that has changed and parts of London immediately south of the river can seem as exciting as anywhere farther north.

The Globe Theatre opened to considerable acclaim in 1997 and the restaurant in the old Oxo Tower has served to consolidate the area's popularity. A spate of new museums and attractions have opened (or are opening) in and around Southwark and the South Bank – from the new Tate Modern and the FA Premier League Hall of Fame to the London IMAX Cinema and the gigantic BA London Eye Ferris wheel. The new pedestrian Millennium Bridge will help bring the two sides even closer together.

This section covers the following areas (from east to west): Bermondsey, Southwark (including Borough and Bankside), Waterloo, the South Bank, Lambeth and Battersea.

Bermondsey (Map 8)

Although parts of Bermondsey still look pretty dejected, there are pockets of refurbishment, even gentrification, especially along the waterfront in the area called Shad Thames, where you might want to visit Terence Conran's Design Museum. Antique lovers will also want to explore the Friday morning antiques market in Bermondsey Square (see the special section 'The Markets of London' after the Shopping chapter).

Design Museum The sparkling white Design Museum (☎ 7403 6933), 28 Shad Thames SE1 (⊖ Tower Hill), has displays on how product design has evolved over time and how it can make the difference between success and failure for items intended for mass production. Try a set of chairs for comfort and then use a computer to help you design a new-look toothbrush. Temporary exhibitions on the 1st floor might tell you, for example, how the Dyson cyclonic cleaner – otherwise known as a newfangled vacuum cleaner – was developed, celebrate 40 years of the Mini car or look at new developments in wheelchair design. The Collection & Review galleries on the 2nd floor look at the past and future development in design of everyday things: from televisions and washing machines to chairs and tableware.

The museum opens daily from 11.30 am to 6 pm. Admission costs £5.25/4 for adults/students & under-18s (family £12). There's a coffee shop and gift shop, while the adjacent Blue Print Café offers sky-high river views and prices to match (see Bermondsey in the Places to Eat chapter).

Bramah Museum of Tea & Coffee The Bramah Museum of Tea & Coffee (☎ 7378 0222), 1 Maguire St, corner of Gainsford St SE1 (⊖ Tower Hill), traces the story of tea and coffee drinking in the UK; nearby Butler's Wharf once handled 6000 chests of tea a day. Teapots abound in every shape you can imagine and many you probably wouldn't – a cactus plant, a ball of wool with knitting needles, a Eurostar train – as well as related silverware and prints.

The museum is open daily from 10 am to 6 pm, and admission costs £4/3 (family £10). In the excellent Tea Room, your cuppa is served with an egg timer so you can get the infusion just right (and, yes, they do reasonable coffee, too).

Just south of the museum in Millennium Square is a **bronze statue of Jacob**, one of the many Courage drayhorses stabled here in the 19th century. These work horses delivered beer all over London from the brewery on Horselydown Lane, where the poor old creatures rested ('horse lie down') before crossing the bridge.

Southwark (Map 8)

Originally settled by the Romans, Southwark (**suth**-erk) became an important thoroughfare for people travelling to London in the Middle Ages. For centuries London Bridge, with its houses and shops, was the only crossing point on the Thames and so travellers congregated in Southwark where many inns opened to cater for them. In Tudor times the City authorities refused to permit theatres to be built in the City and so it was on Bankside in Southwark that the Globe, the Rose, the Swan and the Hope theatres were established. At that time Southwark had a thoroughly raffish air, with plentiful 'stews' (brothels-cum-bathhouses), several prisons and innumerable bear-baiting pits.

Victorian Southwark flourished on the back of the trade passing through the docks. Processing and packaging firms set up nearby, many of them household names in the UK like Crosse & Blackwell, Jacob's and Courage. However, Southwark suffered terribly during WWII and even worse in the postwar years when the docks closed and the trade on which it had prospered moved away.

Although Southwark is still pretty run-down it's on the up and up; some say it's London's new Left Bank. The backstreets are also well worth exploring for their many small museums and attractions, including HMS *Belfast*, the London Dungeon and Winston Churchill's Britain at War

exhibition. In the area known as Borough there's a lovely market (see the special section 'The Markets of London' after the Shopping chapter) and the excellent Old Operating Theatre Museum. The Globe Theatre and Southwark Cathedral in the Bankside area remain the jewels in the crown, although no doubt the new Tate Modern at Bankside will put up fierce competition when it opens.

HMS *Belfast* HMS *Belfast* (☎ 7407 6434, 7940 6328 for a recording), Morgan's Lane, Tooley St SE1 (⊖ London Bridge), is a large, light cruiser built with 16 six-inch guns and launched in 1938. It took its name from the Belfast shipyard Harland & Wolff where it was built. During WWII, the *Belfast* escorted merchant shipping on the Arctic convoy but struck a mine in 1939 and was out of action until 1942. It took part in the 1943 Battle of the North Cape off Norway when the German *Scharnhorst* was sunk during the last large-scale gun battle between ships fought in Europe; only 36 of the 1963 men on board the *Scharnhost* survived. The following year it took part in the Normandy landings, before being moved to Asia to repatriate POWs and internees at the end of the war. It saw 404 days' action during the Korean War.

In 1952 the *Belfast* returned to the UK and was comprehensively refitted before setting off on a round-the-world voyage. In 1963 it returned to Devonport docks and was only saved from the scrap yard when the Imperial War Museum bought it to serve as a branch in 1971. The *Belfast* was towed to Portsmouth for a paint job and a freshening-up in the summer of 1999 – the first time she'd 'put to sea' since she was saved for the nation.

It probably helps to be keen on military manoeuvres, but the *Belfast* is surprisingly interesting anyway for what it shows of the way of life on board a cruiser. Finding your way around the eight zones on nine decks can be rather confusing even with a map to help you, and you need to be prepared for a lot of scrambling up and down steep ladders.

In the Zone 3 Operations Room models and sound effects attempt to bring the Battle of the North Cape to life, while a fixed exhibition, HMS *Belfast* in War and Peace, in Zone 5 gives more details and shows a video of the battle. A second exhibition, the Modern Royal Navy, has information on Britain's nuclear deterrent. Almost anyone should enjoy looking around Zone 7, where you can see the ship's galley, hospital, chapel, dental surgery and laundry. Even more interesting are the mess decks of Zone 4.

HMS *Belfast* is open daily from 10 am to 6 pm, March to October (to 5 pm the rest of the year). Admission costs £4.70/3.60 for adults/seniors & students (family £11.80). Children under 16 years old get in free. You can find out more about the cruiser on its Web site at www.hmsbelfast.org.uk.

London Dungeon Under the arches of London Bridge station, the London Dungeon (☎ 7403 0606, 0891 600066), 28-34 Tooley St SE1 (✆ London Bridge), was supposedly developed after someone's child didn't find Madame Tussaud's Chamber of Horrors frightening enough. Here you can watch people hanging on the Tyburn gallows, listen to Anne Boleyn before her head was separated (by a sword wielded by an executioner imported from Calais – not an axe) from her narrow shoulders, observe Thomas à Becket's murder and wonder at an assortment of ingenious methods of torture. The reconstruction of the French guillotine in action is particularly gruesome but still doesn't hold a candle to the section dealing with Victorian serial killer Jack the Ripper and the five prostitutes he sliced and diced, depicted in gory detail with their entrails hanging out. The Judgement Day exhibit sees spectators condemned to death and put aboard the executioner's barge for a 'final trip' through Traitors' Gate. Love it or leave it, it's your call – but the kids can't get enough.

The dungeon is open daily from 10 am to 5.30 pm, October to March, to 6.30 pm from April to June and in September, and to 9 pm in July and August. Admission costs £9.50/7.95/6.50 for adults/seniors & students/

children aged under 14. Be prepared for long queues in July and August unless you've bought advance tickets from a reputable outlet; there have been complaints from readers about touts selling counterfeit tickets.

Winston Churchill's Britain at War Experience Under another Tooley St railway arch is Winston Churchill's Britain at War Experience (☎ 7403 3171), 64-66 Tooley St SE1 (✆ London Bridge). This aims to educate the younger generation about the effect WWII had on daily life while simultaneously playing on the nostalgia of the war generation who sit in the mock Anderson air-raid shelter listening to the simulated sounds of warning sirens and bombers flying overhead with extraordinary detachment. In general it's a tribute to ordinary people, rather than heroes and statesmen (why Churchill's name is invoked is unclear), and comes off very well.

You descend by lift to a reproduction Underground station fitted with bunks, tea urns and even a lending library (as some of the stations really were) and then progress through rooms that display wartime newspaper front pages, posters and Ministry of Food ration books. Mannequins illustrate the ways in which women tried to get around a shortage of fabric, and there's a model of an iced cardboard wedding cake with a small drawer at the bottom for a tiny piece of real fruit cake. Finally, you emerge amid the wreckage of a shop hit by a bomb, with the smoke still eddying around and a burst pipe gushing with water.

The Britain at War Experience is open daily from 10 am to 5.30 pm, April to September (to 4.30 pm the rest of the year). Admission costs £5.95/3.95/2.95 for adults/seniors & students/children (family £14).

St Olaf House This diminutive office block fronting the Thames on Tooley St (the name of which is a corruption of St Olave's St) was built in 1932 and is one of London's finest Art Deco buildings. Notice the gold mosaic lettering on the front and the bronze relief sculptures.

Old Operating Theatre Museum & Herb Garret While the London Dungeon is all about shock and horror, the Old Operating Theatre Museum nearby (☎ 7955 4791), 9A St Thomas St SE1 (⊖ London Bridge), focuses on the more mundane nastiness of 19th-century hospital treatment. It is at the top of the 32-step tower of St Thomas Church (1703). The garret was used by the apothecary of St Thomas's Hospital to store medicinal herbs and now houses an atmospheric medical museum delightfully hung with bunches of herbs that soften the impact of the horrible devices displayed in the glass cases.

Even more interesting is the 19th-century women's operating theatre attached to the garret. An adjoining building used to house the surgical ward of St Thomas's and the church's roof space provided an ideal position for the theatre – high enough to take advantage of the natural light and isolated enough to provide soundproofing. In the days before the importance of an antiseptic environment was understood, students crowded round the operating table in what looks like a modern lecture hall. A box of sawdust was placed beneath the table to catch the blood and contemporary accounts record the surgeons wearing frock coats 'stiff and stinking with pus and blood'.

The museum is open daily from 10 am to 4 pm, and admission costs £2.90/2/1.50 for adults/seniors & students/children (family £7.25).

Bankside (Maps 6 & 8) This corner of Southwark includes several of south London's most essential attractions.

Southwark Cathedral There was already a church on this site in 1086, but it was rebuilt in 1106 and then for a third time in the 13th century. During the Middle Ages it was part of the Priory of St Mary Overie (from 'St Mary over the Water'), becoming the local parish church in 1539 after the dissolution of the monasteries. By the 1830s it had fallen into decay and much of what you see today is actually Victorian – the nave

was rebuilt in 1897 – although the central tower dates from 1520 and the choir from the 13th century. In 1905 the Collegiate Church of St Saviour and St Mary Overie became Southwark Cathedral (Map 8; ☎ 7407 3708), Montague Close SE1 (⊖ London Bridge), with its own bishop.

You enter via the south-west door and immediately to the left is the ***Marchioness memorial*** to the 51 people who died in 1989 when a pleasure cruiser on the Thames near Southwark Bridge hit a dredger and sank. Against the west wall are a series of **15th-century wooden bosses** taken from the original nave ceiling; one shows a pelican (Christ) nurturing its young (the faithful) with its own breast blood – a common motif in medieval Christianity.

Walk up the north aisle of the nave and you'll come to the brightly coloured and much renovated canopied **tomb of John**

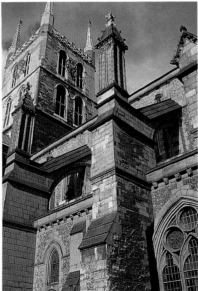

GLENN BEANLAND

Used as a pigsty prior to restoration, Southwark Cathedral is a fascinating mix of styles.

Gower (circa 1330-1408), whose *Confessio Amantis* is considered the first poem written in English.

In the north transept, you'll see several 17th- and 18th-century monuments and a fine 17th-century wooden **sword-rest** from the church of St Olave Old Jewry, demolished in 1888. More interesting is the nearby **memorial tablet to Lionel Lockyer**, a quack doctor celebrated for his pills, and its humorous epitaph. On the eastern side of the north transept is the **Harvard Chapel**, originally the chapel of St John the Evangelist but now named after John Harvard, founder of Harvard University in Cambridge, Massachusetts, who was baptised here in 1607.

In the north choir aisle look out for the macabre **medieval tomb** showing a skeleton in a shroud and for a rare but heavily restored 13th-century **wooden effigy** of a knight in chain-mail armour. Immediately opposite is

a **17th-century monument** to one Richard Humble that shows him kneeling towards the altar with his two little wives behind him. The lovely inlaid chest nearby is the **Nonsuch Chest**, given to the church in 1588.

Cross the retrochoir – used as a bakery and a pigsty in the 16th century – with its four chapels behind the high altar and return along the south choir aisle. To the right is the fine **17th-century tomb of Lancelot Andrewes**, last bishop of Winchester, who helped translate the King James version of the Bible. A few steps farther on and you'll see a **Roman statue of a hunter god** found in a nearby well in 1976 and probably dating from the 2nd or 3rd century AD.

Cross into the choir to admire the Early English arches and vaults, and the **16th-century screen** separating the choir from the retrochoir, a gift of the bishop of Winchester in 1520. The statues in the niches were

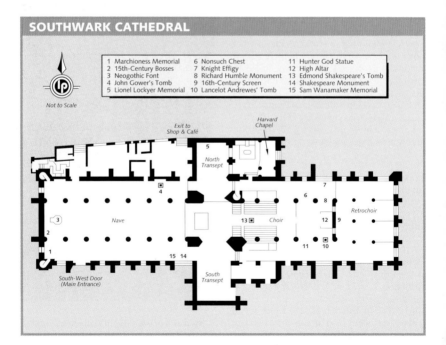

SOUTHWARK CATHEDRAL

1 Marchioness Memorial	6 Nonsuch Chest	11 Hunter God Statue
2 15th-Century Bosses	7 Knight Effigy	12 High Altar
3 Neogothic Font	8 Richard Humble Monument	13 Edmond Shakespeare's Tomb
4 John Gower's Tomb	9 16th-Century Screen	14 Shakespeare Monument
5 Lionel Lockyer Memorial	10 Lancelot Andrewes' Tomb	15 Sam Wanamaker Memorial

Not to Scale

added in 1905. On the choir floor are tablets marking the **tomb of Edmond Shakespeare**, actor-brother of the Bard, who died in 1607. The Jacobean dramatists John Fletcher and Philip Massinger are also buried here.

Return to the south choir aisle and continue to the south transept, noting the fine **organ** designed by Lewis in 1897 (rebuilt in 1952).

Stand beneath the 16th-century crossing tower and look up at the finely **painted ceiling**. The **brass candelabrum** hanging from it dates from 1680. The crown, mitre and dove incorporated in the design are said to have reflected concern at the time about the relationship between Church and State.

Returning along the south aisle of the nave, stop and look at the green alabaster **monument to William Shakespeare**, whose great works were originally written for the Bankside playhouses. The background depicts the Globe Theatre and Southwark Cathedral, while the stained-glass window above shows characters from *A Midsummer Night's Dream*, *Hamlet* and *The Tempest*. Shakespeare is actually buried in Stratford-upon-Avon and this memorial was only erected in 1912. Each year on 23 April a birthday service is held here in his honour. Right beside Shakespeare's monument is a small **memorial to Sam Wanamaker** (1919-93), the American film director and actor who was the force behind the rebuilt Globe Theatre.

The cathedral (free, £2.50 donation requested) is open daily from 8 am to 6 pm. Evensong is sung at 5.30 pm on Tuesday and Friday, 4 pm on Saturday and 3 pm on Sunday. Le Petit Café in the Chapter House, with main dishes from £5.25, is open weekdays from 10 am to 6 pm. Lunch-time concerts usually take place on Monday and Tuesday at 1.10 pm.

Golden Hinde A replica of the boat in which Sir Francis Drake circumnavigated the globe between 1577 and 1580 is moored in tiny St Mary Overie Dock (Map 8; ☎ 7403 0123), Cathedral St SE1. You can go on board and explore the five decks from 9 am to sunset every day (£2.30/1.90/1.50 for adults/seniors

& students/children); buy your tickets at the card and souvenir shop just opposite the Golden Hinde. It's quite fun to see the replica Tudor fittings and cannons, but watch your head on the low ceilings of the gun deck.

Winchester Palace North-west of Southwark Cathedral is Clink St (Map 8), once the heart of a huge palace complex built for the bishop of Winchester, William Giffard, in 1109; it would remain home to the bishops of Winchester for more than 500 years but was converted into a prison for royalists under Cromwell in 1642. Today the scant remains include a fine 14th-century rose window (discovered in a Clink St warehouse in 1814) from the Great Hall and part of the flooring.

Clink Exhibition Clink Prison, a private jail in the park of Winchester Palace – a 28-hectare area known as the Liberty of the Clink and under the jurisdiction of the bishops of Winchester and not the City – was used to detain debtors, whores, thieves, martyrs and even actors. It was burned down during the Gordon Riots in 1780 but hadn't been used for a century in any case. This was the notorious address that gave us the expression 'in the clink', meaning 'in jail'. The small, rather half-hearted Clink Exhibition (Map 8; ☎ 7378 1558), 1 Clink St SE1 (Ө London Bridge), reveals the wretched life of the prisoners who were forced to pay for their own food and accommodation and sometimes had to resort to catching and eating mice. It also looks at the history of prostitution; this was, after all, the heart of the red-light district south of the river.

The exhibition is open daily from 10 am to 6 pm; admission costs £4/3 (family £9).

Vinopolis – City of Wine It might seem an odd attraction in the capital of a country with little in the way of wine-making history and negligible amounts produced from its own vines, but Vinopolis (Map 8; ☎ 0870 444 4777), 1 Bank End, Park St SE1 (Ө London Bridge), in a hectare of Victorian railway vaults in

Bankside, has cashed in on Londoners' love affair with things red, white and rosé. The high-tech exhibits introduce visitors to the history of wine-making, vineyards and grape varietals, regional characteristics and which wine goes with which food.

The centrepiece is the Wine Odyssey in which you travel through the hills of Chianti on a 'scooter', 'fly' over the Hunter Valley and 'visit' Argentina, Chile, California, Spain and South Africa. The tour ends in the Grand Tasting Halls, where you can sample five different wines from all over the world. There's also a wine school offering classes, a branch of the wine retailer Majestic, a gourmet food shop and four restaurants. Vinopolis (entry £10, or £9 if booked in advance) is open daily from 10 am to 5.30 pm year-round. Under-18s must be accompanied by an adult.

Rose Theatre Though nothing of the original Globe Theatre has ever been found, the foundations of the nearby Rose Theatre, built in 1587, were discovered in 1989 beneath an office building at Southwark Bridge. A 25-minute sound-and-light show at the excavation site at 56 Park St SE1 (Map 8; ☎ 7593 0026) takes place daily every 30 minutes, with the first show at 10 am and the last at 5 pm. Entry costs £3/2.50/2 for adults/seniors & students/children.

Shakespeare's Globe & Exhibition The Globe Theatre (Map 8; ☎ 7401 9919), 21 New Globe Walk SE1 (⊖ London Bridge), consists of the reconstructed Globe Theatre and, beneath it, an exhibition focusing on Elizabethan London and the struggle to get the theatre rebuilt.

The original Globe (known as the 'Wooden O' after its circular shape and roofless centre) was erected in 1599 with timber from the Theatre (1576) on Curtain St in Shoreditch. The Globe burned down in 1613 and was immediately rebuilt. In 1642 it was finally closed by the Puritans, who regarded theatres as dreadful dens of iniquity, and it was dismantled two years later. Despite the worldwide popularity of Shakespeare,

SIMON BRACKEN

'If music be the food of love, play on' – open-air Shakespeare at the Globe Theatre.

the Globe was barely a distant memory when American actor (later film director) Sam Wanamaker came searching for the Globe in 1949. Undeterred by the fact that the foundations of the theatre had vanished beneath a row of listed Georgian houses, Wanamaker set up the Globe Playhouse Trust in 1970 and began fund-raising for a memorial theatre. Work started in 1987, but Wanamaker died four years before it opened in 1997.

The new Globe was painstakingly constructed with 600 oak pegs (there's not a nail or a screw in the house), specially fired Tudor bricks and thatching reeds from Norfolk that – for some odd reason – pigeons don't like; even the plaster contains goat hair, lime and sand as it did in Shakespeare's time. Unlike other venues for Shakespearean plays, this theatre has been designed to resemble the original as closely as possible – even if that means leaving the arena open to the skies, expecting the 500 'groundlings' to stand and obstructing much of the view from the seats closest to the stage with two enormous 'original' Corinthian pillars. Still, you should try to see a production – and it's not always Shakespeare; during the 1999 season (the Globe's 400th anniversary), for example, it staged its first commissioned play, *Augustine's Oak* by Peter Oswald, and the first true English opera, *Venus and Adonis*, by John Blow. For ticket details see Theatre in the Entertainment chapter; it's a very popular tourist attraction, with English-speaking foreigners far outnumbering local spectators. There's both a café and a restaurant (☎ 7928 9444).

The Globe is open to visitors daily from 10 am to 5 pm. A visit to the exhibition, which also includes a guided tour of the Globe Theatre itself (except on days with a matinee performance, when tours are in the morning only), costs £6/5/4 for adults/seniors & students/children aged five to 15 (family £14). The theatre's Web site is at www.shakespeares-globe.org.

Millennium Bridge Of all the projects conceived to help usher in the third millennium, this footbridge (Map 8) over the Thames is arguably the most important to the people of London: it is both beautiful and useful and will do much to bring London back to the Thames, its birthplace, and link its two banks. May it last 1000 years!

The Millennium Bridge pushes off from the south bank of the Thames in front of the new Tate Modern and berths on the north bank at the steps of Peter's Hill. A footpath leads up to and across Queen Victoria St to St Paul's Churchyard and the cathedral. The bridge is accessible 24 hours a day and, of course, is free.

Tate Modern The Bankside Power Station, designed by Giles Gilbert Scott after WWII but decommissioned in 1986, is from May 2000 home to the Tate Modern (Maps 6 & 8; ☎ 7887 8000 for information), Queen's Walk SE1 (⊖ Blackfriars or London Bridge). The structure itself – with its two new upper floors shrouded in glass and

brightly lit at night and its landmark central chimney – is quite dramatic, especially when viewed from the opposite bank or the new Millennium Bridge.

This gallery will contain Britain's collection of international 20th-century and modern art and display high-quality works by Picasso, Matisse, Cézanne, Pollock and so on. There's no reason to think that the Tate's reputation for avant-garde exhibitions – firmly established at its Millbank site – won't continue at the new gallery.

The Tate Modern (free) is open daily from 10 am to 5.50 pm. Special exhibitions will have an admission charge.

Bankside Gallery Bankside Gallery (Map 6; ☎ 7928 7521), 48 Hopton St SE1 (⊖ Blackfriars or Waterloo), is home to the Royal Watercolour Society and the Royal Society of Painter-Printmakers. There's no permanent collection here but there are frequently changing exhibitions of watercolours, prints and engravings. It usually opens on Tuesday from 10 am to 8 pm, Wednesday to Friday until 5 pm and on Saturday and Sunday from 1 to 5 pm. Admission costs £3.50/2 for adults/seniors & students. Artists Perspectives on Tuesday at 6.30 pm gives you a chance to meet the artists and discuss their work. The gallery's bookshop is very good.

Museum Of ... The Museum Of ... (Map 6; ☎ 7928 1255), Bargehouse, Oxo Tower Wharf, Bargehouse St SE1 (⊖ Waterloo or Blackfriars), is a new concept for a museum: quirky, changing exhibits that, among other things, focus on what everyday people amass. The Museum of Collectors, for example, which launched the museum in 1999, featured 40 different collections with items as varied as drinks cans from around the world, fishing flies, carrier bags and Dolly Parton memorabilia. The Museum of Me, the next exhibit, allowed visitors to measure the length of their left index finger, change their appearance or appear on stage. The museum (free) is open Wednesday to Sunday from noon to 6 pm.

Waterloo (Maps 6 & 7)

The area immediately around Waterloo station (Map 6) is currently a mess of run-down streets and concrete walkways. However, this is where you'll find the area known as the South Bank, with several important theatres and concert halls. The riverside walk here also provides stunning views across the Thames. A lot of work is being done to brush things up – in the short term that may make matters worse, but in the long term it can only be good news. Emerging from the main exit of Waterloo station you'll see the new circular London IMAX Cinema sitting in the middle of a roundabout. For many years the wretched underpass below Tenison Way suffered the nickname 'Cardboard City' because of the number of homeless people living in its soulless confines. With the arrival of the cinema, they've been moved on.

London IMAX Cinema Part of the British Film Institute, the new £20 million London IMAX Cinema (Map 6; ☎ 7902 1234), Tenison Way SE1 (⊖ Waterloo), is the largest in Europe, with a screen some 10 storeys high and 26m wide. The 485-seat cinema screens the usual 2-D and IMAX 3-D films – documentaries about travel, space and wildlife that thrill and shock and frighten for a while and then get rather dull and repetitive. They last between 40 minutes and 1½ hours. Film showings are daily at noon and then at 1.15, 2.30, 3.45, 5, 6.15, 7.30 and 8.45 pm with an additional screening on Friday and Saturday at 10 pm. Tickets cost £6.50/5.50/4.50 for adults/ seniors & students/children aged five to 16.

The South Bank (Map 6)

North of Waterloo station and across the Thames from Embankment tube station, the South Bank is a labyrinth of arts venues strung out on rain-stained concrete walkways between Hungerford Railway Bridge and just beyond Waterloo Bridge. Almost no one has a good word to say about the indescribably ugly architecture and a complete overhaul is on the cards so expect a lot of work to be going on here. In the meantime the concrete slopes and buttresses host a mixed bag of art lovers, skateboarders and homeless people.

The **Royal Festival Hall** (Map 6) was built in 1951 for the Festival of Britain and now hosts classical, opera, jazz and choral music. Alongside a range of pricey cafés and restaurants and a good music shop, it also has a foyer where free recitals take place most evenings. The smaller **Queen Elizabeth Hall** to the north-east and the **Purcell Room** host similar concerts. A full-scale refurbishment of the Royal Festival Hall began in June 1999; there are discussions about demolishing or redesigning the unloved other two as well as the Hayward Gallery and moving them to a low-rise riverfront building a bit farther south.

Tucked almost out of sight under the arches of Waterloo Bridge is the **National Film Theatre** (NFT; Map 6), built in 1958 and screening some 2000 films a year. The popular, and much newer, **Museum of the Moving Image** (closed for redevelopment until 2003) next door tells the story of film and television. A second-hand book and print market takes place immediately in front of the NFT under the arches of the bridge.

The **Hayward Gallery** (Map 6), built in 1968, usually hosts blockbuster modern art exhibitions, while the **Royal National Theatre**, a love-it-or-hate-it complex of three theatres (Olivier, Lyttleton and Cottesloe), is the nation's flagship theatre. Dismissed by Prince Charles as resembling a 'disused power station', the National was designed in 1976 by the modernist architect Denys Lasdun, a great fan of concrete and horizontal lines. A £42 million modernisation was completed in 1999.

A short walk east along the South Bank is **Gabriel's Wharf** (Map 6), a cluster of twee little craft shops, snack bars and restaurants that forms part of a successful attempt by local residents to resist further large-scale development in the area. From the South Bank Walkway you look across the river to stunning views of St Paul's, Lloyd's of London, Minster Court and so on.

ELLIOT DANIEL

The South Bank arts complex: a cultural cornucopia.

Museum of the Moving Image Tucked away among the South Bank's high-brow arts venues, the Museum of the Moving Image (MOMI; Map 6; ☎ 7401 2636 for a recording; ✪ Waterloo or Embankment) is currently closed while it undergoes extensive redevelopment – it is expected to reopen around 2003. In the meantime there are plans for its collections to be shown at the Science Museum (see the Chelsea, South Kensington & Earl's Court section later in this chapter). You can visit MOMI's Web site at www.bfi.org.uk/museum to get the latest news.

Hayward Gallery The Hayward Gallery (Map 6; ☎ 7928 3144, 7261 0127 for a recording), Belvedere Rd SE1 (✪ Waterloo), is London's premier exhibition space for major international art shows. Some love the grey, concrete fortress-like building, others can't say a nice thing about it. Whichever camp you fall into, you can

hardly deny that it makes an excellent hanging space for contemporary and 20th-century art. But it's future is also in doubt.

Between exhibitions the Hayward is sometimes closed, so check before turning up. In general it's open on Monday and Thursday to Sunday from 10 am to 6 pm, on Tuesday and Wednesday from 10 am to 8 pm. Admission depends on what's showing but assume around £6/4/2.50 for adults/seniors & students/under-18s (family £14). The gallery's Web site at www.hayward-gallery.org.uk is useful.

County Hall Directly across Westminster Bridge from the Houses of Parliament stands County Hall (Map 6; ✪ Westminster or Waterloo), home to London County Council and then the renamed (1965) Greater London Council until its final disagreement with Margaret Thatcher in 1986. The grand building with its curved, colonnaded façade was built in 1922. After more than a decade of wrangling over its future it's finally started to acquire new life with the opening of a vast aquarium in the basement, a new hall of fame honouring great names in English football, two hotels, a Chinese restaurant and a McDonald's.

London Aquarium The London Aquarium (Map 6; ☎ 7967 8000), County Hall, Westminster Bridge Rd SE1 (⊖ Westminster or Waterloo), with its entrance along Albert Embankment, is one of the largest in Europe but curiously disappointing, partly because its location on three levels in the basement is so dark but also because the fish on display are generally of the less colourful variety. There's also an uncomfortable discrepancy between the huge tanks with their sharks and the side tanks, which are so small that it only takes one inconsiderate photographer to block them from view. The new coral-reef display, however, is quite impressive.

The aquarium is open daily from 10 am to 6 pm, closing at 6.30 pm from June to August. Admission costs £8/6.50/5 for adults/seniors & students/children (family

£22), and there's a café and a shop attached. The aquarium also has a Web site at www .londonaquarium.co.uk.

FA Premier League Hall of Fame The Football Association Premier League Hall of Fame (Map 6; ☎ 7928 3636), County Hall, with its main entrance off Westminster Bridge Rd, is a temple to English football divided into five themed sections: the Hall of Legends traces the sport's history to the present day; the Hall of Fame exhibits full-sized wax figures of the first 12 inductees (among them Les Ferdinand, Peter Schmeichel, Alan Shearer, Tony Adams, Eric Cantona and Ruud Gullit) and will grow; the Hall of Fans is dedicated to football fanatics, both the famous and the not-so-famous; Hope and Glory is a soppy film about a young boy's journey from street footballer to Premier League star; and Football Interactive allows visitors to test their skills by computer.

The Hall of Fame is open daily from 10 am to 6 pm. Tickets cost £9.95/7.50/6.50 for adults/seniors & students/children aged four to 15. Its Web site is at www .hall-of-fame.co.uk.

Ancient and modern: Big Ben ponders the stunning BA London Eye from across the Thames.

BA London Eye Just north of County Hall are the **Jubilee Gardens**, the site of the 1951 Festival of Britain. At the south-western corner of the gardens rises the British Airways London Eye (Map 6; ⊖ Waterloo), which, at 135m tall, is the world's largest Ferris wheel. It is a thrilling experience to be in one of the 32 enclosed glass gondolas, enjoying views of some 40km (on clear days) across the capital; the 'Millennium Wheel' (as it's also known) takes 30 minutes to rotate completely. The wheel operates daily from 9 am to dusk, April to October (10 am to 6 pm the rest of the year). Tickets cost £6.95/£4.80 for adults/children. Current plans are for the wheel to remain on site until 2005 and then be moved elsewhere, but we're putting our money on it becoming another Eiffel Tower – a strange one-off that was meant to go but instead turned into a city icon. You can find out the latest on the wheel by visiting www.ba-londoneye.com on the Web.

Lambeth (Maps 2 & 6)

Lambeth is the district immediately south of Westminster Bridge where you'll find Lambeth Palace, with the Museum of Gardening History just beside it, and St Thomas's Hospital, with the Florence Nightingale Museum inside its grounds.

Florence Nightingale Museum Within walking distance of County Hall and attached to St Thomas's Hospital is the Florence Nightingale Museum (Map 6; ☎ 7620 0374), 2 Lambeth Palace Rd SE1 (⊖ Westminster or Waterloo), which tells the story of the feisty war heroine (1820-1910) who led a team of nurses to Scutari in Turkey in 1854 during the Crimean War, where she worked to improve conditions for the soldiers before returning to London to set up a training school for nurses. The museum will be rather wordy for some, but the video about Nightingale's life is certainly interesting.

It's open Tuesday to Sunday from 10 am to 5 pm (last admission at 4 pm) and admission costs £3.50/2.50 (family £7).

Lambeth Palace The red-brick Tudor gatehouse immediately beside the church of St Mary-at-Lambeth leads to Lambeth Palace (Map 2), the London home of the Archbishop of Canterbury. Although the palace is not usually open to the public, the gardens occasionally are; check with a tourist information centre (see Tourist Offices in the Facts for the Visitor chapter) for details.

Museum of Gardening History At the southern end of Lambeth Palace is the Museum of Gardening History (Map 2; ☎ 7401 8865), Lambeth Palace Rd SE1 (⊖ Lambeth North), housed in the church of St Mary-at-Lambeth, which has some lovely stained glass (notice the *Pedlar of Lambeth*, who left the parish an acre of land provided he and his dog were remembered in a church window like this one) and a font for Baptist-style total immersion (the only one in London). The museum was inspired by the work of John Tradescant (1608-62) and his son, also called John, who were gardeners to Charles I and Charles II respectively. The Tradescants roamed the globe and brought back many exotic plants to London, including the pineapple, together with a collection of 'all things strange and rare' that they housed in The Ark, their house on South Lambeth Rd. This collection eventually formed the basis of the Ashmolean Museum in Oxford (see the Excursions chapter).

Although the church tower dates from the 14th century, the nave was rebuilt in 1852 and now provides exhibition space for information on the Tradescants' lives and on the inspirational 20th-century gardener Gertrude Jekyll. A 17th-century replica knot garden – a formal garden of intricate design – has been planted in the small churchyard, which also shelters the tombs of the Tradescants and of William Bligh (1754-1817), the ship's captain cast adrift during the mutiny on the *Bounty* in 1789. The Tradescants' tomb is well worth a look for its carvings: on the eastern side, the Tradescant coat of arms; on the western, a Hydra and a skull; on the southern, broken columns, Corinthian capitals, a pyramid and ruins; and on the northern, a crocodile, shells and a view of some Egyptian buildings.

The museum (free) is open Monday to Friday from 10.30 am to 4 pm and on Sunday until 5 pm (closed Saturday). For more information you can visit its Web site at www.museumgardenhistory.org.

Imperial War Museum The Imperial War Museum (Map 2; ☎ 7416 5320, 0891 600140 for a recording), Lambeth Rd SE1 (⊖ Lambeth North), is housed in a striking building dating from 1815 and given a magnificent copper dome in 1845. Originally this was the site of the third Bethlehem Royal Hospital, commonly known as Bedlam (the first was established outside Bishopsgate in Liverpool St in 1247, the second in Moorfields in 1676). When the hospital moved to Kent in 1926, Viscount Rothermere bought the old building and gave it to the nation to house a museum. Look out for a chunk of the Berlin Wall to the left of the main entrance.

Although there's still plenty of military hardware on show and the core of the museum is a chronological exhibition on the two world wars, these days the museum places more emphasis on the social cost of war: the Blitz, the food shortages and the propaganda. Especially distressing is a small room where film footage of the discovery of the Bergen-Belsen concentration camp is shown. Children under 14 are not admitted without adults. The top floor features war paintings by the likes of Henry Moore, Paul Nash and John Singer Sargent.

Particularly popular exhibits are the Trench Experience, which depicts the grim day-to-day existence of a WWI infantryman in a frontline trench on the Somme, and the Blitz Experience, which lets visitors sit inside a mock bomb-shelter during an air raid and then stroll through ravaged East End streets. Another popular one is Secret History, which takes a look at the work of the secret services, with video footage of the 1980 siege of the Iranian embassy in

Knightsbridge brought to a dramatic end by Balaclava-clad SAS commandos in an 11-minute assault. New exhibits include Conflicts since 1945, which covers the campaigns in Korea, Vietnam, the Gulf and the Balkans, as well as the Cold War and National Service. A new permanent exhibition devoted to the Holocaust opens in the summer of 2000. Temporary exhibits cover such topics as war reporting and fashion in the postwar years. You can find out more about current exhibitions on the museum's Web site at www.iwm.org.uk.

The Imperial War Museum is open daily from 10 am to 6 pm. Admission costs £5.20/4.20 for adults/seniors & students (free for under-17s and for everyone after 4.30 pm). It's particularly popular with school groups; visit early in the morning or late in the afternoon to avoid them.

Next to the museum is the **Tibetan Peace Garden** opened by the Dalai Lama in May 1999.

Battersea (Maps 9 & 10)

South-west along the Thames from Lambeth is Battersea, not the most inspiring of London districts but boasting a fine riverside park with a children's zoo, a pagoda and the looming shell of the old Battersea Power Station.

Battersea Power Station Familiar from a million Pink Floyd album covers, Battersea Power Station (Map 10) is the building with the four smokestacks that somewhat resembles a table turned upside-down visible from Chelsea Bridge. Built by Giles Gilbert Scott with two chimneys in 1933 (the other two were added in 1955), it ceased operating in 1982 and since then there have been innumerable proposals to give it a new life – from a Disney theme park, Warner multiplex cinema and Cirque du Soleil theatre to a new train station and shopping and hotel complex. Meanwhile, the main hall stands exposed to the elements with its insides ripped out, and the power station's future seems as uncertain as ever.

Pigs might fly: the menacing hulk of Battersea Power Station awaits a new life.

DOUG McKINLAY

CHELSEA, SOUTH KENSINGTON & EARL'S COURT (Map 9)

Much of west London is high-class territory; indeed, Kensington & Chelsea enjoys the highest average gross income of all London boroughs (over £485 a week). Go a bit farther west, though, and you'll reach Earl's Court and Barons Court, less prosperous areas that seem to have been dropped here by accident.

Until the 18th century Chelsea was a relatively remote village harbouring the grand country houses of the rich. Cheyne Mews was the site of Henry VIII's Chelsea Manor House, built in 1536 and demolished shortly after the death of its last resident, Hans Sloane, the British Museum benefactor, in 1753. Nowadays, of course, it's well and truly part of London, although its riverside setting ensures that it's still a favoured place for the wealthy to live. During the 1960s Chelsea was fashionable with the trendsetters who frequented King's Rd. The heyday of punk brought a brief, colourful renaissance in the 70s and the Sloane Rangers ruled the 80s from Sloane Square, but even if Chelsea is no longer at the forefront of fashion this is still one of London's classier and most exclusive districts.

Thanks to Prince Albert and the 1851 Great Exhibition (see the boxed text 'Prince Albert & the Great Exhibition' under History in the Facts about London chapter), South Kensington is first and foremost museumland, boasting the Natural History, Science and Victoria & Albert museums all on one road. Albert's newly renovated memorial is due north of this admirable trio.

Earl's Court is a lively, cosmopolitan part of town, with a large, mobile population, particularly Poles (who stay) and Australians (who move on). It's a funny mix of the smart and the scruffy – one minute you're on Earl's Court Rd watching cans of lager being swilled on the street, the next you're on Old Brompton Rd with its gay-bars and too-chic-by-half continental-style cafés.

Battersea Park Stretching out between Albert and Chelsea bridges is Battersea Park (Maps 9 & 10), a 50-hectare area of greenery filled with attractions and distractions, most prominently the **Peace Pagoda** (Map 9), erected in 1985 by a sect of Japanese Buddhists who aim to complete similar pagodas all over the world. Golden statues of the Buddha sit in the niches on all four sides and a pinnacle soars 10m into the air.

Boats can be hired (about £4 an hour) to get around the small lake, and there's a running track. The small **Children's Zoo** (Map 9) is open from 10 am to 5 pm, Easter to October (11 am to 3 pm at the weekend during the rest of the year), and admission costs £1.45/95p/70p for adults/seniors & students/children. On public holidays there is usually a funfair here, the sound carrying over the river. The park is open daily from dawn to dusk.

Chelsea Royal Hospital

Site of the Chelsea Flower Show in May
(☎ 09064 123412 for information), Chelsea
Royal Hospital (☎ 7730 5282), Royal
Hospital Rd SW3 (✆ Sloane Square), is
a superb building (1692) designed by
Sir Christopher Wren during the reign of
Charles II, whose statue (Map 10) in Roman
dress adorns the courtyard facing south
(there are excellent 'framed' views of Battersea Power Station across the Thames
from here). It was a home for veteran soldiers and still houses more than 400 Chelsea
Pensioners – you may see them around town
in their dark blue greatcoats (in winter) or
scarlet frock-coats (in summer).

You can stroll in the grounds (enter from
West Rd) and visit the elegantly simple
Chapel with its altar painting, *The Resurrection* by Sebastiano Ricci, and the **Great
Hall**, a refectory bedecked with flags and
royal portraits. The Royal Hospital (free) is
open Monday to Saturday from 10 am to
noon and 2 to 4 pm; on Sunday it's open in
the afternoon only.

National Army Museum

Right beside the Royal Hospital but designed in the late 1960s with complete dis-
regard for its elegant neighbour, the
National Army Museum (☎ 7730 0717),
Royal Hospital Rd SW3 (✆ Sloane
Square), does its best to inject life into its
military exhibits. Displays deal with the
history of weapons, armies, artillery and
tactics, but the best examine the life and
times of the British soldier from the Battle
of Agincourt (1415) to the present. On the
2nd floor there's a display on women's role
in the armed forces. Outside there is a
memorial, in English and Chinese, to the
Middlesex Regiment 'who defended Hong
Kong with distinction in December 1941'.

The National Army Museum (free) is
open daily from 10 am to 5.30 pm.

Chelsea Physic Garden

The Chelsea Physic Garden (☎ 7352 5646),
66 Royal Hospital Rd SW3 (entrance on
Swan Walk; ✆ Sloane Square), was created

by the Apothecaries' Society, a City livery
company, in 1673 to study the ways in
which botany related to medicine (then
known as the 'physic art'). It's one of the
oldest botanical gardens in Europe (the second oldest in the UK), and its 1.5 hectares
contain many rare trees and plants. Individual corners of the garden are given over to
world medicine and plants suitable for dye-
ing and use in aromatherapy. A number of
notable gardeners have worked here over
the years, including William Aiton, the first
gardener at Kew, and William Forsyth, who
gave his name to forsythia.

The garden is open on Wednesday from
noon to 5 pm and on Sunday from 2 to
6 pm, April to October. During the week
of the Chelsea Flower Show in late May
and the Chelsea Festival in June it opens
Monday to Friday from noon to 5 pm.
Admission costs £4/2 for adults/conces-
sions. Tea and cakes are served from 2.30 to
4.45 pm (5.45 pm on Sunday).

Carlyle's House

From 1834 the great Victorian essayist and
historian Thomas Carlyle (1795-1881) lived
at 24 Cheyne Row SW3 (☎ 7352 7087;
✆ Sloane Square), a three-storey terrace
house built in 1708. Here in the attic he wrote
his famous history of the French Revolution
and many other works. Legend claims that
when the manuscript was complete, a maid
mistakenly threw it on the fire, whereupon
the diligent Thomas duly wrote it all again.

While it's not particularly large, this
charming house has been left much as it was
when Carlyle was living here and Chopin,
Thackeray and Dickens were among the
guests. There's a small garden at the rear.

The house is open Wednesday to Sunday
from 11 am to 5 pm, from late March to
October. Admission costs £3.30/1.65 for
adults/children; National Trust (NT) members get in free.

Chelsea Old Church

As you walk along Cheyne Walk you'll spot
a black and gold **statue of Thomas More**
(1477-1535), the lord chancellor who was

executed for his opposition to Henry VIII's plans to make himself head of the Church of England after his divorce from Catherine of Aragon and marriage to Anne Boleyn. More and his family used to live in Chelsea, in a property appropriated by Henry after his beheading.

Immediately behind the statue is Chelsea Old Church, which dates from the 13th century but was flattened by two bombs in 1941 and later rebuilt. The interior contains many fine Tudor monuments, including the **More Chapel** to the south, which was rebuilt by Sir Thomas in 1528 and retains its wooden ceiling and pillar capitals, examples of the fledgling Renaissance style. At the western end of the south aisle don't miss the only chained books in a London church (chained, of course, to stop anyone making off with them), including a copy of Foxe's *Book of Martyrs* dating from 1684. They were a gift from Hans Sloane.

'Scholar, Saint, Statesman' – Thomas More in contemplative mood.

Celebrated former residents of Cheyne Walk also include *Middlemarch* author George Eliot, who lived and died at No 4; the artist Dante Gabriel Rossetti and the poet Algernon Swinburne, who shared the house at No 16; and JMW Turner, who lived at No 119 under the alias Booth.

Albert & Battersea Bridges

One of the most striking of London's bridges, Albert Bridge is a cross between a cantilever and a suspension bridge that was buttressed to strengthen it as an alternative to closure in the 1960s. It was designed by Roland Mason Ordish in 1873 but later modified by the engineer Joseph Bazalgette (see Victorian London under History in the Facts about London chapter). Painted white and pink and with fairy lights adorning its cables, it can look positively festive at night. The booths at either end survive from the days when tolls were charged to cross it.

The Battersea Bridge featured in the painter Whistler's *Nocturnes* and etchings was an earlier wooden model dating from 1772. It was Bazalgette who once again came up with the designs for the current bridge, which was built in 1890. The cliffhanger climax of the film *Lock, Stock and Two Smoking Barrels* took place here.

King's Rd

In the 17th century Charles II set up a Chelsea love nest for his mistress, an orange-seller at the Drury Lane Theatre called Nell Gwyn. Returning from her house to Hampton Court Palace, he would make use of a farmer's track that inevitably came to be known as the King's Rd.

Even today when the hippies and punks have moved on, King's Rd is still a fashionable place. It begins at Sloane Square, to the north of which runs Sloane St, celebrated for its designer boutiques. At 75 Sloane St is the Cadogan Hotel, where Oscar Wilde was arrested (in room No 118, to be precise) and later jailed for his 'friendship' (the euphemism of the time) with Lord Alfred Douglas in 1895.

Michelin House

Even if you can't afford to eat in Bibendum, Terence Conran's restaurant in the Michelin House, 81 Fulham Rd SW3 (see Chelsea, South Kensington & Earl's Court in the Places to Eat chapter), pass by just to take a look at the superb Art Nouveau architecture. It was built for Michelin between 1905 and 1911 by François Espinasse and completely restored in 1985; the famous roly-poly Michelin Man appears in the modern stained glass. The open-fronted ground floor provides space for upmarket fish and flower stalls, while the lobby is decorated with tiles showing cars of the early 20th century. The Conran Shop (see Furnishings & Household Goods in the Shopping chapter) is also housed here.

Brompton Oratory

Also known as the Oratory of St Philip Neri, this Roman Catholic church was built in the Italian baroque style in 1884. It is open daily from 6.30 am to 8 pm. There are six weekday Masses, one at 6 pm on Saturday and nine on Sunday between the hours of 7 am and 7 pm.

Victoria & Albert Museum

The Victoria & Albert Museum (☎ 7938 8500, 7938 8441 for a recording), Cromwell Rd SW7 (⊖ South Kensington), is a vast, rambling, wonderful museum of decorative art and design, part of Prince Albert's legacy to Londoners in the aftermath of the successful Great Exhibition of 1851 (see the boxed text 'Prince Albert & the Great Exhibition' under History in the Facts about London chapter).

Like the British Museum, this is one that needs careful planning if you're to get the most out of your visit. As soon as you're through the turnstile look at the floor plan and decide what you're most interested in; then stick to that plan unless you want to find the time has flown by and you're still inspecting the plaster casts of classical statues. Alternatively, take one of the free guided tours that introduce you to the galleries. Amazingly, most of the V&A's collection of

V&A Museum Highlights

- Raphael Cartoons
- Music Room from Norfolk House
- Morris, Gamble and Poynter Refreshment Rooms
- Tippoo's Tiger
- Shah Jahan's wine cup
- Throne of Maharaja Ranjit Singh
- Becket Casket
- Ironwork Gallery
- *Board and Bear Hunt* tapestry
- Henry VIII's writing desk
- Burghley Nef
- Gloucester Candlestick
- Pagoda
- Ardabil Carpet

four million items is actually on display, but you've no hope of seeing everything.

Orientation The V&A's main entrance is on Cromwell Rd although you can also enter from Exhibition Rd. Level A is mostly devoted to art and design from India, China, Japan and Korea, and to European art. There's a fine new room devoted to costume – everything from absurd 18th-century wigs and whalebone corsets to the platform shoes that brought Naomi Campbell crashing to the ground on a Paris catwalk.

The Raphael Gallery is devoted to seven cartoons by Raphael (1483-1520), not early satirical drawings but great paintings commissioned by Pope Leo X as designs for tapestries that now hang in the Vatican Museum. The finest are *Christ's Charge to Peter*, *The Miraculous Drought of Fishes* and *Paul Preaching at Athens*. Also on this floor are the V&A's three original refreshment rooms dating from the 1860s. The gorgeous Green Dining Room was designed by William Morris with help from his friend Edward Burne-Jones and is now named after the former. Next to it is the Gamble Room with elegant tiles, marble statuary and friezes with quotations from Ecclesiasticus, a book of the Bible. Finally there's the Poynter Room, designed by Edward Poynter and still with its grill for turning out chops.

On Level B you'll find collections of ironwork, stained glass, church plate and jewellery, together with a wonderful exhibition of musical instruments. In the British Galleries, some of which will be closed for redesign until late 2001, you may get to see the late 16th-century Great Bed of Ware, big enough to sleep five and designed as an early advertising gimmick for an inn in Hertfordshire. The highlights of this floor, though, are the Silver Galleries, even if silver isn't your thing. The goblets, chalices and assorted other gewgaws are displayed in a lovely Victorian gallery approached up a delightful tiled staircase, which was narrowly saved from destruction in the days when full-blown Victoriana was thought the height of bad taste.

On this floor you'll also find displays of textiles, arms and armour and 20th-century furniture, including the famous sofa in the shape of Mae West's lips (unless it's off on loan again). Up on Levels C and D are displays of British art and design, ceramics and porcelain from Europe and Asia.

The Henry Cole Wing, an add-on at the Exhibition Rd side of the museum, contains the largest collection of Constables gathered under one roof. It was a bequest from the artist's Charlotte St studios and contains mostly watercolours and minor oil paintings. Here you'll also find displays of prints and printmaking techniques as well as European paintings and miniatures. Construction is due to begin soon on a new zigzag-shaped extension called the Spiral, designed by Daniel Libeskind and as innovative and striking a modern structure as we've ever seen. When it opens in 2004 it will house temporary exhibitions rotated every two to three months and its two amphitheatres will show films.

The restaurant in the Henry Cole Wing serves snacks and light meals to keep you going; on Sunday there's also a jazz brunch (£8.50 or £9.50 including museum entry) between 11 am and 3 pm.

Hours & Tickets The museum is open daily from 10 am (on Sunday from 11 am) to 5.50 pm (and again on Wednesday from 6.30 to 9.30 pm). Admission costs £6/3 for adults/seniors (free for students and under-18s and for everyone after 4.30 pm); the late Wednesday session costs £3.

For the latest information on what's on at the museum you can visit its Web site at www.vam.ac.uk.

Guided Tours There are free introductory tours of the V&A lasting between one and 1½ hours to some of the museum's galleries between 10.30 am and 4.30 pm.

Natural History Museum

The Natural History Museum (☎ 7938 9123), Cromwell Rd SW7 (⊖ South Kensington), is one of London's finest neogothic buildings. It was designed by Alfred Waterhouse between 1873 and 1880 with a grand cathedral-like main entrance, a gleaming blue and sand-coloured brick and terracotta frontage, thin columns and articulated arches, and carvings of plants and animals crawling all over it.

The Natural History Museum now incorporates the old Geological Museum in Exhibition Rd; the two collections are divided between the adjoining Life and Earth Galleries. Where once the former was full of dusty glass cases of butterflies and stick insects, there are now wonderful interactive displays on themes like Human Biology and Creepy Crawlies,

---

Natural History Highlights

- Entrance to the Earth Galleries
- Simulated Kobe earthquake
- Creepy Crawlies display
- Dinosaurs' Feeding Time
- Minerals and gemstones in the Earth's Treasury
- Diplodocus dinosaur skeleton
- Blue whale model
- Wildlife Garden

alongside the crowd-pulling exhibition on mammals and dinosaurs, which includes animatronic movers and shakers like the new 4m-high Tyrannosaurus Rex. School children flock to see these, but luckily that eaves more space on the wondrous mammal balcony, at the Blue Whale exhibit and in the Ecology gallery (a replica rainforest).

In some ways though it's the Earth Galleries that are the most staggering. Enter from Exhibition Rd and you'll find yourself facing an escalator that slithers up and into a hollowed-out globe. Around its base, single fine samples of different rocks and gems are beautifully displayed. Upstairs there are two main exhibits: Earthquake and the Restless Surface, which explains how wind, water, ice, gravity and life itself impact on the earth. Earthquake is an extraordinary trembling mock-up of what happened to one small grocery shop during the Kobe trembler in Japan in 1995 that killed 6000 people. Excellent exhibitions on lower

Dinosaurs and creepy-crawlies: just some of the delights at the National History Museum.

floors include Earth Today and Tomorrow, which focuses on ecology; the Earth's Treasury, which looks at gems and other precious stones; and From the Beginning, which explores how planets are formed.

The Natural History Museum is open daily from 10 am to 5.50 pm (on Sunday from 11 am). Admission costs £6.50/3.50 for adults/seniors & students. It is free for those under 17, and for everyone after 4.30 pm on weekdays and after 5 pm at weekends. The museum's Web site is at www.nhm.ac.uk. To avoid the crowds it's best to visit early in the morning or late in the afternoon. There's a decent café ith some good selections for vegetarians.

Science Museum

The Science Museum (☎ 7942 4455), Exhibition Rd SW7 (✆ South Kensington), has had a complete makeover since the days when it was a rather dreary place for eggheads and reluctant school children. The ground floor looks back at the history of the Industrial Revolution via examples of its machinery and then looks forward to the exploration of space. There are enough old trains (including Puffing Billy, a steam locomotive dating from 1813) and vintage cars to keep the kids well and truly happy. Up a floor and you can find out about the impact of science on food, up another one and you're into the world of computers and nuclear power. The 3rd floor is the place to come for the old aeroplanes, among them the Vickers Vimy in which Alcock and Brown first flew the Atlantic in 1919, and Amy Johnson's *Gypsy Moth*, in which she flew to Australia in 1930. On the 4th and 5th floors you'll find exhibits relating to the history of medicine.

Look out for a modern version of Foucault's famous pendulum hanging in the hall. As the day wears on the pendulum seems to change direction. In fact, because the earth is moving beneath it, it really stays in the same place all the time. This is how Foucault illustrated how the earth rotates on its own axis.

The basement has imaginative hands-on

Science Museum Highlights

- Boulton & Watt's steam engine
- Foucault's Pendulum
- Apollo 10 Command Module
- Robert Stephenson's *Rocket*
- Gas-drilling rig
- Watson & Crick's DNA model
- Amy Johnson's *Gypsy Moth*
- Alcock & Brown's Vickers Vimy
- Wells Cathedral clock (1392)
- Pasteur's microscope

galleries for children: the Garden is for three to six-year-olds, Things for seven to 11-year-olds. The Secret Life of the Home, a collection of labour-saving appliances that householders have either embraced or shunned, is for everyone. The new Wellcome Wing focuses on contemporary science, medicine and technology and include a 450-seat IMAX cinema.

The Science Museum is open daily from 10 am to 6 pm. Admission costs £6.50/3.50 for adults/seniors & students (free for under-17s, and for everyone after 4.30 pm). You can visit its Web site at www.nmsi.ac.uk.

KNIGHTSBRIDGE, KENSINGTON & HOLLAND PARK (Map 5)

Knightsbridge is where you'll find some of London's best-known department stores, including Harrods and Harvey Nichols (see Department Stores in the Shopping chapter). To the west and north-west is Kensington, another thoroughly desirable London neighbourhood where you'll not get much change from a million pounds if you want to buy a sizeable house. Its main thoroughfare, Kensington High St, is another shoppers' paradise. North of Kensington High St is Holland Park, a residential district of elegant town houses, in the heart of which is the well wooded park, open from 7.30 am to dusk. Here you'll find a hostel in the Jacobean wing of the former Holland House (see YHA/HI Hostels in the Places to Stay chapter), some

delightful formal gardens (at their most glorious in summer), a playground and a restaurant. The old Orangery is often used as an exhibition space for young artists.

Albert Memorial

On the southern edge of Hyde Park facing Kensington Gore, the Albert Memorial (⊖ South Kensington or Gloucester Road) is an over-the-top monument to Queen Victoria's German husband Albert (1819-61), which was unwrapped in 1998 after an eight-year renovation costing £11 million. The 52.5m-high memorial was designed by George Gilbert Scott in 1863 and decorated with 178 figures representing the continents (Asia, Europe, Africa and America) as well as the arts, industry and science. The mosaics are the work of the renowned church artists Clayton and Bell. Albert is shown holding a copy of the catalogue of the 1851 Great Exhibition (see the boxed text 'Prince Albert & the Great Exhibition' under History in the Facts about London chapter). Guided tours (☎ 7495 0916) lasting 35 to 40 minutes depart on Friday and Saturday at 10 and 11 am and cost £3/2/50p for adults/seniors & students/children. The monument is very impressive at night when it is fully illuminated.

Royal Albert Hall

The huge red-brick amphitheatre facing the Albert Memorial on the other side of Kensington Gore is the Royal Albert Hall (☎ 7589 3203, 0891 500252 for a recording; ⊖ South Kensington), completed in 1871 and adorned with a frieze of Minton tiles. The hall was never intended as a concert venue but as a 'Hall of Arts and Sciences'; Queen Victoria added the 'Royal Albert' when she laid the foundation stone, much to the surprise of those attending. The management has been renovating the South Steps, the Queen's Box and the performers' dressing rooms as well as adding or expanding several bars and restaurants; parts may be still closed off.

The hall is best known for the Promenade Concerts (or 'Proms') held here every

The big frieze: the splendidly decorated Royal Albert Hall.

summer since 1947 (see Classical Music in the Entertainment chapter). Unfortunately, the only way to see inside is by attending a concert, and the acoustics are horrible; it is said that the only way a British composer can ever hear his work twice is by playing at the Royal Albert Hall, so bad is the echo reverberating around the oval structure.

Royal Geographical Society
A short distance to the east is the headquarters of the Royal Geographical Society (☎ 7591 3040), 1 Kensington Gore SW7 (⊖ South Kensington), a Queen Anne-style red-brick edifice (1874) easily identified by the statues of explorers David Livingstone (facing Kensington Gore) and Ernest Shackleton (facing Exhibition Rd) outside. There is a reading room (free) open to the public for map research on the ground floor, weekdays from 10 am to 5 pm.

Kensington Palace
Sometime home to Princess Margaret and the late Diana, Princess of Wales, Kensington Palace (☎ 7937 9561), Kensington Gardens W8 (⊖ High Street Kensington), dates from 1605 when it was home to the 2nd Earl of Nottingham. In 1688, when William of Orange arrived to take over as king from James II, he found the old palace at Whitehall confining and too close to the river to suit his asthmatic lungs; Queen Mary complained she could 'see nothing but water or wall'. They bought the house in the park from Nottingham and had it adapted by Sir Christopher Wren and Nicholas Hawksmoor. When George I arrived from Hanover to succeed Queen Anne, the childless last Stuart monarch, he recruited William Kent to modernise the palace. Much of the interior décor you see today is Kent's sometimes clumsy handiwork. Queen Victoria was born in a ground floor room here in 1819, and one room is preserved as a memorial to her, with a painting of her marriage to Prince Albert.

Hour-long tours of the palace take you round the small, wood-panelled State Apartments dating from the time of William and the much grander, more spacious apartments of the Georgian period.

Displayed under low lights in some of the rooms you'll see costumes from the Royal Dress Collection, including skirts so ludicrously wide that they made it impossible for their wearers to sit down and ensured that rooms had to be sparsely furnished.

Most striking of all is the **Cupola Room** where the ceremony of initiating men into the exclusive Order of the Garter took place; you can see the order's crest painted on the trompe l'oeil 'domed' ceiling, which is essentially flat. The room is ringed with marbled columns and niches in which stand gilded statues in the Roman style. In the centre of the room an ugly clock stands on a stepped plinth. It used to play the music of Handel and Corelli but no more.

The **King's Long Gallery** displays some of the royal art collection, including the only known painting of a classical subject by Van Dyck. On the ceiling William Kent painted the story of Odysseus but slipped up by giving the Cyclops two eyes!

The **King's Drawing Room** is dominated by an extraordinarily ugly painting of *Cupid and Venus* by Giorgio Vasari (1511-74), an Italian mannerist painter better known for his history of Italian Renaissance art. Through the window you can see the **Round Pond**, once full of turtles for turtle soup but now popular for sailing model boats, and a statue of the young Queen Victoria, sculpted by her daughter, Princess Louise.

The **King's Staircase** is decorated with striking murals by William Kent who painted himself in a turban on the fake dome. A prominent figure of a Highlander was included at a time when the threat from the Jacobites in Scotland was by no means dead. Also included is a portrait of Peter, the 'wild child' who had been discovered in the woods of Hanover and brought to England to entertain the jaded court.

The **Sunken Garden** near the palace is at its prettiest in summer. Also nearby is the Orangery, designed by Hawksmoor and Vanbrugh and with carvings by Grinling Gibbons. Tea here is a pricey treat (see the boxed text 'Tea for Two or More' in the Places to Eat chapter).

The State Apartments are open daily from 10 am to 5 pm. Admission costs £8/6.70/6.10 for adults/seniors & students/children (family £26.10). The park and gardens are open from 5 am to 30 minutes before dusk.

Linley Sambourne House

Tucked away behind Kensington High St is Linley Sambourne House (☎ 8994 1019), 18 Stafford Terrace W8 (✪ High Street Kensington), home from 1874 to 1910 of the *Punch* political cartoonist Linley Sambourne. This is one of those houses whose owners never redecorated or threw anything away; what you see is the virtually unmodernised home of a reasonably well-to-do Victorian family, all dark wood, Turkish carpets and rich stained glass.

The house is open on Wednesday from 10 am to 4 pm and on Sunday from 2 to 5 pm, March to October. Admission costs £3/2.50/1.50.

Commonwealth Institute

On the southern side of Holland Park just off Kensington High St, an open space with fountains and flagpoles fronts the Commonwealth Institute (☎ 7603 4535; ✪ High Street Kensington), designed in 1962 to resemble a large tent and created from materials gathered from all over the British Commonwealth. It looks as horrid as it sounds. The rather pedestrian interior is being revamped to extol the virtues of the 50-odd countries making up the Commonwealth; its exhibition (the Commonwealth Experience), spread over three floors, has closed for a refit and will reopen in 2002.

Leighton House

Near Holland Park and Kensington but frequently overlooked is Leighton House (Map 9; ☎ 7602 3316), 12 Holland Park Rd W14 (✪ High Street Kensington), a gem of a house designed in 1866 by George Aitchison. It was once the home of Lord Leighton (1830-96), a painter who belonged to the Olympian movement and decorated parts of the house in Middle Eastern style. Finest of all the rooms is the exquisite **Arab Hall**, added in 1879 and densely covered with blue and green tiles from Rhodes, Cairo, Damascus and Iznik (Turkey) and with a fountain tinkling away in the centre. Even the wooden latticework of the windows and gallery came from Damascus. The house contains notable pre-Raphaelite paintings by Burne-Jones, Watts, Millais and Lord Leighton himself. Restoration of the back garden has returned it to its Victorian splendour but work continues apace on the upstairs studio.

Leighton House (free, donations welcome) is open Monday to Saturday from 11 am to 5.30 pm.

NOTTING HILL & BAYSWATER (Map 5)

The great popularity of the Notting Hill Carnival on the last weekend of August reflects the multicultural appeal of this area of west London. In the 1950s Notting Hill became a focus for immigrants from Trinidad. Today it's a thriving, vibrant corner of London separated from the West End and Mayfair by the great expanse of Hyde Park and best visited on Saturday for the Portobello Rd

CHARLOTTE HINDLE

Don't believe the hype: Notting Hill has more to offer than posh accents and floppy haircuts.

Market (see the special section 'The Markets of London' after the Shopping chapter).

There's not a heck of a lot to see in Notting Hill – though you may get a kick out of trying to recognise a few locations from the hit film *Notting Hill*, starring Hugh Grant and Julia Roberts (the place where William Thacker lives in the film – the one with the blue door – is in fact on Westbourne Park Rd, not Portobello Rd). You might also check out how the ambitious refurbishment of the Edwardian **Electric Cinema** at 195 Portobello Rd is progressing (see Cinemas in the Entertainment chapter).

The site of a spring (Baynard's Watering) that supplied the City of London with fresh water in the Middle Ages, Bayswater was given wide berth for centuries due to the proximity of the gallows at Tyburn (see Marble Arch in the following Hyde Park Area section). Today it is a fairly well-to-do and convenient residential area sitting uncomfortably close to scruffy Paddington. Its main thoroughfare is Queensway, which has a decent selection of restaurants, mostly Chinese. Come to Bayswater on Sunday to view the paintings (mostly derivative touristy stuff) on sale on the railings of Hyde Park and Kensington Gardens along Bayswater Rd or to unwind in the Porchester Spa (see Public Baths under Activities later in this chapter).

HYDE PARK AREA (Maps 5 & 6)

At the far western end of Piccadilly, Hyde Park is one of those areas where posh hotels and prestigious shops have long since squeezed out the hoi polloi. If you're driving, you'd do well to avoid the nightmare of the Hyde Park Corner roundabout – although trying to find the right exit from the Underground isn't much easier.

Hyde Park

At 145 hectares, Hyde Park (Map 5) is central London's largest open space. Expropriated from the Church by Henry VIII in 1536, it became a hunting ground for kings and aristocrats, and then a venue for duels, executions and horse racing. In 1851 the Great Exhibition was held here (see the boxed text 'Prince Albert & the Great Exhibition' under History in the Facts about London chapter) and during WWII it became an enormous potato field. More recently, it has served as a concert venue. The park is a riot of colour in spring, and full of lazy, milk-white to pink sunbathers in summer. Boating on the Serpentine is an option for the relatively energetic.

Along with sculptures by Henry Moore and Jacob Epstein, and the statue of Peter Pan by George Frampton, Hyde Park boasts its own art gallery. The **Serpentine Gallery** (Map 5; ☎ 7402 6075, ✆ Hyde Park Corner or Lancaster Gate), beautifully located south of the lake and just west of the main road that cuts through the park, holds temporary exhibitions and specialises in contemporary art, displaying the work of such artists as William Kentridge, Bridget Riley and Andreas Gursky. The gallery (free) is open daily from 10 am to 6 pm.

Near Marble Arch, **Speakers' Corner** (Map 5; ✆ Marble Arch) started life in 1872 as a response to serious riots. Every Sunday anyone with a soapbox – or anything else to stand on – can hold forth on whatever subject takes their fancy. Provided you don't go along expecting Churchillian oratory, it's an entertaining experience.

Hyde Park is open daily from 5.30 am till midnight.

Marble Arch

In the north-eastern corner of Hyde Park is Marble Arch (Map 5; ✆ Marble Arch), a huge arch designed by John Nash in 1827 that was moved here from in front of Buckingham Palace in 1851. There is actually a one-room flat inside.

At the junction of Edgware Rd and Bayswater Rd stood the so-called **Tyburn Tree** (Map 5), the three-legged gallows where up to 50,000 people were executed between 1300 and 1783. Many of them had been dragged to the scaffold from the Tower of London or Newgate Prison in the City. Farther west along Bayswater Rd at 8 Hyde

Stranded at the end of Oxford St, Marble Arch is London's most elegant traffic island.

Park Place is **Tyburn Convent** (☎ 7723 7262), whose chapel contains relics of 105 Catholic martyrs executed at Tyburn during the Reformation (notice the victims' coats of arms on the walls). Free 40-minute tours take place daily at 10.30 am and 3.30 and 5.30 pm.

Apsley House (Wellington Museum)

Striking Apsley House (Map 6; ☎ 7499 5676; ✆ Hyde Park Corner), with the prestigious address of No 1 London but overlooking the nightmarish Hyde Park Corner roundabout, was designed by Robert Adam between 1771 and 1778 for Baron Apsley. It was sold in 1817 to the 1st Duke of Wellington, victor at the Battle of Waterloo and later prime minister. In 1947 the house was given to the nation and today it houses the Wellington Museum (☎ 7499 5676). Unlike most 18th-century London town houses, Apsley House retains many of its original furnishings and collections and still has descendants of the original family in residence.

The ground floor displays an astonishing collection of china, including a dinner service decorated with Egyptian scenes, and some of the Iron Duke's silverware, including the stunning Waterloo Vase and Shield. The stairwell is dominated by Canova's staggering 3.4m-high statue of Napoleon, naked but for the obligatory fig leaf. 'Rather too athletic', opined the subject when it was unveiled. The 1st floor rooms have fine plaster ceilings and a collection of paintings by Velásquez, Goya, Rubens, Brueghel and Murillo. The basement gallery contains Wellington memorabilia, including his medals and some entertaining old cartoons.

The Wellington Museum is open Tuesday to Sunday from 11 am to 5 pm. Admission costs £4.50/3 for adults/concessions.

MARYLEBONE & REGENT'S PARK (Maps 3, 5 & 6)

Marylebone Rd is north of Oxford St and home to the capital's No 1 tourist trap, Madame Tussaud's. It's also close to Regent's Park, which provides a haven of peace in the city as well as being home to London Zoo.

Wallace Collection

The Wallace Collection (Map 6; ☎ 7935 0687), Hertford House, Manchester Square W1 (⊖ Bond Street), is London's finest small gallery and relatively unknown. It houses a treasure trove of high-quality paintings from the 17th and 18th centuries, including works by Rubens, Titian, Poussin and Rembrandt, in a splendid Italianate mansion. There's also a collection of elaborate armour. The exquisite classical building is worth a visit in itself, and the staircase is reckoned to be one of the best examples of French interior architecture; it was intended for the Banque Royale in Paris but was bought by Richard Wallace and installed here in 1874. Vast canvases by Frances Boucher adorn the stairwell.

The collection was bequeathed to the nation at the end of the 19th century. Four new galleries are slated to open in the basement soon, at which time the collection will become a national museum. The courtyard will be roofed over with glass to create a year-round sculpture garden.

The collection (free) is open Monday to Saturday from 10 am to 5 pm, on Sunday from 2 to 5 pm. Free guided tours take place daily; phone for the exact times. You can also check the museum's Web site at www.demon .co.uk/heritage/wallace for details.

Madame Tussaud's

Madame Tussaud's (Map 5; ☎ 7935 6861), Marylebone Rd NW1 (⊖ Baker Street), is the third-most popular sight in London (after the British Museum and the National Gallery), counting some 2.7 million visitors a year. In order to avoid the long queues (particularly in summer), arrive early in the morning or late in the afternoon or – better still – buy your tickets in advance from a ticket agency.

Madame Tussaud's – or Madame Tussaud's Waxworks as it was once known – dates back two and a half centuries and Mme T herself started life modelling the heads of people killed during the French Revolution; the 200 Years exhibition shows her working on a death mask from the head of Marie Antoinette in her original studio.

Much of the modern Madame Tussaud's is made up of the **Garden Party** exhibition where you can have your picture taken alongside stars like Pierce Brosnan. The **Grand Hall** is where you'll find models of world leaders past and present, of the Royal Family (now minus Sarah 'Fergie' Ferguson, the disgraced Duchess of York, and with Diana, Princess of Wales, on the sidelines) and of pop stars like the Beatles. And what happens to those whose 15 minutes of fame has ticked by? Their heads are removed as surely as Marie Antoinette's was and stored in a cupboard – just in case they get another stab at those 15 minutes.

In the **Spirit of London** 'time taxi', you sit in a mock-up of a London black cab and are whipped through a five-minute summary of London's history. The models are great but it's irritating if you land the cab whose commentary is still dealing with the Great Fire as you're passing the Swinging London panorama.

The revamped **Chamber of Horrors** has models of contemporary prisoners like Dennis Nilsen (the 'Muswell Hill Murderer') sitting uneasily alongside representations of historic horrors like the mutilated corpse of one of Jack the Ripper's victims. But it all seems somewhat tame compared with the London Dungeon's blood-fest.

SIMON BRACKEN

Don't go in the shower: an audience with Hitch at Madame Tussaud's.

Madame Tussaud's is open daily from 9 am to 5.30 pm, June to mid-September. During the rest of the year it opens weekdays from 10 am to 5.30 pm and at weekends from 9.30 am. Tickets cost £10/7.50/6.50 for adults/seniors/under-16s. A combined ticket allowing entry to the London Planetarium (see below) as well costs £12.25/9.30/8.

London Planetarium

Attached to Madame Tussaud's, the London Planetarium (Map 5) presents 30-minute spectaculars on the stars and planets livened up with some fairly impressive special effects. While you're waiting for the show to begin you can have a look at waxworks of the great scientists from Copernicus to Stephen Hawkings and find out more about the universe on assorted computer consoles.

The planetarium keeps the same hours as Madame Tussaud's. Entry costs £6/4.60/4 for adults/seniors/under-16s. A combined ticket allowing entry to Madame Tussaud's as well is £12.25/9.30/8.

Baker Street Underground Station

The train (station) spotters among you – and we know you're out there – will be interested (make that ecstatic, positively light-headed) to learn that one of the original stations of the first underground train line in the world (the Metropolitan Railway) lies underfoot at Baker Street station (Map 5) and can be visited simply by buying an Underground ticket or using your travel pass. Baker Street, one of the seven original stations on the line that stretched for all of about 6km (3¾ miles) from Paddington to Farringdon St, opened in 1863. It's on platform Nos 5 and 6 (Circle and Hammersmith & City lines) and was restored to its dimly lit former self in 1983.

Sherlock Holmes Museum

While the Sherlock Holmes Museum (Map 5; ☎ 7935 8866) gives its address as 221b Baker St, the house in which Sherlock Holmes supposedly resided is actually the Abbey National building a bit farther south on the corner with Melcombe St. Fans of the books will enjoy looking at the three floors of reconstructed Victoriana, but the building is too small to cope comfortably with the summer crowds. At £5/3 for adults/under-15s, it's also expensive. The museum is open daily from 9.30 am to 5.30 pm.

Regent's Park

Regent's Park (Map 3; ⊖ Baker Street or Regent's Park), north of Marylebone and south-west of Camden, was, like many other London parks, once used as a royal hunting ground, subsequently farmed and then revived as a place for fun and leisure during the 18th century.

ED HILLYER

Chilling out in one of north London's wide open spaces.

With the London Zoo, the **Grand Union Canal** along its northern side, an **open-air theatre** where Shakespeare is performed during the summer months, ponds and colourful flower beds, football pitches and summer games of softball, Regent's Park is a lively but serene, local but cosmopolitan haven in the heart of the city. The roses in **Queen Mary's Gardens** are particularly spectacular, and there's an adjoining café.

On the western side of the park is the impressive **London Central Islamic Centre & Mosque**, a huge white edifice with a glistening dome. Provided you take your shoes off and dress modestly you're welcome to go inside, although the interior is fairly stark.

To the north of Regent's Park, across Prince Albert Rd, is **Primrose Hill**, which, besides being less touristy and less conventionally pretty, also has a spectacular view over London

London Zoo

One of the oldest zoos in the world, London Zoo (Map 3; ☎ 7722 3333), Regent's Park NW1 (⊖ Camden Town), is – like the London Underground – a victim of its great age; it was 170 years old in 1998. During WWII, most of the wild animals here were put down as it was feared that they might escape if the zoo was bombed. The rest were evacuated to Ireland. Zoo staff took the tropical fish home for supper.

The zoo is saddled with many buildings

that are historically interesting but don't meet the expectations of animal-rights-minded modern visitors. After a long period in the doldrums, the zoo has now embarked on a 10-year, £21 million programme to prepare it for the third millennium. The emphasis is now firmly on conservation and education, with fewer species kept, wherever possible in breeding groups.

The new **Web of Life**, a glass pavilion containing 65 live animal exhibits (from termites and jellyfish to the birds and the bees), has interactive displays and, yes, real-life, on-show breeding groups. It makes a visit to the zoo worthwhile by itself. Elsewhere don't miss the enclosures housing the big cats, the elephants and rhinos, the apes and monkeys, the small mammals and the birds. The revamped Mappin Terraces house the bears; the elegant and cheerful **Penguin Pool** is one of London's foremost modernist structures, designed by Berthold Lubetkin in 1934.

The zoo is open daily from 10 am to 5.30 pm, March to October, and from 10 am to 4 pm, November to February. Admission costs £9/8/7 for adults/seniors & students/ children aged four to 14 (family £28).

The nicest way to get to the zoo is by canal boat from Little Venice or Camden (see Canal Trips in the Getting Around chapter), but you can also walk along the canal towpath.

North London

The northern reaches of central London stretch in a broad arc from St John's Wood in the west to Islington in the east. Those two districts exemplify the great economic divide that exists in the capital: the former is all moneyed gentility, the latter the run-down opposite in areas around Angel, where less than 10% of the area is open public space. In between, Regent's Park and its Primrose Hill northerly extension offer the largest expanse of greenery. The Grand Union (Regent's) Canal winds round the north of the park, offering a pleasant way to avoid the traffic en route to Camden Market. North London's other main attractions are Hampstead Heath, where it's as easy to forget you're in a big city as it is to get completely lost; the Victorian Valhalla of Highgate Cemetery; and – for football fans (but not for long) – Wembley Stadium.

ST JOHN'S WOOD & MAIDA VALE (Maps 2 & 3)

Posh St John's Wood, a leafy suburb of genteel houses to which the comfortably off retreat, is due west of Regent's Park. Art lovers may want to detour here to visit the Saatchi Gallery, one of the more cutting-edge art collections in London, and pop fans will head for 3 Abbey Rd NW8, where the Beatles recorded 80% of their albums, including *Abbey Road* (1969) itself with its cover shot taken on the zebra crossing outside (Map 3). Cricket lovers will instead want to hotfoot it to Lord's Cricket Ground. Slightly south-west are Maida Vale and Little Venice, the place to come for canal trips to London Zoo and Camden (see Canal Trips in the Getting Around chapter).

Saatchi Gallery

The Saatchi Gallery (Map 2; ☎ 7624 8299), 98a Boundary Rd NW8 (✆ Kilburn Park), is the private collection of contemporary art owned by Charles Saatchi, until recently co-chairman of Saatchi & Saatchi, once the world's biggest advertising agency.

This is not the place to come if your tastes run to Constable or Turner. Here you're more likely to find yourself confronting giant pools of oil reflecting the ceiling or models of human figures so lifelike you're almost afraid they'll jump and start talking. It was Saatchi who patronised Damien Hirst, the formaldehyde king, and Rachel Whiteread, who turned an entire house into a work of sculpture only to see it torn down shortly afterwards. The exhibition space is light-filled, airy and large.

The gallery is open Thursday to Sunday from noon to 6 pm; admission costs £4/2.

Lord's Cricket Ground

Daily tours of Lord's Cricket Ground (Map 3; ☎ 7432 1033), St John's Wood Rd NW8 (✆ St John's Wood), take in the famous Long Room, where members watch the games surrounded by portraits of cricket's great and good. There's also a museum that contains cricket memorabilia and offers cricket fans the chance to pose next to the famous little urn containing the Ashes – however many times Australia wins the Ashes, they still remain in English hands. In the grounds look out for the famous weather-vane in the shape of Old Father Time and the lovely modern Mound Stand (see the special section 'London's Contemporary Architecture' after the Facts about London chapter). Tours leave from the Grace Gates on St John's Wood Rd daily at 10 am, noon and 2 pm from April to September, and at noon and 2pm only October to March (there are no tours when major matches are on). They cost £5.80/4.20 and last 1½ hours.

EUSTON & KING'S CROSS (Maps 3 & 4)

Euston Rd links Euston train station to St Pancras and King's Cross stations. This is not an especially inviting area to visit although it's one that you're likely to pass through en route to or from the north of England. Attractions are thin on the ground, although the recently restored St Pancras station is a Victorian masterpiece and the long-awaited British Library has finally opened its doors to readers and visitors alike.

What would have been the most imposing sight at Euston was the vast Great Hall of Philip Hardwick's original Euston station, the world's first, and its portico with four Doric columns at the entrance. It was ripped down in the 1960s before the conservation movement caught on in London and flamboyant Victorian buildings were generally viewed with suspicion. Outrage at this act of vandalism was a spur to the creation of the Victorian Society.

Although some effort has been made to clear up the street prostitution and drug-dealing around King's Cross, this is still a distinctly seedy district best avoided after dark.

St Pancras New Church

The striking Greek Revival St Pancras New Church (Map 3), Upper Woburn Place WC1, has a tower designed to imitate the Temple of the Winds in Athens, a portico with six Ionic columns like the Erechtheion on the Acropolis and a wing decorated with caryatids, again like the Erechtheion. When it was completed in 1822 this was the most expensive new church to have been built in London since St Paul's Cathedral. It's frequently locked but within the porch you can see a large tablet in memory of the 31 people who lost their lives in the King's Cross tube station fire of November 1987.

British Library

After 15 years and £500 million (the most expensive building in the UK after the Millennium Dome), the new British Library (Map 3; ☎ 7412 7000), 96 Euston Rd NW1 (✚ King's Cross St Pancras), designed by Colin St John Wilson, opened its doors in 1998. It is the nation's principal copyright library and stocks one copy of every British publication as well as historical manuscripts, books and maps from the British Museum. As usual, London was split down the middle on the building's architectural merits, those calling it 'stark' and 'prison-like' balanced by those who (like us) think its clean lines,

British Library Highlights

DOUG McKINLAY

- Magna Carta
- Sherborne Missal
- Gutenberg Bible
- Shakespeare's First Folio
- Sforza Book of Hours
- Lindisfarne Gospels
- Leonardo da Vinci notebook
- *Alice's Adventures Under Ground* manuscript by Lewis Carroll
- *Summer Is Icumen In* poem
- Illustrated *Puss in Boots*
- Penny Black stamp

red-brick exterior and vaguely Asian elements complement St Pancras train station next door very nicely indeed.

The library already counts some 325km of shelved books on four basement levels, and will have some 12 million volumes when it reaches the limit of its storage capacity. At the heart of the building is the wonderful **King's Library**, the 65,000 volume collection of the insane George III, given to the nation by his son, George IV, in 1823 and now housed in a six-storey, 17m-high glass-walled tower. To the left as you enter are the library's bookshop and three exhibition galleries.

Subtitled 'Treasures of the British Library', the **John Ritblat Gallery** spans almost three millennia and every continent. Among the most important documents here are the Magna Carta (1215); the Sherborne Missal, the supreme masterpiece of English book painting (1400-07); a Gutenberg Bible

(1455), the first western book printed using movable type; Shakespeare's First Folio (1623); manuscripts by some of Britain's best-known authors (eg Lewis Carroll, Jane Austen, George Eliot and Thomas Hardy); and *Summer Is Icumen In*, the earliest known example of poetry in English (13th century). The Turning the Pages exhibit allows you to browse through several important texts – the Sforza Book of Hours, the Lindisfarne Gospels, the Diamond Sutra and a Leonardo da Vinci notebook – by touching a computer screen.

The **Pearson Gallery of Living Words** groups documents around five themes. The Story of Writing examines the way in which we communicate via the written word and how different forms of writing have developed, using materials from a vast range of periods and cultures. It also looks at the future of writing. In Children's Books, a diorama depicts classic children's stories from Robinson Crusoe to Alice in Wonderland. The Scientific Record contains first editions of works by Charles Darwin, Sir Isaac Newton and William Harvey and examines the vast engineering projects of Isambard Kingdom Brunel, who built – among other things – the Great Western Railway between London and Bristol and designed Paddington station. Bill Bryson, American author of *Notes from a Small Island*, takes visitors around the UK in the late 1990s in the Images of Britain section, which also looks at the journeys and travels of medieval pilgrims. The Art of the Book includes such sumptuous examples as Chinese calligraphy scrolls wrapped in silk, a lavishly illustrated manuscript of the Ramayana and masterpieces of scribes' and printers' artistry from western and Asian manuscripts and printed books.

The library's **Philatelic Exhibition** is based on collections established in 1891 with the bequest of the Tapling Collection and that now consist of over eight million items, including postage and revenue stamps, postal stationery and first-day covers from almost every country and from all periods.

The British Library (free) is open to visitors weekdays from 9.30 am to 6 pm (on Tuesday to 8 pm), on Saturday from 9.30 am to 5 pm and on Sunday from 11 am to 5 pm. The bookshop is particularly good. The library's Web site is at www.bl.uk.

St Pancras Station

Together with the Houses of Parliament, St Pancras train station is the pinnacle of the Victorian Gothic revival. Whether you go for the style or not, beautifully restored St Pancras is something special: there's a dramatic glass-and-iron train shed at the back, engineered by the great Brunel, and a fantastically pinnacled hotel designed by George Gilbert Scott at the front.

Though the train station is still active (it *may* end up as the terminus of Eurostar services to/from continental Europe by 2003), the hotel has been disused for years.

From the sublime to the sleazy: St Pancras station viewed from King's Cross.

ISLINGTON & STOKE NEWINGTON (Maps 1 & 4)

Islington is an up-and-coming area of northeast London that you're most likely to visit in order to eat in one of Upper St's many restaurants or to take in a show at the Almeida Theatre (see Islington in the Places to Eat chapter and Theatre in the Entertainment chapter). Antique-lovers will also want to explore Camden Passage antiques market (not to be confused with the better known Camden Market in Camden Town), which is described in the special section 'The Markets of London' after the Shopping chapter. There's also a fine museum of Italian art here.

Islington's literary associations are legion. George Orwell was living at 27 Canonbury Square the year he published *Animal Farm* (1945). The playwright Joe Orton (1933-67) had been living at 25 Noel Rd for seven years when his lover, Kenneth Halliwell, bludgeoned him to death and then committed suicide.

Stoke Newington likes to pass itself off as 'village London with an international flavour' and that's more or less true; villages can be dirty and noisy (but the causes are usually the dirt you grow things in and the mooing and neighing of farmyard animals) and Stoke Newington Church St is chock-a-block with shops, pubs and ethnic restaurants. Daniel Defoe wrote *Robinson Crusoe* and *Moll Flanders* while living in a house at No 95, and Abney Park Cemetery, the 'poor man's Highgate', might be worth a look.

Estorick Collection of Modern Italian Art

The Estorick Collection (Map 4; ☎ 7704 9522), 39A Canonbury Square N1, with its entrance on Canonbury Rd (⊖ Highbury & Islington), housed in a lovely Georgian town house, focuses on futurism (*futurismo* in Italian), an early 20th-century artistic movement centred in Italy that responded to the pace of technological development. The collection of paintings, drawings, etchings and sculpture, amassed by American writer and art dealer Eric Estorick and his wife Salome, includes works by such greats as Giacomo Balla, Umberto Boccioni, Carlo Carrà, Gino Severini, Luigi Russolo and Ardengo Soffici. It's a fine collection of an arguably minor school of art; you could be forgiven for thinking the museum should be named the Esoteric Collection. The Café Panini, with seating in the back garden, serves lunch and snacks, and there is a branch of the Zwemmer art bookshop.

The Estorick Collection is open Wednesday to Saturday from 11 am to 6 pm and on Sunday from noon to 5 pm. Admission costs £3.50/2.50 for adults/concessions. The collection's Web site is at www .estorickcollection.com.

Abney Park Cemetery

Overgrown and spooky Abney Park Cemetery (Map 1; ☎ 7275 7557), Stoke Newington Church St N16 (Stoke Newington station; bus No 73), once the burial ground for nonconformists and laid out in 1840, contains – among many others – the tomb of General William Booth, founder of the Salvation Army. The cemetery (free) is open daily from 8 am till dusk, April to September.

CAMDEN & KENTISH TOWN (Map 3)

From Euston station you can walk up Eversholt St to Camden, a tourist mecca that is especially lively at weekends. Some two decades ago Camden Town was home to a large Irish community, but yuppification has changed all that and nowadays parts of it, at the Chalk Farm end in particular, blend in more with the sedate middle-class character of Hampstead to the north. Not that you'll notice if you just come for the market.

North of Camden, Kentish Town has been solidly working class since the 1860s with the arrival of the Midland Railway. Still, it has a few claims to fame. Karl Marx, the artist Ford Madox Ford and George Orwell all lived here at various stages, and it's now home to the London office of Lonely Planet.

Camden High St groans under the weight of its quirky shops and off-the-wall boutiques.

Camden Market

In just over 20 years Camden Market has developed into London's most visited 'unticketed' tourist attraction, with some 10 million visitors a year. What started out as a collection of attractive craft stalls by Camden Lock on the Grand Union Canal now extends most of the way from Camden Town tube station to Chalk Farm tube station to the north. How much you like it probably depends on your tolerance for crowds, but the junky stalls at the Camden end and the sight of people gorging themselves on sausages and chips out of polystyrene boxes is not a pretty sight.

The best time to see the market in full swing is at weekends – Sunday is particularly busy. But if crowds and mayhem aren't your idea of fun, a few of the stalls open throughout the week, increasing in number on Thursday and Friday.

If you arrive at Camden Town tube station, take the right-hand exit and turn right again on to Camden High St (which becomes Chalk Farm Rd). For more details see the special section 'The Markets of London' after the Shopping chapter.

To escape the crowds, head for the canal towpath, which is a lovely walk, especially heading west past London Zoo to Little Venice in Maida Vale. For details of boat trips see Canal Trips in the Getting Around chapter.

Jewish Museum

This Jewish Museum (☎ 7284 1997), Raymond Burton House, 129-131 Albert St NW1 (⊖ Camden Town), examines Judaism in the Ceremonial Art Gallery and the story of the Jewish community in Britain in the History Gallery. There's also a gallery for temporary exhibitions. It's open Sunday to Thursday from 10 am to 4 pm. Admission costs £3/2/1.50 for adults/seniors/students & children up to 13 years (family £7.50).

The museum's branch in Finchley (Map 1; ☎ 8349 1143), 80 East End Rd N3 (⊖ Finchley Central), houses the museum's social-history collections and hosts changing exhibitions. Its permanent collection includes reconstructions of tailoring and cabinet-making workshops and an East End immigrant home as well as a Holocaust exhibition focusing on the experience of one Jewish Briton who survived Auschwitz. It is open Monday to Thursday from 10.30 am to 5 pm and on Sunday to 4.30 pm. Admission costs around £2/1 (free for children) but depends on what's being exhibited.

You can visit the museum's Web site at www.jewmusm.ort.org.

HAMPSTEAD & HIGHGATE (Map 11)

Perched on a hill 6.5km north of the City, Hampstead is an exclusive suburb, attached to an enormous, rambling heath, that just about gets away with calling itself a village. You can lose yourself on Hampstead Heath and forget that you're in one of the world's largest, noisiest cities.

Famous people have been making their home in Hampstead since the 17th century, among them the poets Coleridge, Keats and Pope; Charles II's mistress, Nell Gwyn; General Charles de Gaulle during WWII in a convent at 99 Frognal; Sigmund Freud; painters John Constable and William Hogarth. More recent inhabitants include actress-turned-politician Glenda Jackson, Noel Gallagher of Oasis and Boy George.

Hampstead Heath

Hampstead Heath (✆ Hampstead; Gospel Oak or Hampstead Heath station) covers 320 hectares, most of it woods, hills and meadows, and is home to some one hundred species of bird. Some sections of the heath are laid out for sports like football and cricket. There are several bathing ponds, but they're only recommended for strong, competent swimmers (see Swimming in the Activities section later in this chapter). Walk up Parliament Hill or the hill in North Wood, and on a clear day you'll see Canary Wharf and even the Millennium Dome.

For a drink after walking, the two best-known pubs are the Spaniard's Inn and Jack Straw's Castle (see Pubs & Bars in the Entertainment chapter); both played their part in famous uprisings. Jack Straw's Castle is named after Wat Tyler's brother-in-arms of the Peasants' Revolt (though the building only dates from the 1970s), while some of the Gordon Rioters of 1780 popped into the Spaniard's Inn for a quick one before continuing on to attack Kenwood House.

By night Hampstead Heath is a gay cruising ground and the activities therein are generally overlooked by the authorities. In 1999 the local council approved a plan to renovate a Victorian **lavatory** built in 1897 on South End Green, just opposite Hampstead Heath station. This was gay playwright Joe Orton's toilet of choice for cottaging (cruising for gay sex). Author George Orwell worked in a bookshop opposite the lavatories and doubtless used them once or twice for what they were intended.

Kenwood House This magnificent neo-classical mansion (✆ 8348 1286), Hampstead Lane NW3 (✆ Archway or Golders Green, then bus No 210), on the northern side of the heath, was remodelled by Robert Adam from 1764 to 1779. It is crammed with paintings by Gainsborough, Reynolds, Turner, Lely, Hals, Vermeer and Van Dyck, and outside has sculptures by Henry Moore (eg *Two Piece Reclining Figure*, 1964) and Barbara Hepworth; it is arguably the finest small collection of European art in London. Adam's Great Stairs and his Library, one of 14 rooms open to the public, are especially fine. Kenwood House (free) is open daily from 10 am to 6 pm, April to September, closing at 5 pm in March and October and 4 pm the rest of the year. There's a pub-restaurant called the Brew House and the Garden Café for light snacks and tea.

Keats' House

A stone's throw from the lower reaches of the heath, this elegant Regency house (✆ 7435 2062), Wentworth Place, Keats Grove NW3 (✆ Hampstead; Hampstead Heath station), was home to the golden boy of the Romantic poets. Never short of generous mates, Keats was persuaded to take refuge here by Charles Armitage Brown from 1818 to 1820 and it's here that he met his fiancée Fanny Brawne. Sitting under a plum tree in the garden in 1819, Keats wrote his most celebrated poem, *Ode to a Nightingale*. Apart from many mementoes, including original manuscripts and Keats' collection of works by Shakespeare and Chaucer, you can also peek at some of his love letters.

The house (free, donations welcome) is open Monday to Friday from 10 am to 1 pm and 2 to 6 pm, closing at 5 pm on Saturday and all morning on Sunday, from April to

RACHEL BLACK

A poetic hideaway: Keats' House in Hampstead.

small art gallery. Admission is free, but it's only open Wednesday to Sunday from noon to 5 pm. The Buttery basement tearoom serves a decent lunch for £5 from 11 am to 5.30 pm.

Fenton House

One of Hampstead's oldest houses, Fenton House (☎ 7435 3471), Windmill Hill, Hampstead Grove NW3 (⊖ Hampstead), is a late 17th-century merchant's residence with a large walled garden and a fine collection of keyboard instruments, including a harpsichord from 1612 played by Handel. It's open at weekends from 2 to 5 pm in March; and Wednesday to Friday from 2 to 5 pm and at weekends from 11 am to 5 pm, April to October. Admission costs £4.10/2.05 for adults/children (family £10.25, free for NT members).

Freud Museum

Sigmund Freud lived at 20 Maresfield Gardens NW3 (Map 3; ☎ 7435 2002; ⊖ Finchley Road) for the last 18 months of his life after it became clear that it would no longer be safe for him to remain in Nazi-occupied Vienna in 1938. The house, on a quiet, tree-lined residential street, contains the psychiatrist's original couch, together with all his Greek and Asian artefacts and, of course, his books. A photo shows how carefully he attempted to reproduce his Viennese home in the unfamiliar surroundings of London. Later the house was occupied by Freud's daughter, Anna, a child psychologist of note.

The Freud Museum is open Wednesday to Sunday from noon to 5 pm. Admission costs £4/2. A small shop sells all sorts of histories, biographies and books to do with all aspects of the psyche. You can visit the museum's Web site at www.freud.org.uk.

Highgate Cemetery

This is the final resting place for Karl Marx, the novelist Mary Anne Evans (aka George Eliot), Michael Faraday and lots of other ordinary mortals. Highgate Cemetery (☎ 8340 1834), Swain's Lane N6 (⊖ Highgate), has 20 wild, hectic hectares

October. The rest of the year it opens from 1 to 5 pm only on weekdays and from 2 to 5 pm at weekends.

No 2 Willow Rd

Fans of modern architecture may want to visit the nearby National Trust (NT) property at 2 Willow Rd (☎ 7435 6166; ⊖ Hampstead; Hampstead Heath station), the central house in a block of three designed by 'structural rationalist' Ernő Goldfinger in 1939 as his family home. Though the architect was following Georgian principles in creating it, many people think it looks uncannily like the sort of mundane 1950s architecture you see everywhere. They may look similar now, but 2 Willow Rd was in fact a forerunner; the others were just imitations – and mostly bad ones at that. The interior, with its cleverly designed storage space and collection of artworks by Henry Moore, Max Ernst and Bridget Riley, is certainly interesting and accessible to all. It is open for hour-long guided tours on Thursday, Friday and Saturday from noon to 5 pm, April to October. Admission costs £4.10/2.05 for adults/children (free for NT members).

Burgh House

In New End Square you can visit this late 17th-century Queen Anne mansion (☎ 7431 0144; ⊖ Hampstead), which houses the **Hampstead Museum** of local history and a of absurdly overdecorated Victorian graves, catacombs, and sombre family tombs linked in a ring, based on ancient Egyptian burial sites, all flanked by spooky cypresses.

It's divided into two parts. The only way to see the wonderfully atmospheric western section is on a tour (£3/1 for adults/children aged eight to 16) on weekdays at noon and at weekends on the hour from 11 am to 4 pm, April to October. The tours leave at weekends only, on the hour from 11 am to 3 pm, from November to March.

Marx's tomb (and that of his 'neighbour', the philosopher Herbert Spencer) can be found in the comparatively uninteresting eastern part, which is open on weekdays from 10 am to 5 pm and at weekends from 11 am, April to October, and from 10 am (11 am at weekends) to 4 pm the rest of the year. Admission costs £1.

WEMBLEY & NEASDEN (Map 1)

Visiting football fans will want to hurry out to Wembley in north-west London to see the stadium before it and its famous twin towers bite the dust. Neasden, on the other hand, offers something much more otherworldly: an enormous Hindu temple.

Wembley Stadium

Tours of Wembley Stadium (☎ 8902 8833; ⊖ Wembley Park), which will continue until August 2000 when the existing structure will be razed and the construction of a new state-of-the-art £320 million stadium begins, include the opportunity to walk down the players' tunnel as well as to go up and receive the FA Cup to the (taped) roar of the crowd. Tours take place daily between 10 am and 4 pm (3 pm from October to March) and cost £7.45/5.25 for adults/children (family £22.50).

Shri Swaminarayan Mandir

In the unlikely setting of Neasden, Britain's Hindu community has built Europe's first traditional mandir, or temple, an astonishing sight with its icing-sugar towers and pinnacles. Shri Swaminarayan Mandir

(☎ 8965 2651), 105-115 Brentfield Rd NW10 (⊖ Neasden or Stonebridge Park), was constructed out of Bulgarian limestone and Italian marble, all shipped to India to be carved traditionally and then shipped back to London for erection. Some of the carvings on the pillars seem relatively crude, but the *mandapa* (dome) is a masterpiece, so finely carved it looks more like lace than marble. The work took three years to complete and cost around £7.5 million, with much of the labour provided by volunteers. The temple opened in 1995.

You can visit the temple from 9 am to 6 pm but the best times to go are from 9 am to noon and 4 to 6 pm when the *murtis*, the representations of gods and saints, are on view. You must leave your shoes in racks near the door, and women in short skirts will be asked to wrap up in a sheet. Admission to the exhibition centre costs £2/1.50 for adults/children.

WALTHAMSTOW (Map 1)

Walthamstow, in north-east London, was a village on the outskirts of the city when the designer William Morris was born here in 1834 on Forest Rd, where a fire station now stands.

William Morris Gallery

The William Morris Gallery (☎ 8527 3782), Lloyd Park, Forest Rd E17 (⊖ Walthamstow Central, then bus No 97, 97A or 215), is housed in a delightful Georgian house where the Morris family lived from 1848 to 1856. The downstairs rooms tell the story of Morris' life and his working relationship with pre-Raphaelite artists like Burne-Jones. They're also full of gorgeous Morris-designed wallpapers, chintzes and furniture, together with tiles and stained glass designed by his friends. The upstairs gallery houses a selection of pre-Raphaelite paintings and an exhibition about the designer AH Mackmurdo (1851-1942) and the Century Guild. The gallery (free) is open Tuesday to Saturday from 10 am to 1 pm and 2 to 5 pm and at the same times on the first Sunday of each month.

East London

The eastern reaches of central London are taken up by the East End – the London of old Hollywood films and Christmas pantomimes – and the sprawl of the Docklands, an odd mix of the old and decaying and the shockingly new.

EAST END (Maps 2, 4 & 8)

The East End districts of Shoreditch, Hoxton, Spitalfields and Whitechapel may lie within walking distance of the City, but the change of pace and style is extraordinary. Traditionally this was working-class London, an area settled by wave upon wave of immigrants, giving it a curious mixture of Irish, French Huguenot, Bangladeshi and Jewish culture, all of which can still be felt to varying degrees

today. Run-down and neglected in the early 1980s, the East End is starting to look up in places, especially where it rubs right up against the City and Liverpool Street station in Spitalfields, the *nouveau* trendy district of Hoxton and the area around Old St.

For anyone interested in modern, multicultural London, it's well worth venturing a look at the East End. Alongside a couple of interesting museums you'll find some of London's best-value Asian cuisine in Whitechapel and, to a lesser extent, Brick Lane (see East End & the Docklands in the Places to Eat chapter) as well as some of its most colourful markets (see the special section 'The Markets of London' after the Shopping chapter). You may also want to pop into the Whitechapel Art Gallery to see what's on or to eat in its excellent café; see the East End walking tour in this section.

Cockney Rhyming Slang

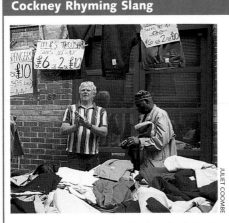

"Ave a butcher's at that ...' (butcher's hook: look)

Many visitors arrive in London expecting to find a city populated by people conversing in Cockney. Traditionally Cockneys were people born within range of Bow Bells – the church bells of St Mary-le-Bow. Since few people live in the City, that meant most Cockneys were East Enders.

The term Cockney is often used to describe those speaking what is also called Estuary English (in which 't's and 'h's are regularly dropped). In fact the true Cockney language also uses something called rhyming slang, which may have developed among London's costermongers (street traders) as a code to avoid police attention. This code replaced common nouns and verbs with rhyming phrases. So 'going up the apples and pears' meant going up the stairs, the 'trouble and strife' was the wife, and 'would you Adam and Eve it?' meant would you believe it? Over time the second of the two words tended to be dropped so the rhyme vanished. Few – if any – people still use pure Cockney. You're more likely to come across it in residual phrases like 'use your loaf' ('loaf of bread' for head), 'ooh, me plates of meat' (feet) or ''e's me best china' ('china plate' for mate).

EAST END

This walk takes you through the streets of Spitalfields and Whitechapel. Come out of Liverpool Street train station and have a look at the high-rise **Broadgate Centre (1)**. Cross Bishopsgate and walk north, past the turning for Spital Square, where the medieval hospital (or 'spittle') originally stood. Turn right into Folgate St, lined with fine Georgian houses. It was in this area that Protestant Huguenots chose to settle in the late 17th century, bringing with them their skills as silk weavers.

At 18 Folgate St is the **house of Dennis Severs (2)** (☎ 7247 4013), an American expatriate who has restored it to its 18th-century splendour and now opens the gas-lit house for tours from 2 to 5 pm on the first Sunday of each month (£7) and in the evening on the first Monday (£10).

Turn right (south) along Commercial St and soon you'll see the covered **Spitalfields Market (3)** on the right. During the week this is a quiet, empty space ringed with interesting small shops and restaurants, but on Sunday one of London's more interesting and varied markets takes place in the arena (see the special section 'The Markets of London' after the Shopping chapter).

On Commercial St, virtually opposite the market, you can't miss the striking façade of **Christ Church, Spitalfields (4)** (☎ 7247 7202), a magnificent English-baroque structure designed by Nicholas Hawksmoor and completed in 1729 for the Huguenot weavers who lived in the area. Ongoing restoration work is coming to an end, and it's worth timing your visit for the brief opening hours (Monday to Friday from noon to 2.30 pm).

Turn down Fournier St, to the left (north) of Christ Church, admiring the beautifully restored Georgian houses with their wooden shutters. Most of them were built between 1718 and 1728 for wealthy London merchants, only to be taken over by silk weavers and their families.

At the Brick Lane end of Fournier St is one of the most interesting buildings in the whole of Spitalfields. The **New French Church (5)** was built for the Huguenots in 1743. In 1899 the church became the Great Synagogue for Jewish refugees from Russia and Central Europe. In 1975 it changed religion yet again, becoming the Great Mosque of the Bengali community who moved in.

Turn left (north) into Brick Lane, a wonderful street of small curry and balti houses intermingled with shops where you can buy brightly coloured fabrics, all the ingredients for cooking your own curries and the paraphernalia of Islam. In 1550 this was just a country road leading to brickyards; by the 18th century it had been paved and lined with a mixture of houses and cottages inhabited by the Spitalfields weavers. These days many of the Bengalis also make a living from the clothes trade and all the street names are in Bengali too.

Cross over Hanbury St and on the left you come to **Truman's Brewery (6)**, the biggest brewery in London by the mid-18th century. The Director's House standing to the left dates from 1740. The brewery closed in 1989 and there's a modern café-bar on the site. The old **Vat House (7)**, which dates from the turn of the 19th century and has a

distance: about 2.5km

start: Liverpool St
⊖ Liverpool Street

finish: Whitechapel Rd
⊖ Whitechapel

hexagonal bell tower, is across the road. Next to it stand the Engineer's House of 1830 and a row of former stables, all given new uses.

Head back down Brick Lane (south) to where it joins Whitechapel High St. If you need a break and something to eat it's worth turning right to the **Whitechapel Art Gallery (8)** (☎ 7522 7888) at Nos 80 to 82. It's open Tuesday to Sunday from 11 am to 5 pm (on Wednesday to 8 pm) and has a pleasant café upstairs (see East End & the Docklands in the Places to Eat chapter).

Whitechapel High St leads eastwards into Whitechapel Rd. At Nos 32 to 34 you'll see the **Whitechapel Bell Foundry (9)** (☎ 7247 2599), which has been standing on this site since 1738, although an earlier foundry nearby is known to have been in business in 1570. The clock bell at St Paul's Cathedral, Big Ben and the Liberty Bell in Philadelphia were all cast here. It can be visited by guided tour only on Saturday at 10 am (£7, children under 14 years not allowed).

You have now entered **Jack the Ripper country**. Although the serial killer's actual identity remains a mystery to this day, that seems only to have added to the interest in him and his crimes. What is certain is that in 1888 he murdered five prostitutes in the wretched backstreets of the Victorian East End; Mary Anne Nichols died in Bucks Row (now Durward St) north of Whitechapel, Annie Chapman in Hanbury St near the Ten Bells pub near Christ Church, Elizabeth Stride in Berner St (now Henriques St) south of Commercial Rd, Catherine Eddowes in Mitre Square near Aldgate and Mary Kelly in Miller's Court.

From here you can walk along Fieldgate St, where you'll find some good Pakistani restaurants (again see the Places to Eat chapter) and the **Fieldgate Great Synagogue (10)**, now part of a modern mosque. Alternatively continue east on Whitechapel Rd to the junction with Cambridge Heath Rd and you'll see the **Blind Beggar pub (11)**, notorious as the place where Ronnie Kray shot George Cornell in 1966 in a gang war over control of the East End's organised crime. The Whitechapel tube is a short distance west of the pub.

The East End: multi-cultural London at its vibrant best.

ED HILLYER

Geffrye Museum

The 14 almshouses that contain the Geffrye Museum (Map 4; ☎ 7739 9893), 136 Kingsland Rd E2 (✆ Old Street, then bus No 243; Dalston Kingsland station), were originally built to provide homes for the elderly poor by Robert Geffrye, a late 16th-century mayor of London who had made a fortune from the slave trade. Today it's devoted to domestic interiors, with each room furnished to show how the homes of the relatively affluent middle class would have looked from Elizabethan times right through to the end of the 19th century. The original chapel also survives. A new postmodernist extension (1998), designed by Nigel Coates, contains several new 20th-century rooms (a flat from the 1930s, a room in the contemporary style of the 1950s, a 1990s converted warehouse) as well as a gallery for temporary exhibits, design centre, shop and restaurant. There's also a lovely herb garden at the museum.

The museum (free) is open Tuesday to Saturday from 10 am to 5 pm, and on Sunday from noon to 5 pm. Its Web site is at www.geffrye-museum.org.uk.

Bethnal Green Museum of Childhood

The Bethnal Green Museum of Childhood (Map 2; ☎ 8980 2415), Cambridge Heath Rd & Old Ford Rd E2 (✆ Bethnal Green), is guaranteed to bring back memories of childhood. Set in a rather grungy 19th-century building, it's full of dolls, dolls' houses, train sets, model cars, children's clothes, board games, books, toy theatres and puppets from the 17th century to today. The upstairs gallery attempts to provide a context for the toys by tracing the stages of childhood from life as a baby to leaving home.

The museum (free) is open from Monday to Thursday and on Saturday from 10 am to 5.50 pm, from 2.30 pm on Sunday.

THE DOCKLANDS (Maps 8 & 12)

The Port of London was once the world's greatest port, the hub of the British Empire and its enormous global trade. In the 16th century there were 20 cargo quays to the east of London. By the 18th and 19th centuries these were hard-pressed to cope with the quantity of cargo flowing through, and

ANDREW HUMPHREYS

It's a fishy business: Billingsgate Fish Market and Canary Wharf in the heart of the Docklands.

new docks were opened: West India Dock in 1802, London Dock in 1805, East India Dock in 1806 and Victoria Dock in 1855.

But even these proved inadequate as goods from the empire poured in and out and a new wave of dock building kicked off, with Millwall on the Isle of Dogs in 1868, followed by the Royal Albert in 1880 and Tilbury in 1886. Each dock catered for a specific type of cargo – from rum and rubber to wool and ivory. A new dock – the King George V – opened as late as 1921.

After the Blitz of WWII the docks were in no state to cope with the postwar technological and political changes as the empire evaporated. At the same time, enormous new bulk carriers and container ships demanded deep-water ports and new loading and unloading techniques. From the mid-1960s dock closures followed each other as fast as they had opened and the number of dock workers dropped from as many as 50,000 in 1960 to about 3000 by 1980. Almost 12% of the total land area of London now stood derelict.

In 1981 the London Docklands Development Corporation (LDDC) was set up to rejuvenate the area by encouraging new office and housing development. The builders moved in, the Docklands Light Railway (DLR) was built to link the area with the rest of London, new offices were constructed and new toy-town houses were thrown up beside new marinas. Places like **Tobacco Dock** in Wapping (Map 8) were transformed into shopping centres full of delicatessen food and designer clothes. But a lack of thought for aesthetics and no planning for open green areas or public spaces left the local community poorly catered for.

When the recession of the early 1990s hit, the Docklands bubble burst. Offices stood empty, people lost their jobs, flats wouldn't sell and shopping arcades emptied as trendy shops hung up 'For Sale' signs. Over it all towered the flagship development of Canary Wharf on the Isle of Dogs (Map 12), bankrupted by the recession and falling property prices well before the IRA bomb of 1996 devastated the area immediately around it.

JULIET COOMBE

The *Traffic Light Tree* near Canary Wharf: waiting for London's first 75-road junction.

Things have partly turned around since then and 1 Canada Square – the official name of **Canary Wharf Tower** – is full of newspaper people; as the home of the *Telegraph* and *Independent*, it has been described as a 'vertical Fleet St' and is a striking focal point visible in every direction. Sadly, Tobacco Dock remains an empty shell, waiting yet another reincarnation.

Getting around was always the Docklands' Achilles heel. The DLR has got over its teething problems and has even been extended under the Thames (see DLR & Train in the Getting Around chapter). What's more the Jubilee Line extension means that for the first time the Isle of Dogs is served by the Underground.

The Docklands today is a world of contrasts. Eye-catching bridges across docks and futuristic buildings dominate the skyline; it really is today's view of London's future. But it is also an area rich in history. To see both sides, try the Wapping & the Isle of Dogs walking tour next in this section.

WAPPING & THE ISLE OF DOGS

The obvious starting point for a tour of the Docklands is Tower Hill. If you pass under Tower Bridge from the Tower of London on foot you'll come to **St Katharine's Dock (1)**, created in 1828 after up to 1000 houses and a 12th-century church were cleared away. It was the first of the docks to be renovated following its closure in 1968. It's a pleasant – if touristy – haven away from the bustle around the Tower, with a marina and the Dickens Inn (see Pubs & Bars in the Entertainment chapter).

distance: about 6km

start: Tower Hill
⊖ Tower Hill

finish: Island Gardens
DLR: Island Gardens

If you head east along the river from St Katharine's Dock you'll come to Wapping and **Wapping High St**. A quiet cobbled road flanked by restored warehouses, it was described by John Stow in his *Survey of London* (see Tudor London under History in the Facts about London chapter) as 'a filthy strait passage, with alleys of small tenements or cottages'. As you walk along the street glance to the left down Scandrett St to see the remnants of what was a small community, with a church, a school and – inevitably – a pub.

Your first real port of call though is **Execution Dock (2)** near the old river police station at Wapping New Stairs. This is where convicted pirates were hanged and their bodies chained to a post at low tide, to be left until three tides had washed over them. A nearby pub (see Pubs & Bars in the Entertainment chapter) recalls one of the more famous executions – that of Captain William Kidd in 1701.

From Wapping High St, head north along Wapping Lane and across The Highway to **St George-in-the-East (3)**. It was badly damaged during the Blitz and the shell of the original church, designed by Nicholas Hawksmoor in 1726, now encloses a smaller modern church.

Cannon St Rd leads north to Cable St, where ropes were manufactured in the late 18th century. It was once as long as the standard English measure for cable (180m or 600 feet). Head east along Cable St to the **Town Hall building (4)** (now a library). On the outside wall a large mural commemorates the battle that took place here in October 1936 when the British Fascist Oswald Mosley led a bunch of his Blackshirts into the area to intimidate the local Jewish population.

From here you can enter the **Limehouse** district by following Commercial Rd eastwards or catching the DLR two stops to Westferry. Limehouse became the centre of London's Chinese community – its first Chinatown – after some 300 sailors settled here in 1890. The protagonist of Oscar Wilde's *Picture of Dorian Gray* (1891) passed by this way in search of opium. Today the only reminders are street names like Ming and Mandarin Sts and some Chinese restaurants on Commercial Rd. Nearby is **St Anne's, Limehouse (5)**, Three Colt St, Hawksmoor's earliest church (1724) and boasting the highest church clock in London.

A couple of stops after Westferry on the DLR is Canary Wharf on the Isle of Dogs. Etymologists are still out to lunch over the origin of the island's name. Most likely it's a corruption of the Flemish *dijk* (dike), recalling the island's muddy banks.

Canary Wharf is dominated by Cesar Pelli's 500m **tower (6)** (1991), described as a 'square prism with a pyramidal top'. Unfortunately, there is no public access to this steel and glass colossus. Instead, check out **Cabot Square**, at the centre of the Canary Wharf complex, which features a shopping centre and hosts arts and cultural events. Norman Foster's new Jubilee Line Underground station here is very impressive indeed (see the special section 'London's Contemporary Architecture' after the Facts about London chapter).

There are plans to open a **Docklands Museum**, focusing on the history of the Thames, its port and its industries, in 2001, as well as a new visitor centre (to replace the one further south at Limeharbour) in Sugar House, a 19th-century warehouse at **West India Quay**, to the north of Canary Wharf.

To the west of the complex, in the centre of Westferry Circus round-about, is a magnificent modern sculpture by Pierre Vivant called *Traffic Light Tree* **(7)**, composed of 75 sets of flashing red, amber and green lights and looking very much like a Christmas tree gone mad. To the south, a twisting, futuristic **footbridge (8)**, its masts and cables evoking a ship at sea, links Heron Quays with South Quay.

Farther south is the **London Arena (9)**, Limeharbour E14 (DLR Crossharbour & London Arena), a huge venue for fairs, conferences and concerts. If you want to see how much of the Isle of Dogs once looked, check out **Mudchute Park Farm (10)**, a short distance to the south-east (see the boxed text 'Old MacDonald's London Farms' under Flora & Fauna in the Facts about London chapter).

The last DLR station on the Isle of Dogs is **Island Gardens**, from where there are exquisite views of Greenwich's architectural heritage. If you'd like to carry on south to Greenwich, take the new DLR ex-tension to Cutty Sark station or, alternatively, use the historic 390m-long **foot tunnel (11)** running under the Thames. The lifts down to the tunnel are open Monday to Saturday from 7 am to 7 pm and on Sunday from 10 am to 5.30 pm. Otherwise you're facing between 88 and 100 steps down and – shudder – up.

The Docklands: the cutting edge of economic regenera-tion or a prime example of spec-ulators' folly? Time will tell.

ED HILLYER

South London

For tourists a major reason to venture south of the Thames (see the boxed text on this page) is to visit Greenwich, but you can also have fun exploring Brixton's colourful market or visiting the excellent Horniman Museum in Forest Hill or the Dulwich Picture Gallery designed by John Soane.

GREENWICH (Map 13)

Packed with splendid architecture, Greenwich has strong connections with the sea, science, sovereigns and – of course – time.

Greenwich (**gren**-itch) lies to the southeast of central London, where the Thames widens and deepens, and there's a sense of space that is rare in the city. Quaint and village-like, and boasting the magnificent *Cutty Sark* clipper ship, the fabulous National Maritime Museum and now the Millennium Dome, Greenwich is a delightful place that has been on UNESCO's list of World Heritage Sites since 1997. A trip there will be one of the highlights of any visit to London,

and you should certainly allow a day to do it justice, particularly if you want to head down the river to the Thames Flood Barrier.

Greenwich is home to an extraordinary interrelated cluster of classical buildings; all the great architects of the Enlightenment made their mark here, largely due to royal patronage. Henry VIII and his daughters Mary and Elizabeth were all born here. Charles II was particularly fond of the area and had Sir Christopher Wren build both the Royal Observatory and part of the Royal Naval College, which John Vanbrugh then completed in the early 17th century.

It's worth timing your visit for the weekend arts & crafts and antiques markets; see the special section 'The Markets of London' after the Shopping chapter.

Virtually everything in Greenwich can be easily reached from the Cutty Sark DLR station. A shuttle bus (£1.50) linking Greenwich Pier with the Royal Observatory, Fan Museum and Ranger's House runs from 11 am to 5 pm, April to October.

Information

The tourist information centre (☎ 8858 6376, 0870 608 2000, fax 8853 4607), 46 Greenwich Church St SE10 (DLR Cutty Sark), is open daily from 10.15 am to 4.45 pm, April to October, and Monday to Thursday, 11 am to 4 pm, and Friday to Sunday, 10.15 am to 4.45 pm, the rest of the year. Its Web site is at www.greenwich2000.co.uk.

Guided walks (☎ 8858 6169) to selected sites in Greenwich depart daily from the tourist information centre at 12.15 pm (the Meridian Walk) and 2.15 pm (the Royal Greenwich Walk). They cost £4/3 for adults/concessions. There are tours with different themes at other times of the day as well.

Cutty Sark

The *Cutty Sark* clipper ship (☎ 8858 3445) is in Cutty Sark Gardens at the top of King William Walk, right beside Greenwich Pier. It was the fastest ship that had ever sailed the seven seas when launched in 1869, though it was built just as steam and the opening of

---

The North-South Divide

Londoners still talk as if the Thames was the huge barrier between north and south that it was in the Middle Ages. In fact, the psychological gulf between the two banks is as wide as ever; most people in north London (and that's most Londoners) refuse to believe there's anything of importance across the river. One of the standard questions in Londoner-to-Londoner interviews is 'When was the last time you crossed the river?' (which usually means 'went south') and jokes abound about having to get a visa before crossing the Thames. One wag even called the south the 'B-list side of the Thames', referring – we hope – to the number of place names beginning with that letter (Battersea, Borough, Brixton etc) and not making a value judgement.

DENNIS JOHNSON

Looking down on Greenwich's classical ensemble from the Royal Observatory.

the Suez Canal were making sailing ships redundant. It remains the sole surviving example of the clippers that dominated mid-19th-century trade in tea and wool across both the Pacific and Atlantic oceans and was still carrying cargoes when she was restored in 1922 and retired to Greenwich in 1954.

You can stroll on the decks and peep in the teak-panelled cabins, then read up on the history below deck and inspect maritime prints, paintings and the world's largest collection of ship's figureheads in the hold.

The *Cutty Sark* is undergoing a £2 million restoration, but you can still visit Monday to Saturday from 10 am to 6 pm and on Sunday from noon, April to October. The rest of the year it's open Monday to Saturday from 10 am to 5 pm, on Sunday from noon. Admission costs £3.50/2.50 (family £8.50).

Gipsy Moth IV

Just next to the *Cutty Sark* is the *Gipsy Moth IV* (☎ 8858 3445), the 16m-long sailing ketch in which Sir Francis Chichester made the world's first single-handed circumnavigation of the globe (1966-67). Chichester was 64 at the time and endured 226 days in this bathtub-sized craft. He was knighted close to where the boat is now dry-docked by Elizabeth II, using the same sword that Elizabeth I used to knight Francis Drake. Unfortunately visitors are no longer allowed on board.

Old Royal Naval College

If you walk south along King William Walk from the *Cutty Sark* you'll come to the entrance of the Old Royal Naval College (☎ 8858 2154) on the left. This Wren masterpiece has been largely taken over by the University of Greenwich since the Royal Navy baled out in 1998, but the buildings on the south side allow visitors to view the fabulous Painted Hall and the Chapel.

Work on the college began on the site of the old Greenwich Palace in 1692 when William and Mary ordered the building of a naval hospital for those wounded in the victory over the French at La Hogue. Intended as a retirement home for navy veterans, just as the Chelsea Royal Hospital was for army veterans, it was designed in two separate halves so as not to spoil the view of the river from the Queen's House, Inigo Jones' miniature masterpiece to the south.

You can visit the **Chapel** in the Queen Mary Building, which was completed in 1742, almost two decades after Wren's death, only to be gutted by fire in 1779. When it was redecorated it was in the lighter, airier rococo style. The eastern end of the chapel is dominated by a painting by the 18th-century American artist Benjamin West showing *St Paul at Malta*. The 'marble' Corinthian columns are actually made of Coade stone, an artificial material manufactured at a site beside Westminster Bridge in the 19th century. The secret of its composition is now lost. Sung Eucharist takes place in the Chapel on Sunday at 11 am.

Even more wonderful is the **Painted Hall**, which is made up of the Great Hall and the Upper Hall, across Upper Grand Square in the King William Building. As soon as you step inside the Great Hall, your eyes will be drawn towards the ceiling to marvel at the painting by James Thornhill (the mirrors on wheels will help you inspect the ceiling without suffering a crick in your neck). It shows William and Mary enthroned amid symbols of the Virtues. Beneath William's feet, you can see the defeated French king Louis XIV grovelling with a furled flag in hand. Up a few steps is the Upper Hall, where George I is depicted with his family on the western wall. In the bottom right-hand corner Thornhill drew himself into the picture, pointing at the sovereign.

Wren designed the hall as the hospital dining room, but it soon proved too small and was vacated. Until 1806 it stood empty until Admiral Nelson's body was brought here to lie in state.

The college (free) is open daily from 2 to 5 pm. The Queen Elizabeth Anteroom Café is in the basement.

National Maritime Museum

Farther south along King William Walk, you'll come to the National Maritime Museum (☎ 8312 6565), Romney Rd SE10, a massive collection of boats, maps, charts, uniforms and marine art designed to tell the long and convoluted history of Britain as a seafaring nation.

As part of a major redevelopment, the brightly lit central courtyard, Neptune Court, has been covered with a huge single-span glass roof to provide easy access to some 16 new themed galleries on two of the museum's three levels. The galleries have interactive displays and video art that focus on such things as marine ecology and the future of the sea, the tea trade and slavery, and imperialism and white settlement.

Videos in the Nelson Gallery on the 3rd level tell the story of the battles of the Nile and Trafalgar, and there's an impressive display of Nelson memorabilia, including his tunic with a hole from the bullet that killed him and the actual bullet itself. All Hands is an on-board interactive display for children on gunnery, signalling and deep-sea diving.

The museum is open daily from 10 am to 5 pm. Admission costs £7.50/6 for adults/seniors & students; it is free for children. A ticket allowing entry to the museum and the Royal Observatory is £9.50/7.60. The museum's Web site is at www.nmm.ac.uk.

Queen's House

The Palladian Queen's House (☎ 8858 4422) is attached to the National Maritime Museum on its eastern side. Inigo Jones started work on the house for Anne of Denmark, wife of James I, in 1616, but it wasn't completed until 1635 when it became the home of Charles I and his queen, Henrietta Maria. Throughout 2000 it will house a special exhibit called The Story of Time.

Rooms open off the **Great Hall**, which originally had a ceiling painted by Orazio Gentileschi and his daughter Artemisia, one of the few early female artists to achieve much celebrity. Sadly the original was later moved. Most of the original furniture has also been lost and replaced with 17th-century copies so the rooms are perhaps not as exciting as the building's exterior might lead you to expect. You may recognise the Great Hall; it featured in the Ang Lee film *Sense and Sensibility* (1995) starring Emma Thompson.

The Queen's House is open daily from 10 am to 5 pm. Admission costs £7.50/6.

St Alfege Church

Designed by Nicholas Hawksmoor in 1714 to replace a 12th-century one, this church is dedicated to St Alfege, archbishop of Canterbury, who was martyred on the site by Vikings in 1012.

Fan Museum

The delightful Fan Museum (☎ 8305 1441), in an 18th-century Georgian town house at 12 Croom's Hill, exhibits a collection of fans from around the world dating back to the 17th century and examines their role and importance through history. It also has some wonderful temporary exhibits. The museum is open Tuesday to Saturday from 11 am to 5 pm and on Sunday from noon. Admission costs £3.50/2.50. At the back there's a Japanese-style garden with an Orangery serving afternoon set-teas (£4.50/3.50 for full/half tea) on Tuesday and Sunday only from 3 to 5 pm.

Greenwich Park

Greenwich Park is London's largest and one of its loveliest, with a grand avenue, wide-open spaces, a rose garden and rambling, picturesque walks. It's partly the work of Le Nôtre, who landscaped the palace gardens of Versailles for Louis XIV. It contains several historic sights as well as a café and an enclosed deer park called the **Wilderness**.

If you continue south of the park past the Ranger's House and down Chesterfield Walk (or south on Blackheath Ave and through Blackheath Gate) and then cross Shooters Hill Rd, you come to **Blackheath**, a 110-hectare expanse of open common where Wat Tyler camped in 1381 before marching on London and where Henry VII fought off Cornish rebels in 1497. Later it became a highwaymen's haunt, and it was not until the area's development in the late 18th century – the lovely Paragon crescent on the edge of the heath was built to entice people to move to the area – that Blackheath was considered safe. It's now a very pleasant place indeed, with restaurants and bars flanking it.

Royal Observatory In 1675 Charles II had the Royal Observatory (☎ 8858 4422) built on a hill in the middle of the park, intending that astronomy be used to establish longitude at sea. The Octagon Room, designed by Wren, and the nearby Sextant Room are where John Flamsteed (1646-1719), the first

The Longitude Solution

It was the challenge of the century. Establishing latitude – the imaginary lines that girdle the earth – was child's play; any sailor could do that by looking at the height of the sun or the stars. Finding longitude, however, was an entirely different matter and had stumped astronomers from the Greeks to Galileo.

As it takes 24 hours for the earth to complete one revolution of 360°, one hour is 1/24 of a revolution – or 15°. By the 16th century astronomers knew that longitude could be found by comparing local time with the reading of a clock set at the time of a home port or another place of known longitude. But that meant two *reliable* clocks, ones that would keep accurate time as the ship pitched and shook and the temperature rose or fell. Such technology was unavailable in the 17th century.

Reading longitude inaccurately lengthened sea voyages, cost shipping companies money and increased the number of sailors' deaths due to scurvy and accidents, as islands, rocks and reefs appeared out of nowhere. In 1714 Parliament offered a prize of £20,000 – a king's ransom in the 18th century – to anyone who could discover a method of finding longitude accurate to within 48km (30 miles). It's a long story (one wonderfully told in *Longitude* by Dava Sobel) but the English inventor John Harrison was eventually awarded the prize for a marine chronometer tested from 1761 to 1762 by the Royal Observatory at Greenwich.

In 1884 the observatory's contribution in solving the longitude riddle was acknowledged when an international conference in Washington designated 'the meridian passing through the centre of the transit instrument at the Observatory of Greenwich as the initial meridian for longitude', or the prime meridian. Greenwich Mean Time (GMT) was then accepted worldwide as the universal measurement of standard time.

astronomer royal, made his observations and calculations. This is one of the few Wren interiors known to have survived intact.

The globe is divided between east and west at the Royal Observatory, and you can place one foot either side of the meridian line and straddle the two hemispheres. For a small fee a machine will generate a certificate confirming that you've done just that.

The observatory is open daily from 10 am to 5 pm. Admission costs £5/4 for adults/seniors & students; it is free for children. A ticket allowing entry to the observatory as well as the National Maritime Museum costs £9.50/7.60.

Attached to the observatory is the Greenwich Planetarium, where you can see the night sky projected on a dome for £2/1.50. There are showings during the week at 2.30 pm and at weekends at 2 and 3 pm.

Ranger's House South-west of the observatory is the Ranger's House (☎ 8853 0035), a stately home built for Admiral Francis Hosier in 1700 and later used to house the park's ranger. Inside there's not a great deal to detain you, although the Jacobean and Stuart portraits, including some by Lely and Kneller, are striking for their size if nothing else. You can also ascend to Admiral Hosier's rooftop gazebo.

The Ranger's House is open daily from 10 am to 6 pm, April to September, closing at 5 pm in October; and Wednesday to Sunday from 10 am to 4 pm, November to March. Admission costs £2.50/1.90/1.30 for adults/seniors & students/children (free for EH members).

Getting There & Away

Greenwich is now most easily accessible on the DLR; Cutty Sark is the station closest to the information office and most of the sights. If you happen to be in the Docklands before you visit, you can catch the DLR to Island Gardens and walk through the historic foot tunnel to the south side of the river (see the Wapping & the Isle of Dogs walking tour in the Docklands section earlier in this chapter).

There are fast, cheap trains from Charing Cross to Greenwich station via London Bridge about every 15 minutes. Maze Hill station is more convenient for most of the sights than Greenwich station.

The most pleasant way to get to/from Greenwich if the weather is fine is by boat. For details, see Organised Tours in the Getting Around chapter.

AROUND GREENWICH (Map 1)
Millennium Dome

The all-singin', all-dancin' Millennium Dome (Map 1; ☎ 0870 606 2000; ⊖ North Greenwich), which opened on the first day of 2000, is the most ambitious building erected in London since St Paul's Cathedral was completed in 1710. And at more than £750 million, it's also the most expensive, with more than half the cost being paid for with funds from the National Lottery.

The comparison with St Paul's is not a facile one; with its enormous cupola of white fibreglass – the largest in the world – and 12 supporting masts of yellow steel the Millennium Dome is (vaguely) reminiscent of the marble dome and spires/towers of that great paean to Christianity. But this dome celebrates things spiritual in only one 'zone', while the rest deal with the temporal world of progress, development and, of course, mammon.

The dome's design (not to mention cost) was controversial from the outset, but many people (including us) believe it is everything modern architecture should be: innovative, complementary and startlingly beautiful. It was designed by Richard Rogers.

Inside, though, it's a bit of a hotchpotch and divided into 14 themed (and commercially sponsored) 'zones' – from Body, which explores the world of human biology and medical science, and Faith, looking at the spiritual and moral aspects of the human experience, to the multimedia and digital Play zone and Living Island, complete with a mock-up of a British seaside town.

In the centre of the dome there is a show based on the theme of creation – with some 200 live performers plus state-of-the-art visual effects and high-tech gadgetry –

ELLIOT DANIEL

The Millennium Dome: the very latest in tent technology.

Getting There & Away The easiest way to reach the Millennium Dome is to take the Jubilee Line to North Greenwich, the largest underground station in Europe, which is 50m from the dome. There is also a bus shuttle linking North Greenwich with Charlton train station, which can be reached from Charing Cross and London Bridge stations.

City Cruises (☎ 7237 5134) operates a river service from Festival Pier on the South Bank to Millennium Pier (formerly the Phoenix Jetty) at the dome via Blackfriars. The journey takes 45 minutes and boats go every 15 to 30 minutes. Fares are £6.75/8.40 single/return for adults and £4/5.20 for children. White Horse Fast Ferries (☎ 7231 9221) runs a 10-minute shuttle boat between Greenwich and Millennium piers every 10 minutes throughout the day.

Thames Flood Barrier

The Thames Flood Barrier between Greenwich and Woolwich was built from 1972 to 1982 to protect London from flooding. It consists of 10 separate movable gates supported between seven concrete piers with silver roofs that house the operating machinery. They make a surreal sight, straddling the river in the lee of a giant warehouse.

The reason why London needs such a barrier is that the water level has been rising by as much as 75cm per century, while the river itself has been narrowing; in Roman times it was probably around 800m wide at the site of today's London Bridge while now it's barely 250m, with constant pressure to develop the foreshores. The Thames tide rises and falls quite harmlessly twice a day, and once a fortnight there's also a stronger 'spring' tide. The danger comes when the spring tide coincides with an unexpected surge, which pushes tons of extra water upriver. The barrier has been built to prevent that water pouring over the riverbanks and flooding nearby houses.

The barrier's visitor centre (☎ 8305 4188), 1 Unity Way SE18, is open Monday to Saturday from 10 am to 5 pm (10.30 am to 5.30 pm on Sunday) and tells the story of

playing up to three times a day. Performances also take place in the piazza.

The futuristic Skyscape building next to the dome contains two 2500-seat cinemas as well as the largest live performance theatre in the UK. Films screened and performances staged here require a separate ticket.

The Millennium Dome is open daily from 10 am to 5.30 pm (and again from 6 to 11 pm when a second session is scheduled). Tickets are expensive at £20/18/16.50 for adults/ seniors/students & children aged five to 15 (family £57). The average visit is expected to last five hours. Audioguides in seven different languages are available free. At present it's planned that the dome will remain open only until the end of 2000 and then be converted for another use, such as a sports centre and stadium, TV and film studios, a conference centre or even a theme park.

Further details on the dome are available on its Web site at www.dome2000.co.uk.

Since 1982, the Thames Flood Barrier has been raised over 20 times to prevent London flooding.

the Thames through history, of the building of the barrier and of recent attempts to clean the river up. An audiovisual show lasts 20 minutes. Admission costs £3.40/2 (family £7.50), although if you just want to see the barrier there's no charge. There's a small, reasonably priced terrace restaurant here and picnic tables outside.

The barrier's mechanisms are checked roughly once a month. If you'd like to see this wonder in action, ring the visitor centre for exact dates and times.

Getting There & Away You can get to within 20 minutes' walk of the barrier by taking a train to Charlton station from Charing Cross or London Bridge. When you get there, turn left (north) out of the station onto Charlton Church Lane, cross Woolwich Rd and follow Anchor & Hope Lane to the Thames Path. Head east along the path for about 800m to the barrier. It's not the path's prettiest stretch, but it's better than walking along busy Woolwich Rd.

To visit the barrier from Greenwich catch

bus No 177 or 180 along Romney Rd and get off at the Victoria pub, 757 Woolwich Rd. From there Westmoor St leads north to the visitor centre.

A slower – but nicer – way to get to the barrier from Greenwich is by boat. From late March to October boats run by Campion Launches (☎ 8305 0300) leave Greenwich Pier at 11.15 am and 12.30, 2 and 3.30 pm and take 35 minutes to get there (the last departure doesn't leave time to take in the visitor centre), passing the Dome along the way. Single tickets cost £3.25/2.75/2 and returns £4.75/4.25/2.75 (family £14). In winter the 11.15 am service doesn't operate and in January there are no boats at all. You can also get here from Westminster Pier via Canary Wharf and the Millennium Dome with Thames Cruises (☎ 7930 3373) from three to seven times a day from April to October. Single fares are £5.75/4.55/3.20, returns £6.95/5.75/3.70.

If you're up to hoofing it, the barrier is 5.25km (3¼ miles) from Greenwich via the Thames Path.

Eltham Palace

Eltham Palace (☎ 8294 2548), Court Rd SE9 (Eltham station), is an unusual hybrid: part Tudor, part 1930s Art Deco. It started life as a royal palace in 1305 and was for a time the boyhood home of Henry VIII. But the Tudors abandoned it in 1526 in favour of Greenwich and it fell into disrepair. From 1933 to 1937 a member of the Courtauld clan (of Courtauld Institute fame) built a country home onto the palace remains. It was occupied by the Army from WWII until 1995, when English Heritage took it over.

Of what little remains from the Tudor period, the Great Hall's hammer-beam roof is said to be third only to the ones at Westminster Hall and Hampton Court Palace. However, the main draw is the Art Deco fixtures restored to the way they were when the Courtaulds lived here: from an enormous circular carpet with geometric shapes in the domed entrance hall and a burlwood-veneer fireplace to the black-marble dining room with a silver-foil ceiling. You can almost see Mae West lounging on a settee and demanding a peeled grape.

Eltham Palace is open daily from 10 am to 6 pm, April to September, closing at 5 pm in October; and Wednesday to Sunday from 10 am to 4 pm, November to March. Admission to both the house and gardens costs £5.50/4.10/2.75 for adults/seniors & students/children (free for EH members). For just the gardens it's £3.30/2.50/1.65.

DULWICH & FOREST HILL (Map 1)

Tucked away in the wide expanse of south London that the tube fails to reach, Dulwich (**dull**-itch) is a leafy, quiet suburb with some fine architecture and an air of gentility. You might want to venture out here to see the Dulwich Picture Gallery, a work of that idiosyncratic 19th-century architect John Soane.

A bit farther off the beaten track and lacking Dulwich's cohesiveness, Forest Hill boasts one attraction well worth venturing onto a suburban train to reach: the Horniman Museum.

Dulwich Picture Gallery

John Soane designed the Dulwich Picture Gallery (☎ 8693 5254), College Rd SE21 (North Dulwich station), the country's oldest public art gallery, in 1811 to house paintings collected by dealer Noel Desenfans and painter Francis Bourgeois. Perhaps uniquely, the gallery doubles as this august pair's mausoleum, lit by a moody *lumière mystérieuse* created with stained glass. The gallery, which has just emerged from a major refurbishment and extension, contains masterpieces by Rembrandt, Rubens, Reynolds, Gainsborough, Lely and others. Temporary exhibitions by modern artists generally get more space.

The gallery is open Tuesday to Friday from 10 am to 5 pm, and at weekends from 11 am. Admission costs £3/1.50 (£5 for special exhibitions) but is free on Friday. To get there from North Dulwich station, turn left out of the station, cross over East Dulwich Grove and walk down Dulwich Village until the road divides. Take the left fork (College Rd); the entrance is on the right, opposite Dulwich Park.

Horniman Museum

The Horniman Museum (☎ 8699 1872, 8699 2339 for a recording), 100 London Rd SE23 (Forest Hill station), is an extraordinary little place, comprising the original collection of Frederick John Horniman, the son of a wealthy tea merchant, who, in 1901, had the Art Nouveau building with clock tower and mosaics specially designed to house it. The main ethnographic hall has undergone major renovation and has emerged as African Worlds, the first permanent gallery of African, Afro-Caribbean and Brazilian art and culture in the UK. The Music Room has a superb collection of musical instruments, each displayed with computerised recordings and headsets, and a wonderful room devoted to nomad life, with reconstructed tents and yurts. The small Living Waters Aquarium sits rather oddly with the other exhibits, but the way it follows the line of the steps is rather fun. The museum is a great place to take kids.

The museum (free) is open Monday to Saturday from 10.30 am to 5.30 pm and on Sunday from 2 pm. To get there from Forest Hill station, turn left out of the station along Devonshire Rd and then right along London Rd. The Horniman is on the right.

BRIXTON

There was a settlement on the site of today's Brixton (see the map under Brixton in the Places to Eat chapter), the southern terminus of the Victoria Line, as early as a year after the Norman Invasion, but it was an isolated, far-flung village until the 19th century, when the new Vauxhall Bridge (1810) and the railways (1860) linked it with central London. After WWII immigrants from the West Indies settled in large numbers here, giving Brixton a palpable Caribbean flavour that can still be found in the exotic fruits and vegetables on sale at Brixton Market (see the special section 'The Markets of London' after the Shopping chapter), the reggae blaring from car radios and boom boxes and the never-say-die all-night dance clubs.

Economic decline and hostility between the police and blacks (who accounted for only 29% of the population of Brixton at the time) led to the riots of the 1980s (see The Thatcher Years under History in the Facts about London chapter). Since then the mood has been decidedly upbeat. Soaring property prices have sent house-hunters foraging in these parts, and pockets of gentrification sit alongside the more run-down streets. Whatever edge is left from the dark days of the 80s has only added to the excitement of the restaurants and clubs (see Brixton in the Places to Eat chapter and Clubs in the Entertainment chapter) that have sprung up in recent years like mushrooms after rain.

WANDSWORTH (Map 1)

This poorer, working-class sibling of the more affluent Battersea (immediately down river) was synonymous with quality headgear as early as the 13th century. When the Roman Catholic hierarchy in Rome began to order their mitres and birettas from the newly established Huguenot milliners in the 18th century, Wandsworth hats became famous throughout Europe. You can learn more about this history at the Wandsworth Museum but if your interests lie in things wet and cool, head for Young's Ram Brewery, one of the few working breweries still extant in London.

Young's Ram Brewery

Young's Ram Brewery (☎ 8875 7005), corner of Wandsworth High & Ram Sts SW18 (Wandsworth Town station), is where to go when you're 'museumed out' and want to digest history with a cup of good cheer. Beer (as in 'ale' or 'bitter', not lager – see the boxed text 'Beer: The National Drink' in the Entertainment chapter) has been brewed at this site since the late 16th century, and tours of the brewery lasting 1½ hours leave from Monday to Saturday at 10 am, noon and 2 and 4 pm (the visitor centre is open from 10 am to 6 pm). Admission costs £5.50/4.50/3 for adults/seniors & students/ those aged 14 to 17 (who must be accompanied by an adult). Tours include a pint in the old pub attached. Tours of the stables, where a herd of working shires make their home, are also available and cost £3.50/2 for adults/those aged six to 18 (family £9). To get here from Wandsworth Town station (trains from Waterloo), walk west on Old York Rd, cross over to Armoury Way and then go south along Ram St.

Wandsworth Museum

It's small and it ain't the British Museum, but the Wandsworth Museum (☎ 8871 7074), The Courthouse, 11 Garratt Lane SW18 (Wandsworth Town station), a short distance south of Wandsworth High St and the brewery, is quirky and welcoming. Most of the exhibits are of local interest and trace the history of the borough from medieval times to the present day. The museum (free) is open Tuesday to Saturday from 10 am to 5 pm, on Sunday from 2 pm.

WIMBLEDON

This leafy southern suburb will be forever associated in most minds with the lawn tennis championships that have been taking place here every June since 1877. The rest of the year you can still visit the Wimbledon Lawn Tennis Museum. Wimbledon Common is a great place for a picnic.

Wimbledon Lawn Tennis Museum

This museum (☎ 8946 6131), Gate 4, Church Rd SW19 (⊖ Southfields or Wimbledon Park), is of specialist interest, dwelling as it does on the minutiae of the history of tennis playing, traced back here to the invention of the all-important lawnmower in 1830 and of the India-rubber ball in the 1850s. Nonetheless it's a state-of-the-art presentation, with plenty of video clips to let fans of the game relive their favourite moments.

It's open Tuesday to Saturday from 10.30 am to 5 pm and on Sunday from 2 pm. During the tournament the museum is only open to those attending the event. Admission costs £4/3. There's a tea room and a shop selling all kinds of tennis memorabilia.

Wimbledon Common

Running on into Putney Heath, Wimbledon Common covers 440 hectares of south London, a wonderful expanse of open space for walking, nature trailing and picnicking. There are a few specific sights on the common, most unexpectedly **Wimbledon Windmill** (☎ 8947 2825), Windmill Rd SW19 (⊖ Wimbledon), a fine smock windmill dating from 1817. It was during a stay in the mill in 1908 that Baden-Powell was inspired to write parts of his *Scouting for Boys*. The mill is open at weekends from 2 to 5 pm, April to October. Admission costs £1/50p. On the south side of the common, the misnamed **Caesar's Camp** is a prehistoric earthwork that proves that Wimbledon was settled before Roman times.

Buddhapadipa Temple

Popping up unexpectedly in a residential neighbourhood 1km from Wimbledon village is as authentic a Thai temple as ever graced this side of Bangkok. Buddhapadipa Temple (☎ 8946 1357), 14 Calonne Rd SW19 (⊖ Wimbledon), was built by an association of young Buddhists in Britain and opened in 1982. The *wat* (temple compound) boasts a traditional *bot*, or consecrated chapel, decorated with traditional scenes by two leading Thai artists. Remember to take your shoes off before entering the bot. To get there take the tube or train to Wimbledon and then bus No 93 up to Wimbledon Parkside. Calonne Rd leads off it on the right. The temple is open on Saturday from 1 to 6 pm and on Sunday from 8.30 to 10.30 am and 12.30 to 6 pm, but the complex keeps longer hours: daily from 8 am to 9.30 pm in summer, to 6 pm in winter.

West London

There are many reasons why visitors may consider a foray into the hinterland of west London, including Fulham Palace, Kew Gardens, Syon House, Richmond Park or even a boozy afternoon at one of the riverfront pubs in Hammersmith. But the main one should be to visit Hampton Court, the mother of all palaces.

HAMMERSMITH & FULHAM (Maps 1 & 2)

Hammersmith is not an especially inviting borough, dominated as it is by a hideous flyover and chaotic roundabout. There are no specific sights, although you might want to visit the Riverside Studios or the popular Lyric Theatre. With time to spare there's a good set of riverfront pubs on the Chiswick side of Hammersmith Bridge plus a pleasant 3.5km walk along the Thames from the shopping centre beside the bridge to Chiswick itself.

Fulham is more immediately agreeable than Hammersmith; its main draw is Fulham Palace.

Riverside Studios

Riverside Studios (Map 1; ☎ 7420 0100, 8237 1111 for a recording), Crisp Rd W6 (⊖ Hammersmith), is west London's equivalent of the ICA, a mixed-media arts centre with two good-sized auditoriums that present films, theatre, modern dance and about a dozen art shows per year. It's open Monday to Saturday from 9 am to 11 pm, on Sunday from noon.

Fulham Palace

In Bishop's Park, next to the Thames on the Fulham side of Putney Bridge, stands Fulham Palace (Map 2; ☎ 7736 3233), Bishop's Avenue SW6 (✆ Putney Bridge), summer home of the bishops of London from 704 to 1973. It originally boasted a long moat, making it the largest moated site in Europe. The oldest part to survive is the little red-brick Tudor gateway, but the main building you see today dates from the mid-17th century and was remodelled in the 19th century. There's a pretty walled garden and, detached from the main house, a Tudor Revival chapel designed by Butterfield in 1866.

The museum describes the history of the palace and is open Wednesday to Sunday from 2 to 5 pm. Admission costs 50/25p. On the second Sunday of every month 90-minute tours (£2) take place at 2 pm, taking in the Great Hall, the chapel, Bishop Sherlock's dining room and the museum.

CHISWICK (Map 1)

Despite the abomination of the A4, which cuts off the riverside roads from the centre, Chiswick (**chiz**-ick) is still a pleasant suburb, with cafés and restaurants with pavement tables on Chiswick High Rd. Most people come to Chiswick to visit Chiswick House and the home of the artist Hogarth. There's also a very pleasant riverside walk all the way to Hammersmith.

Chiswick House

Chiswick House (☎ 8995 0508), Chiswick Park W4 (✆ Turnham Green), is a fine Palladian pavilion with an octagonal dome and colonnaded portico. It was designed by the 3rd Earl of Burlington (1694-1753) when he returned from his grand tour of Italy, fired up with enthusiasm for all things Roman. Lord Burlington used it to entertain friends and to house his library and art collection.

Inside, the ground floor has details of the restoration work that took place recently and also accommodates several statues brought in from the park to protect them. Upstairs some of the rooms have been completely restored to a grandeur some will find overpowering. The dome of the main salon has been left ungilded and the walls are decorated with eight enormous paintings. In the Blue Velvet Room look for the portrait of Inigo Jones, the architect much admired by Lord Burlington, over one of the doors. The ceiling paintings are by William Kent, who also decorated the Kensington Palace State Apartments.

Lord Burlington also planned the house's original gardens, now Chiswick Park, but they have been much altered since then. The restored Cascade waterfall is bubbling again after being out of action for years.

Chiswick House is open daily from 10 am to 6 pm, April to September, closing at 5 pm in October; and Wednesday to Sunday from 10 am to 4 pm, November to March. Admission costs £3/2.30/1.50 for adults/seniors & students/children (free for EH members).

The house is about 1.5km from the tube station, but bus No E3 from under the bridge outside the station will drop you nearby.

Hogarth's House

Robbed of its setting by the thundering traffic on the A4, Hogarth's House (☎ 8994 6757), Hogarth Lane, Great West Rd W4 (✆ Turnham Green), nevertheless offers an opportunity to see inside a small 18th-century house.

William Hogarth lived here from 1749 to 1764 and although very little original furniture remains, the pistachio-coloured walls are decorated with his evocatively named engravings of life in Georgian London (see the boxed text 'Of Rakes & Harlots: Hogarth's World' under Arts in the Facts about London chapter).

The house (free) is open Tuesday to Friday from 1 to 5 pm (6 pm at weekends), closing an hour earlier November to March.

JULIET COOMBE

Flower-fest: Kew Gardens has the world's largest collection of orchids.

KEW (Map 1)

Kew will be forever associated with Kew Gardens, headquarters of the Royal Botanical Society and boasting one of the world's finest plant collections. But central Kew Green is itself a pretty place where cricket is played in summer.

Kew Gardens

The Royal Botanic Gardens at Kew (☎ 8332 5000, 8940 1171 for a recording), Kew Rd, Kew (✆ Kew Gardens), is one of the most visited sights on the London tourist itinerary, which means it can get very crowded during summer, especially at weekends. Spring is probably the best time to visit, but at any time of year this 120-hectare expanse of lawns, formal gardens and greenhouses has delights to offer. As well as being a public garden, Kew is an important research centre, and it maintains its reputation as the most exhaustive botanical collection in the world. Its Web site is at www.kew.org.

Orientation The wonderful plants and trees aside, there are several specific sights within the gardens. Assuming you come by tube and enter via **Victoria Gate**, you'll come almost immediately to a large pond overlooked by the enormous **Palm House**,

a hothouse of metal and curved sheets of glass designed by Decimus Burton and Richard Turner from 1844 to 1848 and housing all sorts of exotic tropical greenery. Just north-west of the Palm House is the tiny but irresistible **Water Lily House** (open March to December), dating from 1852.

If you head north, you'll come to the stunning **Princess of Wales Conservatory**, opened in 1987 and housing plants in 10 different computer-controlled climatic zones – everything from a desert to a cloud forest. Beyond that is the **Kew Gardens Gallery** bordering Kew Green, which houses exhibitions of paintings and photos mostly of a horticultural theme.

Heading west from the gallery you'll arrive at the red-brick **Kew Palace**, a former royal residence once known as Dutch House, dating from 1631. It was very popular with George III and his family (his wife Charlotte died here in 1818). The gardens surrounding the palace are especially pretty. The palace has been closed for extensive renovations.

If you cut south from the palace across the lawns you'll pass a long **lake** running roughly west to east. To the south west is **Queen Charlotte's Cottage**, a wooden summerhouse used, again, by George III and his family and surrounded by bluebells in spring. It is open at weekends in summer only. Due east of the cottage is the **Japanese Gate** and then the celebrated **Pagoda**, designed by William Chambers in 1761.

Heading north again you'll arrive at the 180m-long **Temperate House**, another wonderful iron and glass hothouse (although not so hot this time) designed by Burton in 1860 but not completed until 1899. On the western side the small, all-glass **Evolution House** shows how plants have evolved over the millennia.

Due east of Temperate House is the **Marianne North Gallery**. Marianne North was one of those indomitable Victorian female travellers who roamed the continents from 1871 to 1885, painting their plants and trees along the way. The results of her labour now cover the walls of this small purpose-built gallery.

The **Orangery** near Kew Palace contains a licensed self-service restaurant, café and shop.

Hours & Tickets Kew Gardens opens daily at 9.30 am but closes at different times throughout the year: at 4.30 pm, November to January; at 5 pm, February; at 6 pm, March; Monday to Saturday at 6.30 pm and on Sunday at 8 pm, April to August; at 6 pm, September to October. Note that most of the hothouses close at 5.30 pm in summer, earlier in winter. Admission costs £5/3.50/2.50 for adults/seniors & students/children aged five to 16 (family £13). Late entry (45 minutes before the conservatories close) is £3.50.

Getting There & Away You can get to Kew Gardens by tube or train. Come out of the station and walk straight (west) along Station Parade, cross Kew Gardens Rd and continue straight along Lichfield Rd. This will bring you to Victoria Gate.

Alternatively, from March to September (with reduced services in October), boats run by the Westminster Passenger Services Association (☎ 7930 4721) sail from Westminster Pier to Kew Gardens up to eight times a day, with the first boat departing at 10.15 am and the last at 2.30 pm. The boats, which go via Putney, take 1¾ hours and single tickets cost £6/5/3 for adults/seniors/children, returns £10/8/5.

RICHMOND & TWICKENHAM (Map 1)

If anywhere in London could be described as a village, Richmond – with its delightful green and riverside vistas – is it. There are plenty of good places to eat and drink. Of Richmond Palace south of the Old Deer Park, where Elizabeth I died in 1603, only a red-brick gatehouse with the name Henry VII on it and a courtyard survive. Best of all Richmond Park is the largest and most rural of the royal parks. You can get to Richmond on foot from Kew by following the river towards Twickenham, just across the bridge from Richmond.

Twickenham will always be associated with rugby. Otherwise there's not much to detain you here unless you want to visit the fine Marble Hill House overlooking the Thames.

Richmond Park

One of London's finest and wildest parks, Richmond Park covers 1000 hectares and is home to all sorts of wildlife including herds of red and fallow deer, and more elusive foxes and badgers. It's a great place for birdwatchers too, with a wide range of habitats, from neat gardens to woodland and assorted ponds. The philosopher Bernard Russell (1872-1970) grew up in Pembroke Lodge, now a tearoom with fine views from the terrace at the back. Edward VIII was born in the 18th-century White Lodge. The Isabella Plantation is at its most spectacular in April and May when the rhododendrons and azaleas are in bloom.

The park is open daily from dawn to 30 minutes before dusk.

Getting There & Away It's easiest to get to the park with your own transport, although parking can be tricky at weekends. To get there from Richmond station, turn left along George St, which winds

MARK HONAN

The green, green grass of home: munching away in Richmond Park.

round towards Richmond Bridge and then forks. Take the left fork up Richmond Hill, pausing to soak up views so magnificent that they spurred Gainsborough and Turner to canvas, until you reach the Royal Star & Garter Home, for men disabled in 20th-century conflicts from WWI to the Gulf War. Across the road (a dangerous crossing) is Richmond Gate and the park.

Ham House

This 'Hampton Court in miniature' was built in 1610 and became home to the 1st Earl of Dysart, an unlucky individual who had been employed as 'whipping boy' to Charles I, taking the punishment for all the king's wrongdoings. Inside it's furnished with all the grandeur you might expect; the Great Staircase is a magnificent example of Stuart woodworking. Look out for ceiling paintings by Antonio Verrio, who also worked at Hampton Court Palace, and for a miniature of Elizabeth I by Nicholas Hilliard. Other notable paintings are by Constable, Reynolds and Kneller. The grounds of Ham House slope down to the Thames, but there's also a pleasant 17th-century formal garden.

Ham House (☎ 8940 1950) is open Saturday to Wednesday from 1 to 5 pm, from late March to October. The gardens are open on the same days from 10.30 am to 6 pm. Admission costs £5/2.50 for adults/children

(free for NT members; family £12.50). Entry to just the garden is £1.50/75p (family £3.75). To get there take a train or tube to Richmond and then bus No 371.

Museum of Rugby

A state-of-the-art museum that will appeal to sports lovers but leave everyone else less than impressed, the Museum of Rugby, also known as the Twickenham Experience (Map 1; ☎ 8892 2000), Twickenham Rugby Stadium, Rugby Rd, Twickenham (⊖ Hounslow East, then bus No 281; Twickenham station), is tucked behind the east stand of the stadium. Relive those highlights of old matches in the video theatre and then take a tour of the grounds.

The museum is open Tuesday to Saturday from 10.30 am to 5 pm and on Sunday from 2 pm. Combined tickets to the museum and a tour round the stadium (not scheduled on or around match days) cost £5/3 (family £15).

Marble Hill House

Marble Hill House (Map 1; ☎ 8892 5115), Richmond Rd, Twickenham (St Margaret's station), is an 18th-century Palladian love nest, built originally for George II's mistress Henrietta Howard and later occupied by Mrs Fitzherbert, the secret wife of George IV. The poet Alexander Pope had a hand in designing the park, which stretches down to the Thames. Inside you'll find an exhibition about the life and times of Henrietta, and a collection of early Georgian furniture.

Marble Hill House is open daily from 10 am to 6 pm, April to September, closing at 5 pm in October; and Wednesday to Sunday from 10 am to 4 pm, November to March. Admission costs £3/2.30/1.50 for adults/seniors & students/children (free for EH members).

From St Margaret's station, turn right along St Margaret's Rd. Then take the right fork along Crown Rd and turn left along Richmond Rd. Turn right along Beaufort Rd and walk across Marble Hill Park to the house.

HAMPTON

Out in London's south-western outskirts, the wonderful Hampton Court Palace (see the Around London map in the Excursions chapter) is pressed up against 400-hectare Bushy Park, a semi-wild expanse with herds of red and fallow deer.

Hampton Court Palace

In 1514 Cardinal Thomas Wolsey, lord chancellor of England, decided to build himself a palace in keeping with his sense of self-importance. Unfortunately, even Wolsey couldn't persuade the pope to grant Henry VIII a divorce from Catherine of Aragon and relations between king and chancellor rapidly soured. Given that background, you only need to take one look at Hampton Court Palace (☎ 8781 9500; Hampton Court station) to realise why Wolsey felt obliged to present it to Henry, a monarch not too fond of anyone trying to muscle in on his mastery of all he surveyed. The hapless Wolsey was charged with high treason but died before he could come to trial in 1530.

As soon as he acquired the palace, Henry set to work expanding it, adding the Great Hall, the Chapel Royal and the sprawling kitchens. By 1540 this was one of the grandest and most sophisticated palaces in Europe. In the late 17th century, William and Mary employed Sir Christopher Wren to build extensions. The result is a beautiful blend of Tudor and 'restrained baroque' architecture.

Today the palace is England's largest and grandest Tudor structure, knee-deep in history, and with superb gardens and a famous 300-year-old maze. You should set aside plenty of time to do it justice, bearing in mind that if you come by boat from central London the trip will have eaten up half the day already.

Orientation Tickets are on sale in an office to the left of the main **Trophy Gate**. Here you should pick up a leaflet listing the daily programme, which will help you plan your visit; this is important as many of the free guided tours require advance booking.

As you walk up the path towards the palace you'll have a fine view of the lengthy red-brick façade with its distinctive, twisted Tudor chimneys and sturdy gateway. Passing through the main gate you arrive first in the **Base Court** and then the **Clock Court**, named after the fine 16th-century astronomical clock that still shows the sun revolving round the earth. The **Fountain Court** is next. From the Clock Court you can follow signs to the six main sets of rooms in the complex.

The stairs inside Anne Boleyn's Gateway lead up to **Henry VIII's State Apartments**, including the Great Hall, the largest single room in the palace, decorated with tapestries and a spectacular hammer-beam roof from which tiny painted faces peep down. A hallway hung with antlers leads to the **Great Watching Chamber** where guards controlled access to the king; this is the least altered of all the rooms dating from Henry's day. Leading off from the chamber is the smaller Pages' Chamber and the Haunted Gallery. Arrested for adultery and detained in the palace in 1542, Henry's fifth wife Catherine Howard managed to evade her guards and ran screaming down the corridor in search of the king. Her woeful ghost is said to do the same thing to this day.

Farther along the corridor you'll come to the beautiful **Chapel Royal**. A Royal Pew forming part of the state apartments looks down over the altar below. The blue and gold vaulted ceiling was originally intended for Christ Church, Oxford, but was installed here instead, while the 18th-century reredos was carved by Grinling Gibbons.

Also dating from Henry's day are the **Tudor Kitchens**, again accessible from Anne Boleyn's Gateway and originally able to rustle up meals for a royal household of some 1200 people. The kitchens have been fitted out to look as they might have done in Tudor days and palace 'servants' turn the spits and stuff the bustards. Don't miss the Great Wine Cellar, which could originally cope with the 300 barrels of ale and the same again of wine consumed here annually in the mid-16th century.

RACHEL BLACK

Save the maze until last, in case you get stuck and miss out on Hampton Court Palace itself.

Returning again to the Clock Court and passing under the colonnade to the right you reach the **King's Apartments** built by Wren for William III towards the end of the 17th century. These apartments were badly damaged by fire in 1986 but have now been extensively restored.

A tour of the apartments takes you up the grand King's Staircase painted by Antonio Verrio in about 1700 and flattering the king by comparing him to Alexander the Great. You'll emerge into the **King's Guard Chamber**, which is decked out with guns, bayonets and swords and leads to the King's Presence Chamber. This room is dominated by a throne backed with scarlet hangings and by an equestrian portrait of William III by Godfrey Kneller.

Next on the tour is the King's Eating Room where William would sometimes have dined in public, beyond which you'll find the King's Privy Chamber where ambassadors were received; the chandelier and throne canopy have been carefully restored after suffering terrible damage in the 1986 fire. Beyond this is the King's Withdrawing Room, where more intimate gatherings took place, and the **King's Great Bedchamber**, a

splendid room, its bed topped with ostrich plumes, where the king was ceremonially dressed each morning. William actually slept in the Little Bedchamber beyond.

The back stairway beyond the King's Closet leads to three more wood-panelled closets furnished with paintings and more carvings by Grinling Gibbons. You then walk through an orangery to the King's Private Drawing Room and Dining Room, which is decorated with Kneller's paintings of the *Hampton Court Beauties*.

William's wife, Mary II, had her own separate **Queen's Apartments**, which are accessible up the Queen's Staircase, decorated by William Kent. When Mary died in 1694 work on these rooms was incomplete; they were finished George II's reign. The rooms are shown as they might have been when Queen Charlotte used them for entertaining between 1716 and 1737.

In comparison with the King's State Apartments, those for the queen seem rather austere, although the Queen's Audience Chamber has a throne as imposing as the king's. Pass through the Queen's Drawing Room and you come to the **State Bedchamber** where the queen took part in levees rather than sleeping. The Queen's Gallery is hung with a set of 18th-century tapestries depicting the adventures of Alexander the Great.

Also upstairs and ringing Wren's graceful Fountain Court are the **Georgian Rooms** used by George II and Queen Charlotte on their last visit to the palace in 1737. The first rooms you come to were designed to accommodate George's second son, the Duke of Cumberland, whose bed is woefully tiny for its grand surroundings. The Wolsey Closet was restored and repanelled in 1888 to give an idea of what one of the palace's smaller rooms might have looked like in Tudor times. The Communications Gallery was built for William III and is decorated with Peter Lely's portraits of the *Windsor Beauties*, the most beautiful women at the court of Charles II. Beyond that is the Cartoon Gallery where the Raphael Cartoons now in the Victoria & Albert Museum used to hang; nowadays you have to make do with late 17th-century copies.

Beyond the Cartoon Gallery are the queen's private rooms: her drawing room and bedchamber, where she and the king would sleep if they wanted to be alone. Particularly interesting are the Queen's Bathroom, with its tub set on a floor cloth to soak up any spillage, and the Oratory, with its 16th-century Persian carpet.

Once you're finished with the palace interior there are still the wonderful gardens to appreciate. Look out for the **Real Tennis Court**, dating from the 1620s and designed for real tennis, a rather different version of the game from that played today. The **Privy Gardens** have recently been restored and are spectacular. Here you'll find the Great Vine planted in 1768 and still producing around 300kg of grapes a year; the Lower Orangery housing Andrea Mantegna's nine *Triumphs of Caesar* paintings, bought by Charles I in 1629; and the Banqueting House designed for William III and painted by Antonio Verrio. Look out, too, for the iron screens designed by Jean Tijou.

No one should leave Hampton Court

without losing themselves in the famous 800m-long, hornbeam and yew **maze**, planted in 1690. In case you're wondering, the average visitor takes 20 minutes to reach the centre.

Hours & Tickets Hampton Court Palace is open daily from 9.30 am (10.15 am on Monday) to 6 pm, mid-March to October. During the rest of the year it opens at the same times but closes at 4.30 pm. An all-inclusive ticket costs £10/7.60/6.60 for adults/seniors & students/children (family £29.90), but if you just want to visit the Privy Gardens you pay £2.10/1.30 and £2.30/1.50 for the maze. Admission to the real tennis court is free. Carriage rides round the gardens cost £14 (up to six people) and are available from 10 am to 5 pm.

Getting There & Away There are trains every 30 minutes from Waterloo to Hampton Court station.

The palace can also be reached by Westminster Passenger Services Association river boat (☎ 7930 4721) from Westminster Pier to Hampton Court Pier from April to September, with reduced sailings in October. Ferries depart at 10.30 am, 11.15 am and noon and take about 3½ hours to complete the journey via Putney, Kew and Richmond. Tickets cost £8/7/4 one way for adults/seniors/children and £12/10/7 return.

ISLEWORTH, BRENTFORD & EALING (Map 1)

Isleworth is a quiet suburb by the Thames without much to draw a visitor except for Osterley House and its fine park. Brentford, equally nondescript, links Kew to Osterley and Ealing and boasts magnificent Syon House. Ealing is reasonably leafy and has Pitshanger Manor, the country retreat designed by John Soane.

Osterley Park & House
Set in 120 hectares of landscaped park and farmland, Osterley House (☎ 8568 7714) started life in 1575 as the country retreat of Thomas Gresham, the man responsible for

the Royal Exchange, but was extensively remodelled in the 18th century by Robert Adam. The wonderful plasterwork, furniture and paintings are all worth seeing, but many people rate the downstairs kitchen as being even more interesting.

It's open Wednesday to Sunday from 1 to 4.30 pm, April to October, and admission costs £4.10/2.05 for adults/children (free for NT members; family £10.25). A discount for Travelcard-holders encourages people to arrive by public transport. The Tudor Grand Stables are open on Sunday in summer. The park, with its ornamental lake, is open from 9 am to sunset and entry is free. To get there from Osterley tube station, walk along the Great West Rd and turn left into Thornbury Rd, which will bring you to the park entrance.

Syon House

Syon House (☎ 8560 0881), Syon Park, Brentford (⊖ Gunnersbury; Syon Lane station), is a superb example of the English stately home. The house where Lady Jane Grey ascended the throne for her nine-day reign in 1554 was remodelled by Robert Adam in the 18th century and has plenty of Adam furniture and oak panelling. The

interior was designed along gender-specific lines, with pastel pinks and purples for the ladies' gallery, and mock Roman sculptures for the men's dining room. The gardens, including a lake and the Great Conservatory, were landscaped by Capability Brown.

Syon House is open on Wednesday, Thursday and Sunday only from 11 am to 5 pm, mid-March to October. The gardens are open daily from 10 am to between 3.30 and 5.30 pm year-round. Admission to the house, the gardens and the Great Conservatory costs £5.80/4 (family £14); entry to just the gardens is £3/2 for adults/seniors & students (family £6).

Pitshanger Manor

Pitshanger Manor (☎ 8567 1227), Walpole Park, Mattock Lane W5 (⊖ Ealing Broadway), was bought by the architect John Soane in 1800 and rebuilt in the Regency style. Parts of the manor now house a collection of pottery designed by the Martin Brothers of Southall in the late 19th century. Not everyone will care for their grotesque designs, although the owl jars with swivel heads are undoubtedly fun.

The manor is open (free) Tuesday to Saturday from 10 am to 5 pm.

ELLIOT DANIEL

An Englishman's Castle: Syon House, still the home of the Duke of Northumberland.

THINGS TO SEE & DO

Other Attractions

MUSEUMS & PUBLIC BUILDINGS

As well as those described earlier, London has many smaller museums and buildings open to the public. Some are of specialist interest and have very restricted opening hours. These include:

Alexander Fleming Laboratory
(Map 5; ☎ 7725 6528) St Mary's Hospital, Praed St W2 (✪ Paddington). Reconstruction of the laboratory where Fleming discovered penicillin in 1928. Open (free) Monday to Thursday from 10 am to 1 pm.

Brunel's Engine House
(Map 8; ☎ 7231 3840, 8806 4325) Railway Ave & Tunnel Rd SE16 (✪ Rotherhithe). Engine house designed by Brunel to drain the Thames Tunnel, the world's first major one underwater (1825-43), which now serves as a railway tunnel. Open on the first Sunday of the month from 1 to 5 pm. Admission costs £2/1.

Faraday Museum
(Map 7; ☎ 7409 2992), Royal Institution, 21 Albemarle St W1 (✪ Green Park). This shrine to Michael Faraday (1791-1867), a pioneer in electromagnetism and inventor of the electric battery, recreates his old laboratory at the Royal Institution, where he taught. Open weekdays from 10 am to 6 pm. Admission costs £1.

Gunnersbury Park Museum
(Map 1; ☎ 8992 1612) Popes Lane W3 (✪ Acton Town). Large Regency house containing a local history museum and a collection of carriages. Open (free) daily from 1 to 5 pm (6 pm at weekends, 4 pm from November to March).

House Mill
(Map 1; ☎ 8980 4626) Three Mill Lane E3 (✪ Bromley-by-Bow). The UK's largest surviving tidal mill (1776), used for making flour and powering a distillery. Guided tours on alternate Sundays only from 2 to 4 pm, from mid-May to October. Admission costs £2/1. There's a craft market here on the first Sunday of every month.

John Wesley's House & Museum of Methodism
(Map 4; ☎ 7253 2262) 49 City Rd EC1 (✪ Old Street). Well-kept chapel, museum and house filled with Wesley memorabilia. Open Monday to Saturday from 10 am to 4 pm, on Sunday from noon to 2 pm. Admission costs £4/2.

Karl Marx Memorial Library
(Map 4; ☎ 7253 1485) 37a Clerkenwell Green EC1 (✪ Farringdon). Library where Lenin edited the Russian-language newspaper *Iskra*. Open Monday to Thursday 1 to 8 pm (till 6 pm on Monday) and on Saturday 10 am to 1 pm. Tours of the house (£1/50p) depart daily at 11 am and 1, 3 and 5 pm.

Kew Bridge Steam Museum
(Map 1; ☎ 8568 4757) Green Dragon Lane, Brentford (Kew Bridge station). Restored 19th-century pumping station with five Cornish beam engines, two of which steam away at weekends. Open daily from 11 am to 5 pm. Admission costs £3.80/2.50/2 for adults/ seniors & students/children aged five to 15 at weekends and £1 less during the week (family £10.50, £7 weekdays).

London Canal Museum
(Map 4; ☎ 7713 0836) 12-13 New Wharf Rd N1 (✪ King's Cross). Victorian warehouse with small museum about life on the canals. Open Tuesday to Sunday from 10 am to 4.30 pm. Admission costs £2.50/1.25 for adults/seniors, students & children. Its Web site is at www.charitynet.org/~ LCanalMus.

Musical Museum
(Map 1; ☎ 8560 8108) 368 High St, Brentford (Kew Bridge station). Converted church housing a collection of mechanical musical instruments. Open for 90-minute tours at weekends from 2 to 5 pm (and on Wednesday in July and August), April to October. Admission costs £3.20/2.50.

North Woolwich Old Station
(Map 1; ☎ 7474 7244) Pier Rd E16 (North Woolwich station). Small preserved train station likely to interest rail fanatics. Open (free) on Friday and Sunday from 2 to 5 pm, and on Saturday from 10 am, April to September.

Petrie Museum of Egyptian Archaeology
(Map 3; 7504 2884) University College London, Malet Place WC1 (✪ Euston Square or Goodge Street). Wonderful collection of Egyptian artefacts, particularly mummy portraits. Open (free) Tuesday to Friday from 1 to 5 pm, on Saturday from 10 am to 1 pm.

Pollock's Toy Museum
(Map 6; ☎ 7636 3452) 1 Scala St W1 (✪ Goodge Street). Collection of old model theatres open Monday to Saturday from 10 am to 5 pm. Admission costs £3/1.50 for adults/ under-18s.

Ragged School Museum
(Map 2; ☎ 8980 6405) 48-50 Copperfield Rd E3 (✪ Mile End). Small East End museum with information on the Dr Barnado homes

for children and on education. Open (free) Wednesday and Thursday from 10 am to 5 pm, and on the first Sunday of the month from 2 pm.

Royal Air Force Museum
(Map 1; ☎ 8205 2266) Grahame Park Way, Hendon NW9 (✆ Colindale). Huge museum in the old Hendon Aerodrome displaying 70 planes and flying machines alongside a flight simulator. It's open daily from 10 am to 6 pm and costs £6.50/3.25.

Sutton House
(Map 2; ☎ 8986 2264) 2 & 4 Homerton High St, Hackney E9 (Hackney Central station). Tudor red-brick house with 18th-century additions and gardens. Open on Wednesday and Sunday from 11.30 am to 5.30pm and on Saturday from 2 pm, February to November. Admission costs £3/50p adults/children (family £4.50; free for NT members).

GALLERIES

Along with the galleries described earlier in this chapter, London has many smaller, often commercial galleries that host changing exhibitions throughout the year. The free monthly publication *Galleries*, available at many galleries, will tell you exactly what's on where. If you're having trouble tracking it down call ☎ 8740 7020 for guidance or try visiting www.artefact.co.uk on the Web.

The galleries in the following list are just suggestions. Go for a stroll up and down Cork St, New Bond St or Old Bond St (all W1) and you'll find several other possibilities.

Agnew's
(☎ 7629 6176) 43 Old Bond St W1 (✆ Bond Street)

Berkeley Square Gallery
(☎ 7493 7939) 23A Bruton St W1 (✆ Green Park)

Brixton Artists' Collective
(☎ 7733 6957) 35 Brixton Station Rd SW9 (✆ Brixton)

Chinese Contemporary
(☎ 7734 9808) 11 New Burlington Place W1 (✆ Piccadilly Circus)

Colnaghi
(☎ 7491 7408) 15 Old Bond St W1 (✆ Bond Street)

Crafts Council
(☎ 7278 7700) 44A Pentonville Rd N1 (✆ Angel)

London's Top 10 Free Sights

London can be frighteningly expensive, but there's no need to despair; there are plenty of places you can visit without having to part with a penny. Our 10 favourites – in no particular order – are:

- British Museum (page 147)
- Geffrye Museum (page 212)
- Kenwood House (page 206)
- Museum Of ... (page 181)
- Museum of Gardening History (page 185)
- National Gallery (page 124)
- National Portrait Gallery (page 125)
- Sir John Soane's Museum (page 152)
- Tate Britain (page 134)
- Wallace Collection (page 198)

Fine Art Society
(☎ 7629 5116) 148 New Bond St W1 (✆ Bond Street)

Lamont Gallery
(☎ 8981 6332) 67 Roman Rd E2 (✆ Bethnal Green)

London Glass-Blowing Workshop
(☎ 7403 2800) 7 The Leather Market, Weston St SE1 (✆ Borough or London Bridge)

London Institute Gallery
(☎ 7514 6238) 65 Davies St W1 (✆ Bond Street)

Lothbury Gallery
(☎ 7726 1642) 41 Lothbury EC2 (✆ Bank)

Mall Galleries
(☎ 7930 6844) The Mall SW1 (✆ Charing Cross)

Marlborough Fine Art
(☎ 7629 5161) 6 Albemarle St W1 (✆ Green Park)

October Gallery
(☎ 7242 7367) 24 Old Gloucester St WC1 (✆ Holborn)

Photographers' Gallery
(☎ 7831 1772) 5 Great Newport St WC2 (✆ Leicester Square)

Spink & Son
(☎ 7930 7888) 5 King St SW1 (✆ Piccadilly Circus)

Activities

CLIMBING

Well, it ain't Everest or even the Matterhorn but the Castle Climbing Centre (Map 1; ☎ 8211 7000), Green Lanes N4 (✆ Manor House or bus No 171A or 141), is the country's foremost climbing centre for everyone from beginners to experienced climbers. It's open weekdays from 2 to 10 pm, at weekends from 10 am to 7 pm. Admission costs £6/3.50. A similar place is the Mile End Climbing Wall (Map 2; ☎ 8980 0289), Haverfield Rd E3, off Grove Rd (✆ Mile End), open Monday to Thursday noon to 9.30 pm, on Friday to 9 pm and at weekends from 10 am to 6 pm.

DOUG McKINLAY

A far more discerning way of getting around than the tube ...

GOLF

If you can't bring yourself to leave the clubs behind, the capital has a couple of leafy golf courses on its outskirts. Brent Valley Golf Course (☎ 8567 1287) is at Church Rd, Cuckoo Lane W7 (Hanwell station). Richmond Park Golf Course (☎ 8876 3205) is at Roehampton Gate SW15 (Barnes station).

HORSE RIDING

If you'd like to go riding in Hyde Park, which has 8km of bridle paths, horses can be hired for £27 per hour (£230 for 10 hours of riding) from Hyde Park Stables (Map 5; ☎ 7723 2813), 63 Bathurst Mews W2 (✆ Lancaster Gate). Riding lessons cost £30 per hour (£260 for a course of 10 hours). It is open weekdays from 10 am to 6 pm and at weekends from 8.45 am to 4.15 pm.

Mudchute Park Farm (Map 12; ☎ 7515 0749), Pier St E14 (DLR Mudchute), is open Tuesday to Sunday from 9 am to 5 pm. It costs £18/16 for an adult/child to ride for an hour. Another place in East London with horses is the Docklands Equestrian Centre (Map 1; ☎ 7511 3917), 2 Claps Gate Lane E6 (DLR Beckton), open Monday to Thursday from 5 to 7.30 pm and in the morning at weekends.

ICE-SKATING

The Broadgate Ice Rink (☎ 7505 4608), Broadgate Centre, Eldon St EC2 (Map 8; ✆ Liverpool Street), is the only open-air rink in the UK and opens in winter only. Entry costs £5/3 and then it's another £2/1 to hire skates.

For a rink open year-round, you'll have to go farther afield. Streatham Ice Rink (☎ 8769 7771), 386 Streatham High Rd SW16 (Streatham station), is a large rink where you can also take lessons. It is open 10 am to 7 pm (to 4 pm during school terms). Entrance costs £6.50 (£5.20 in termtime) and includes skate rental. The Lee Valley Ice Centre (Map 1; ☎ 8533 3154), Lea Bridge Rd E10 (Clapton station, then bus No 48, 55 or 56) is open daily from noon till 4 pm and costs £5.40/4.40 for adults/children, including skates.

PUBLIC BATHS

If you're visiting London during a hot, muggy summer you may well want to find a place to cool off. Medieval and Tudor London boasted innumerable public baths, which were called 'stews' and had a distinctly dodgy reputation. Even in the late 19th century the capital still boasted more than a dozen public baths, but today hardly

Park life: London's green open spaces are chock-a-block with exercise fanatics doing their thing.

any survive. Those that do are well worth seeking out.

The Porchester Spa (Map 5; ☎ 7792 3980), Porchester Centre, Queensway W2 (⊖ Bayswater), where a small plunge-pool sits in the middle of a tiled Art Deco lounge, was built in 1926. You can relax here and then take advantage of the Turkish hot rooms, Russian steam rooms, Finnish sauna, whirlpool bath and swimming pool. A full range of massages (£30 to £35) is available. The spa is open daily from 10 am to 10 pm (last admission at 8 pm). Monday, Wednesday and Saturday are for men, Tuesday, Thursday and Friday (and Sunday until 4 pm) for women. From 4 to 10 pm on Sunday couples can use the facilities. Admission costs £18.20 (£26 per couple).

A cheaper possibility but not as classy as the Porchester is the Ironmonger Row Baths (Map 4; ☎ 7253 4011), 1 Ironmonger Row EC1 (⊖ Old Street), the closest London gets to a real Turkish bath. Monday, Wednesday, Friday and Sunday are for women, Tuesday, Thursday and Saturday for men. The baths open Monday to Friday from 7.30 am to 8 pm, on Saturday from 9 am to 5 pm and on Sunday from noon to 6 pm. Admission costs £10 (£6.20 in the morning). There's a steam room, sauna, small plunge-pool and swimming pool.

A women-only option is the Sanctuary (Map 7; ☎ 7420 5151), 11-12 Floral St WC2 (⊖ Covent Garden), but with a day's membership costing £53 (£32 Wednesday to Friday between 5 and 10 pm only) this is definitely for that *very* special treat. It is open Sunday to Tuesday from 10 am to 6 pm, Wednesday to Friday from 9.30 am to 10 pm, and on Saturday from 9 am to 8 pm. It has a sauna, steam room, whirlpool and twin pools all day.

SKIING

It represents a *very* loose use of the term 'skiing' as we know it, but you can slalom down a 200m slope made out of a substance that looks like the bottom of a bathmat at Beckton Alps Ski Centre (Map 1; ☎ 7511 0351), Alpine Way E6 (⊖ East Ham, then bus No 101; DLR Beckton). It's open daily from 10 am to 10 pm, September to April, and Friday to Tuesday from noon to 10 pm the rest of the year. Use of the slope for two hours costs £8.50.

A similar place is the Bromley Ski Centre (☎ 01689-876812), Sandy Lane, St Paul's Cray, Orpington (Orpington station). It is open Tuesday to Thursday from noon to 10 pm, on Friday from 10 am to 10 pm, on Saturday from 9 am to 6 pm and on Sunday from 10 am to 6 pm. Adults pay

£7.50/10 for one hour/two hours on the slope, children £6/8.50.

SWIMMING

Almost every London borough has its own swimming pool, and many have several; to find the address of the one nearest to you look in the telephone directory or the *Yellow Pages* or call Sportsline on ☎ 7222 8000. One particularly popular and central pool is at the Oasis Sports Centre (Map 7; ☎ 7831 1804), 32 Endell St WC2 (☻ Tottenham Court Road), with both an indoor pool (weekdays from 6.15 am to 6.30 pm) and an outdoor pool (weekdays from 7.30 am to 9 pm). Both pools are open from 9 am to 5 pm at weekends. Admission costs £2.80.

From late June to August you can swim at the outdoor Serpentine Lido (Map 5; ☎ 7298 2100), beside the Serpentine in Hyde Park, daily from 10 am to 5.30 pm. Admission costs £2.50/50p for adults/children (family £5.50). The Parliament Hill Lido (Map 11; ☎ 7485 3873), Gordon House Rd NW5 (Gospel Oak station), is open daily from 7 am to 6 pm (with an hour's closure from 9 to 10 am), May to September. Hardier souls may head to the nearby Highgate Ponds on the eastern edge of Hampstead Heath and the Hampstead Ponds on the western side (Map 11; ☎ 7485 4491; Hampstead Heath or Gospel Oak station). Of the three Highgate Ponds, one is for men only, one just for women (both open from 7 am to 9 pm year-round) and the third mixed (open from 7 am to 7 pm, May to September). Unsurprisingly the ponds are hugely popular in summer.

TENNIS

Although most London parks have tennis courts, they are often booked up for weeks ahead. The Lawn Tennis Association (☎ 7381 7000), Queen's Club, Palliser Rd W14, produces the useful *Where to Play Tennis in London*, which they'll send you on receipt of a stamped addressed envelope. Alternatively, call Sportsline on ☎ 7222 8000.

WATERSPORTS

You can go boating on the Serpentine in Hyde Park, but for a wider range of watersports, the Docklands is the place to go. For details of what's available contact the Docklands Watersports Club (Map 1; ☎ 7511 7000), King George V Dock, Woolwich Manor Way E16 (DLR Gallions Reach). It's open Tuesday to Thursday from 10 am to dusk, April to October, and Thursday to Sunday for the same hours in winter. Hiring a jet ski costs £30/55 for 30/60 minutes and includes tuition.

Other places where you can jet ski, water ski and windsurf (boards from about £8 an hour) include:

Docklands Sailing & Watersports Centre
(Map 12; ☎ 7537 2626) 235A Westferry Rd, Millwall Docks E14 (DLR Crossharbour & London Arena)
Peter Chilvers Windsurfing Centre
(Map 1; ☎ 7474 2500) Royal Victoria Dock, Gate 6, Tidal Basin Rd E16 (DLR Royal Victoria). Open Tuesday to Sunday from 10 am to dusk.
Royal Victoria Dock Watersports Centre
(Map 1; ☎ 7511 2326) Royal Victoria Dock, Gate 5, Tidal Basin Rd E16 (DLR Royal Victoria)
Surrey Docks Watersports Centre
(Map 12; ☎ 7237 5555) Greenland Dock, Rope St SE16 (☻ Surrey Quays)

Courses

No matter whether you want to study sculpture or Sanskrit, circus skills or computing, someone somewhere in London is going to be running a course that will meet your needs, and your starting point for information should be *Floodlight* (£3.50), published in July and listing most of the regular courses around town. Another – and cheaper – source is *On Course* (£1.95), issued twice a year.

LANGUAGE

Every year thousands of people come to London to study English and there are centres offering tuition throughout the city.

The problem for the prospective student is to identify a reputable one, which is where the resources of the British Council (Map 7; ☎ 7930 8466), 10 Spring Gardens SW1 (✆ Charing Cross), come in. It produces a free list of accredited colleges that meet minimum standards for facilities, qualified staff and pastoral back-up. They can also offer general advice to overseas students on educational opportunities in the UK. Most colleges offer courses leading to the full range of Cambridge or IELTS exams and most will help their students find accommodation. The British Tourist Authority also produces a brochure for people wanting to study in England.

The following are recognised schools you might find useful. All offer courses aimed at every level that can be studied full-time or part-time and lead to University of Cambridge qualifications. They also offer intensive summer courses and private tuition. A four-week full-time course is likely to cost from £150 to £200, while a 12-week course will cost between £300 and £400, depending in part on how many hours you'll be studying.

Central School of English
(☎ 7580 2863) 1 Tottenham Court Rd W1 (✆ Tottenham Court Road)

English in Central London
(☎ 7437 8536) Peter St W1 (✆ Piccadilly Circus)
Frances King School of English
(☎ 7838 0200) 195 Knightsbridge SW7 (✆ Knightsbridge)
Hampstead School of English
(☎ 7794 3533) 553 Finchley Rd NW3 (✆ Golders Green)
Holborn English Language Services
(☎ 7734 9989) 14 Soho St W1 (✆ Tottenham Court Road)
Kingsway College
(☎ 7306 5700) Vernon Square WC1 (✆ King's Cross)
London Study Centre
(☎ 7731 3549) Munster House, 676 Fulham Rd SW6 (✆ Fulham Broadway)

COOKING

The Butlers Wharf Chef School (☎ 7357 8842), Cardamom Building, Butlers Wharf, 31 Shad Thames SE1 (Map 8; ✆ Tower Hill), has cookery demonstration classes in the evening – usually on Tuesday from 6 to 8 pm. They cost £20, including a glass of wine, recipes and notes.

The long-established Leith's School of Food & Wine (Map 5; ☎ 7229 0177), 21 St Alban's Grove W8 (✆ High Street Kensington), has courses ranging from a short demonstration (£45) to a year-long diploma in food and wine costing £9200.

Places to Stay

Where you choose to stay in London is going to affect the kind of time you have in the city. You want ethnic London? Stay in Notting Hill. If your idea of the British capital is one of stately Georgian houses, crescents and private parks in the centre of leafy squares, book a place in Chelsea or South Kensington. Culture vultures or those with literary aspirations should choose a place in Kensington or Bloomsbury. You want workaday London with barrow boys, girls in white-heeled shoes and archetypal Cockney accents? Choose somewhere in the East End. And if you want to hang out with your 'mites', Earl's Court (aka Kangaroo Valley) or Shepherd's Bush is for you.

Unfortunately, though, wherever you stay accommodation in London is going to take a great wad out of your pocket. Demand can outstrip supply – especially at the bottom end of the market – so it's worth booking at least a few nights' accommodation before arriving, particularly in July and August. Remember too that single rooms are in short supply, and places are reluctant to let a double room, even during quiet periods, to one person without charging a hefty supplement or even the full double rate.

The London Tourist Board publishes *Where to Stay & What to Do in London* (£4.99), which lists approved hotels, B&Bs, guesthouses and apartments. It also produces a separate (and free) pamphlet called *Accommodation for Budget Travellers*.

Booking Offices

It's possible to make same-day accommodation bookings for free at most of the tourist information centres. The telephone bookings hotline (open Monday to Friday

Effortless grandeur: stay in luxury at the Savoy (but check your credit-card balance first).

from 8.30 am to 6 pm) is ☎ 7932 2020 and costs £5 per booking. The British Hotel Reservation Centre (☎ 0800 282888) on the main concourse of Victoria train station is open from 6 am to 11.30 pm and charges £3 per booking.

Thomas Cook also operates a hostel and hotel reservation service, charging £5 per booking. There are kiosks at the Britain Visitor Centre (Map 7; walk-ins only) as well as Paddington (☎ 7837 5681), Charing Cross (☎ 7976 1171), Euston (☎ 7388 7435), King's Cross (☎ 7828 4646) and Victoria (☎ 7828 4646) train stations; at Earl's Court (☎ 7723 0184) and South Kensington (☎ 7581 9766) tube stations; and at the Gatwick airport train station (☎ 01293-529372).

The Youth Hostel Association (YHA) operates its own central reservations system (☎ 7373 3400, fax 7373 3455, email yhalondonreservations@compuserve.com). Although you still pay the individual hostel directly, the staff will know what beds are available where and when, and they're much easier to contact than the hostels during busy periods like July and August.

If you want to stay in a B&B, bookings for a minimum of three days can be made free through London Homestead Services (☎ 8949 4455, fax 8549 5492), Coombe Wood Rd, Kingston-upon-Thames KT2 7JY. Bed & Breakfast (GB) (☎ 01491-578803), PO Box 66, Henley-on-Thames RG9 1XS, specialises in central London as does Accommodation Line (☎ 7409 1343, fax 7409 2606), 1st floor, 46 Maddox St, London W1R 9PB. Host & Guest Service (☎ 7385 9922, fax 7386 7575), 103 Dawes Rd, London SW6 7DU, will look for student accommodation as well.

Among the best Web sites for locating and booking accommodation in London are www.s-h-systems.co.uk/map5.html and www.demon.co.uk/hotel-uk/lonindex.html for hotels, www.eurotrip.com for hostels, www.lon.ac.uk/accom/vacation.htm for University of London halls of residence and www.loot.com for all types of accommodation throughout the capital.

PLACES TO STAY – BUDGET
Camping

Camping is not a realistic option in the centre of the capital but there are a few possibilities within striking distance.

Tent City Acton *(Map 1; ☎ 8743 5708, fax 8749 9074, Old Oak Common Lane W3; ✪ East Acton).* This site in far west London is the cheapest option short of camping rough and is delightfully situated within break-out distance of Wormwood Scrubs prison. One of 320 beds in dormitory-style tents costs £6. It's open from June to mid-September, and you should book. There are also about 200 pitches for tents only.

Tent City Hackney *(Map 1; ☎ 8985 7656, Millfields Rd E5; Hackney Central station, then bus No 236 or 276).* A north-east London branch of the previous place, Tent City Hackney has a hostel tent with 90 beds and 200 tent pitches for £5 per person. It's open June to August.

Lee Valley Leisure Centre *(Map 1; ☎ 8345 6666, fax 8803 6900, Lee Valley Regional Park, Meridian Way N9; Northumberland Park station).* This site to the north-east has more than 200 pitches for tents and caravans. It's open year-round and the nightly charge is £5.35/2.25 adults/children; electricity hook-up is £2.30 extra.

Abbey Wood Caravan Park *(☎ 8311 7708, fax 8311 6007, Federation Rd SE2; Abbey Wood station).* South of the river and east of Greenwich, Abbey Wood has 360 pitches and is open year-round. Tent/caravan pitches cost £3.50/8.50 plus £4/1.20 per adult/child. Electricity is £1.45.

YHA/HI Hostels

Seven hostels in the central London area – and another two within easy commuting distance – are members of Hostelling International (HI), known as the Youth Hostels Association (YHA) in Britain. Joining the YHA gives you access to a network of hostels throughout the UK and the rest of the world, and you don't have to be 'young' to do so. Annual membership costs £11/5.50 for those over/under 18 years of age. If you are not a member but wish to stay at a YHA hostel, you'll be given a card to fill up with six nightly stamps, each costing £1.70 in addition to the nightly rate. When the card's full, you've become a member.

You can join the YHA at the YHA

Adventure Shop (Map 7; ☎ 7836 8541), 14 Southampton St WC2 (✆ Covent Garden), or by credit/debit card or cheque by contacting the YHA at Membership Department, Youth Hostels Association of England & Wales (☎ 01727-845047, 855215, fax 844126, email customerservices@yha.org .uk), Trevelyan House, 8 St Stephen's Hill, St Albans AL1 2DY). The YHA's Web site is at www.yha.org.uk.

You can also join HI – or its local affiliate – in your home country. National offices include:

Australia
(☎ 02-9565 1699, fax 9565 1325, email yha@yha.org.au)
Australian Youth Hostels Association, Level 3, 10 Mallett St, Camperdown, NSW 2050
Canada
(☎ 613-237 7884, fax 237 7868)
Hostelling International Canada, Suite 400, 205 St Catherine St, Ottawa, Ontario K2P 1C3
Ireland
(☎ 01-830 4555, fax 830 5808, email anoige@iol.ie)
An Óige/Irish Youth Hostel Association, 61 Mountjoy St, Dublin 7
New Zealand
(☎ 03-379 9970, fax 365 4476, email info@yha.org.nz)
Youth Hostels Association of New Zealand, PO Box 436, 3rd floor, Union House, 193 Cashel St, Christchurch 1
Northern Ireland
(☎ 028-9032 4733, fax 9043 9699)
Youth Hostel Association of Northern Ireland, 22-32 Donegall Rd, Belfast BT12 5JN
Scotland
(☎ 01786-891400, fax 891333, email admin@syha.org.uk)
Scottish Youth Hostels Association, 7 Glebe Crescent, Stirling FK8 2JA
South Africa
(☎ 021-424 2511, fax 424 4119, email info@hisa.org.za)
Hostelling International South Africa, PO Box 4402, St George's House, 73 St George's Mall, Cape Town 8001
USA
(☎ 202-783 6161, fax 783 6161, email hiayhserv@hiayh.org)
Hostelling International/American Youth Hostels, Suite 840, 733 15th St, NW, Washington DC 20005

The biggest advantages of staying in hostels are price (although the difference between a very cheap B&B and an expensive hostel is not always so great) and the chance to meet other travellers. The disadvantages are that you usually sleep in bunk beds in single-sex dormitories and may find the atmosphere somewhat institutional. The rates always include bed linen and sometimes breakfast.

The seven hostels in central London can get very crowded in summer. An eighth lies to the north-east of the city in Epping Forest and at a push you could even try the YHA hostel in Windsor (see the Excursions chapter for transport details). All the hostels take advance credit-card bookings by phone and will hold some beds for those who show up on the day (arrive early and be prepared to queue). Most offer 24-hour access, facilities for self-catering and relatively cheap meals (eg £3.10 for a full English or continental breakfast, £3.50 for a large packed lunch, £4.60 for a three-course evening meal).

City of London (Map 6; ☎ 7236 4965, fax 7236 7681, email city@yha.org.uk, 36 Carter Lane EC4; ✆ St Paul's). This excellent hostel (193 beds) stands in the shadow of St Paul's Cathedral. Rooms have mainly two, three or four beds though there are a dozen rooms with five to eight beds. There's a licensed cafeteria but no kitchen. Rates per person go from £19.70 to £26 (£17.80 to £22.30 for juniors), depending on the room type. Remember: this part of town is pretty quiet outside working hours.

Earl's Court (Map 9; ☎ 7373 7083, fax 7835 2034, email earlscourt@yha.org.uk, 38 Bolton Gardens SW5; ✆ Earl's Court). This hostel (154 beds) is a Victorian town house in a shabby, though lively, part of town. Rooms are mainly 10-bed dorms with communal showers. There's a café, a kitchen for self-catering and a small garden courtyard for summer barbecues. Rates for adults/children are £19.45/ 17.15 for B&B.

Hampstead Heath (Map 11; ☎ 8458 9054, fax 8209 0546, email hampstead@yha.org.uk, 4 Wellgarth Rd NW11; ✆ Golders Green). This hostel (190 beds) has a beautiful setting with a well-kept garden, although it's rather isolated. The dormitories are comfortable and each room has a washbasin. There's a licensed café and a kitchen. Rates are £16.25/13.90.

Holland House (Map 5; ☎ 7937 0748, fax 7376 0667, email hollandhouse@yha.org.uk, Holland Walk, Kensington W8; ✚ High Street Kensington). This hostel (201 beds) is built into the Jacobean wing of Holland House in the middle of Holland Park. It's large, very busy and rather institutional, but the position can't be beaten. There's a café and kitchen. Rates are £19.45/17.15.

Oxford St (Map 7; ☎ 7734 1618, fax 7734 1657, 14 Noel St W1; ✚ Oxford Circus or Tottenham Court Road). This most central of the hostels (75 beds) is basic but clean and welcoming. It has a large kitchen but no meals are served apart from breakfast (£2.30). Rates are £19.45/15.90 in rooms with three or four beds and £21.10 per person in twin rooms, which make up the majority.

Rotherhithe (Map 8; ☎ 7232 2114, fax 7237 2919, email rotherhithe@yha.org.uk, 20 Salter Rd SE16; ✚ Rotherhithe). The YHA flagship hostel (320 beds) in London was purpose-built in 1993. It's right by the River Thames and recommended, but the location is a bit remote and quiet. Most rooms have four or six beds, though there are also 22 doubles (four of them adapted for disabled visitors); all have an attached bathroom. There's a bar and restaurant as well as kitchen facilities and a laundry. B&B rates are £22.15/18.65.

St Pancras International (Map 3; ☎ 7388 9998, fax 7388 6766, email stpancras@yha.org.uk, 79-81 Euston Rd N1; ✚ King's Cross St Pancras). This central place (153 beds) is London's newest YHA hostel. The area isn't great, but the hostel itself is up-to-date, with kitchen, restaurant, lockers, cycle shed and lounge. Rates are £22.15/18.65 (or £23.50/25 per person for a twin/premium room).

Epping Forest (☎/fax 8508 5161, Wellington Hill, High Beach, Loughton, Essex; ✚ Loughton). This small hostel (36 beds) is 21km from central London and a good 3km walk (or £3 taxi ride) from the nearest tube station, so it's only worth considering if everything else is full. Rates are £8.35/5.65. The hostel is open to individual travellers from late March to early November.

Windsor (☎ 01753-861710, fax 832100, email windsor@yha.org.uk, Edgeworth House, Mill Lane; Windsor & Eton Central station). This far-flung hostel (74 beds), some 35km from central London but only 16km from Heathrow, is in a Queen Anne building with a fine garden and has its own kitchen. Beds cost £10.15/6.85, mainly in nine-bed dorms. Reception is closed from 10 am to 1 pm.

Independent Hostels

London's independent hostels tend to be more relaxed and cheaper than the YHA ones though standards can be pretty low; some of the places we looked at were downright grotty. Expect to pay a minimum of £10 per night in a basic dormitory.

Most hostels have at least three or four bunk beds jammed into each small room, a kitchen and some kind of lounge. Some have budget restaurants and a bar attached. Be careful with your possessions and deposit your valuables in the office safe, safe-deposit box or secure locker if provided. Check that fire escapes and stairwells are accessible.

Ashlee House (Map 4; ☎ 7833 9400, fax 7833 9677, email ashleehouse@tsnxt.co.uk, 261-265 Gray's Inn Rd WC1; ✚ King's Cross St Pancras). This most welcome newcomer is a clean and well maintained backpackers' hostel on three floors close to King's Cross station. Dorm rooms (most with bunks) can be very cramped, but there's double-glazing on the windows, a laundry and a decent-sized kitchen. Rooms with between four and 16 beds cost between £17 and £13 per person in the low season and between £19 and £15 in the high season. There are a few twins for £44 (£48) and one single for £34 (£36).

Backpackers Village (Map 8; ☎ 7407 1856, 161 Borough High St SE1; ✚ Borough or London Bridge). This new hostel (150 beds), part of the St Christopher's stable (see later in this section), has dorms with four/eight beds for £14/12 and a lovely roof garden with sauna, solarium and excellent views of the Thames.

Barmy Badger Backpackers (Map 9; ☎/fax 7370 5213, email barmy_badger.b@virgin.net, 17 Longridge Rd SW5; ✚ Earl's Court). This new kid on the block is a basic dormitory with dorm beds from £13 per person, including breakfast. Twins without/with facilities cost £28/30. There's a big kitchen and safe-deposit boxes.

Court Hotel (Map 9; ☎ 7373 0027, fax 7912 9500, 194-196 Earl's Court Rd SW5; ✚ Earl's Court). This place is under Australasian management and has well equipped kitchens and TVs in most rooms. Dorm beds cost £11 to £14, singles/doubles are £26/35 a night (£160/210 a week).

Curzon House Hotel (Map 9; ☎ 7581 2116, fax 7835 1319, 58 Courtfield Gardens SW5;

Gloucester Road). This relaxed, friendly place in Earl's Court is one of the better private hostels around. Dorm beds are £16 per person, singles/doubles with facilities £26/36. Rates include breakfast and use of the kitchen.

Eurotower (Map 2; ☎ 7720 5191, fax 7720 5178, email eurotower@moose.co.uk, Courland Grove, Larkhall Lane SW4; ✪ Stockwell). This large place (over 400 beds) in Clapham gets good reports; it's not in the most convenient part of London but transport links are good. A place in a dorm room with four beds costs £10 per person including breakfast, or a very competitive £40/60 per week in the low/high season. There's a free pick-up service from Victoria Coach Station and the hostel has a bar, a restaurant, pool tables, tennis courts and a barbecue area. Lockers are provided.

The Generator (Map 4; ☎ 7388 7666, fax 7388 7644, email generator@lhdr.demon.co.uk, Compton Place, 37 Tavistock Place WC1; ✪ Russell Square). The Generator in Bloomsbury is one of the grooviest budget places in central London and the futuristic décor looks like an updated set of Terry Gilliam's film Brazil. Along with 207 rooms (830 beds), it

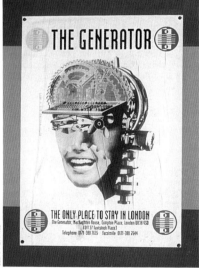

The Generator: neon-lit hostel accommodation in a converted police barracks.

ELLIOT DANIEL

has a bar open to 2 am, a large lounge for eating, watching TV or playing pool, a room with Internet kiosks, safe-deposit boxes and a large eating area, but no kitchen. Depending on the season, a place in a dorm with seven or eight beds costs from £18 to £19.50 and with three to six beds £19 to £21. Singles are £36 to £37 while twins are £45 to £49. All prices include breakfast.

Hyde Park (Map 5; ☎ 7229 5101, fax 7229 3170, email astorhotels@msn.com, 2-6 Inverness Terrace W2; ✪ Bayswater). This Bayswater hostel (50 beds) run by the Astor group is hardly the cleanest or most comfortable place in town, but the building has some character and is conveniently located. There's a café, a laundry and Internet access. Rooms with four/six beds cost £15/14 per person; with eight or 10 beds they're £12.50, including breakfast.

International Students House (Map 3; ☎ 7631 8300, fax 7631 8315, 229 Great Portland St W1; ✪ Great Portland Street). This Marylebone hostel feels more like a university hall of residence. The single and double rooms are ordinary but clean, and there are excellent facilities and a friendly, relaxed atmosphere. It's open year-round. Prices range from £9.99 for a place in an eight-bed dorm without breakfast to £29.50 for a single with washbasin and breakfast. En suite singles/doubles cost £30/47.

Leinster Inn (Map 5; ☎ 7229 9641, fax 7229 5255, email astorhotels@msn.com, 7-12 Leinster Square W2; ✪ Bayswater). In a large old house north-west of Bayswater tube station and close to Portobello Market, this is the largest of the Astor hostels (100 beds). It has a bar, café and laundry. Rates in dorms with up to 10 beds are £13.50, doubles are £22 to £25 per person.

Museum Inn (Map 6; ☎ 7580 5360, fax 7636 7948, 27 Montague St WC1; ✪ Russell Square or Tottenham Court Road). This hostel run by the Astor group has an excellent location opposite the British Museum though we've had several complaints from readers about bookings not being honoured and rude staff. It has a small kitchen and TV lounge; Internet access costs £4 an hour. A basic breakfast is included in the price: £17 per person in one of the five twins, £16/15 in a triple/quad, £14 to £15 in a dorm with eight to 10 beds.

Quest Hotel (Map 5; ☎ 7229 7782, fax 7727 8106, email astorhotels@msn.com, 45 Queensborough Terrace W2; ✪ Bayswater). This Astor hostel one block to the east of the Hyde Park is just as well situated, but with fewer rooms it gets pretty crowded, which may account for the bad-tempered staff. However, the monthly theme parties are popular and there's a kitchen for self-catering. Dorms with four to eight beds cost £15, doubles £18 per person, including breakfast.

St Christopher's Inn (Map 8; ☎ 7407 1856, 121 Borough High St SE1; ✆ London Bridge). This hostel (84 beds), on the corner of Kentish Buildings, is convenient if you want to explore up-and-coming Borough and Bankside, but book ahead in summer. Beds in eight-bed dorms cost £12, including continental breakfast; it's £14/13 in a four/six-bed dorm and £17 per person in a twin. There's a pub beneath the hostel, a small concrete veranda and a lounge. The annexe at No 59 of the same street has six or eight beds in each room and a laundry. The Orient Expresso café below it is open Monday to Thursday from 7.30 am to 7 pm, on Friday from 7.30 am to 4 am, on Saturday from 10 am to 6 am and on Sunday from 10 am to 7 pm.

Windsor House (Map 9; ☎ 7373 9087, 12 Penywern Rd SW5; ✆ Earl's Court). Windsor House has cheap dorm beds for £10, singles for £22 to £28, doubles for £38 and triples for £48, all including breakfast.

Student Accommodation

University halls of residence are let to non-students during the holidays, usually from the end of June to mid-September and sometimes over the Easter break. They're a bit more expensive than the hostels, but you usually get a single room (there are a few doubles) with shared facilities, plus breakfast.

University catering is usually reasonable and includes bars, self-service cafés, take-away places and restaurants. Full-board, half-board, B&B and self-catering options are usually available.

The London School of Economics and Political Science (☎ 7955 7531), Room B508, Page Building, Houghton St, London WC2A 2AE, lets half a dozen of its halls in summer and sometimes during the Easter break. At the time of writing, two popular halls – *Butler's Wharf Residences (Map 8; ☎ 7407 7164, fax 7403 0847, 11 Gainsford St SE1; ✆ Tower Hill)* and *Carr Saunders Hall (Map 6; ☎ 7323 9712, fax 7580 4718, 18-24 Fitzroy St W1; ✆ Warren Street)* – were undergoing major refits, though they most certainly will have reopened by the time you read this.

The other LSE halls are:

Bankside Residence (Map 8; ☎ 7633 9877, 24 Sumner St SE1; ✆ Blackfriars). This hall, with its enviable location near the Globe Theatre and the new Tate Modern at Bankside, has beds in four-bed rooms for £20 to £35 and entire quads for £80, including breakfast.

High Holborn (Map 7; ☎ 7379 5589, fax 7379 5640, 178 High Holborn WC1; ✆ Holborn). This central hall has self-catering twins for £44 to £55 (£55 to £65 with *en suite* bathrooms).

Passfield Hall (Map 3; ☎ 7387 3584, fax 7387 7743, 1-7 Endsleigh Place WC1; ✆ Euston). This hall is composed of 10 late-Georgian houses in the heart of Bloomsbury. B&B costs from £25 to £26.50 for a single, £43 to £48 for a twin and £55 to £60 for a triple.

Rosebery Avenue Hall (Map 4; ☎ 7278 3251, fax 7278 2068, 90 Rosebery Ave EC1; ✆ Angel). B&B costs from £25 to £31 for a single, £34 to £46 for a twin (£57 with facilities) and £55 for a triple.

Other universities and colleges let out their halls of residence outside of term-time:

Finsbury Residences (Map 4; ☎ 7477 8811, fax 7477 8810, 15 Bastwick St EC1; ✆ Barbican or Old Street). These comprise two modern halls belonging to City University. B&B is £21/18 per adult/student. It's open over Christmas, Easter and in the summer.

Goldsmid House (Map 6; ☎ 7493 8911, fax 7491 0586, 36 North Row W1; ✆ Marble Arch). This centrally located hall has 10 singles (£15) and 120 twins (£20) available from mid-June to mid-September.

Imperial College of Science, Technology & Medicine (Map 5; ☎ 7594 9507, fax 7594 9504, email reservations@ic.ac.uk, Watts Way, Prince's Gardens SW7; ✆ South Kensington). This college is two minutes from some of London's greatest museums. It's open at Easter and in summer (July to late September), and B&B with shared bathroom costs £29.50/47 for a single/twin. The college also has rooms with private bathrooms in Pembridge Gardens, Notting Hill W2 (✆ Notting Hill Gate), for £38/54 in summer only.

John Adams Hall (Map 3; ☎ 7387 4086, fax 7383 0164, email jah@ioe.ac.uk, 15-23 Endsleigh St WC1; ✆ Euston). John Adams is quite a grand residence in a row of Georgian houses. It's open at Easter and from July to

September. B&B costs £20/35 or £21.40/37 for a single/double, depending on the time of year.

King's Campus Vacation Bureau *(☎ 7928 3777, fax 928 5777, Riddell House, St Thomas's Campus, Lambeth Palace Rd SE1; Waterloo)*. This bureau administers bookings for four central King's College halls of residence, including one on Stamford St SE1 (Map 6) with apartments for £32.50 per person. Its ***Hampstead Campus*** *(Map 11; ☎ 7435 3564, fax 7431 4402, Kidderpore Ave NW3; Finchley Road)*, for example, has 392 beds from £16.50/28 per single/double and is open from June to September.

Ramsay Hall *(Map 6; ☎ 7387 4537, fax 7383 0843, 20 Maple St W1; Goodge Street or Warren Street)*. This hall in the shadow of the unspeakable Telecom Tower is one of seven University College student houses and halls open at Easter (£23 per person) and in summer (£21).

Regent's College *(Map 3; ☎ 7487 7495, fax 7487 7425, Inner Circle, Regent's Park NW1; Baker Street)*. The college is in a converted Regency manor house right in the middle of beautiful Regent's Park. It's open from mid-May to mid-August. Singles/doubles/triples cost £32/46/54.

University of Westminster *(Map 5; ☎ 7911 5000, fax 7911 5141, 35 Marylebone Rd NW1; Baker Street)*. Westminster has beds in singles or doubles for £20/130 per night/week for people under 26, £25/165 for those over 26. Continental breakfast costs another £3.

YMCAs

YMCA England (☎ 8520 5599), 640 Forest Rd, London E17 3DZ, can supply you with a list of all its hostels in the Greater London area. The main ones are:

Barbican YMCA *(Map 8; ☎ 7628 0697, fax 7638 2420, email admin@barbican.ymca.org.uk, 2 Fann St EC2; Barbican)*. 240 beds, singles/doubles £23/40 with breakfast.

Central Club YMCA *(Map 7; ☎ 7636 7512, fax 7636 5278, 16-22 Great Russell St WC1; Tottenham Court Road)*. 240 beds, singles/doubles £36.75/68.75 (£39/73 with breakfast).

Indian Student YMCA *(Map 6; ☎ 7387 0411, fax 7383 4735, email indianymca@aol.com, 41 Fitzroy Square W1; Warren Street)*. Bed plus breakfast and supper costs £33/45 for a single/double.

London City YMCA *(Map 4; ☎ 7628 8832, fax 7628 4080, 8 Errol St EC1; Barbican)*. 111 beds, B&B £25 per person.

B&Bs, Guesthouses & Hotels

This may come as a shock, but anything below £30/50 for a single/double with shared facilities and below £40/60 with private bathroom is considered 'budget' in London.

B&Bs are an institution in the British Isles and among the cheapest private accommodation around. At the bottom end (hovering around £30 minimum) you get a bedroom in a private house, a shared bathroom and a cooked breakfast. In central London most cheaper accommodation is in guesthouses, often just large converted houses with half a dozen rooms, which tend to be less personal than B&Bs. Double rooms often have twin beds so you don't have to be intimate to share a room.

Don't be afraid to ask for the 'best' price or a discount if you're staying out of season or for more than a couple of nights, or if you don't want a cooked breakfast. In July, August and September prices can jump by 25% or more, and it's advisable to book ahead. Be warned: some of the cheaper B&Bs don't accept credit cards.

Pimlico & Victoria (Map 10) Victoria
may not be the most attractive part of London, but you'll be very close to the action and the budget hotels are better value than those in Earl's Court. Pimlico is more residential though convenient for the Tate Britain at Millbank.

Luna-Simone Hotel *(☎ 7834 5897, fax 7828 2474, 47 Belgrave Rd SW1; Victoria)*. If all London's budget hotels were like this central, spotlessly clean and comfortable place, we would all be happy campers (or perhaps not). Singles/doubles without bathroom start at £28/46; a double with facilities ranges from £55 to £70. A full English breakfast is included, and there are free storage facilities if you want to leave bags while travelling. If the Luna-Simone is full, there are a lot more B&Bs on Belgrave Rd.

Brindle House Hotel *(☎ 7828 0057, fax 7931 8805, 1 Warwick Place North SW1; Victoria)*. This recently renovated place is in an old building in a quiet street; the rooms are small but clean. Singles are £34 (shared facilities), doubles are £48/44 (with/without bathroom), triples are £69.

Romany House Hotel (☎ 7834 5553, fax 7834 0495, 35 Longmore St SW1; ✚ Victoria). Part of this hotel is built into a 15th-century cottage that boasts tales – real or imagined – of highwaymen. You'll share a bathroom, but breakfasts are good and singles/doubles are from £27/37.

The West End & Covent Garden (Map 7) Cheapies in the town centre are like gold dust; you'll almost always get more for your money elsewhere.

Regent Palace Hotel (☎ 7734 7000, fax 7734 6435; ✚ Piccadilly). Ripe for a makeover but pretty cheap for its position right beside Piccadilly Circus, this enormous hotel has rooms – none with bathroom – for £54 Sunday to Thursday and £79 at weekends without breakfast.

Manzi's (☎ 7734 0224, fax 7437 4864, 1-2 Leicester St WC2; ✚ Leicester Square). This cheapie above a seafood restaurant just north of Leicester Square is no great shakes but as central as you're going to get for singles/doubles at £55/75.

Bloomsbury (Maps 4 & 6) Bloomsbury is very convenient, especially for the West End. There are lots of places on Gower and North Gower Sts.

Hotel Cavendish (Map 6; ☎ 7636 9079, fax 7580 3609, 75 Gower St WC1; ✚ Goodge Street). This is a clean and pleasant family-run place, with singles/doubles without bath for £32/47 and with *en suite* facilities for £42/62, including breakfast. Its nearby sister hotel, *Jesmond Hotel (Map 6; ☎ 7636 3199, fax 7323 4373, 63 Gower St WC1; ✚ Goodge Street),* is similar and charges the same rates.

Repton Hotel (Map 6; ☎ 7436 4922, fax 7636 7045, 31-32 Bedford Place WC1; ✚ Russell Square). This hotel is pretty good value for a mid-range place (see the Mid-Range section), but there are also two dormitories with six beds each at £15 a head.

Alhambra Hotel (Map 4; ☎ 7837 9575, fax 7916 2476, 17-19 Argyle St WC1; ✚ King's Cross St Pancras). One of the better finds in this area and very convenient for King's Cross St Pancras tube and the two main-line stations, the Alhambra is a simple but spotlessly clean place with 55 rooms and a charming French owner. Simple singles/doubles/triples are £28/38/55; with shower they're £35/45/60. Particularly

good value is the quad with shower and toilet for £85. All prices include English breakfast.

Cambria House (Map 4; ☎ 7837 1654, fax 7837 1229, 37 Hunter St WC1; ✚ Russell Square). Run by the Salvation Army, Cambria House is one of the best deals around; singles/doubles with washbasin and shared bathroom are £29/45.50 a night or £193/303 a week. *En suite* doubles are £56.50/376 a night/week. Prices include full English breakfast.

Southwark (Map 6) County Hall doesn't just contain fish tanks and football tributes (see South Bank in the Things to See & Do chapter); it also has a couple of hotels, including a budget option.

Travel Inn Capital (☎ 7902 1600, fax 7902 1619, Belvedere Rd SE1; ✚ Westminster). This is one of those one price, one room deals (in this case £59.95 for up to two adults and two children). It's fairly bare bones, and there are more rules than in a Victorian grammar school, but the rooms are large and – by London standards anyway – reasonable.

JULIET COOMBE

County Hall, the grand location of the Travel Inn Capital.

Earl's Court (Map 9) These days African, Arab and Indian immigrants are more conspicuous than Australian visitors in this area, but most people seem to be in transit and it shows in the grubby streets (although some smartening up is taking place). It's not really within walking distance of many places of interest, but Earl's Court tube station is a busy interchange, so getting around is easy.

St Simeon (☎ 7373 0505, fax 7589 6412, 38 Harrington Gardens SW7; ✚ Gloucester Road). This less-than-salubrious place is within striking distance of the South Kensington museums and has dorms (£12/15 in a room with five/three beds) as well as basic singles (£25) and doubles (£36 to £40, depending on the season). All rates include breakfast.

Boka Hotel (☎ 7370 1388, fax 7912 0515, 33 Eardley Crescent SW5; ✚ Earl's Court). Guests have access to the kitchen in this relaxed place. Simple singles go for £20 to £30, doubles £30 to £42, depending on the season. Doubles with bathroom are £40 to £52. There are also dorms with three or four beds costing between £10 and £16.

Regency Court Hotel (☎ 7244 6615, 14 Penywern Rd SW5; ✚ Earl's Court). This hotel has undergone a much needed renovation and its 20 bright rooms, all with *en suite* facilities, cost £30 to £35 for singles and £40 to £45 for doubles.

Shellbourne Hotel (☎ 7373 5161, fax 7373 9824, 1 Lexham Gardens W8; ✚ Gloucester Road). The rooms here are tatty but clean and well equipped for their price, complete with TVs, showers and direct-dial phones. Singles/doubles/triples with full breakfast are £35/47/60. We've had complaints from readers about service, though.

York House Hotel (☎ 7373 7519, fax 7370 4641, 27-28 Philbeach Gardens SW5; ✚ Earl's Court). This place is good value for what and where it is – on a quiet crescent – and the welcome is warm. The rooms are basic, although some have showers. Singles/doubles without facilities are £32/55; with shower and toilet they're £45/69.

Merlyn Court Hotel (☎ 7370 1640, fax 7370 4986, 2 Barkston Gardens SW5; ✚ Earl's Court). This unpretentious place has a nice atmosphere and a lovely location close to the tube. Small but clean singles/doubles with bathroom cost £53/60; without they're £30/45. Triples with/without bathroom are £70/65.

Holland Park (Map 5) Holland Park is a quiet, leafy district convenient for Notting Hill.

Kensington Guesthouse (☎ 7229 9233, fax 7221 1077, email hotelondon@aol.com, 72 Holland Park Avenue W11; ✚ Holland Park). This place gets the thumbs up from several readers. It has twins with shared facilities for £52 and with private bathroom for £58. Triples/quads are £63/70. All rooms have cooking facilities.

Bayswater, Paddington & Notting Hill (Map 5) Bayswater is an extremely convenient location though some of the streets immediately to the west of Queensway, which has a decent selection of restaurants, are run down and depressing. Paddington can be pretty seedy, especially right around the station, but there are lots of cheap hotels and it's a good transit location; you can reach Heathrow in 15 minutes from here (see the Airports section in the Getting Around chapter). Notting Hill is the opposite – it's upbeat and fun, but budget accommodation is at a premium.

Sass House Hotel (☎ 7262 2325, fax 7262 0889, 10-11 Craven Terrace W2; ✚ Lancaster Gate). This place is fairly threadbare but friendly. Doubles with shower, toilet and continental breakfast start at £46 and a quad costs £72.

Oxford Hotel (☎ 7402 6860, fax 7706 7475, 13 Craven Terrace W2; ✚ Lancaster Gate). This neighbouring hotel is also reasonable value; singles and doubles with TV cost £60, which drops to £48 if you stay for eight days or more.

Elysée Hotel (☎ 7402 7633, 25 Craven Terrace W2; ✚ Lancaster Gate). This recently refurbished hotel has doubles from £49.50.

Royal Hotel (☎ 7229 7225, 43 Queensborough Terrace; ✚ Bayswater). The dormitory accommodation here once attracted backpackers, but it's now just another budget guesthouse with affordable rates: £28/34.50 for a double/triple with shared facilities and £30/37.50 with shower.

Manor Court Hotel (☎ 7792 3361, fax 7229 2875, 7 Clanricarde Gardens W2; ✚ Queensway). Though not a spectacular place, this hotel is in a good location just off Bayswater Rd. Singles with private shower or toilet are £30 to £35, doubles £45 to £50, depending on the season.

Garden Court Hotel (☎ 7229 2553, fax 7727 2749, 30-31 Kensington Gardens Square W2; ✆ Bayswater). One of Bayswater's best options and just barely in this category, the Garden Court is a well run and maintained family hotel cobbled from two town houses (1870), and all its 34 rooms have phone and TV. Singles/doubles without bathroom are £34/52, with bathroom £48/74.

Norfolk Court & St David's Hotel (☎ 7723 4963, fax 7402 9061, 16-20 Norfolk Square W2; ✆ Paddington). Right in the centre of the action, this place with the long-winded name is clean, comfortable and friendly with the usual out-of-control décor. Basic singles/doubles have washbasin, colour TV and phone and cost £35/45; doubles with shower and toilet are £60, including a huge breakfast.

Cardiff Hotel (☎ 7723 9068, fax 7402 2342, 5-9 Norfolk Square W2; ✆ Paddington). On the same lovely square, which is a green oasis in summer, the family-run Cardiff has singles/doubles from £40/55 to £49/72.

Balmoral House Hotel (☎ 7723 7445, fax 7402 0118, 156 & 157 Sussex Gardens W2; ✆ Paddington). This immaculate and very comfortable hotel, with two properties directly opposite one another, is one of the better places to stay along Sussex Gardens, a street lined with small hotels but unfortunately a major traffic artery. Singles without/with bathroom cost £35/45, doubles with facilities are £65 (breakfast included and all rooms have TVs).

Europa House Hotel (☎ 7723 7343, fax 7224 9331, email europahouse@enterprise.net, 151 Sussex Gardens; ✆ Paddington). This is another excellent choice, where you're always assured a warm welcome (something not as common as you'd think at small London hotels). Singles cost from £35 to £45, doubles £52 to £65 and all rooms have bathroom, TV and phone.

Portobello Gold Hotel (☎ 7460 4910, fax 7460 4911, 95 Portobello Rd W11; ✆ Notting Hill Gate). This somewhat scruffy hotel has a pleasant restaurant and bar on the ground floor and an Internet café upstairs (see Email & Internet Access in the Facts for the Visitor chapter). Singles/doubles without facilities are £39/55; with shower and toilet they're £54/70.

Marylebone (Map 5) Marylebone is very handy for some of London's most popular sights, such as Madame Tussaud's and the London Planetarium.

Glynne Court Hotel (☎ 7262 4344, fax 7724 2071, 41 Great Cumberland Place W1; ✆ Marble Arch). Fairly typical for this price range and location, the Glynne Court has 15 singles/doubles starting at £50/65, including continental breakfast. All rooms come with TV and phone.

Hampstead & Kentish Town (Map 11)
Hampstead's trump card is the sprawling expanse of Hampstead Heath. Kentish Town is not exactly central, but it's easy to get to on the Northern Line and very handy for Camden.

Charlotte Guest House (☎ 7794 6476, fax 7431 3584, 221 West End Lane NW6; ✆ West Hampstead). This is a traditional B&B in the quiet suburb of West Hampstead. Singles/doubles are £30/40 with shared facilities and £40/50 en suite.

Five Kings Hotel (☎ 7607 3996, 59 Anson Rd N7; ✆ Tufnell Park). Singles/doubles with breakfast cost £23/36.

PLACES TO STAY – MID-RANGE
The B&Bs, guesthouses and small hotels in this category offer singles/doubles from £50/70 for a single/double without private facilities and £70/90 with your own bathroom. Before booking, it's worth checking whether a package including transport and accommodation from home is cheaper.

Pimlico & Victoria (Map 10)
Pimlico is an attractive area with some good-value accommodation. Victoria is extremely convenient for transport, though it doesn't have a lot of character and can be very noisy.

Hamilton House Hotel (☎ 7821 7113, fax 7630 0806, 60 Warwick Way SW1; ✆ Victoria). Hamilton House has simple singles/doubles for £49/62; those with private bathroom, TV and phone are £69/75.

Windermere Hotel (☎ 7834 5163, fax 7630 8831, email windermere@compuserve.com, 142-144 Warwick Way SW1; ✆ Victoria). With 22 small but individually designed rooms in a sparkling white mid-Victorian town house and its own restaurant, the Windermere has singles/doubles with shared bathroom for £64/74; those with their own facilities start at £77/93.

PLACES TO STAY

Winchester Hotel (☎ 7828 2972, fax 7828 5191, 17 Belgrave Rd SW1; ✆ Victoria). This clean, comfortable and welcoming place is also good value for the area: doubles and twins with private bathroom and TV cost £70.

Woodville House (☎ 7730 1048, fax 7730 2574, 107 Ebury St SW1; ✆ Victoria). The Woodville has 12 simple but comfortable rooms with shared bathroom, use of a kitchen and a lovely back patio. Basic singles/doubles cost £42/62. It's a friendly, good-value place.

Morgan House (☎ 7730 2384, fax 7730 8842, 120 Ebury St SW1; ✆ Victoria). This hotel is owned by the same people who run the nearby Woodville House. Singles/doubles without facilities are £42/62, those with bathroom £68/80. You'll find many more places to stay on this street.

Covent Garden (Map 7)
Nothing could be more central than Covent Garden but the buzz continues well into the wee hours.

Fielding Hotel (☎ 7836 8305, fax 7497 0064, 4 Broad Court, Bow St WC2; ✆ Covent Garden). This place, on a pedestrianised street a block away from the Royal Opera House, is remarkably good value, clean and well run. All rooms have private bathroom, TV and phone. Singles/doubles start at £73/95.

Bloomsbury (Maps 3 & 6)
Tucked away in leafy Cartwright Gardens (Map 3) to the north of Russell Square, within walking distance of the West End, you'll find some of London's best-value hotels. The hotels along nearby Gower St (Map 6) are also pretty good value, but not all of them have double-glazing, which is essential if you're sensitive to traffic noise.

Jenkins Hotel (Map 3; ☎ 7387 2067, fax 7383 3139, email reservations@jenkinshotel.demon .co.uk, 45 Cartwright Gardens WC1; ✆ Russell Square). This no-smoking place has attractive, comfortable, stylish rooms, with washbasin, TV, phone and fridge. Basic singles/doubles are £49/64; those with private facilities are £64/74 (all prices include breakfast). Guests get to use the tennis courts in the gardens across the road.

Crescent Hotel (Map 3; ☎ 7387 1515, fax 7383 2054, 49-50 Cartwright Gardens WC1; ✆ Russell Square). This friendly, family-owned operation, maintained at a very high standard, has basic singles from £42 to £45 and en suite singles/doubles from £60/75 to £65/85.

Euro Hotel (Map 3; ☎ 7387 4321, fax 7383 5044, 53 Cartwright Gardens WC1; ✆ Russell Square). With simple singles/doubles for £46/63 and those with shower and toilet £68/82.50, the Euro can be recommended.

Arran House Hotel (Map 6; ☎ 7636 2186, fax 7436 5328, 77-79 Gower St WC1; ✆ Goodge Street). This welcoming place has a lovely garden and laundry facilities. Singles range from £40 with no facilities to £58 with shower, doubles from £50 to £55, triples from £68 to £72. Prices include breakfast. The front rooms are sound-proofed, and all have TV and phone.

Ridgemount Hotel (Map 6; ☎ 7636 1141, fax 7636 2558, 65-67 Gower St WC1; ✆ Goodge Street). Readers have sent favourable comments about the old-fashioned Ridgemount. Basic singles/doubles are £31/46; with shower and toilet they're £41/58 (including breakfast). It also has a laundry room (£2 per wash).

Repton Hotel (Map 6; ☎ 7436 4922, fax 7636 7045, 31-32 Bedford Place WC1; ✆ Russell Square). This hotel is pretty good value for a mid-range place considering that Bedford Place is much more tranquil than nearby Gower St. Singles/doubles with TV, phone and bathroom are £49/69.

St Margaret's Hotel (Map 6; ☎ 7636 4277, fax 7323 3066, 26 Bedford Place WC1; ✆ Russell Square or Holborn). This family-run hotel is in a classic Georgian town house. It's not particularly inspiring, but it is clean and all rooms have TV and phone. Singles/doubles (some with private bathroom) are £46.50/58.50.

Ruskin Hotel (Map 6; ☎ 7636 7388, fax 7323 1662, 23-24 Montague St WC1; ✆ Holborn or Russell Square). The location of this fairly basic place is very good. Singles/doubles without bathroom are £42/60, doubles with facilities £75.

Haddon Hall (Map 6; ☎ 7636 2474, fax 7580 4527, 39 Bedford Place WC1; ✆ Russell Square or Holborn). This is the nearby sister hotel of the Ruskin and is much the same. Simple singles/doubles without bathroom are £42/57, doubles with bathroom £69.

Morgan Hotel (Map 7; ☎ 7636 3735, fax 7636 3045, 24 & 40 Bloomsbury St WC1; ✆ Tottenham Court Road). This place has 20 small but nicely decorated *en suite* rooms at two different locations near the British Museum. Singles/doubles with private facilities start at £52/78; larger singles are £62.

Chelsea, South Kensington & Earl's Court (Map 9)

Classy Chelsea and 'South Ken' offer easy access to the museums and some of London's best shops. Mid-range places in Earl's Court are usually perfectly acceptable; if the one you've set your heart on is full, there will be plenty more nearby.

Wilbraham Hotel (☎ 7730 8296, fax 7730 6815, Wilbraham Place, Sloane St SW1; ✆ Sloane Square). A short distance north of Sloane Square, the Wilbraham boasts many original Victorian features in its public areas and 50 rooms, but Sloane St can be noisy at night. Singles/doubles with amenities start at £68/75.

Annandale House Hotel (☎ 7730 5051, fax 7730 2727, 39 Sloane Gardens SW1; ✆ Sloane Square). This discreet, traditional hotel just south of Sloane Square is perhaps a better choice for the noise-sensitive. Rooms, all with *en suite* facilities, phone and TV, cost £40 to £60 for singles and £80 to £95 for doubles.

Hotel 167 (☎ 7373 0672, fax 7373 3360, 167 Old Brompton Rd SW5; ✆ Gloucester Road). This small hotel is stylish and has an unusually uncluttered and attractive décor. All 19 rooms have private bathroom. Singles are from £72, doubles from £90 to £99.

Swiss House Hotel (☎ 7373 2769, fax 7373 4983, email recep@swiss-hh.demon.co.uk, 171 Old Brompton Rd SW5; ✆ Gloucester Road). The Swiss House is a clean and welcoming hotel that has something of a country feel about it. And it's good value: singles with shower start at £44, twins with shower and toilet at £77, including continental breakfast.

London Town Hotel (☎ 7370 4356, fax 7370 7923, 15 Penywern Rd SW5; ✆ Earl's Court). This pleasant place has singles/doubles with bathroom and TV from £68/90.

Kensington (Map 5)

These hotels are well placed for Kensington Gardens, Notting Hill and Kensington High St.

Vicarage Hotel (☎ 7229 4030, fax 7792 5989, email reception@londonvicaragehotel.com, 10 Vicarage Gate W8; ✆ High Street Kensington). The Vicarage is pleasant and well kept, with good showers and rooms slightly larger than normal. Singles/doubles with shared facilities are £43/68, doubles with private bathroom £95.

Abbey House (☎ 7727 2594, 11 Vicarage Gate W8; ✆ High Street Kensington). Abbey House is a particularly good-value small hotel, with pretty décor and very high standards. Singles/doubles/triples with washbasin and shared bathrooms are £40/65/78, including English breakfast.

Bayswater, Paddington & Notting Hill (Map 5)

Bayswater is residential and convenient for busy Queensway. Though central, Paddington is a bit scruffy at the best of times. Notting Hill has become increasingly trendy and expensive, but it is still a great place to stay, with lots of good bars and restaurants.

Pavilion Hotel (☎ 7262 0905, fax 7262 1324, 34-36 Sussex Gardens W2; ✆ Paddington). This place boasts 30 individually themed rooms (Moorish, 1970s, chinoiserie, all-red) to reflect its slogan/motto: 'Fashion, Glam & Rock 'n' Roll'. If you're feeling somewhat B-list, you might look elsewhere. Singles/doubles from £60/90 include breakfast.

Gresham Hotel (☎ 7402 2920, fax 7402 3137, email sales@the-gresham-hotel.co.uk, 116 Sussex Gardens W2; ✆ Paddington). This less-than-welcoming place is nevertheless a stylish small hotel with bright and cheery rooms. Expect to pay £60/75 for a single/double.

Inverness Court Hotel (☎ 7229 1444, fax 7706 4240, Inverness Terrace W2; ✆ Queensway). This impressive hotel was commissioned by Edward VII for his 'confidante' (ie mistress), the actress Lillie Langtry, and comes complete with a private theatre, now the cocktail bar. The panelled walls, stained glass and huge open fires of the public areas give it a Gothic feel but most of the 183 rooms – some of which overlook Hyde Park – are modern and pretty ordinary. Singles/doubles cost £79/97.

Gate Hotel (☎ 7221 0707, fax 7221 9128, email gatehotel@aol.com, 6 Portobello Rd W11; ✆ Notting Hill Gate). The rooms in this old town house with classic frilly English décor and lovely floral window boxes all have private facilities and cost £45 to £60 for singles and £75 to £78 for doubles, including continental breakfast.

Hillgate Hotel (☎ 7221 3433, fax 7229 4808, email hillgate@lth-hotels.com, 6-14 Pembridge Gardens W2; ✆ Notting Hill Gate). Set in a quiet street off Notting Hill Gate, the Hillgate's 70 rooms spread over five Victorian terrace houses. *En suite* singles/doubles are £78/104.

Marylebone (Map 5)

Wigmore Court Hotel (☎ *7935 0928, fax 7487 4254, email info@wigmore-court-hotel.co.uk, 23 Gloucester Place W1;* ⊖ *Marble Arch).* This hotel with over-the-top décor (pink, pink, pink) is a well organised place whose guests have access to a kitchen and self-service laundry, but there is no lift. Singles/doubles without bath are £48/70; with *en suite* facilities expect to pay from £58/95.

Edward Lear Hotel (☎ *7402 5401, fax 7706 3766, 28-30 Seymour St W1;* ⊖ *Marble Arch).* Once the home of the eponymous Victorian painter and poet, the rooms in this small, comfortable place have TV, tea & coffee facilities and phone. Singles/doubles without bathroom cost from £45/60, with bathroom £79/109.

Bryanston Court (☎ *7262 3141, fax 7262 7248, email hotel@bryanstonhotel.com, 56-60 Great Cumberland Place W1;* ⊖ *Marble Arch).* This place has something of a club atmosphere, with leather armchairs, sepia-toned lighting and a formal feel (though it's a Best Western hotel). All rooms have private bathroom, TV and phone and singles/doubles cost £85/110.

Hampstead (Map 11)

Classy Hampstead retains a village atmosphere although it can feel cut off from central London.

La Gaffe (☎ *7794 7526, fax 7794 7592, 107 Heath St NW3;* ⊖ *Hampstead).* This rather eccentric place is nonetheless a comfortable hotel in an 18th-century cottage, with singles/doubles with bathroom from £60/85.

PLACES TO STAY – TOP END

In this section you'll find the pricier hotels, where doubles cost from £100 to £130 – and more. Of course, in this category you can always count on a private bath/shower and toilet.

Victoria (Map 10)

The following place is (probably) as close as you'll ever get to staying with the Queen.

Rubens at the Palace (☎ *7834 6600, fax 7233 6037, email reservations@rubens.redcarnat ionhotels.com, 39 Buckingham Palace Rd SW1;* ⊖ *Victoria).* This branch of the Rubens chain has a brilliant position overlooking the walls of the Royal Mews and Buckingham Palace. Singles/doubles start at £110/140 without breakfast. It's popular with groups.

Mayfair (Map 6)

If you want a deluxe hotel at top-end prices in one of London's most exclusive neighbourhoods, choose the following hotel.

Chesterfield (☎ *7491 2622, fax 7491 4793, email reservations@chesterfield.viewinn.co.uk, 35 Charles St W1;* ⊖ *Green Park).* With 111 rooms and just a block west of Berkeley Square, the Chesterfield has some fine outlets, particularly the Conservatory restaurant and the Library bar. Singles/doubles start at £129/140.

The West End & Covent Garden (Map 7)

There are tremendous advantages to staying in the centre of town. Unfortunately, such a privilege doesn't come cheaply.

Hazlitt's (☎ *7434 1771, fax 7439 1524, 6 Frith St W1;* ⊖ *Tottenham Court Road).* Built in 1718 and comprising three original Georgian houses, this is one of central London's finest hotels, with efficient personal service. All 23 rooms are named after former residents or visitors to the house and are individually decorated with antique furniture and prints. Singles/doubles start at £130/170. Booking is advisable – especially since Bill Bryson let the cat out of the bag and introduced it to the world in his best-selling *Notes from a Small Island.*

Strand Palace (☎ *7836 8080, fax 7836 2077, Strand WC2;* ⊖ *Charing Cross).* This monstrous place (783 rooms) has improved following recent renovation. Its position, close to Covent Garden, is excellent and there are a number of snappy bars and restaurants, but the prices (from £135/152 for a single/double without breakfast) are still pretty steep.

Bloomsbury (Map 6)

This hotel is handy for both the shopping on Oxford St and the British Museum.

Academy Hotel (☎ *7631 4115, fax 6636 3442, 17-25 Gower St WC1;* ⊖ *Goodge Street).* The Academy is in a rather busy street, although double-glazing keeps the noise down. Its 47 rooms are pale and pretty, and there's a pleasant back garden. Singles cost £100, doubles from £125 to £145.

Clerkenwell (Map 6)

A lovely new hotel has arrived in a part of London seemingly devoid of quality accommodation.

The Rookery (☎ 7336 0931, fax 7336 0932, email reservations@rookery.co.uk, Peter's Lane, Cowcross St EC1; ✆ Farringdon). This 33-room hotel has been built within a row of once derelict 18th-century Georgian houses and fitted out with period furniture (including a museum-piece collection of Victorian baths, showers and toilets), original wood panelling shipped over from Ireland and open fires. Its singles/doubles start at £140/170.

Chelsea, South Kensington & Earl's Court (Map 9)

Gracious Chelsea and South Kensington present London at its elegant best. Two of the following hotels are in Lexham Gardens, which feels more like Kensington than Earl's Court.

Blakes (☎ 7370 6701, fax 7373 0442, email blakes@easynet.co.uk, 33 Roland Gardens SW7; ✆ Gloucester Road). For classic style, one of your first choices in London should be this place: five Victorian houses knocked into one and decked out with four-poster beds, rich fabrics and antiques on stripped floorboards. Singles/doubles start at £130/160.

Five Sumner Place (☎ 7584 7586, fax 7823 9962, email no.5@dial.pipex.com, 5 Sumner Place SW7; ✆ South Kensington). On a quiet leafy road just off Old Brompton St, this hotel has 13 comfortable and well equipped rooms (all with bathroom, TV, phone, drinks cabinet and more), and there's an attractive conservatory and courtyard garden. Singles/doubles start at £75/120.

Number Sixteen (☎ 7589 5232, fax 7584 8615, email reservations@numbersixteenhotel.co.uk, 16 Sumner Place SW7; ✆ South Kensington). Number Sixteen has all the attributes of the almost opposite Five Sumner Place – and then some. It's a smart hotel with a cosy lounge and library, with singles from £90 to £125, doubles £160 to £195.

Amber Hotel (☎ 7373 8666, fax 7835 1194, 101 Lexham Gardens W8; ✆ Earl's Court). This hotel is pretty good value for its location halfway between Kensington and Earl's Court. Fully equipped singles/doubles are £99/105.

London Lodge Hotel (☎ 7244 8444, fax 7373 6661, 134-136 Lexham Gardens W8; ✆ Earl's

JULIET COOMBE

The Rookery's back-garden mural, recalling the days when cows sauntered along Cowcross St.

Court). Singles/doubles at this hotel are £119/139. There's a restaurant and bar called Stephanie's downstairs.

Kensington & Knightsbridge (Map 5)

The theme of top-end hotels in this part of London seems to be antiques – particularly the Victorian kind.

The Gore (☎ 7584 6601, fax 7589 8127, email reservations@gorehotel.co.uk, 189 Queen's Gate SW7; ✆ High Street Kensington or Gloucester Road). This splendid hotel is a veritable palace of polished mahogany, Turkish carpets, antique-style bathrooms, aspidistras and portraits and prints (some 4500 of them). The attached Bistrot 190 is a fine place for brunch. Singles/doubles cost from £125/163.

Basil St Hotel (☎ 7581 3311, fax 7581 3693, email thebasil@aol.com, Basil St SW3; ✆ Knightsbridge). This antique-stuffed hideaway in the heart of Knightsbridge is perfectly placed for carrying back the shopping from Harrods, Harvey Nichols or Sloane St. Its singles/doubles start at £125/185.

Bayswater & Notting Hill (Map 5)

You'll get more for your pound at top-end places in these two areas than you would to the south and east.

Queen's Park Hotel (☎ 7229 8080, fax 7792 1330, email parksales1@compuserve.com, 48 Queensborough Terrace W2; ⊖ Bayswater). With 86 rooms, the Queen's Park is a somewhat functional top-end place popular with groups, but the rates are good for the location: £95/120 for singles/doubles.

Abbey Court (☎ 7221 7518, fax 7792 0858, 20 Pembridge Gardens W2; ⊖ Notting Hill Gate). The Abbey Court has individually decorated rooms, some with fine views over the rooftops. Singles/doubles start at £93/125. The breakfast room with an old Victrola and garden courtyard view is particularly fine.

Portobello (☎ 7727 2777, fax 7792 9641, 22 Stanley Gardens W11; ⊖ Notting Hill Gate). This beautifully appointed place is in a great location and one of the most attractive hotels in London. Most people consider the £115/155 for a single/double to be money well spent.

Marylebone (Map 6)

Durrants Hotel (☎ 7935 8131, fax 7487 3510, George St W1; ⊖ Marble Arch). This luxurious, sprawling hotel, just behind the Wallace Collection and excellently placed for shopping, was, amazingly, once a country inn and still retains something of the feel of a gentleman's club. Comfortable singles/doubles with bathroom start at £97.50/130, but breakfast is extra.

Hampstead (Map 11)

Sandringham Hotel (☎ 7435 1569, fax 7431 5932, 3 Holford Rd NW3; ⊖ Hampstead). The Sandringham is a delightful and warm 17-room place close to the heath whose top-floor rooms overlook the city. Singles/doubles start at £70/120. Breakfast costs from £6.50 extra.

East End & the Docklands (Map 8)

Until the massive overhaul of the historic 266-room Great Eastern Hotel (once the site of the Bethlehem Royal Hospital or 'Bedlam') on Liverpool St is finished, the top-end pickings in this part of town are very few indeed.

Thistle Tower Hotel (☎ 7481 2575, fax 7488 4106, email tower.businesscentre@thistle.co .uk, St Katharine's Way E1; ⊖ Tower Hill). Just beyond the limits of the City, this 802-room place has a superb, central waterside

JULIET COOMBE

Sailing by: echoes of Britain's maritime history outside the Thistle Tower Hotel.

position in St Katharine's Dock. It's a dreadful eyesore of a building, though, marring the architectural harmony of its neighbours, the Tower of London and Tower Bridge, but you're not going to see much of the outside from within, are you? Small singles/doubles start at £165/185.

RCA City Hotel *(☎ 7247 3313, fax 7375 2949, email royalcourt@dial.pipex.com, 12 Osborn St E1; ✪ Aldgate East).* This place has studios for one or two people from £95 to £113 and suites accommodating two to four with kitchen for £143 to £179.

PLACES TO STAY – DELUXE

Some of central London's hotels are so luxurious and well established that they're tourist attractions in their own right. Despite their often olde-worlde splendour – verging on the baroque/rococo in some cases – all are geared for the needs of business travellers.

Brown's *(Map 7; ☎ 7493 6020, fax 7493 9381, email brownshotel@ukbusiness.com, 30 Albemarle St W1; ✪ Green Park).* A stunner of a five-star hotel, 118-room Brown's was created from 11 houses joined together and was the first hotel in London to have a lift, a telephone and electric lighting. Service is tip-top. Rooms start at £250.

Claridges *(Map 6; ☎ 7629 8860, fax 7499 2210, email info@claridges.co.uk, Brook St W1; ✪ Bond Street).* Claridges is one of the greatest of London's five-star hotels, a leftover from a bygone era. Many of the Art Deco features of the public areas and suites were designed in the late 1920s and some of the 1930s-vintage furniture once graced the staterooms of the decommissioned SS *Normandie*. Expect to pay £265/320 for a single/double.

The Connaught *(Map 6; ☎ 7499 7070, fax 7495 3262, email info@the-connaught.co.uk, Carlos Place W1; ✪ Green Park).* The Connaught continues to refuse to cut its clothes to suit this year's fashion and concentrates instead on a style appropriate to a hotel that has one of the best restaurants in London. The rooms are similarly old-fashioned in that grand way. Singles/doubles start at £265/300.

Covent Garden Hotel *(Map 7; ☎ 7806 1000, fax 7806 1100, 10 Monmouth St WC2; ✪ Covent Garden).* As now as the new millennium but in a reserved, British sort of way, this 50-room hotel prefers to use antiques (don't miss the beautiful marquetry desk in the drawing room), gorgeous fabrics and a kind of 'theatreland'

theme to stake out its individuality. There's a good bar/restaurant called Brasserie Max. Its singles/doubles start at £175/200.

The Halkin *(Map 6; ☎ 7333 1000, fax 7333 1100, email sales@halkin.co.uk, 5 Halkin St SW1; ✪ Hyde Park Corner).* The Halkin is for business travellers of a minimalist bent: lots of burlwood, marble and round things. Bedrooms are wood-panelled and stylishly uncluttered; staff strut about in Armani uniforms. Room rates start at £255.

The Hampshire *(Map 7; ☎ 7839 9399, fax 7930 8122, Leicester Square WC2; ✪ Leicester Square).* This centrally located hotel attracts rich, retired Americans and top-flight businesspeople. Standard rooms start at £280.

The Hempel *(Map 5; ☎ 7298 9000, fax 7402 4666, email the-hempel@easynet.co.uk, 31-35 Craven Hill Gardens W2; ✪ Lancaster Gate or Queensway).* We've visited, inspected and/or stayed in lots and lots of hotels in our day, but we've never seen anything quite like the Hempel, a minimalist symphony in white and natural tones where Kyoto meets *2001: A Space Odyssey* and puts a spin on it. We can only say 'Wow!' at the design, the service and the room rates – from £220. The I-Thai, serving Italian *and* Thai cuisine, is one of London's more unusual (and successful) fusion restaurants.

The Metropolitan *(Map 6; ☎ 7447 1000, fax 7447 1100, email sales@metropolitan.co.uk, 19 Old Park Lane W1; ✪ Hyde Park Corner).* In the same stable as the Halkin, the 155-room Metropolitan is another of the new minimalist hotels – 'stripped of nonessentials' (as they boast) and decorated in shades of cream and Granola – that attracts a super-trendy, well-heeled crowd. More rock star than royal, really. The hotel's Japanese restaurant, Nobu, consistently gets rave reviews, and the Met Bar is one of the more difficult night spots in London to get into. Singles/doubles start at £205/265.

One Aldwych *(Map 7; ☎ 7300 1000, fax 7300 1001, email sales@onealdwych.co.uk, 1 Aldwych WC2; ✪ Covent Garden or Charing Cross).* What was once Art Nouveau newspaper offices is now a minimalist, 105-room hotel with modern art everywhere the eye rests and a merry, upbeat atmosphere. Singles/doubles start at £245/265.

Park Lane Hotel *(Map 6; ☎ 7499 6321, fax 7499 1965, Piccadilly W1; ✪ Green Park).* There's vintage Art Deco on display in the Palm Room of the Park Lane, which needs triple-glazing to keep the noise of the modern world outside its hallowed halls. Most rooms have been refurbished in a light, modern style and it's now

Putting on the Ritz: the epitome of West End sophistication.

part of the Sheraton group; perhaps the public areas will get a much needed upgrade as well. Singles/doubles start at £260/280.

The Ritz (Map 6; ☎ 7493 8181, fax 7493 2687, email enquire@theritzhotel.co.uk, 150 Piccadilly W1; ✪ Green Park). What can you say about a hotel that has lent its name to the English lexicon? Arguably London's most celebrated hotel, the ritzy Ritz has a spectacular position overlooking Green Park and is the royal family's 'home away from home'. Rooms cost from a budget-busting £245 to £385 for a junior suite. The Long Gallery and the Restaurant are decked out like a rococo boudoir, and the food is said to have been recently dragged into the 20th century.

St Martins Lane (Map 7; ☎ 7300 5500, 0800 634 5500, 45 St Martin's Lane; ✪ Leicester Square). London's newest designer hotel, providing what it calls a 'slice of New York urban chic' just a stone's throw from Covent Garden,

St Martins was created by international hotelier Ian Schrager and French designer Philippe Starck. It's the place to check into if you want to bump into supermodels in the lift and have great views of the pulsating West End. Indulging in its late-90s minimalism costs from £229/253 for a single/double.

The Savoy (Map 7; ☎ 7836 4343, fax 7240 6040, email info@the-savoy.co.uk, Strand WC2; ✪ Charing Cross). This hotel stands on the site of the old Savoy Palace, which was burned down during the Peasants' Revolt of 1381. The 207 rooms are so comfortable and have such great views that some people have been known to take up permanent residence. Singles/doubles start at £265/290. The forecourt is the only street in the British Isles where motorists drive on the right.

The Waldorf (Map 7; ☎ 7836 2400, fax 7836 7244, Aldwych WC2; ✪ Charing Cross). Now part of the Meridien chain, the Waldorf is another grand old dame glorying in her Edwardian splendour, which is typified by the wonderful Palm Court, the splendid lounge where tea dances are held at weekends. Singles/doubles start at £210/240.

SPECIALIST HOTELS
Gay Hotels

Philbeach Gardens (Map 9) is a pleasingly quiet yet central side street with a couple of hotels catering for a gay clientele.

Philbeach Hotel (☎ 7373 1244, fax 7244 0149, 30 Philbeach Gardens SW5; ✪ Earl's Court). This is an especially fine hotel popular with both gays and lesbians. It has a lovely garden restaurant called Wilde about Oscar and a super new bar in the basement. Basic singles/doubles are £45/58; with shower they're £55/75.

New York Hotel (☎ 7244 6844, fax 7370 4961, 32 Philbeach Gardens SW5; ✪ Earl's Court). This much more reserved, less welcoming hotel next door to the Philbeach caters for a male gay clientele and charges £50 for a single with shared bathroom and from £55/70 for *en suite* singles/doubles. It has a Jacuzzi and a garden.

Children's Hotels

Visitors who want a break from the ankle-biters will find the following hotel useful.

Pippa's Pop-Ins (Map 9; ☎ 7385 2458, fax 7385 5706, 430 Fulham Rd SW6; ✪ Fulham Broadway). This unique hotel gives parents a break from their children. It offers 24-hour childcare by trained nannies and entertainment for children aged two to 12; overnighters get midnight snacks as well as dinner, bed and breakfast. A stay here costs £60/70 for a weekday/weekend night and £100 for a full 24 hours.

LONG-TERM RENTALS
Serviced Apartments

Families or groups may prefer to rent a flat rather than stay in a hotel or B&B. Several agencies can help track something down. Holiday Serviced Apartments (☎ 7373 4477, fax 7373 4282, email reservations@ holidayapartments.co.uk), 273 Old Brompton Rd SW5 (⊖ Gloucester Road), and Aston's Budget & Designer Studios (☎ 7590 6000, fax 7590 6060), 39 Rosary Gardens SW7 (⊖ Gloucester Road), have a range of holiday flats on their books. Crystal Premier Cities (☎ 8241 5040) has two-bed apartments (eg One Thirty Apartments in Queen's Gate SW7) from £35 per person per night.

The Imperial College of Science, Technology & Medicine (see the earlier Student Accommodation section) has two-bedroom apartments and mews houses in the South Kensington area from £300 per week. They are available year-round.

Finding a Flat

At the bottom end of the rental market, bedsits are single furnished rooms, usually with a shared bathroom and kitchen, although some have basic cooking facilities. The next step up is a studio, which normally has a separate bathroom and kitchen; one-bedroom flats are more expensive again. Shared houses and flats generally offer the best value. Most landlords demand a security deposit (normally one month's rent) plus a month's rent in advance.

Rents vary dramatically according to the part of the city you're considering – one of the best ways to get an idea of current prices is to look in a paper like *Loot*, which has a huge selection of small ads. Rooms, flats and flat-shares are also advertised in *TNT*, *Time Out*, the *Evening Standard* (including the *Homes & Property* supplement on Wednesday), the *Pink Paper* and *Boyz*.

For help in finding a flat call into the foyer of Capital Radio (☎ 7484 4000), 29-30 Leicester Square WC2 (⊖ Leicester Square), and pick up their flat-share list; new lists appear at 4 pm every Thursday and the best places go fast. A supplement called *Space* in Friday's *Guardian* reproduces this list.

If you prefer to use an agency, make sure that it doesn't charge fees to tenants. The Jenny Jones Agency (☎ 7493 4381), 40 South Molton St W1 (⊖ Bond Street), charges the landlord.

Places to Eat

London is the UK's undisputed culinary capital, and the growth in the number of restaurants and cafés – some 8500 at the last count, representing 70 different cuisines – has made the city much more international. No matter what you fancy eating, there's bound to be a restaurant serving it.

Yes, things have improved remarkably since the 1970s. But then again the only way was up from caffs serving greasy breakfasts and fish and chips deep-fried in rancid-smelling oil.

Now food in all its guises has become the new sex in London and everyone wants a piece of the action. Just don't count on value for money. We can't remember the number of times we've eaten over-refined

Italian food or the ubiquitous Modern European/British, dropped £35 a head and wondered why we'd bothered. For that kind of money, this would be inconceivable in cities like New York (US$56), Paris (350FF) or Sydney (A$85). On the other hand we've had Pakistani food in Whitechapel, Turkish in Dalston and Indonesian in Brixton that has made our hearts and tastebuds sing and our wallets only a little bit lighter.

Eating out in London can be a real hit or miss affair. What we've done in this chapter is separate the wheat from the chaff. The restaurants, pubs and cafés appearing below range from pretty good (convenient location, cheap price, unusual cuisine) to fantabulous (worth a big splurge or a lengthy journey). Hopefully this list will lead you in the right direction and you won't walk out wondering why you bothered. *Bon appétit!*

Restaurants and other eateries in London have extremely varied opening hours. Many in Soho are closed on Sunday, for example, and in the City the entire weekend. We have tried to note when restaurants stray from the standard 'open daily for lunch and dinner', but it's always safest to call and check.

Of the many guides to London restaurants, Lonely Planet's *Out to Eat – London* includes an enormous selection of the city's best eateries. Also available is the *Time Out Eating & Drinking Guide*; see Newspapers & Magazines in the Facts for the Visitor chapter for details.

FOOD
Cuisines

London is the capital of a nation that gave the world beans on toast, mushy peas and chip butties (french fries between two slices of buttered white bread). But that's hardly the whole story and with the emergence of Modern British cuisine it will get even longer (see the boxed text 'Eel,

ED HILLYER

A Beefeater eating beef – or whatever else is in his burger.

Eels, Liquor & Spotted Dick: English Food in Perspective

English food will never win any awards on the world culinary stage, but when well prepared – be it a Sunday lunch of roast beef and Yorkshire pudding (light batter baked until fluffy and eaten with gravy) or a cornet of fish and chips eaten on the hoof – it can have its moments.

Pubs generally serve low-cost traditional dishes of varying quality such as pies: pork pies, Cornish pasties (filled with minced beef or mutton, diced potatoes and onions) and steak and kidney pie. (Shepherd's pie, on the other hand, has no crust but is a baked dish of minced lamb and onions topped with mashed potatoes.) On a pub menu you'll also usually find bangers and mash (sausages served with mashed potatoes and gravy), sausage rolls (sausage meat cooked in pastry) and the crowd-pleasing ploughman's lunch (thick slices of bread served with Cheddar or Cheshire cheese, chutney and pickled onions). The catalogue of calorific desserts includes bread and butter pudding, steamed pudding (a cake with beef suet a key ingredient) served with treacle (molasses) or jam, and the frighteningly named spotted dick, a steamed suet pudding with currants and raisins.

The most English of dishes, though, is fish and chips: cod, plaice or haddock dipped in batter, deep-fried and served with chips (french fries) doused in vinegar and sprinkled with salt. With the arrival of American-style fast-food joints, authentic 'chippies' are becoming rarer but we still like the Rock & Soul Plaice in Covent Garden, the North Sea Fish Restaurant in Bloomsbury and the Upper St Fish Shop in Islington.

From the middle of the 19th century until just after WWII the staple lunch for many Londoners was a pie filled with spiced eel (then abundant in the Thames) and served with mashed potatoes and liquor, a parsley sauce. Nowadays the pies are usually meat-filled and the eel served smoked or jellied as a side dish. The best places to try this are Manze's near Bermondsey Market, R Cooke in Waterloo and Castle's in Camden Town.

Many 'gastropubs' and trendy restaurants now serve what is called Modern British cuisine. Though it can sometimes be difficult telling the difference between it and Modern European food, Modern British is a lot more than 'staples like bangers and mash with the grease removed', as one philistine colleague described it. It can be anything from game served with a traditional vegetable like Jerusalem artichoke (try St John in Clerkenwell) and smoked haddock with melted Cheddar (Fish! in Borough) to smoked Norfolk eel with little buckwheat pancakes and calf's liver with Italian bacon and English field mushrooms (Ransome's Dock in Battersea).

PLACES TO EAT

Liquor & Spotted Dick: English Food in Perspective').

London has a considerable population of immigrants from the former British Empire as well as refugees from around the globe, so a wide variety of ethnic food is now consumed by everyone – from the tandooris of the Indian subcontinent and the kebabs of Turkey and Cyprus to the chicken Kievs of Ukraine and the noodles and dim sum of Hong Kong and China. Pizza and pasta are the staples of every high street in London and curry remains the takeaway of choice.

Vegetarian Food

Vegetarianism is an accepted part of London's restaurant scene and most places offer at least something for those who don't eat meat. *Cranks* is the best-known restaurant chain, with an outlet in Soho *(Map 7; ☎ 7437 9431, 8 Marshall St W1; ✪ Oxford Circus)* and one near Leicester Square *(Map 7; ☎ 7836 5226, 17-19 Great Newport St WC2; ✪ Leicester Square)*. A full meal costs around £10, and breakfast is £2.25. The listings in this chapter include many other vegetarian places.

London abounds with off-licences where you can stock up with plonk for the evening.

Kosher Food

Searching for a kosher meal in central London has been a joyless task ever since Bloom's closed its main deli-restaurant in Whitechapel in 1994. The best places to look are Golders Green, Stamford Hill and much farther out like Edgware in Middlesex and Ilford in Essex.

The following is a short list of kosher-supervised restaurants accessible by tube. All are closed after lunch on Friday and all day Saturday.

Reubens (Map 5; ☎ 7486 0035, 79 Baker St W1; ✪ Baker Street). This newly reopened café-restaurant has all the Ashkenazi favourites: gefilte fish (£2.25), *latkes* (potato pancakes; £1.10) and sandwiches (from £1.95 to £3.50).
Solly's (☎ 8455 2121, 148a Golders Green Rd NW11; ✪ Golders Green). Middle Eastern/Sephardic dishes like *felafel*, North African *merguez* sausage and *tahini* are served in the café downstairs for under £4 while the huge Solly's Exclusive restaurant upstairs does full meals (four course set meal £20).
Carmelli (☎ 8455 2074, 128 Golders Green Rd NW11; ✪ Golders Green). Here real kosher bagels, *challah*, dark rye bread (pumpernickel) and onion *platzels* are available as well as cakes, pastries and savoury snacks.
Kaifeng (☎ 8203 7888, 51 Church Rd NW4; ✪ Hendon Central). Chinese kosher cuisine is available here with starters around £5.95 and main courses from £11.50 to £15.95.

If you require further information, contact the London Beth Din Kashrut Division (☎ 8343 6255, fax 8343 6254, email info@kosher.org.uk), which publishes a guide to kosher food throughout the UK called *The Real Jewish Food Guide* (£6.95).

DRINKS

In general, off-licences and pubs have an impressive range of lagers, bitters, ales and stouts (see the boxed text 'Beer: The National Drink' in the Entertainment chapter). Cider, a fermented drink as strong as beer and not the unfiltered apple juice it is in the USA, also has its fans. The most common brands are Scrumpy Jack and the drier Woodpecker, but there are wonderful 'boutique' ciders available from presses in Norfolk and Kent.

Good wine – of whatever nationality – is widely available in London and very reasonably priced (except in pubs and restaurants). In supermarkets an ordinary but quite drinkable bottle can still be found for around £4.

The most popular nonalcoholic drink in the UK has traditionally been tea – whether casually drunk from a mug or ceremoniously taken at 'high tea' (see the boxed text 'Tea for Two or More'). But judging from the preponderance of US-style coffee-shop chains like Aroma, Costa, Coffee Republic and the Seattle Coffee Company, that allegiance might be shifting.

TRAFALGAR SQUARE (Map 7)

You won't find a tremendous number of eateries directly on the square, but there are a couple of cafés within striking distance and the *Brasserie* (☎ 7747 2885) on the 1st floor of the National Gallery's Sainsbury Wing gets good reviews.

International

Café in the Crypt (☎ 7839 4342, St Martin-in-the-Fields, Duncannon St WC2; ✪ Charing Cross). The food in this atmospheric crypt is good, with plenty of offerings for vegetarians, but the place can be hectic and noisy at lunch time. Most main dishes are from £5 to £6 and

JULIET COOMBE

PLACES TO EAT

there are 'quick meals' from £3.95. It's open from 10 am to 8 pm (6 pm on Sunday).

ICA Café (Map 6; ☎ 7930 8619, ICA, The Mall SW1; ✆ Charing Cross). You can lunch at this bohemian magnet for less than £10 but for considerably more in the evening (£36 for two with wine). It's no-smoking, there are lots of vegetarian dishes, and it's licensed to serve alcohol until 1 am.

WESTMINSTER & PIMLICO (Map 10)

We wonder where all those MPs lunch, given the dearth of restaurants in Westminster, but Pimlico has a wide assortment.

Modern British

Grumbles (☎ 7834 0149, 35 Churton St SW1; ✆ Victoria). This pleasant wine bar serves, among other things, stuffed aubergine for £6.75, fish pie for £8.45 and sirloin steak for £9.95.

International

The Footstool (Map 2; ☎ 7222 2779, St John's, Smith Square SW1; ✆ Westminster). Housed in the crypt of an 18th-century church (now a concert hall), the Footstool offers a buffet with soups for £3.30 and casseroles for £6.50 and a more formal restaurant for à la carte lunches (main courses from £9.95 to £11.25) and post-concert set dinners (£10.95 for two courses).

Tea for Two or More

Given the important role that tea has always played in English culture and society, it should be no surprise that going out for 'afternoon tea' is something dear to the heart of many Londoners. A traditional set tea comes with a selection of delicate sandwiches (cucumber and smoked salmon are favourites), scones with cream and jam, and rich desserts. Oh, and lots and lots of tea too.

The following are some of the best places to go for afternoon tea:

Brown's Hotel (Map 7; ☎ 7493 6020, 30 Albemarle St W1; ✆ Green Park) dispenses tea in the Drawing Room daily from 3 to 6 pm, with a pianist to soothe away any lingering stress from the bustling streets outside. A sizeable tea will set you back £17.95 a head.

The landmark *Claridges Hotel (Map 6; ☎ 7629 8860, Brook St W1; ✆ Bond Street)* serves tea in its grand 18th-century foyer daily from 3 to 5.30 pm. It'll cost you £18.50 a head for a set tea or £25 if you want champagne thrown in.

The celebrated *Fortnum & Mason (Map 7; ☎ 7734 8040, 181 Piccadilly W1; ✆ Piccadilly Circus)* serves afternoon tea for £13.50 and high teas for £16.50 and £18.50 (with champagne) from Monday to Saturday between 3 and 5 pm.

Tea at the *Waldorf (Map 7; ☎ 7836 2400, Aldwych WC2; ✆ Charing Cross)* is served in the splendidly restored Palm Court on weekdays between 3 and 5.30 pm for £18 and £21 (with champagne). On Saturday from 2.30 to 5.30 pm and on Sunday from 4 to 6.30 pm you can take part in the old-fashioned ritual of tea dancing (£25/28) and booking is essential.

The graceful *Orangery (Map 5; ☎ 7376 0239; ✆ High Street Kensington or Queensway)* in Kensington Gardens is a superb place to have a relatively affordable set tea; prices range from £6.50 with cucumber sandwiches or scones to £12.50 with champagne. It's open daily from 10 am to 6 pm, April to September (to 4 pm the rest of the year).

The Ritz (Map 6; ☎ 7493 8181, 150 Piccadilly W1; ✆ Green Park) is probably the best-known place to take tea, although these days it's become something of a production-line process – the splendour of the florid pink and gold surroundings notwithstanding. Afternoon tea is served daily between 2 and 6 pm and costs £24.50 per person. You need to book a month ahead for weekdays and a ridiculous three months ahead for weekends; reserved sittings are at 3.30 and 5 pm. A strict dress-code applies.

The Savoy (Map 7; ☎ 7836 4343, Strand WC2; ✆ Charing Cross) serves tea in its enormous Thames Foyer daily between 3 and 5.30 pm. It costs £18.50 (or £28 including champagne).

PLACES TO EAT

Restaurant Services

Restaurant Services (☎ 8888 8080) is a free switchboard service open weekdays from 9 am to 7 pm with which you can specify a certain cuisine (eg Thai), or even atmosphere, in a certain price range (say £15 per head) and within a postcode (WC2, for example) and they'll come up with a suitable list for you and even book a table. For a group of up to six people, they'll reply the same day; for more than that you should phone a day or two in advance. The service's Web site is at www .restaurant-services.co.uk.

You might also look at the Web site www.simplyfood.co.uk, which offers information on food and wine and has links with restaurants.

Italian

UNo 1 (☎ 7834 1001, 1 Denbigh St SW1; ✛ Victoria). Pastas cost from £5.50 to £8 in this cheery dining room decorated in reds and yellows.

O Sole Mio (☎ 7976 6887, 39 Churton St SW1; ✛ Victoria). This standard, decent-value Italian restaurant has pizzas and pastas for around £6.

Olivo (☎ 7730 2505, 21 Eccleston St SW1; ✛ Victoria). This Modern Italian place produces unfussy pastas and main dishes like grilled swordfish with rocket (£12.50). Colourful surroundings and set lunches for £15/17 for two/three courses make it a winner.

Oliveto (☎ 7730 0074, 49 Elizabeth St SW1; ✛ Victoria or Sloane Square). This is Olivo's smaller (and cheaper) branch a short distance to the south-west.

Asian

Mekong (☎ 7630 9568, 46 Churton St SW1; ✛ Victoria). Mekong is a popular neighbourhood Vietnamese restaurant with set meals for £13 (minimum of two people).

Jenny Lo's Tea House (☎ 7259 0399, 14 Eccleston St SW1; ✛ Victoria). This was started by the daughter of the late Kenneth Lo, whose *Ken Lo's Memories of China* (☎ 7773 7734, 67-69 Ebury St SW1; ✛ Victoria) brought Chinese food to a new level in London. Jenny Lo's is a simple place with soup and fried noodles from £3.50 to £6.50 and rice dishes from £4.50.

ST JAMES'S & MAYFAIR (Maps 6 & 7)

This is an expensive part of London and not well stocked with budget places to eat.

Modern European

Quaglino's (Map 7; ☎ 7930 6767, 16 Bury St SW1; ✛ Green Park or Piccadilly Circus). Quaglino's has remained popular since its relaunch back in 1993. The food (starters from £4.50 to £6.50, main courses £11 to £16.50) is good but still manages to be outdone by the atmosphere, which is busy, fun and relatively glamorous.

American

Hard Rock Café (Map 6; ☎ 7629 0382, 150 Old Park Lane W1; ✛ Hyde Park Corner). This, the original Hard Rock Café, has been here since 1971 and is as popular as ever – just check out the queues that form every day of the year (no bookings taken). It serves a tried and tested diet of burgers and fries (from £7.25) and some decent Tex-Mex dishes. The rock memorabilia is memorable.

Middle Eastern

Sofra (Map 6; ☎ 7493 3300, 18 Shepherd Market W1; ✛ Green Park). A branch of a chain of Turkish eateries, Sofra's offerings include a set array of *mezes* (mixed hors d'oeuvres; £9.95). There's a good choice for vegetarians too. There's another branch at 36 Tavistock St WC2 (Map 7; ☎ 7240 3773; ✛ Covent Garden).

Indian

Rasa W1 (Map 6; ☎ 7629 1346, 6 Dering St W1; ✛ Bond Street). This is a larger, posher and more expensive branch of the South Indian vegetarian restaurant Rasa in Stoke Newington. See the Stoke Newington & Finsbury Park section for details.

THE WEST END: PICCADILLY, SOHO & CHINATOWN (Map 7)

These days Soho is London's gastronomic heart with numerous restaurants and cuisines to choose from. The liveliest streets tend to be Greek, Frith, Old Compton and Dean Sts. Gerrard and Lisle Sts are chock-a-block with Chinese eateries of every description.

English/Modern British

Franx Snack Bar *(☎ 7836 7989, 192 Shaftesbury Ave WC2; ⊖ Tottenham Court Road)*. Franx is as authentic a London 'caff' as you'll find in these parts, with eggs and bacon and other one-plate specials for around £3.

French House Dining Room *(☎ 7437 2477, 49 Dean St W1; ⊖ Leicester Square)*. The short menu at this restaurant above an old-fashioned Soho pub changes frequently and offers robust English/Modern British food like roast duck for £12 and sweetbreads with shallots and red chard (£10.50). Expect to pay around £5 for starters and from £8 to £12 for main courses. It has an excellent range of British cheeses.

The Ivy *(☎ 7836 4751, 1 West St WC2; ⊖ Leicester Square)*. With its liveried doorman and celebrity clientele, the Ivy is a showbizzy event in itself. The English menu includes dishes like shepherd's pie (£9.75), steak tartare (£7.75), kedgeree (£9.95) and Cumberland sausages with onions and mash.

International/Modern European

Stockpot *(☎ 7287 1066, 18 Old Compton St W1; ⊖ Leicester Square)*. This old stand-by does a long list of basic dishes (including a number of vegetarian options) like fish and chips (£4.50), spaghetti bolognese (£3) and chicken Provençale (£3.90). It has branches at 6 Basil St SW3 (Map 5; ☎ 7589 8627; ⊖ Knightsbridge) and 273 King's Rd SW3 (Map 9; ☎ 7823 3175; ⊖ Sloane Square).

Star Café *(☎ 7437 8778, 22 Great Chapel St W1; ⊖ Tottenham Court Road)*. This reliable cheapie dating from the 1930s serves up bangers and mash, fried breakfasts and pastas for under £5. It's open weekdays only from 7 am to 6 pm.

New Piccadilly *(☎ 7437 8530, 8 Denman St W1; ⊖ Piccadilly Circus)*. Entering the New Piccadilly is a step back in time; apart from the prices nothing has changed since it first opened in the 1950s, and even those haven't increased by as much as you'd expect: pastas and pizzas are around £4, chicken and steaks come in at around £5.

Capital Radio Café *(☎ 7484 8888, 29-30 Leicester Square W1; ⊖ Leicester Square)*. This is a stylish theme-café, with radio broadcasts *in situ* and high prices (salads from £7.95, designer sandwiches from £6.95). The menu mixes Italian, American, Greek, Thai and Chinese dishes with postmodern abandon.

Soup *(☎ 7287 9100, 1 Newburgh St W1; ⊖ Oxford Circus)*. Another of those upmarket 'soup kitchens' that are all the rage in New York and are now finding their way to London, Soup has a wide variety of choices – from pea and mushroom claret to Indonesian crab *laksa*. Prices start at £2.95 for a small cup and go up to £9.50 for a 1L container. A similar place is ***Soup Works*** *(☎ 7248 7687, 9 D'Arblay St W1; ⊖ Oxford Circus)*.

Garlic & Shots *(☎ 7734 9505, 14 Frith St W1; ⊖ Leicester Square)*. Whether or not you'll want to risk eating at this place depends on your tolerance for garlic – and your plans for later in the evening. Everything, including the cheesecake, ice cream and vodka, is spiked with the stuff. Main courses clock in at £9 to £13. It's open daily for dinner only.

Quo Vadis *(☎ 7437 9585, 26-29 Dean St W1; ⊖ Leicester Square)*. The French menu here is by the ubiquitous Marco Pierre White and the prices aren't too stratospheric for the location: £14.95/17.95 for a set two/three course lunch, which is also available between 6 and 7 pm. Don't come looking for artist Damien Hirst's quirky sculptures (eg dead cows preserved in formaldehyde), though; they were removed after a clash of egos and with typical humility MPW has replaced them with his own works (next thing we know, Hirst will be cooking). Karl Marx lived upstairs in two small rooms (now the restaurant's wine and cocktail bar) from 1851 to 1856.

Listen to the radio while you tuck in at the Capital Radio Café.

Mezzo (☎ 7314 4000, 100 Wardour St W1; ✆ Piccadilly Circus). Another of Terence Conran's ventures that attracts London's media crowd and media wannabes, Mezzo is so big you might lose your way coming back from the loo. The main restaurant in the basement is a fun, very modern place to eat, with starters from £5.50 and main courses from £11.50. *Mezzonine* on the ground floor is more casual and cheaper. At weekends orders are taken as late as 1 am.

Atlantic Bar & Grill (☎ 7734 4888, 20 Glasshouse St W1; ✆ Piccadilly Circus). This buzzy, atmospheric place boasts high ceilings, a large dining area and two bars. Food is expensive (from £6.50 to £10.50 for starters, £14.50 to £19 for main courses) and booking is a must at weekends. Set lunch is £14.50 for three courses.

Sugar Club (☎ 7437 7776, 21 Warwick St W1; ✆ Oxford Circus). Chef Peter Gordon is a New Zealander who concentrates on Pacific Rim dishes – like grilled kangaroo loin with coriander and mint, and roast pigeon breast on wok-fried black beans – that cleverly mix and match traditions of east and west. They don't come cheap; starters cost from £4.60 to £8.60, main courses £11.50 to £18.

Stargazer (☎ 7636 1057, 11 Rathbone St W1; ✆ Tottenham Court Road). This wine bar and restaurant (global food at about £20 a head) in Fitzrovia is a good place to come to catch a look at all the media wannabes in Charlotte St.

Bam-Bou (Map 6; ☎ 7323 9130, 1 Percy St W1; ✆ Tottenham Court Road). This chichi place, just around the corner from Stargazer, is a gastronomic hybrid of French and Asian (curried frogs' legs, *sauté de bœuf* with lime etc) that has got very mixed reviews. Count on £30 a head.

American

Sports Café (☎ 7839 8300, New Zealand House, 80 Haymarket SW1; ✆ Piccadilly Circus). There's no escaping sport at this restaurant with a dance floor, a ski simulator, a basketball court and a lot of sporting memorabilia. Indeed, table-side TVs keep you occupied with the latest games, matches and races while you await your burger and chips (around £8). There's a cheap lunch available for £4.95 and an early-bird dinner menu (from 5 to 7 pm) lets two eat for the price of one.

Planet Hollywood (☎ 7287 1000, 13 Coventry St W1; ✆ Piccadilly Circus). Be prepared to queue at this international favourite for standard American and Californian fare (eg burgers from £8.45, Cajun salmon for £12.50).

Rainforest Café (☎ 7434 3111, 20 Shaftesbury Ave W1; ✆ Piccadilly Circus). The greenie's Hard Rock Café, with live birds and animatronic wild beasts roaring and hooting, waterfalls cascading and thunder crashing among larger-than-life (alas, fake) banyan trees, the Rainforest Café serves American food like burgers (£9.95) with a splash of Tex-Mex/Caribbean. It's frenetic but the kids are going to love it.

French

L'Odéon (☎ 7287 1400, 65 Regent St W1; ✆ Piccadilly Circus). This upmarket restaurant is worth a visit just for the views of Regent St from its lofty windows. The food also comes in for good reports, especially if you go for the £15.50/19.50 two/three course set lunch or dinner (from 5.30 to 7 pm only).

The Criterion (☎ 7930 0488, 224 Piccadilly W1; ✆ Piccadilly Circus). This place right on Piccadilly Circus has a spectacular interior – all chandeliers, mirrors, marble and sparkling mosaics – that one breathless wag compared to the inside of a Fabergé egg. The menu offers Marco Pierre White's fashionable Modern French food (eg sautéed goat's cheese and roasted peppers), but there are also some English classics like fish and chips. You won't see much change from £35 per person at dinner, but set two/three-course lunches (also available from 6 to 6.30 pm) cost just £14.95/17.95.

Italian

Pollo (☎ 7734 5917, 20 Old Compton St W1; ✆ Leicester Square). This cheapie attracts a student crowd with its pastas, *risottos*, pizzas and chicken dishes for under £4.

Pizza Express (☎ 7439 8722, 10 Dean St W1; ✆ Tottenham Court Road). This branch of the huge pizza chain is unusual: at street level you get cheap, good-quality pizzas (about £6) and a glass of house wine for £2.50; downstairs you can eat to the accompaniment of excellent jazz (admission is £8 to £20).

Kettners (☎ 7734 6112, 29 Romilly St W1; ✆ Leicester Square). If you fancy something with fewer links than the Pizza Express chain, Kettners serves pizzas (from £6.50) and burgers of a similar standard and price but in a wonderful atmosphere of gently fading grandeur with a piano tinkling softly in the background.

Spiga (☎ 7734 3444, 84-86 Wardour St W1; ✆ Tottenham Court Road). This is where to head if you want authentic pizza (from £6), pasta or an Italian main dish in sleek, pleasant surroundings but don't want to pay the earth for it. It has a cheaper branch called *Spighetta* (*Map 6;* ☎ *7486 7340, 43 Blandford St W1;* ☻ *Baker Street*) in Marylebone.

Spanish

There are a couple of decent Spanish eateries with *tapas* (£2 to £6.95) that tourists never get to on Hanway St (☻ Tottenham Court Road), a narrow street running north off Oxford St, including *Costa Dorada* (☎ *7636 7139*) at Nos 47 to 55 and its sister restaurant, the cheaper *Sevilla Mia* (☎ *7637 3756*), a hole-in-the-wall basement eatery at No 22.

Hungarian

Gay Hussar (☎ *7437 0973, 2 Greek St W1;* ☻ *Tottenham Court Road*). This is the Soho of the 1950s, when dining was still done in the grand style in rooms with brocade and sepia prints on the walls. And they serve portions only the Hungarians can: try the roast duck (£16) with all the trimmings or the 'Gypsy quick dish' of pork medallions, onions and green peppers (£13.50). You won't need to eat again for a while.

Indian

Gopal's of Soho (☎ *7434 0840, 12 Bateman St W1;* ☻ *Tottenham Court Road*). Gopal's is cramped and run-down but it offers reasonably authentic food at affordable prices. *Thalis* (set meals served on circular metal trays) are good value: £11.75 for vegetarian and £1 more for the meat equivalent.

Rasa Samudra (☎ *7637 0222, 5 Charlotte St W1;* ☻ *Goodge Street*). This place just north of Oxford St is from the same people who gave you the South Indian vegetarian restaurants Rasa in Stoke Newington and Rasa W1 in Mayfair (see the Stoke Newington & Finsbury Park and St James's & Mayfair sections), but here they've moved on from catering for veggies and emphasise seafood.

Chinese

If you're with several people and want a proper sit-down meal in Chinatown (☻ Leicester Square) but are overwhelmed by the choice, consider any of the following three. They've been tested again and again and have always come up trumps:

Fung Shing (☎ *7437 1539, 15 Lisle St WC2*)

Gerrard's Corner (☎ *7437 0984, 30 Wardour St WC2*)

London Hong Kong (☎ *7287 0324, 6-7 Lisle St WC2*)

A particularly good way to sample the best of Chinese cuisine is to try Cantonese dim sum where you select numerous small dishes and wash them down with a pot of jasmine tea.

Chuen Cheng Ku (☎ *7437 1398, 17 Wardour St W1*). This place is ideal for the uninitiated as all the dishes (dumplings, noodles, paper-wrapped prawns etc) are trundled around on trolleys.

Poons (☎ *7437 4549, 27 Lisle St WC2*). This hole-in-the-wall eatery is where the upmarket Poons empire started. It offers OK food at very good prices and specialises in dried duck and pork (£4.20 per plate). Be prepared to queue at busy times and to be hustled out again pretty quickly.

Wong Kei (☎ *7437 3071, 41-43 Wardour St W1*). Wong Kei is famous for the rudeness of its waiters. Some find this adds to the experience, but even if you don't – like us – you might be

PLACES TO EAT

RICHARD I'ANSON

Soho's Chinese eateries range from 'greasy chopsticks' to imperial banquet houses.

A familiar sight in the Soho backstreets: sizzling displays of succulent duck.

From yakitori to sashimi, tempura to sushi – mouth-watering Japanese goodies in Soho.

tempted by the cheap Cantonese food (main dishes from £4.50 to £7.50, rice dishes from £3, set menus from £6).

Mr Wu (☎ 7839 6669, 6-7 Irving St WC2). Mr Wu offers a 10 course all-you-can-eat Chinese lunch or dinner buffet for £4.50. It's not gourmet but it's filling. There's another branch at 26 Wardour St W1 (☎ 7287 3885).

Mr Au (☎ 7437 7472, 47-49 Charing Cross Rd WC2). Similar place to Mr Wu, same price, same deal – only the name is different.

1997 Special Zone (☎ 7734 2868, 19 Wardour St W1). If you've got a craving for Peking duck (£8.50) or comforting soup noodles (£4.50) at 4 am, head for 1997 SZ; it's open 24 hours.

Japanese & Korean

Ikkyu (☎ 7439 3554, 7-9 Newport Place WC2; ⊖ Leicester Square). This Chinese-owned restaurant with Japanese cooks has à la carte sushi, sashimi and noodle dishes, but the great draws for budget travellers are the four different set lunches (from £5.50 to £13.50) and the all-you-can-eat Japanese buffet available from 6 to 10.30 pm for £12.50 (£6.50 for children aged under 12).

Tokyo Diner (☎ 7287 8777, 2 Newport Place WC2; ⊖ Leicester Square). The Tokyo Diner is a good-value place to stop for a quick bowl of noodles or a plate of sushi before the cinema or theatre. A meal is likely to cost from £8 to £10, although their set bento boxes start at £10.50.

Zipangu (☎ 7437 5042, 8 Little Newport St WC2; ⊖ Leicester Square). This is another budget choice for Japanese food, with similar prices and fare to the Tokyo Diner.

Soba (☎ 7734 6400, 38 Poland St W1; ⊖ Oxford Circus). Soba is always our first choice for an easy (and cheap) bowl of Japanese noodles for around £5.

Satsuma (☎ 7437 8338, 56 Wardour St W1; ⊖ Leicester Square). This place is similar to Soba but a wee bit more upmarket.

Yo! Sushi (☎ 7287 0443, 52-53 Poland St W1; ⊖ Oxford Circus). Yo! Sushi is one of London's livelier sushi bars, where diners sit around the bar and the dishes come to them on a 60m-long conveyor belt (drinks, on the other hand, arrive on a robotic trolley). Sushi costs from £1.50 to £3.50; you should be able to get away with around £10 a head. There are branches at Selfridges department store (☎ 7318 3885; ⊖ Oxford Circus), 400 Oxford St W1, where you can eat your fill for £18, and on the 5th floor of Harvey Nichols (☎ 7235 5000; ⊖ Knightsbridge), Brompton Rd SW1.

Wagamama (☎ 7292 0990, 10A Lexington St W1; ⊖ Piccadilly Circus). This brash and spartan place does great Japanese food but is hardly the place for a quiet dinner. You have to share long tables and, having queued to get in, may feel pressured to move on again quickly. Main dishes range from £5 to £7.50 while Japanese-style set menus are from £8 to £9.50. Wagamama has several branches: 4a Streatham St WC1 (☎ 7323 9223; ⊖ Tottenham Court Road); 101a Wigmore St W1 (☎ 7409 0111; ⊖ Oxford Circus); and 9-11 Jamestown Rd NW1 (☎ 7428 0800; ⊖ Camden Town).

Nam Dae Moon (☎ 7836 7235, 56 St Giles High St WC2; ⊖ Tottenham Court Road). With bulgogi or kalbi (£7.50) grills and spicy kimchee, Nam Dae Moon is as authentic a Korean restaurant as you'll find in the West End. Try the noodles with squid and dried fish (£5.50) or the pibimbap (£7.50), a rice, meat and vegetable concoction that gets stirred together with a raw egg.

South-East Asian

Melati (☎ 7437 2745, 21 Great Windmill St W1; ⊖ Piccadilly Circus). This Indonesian/Malaysian/Singaporean restaurant has good food and a respectable range of vegetarian options. Various noodle and rice dishes cost from £6 to £8 and the fish in chilli sauce (£7.25) is excellent.

Chiang Mai (☎ 7437 7444, 48 Frith St W1; ⊖ Tottenham Court Road). A top-class, rather expensive Thai restaurant (it's a branch of the Thai Bistro in Chiswick), Chiang Mai has a separate vegetarian menu and a wide range of soups. Set vegetarian or meat and fish menus start at just under £25 per person.

Cam Phat (☎ 7437 5598, 12 Macclesfield St W1; ⊖ Leicester Square). Cam Phat is a cheap and cheerful Vietnamese place that serves well prepared dishes like roast pork with vermicelli noodles (£4.50) and *pho* (£3.50), the Vietnamese soup staple of beef and noodles in a stock flavoured with lemon grass.

Middle Eastern

Gaby's (☎ 7836 4233, 30 Charing Cross Rd WC2; ⊖ Leicester Square). This snack bar beside Wyndham's theatre has been here forever and attracts queues for staples like *hummus* and felafel (£3.20) and *couscous royale* (£7.50).

Momo (☎ 7434 4040, 25 Heddon St W1; ⊖ Piccadilly Circus). The kasbah comes to London at this trendy and expensive Moroccan restaurant, with couscous for £12.50 to £16.50 and *tajines* from £9.75 to £15. Set lunches cost £12.50/15.50 for two/three courses.

Vegetarian

Mildred's (☎ 7494 1634, 58 Greek St W1; ⊖ Tottenham Court Road). Mildred's is so small (and popular) that you may have to share a table. It's worth it, however, because the vegetarian food – including stir-fried vegetables and beanburgers – is both good and well priced (from £5 to £7 for a large main course).

Govinda's (☎ 7437 5875, 10 Soho St W1; ⊖ Tottenham Court Road). Govinda's serves pure vegetarian food cooked with love and devotion (the latter to Krishna, to whom the temple next door is dedicated). Almost everything is under £3.

Cafés

Pâtisserie Valerie (☎ 7437 3466, 44 Old Compton St W1; ⊖ Tottenham Court Road or Leicester Square). You can't beat this Soho institution for coffee or tea and something sweet (calorie-crunching cakes around £2.50), though you'll be lucky to get a seat. It also does filled croissants and club sandwiches (from £4 to £5.50). There are branches at 79 Regent St W1 (☎ 7439 0090; ⊖ Piccadilly Circus) and 215 Brompton Rd SW5 (☎ 7823 9971; ⊖ Knightsbridge).

Maison Bertaux (☎ 7437 6007, 28 Greek St W1; ⊖ Tottenham Court Road). Bertaux has been turning out confections for 130 years, and they're still as exquisite as ever.

Monmouth Coffee House (☎ 7836 5272, 27 Monmouth St WC2; ⊖ Covent Garden). Essentially a shop selling beans from every coffee-growing country in the world, Monmouth has seating for eight where you can sample their blends: from Nicaraguan and Guatemalan to Kenyan and Ethiopian.

Bar Italia (☎ 7437 4520, 22 Frith St W1; ⊖ Leicester Square). This great favourite is open round the clock and has a wonderful 1950s décor. It's always packed and buzzing (from the caffeine, no doubt); your best chance for a seat might be sometime after 1 am.

CHARLOTTE HINDLE

Caffè latte, cappuccino, espresso ... linger over a coffee, Continental style.

RICHARD I'ANSON

Underneath the arches: lunch time in Covent Garden.

COVENT GARDEN & THE STRAND (Map 7)

Right beside Soho and technically part of the West End, Covent Garden is also densely packed with places to eat. The following are all accessible from Covent Garden tube station unless indicated otherwise.

English

Rock & Sole Plaice (☎ 7836 3785, 47 Endell St WC2). This no-nonsense fish and chips shop has basic Formica tables and delicious cod or haddock in batter (£3.50 or £4.50 with chips). It's unlicensed but you can BYO (bring your own).

Porters (☎ 7836 6466, 17 Henrietta St WC2). Porters specialises in pies, long a staple of English cooking but not regularly found on modern menus. Unusual ones like lamb and apricot or chicken and broccoli go for £7.95. Steak and kidney pudding is £8.

Simpson's-in-the-Strand (☎ 7836 9112, 100 Strand WC2). For traditional English roasts, Simpson's is where to go – it's been dishing up hot meats in a fine panelled dining room since 1848 (when it was called Simpson's Divan and Tavern). Steak and kidney pudding will set you back £13.80, lamb and redcurrant jelly is £18.50 and duck and apple sauce £15.50.

Rules (☎ 7836 5314, 35 Maiden Lane WC2). This very posh, very British (and rather stuffy) place has a wonderful Edwardian interior and waiters dressed in starched white aprons. The menu is inevitably meat-oriented but fish dishes are also available. Puddings are traditional: trifles, pies and an abundance of custard. The quality and feel of the place make up for the steep prices (main courses from £14.95).

American

Joe Allen (☎ 7836 0651, 13 Exeter St WC2). This long-established American-style eatery is a star-spotter's paradise. There's a real buzz here and it gets crowded, so book. Starters and main dishes (lamb chops, grilled halibut etc) are varied, with some vegetarian choices. A three course meal will be from £20 to £25 though there are cheap two/three-course lunch menus for £11/13 and pre-theatre dinners for £12/14.

French

Café des Amis du Vin (☎ 7379 3444, 11-14 Hanover Place WC2). This brasserie is handy for pre or post-theatre meals with good, affordable French fare. Starters are from £4.95 to £6.50, main courses from £9.85 to £13.50 and set lunches of two/three courses £9.95/12.50.

Italian

Orso (☎ 7240 5269, 27 Wellington St WC2). An established Italian eatery popular with media types, Orso is relatively expensive for dinner (about £25 per head) but does a cheaper two/three course lunch for £14/16 including – as any journalist would expect – a Bloody Mary or a glass of champagne.

Middle Eastern

Sarastro (☎ 7836 0101, 126 Drury Lane WC2). Any place that bills itself as 'The Show after the Show' has got to be more concerned with gimmicky entertainment than food but Sarastro, which serves Turkish-ish food (starters from £3 to £7, main courses from £8.50 to £14), and its baroque décor, opera music and 'master of ceremonies', Big Boss Richard, make for a night to remember.

Asian

Mongolian Barbecue (☎ 7379 7722, 12 Maiden Lane WC2; ✚ Leicester Square). 'All you Khan eat' (their joke, not ours) for £10.95.

Tibetan Restaurant (☎ 7839 2090, 17 Irving St WC2; ✚ Leicester Square). Not surprisingly, the Tibetan specialises in the esoteric cuisine hailing from the rooftop of the world (a bit like Chinese mixed with Indian, with a pat of yak butter thrown in for authenticity). A host of three-course set menus (including vegetarian ones) cost from £8.50 to £13.50.

Other Cuisines

Belgo Centraal (☎ 7813 2233, 50 Earlham St WC2). Taking the lift down to the basement and walking through the kitchens is all part of the fun at Belgo, where the waiters dress up as 16th-century monks. This being a Belgian restaurant, *moules et frites* (mussels and chips/french fries) and spit roasts are the specialities and beer (100 different flavoured Pilsners, including banana, peach and cherry) is the drink. There's a set lunch menu for £5; a set dinner of a starter, mussels and chips and a beer costs £13.95. On weekdays from 5.30 to 7 pm you can try the 'Beat the Clock' menu – the time you sit down decides the price you pay for your main dish (sit down at 6.15 pm and you pay £6.15, with the minimum charge, of course, being £5.30).

Café Pacifico (☎ 7379 7728, 5 Langley St). Pacifico serves Mexican food in a cheerful dining room, with main courses for £6.25 to £8.95 and great margaritas. The same people own *La Perla de Pacifico* (☎ 7240 7400, 28 Maiden Lane WC2), with healthy lunches and not quite so healthy rare and premium tequilas and mescals (from £2.50 to £5.75).

Calabash (☎ 7836 1973, 38 King St WC2). This simple eatery in the Africa Centre serves food from all over Africa and has a menu for the uninitiated describing each dish. Typical dishes are *egusi* (£6.95), a Nigerian meat stew with tomatoes and spices, and *yassa* (£6.50), chicken marinated with lemon juice and peppers, hailing from Senegal. There are also beers from all over Africa and wines from Algeria, Zimbabwe and South Africa.

Vegetarian

Food for Thought (☎ 7836 0239, 31 Neal St WC2). This tiny, no-smoking vegetarian café features dishes like West Indian curry for £3.80 and stir-fried vegetables with brown rice for £3.30.

Cafés

There's a cluster of enjoyable New Age cafés – some of them vegetarian – in Neal's Yard, including those listed below. All offer a similar diet of wholesome dishes like cheese breads and home-made noodles in pleasing surroundings, but space fills up quickly. Lunch in any of these places should cost about £5 to £6 if you choose carefully.

Neal's Yard Beach Café (☎ 7240 1168, 13 Neal's Yard WC2)

World Food Café (☎ 7379 0298, 14 Neal's Yard WC2)

Neal's Yard Salad Bar (☎ 7836 3233, 2 Neal's Yard WC2).

BLOOMSBURY (Maps 4, 6 & 7)

Though usually thought of as B&B land, Bloomsbury has a large number of restaurants, many of them reasonably priced.

English

North Sea Fish Restaurant (Map 4; ☎ 7387 5892, 7-8 Leigh St WC1; ✚ Russell Square). The North Sea sets out to cook fresh fish and potatoes – a simple ambition in which it succeeds admirably. Cod, haddock and plaice, deep-fried or grilled, and a huge serving of chips will cost you between £6.95 and £7.95.

Italian

Mille Pini (Map 6; ☎ 7242 2434, 33 Boswell St WC1; ✚ Russell Square or Holborn). This well regarded place is a true, old-fashioned Italian restaurant and pizzeria with reasonable prices. You'll waddle out, but will only have spent about £6/10 for a two course lunch/dinner.

Vegetarian

The Greenhouse (Map 6; ☎ 7637 8038, 16 Chenies St WC1; ✚ Goodge Street). Below the Drill Hall Theatre, the Greenhouse is popular and very busy, so expect to share a table. Vegetable bakes cost around £3.95, casseroles from £2.25 and quiches £2.10.

Museum St Café (Map 7; ☎ 7405 3211, 47 Museum St WC1; ✚ Tottenham Court Road). This place is packed at lunch time (it opens at 8 or 9 am and closes after tea) and is totally no-smoking. Mediterranean-inspired main courses (from £7.50) include warm goat's cheese salad and *frittata* with rosemary potatoes. Set tea (served from 3 to 6 pm) costs £8.

Mandeer (*Map 7;* ☎ *7242 6202, 8 Bloomsbury Way WC1;* ✪ *Tottenham Court Road*). Vegetarian Indian – this time Ayurvedic – with main dishes from £3.75 to £5.25 and thalis for £10.95.

Cafés

If you're visiting the British Museum it's worth knowing that Museum St (Map 7; ✪ Tottenham Court Road) is packed with cafés and simple lunch places where you'll get better value for your money than in the museum café.

Coffee Gallery (☎ *7436 0455, 23 Museum St WC1*). This tremendously popular place serves pasta dishes and main courses like grilled sardines and salad in a bright, cheerful room with modern paintings on the walls.

Garden Café (☎ *7637 4309, 32 Museum St WC1*). Head for the Garden for cakes.

Ruskins Café (☎ *7405 1450, 41 Museum St WC1*). This place does soup and filled jacket potatoes from £2.95.

HOLBORN & CLERKENWELL (Maps 4 & 6)

Holborn has a few restaurants and night spots to recommend it but is generally dead after dark. On the other hand, Clerkenwell has well and truly arrived on the eating-out map. These places are mostly accessible from Farringdon tube station.

English

Ferrari's Cafe (*Map 6;* ☎ *7236 7545, 8 West Smithfield EC1*). This 24-hour greasy spoon opposite the market at Smithfield has fry-ups substantial enough to keep the market folk going through the morning for under £5.

St John (*Map 6;* ☎ *7251 0848, 26 St John St EC1*). St John is the place to come if you fancy sampling old-fashioned British staples in new guises, like tripe and sausage soup (£5), pigeon and Jerusalem artichoke (£11.80) and sweetbreads, peas and broad beans (£12.80). While there are some fish dishes, this place is all about meat, and offal in particular (after all, it is right next to Smithfield Market).

French

Mange-2 (*Map 6;* ☎ *7250 0035, 2-3 Cowcross St EC1*). Primarily a business location at lunch,

Mange-2 quietens down at dinner. Many of the middle-of-the-road French dishes are based on fish (although not exclusively so) and there is some excellent seafood. Who could resist seafood quenelles in lobster sauce (£13.75)? There's a two course set meal for £17.95.

Novelli EC1 (*Map 4;* ☎ *7251 6606, 31 Clerkenwell Green EC1*). This is the less expensive cousin of chef/owner Jean-Christophe Novelli's flagship *Maison Novelli* restaurant next door. It too serves sublime Modern French food in a brasserie looking on to Clerkenwell Green. Count on about £25 per person.

Club Gascon (*Map 6;* ☎ *7253 5853, 57 West Smithfield EC1*). Right next to glorious St Bartholomew's-the-Great (of *Four Weddings and a Funeral* fame), Club Gascon serves the food of south-west France. It's in the same league as Novelli. Book well in advance.

Italian

Spaghetti House (*Map 6;* ☎ *7405 5215, 20 Sicilian Ave WC1;* ✪ *Holborn*). This basic Italian eatery in a pedestrianised short cut between Southampton Row and Vernon Place has outside seating in warm weather. Pasta dishes kick off at £5.95, and there's a set menu for £7.50.

Spanish

Moro (*Map 4;* ☎ *7833 8336, 34-36 Exmouth Market N1*). As its name implies, this place serves 'Moorish' cuisine, a fusion of Spanish, Portuguese and North African flavours. Try the crab *brik* (£6.50), a crispy deep-fried packet served with piquant *harissa*, and the wood-roasted red mullet (£12.50) with sharp Seville orange. Starters go for £4 to £6.50, main courses from £9.50 to £13.50.

Gaudí (*Map 6;* ☎ *7608 3220, 63 Clerkenwell Rd EC1*). This restaurant takes its cue from the Catalan architect's designs to provide a backdrop for a classy restaurant specialising in what has been dubbed New Spanish cuisine. Fish plays a big, if not exclusive, role, and first courses start at about £6, main courses at £14. Set lunch midweek costs £12.50/15 for two/three courses. It's got a good Spanish wine list.

Asian

East One (*Map 4;* ☎ *7566 0088, 175-179 St John St EC1*). East One is another of those Asian do-it-yourself places, where an all-you-can-eat stir-fry costs £10/12.50 for lunch/dinner.

Cicada (Map 4; ☎ *7608 1550, 132-136 St John St EC1).* Cicada is a lovely, modern restaurant that mingles Asian tastes and flavours with great success. Starters cost from about £5, main dishes from £6 to £10.

Other Cuisines
My Old Dutch (Map 7; ☎ *7242 5200, 131-132 High Holborn WC1;* ✪ *Holborn).* This long-lived restaurant serves over 100 different plate-sized sweet and savoury pancakes (from £3.70 to £5.95) and waffles (£3.45 to £4.45) seven days a week. There's a branch at 221 King's Rd SW3 (☎ *7376 5650;* ✪ *Sloane Square*).

Vegetarian
The Greenery (Map 6; ☎ *7490 4870, 5 Cowcross St EC1).* This small vegetarian café, hanging on for the moment amid all the gentrification of Clerkenwell, has salad platters for £3.95 and chickpea and coriander *chapatis* for £1.80.

THE CITY (Maps 6 & 8)
The City can be an irritating place in which to try to find a decent, affordable restaurant that stays open after office hours. The following are the pick of the crop.

English
Sweeting's (Map 8; ☎ *7248 3062, 39 Queen Victoria St EC4;* ✪ *Mansion House).* Sweeting's is an old-fashioned place, with a mosaic floor and waiters in white aprons standing behind narrow counters serving up all sorts of traditional fishy delights. Something like wild smoked salmon costs £8.50; main courses run from £8 to £19. Oysters are sold in season (ie from September to April) and cost £11.25 a half-dozen.

Ye Olde Cheshire Cheese (Map 6; ☎ *7353 6170, Wine Office Court EC4;* ✪ *Blackfriars).* Rebuilt six years after the Great Fire and popular with Dr Johnson, Thackeray, Dickens and the visiting Mark Twain, the Cheshire Cheese is touristy but the traditional Chop Room is a good place to take visitors.

International/Modern European
Wine Library (Map 8; ☎ *7481 0415, 43 Trinity Square EC3;* ✪ *Tower Hill).* This is a great place to go if you want a light but boozy lunch. Buy a bottle of wine retail (no mark-up; £2 corkage fee) from the large selection on offer

Ye Olde Cheshire Cheese, a magnet for literary types through the ages.

and then snack on pâtés, cheeses and salads for £9.95. The shop is open weekdays from 10 am to 6 pm and for lunch from 11.30 am to 3 pm.
Searcy's (Map 8; ☎ *7588 3008, Level 2, Arts Centre Building, Barbican Centre EC2;* ✪ *Barbican).* This brasserie in the bowels of the Barbican is a great place for a pre or post-performance meal. Unless you're up for a bill topping £35 a head you'll have to stick with the two/three course set meal for £18.50/21.50.

Italian & Pizza
Da Vinci (Map 6; ☎ *7236 3938, 42-44 Carter Lane EC4;* ✪ *St Paul's).* Here's a rare bird indeed: an affordable neighbourhood Italian place in the City. Starters are from £3.95 to £6.95, pastas £3.80 to £5.95 and main courses £8.50 to £14. A two course set lunch is £11.50 and there's a 'cheap lunch' for £4.50 available from 11.30 am to 1 pm.
Caravaggio (Map 8; ☎ *7626 6206, Bank-side House, 107-112 Leadenhall St EC3;* ✪ *Aldgate or Bank).* This probably wouldn't rate a listing if it were anywhere else, but relatively authentic Italian food is not easy to find in the City. Count on £30 per person all in.

Indian

Café Spice Namaste (Map 8; ☎ 7488 9242, 16 Prescot St E1; ✛ Tower Hill). One of our favourite Indian restaurants in London, the Namaste serves Goan and Keralan cuisine (with South-East Asian hints) in an old courthouse that has been decorated in 'carnival' colours. Try *frango piri-piri* (£7.75), a fiery hot chicken *tikka* marinated in red *masala*, or the *muglai maas* (£10.25), Kashmiri lamb in a nut-based sauce. There are plenty of vegetarian side and main dishes.

Asian

Dim Sum (Map 6; ☎ 7236 1114, 5-6 Deans Court EC4; ✛ St Paul's). A budget traveller's delight and convenient to St Paul's and the City of London YHA hostel, Dim Sum serves Peking and Szechuan dishes for £3 to £6, but the best deal is the £9.99 all-you-can-eat buffet (minimum four people) available weekdays from 6 to 10.30 pm.

Saigon Times (Map 8; ☎ 7621 0022, 20-22 Leadenhall Market EC3; ✛ Monument). This 'French Oriental' bar and restaurant right inside ornate Leadenhall Market serves three meals a day weekdays only but keeps City hours: 7.30 am to 9.30 pm. It gets mixed reviews but we like the French waiters.

Vegetarian

The Place Below (Map 8; ☎ 7329 0789, St Mary-le-Bow Church, Cheapside EC2; ✛ St Paul's or Mansion House). This pleasant vegetarian restaurant in a church crypt is open weekdays from 7.30 am to 2.30 pm. Salads cost £6.95, pasta £6.50 and soup £2.95, but if you arrive between 11.30 am (when lunch begins) and noon you'll get £2 off most main dishes.

BERMONDSEY (Map 8)

This area's culinary highlights include Terence Conran's gastronomic palaces at Shad Thames, but there are several other places of note.

Modern British

Butlers Wharf Chop House (☎ 7403 3403, Butlers Wharf Building, 36E Shad Thames SE1; ✛ Tower Hill). Furniture retailer and restaurateur Terence Conran, who set up the Design Museum in the little enclave called Shad Thames, also located some of his excellent though expensive restaurants nearby. This one serves lamb, beef and its signature steak, kidney and oyster pudding. Set meals cost £18.75/22.75 for two/three courses.

Modern European

The Apprentice (☎ 7234 0254, Cardamom Building, Butlers Wharf, 31 Shad Thames SE1; ✛ Tower Hill). This restaurant is so named because trainees practise here at the Butlers Wharf Chef School. Prices are lower than at the neighbouring restaurants, with a set lunch for £9.50/12.50 for two/three courses and a three course set dinner for £17.50. It's open for lunch and dinner (to 8.30 pm) weekdays only.

Blue Print Café (☎ 7378 7031, Design Museum, Butlers Wharf SE1; ✛ Tower Hill). Modern European cooking is the order of the day at this flagship Conran restaurant, with starters from £5 to £6.50 and main courses from £11 to £16.50. There are spectacular views of the river from here.

Le Pont de la Tour (☎ 7403 8403, Butlers Wharf Building, 36D Shad Thames SE1; ✛ Tower Hill). This is where movers and shakers like Prime Minister Tony Blair dine on French-ish food, peruse the 30 page wine list and enjoy the river setting. Set lunch is £28.50; at dinner starters are from £8.50 to £15, main courses £17.50 to £20.

Italian & Mediterranean

Cantina del Ponte (☎ 7403 5403, Butlers Wharf Building, 36C Shad Thames SE1; ✛ Tower Hill). This is a more affordable riverside Conran restaurant serving Italian/Mediterranean food. Starters are from £5 to £6.95, main courses £12.50 to £13.95, with pizzas £6.10 to £7.95 and pastas £7.50 to £12.50. At lunch during the week and at dinner on Sunday there's a two/three course meal for £12/15. There's fabulous outside seating in warm weather.

SOUTHWARK (Map 8)

Options in this part of town range from workers' caffs and pie shops to some more exotic – and expensive – choices.

English/Modern British

Manze's (☎ 7407 2985, 87 Tower Bridge Rd SE1; ✛ London Bridge). This pie shop, the oldest still trading in London, has been going strong for over a century and is handy for Bermondsey Market. In its pleasantly tiled interior jellied eels cost £1.80, pie and mash £2.05, and pie and liquor £1.40.

Fish! Fresh fish of every description, from the everyday to the exotic.

Borough Café (11 Park St SE1; ✆ London Bridge). Close to Borough Market, this is the quintessential London market caff, where you can eat a full meal for less than £4 weekdays from 4 am to 3 pm and on Saturday to 11 am.

Fish! (✆ 7836 3236, Cathedral St SE1; ✆ London Bridge). Situated in an all-glass Victorian pavilion overlooking Borough Market and Southwark Cathedral, Fish! serves fresher-than-fresh fish and seafood prepared simply: steamed or grilled swordfish, cod, skate, squid (or whatever is ticked off on the placemat) served with one of five sauces. Expect to pay anything from £8.50 to £15.95 for a main course.

Other Cuisines

Fina Estampa (✆ 7403 1342, 150 Tooley St SE1; ✆ Tower Hill or London Bridge). Come here for solid, home-cooked Peruvian fare – and lots of it. Try *cebiche*, white fish marinated in lemon juice (£5.95), to start and either *seco* (lamb or chicken in coriander sauce; £10.95) or *carapulcra* (dried Peruvian potatoes served with pork, chicken and yucca; £10.95). The *pisco* cocktails (£3.50) are deadly.

WATERLOO & LAMBETH (Map 6)

This part of south London is not immediately attractive as a place for eating out, although the cafés and restaurants in the Festival Hall, the Royal National Theatre and the National Film Theatre are popular places to meet, with reasonable food.

English

R Cooke Eel & Pie Shop (✆ 7928 5931, 84 The Cut SE1; ✆ Waterloo). Cooke's serves excellent pies (£1.60) and eel and mash (£2.35) in a lovely old café. It's open Tuesday to Saturday from 10.30 am to 2.30 pm.

Marie's Café (✆ 7928 1050, 90 Lower Marsh SE1; ✆ Waterloo). Marie's is a typical caff with above-average fry-ups (including great mushrooms) as well as – wait for it – Thai dishes.

International/Modern European

Livebait (✆ 7928 7211, 43 The Cut SE1; ✆ Waterloo). This green-and-white-tiled restaurant that is trying to look more proletarian than it really is serves up fish dishes in all their guises (eg *lasagne ai frutti di mare* £7.95, halibut Wellington £17.10) but can't hold a candle to Fish! in Borough Market (see the previous Southwark section). The atmosphere is so casual it borders on the cavalier. There's a branch at 21 Wellington St WC2 (✆ 7836 7161; ✆ Covent Garden).

Bar Central (✆ 7928 5086, 131 Waterloo Rd SE1; ✆ Waterloo). Its name notwithstanding, Bar Central is actually a quiet, intimate restaurant with a small bar. The 'global' (ie a bit from everywhere) main courses cost from £8 to £12.50.

Oxo Tower Restaurant & Brasserie (✆ 7803 3888, Barge House St SE1; ✆ Waterloo). The conversion of the old Oxo Tower on the South Bank into housing with this restaurant on the 8th floor helped spur much of the restaurant renaissance south of the river. The food – a bit Mediterranean, a bit French, some Pacific Rim – is satisfactory in that Fifth Floor (see the later Kensington & Knightsbridge section) sort of way (it's owned by the Harvey Nichols department store). Starters cost from £5.50 to £13.50, main courses average £18 and there's a three course set lunch for £24.50. If you can't get in there's always the cheaper *Bistrot 2 Riverside (✆ 7498 8200)* on the 2nd floor of the tower.

DOUG McKINLAY

PLACES TO EAT

People's Palace (☎ 7928 9999, Royal Festival Hall; ✪ Waterloo). Easy to miss inside the Royal Festival Hall and boasting some enviable fine views of the Thames and the City, this rather deceptively named 3rd floor restaurant serves such delights as beetroot tart *tatin* and roast rabbit. Expect to pay a minimum of £20 per person.

Italian
The Gourmet Pizza Company (☎ 7928 3188, Gabriel's Wharf, 65 Upper Ground SE1; ✪ Waterloo). It may not look like much but there are always queues here, waiting for such unusual toppings as Thai chicken (£7.95) and Cajun chicken with prawns (£8.45) along with the more usual cheese and tomato (£4.95) and Italian sausage (£7.25).

Pizzeria Castello (☎ 7703 2556, 20 Walworth Rd SE1; ✪ Elephant & Castle). Ask any south Londoner to direct you to the best pizzeria on this side of the Thames and you'll find yourself here. Castello has been going for years, is family owned, very friendly and prices are low (under £6). Book or count on a long wait for a table.

Chinese
The Four Regions (☎ 7928 0988, County Hall, Westminster Bridge Rd SE1; ✪ Waterloo or Westminster). The inspiration for the dishes at this restaurant purports to come from the four main culinary regions of China: Canton, Szechwan, Peking and Shanghai. But such a mishmash is always suspect – can't they do just one well? It gets so-so reviews; many people come for the views and the promise that this restaurant doesn't use any monosodium glutamate (MSG) in its dishes. Main courses are £6 or £7, set meals cost from £18 to £28 per person (minimum two people).

Other Cuisines
Cubana (☎ 7928 8778, 48 Lower Marsh SE1; ✪ Waterloo). This popular (though hardly authentic) theme restaurant has tapas for £2.95 to £4.25, main courses (with three vegetarian choices) from £6.45 to £8.95 and dozens of rum cocktails from £4.25.

Mesón Don Felipe (☎ 7928 3237, 53 The Cut SE1; ✪ Waterloo). This tapas place gets recommended more often than most for its wide choice, affordability (£3 to £4 per dish) and attractive surroundings.

CHARLOTTE HINDLE

Cubana: brightening up Waterloo with a taste of Latin America.

Cafés
Konditor & Cook (☎ 7620 2700, 66 The Cut SE1; ✪ Waterloo). This place at the Young Vic Theatre serves meals Monday to Friday from 8.30 am to 11 pm and on Saturday from 10.30 am, but we come here for the pastries and cakes made by Konditor & Cook, arguably the best bakery in London.

BATTERSEA (Map 9)
This part of south London, with its lovely park and expensive mansion blocks, tends to have more upmarket restaurants than areas to the east and west. South of Clapham Junction, Battersea Rise is a street of restaurants, including the meatier-than-meaty Argentinian *La Pampa Grill (Map 2; ☎ 7924 4774)* at No 60 and, at the other end, *Le Bouchon Bordelais (☎ 7738 0307)* at No 9.

Modern British

Ransome's Dock (☎ 7223 1611, 35-37 Parkgate Rd SW11; ⊖ Sloane Square then bus No 19, 49, 239, 319 or 345). Diners flock here not because it's on a narrow inlet of the Thames but for the superbly prepared Modern British food: smoked Norfolk eel with little buckwheat pancakes and crème fraîche (£7.50), noisettes of English lamb (£16) and melt-in-your-mouth calf's liver with Italian bacon and field mushrooms (£13.50).

Buchan's (☎ 7228 0888, 62-64 Battersea Bridge Rd SW11; bus No 19, 49, 319 or 345). This wine bar and restaurant specialises in Scottish fare like haggis and the accompanying neeps and tatties, smoked salmon and so on. But with the range of Caledonian dishes being fairly limited, it ventures into the Modern British arena. Expect to pay about £25 per person.

WANDSWORTH & PUTNEY (Map 1)

Visitors wouldn't normally stray this far south for a meal, but there are a couple of reasons for doing so.

Italian

Del Buongustaio (☎ 8780 9361, 283 Putney Bridge Rd SW15; ⊖ East Putney). People constantly sing the praises of this Italian local with southern specialities and a menu that changes each month. Top marks for the welcoming, professional service too. Count on about £25 per person.

Indian

Bombay Bicycle Club (☎ 8673 6217, 95 Nightingale Lane SW12; Wandsworth Common station; ⊖ Clapham South). This place has the best Indian food south of the river. It also has a takeaway branch in Battersea at 28 Queenstown Rd SW8 (Map 10; ☎ 7720 0500; Queenstown Road station).

CHELSEA, SOUTH KENSINGTON & EARL'S COURT (Map 9)

These three areas boast an incredible array of eateries – from Michelin-starred restaurants and upmarket 24-hour burger joints to Polish cafés and French pâtisseries – to suit all budgets.

Modern British

Bibendum (☎ 7581 5817, 81 Fulham Rd SW3; ⊖ South Kensington). This Conran establishment is in one of London's finest settings for a restaurant, the Art Nouveau Michelin House (1911). The popular Bibendum Oyster Bar (£3.60 to £10.20 a half-dozen) is on the ground floor, where you really feel at the heart of the architectural finery. Upstairs it's all much lighter and brighter. A full meal with wine is likely to set you back around £55 a head.

Foxtrot Oscar (☎ 7352 7179, 79 Royal Hospital Rd SW3; ⊖ Sloane Square). This place – bar first, restaurant second – serves passable dishes, but the desserts are noteworthy. There's a branch at 16 Byward St EC3 (☎ 7481 2700; ⊖ Tower Hill).

International/Modern European

Chelsea Kitchen (☎ 7589 1330, 98 King's Rd SW3; ⊖ Sloane Square). This spartan place has some of the cheapest food in London, with a set meal costing under £5 (£3.80 at lunch).

Benjy's (☎ 7373 0245, 157 Earl's Court Rd SW5; ⊖ Earl's Court). Though Benjy's is nothing more than a fairly traditional café, it's always busy and the food is cheap and filling. Serious breakfasts, with as much tea or coffee as you can drink, are around £3.50, while lunch is £4.95.

Blanco's (☎ 7370 3101, 314 Earl's Court Rd SW5; ⊖ Earl's Court). Blanco's is a lively, authentic tapas bar (from £2.25 to £4.95) with good Spanish beer. It stays open until midnight.

Troubadour (☎ 7370 1434, 265 Old Brompton Rd SW10; ⊖ Earl's Court). Boasting an illustrious past as a coffee shop and folk music venue, the Troubadour has hosted Bob Dylan, Eric Clapton, John Lennon and the Stones, among others. These days it still occasionally has bands, plus good-value food, with soups at £3.50, bangers and mash £4, a full breakfast £4.25 and a set meal with a drink £4.50.

Oriel (☎ 7730 2804, 50-51 Sloane Square SW1; ⊖ Sloane Square). With its comfortable wicker chairs and mirrors, and tables overlooking Sloane Square, the Oriel makes the perfect place to meet before going shopping in King's Rd or Sloane St. Main dishes cost from £5 to £10, lighter fare like pasta and salads from £6 to £8.50.

The Collection (☎ 7225 1212, 264 Brompton Rd SW3; ⊖ South Kensington). The Collection has a wonderful location in a converted gallery, with the main restaurant on a balcony overlooking the bar – great for people-watching. Starters are from £3.50 to £7, main courses £11 to £14.50, and there are set meals for £10/13 for two/three courses.

Aubergine (☎ 7352 3449, 11 Park Walk SW10; ⊖ Sloane Square). One of the most popular restaurants in Chelsea, Aubergine was knocked sideways when its celebrity chef walked out to start his own restaurant in 1998, which he humbly named *Gordon Ramsay* (☎ 7352 4441, 68-69 Royal Hospital Rd SW3; ⊖ Sloane Square). By all accounts it has weathered the storm; some say it's even better. There is no à la carte ordering: the set three course dinner costs £39.50 while a seven course *dégustation* one is £50. Set lunches with two/three courses are a more affordable £15/18.

American

Henry J Bean's (☎ 7352 9255, 195 King's Rd SW3; ⊖ Sloane Square or South Kensington). This popular American bar and restaurant has a garden complete with fans and heaters. Main dishes cost from £5 to £7.

Cactus Blue (☎ 7823 7858, 86 Fulham Rd SW3; ⊖ South Kensington). This lovely Southwestern (let's just call it fancy Cal-Mex) restaurant has starters from £3.95 to £5.95, main courses from £8.25 to £13.95. The list of tequilas and wine from Mexico is impressive.

French

A large number of French people live in South Kensington, and you'll find a lot of French-operated businesses there, particularly along Bute St, just south-west of South Kensington tube station, including a delicatessen called *La Grande Bouchée* (☎ 7589 8346) at No 31; the *Pâtissier-Chocolatier*, with fine cakes and sweets, at No 24a; and the *Rôtisserie Jules* (☎ 7584 0600) at Nos 6 to 8, a simple French-style cafeteria with flame-roasted chicken (from £4.95 to £9.75) and *gigot d'agneau*.

Around the corner, *FrancoFill* (☎ 7584 0087, 1 Old Brompton Rd SW7) is a delightful café-restaurant serving meals for around £10 while *Marius Le Gourmet* at No 40 on the same street has excellent pastries. Another excellent choice for lunch is the French Institute's *Brasserie de l'Institut* (☎ 7838 2144, 17 Queensberry Place SW7),

with starters from £3.50 to £5.50, salads for £4.95 to £5.95 and main courses for £4.50 to £7. A three course lunch with oysters or *foie gras* is £10.95.

Italian & Mediterranean

Spago (☎ 7225 2407, 6 Glendower Place SW7; ⊖ South Kensington). This excellent-value restaurant with a good range of pastas and pizzas from £4.50 is convenient for the South Kensington museums. It is open daily for dinner only, and there is live music on Saturday. Its branch, *Spago 2* (Map 5; 45 Kensington High St W8; ⊖ High Street Kensington), is open all day.

Pizza Express (☎ 7351 5031, 152-154 King's Rd SW3; ⊖ Sloane Square). This branch of the chain is worth a visit just to have a look at its location: it's in the Pheasantry building, with an ornate façade and portico dating from the mid-18th century.

Daphne's (☎ 7589 4257, 112 Draycott Ave SW3; ⊖ South Kensington). This place, popular with celebrities and their followers, is small enough to be intimate but large enough not to be claustrophobic. It serves delicious Mediterranean-style food, with main courses from £12.50 to £18.50, pastas from £9.

Asian

New Culture Revolution (☎ 7352 9281, 305 King's Rd SW3; ⊖ Sloane Square). This trendy, good-value dumpling and noodle bar has main dishes at around £6. There are other branches at 43 Parkway NW1 (Map 3; ☎ 7267 2700; ⊖ Camden Town) and 42 Duncan St N1 (Map 4; ☎ 7833 9083; ⊖ Angel).

Krungtap (☎ 7259 2314, 227 Old Brompton Rd SW10; ⊖ Earl's Court). Krungtap (the Thai name for Bangkok) is a busy, friendly café open for dinner only. Most dishes are in the £3.50 to £5 range.

Mr Wing (☎ 7370 4450, 242-244 Old Brompton Rd SW5; ⊖ Earl's Court). This is one of London's more interesting Chinese restaurants, with a jungle-style basement and live jazz Thursday to Saturday at 8.15 pm. The food is pricey for Chinese (starters around £4.95, main courses from £10.95 to £12.95).

Other Cuisines

Daquise (☎ 7589 6117, 20 Thurloe St SW7; ⊖ South Kensington). This place is a real dinosaur – but a loveable little tyrannosaurus indeed – and close to the museums. It's a rather

Eating on a Budget

London restaurant prices may look terrifying – and they are – but there are still ways to eat without breaking the bank.

The best way to keep prices down, of course, is to cater for yourself. If you're staying in a hostel you will probably have access to cooking facilities, but – weather providing – London's parks also provide excellent picnic sites. Beware of some of the smaller grocer's shops where prices are marked up considerably; look instead for a branch of Tesco Metro, part of Britain's most successful supermarket chain, which has branches in Covent Garden at 22-25 Bedford St WC2; opposite Liverpool Street station at 158-164 Bishopsgate EC2; in the City at 80B Cheapside EC2; at 311 Oxford St W1; in Notting Hill at 224-226 Portobello Rd W11; and in Canary Wharf at 15 Cabot Place E14. Branches of Safeway, Asda and Sainsbury's are equally competitively priced. Waitrose is more upmarket and expensive.

If breakfast is not included in your hotel or hostel and you're within striking distance of Oxford St (Maps 6 & 7), the department stores there (see the Shopping chapter for details) do big, sustaining breakfasts for very reasonable prices. BHS at Nos 252 to 258 serves a breakfast of six items (£1.99) and one with 10 items (£3.99) up to 11.30 am. Nearby Debenhams at Nos 334 to 348 does a six item breakfast (£1.65) Monday to Saturday until 11 am.

In the restaurant and café listings in this chapter the first few choices under International, English and/or Vegetarian are almost always budget options with individual prices (or at least a range) listed. Also check the listings for the various international cuisines; Indian (around Brick Lane and in Drummond St near Euston) and Chinese (especially in Soho) are always safe bets. Japanese-style noodle bars, where you can eat for £5, are becoming a way of life in London. Be on the lookout too for a new breed of budget eatery: upmarket soup kitchens like Soup near Oxford Circus.

---

shabby-looking Polish café-diner, with a good range of vodkas and extremely reasonably priced food. Starters like borscht cost from £2.50 to £4, main courses (a 'hunter's stew' called *bigos*, for example) are from £5.50 to £9.50 and a set lunch £6.80.

Nando's (☎ 7259 2544, 204 Earl's Court Rd SW5; ⊖ Earl's Court). This almost-fast-food chain serves Portuguese-style flame-grilled chicken dishes. A quarter/half-chicken with coleslaw and rice or chips is £4.35/6.35; there's a vegetarian burger/pita for £2.65/3.20. Among the many branches is one at 57 Chalk Farm Rd NW1 (Map 3; ☎ 7424 9040; ⊖ Camden Town).

KENSINGTON & KNIGHTSBRIDGE (Maps 5 & 9)

The restaurants, cafés and bars in these posh 'villages' of west and south-west London cater for a very well-heeled clientele, but there's always something good (and affordable) off the high streets.

International/Modern European

Arcadia (Map 5; ☎ 7937 4294, 35 Kensington Court W8; ⊖ High Street Kensington). Arcadia is one of the more interesting of a cluster of restaurants and cafés in Kensington Court. Its interior, with a pair of macaws preening and showing off amid the mirrors and the murals, is classy and distinctive, and the menu features dishes like rack of lamb with sautéed spinach, best sampled via the set two/three-course lunches at £12.95/15.95.

Fifth Floor (Map 5; ☎ 7235 5250, Harvey Nichols, 109-125 Knightsbridge SW1; ⊖ Knightsbridge). This restaurant, bar and café is the perfect place to drop after you've shopped. It's expensive, averaging £30 per head at dinner, but there's a three course set lunch for £23.50 served weekdays between noon and 3 pm (at weekends to 3.30 pm).

Launceston Place (Map 9; ☎ 7937 6912, 1a Launceston Place W8; ⊖ High Street Kensington). Sister restaurant to Kensington Place in Notting Hill (see the following section) but as different from it as night from day, Launceston

Place is tucked away in the quiet backstreets of Kensington. It's a pretty, subdued, intimate restaurant, perfect for *dîner à deux*. The Modern European food is expensive (starters from £6, main courses from £15) but there are two/three-course lunches for £14.50/17.50.

American

Sticky Fingers (Map 5; ☎ 7938 5338, 1A Phillimore Gardens W8; ✚ High Street Kensington). Sticky Fingers is where ex-Rolling Stone Bill Wyman has chosen to hang up his gold discs and other memorabilia, but it's still a rather good burger bar, with prices kicking off at £7.50 (salads are from £6.95 to £9.95).

Italian

Pizza on the Park (Map 6; ☎ 7235 5273, 11 Knightsbridge SW5; ✚ Hyde Park Corner). This place is as popular for its nightly jazz in the basement as for its pizza. There's also a spacious restaurant upstairs and, if you're lucky, a few tables overlooking Hyde Park. Pizzas average £6.50. Breakfast is available all day from 8.15 am (£4 for continental, £4.95 for English) and afternoon tea (£6.95) at 3.15 pm.

Bellini's (Map 5; ☎ 7937 5520, 47 Kensington Court W8; ✚ High Street Kensington). This stylish restaurant with a few pavement tables and views of a flower-bedecked alley serves two/three-course lunches for £6.75/7.90.

Montpeliano (Map 5; ☎ 7589 0032, 13 Montpelier St SW7; ✚ Knightsbridge). This expensive Italian place comes highly recommended by local residents.

Asian

Vong (Map 5; ☎ 7235 6000, Berkeley Hotel, Wilton Place SW1; ✚ Knightsbridge). This super-trendy Thai restaurant is a place to be seen in, though most people will find the food, with its French accents, as enjoyable and memorable as the décor is spartan. Expect to pay £30 a head though there's an early and late night dinner menu for £17.50.

Other Cuisines

Wódka (Map 5; ☎ 7937 6513, 12 St Alban's Grove W8; ✚ High Street Kensington). This Polish place lies in a quiet residential area away from the hustle and bustle of Kensington High Street. *Blinis* (filled pancakes) range from £4.90 to £8.90 (average £6.50) and a large array of clear and flavoured vodkas (£2.25 to £2.75 a shot) is available.

Ognisko Polskie (Map 9; ☎ 7589 4635, 55 Prince's Gate SW7; ✚ South Kensington). This is the Polish of another world and time, with reasonably priced food (about £20 per person) served in a baroque dining room filled with portraits, chandeliers and mirrors.

NOTTING HILL & BAYSWATER (Map 5)

Notting Hill, so popular ever since *that* film, has all sorts of interesting places to eat, and there are literally dozens of places lining Queensway and Westbourne Grove, with everything from cheap takeaways to good quality restaurants.

English/Modern British

Sausage & Mash Café (☎ 8968 8898, 268 Portobello Rd W10; ✚ Ladbroke Grove). Under the elevated Westway, this is just the ticket if you're looking for cheap English stodge (£5) in upbeat surroundings.

Geales (☎ 7727 7969, 2 Farmer St W8; ✚ Notting Hill Gate). This popular fish restaurant prices everything according to weight and season. Fish and chips costs about £8.50 and it's worth every penny.

Veronica's (☎ 7229 5079, 3 Hereford Rd W2; ✚ Bayswater). This place is doing its best to establish that England does have a culinary heritage, with some fascinating dishes dating back to as early as the 14th century. Starters range from £4 to £7.50, main courses from £10.50 to £18.50, and there are two/three-course set menus for £12.50/16.50 available at lunch weekdays and at dinner Monday to Thursday.

International/Modern European

Kensington Place (☎ 7727 3184, 201-207 Kensington Church St W8; ✚ Notting Hill Gate). This restaurant has an impressive glass frontage and a design-conscious interior, but seating seems cramped and the acoustics are bad. Starters cost from £5 and main courses from £12.50; a meal is likely to cost around £25 a head unless you settle for the set three course lunch for £14.50.

Bali Sugar (☎ 7221 4477, 33a All Saints Rd W11; ✚ Westbourne Park). Bali Sugar has moved into where its parent restaurant, the Sugar Club (see the earlier West End section), used to be. The food is described as 'fusion' (average £27 per person) and leans slightly on the Asian side.

An alfresco lunch-break on Portobello Rd.

Anonimato (☎ *7243 2808, 12 All Saints Rd W11;* ✆ *Westbourne Park).* This neighbouring restaurant, in an area that was once one of the dodgier parts of Notting Hill, serves similar 'global' food (about £22), but with many dishes verging on the Mediterranean/Spanish. It is open for dinner only from Monday to Saturday.

Pharmacy (☎ *7221 2442, 150 Notting Hill Gate W11;* ✆ *Notting Hill Gate).* This is the over-publicised restaurant and bar with a chemist theme designed by *enfant terrible* artist Damien Hirst. At first glance it appears to be little more than a showroom for trendies and fashion victims, but the food (mostly fish) is very good (though at £35 per person very expensive). Set lunches cost £13.50/15.50 for two/three courses.

French

Novelli W8 (☎ *7229 4024, 122 Palace Gardens Terrace W8;* ✆ *Notting Hill Gate).* Novelli serves superb quality French food, with main courses from £11 to £14 in a romantic hideaway restaurant once known as the Ark. Midweek set lunch menus cost £12.50/15 for two/three courses. Chef/owner Novelli has an equally popular restaurant and brasserie in Clerkenwell (see the earlier Holborn & Clerkenwell section).

Italian

Osteria Basilico (☎ *7727 9372, 29 Kensington Park Rd W11;* ✆ *Notting Hill Gate or Ladbroke Grove).* This neighbourhood restaurant offers a good mix of Italian rustic charm and West London chic, with an authentic menu and a lively, relaxed atmosphere. The tables by the window are best, but you will need to book. Pasta (from £5.80 to £6.80) and fish dishes (£7.90 to £10.50) are recommended.

Assagi (☎ *7792 5501, 39 Chepstow Place W2;* ✆ *Notting Hill Gate).* Assagi, a posh neighbourhood Italian place above the Chepstow pub, serves elaborate starters (from £6.95 to £8.95) but pared down main courses like liver, veal chops and roast lamb (£12.95 to £18.50).

L'Accento (☎ *7243 2201, 7243 2664, 16 Garway Rd W2;* ✆ *Bayswater).* This highly stylish restaurant offers a two course set menu for £11.50, which could include mussel stew in white wine with fresh herbs, followed by roast leg of lamb with balsamic vinegar. Once you step away from this menu, though, L'Accento becomes a lot more expensive (starters from £4.50 to £7, main courses £11 to £13).

Greek & Middle Eastern

Costas Fish Restaurant (☎ *7229 3794, 12-14 Hillgate St W8;* ✆ *Notting Hill Gate).* This reliable Greek fish restaurant has meze with dips from £1.50, *souvlakia* for under £5 and a huge array of fresher-than-fresh fish at market prices (eg haddock £5.50), which some maintain is better than at its closest competitor, Geales.

Kalamaras Micro (☎ *7727 5082, 66 Inverness Mews W2;* ✆ *Bayswater).* The surroundings aren't mega, but the food is macro in this Greek spot in a quiet mews off Queensway. Main courses average about £7.50 and you can BYO.

Manzara (☎ 7727 3062, 24 Pembridge Rd W11; ✆ Notting Hill Gate). This simple place offers cheap but fresh and well prepared Turkish food for less than £10.

Indian

Modhubon Tandoori (☎ 7727 3399, 29 Pembridge Rd W11; ✆ Notting Hill Gate). This place has been recommended for its inexpensive Indian food. Main dishes are under £5, set lunch is £3.95 and an eat-as-much-as-you-like Sunday buffet is £7.50.

Khan's (☎ 7727 5420, 13-15 Westbourne Grove W2; ✆ Bayswater). Khan's is a vast and popular Indian restaurant where diners eat amid palms and pillars and get out quickly. It's fairly authentic, the décor is smart and it's good value but it's really just for a quick curry. There are vegetarian dishes from £2.60 and a selection of meat curries from £3.20.

The Standard (☎ 7229 0600, 21-23 Westbourne Grove W2; ✆ Bayswater). A neighbour of Khan's, the Standard serves excellent and very good-value Indian food. Count on about £10 per person.

Asian

Inaho (☎ 7221 8495, 4 Hereford Rd W2; ✆ Bayswater). This tiny Japanese restaurant has a *tempura* set dinner comprising an appetiser, soup, mixed salad, *yakitori*, sashimi, tempura, rice and seasonal fruits for £20 and a *teriyaki* equivalent for £22. A *tonkatsu* is £7, and rice and noodle dishes cost from £4 to £6.

Tawana (☎ 7229 3785, 3 Westbourne Grove W2; ✆ Bayswater or Royal Oak). Tawana is a decent Thai place with small/large dishes around £4.95/6.95.

Other Cuisines

Nachos (☎ 7221 5250, 147-149 Notting Hill Gate W11; ✆ Notting Hill Gate). This popular Mexican joint serves better than average food at decent prices. A couple of enchiladas will cost you £8.75, *fajitas* (strips of grilled meats in salsa) £10.45.

Mandola (☎ 7229 4734, 139-141 Westbourne Grove W2; ✆ Bayswater). Mandola offers something entirely different: vegetarian Sudanese dishes like *tamia* (£4.50), a kind of falafel, or *fifilia* (£6.95), a vegetable curry. Meat dishes like chicken *halla* are around £7. Try the unusual *shorba fude* (£3.15), a meat and peanut soup.

Belgo Zuid (☎ 8982 8400, 124 Ladbroke Grove W11; ✆ Ladbroke Grove). The spectacular interior of this branch of Belgo Centraal (see the earlier Covent Garden & the Strand section) opposite the tube station is worth a visit in itself.

Cafés

Café Grove (☎ 7243 1094, 253A Portobello Rd; ✆ Ladbroke Grove). Head here for gigantic and imaginative breakfasts (chilli sausages, pints of cappuccino) as well as cheap and cheerful vegetarian food at around £5. The large balcony overlooking the market is great for watching all the action on a weekend morning.

Churrería Española (☎ 7727 3444, 179 Queensway W2; ✆ Bayswater). This unexpected café serves that old Spanish breakfast favourite: hot chocolate and *churros* (deep-fried sweet fritters) for £1.75. Cooked English breakfast is £3.50.

MAIDA VALE (Map 5)

Little Venice, a rather ambitiously named area of Maida Vale, near St John's Wood, is nonetheless charming and holds a couple of secret 'finds' for food lovers.

Modern European

Jason's (☎ 7286 6752, Jason's Wharf W9; ✆ Warwick Avenue). While boating along the Grand Union Canal you might want to stop for lunch at Jason's, opposite 60 Blomfield Rd, which serves superb fresh-fish dishes (from £14.50 to £16.75) with a Mauritian, Indian and Chinese slant. A two/three course set lunch midweek costs £16.50/21.50 and there's outside seating.

Italian

Green Olive (☎ 7289 2469, 5 Warwick Place W9; ✆ Warwick Avenue). This neighbourhood Italian place has crackingly creative food and comes highly recommended by the Maida Vale cognoscenti. Set meals are £20.50/23.50/26 for two/three/four courses. Avoid the basement.

EUSTON (Map 3)

While 'Euston' and 'good food' do not usually a valid phrase make, a street a short distance south-west of the station is a mecca for veggies looking for a little bite in their legumes.

Café Grove: perfect for a groovy breakfast before diving into Portobello Rd Market.

Vegetarian

Drummond St (✆ Euston Square or Euston) has a number of good South Indian vegetarian restaurants. *Diwana* (✆ 7387 5556) at No 121, the first (and some say still the best) of its kind on the street, specialises in Bombay-style *bel poori* (a kind of 'party mix' snack) and *dosas* and has an all-you-can-eat lunchtime buffet for £3.95. Nearby at No 124, *Chutneys* (✆ 7388 0604) has a better lunch buffet (available all day on Sunday) for £4.95. The latter's cousin, *Ravi Shankar* (✆ 7388 6458) at Nos 133 to 135, is perhaps the most relaxed for an evening meal with starters from £1.95 and main courses from £3.50.

CAMDEN & KENTISH TOWN (Map 3)

Camden High Street is lined with good places to eat, although to watch the Sunday day-trippers snacking on takeaway sausages and chips you'd hardly believe it.

English

Castle's (✆ 7485 2196, 229 Royal College St NW1; ✆ Camden Town). Castle's is another member of that almost extinct species: a real live pie and mash caff with Formica tables and plastic chairs. A pie with liquor and mash is £1.60, jellied eel is £1.65.

International

Ruby in the Dust (✆ 7485 2744, 102 Camden High St NW1; ✆ Camden Town). This atmospheric, cheerful branch of a bar/café chain has Mexican snacks, soup for £3 and main courses like bangers and mash or fish and chips for £6.65.

Sauce barorganicdiner (✆ 7482 0777, 214 Camden High St NW1; ✆ Camden Town). This oddly named basement café/restaurant serves dishes prepared only with ingredients certified by the UK and the EU as organic. Try the crab cakes with sweet chilli sauce or even the hamburgers. Starters cost from £3.50 to £5.50, main courses £6.50 to £10.50 and they do a great all-day breakfast for £6.50.

French

Café Delancey (✆ 7387 1985, 3 Delancey St NW1; ✆ Camden Town). The granddaddy of French-style brasseries in London, Café Delancey offers the chance to get a decent cup of coffee with a snack or a full meal in relaxed European-style surroundings complete with newspapers. Main dishes are from £8 to £13, wine starts at £6.90 for a half-bottle. The cramped toilets, bickering staff and Charles Aznavour crooning in the background seem suitably Parisian too.

Italian

Marine Ices (✆ 7485 3132, 8 Haverstock Hill NW3; ✆ Chalk Farm). As its name suggests, Marine Ices started out as a Sicilian ice-cream parlour but these days it does some savoury dishes, including pizzas from £5.20 and pastas from £5.95. Try some of the excellent ice cream – sundaes start at £2.40.

Pizza Express (✆ 7267 0101, 187 Kentish Town Rd NW5; ✆ Kentish Town). This is a Pizza Express branch with a difference: a converted university building with a balcony bar overlooking a large dining room and open kitchen. Pizzas cost around £6, and the house wine is £9.50/2.50 a bottle/glass. There's sometimes live jazz at weekends.

Spanish

El Parador (✆ 7387 2789, 245 Eversholt St NW1; ✆ Mornington Crescent). El Parador is a quiet Spanish place where the selection of some 15 vegetarian dishes and tapas includes *empanadillas de espinacas y queso* (a spinach and cheese dish) for £3.80, with meat and fish dishes just a little more expensive (£4.60).

JULIET COOMBE

PLACES TO EAT

Bar Gansa (☎ 7267 8909, 2 Inverness St NW1; ✆ Camden Town). This arty bar/café has tapas for around £3 and more elaborate Spanish main courses from £6.50 to £7.95. Service is good and the Spanish staff are very friendly. Breakfast costs £3.95. It serves drinks to 12.30 am (1 am on Friday and Saturday).

Asian

Lemon Grass (☎ 7284 1116, 243 Royal College St; ✆ Camden Town). Lemon Grass is one of the better Thai eateries in Camden with authentic food and charming décor and staff. Main dishes are around £6.

Taste of Siam (☎ 7380 0665, 45 Camden High St NW1; ✆ Mornington Crescent). Not as good or authentic as Lemon Grass, this place is cheaper (count on about £13 a head) and more centrally located.

Silks & Spice (☎ 7267 5751, 28 Chalk Farm Rd NW1; ✆ Camden Town). This Thai/Malay restaurant does express 'lunches' (from £4.95 to £5.95) from noon to 7 pm.

Thanh Binh (☎ 7267 9820, 14 Chalk Farm Rd NW1; ✆ Camden Town). A quiet little eatery opposite Camden Market, Thanh Binh serves decent Vietnamese dishes for between £4.50 and £6.50 and there's a set lunch for £5.

Asakusa (☎ 7388 8533, 265 Eversholt St NW1; ✆ Mornington Crescent). For affordable Japanese – not necessarily an oxymoron – in Camden Town, head for Asakusa where set menus like prawn tempura with *miso* soup and rice are under £7. It's open for dinner only from 6 to 11 pm.

China Blues (☎ 7482 4104, 29 Parkway NW1; ✆ Camden Town). Fancy noodles and a bit of romance? China Blues is a pan-Asian restaurant (*satays*, sweet and sour chicken etc) with a jazz singer and an accompanying pianist. We almost swooned into our *gwei tiao* noodles. Starters are around £5, main courses average £8.50.

Other Cuisines

Trojka Russian Tea Room (☎ 7483 3765, 101 Regent's Park Rd NW1; ✆ Chalk Farm). Also known as the Primrose Brasserie, Trojka serves good-value Eastern European/Russian dishes like herrings with dill sauce (£3.50) and salt beef (£6.50) in an attractive, sky-lit restaurant. It has a house wine but it's also BYO (£3 corkage).

Lemonia (☎ 7586 7454, 89 Regent's Park Rd NW1; ✆ Chalk Farm). This upmarket and very popular Greek restaurant offers good-value food and a lively atmosphere. Meze costs £12.25 per person and both the vegetarian and meat *moussakas* for £7.50 are particularly tasty. There's a set weekday lunch for £7.50.

Belgo Noord (☎ 7267 0718, 72 Chalk Farm Rd NW1; ✆ Chalk Farm). This branch of Belgo Centraal near Covent Garden has almost exactly the same design and food. See the earlier Covent Garden & the Strand section.

African & Caribbean

Selam (Map 11; ☎ 7284 3947, 12 Fortess Rd NW5; ✆ Kentish Town). This – would you believe? – Eritrean restaurant serves its food Ethiopian-style. Dishes of lamb cooked with red chillies, chicken legs and hard-boiled eggs and a 'ratatouille' of root vegetables (£5 to £7.50) are placed on a platter-sized piece of spongy *injera* bread; you use rolled-up pieces of it to eat with your fingers. Solves the washing-up problem ...

Wazobia (☎ 7284 1059, 257 Royal College St NW1; ✆ Camden Town). This charmingly laid-back West African place serves Nigerian-style pepper soups (£3) and hearty stews (£7). Service is good and the welcome warm.

Cottons Rhum Shop, Bar & Restaurant (☎ 7482 1096, 55 Chalk Farm Rd NW1; ✆ Chalk Farm). Come to Cottons for authentic Caribbean favourites like jerk chicken and curried goat (£7.95 to £9.95), but beware of those potent rum-based cocktails (from £4); they'll knock your socks – and most everything else – off.

Mango Room (☎ 7482 5065, 10 Kentish Town Rd NW1; ✆ Camden Town). Mango Room is a more upmarket and refined choice than Cottons for island food, with delightful starters like fluffy crab and potato balls (£3.50) and unusual main courses like a platter of cooked vegetables (£7.40) including *ackee*, a yellow-skinned Jamaican fruit that has an uncanny resemblance to scrambled eggs.

Cafés

The Curly Dog Café (☎ 7483 0433, 75A Gloucester Ave NW1; ✆ Camden Town). This cosy little place near the Engineer pub is great for lunch, tea or a quick snack.

ISLINGTON (Map 4)

Islington is an excellent place for a night out. At the last count there were more than 60 cafés and restaurants between Angel and Highbury Corner, with most of the action on Upper St.

English

Upper St Fish Shop (☎ 7359 1401, 324 Upper St N1; ❸ Highbury & Islington). This legendary fishmonger's doles out classy fish and chips for £7 to £7.50 and seafood like half a dozen Irish oysters for around £6.

Modern European

Lola's (☎ 7359 1932, The Mall, 359 Upper St N1; ❸ Angel). This award-winning restaurant is celebrated for its lovely décor, changing menu and popular Sunday brunch with live jazz. Starters range from £4.75 to £7, main courses from £10.50 to £14.

Granita (☎ 7226 3222, 127 Upper St N1; ❸ Angel or Highbury & Islington). Minimalist to the point of sterility, Granita remains the territory of movers and shakers; it was here that Tony Blair and his chancellor-to-be, Gordon Brown, plotted the future of the Labour Party before their landslide victory in 1997. The food is Mediterranean but not strictly so and should cost about £20 per person (excellent-value two/three-course lunches are £11.95/13.95).

French

Le Sacré Coeur Bistro (☎ 7354 2618, 18 Theberton St N1; ❸ Angel). This cramped little restaurant has reliable French food like moules-frites for £6.95 and a weekday £5.50/6.95 fixed-price menu with two/three courses (£6.95/8.50 at weekends).

Italian

Casale Franco (☎ 7226 8994, 134-137 Upper St N1; ❸ Angel). This great little find serves some of the best pizza in north London (from £7.50).

Other Cuisines

Inter Mezzo (☎ 7607 4112, 207 Liverpool Rd N1; ❸ Angel). This Turkish meze bar and restaurant gets our vote as one of the best value and friendliest eateries in town. Set lunches are £5.90/6.90 for two/three courses, dinners £8.90/10.90. TJ's Special Seafood Pot (£8.50), chock-a-block with things from the sea in a spicy broth, is to die for and enough for two.

Cuba Libre (☎ 7354 9998, 72 Upper St N1; ❸ Angel). This place has tapas and more filling dishes like moros y christianos (beans and rice); expect to pay around £18. There's a popular bar with extended hours at the back (see

Islington under Pubs & Bars in the Entertainment chapter).

Anna's Place (☎ 7249 9379, 90 Mildmay Park N1; Canonbury station; ❸ Highbury & Islington). This lovely Swedish restaurant just off Newington Green was once one of our locals and we were never disappointed with the constantly changing menu of gravlax, herring, smoked fish and even reindeer in season. The service is excellent, the welcome always warm. Count on about £20 a head.

Vegetarian

Ravi Shankar (☎ 7833 5849, 422 St John St EC1; ❸ Angel). This small, inexpensive restaurant has some of the best Indian vegetarian food in London. There's another branch near Euston station (see the earlier Euston section).

STOKE NEWINGTON & FINSBURY PARK (Map 1)

A thoroughly cosmopolitan area of north London, Finsbury Park has a good mix of restaurants at very reasonable prices. Church St in Stoke Newington is lined with ethnic restaurants.

Italian

La Porchetta (☎ 7281 2892, 147 Stroud Green Rd N4; ❸ Finsbury Park). La Porchetta serves such tasty home-made pizzas and pastas that there's invariably a queue at the door in the evenings. The fiorentina and Gorgonzola pizzas (both £4.70) are particularly delicious and the calzone (£5) will keep you going all day.

Middle Eastern

Mangal (☎ 7275 8981, 10 Arcola St E8; Dalston Kingsland station; bus No 67, 76, 149 or 243). This hole-in-the-wall Turkish eatery is London's worse-kept little secret 'find'. It serves the freshest kebabs and other grilled food cooked over a smoking ocakbasi (wood-fired brazier) and served with excellent salads. It's BYO only (though there's an off-licence around the corner) and you'll get away with about £8 per person.

Mangal II (☎ 7254 7888, 4 Stoke Newington Rd N16; Dalston Kingsland station). Mangal's more upmarket (and expensive) sister restaurant a short distance away has plates of mixed meze for £4, kebabs and other main dishes for £7 to £8.50.

Other Cuisines

Lucky Village (☎ 7254 0928, 137 Stoke Newington High St N16; Stoke Newington station; bus No 73). Some people come here just to say they've tried Georgian cuisine, but we like the Russian-influenced starters like blinis (under £4)and the main dishes flavoured with walnuts (around £7.50).

Vegetarian

Rasa (☎ 7249 0344, 55 Stoke Newington Church St N16; Stoke Newington station; bus No 73). This no-smoking South Indian vegetarian restaurant gets rave reviews (and attracts queues) for dishes not often seen (or tasted) outside private homes. Count on spending about £15 a head.

Jai Krishna (☎ 7272 1680, 161 Stroud Green Rd N4; ⊖ Finsbury Park). Jai Krishna is a much simpler Indian vegetarian café than Rasa and you won't be writing home about the décor, but the prices – *masala dosa* for £3.50, a mixed thali for £5.75 – are noteworthy.

HAMPSTEAD (Map 11)

Hampstead, the well-to-do 'village' south-west of Hampstead Heath, has loads of good restaurants within easy walking distance of Hampstead tube station.

Italian

La Gaffe (☎ 7794 7526, 107 Heath St NW3). This comfortable, family-run restaurant in an 18th-century cottage has been going forever.

Pizza Express (☎ 7433 1600, 70 Heath St NW3). If you want your pizza more industrial, head south from La Gaffe to this fancy branch of the popular chain.

Other Cuisines

Al Casbah (☎ 7435 7632, 45 Hampstead High St NW3). Al Casbah is a small, friendly Moroccan restaurant with couscous and tajines for £8.50 to £12.50.

Viva Zapata (☎ 7431 9134, 7 Pond St NW3). If you're really famished, head for Zapata for a grazing at their £5 Mexican buffet. Ordering à la carte should cost about £15 for two.

Jin Kichi (☎ 7794 6158, 73 Heath St NW3). A lot of Japanese live in Hampstead and this cramped little place is where they dine out; some say it's the best Japanese restaurant in London. Set courses cost from £7 to £11.50.

Cafés

Café Base (☎ 7431 3241, 70-71 Hampstead High St NW3). This bright and clean café has unusual *ciabatta* sandwiches and wraps for £2.60 to £4.95 and salads and pastas for £2.95 to £3.95.

The Coffee Cup (☎ 7435 7565, 74 Hampstead High St NW3). If you prefer greasy fried breakfasts (£5.90) and indifferent pasta dishes (£4.70) head next door to this rather unsalubrious café.

EAST END & THE DOCKLANDS (Maps 4 & 8)

From the Indian and Bangladeshi restaurants of Brick Lane to the trendy Modern British/European eateries of Hoxton and Shoreditch, the East End has finally made it onto the culinary map of London. The Docklands, however, remains in general the territory of expense accounts and quick lunches.

Modern British

Great Eastern Dining Room (Map 4; ☎ 7729 0022, 93 Great Eastern St EC2; ⊖ Old Street). This is a prime example of the new breed of eatery in London – particularly in trendy places like Clerkenwell and Hoxton. It's a large, open-plan, simple restaurant serving starters like fish soup with *rouille* (garlic-mayonnaise sauce; £3.95) and main courses like roast cod fillet (£9.95). It's open Monday to Friday from 7.30 am to 5.30 pm.

American

Babe Ruth's (Map 8; ☎ 7481 8181, 172-176 The Highway E1; ⊖/DLR Shadwell). Babe Ruth's is a remarkably popular sports restaurant/bar with an American theme and American food (huge but relatively expensive portions of pizzas, burgers etc). Kids will love the miniature basketball court and video games.

Italian

Il Bordello (Map 8; ☎ 7481 9950, 75 Wapping High St E1; ⊖ Wapping). You wouldn't go out of your way to eat at this neighbourhood Italian place, but if you're drinking at the Captain Kidd (see East End & the Docklands under Pubs & Bars in the Entertainment chapter), it's a convenient blotter stop for above-average pizzas (from £6.25 to £7.75), pasta (£5.75 to £7.50) and meat and fish main courses (£9.95 to £12.95).

Spanish

Mesón Los Barriles (Map 8; ☎ 7375 3136, 8a Lamb St E1; ⊖ Liverpool Street). This tapas bar and restaurant inside Spitalfields Market has an excellent selection of fish and seafood. Tapas range from £2 to £4.90, main courses average £6.50.

Indian

Brick Lane (Map 8; ⊖ Aldgate East or Shoreditch) is lined wall-to-wall with cheap Indian and Bangladeshi restaurants – not all of them very good – and frequented by City types who talk loudly on their mobile phones, drink too much Kingfisher and not infrequently lose their dinner on the pavement upon exit. *Aladin* (☎ 7247 8210) at No 132, a favourite of Prince Charles, and *Nazrul* (☎ 7247 2505) at No 130 may be worth a try; both are unlicensed but you can BYO and should eat for around £8. More upmarket (and expensive) are *Le Taj* (☎ 7247 4210) at No 134 and *Sheraz* (☎ 7247 5755) at No 13. Some people swear by nearby *Salique's* (☎ 7377 2137, 32 Hanbury St E2) with curries from £3.75 and tandoori and balti dishes from £4.50; we were less than impressed. You'll also find lots of bakeries and pastry shops along Brick Lane, like *Ambla* (☎ 7247 8569) at No 55, selling luridly coloured, sickly-sweet confectionery.

We suggest that you give Brick Lane and its drunken denizens the brush-off and head south to Whitechapel (⊖ Whitechapel) for Pakistani food. *New Tayyab* (☎ 7247 9543, 83 Fieldgate St E1) has some of the most authentic Indian and Pakistani food this side of the subcontinent. Choose your *seekh* kebabs, lamb chops or one of several *karahi* (a small wok) dishes, add a vegetable and one of several *dahls* and you'll eat for less than £10. This place is BYO only.

Two other decent (but not as good) Pakistani choices nearby are *New Lahore* (☎ 7791 0112, 218 Commercial Rd E1) and *Lahore Kebab House* (☎ 7481 9738, 2 Umberston St E1). They serve the same sort of dishes and, if you're really skint, rich brown dahl and tandoori *rotis* cost just £3.50.

JULIET COOMBE

**Sizing up the restaurant options
on Brick Lane.**

South-East Asian

Viet Hoa (Map 4; ☎ 7729 8293, 70-72 Kingsland Rd E2; bus No 67 or 149). This simple canteen-style eatery serves excellent and authentic Vietnamese dishes. A full meal should cost you less than £10 and it's always full.

Vegetarian

Whitechapel Art Gallery Café (Map 8; ☎ 7522 7878, 80-82 Whitechapel High St E1; ⊖ Aldgate East). This vegetarian place upstairs from the gallery serves dishes like spinach Florentine and salad for £4.65 and soups for £2.35. It's open Tuesday to Sunday from 11 am to 5 pm (on Wednesday to 8 pm).

Cafés

Brick Lane Beigel Bake (Map 4; ☎ 7729 0616, 159 Brick Lane E2; ⊖ Shoreditch). More of a delicatessen than a café, the Beigel Bake is at the Bethnal Green Rd end of Brick Lane and open 24 hours. You won't find fresher or cheaper bagels anywhere in London – just ask any taxi driver or the author who ate them for lunch for almost two years while writing up Lonely Planet guides in an office round the corner. Filled bagels are a snip at 45p to

PLACES TO EAT

NEIL SETCHFIELD

The best bagels in London (plus countless Indian and Bangladeshi restaurants).

65p (the salmon and cream cheese version is a whopping 95p) and a salt beef bagel is £1.60. Note that the Beigel Bake is not kosher-supervised.

Evering Bakery Bagel Shop *(Map 4; ☎ 7729 0826, 155 Brick Lane E2; ✆ Shoreditch).* We're going to get it in the neck for this, but just between you and us and the lamppost, this bakery just next door has better fillings than the Beigel Bake.

GREENWICH (Map 13)

Beautiful Greenwich has both old-style eateries and trendy new restaurants from which to choose. And don't forget the market from Friday to Sunday. The new Cutty Sark DLR station is convenient for all of the following recommendations unless noted otherwise.

English

Goddards Ye Olde Pie Shop *(45 Greenwich Church St SE10).* Goddards is truly a step back into the past: a real London caff with wooden benches and things like steak and kidney pie (£2.40) with liquor and mash, and shepherd's pie (£2.20) with beans and a rich brown gravy. Sweet pies are from 50p. It's open most days except Monday from 11 am to 3 or 4 pm.

International/Modern European

Beachcomber *(☎ 8853 0055, 34 Greenwich Church St SE10).* This old stalwart festooned

with flower baskets and potted plants does set two/three/four-course lunches for £5.90/7.95/9.90 and full breakfasts for £3.90. It's a very pleasant place on a sunny afternoon.

North Pole *(☎ 8853 3020, 131 Greenwich High Rd SE10; DLR Greenwich; Greenwich station).* This pleasant place has a bar/pub on the ground floor and an excellent, if somewhat stuffy, restaurant on the 1st floor. Starters cost from £3.80 to £6.20, main courses £9.50 to £14. There's a decent Sunday brunch from noon to 6.30 pm and a 25% discount on dinner on Monday.

Asian

Hatomana *(☎ 8293 5263, 10-11 Nelson Rd SE10).* Come to this simple place for cheap Japanese noodles and rice dishes (£2.80 to £4.50).

Vietnam *(☎ 8858 0871, 18 King William Walk SE10).* Vietnam has inexpensive lunch plates like spring rolls with noodles or rice (£3.95) available from noon to 5 pm.

Cafés

Greenwich Church St has a couple of decent and inexpensive cafés, including ***Il Batello*** *(☎ 8858 5124)* at No 39 and ***Peter de Wit's*** *(☎ 8305 0048)* at No 21 with cream teas for £3.80. In the covered market at No 8 the ***Meeting House Café*** *(☎ 8305 0403)* does ploughman's lunches and quiches (£2.75) as well as milk shakes (£1.50). There's a minimum £2 charge at weekends when it closes at 5 pm.

BRIXTON

If you're coming to Brixton for its market (✆ Brixton), don't restrict yourself to the eateries in the covered market itself. The surrounding streets (eg Atlantic Rd, Coldharbour Lane) have a number of excellent places.

English

The Phoenix *(☎ 7733 4430, 441 Coldharbour Lane SW9).* This is a classically reliable English caff just outside the covered market serving all the old favourites: bangers and mash, pies of all sorts and – of course – chips with everything.

Kim's Café *(☎ 7978 8515, 15 Market Row SW9).* A similar place inside the market, Kim's does fried breakfasts – chips extra – from £3.50.

Modern European

Helter Skelter (☎ 7274 8600, 50 Atlantic Rd SW9). With its bright designer décor (excluding the original ceramic tiles on the walls) and Modern European specialities on the menu, Helter Skelter is something of an oasis in the greater area of Brixton Market. Starters cost from £4.80 to £5.50, main courses £9.50 to £12.50. There is a fair number of vegetarian choices as well.

Italian

Eco Brixton (☎ 7738 3021, 4 Market Row SW9). This is the sister restaurant of Clapham's *Eco (☎ 7978 1108, 162 Clapham High St; ⊖ Clapham Common),* which has arguably the best pizzas (from £5.30), antipasto (£7.20) and cappuccino in south London. It's open daily (except Wednesday and Saturday) to 5 pm.

Other Cuisines

El Pilon Quindiano (☎ 7326 4316, Granville Arcade SW9). This Colombian café serves such authentic delicacies as *arepa* (small maize pancakes with various fillings), yucca and *empañadas* for around £3. A full lunch costs £6. This is the place to come if you want to try cheap South American dishes.

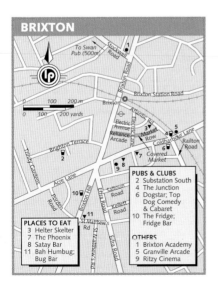

BRIXTON

PLACES TO EAT
3 Helter Skelter
7 The Phoenix
8 Satay Bar
11 Bah Humbug;
   Bug Bar

PUBS & CLUBS
2 Substation South
4 The Junction
6 Dogstar; Top
   Dog Comedy
   & Cabaret
10 The Fridge;
   Fridge Bar

OTHERS
1 Brixton Academy
5 Granville Arcade
9 Ritzy Cinema

Satay Bar (☎ 7326 5001, 447-450 Coldharbour Lane SW9). One of our favourite Asian eateries, the Satay Bar serves surprisingly authentic Indonesian food: *rendang ayam* (£5.95), laksa (£5.25) mixed satays (£5.95) and *mee goreng* (£4.25). *Rijsttafel* is £11.95 per person. Even more authentic are all the doors that open on to the busy street – you could easily be in a *warung* in Yogyakarta.

Vegetarian

Café Pushkar (☎ 7738 6161, 16B Market Row SW9). This small, cosy vegetarian place serves various soups (£2.45), quiche and salad (£4.20) and good cakes (from £1.50).

Bah Humbug (☎ 7738 3184, St Matthew's Peace Garden, Brixton Hill SW2). In the crypt of St Matthew's Methodist Church, Bah Humbug is one of the best vegetarian restaurants in London with quite a global range – from Thai vegetable fritters (£3) to Cantonese mock duck and masala curry (under £6.50).

HAMMERSMITH & FULHAM

Hammersmith is not an especially inviting borough, though we can think of worse ways of spending a sunny afternoon than sipping at one of the riverside pubs along the Upper Mall. Fulham is more agreeable, with Fulham Road in particular a good place for a meal and a night out.

English/Modern British

Chelsea Bun (Map 9; ☎ 7352 3635, 9A Lamont Rd SW10; ⊖ Fulham Broadway or Earl's Court). This London version of an American diner is a great-value place in the area known as World's End. Breakfast is served all day, and there's seating on an upstairs veranda. Main dishes cost between £4 and £7.

Ed's Easy Diner (Map 9; ☎ 7352 1956, 362 King's Rd SW3; ⊖ South Kensington). If you prefer your diner to be more New World-ish, check out Ed's. You could be in Cleveland.

International/Modern European

Kartouche (Map 9; ☎ 7823 3515, 329-331 Fulham Rd SW10; ⊖ South Kensington, then bus No 14 or 211). This eclectic restaurant, which serves bits and pieces borrowed from most of the world's cuisines (from Caesar salad and Thai fish cakes to Tuscan *pappardelle* pasta), remains something of a favourite among

PLACES TO EAT

Chelsea's young bloods, but it's noisy and the décor is kitsch in the extreme; we wonder what all the fuss is about. Starters are from £4.95 to £6.50, main courses average £11. There's an early two-course set dinner for £12.50 and a Sunday lunch for £10.50.

Shoeless Joe's (Map 9; ☎ 7610 9346, 555 King's Rd SW6; ✆ Fulham Broadway). Owned by members of the England rugby team, Joe's is yet another sports theme bar and grill (meat and fish main courses around £10), but with a more imaginative approach than is usual at this sort of place. There's a new, much more central branch in Temple Place WC2 (☎ 7240 7865; ✆ Temple).

Vingt-Quatre (Map 9; ☎ 7376 7224, 325 Fulham Rd SW10; ✆ South Kensington, then bus No 14 or 211). This extremely popular 24-hour place is where to go if you're looking for a late-night meal. It has a proper menu at lunch and dinner (starters from £3.25 to £4.75, main courses £6.75 to £9.95) but also serves more basic dishes like burgers (£6.95), steak and chips, and salads after midnight (at which time the bar closes). We only wonder why there aren't more places like Vingt-Quartre in London as there are in most other world capitals.

Bluebird (Map 9; ☎ 7559 1000, 350 King's Rd SW3; ✆ Fulham Broadway). Yet another Conran venture, Bluebird is a large complex with a vast restaurant and bar above an upmarket food hall, flower market and the *Café Bluebird* (☎ 7559 1222). The restaurant is fantastically expensive (about £40 per person), though there are set two/three-course meals available at lunch and before 7 pm for £12.75/15.75.

Ready to wok: improvised stir-fries at Tiger Lil's.

Italian

The River Café (☎ 7381 8824, Thames Wharf, Rainville Rd W6; ✆ Hammersmith). The very buzzy, see-and-be-seen River Café owes its fame as much to the cookbooks it has spawned as to the food actually served here, but it does have the best Modern Italian cuisine in London. Main dishes start at £16.50 and you're unlikely to have much change from £40 once you've added a starter or dessert and wine.

Greek

Wine & Kebab (Map 9; ☎ 7352 0967, 343 Fulham Rd SW10; ✆ South Kensington, then bus No 14 or 211). The Wine & Kebab sounds like a takeaway place but there's more to it than that. It's an attractive, very pleasant Greek restaurant with starters like *avgolemono* and *dolmades* for £2.95 to £3.95 (mixed meze is £7.50) and main courses for between £8.50 and £10.50.

Indian

The two upmarket Indian places in this neck of the woods are expensive (from £25 to £30 per person) but worthwhile. If you've got a rich uncle or aunt in town, consider them.

Chutney Mary's (Map 9; ☎ 7351 3113, 535 King's Rd SW10; ✆ Fulham Broadway; bus No 11 or 22). Mary's does regional Indian and Anglo-Indian food and hosts a great jazz brunch on Sunday.

Vama (Map 9; ☎ 7351 4118, 438 King's Rd SW10; ✆ Fulham Broadway; bus No 11 or 22). Vama serves unusual dishes from the North-West Frontier and other regions of India in a lovely dining room that feels like an upmarket Italian restaurant (as it was in a previous life).

Asian

Tiger Lil's (Map 9; ☎ 7376 5003, 500A King's Rd SW10; ✆ Fulham Broadway). One of three branches of an Asianesque restaurant chain – the others are at 16A Clapham Common Southside SW4 and 270 Upper St N1 (Map 4) – Lil's allows you to create your own meal by selecting from 16 ingredients and taking them to the energetic chefs who cook them for you in a gigantic wok (£5 per go, £11/5.50 for unlimited plates for adults/children aged under 10). The food is so-so but you won't go away hungry.

Jim Thompson's (Map 9; ☎ 7731 0999, 617 King's Rd SW6; ✆ Fulham Broadway). Named after the American who kick-started the mass production of silk in Thailand after WWII and then mysteriously vanished in Malaysia's Cameron Highlands, Jim Thompson's offers mixed South-East Asian fare – from Burma to Singapore – rather than straightforward Thai food. What with the dense greenery and swathes of Thai silk, you could easily imagine yourself in some Bangkok *soi*. Count on about £17 for a full meal.

The Blue Elephant (Map 9; ☎ 7385 6595, 4-6 Fulham Broadway SW6; ✆ Fulham Broadway). This Fulham institution serves upmarket (and very pricey) Thai food in jungle-like surroundings – you can't see the trees for the forest. The best time to come is between noon and 2.30 pm on Sunday when they do a fab Sunday set brunch for £16.75.

Bonjour Vietnam (Map 9; ☎ 7385 7603, 593-599 Fulham Rd SW6; ✆ Fulham Broadway). This place serves passable à la carte Vietnamese dishes that will add up to about £20 per person at dinner, but it's the weekday lunch-time all-you-can-eat buffet for £14 that pulls people in.

Vegetarian

The Gate (☎ 8748 6932, 51 Queen Caroline St W6; ✆ Hammersmith). This may be the place to convert your carnivorous counterparts to the kinder, gentler world of vegetarianism. The beautifully presented, unusual main courses go for around £8.50; the dining room with its high ceilings and wall of glass is equally fine.

CHISWICK

Chiswick High Rd and lovely Turnham Green Terrace are happy hunting grounds for eateries. There are restaurants and cafés to suit all purses and purposes and most known cuisines are on offer.

Modern British

The Chiswick (☎ 8994 6887, 131 Chiswick High Rd W4; ✆ Turnham Green). Despite its unimaginative name and rather spartan décor, the Chiswick offers outstanding Modern British cuisine, its menu making free with all sorts of combinations of wood pigeon, onion marmalade, lamb and couscous. Main courses average £10, but there's a two/three course lunch for £9.50/13 available until 8 pm.

International

Mackintosh's Brasserie (☎ 8994 2628, 142 Chiswick High Rd; ✆ Turnham Green). A popular place with tables on the pavement terrace in good weather, Mackintosh's offers a fairly conventional mix of burgers, salads and grills, but portions are large and puddings a treat, especially the Key lime pie (£3.50) and *amaretto* chocolate cheesecake (£3.95).

Asian

Thai Bistro (☎ 8995 5774, 99 Chiswick High Rd W4; ✆ Turnham Green). This was one of London's first Thai restaurants and owner Vatcharin Bumichitr has drawn up the main and vegetarian menus from his own cookbooks, including the seminal *The Taste of Thailand*. It remains worlds apart from all those 'above pub' Thai eateries elsewhere in London, both with its stylishly simple black and white décor and with its authentic dishes: *tom ka gai* (chicken in spicy coconut broth; £4.20), *pad thai* and *gwei tiao* noodles (£5.95).

Other Cuisines

Springbok Café (☎ 8742 3149, 42 Devonshire Rd W4; ✆ Turnham Green). Fancy a little big game? This colourful restaurant will do you zebra *carpaccio*, an impala loin fillet or chargrilled ostrich – among, of course, the more usual offerings. Starters are around £4.50, main courses from £8.75 to £12.25. It's got an excellent South African wine list.

KEW

A short distance north of Victoria Gate, the main entrance to Kew Gardens, is a historic café.

Cafés

Newens Maids of Honour (☎ 8940 2752, 288 Kew Rd; ✆ Kew Gardens). This old-fashioned tearoom that wouldn't seem out of place in a Cotswold village owes its fame to a special dessert supposedly concocted by Henry VIII's second wife, the ill-fated Anne Boleyn, from puff pastry, lemon, almonds and curd cheese. A 'maid of honour' will cost you £1.35, but don't plan on sampling it on Monday afternoon or Sunday when the tearoom is closed (otherwise it's open from 9.30 am to 6 pm). Set teas (£4.65) are served from 2.30 to 5.30 pm.

PLACES TO EAT

RICHMOND

There are several places to eat along Richmond's high street, which runs south-west from the train/tube station towards the river, but many of the more interesting places are clustered together around Hill Rise, just east of Richmond Bridge.

International

Crusts *(☎ 8940 1577, 2 Hill Rise; ✆ Richmond).* This long-standing café, with appealingly homely décor and tables outside on a platform overlooking a busy roundabout, serves burgers (£5.95) and steaks (from £9.95).

French

Chez Lindsay *(☎ 8948 7473, 11 Hill Rise; ✆ Richmond).* An inviting neighbourhood French restaurant, Chez Lindsay specialises in crepes (£5.80 to £7.95) chased with cider, as done in Brittany, the birthplace of these flat, filled pancakes. A two course set lunch is £4.99, three courses at dinner are £9.99.

Other Cuisines

Kozachok *(☎ 8948 2366, 10a Red Lion St; Richmond station).* We can't vouch for the authenticity of the food, but Kozachok serves an array of Russian and Ukrainian dishes – from borscht (£3.50) and blinis (from £2.95 to £5.50) to chicken Kiev (£8.50) and *kasha* (buckwheat groats) with mushrooms, onions and sour cream. There are 26 different clear and flavoured vodkas on offer – from apricot to *zubrówka* (bison's grass). It's open for dinner only.

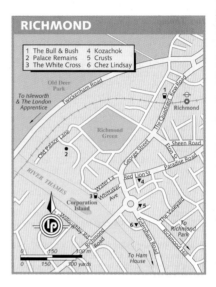

RICHMOND

1 The Bull & Bush	4 Kozachok
2 Palace Remains	5 Crusts
3 The White Cross	6 Chez Lindsay

Entertainment

LISTINGS

To find out what's on, buy a copy of the comprehensive entertainment listings magazine *Time Out* (£1.80), which is published every Wednesday (though available Tuesday) and covers a week of events to the following Wednesday. In many ways *Hot Tickets*, free with the *Evening Standard* newspaper on Thursday, is a better source – briefer and more eclectic.

Alternatively you can use the London Tourist Board (LTB)'s Visitorcall service to find out what's on. See Tourist Offices in the Facts for the Visitor chapter for details.

PUBS & BARS

Pubs are perhaps the most distinctive contribution the English have made to urban social life, and nothing really compares to a good one. What that constitutes – beyond a wide range of beers (see the boxed text 'Beer: The National Drink') – is very subjective and almost indefinable: a warm

RICHARD I'ANSON

One of the innumerable olde-worlde pub signs you'll see as you stroll around the city.

Beer: The National Drink

In public houses – universally known as pubs – it is possible to order wine or even a cocktail. The *raison d'être* of these establishments, however, is first and foremost to serve beer – be it lager, ale or stout, in a glass or in a bottle. On draught it is served by the pint (570mL) or half-pint (285mL). The percentage of alcohol varies from 3% to a gobsmacking 8%.

Most beers are made from malted barley and flavoured with hops. The term lager refers to the amber-coloured bottom-fermented beverage found the world over. In general lagers are highly carbonated, of medium hop-flavour and drunk cold. In London, the best-known British brands are Tennent's and Carling, but there's nothing special about them.

Ale is a top-fermented beer whose flavours can run the gamut from subtle to robust; proponents of 'real ale', made according to traditional recipes and methods, use the language of oenologists to describe them. Ales can be very slightly gassy or completely still, have a strong hop-flavour and are drunk at slightly above room temperature. Real ale is sometimes pulled from barrels. Among the multitude of ales on offer in London pubs, London Pride, Courage Best, Burton Ale, Adnam's, Theakston (in particular Old Peculier), Marston's Pedigree and Old Speckled Hen are among the most popular. If in doubt, just ask for 'a bitter' and you'll be served the house ale. Stout, the best-known brand of which is Guinness, is a slightly sweet, dark beer whose distinct flavour comes from malt that is roasted before fermentation.

welcome, a sense of bonhomie, the feel of a 'local' (ie people in the neighbourhood – and not just a bunch of faceless transients and tourists – patronise the place) and so on. Pubs have complex opening hours, but in general they are open Monday to Saturday from 11 am to 11 pm and on Sunday from noon to 10.30 pm. Some neighbourhood pubs and ones in the country still close in the afternoon (which used to be the law) between 3 and 7.30 pm, especially on Sunday.

These days traditional pubs can be thin on the ground in London. In many areas spruced-up chain pubs – look for words such as 'slug', 'lettuce', 'rat', 'firkin' and 'parrot' in their names – have taken over the role of the local. American-style bars, with bottled beer, luridly coloured designer drinks and bar staff who expect a tip, have also arrived in a big way. The stylish décor, late opening hours and more upbeat atmosphere seem to attract the upwardly mobile twenty and thirtysomethings. One such chain that has been trying to lure back drinkers tired of smoky, noisy, old-style pubs by creating no-smoking areas and, in some cases, removing jukeboxes is Wetherspoon. A clue is the word 'moon' in their pub names.

Sampling a range of pubs and bars is part of the fun of visiting London. The following list includes most of our favourites, but there's no substitute for individual research. For more suggestions look in the *Evening Standard Pub Guide* (£9.99) or the *Time Out Pubs & Bars Guide* (£5.99).

Trafalgar Square (Map 7)
Sherlock Holmes (10 Northumberland St WC2; ✪ Charing Cross). Tucked away just off Northumberland Ave, this pub filled with Holmes memorabilia doesn't get quite as busy as it otherwise might and is never touristy.

Westminster & Pimlico (Maps 6 & 10)
Westminster Arms (Map 6; 9 Storey's Gate SW1; ✪ Westminster). This pleasant, atmospheric place is great for a quick one after a tiring tour of Westminster Abbey, which is a two-minute walk away. Think of the convenience.

The Orange Brewery (Map 10; 37-39 Pimlico Rd SW1; ✪ Sloane Square). This place is for serious aficionados of the amber liquid: it's ·got a microbrewery in the basement churning out all-natural pints of beer and stout that you can sample for less than £2 a go. Should you get carried away (and we know you will) there's food available all day to play the important blotter role.

St James's & Mayfair (Maps 6 & 7)
I Am the Only Running Footman (Map 6; 5 Charles St W1; ✪ Green Park). No matter how hard you look, you're not going to find another pub with a name like this one. It's an olde-worlde place that has been extensively refitted; the eponymous running footman – the guy employed by a wealthy 18th-century gentleman to run in front of his carriage lighting the way and shifting any obstacles (including people) – probably wouldn't recognise it.

Che (Map 6; 23 St James's St W1; ✪ Green Park). This ever-so-trendy cigar bar-cum-restaurant has an enviable collection of vintage rums, tequilas and whiskies.

Windows on the World (Map 6; Hilton Hotel, 29th floor, Park Lane W1; ✪ Hyde Park Corner). No doubt the staff would throw up their hands in horror at being associated with pubs, but anyone smartly dressed and not suffering from vertigo might like to buy a pricey drink (£3.50 for a bottle of lager, from £6.25 for cocktails) to enjoy the views over Hyde Park.

West End: Piccadilly, Soho & Chinatown (Map 7)
Scruffy Murphy's (15 Denman St W1; ✪ Piccadilly Circus). This little place is the most authentic – snugs, brogues, Guinness and drunks – of the Irish pubs in Soho.

Waxy O'Connors (14-16 Rupert St W1; ✪ Leicester Square). This is a large, multi-level Irish pub with a quirky, Gothic interior.

The Salisbury (90 St Martin's Lane WC2; ✪ Leicester Square). Brave the crowds at this centrally located pub just to see the beautifully etched and engraved windows and other Victorian features that have somehow escaped the developer's hand.

Denim (4A Upper St Martin's Lane WC2; ✪ Leicester Square). Denim is an ultra-trendy bar for the glitterati, with hugely expensive drinks, a wall of blank TV screens and a restaurant on the mezzanine level. Clearly a place to be seen entering.

Lupo (50 Dean St W1; ⊖ Leicester Square). This place looks small and cramped from the outside but enter and you'll discover the comfortable rooms go on forever and ever. It's a great place to escape to in Soho.

French House (49 Dean St W1; ⊖ Leicester Square). The French House was the headquarters of the Free French Forces during WWII and De Gaulle is said to have drunk here frequently (as have writers like Dylan Thomas and actors like Peter O'Toole, who only does shandies, we're told). It's very popular despite only serving half-pints.

Coach & Horses (29 Greek St W1; ⊖ Leicester Square). The Coach is a small, busy pub with a regular clientele but is nonetheless hospitable to visitors. It was made famous by the much missed alcoholic *Spectator* columnist Jeffrey Bernard.

Riki-Tik (23-24 Bateman St W1; ⊖ Tottenham Court Road). Famous for its flavoured vodka shots (Rolo and Toblerone may not be to everyone's taste) and half-price jugs of cocktails before 8 pm from Wednesday to Saturday and all day on Monday and Tuesday, Riki-Tik commendably bans suits.

O Bar (83-85 Wardour St W1; ⊖ Piccadilly Circus). This upbeat bar has two main drinking floors with a DJ downstairs nightly (£5 cover charge). It also serves half-price pitchers of cocktails till 8 pm (till closing on Monday, to midnight on Wednesday). There's another O Bar in Camden Town (Map 3; ☎ 7383 0330, 111-113 Camden High St NW1; ⊖ Camden Town).

Mash (19-21 Great Portland St W1; ⊖ Oxford Circus). Just across Oxford St and really in an area called Fitzrovia (but let's not get technical), Mash is a thoroughly groovy in-house brewery (£2.80 a pint) decorated to resemble how some imaginative designer in the 1960s may have envisaged the 1990s. The restaurant upstairs (about £20 for a full meal) is based on the something-for-everybody concept.

Point 101 (101 New Oxford St WC1; ⊖ Tottenham Court Road). The Point is a spartan but hugely popular spot below that skyscraping monstrosity called Centre Point. We hear it's great for scoring (or pulling, as they say here).

Covent Garden & the Strand (Map 7)

Cork & Bottle Wine Bar (44-46 Cranbourn St WC2; ⊖ Leicester Square). Hidden downstairs on the left as you head to Leicester Square from the tube station, the Cork & Bottle is always packed to the hilt after work, but the food's good, the wine list commendable and there are several hideaway alcoves.

Lamb & Flag (33 Rose St WC2; ⊖ Covent Garden). Everyone's 'find' in Covent Garden and therefore always jammed, the pleasantly unchanged Lamb & Flag was once known as the Bucket of Blood – either because of the fighters who favoured it as a local or because the poet John Dryden was attacked outside in 1679 for having written less-than-complimentary verses about Charles II's mistress. That'll teach him.

Walkabout Inn (33 Maiden Lane WC2; ⊖ Covent Garden). The Walkabout Inn is a popular Australian-themed bar with live music and cheap midweek drink specials. Expect it to be packed to the rafters from Thursday to Sunday. There's a branch in Shepherd's Bush at 58 Shepherd's Bush Green W12 (⊖ Shepherd's Bush).

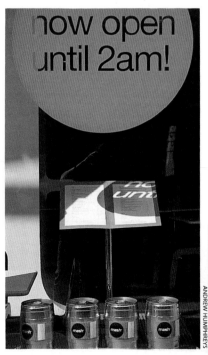

Mash, one of the new breed of London bars with in-house breweries.

A pub with a view: the perfect spot for taking in the Covent Garden street performers.

Punch & Judy *(40 The Market WC2;* ✪ *Covent Garden).* Inside the central market hall itself, this is not the most beautiful (or cheapest) of pubs, but it is extremely well positioned and has a balcony that lets you look down on the buskers.

Freud *(198 Shaftesbury Ave WC2;* ✪ *Covent Garden).* Freud is a small basement bar/café/gallery with the sort of beige walls that could look just plain dirty but there are purposefully arty pictures to complement the heavy church candles. The beers and cocktails aren't cheap, but the food and bar snacks are a cut above.

Gordon's Wine Bar *(47 Villiers St WC2;* ✪ *Embankment or Charing Cross).* This atmospheric wine bar (no beer) in ancient vaults beneath the street is as close as you'll get to drinking in the London Dungeon. The cold buffets are marvellous, but you'll need to nip in quickly after work to get a table.

Bloomsbury (Map 6)

The Lamb *(94 Lamb's Conduit St WC1;* ✪ *Russell Square).* The Lamb is unprepossessing from the outside but the interior is full of Victorian wood and snugs.

The Queen's Larder *(1 Queen Square WC1;* ✪ *Russell Square).* In a lovely square southeast of Russell Square, the Queen is a handy retreat, with outside benches and pub grub.

The Swan *(7 Cosmo Place WC1;* ✪ *Russell Square).* This neighbour of the Queen is less authentic but has a good selection of beers.

Museum Tavern *(Map 7; 49 Great Russell St WC1;* ✪ *Tottenham Court Road).* After a hard day's work in the British Museum Reading Room, Karl Marx used to repair to this capacious pub, where you too can sup your pint and reflect on dialectical materialism if so inclined.

Holborn & Clerkenwell (Maps 4 & 6)

Princess Louise *(Map 7; 208 High Holborn WC1;* ✪ *Holborn).* This is a delightful and eternally popular example of Victorian pub décor with fine tiles, etched mirrors, columns, plasterwork and an open fire in winter but we wish it would stop bragging about the *Evening Standard* Pub of the Year Award it won way back in 1986.

The Eagle *(Map 4; 159 Farringdon Rd EC1;* ✪ *Farringdon).* The Eagle was one of the first of the new-style 'gastropubs' to arrive on the scene and serves delicious Mediterranean food and a good range of beers.

The Castle *(Map 6; 34 Cowcross St EC1;* ✪ *Farringdon).* This is the only pub in London that is also a licensed pawnbroker's (look for the symbol of the three gold balls hanging above the bar inside). This dual function dates from a time when George IV was in urgent need of a float to pay off his gambling debts and got one from the innkeeper.

Three Kings of Clerkenwell *(Map 4; 7 Clerkenwell Close EC1;* ✪ *Farringdon).* A friendly, family-run pub a stone's throw from Clerkenwell Green, the Three Kings is festooned with papier-mâché models, including a giant rhino head above the fireplace.

The City (Maps 6 & 8)

The City is a notorious black spot at weekends, when the suits are all watering themselves at pubs closer to home, but some of the following places can oblige.

Ye Olde Cheshire Cheese *(Map 6; Wine Office Court EC4;* ✪ *Blackfriars).* The entrance to this historic pub is via a picturesque alley at 145 Fleet St. Cross the threshold and you'll find yourself in a wood-panelled interior (the oldest bit dates from the mid-17th century) with sawdust on the floor and divided up into various bars and eating areas (see the City section in the Places to Eat chapter).

Ye Olde Mitre *(Map 6; 1 Ely Court EC1;* ✪ *Chancery Lane).* One of our absolute favourites, the Mitre is one of London's oldest and most historic pubs, although the 18th-century-sized rooms can be a bit tight for late-20th-century punters like us.

The Bleeding Heart *(Map 6; Bleeding Heart Yard EC1;* ✪ *Chancery Lane).* Just around the corner from the Mitre, off Greville St, this bar/restaurant has excellent wines, great French food and a lot of history.

Jamaica Wine House *(Map 8; St Michael's Alley EC3;* ✪ *Bank).* The 'Jam Pot' is an authentic Victorian pub (yes, everything's real) on the site of what was the first coffee house in London (see Georgian London in the Facts about London chapter), which were often just fronts for brothels.

Hamilton Hall *(Map 8; Liverpool Street station, Bishopsgate EC2;* ✪ *Liverpool Street).* This is a huge warehouse of a pub; most punters here are drinking quickly to get enough down before their train departs. It started life as the ballroom of the Great Eastern Hotel (1901) and you can tell: plaster cherubs, gilt mirrors and shelves of old books line the turquoise and gold-coloured walls.

Railway Tavern *(Map 8; 15 Liverpool St EC2;* ✪ *Liverpool Street).* If you need a pub in this area and want something a little less frenetic than Hamilton Hall, try the Railway, with its booths, partitions and Pizza Hut franchise.

Liberty Bounds *(Map 8; Byward St EC3;* ✪ *Tower Hill).* Down by Tower Hill, the Liberty Bounds is a large sterile Wetherspoon pub but has great views of the Tower.

Cock Tavern *(Map 6; East Poultry Ave EC1;* ✪ *Farringdon).* This legendary pub will serve you a pint between 6.30 and 10.30 am when it feeds and waters the workers from Smithfield Market.

South of the Thames

Rotherhithe This is the place to go if you want to enjoy a pint while watching the Thames flow by. The three places listed below are on Map 8 and are convenient for Rotherhithe tube station.

Spice Island *(163 Rotherhithe St SE16).* This enormous place, a stone's throw west of the Rotherhithe YHA hostel, has bars on two floors, a restaurant and a large heated terrace overlooking the river. Of the three here, it's got the least history but the best views.

The Mayflower *(117 Rotherhithe St SE16).* This 15th-century pub was originally called the Spread Eagle but was renamed after the ship that took the Pilgrims to America in 1620 because the ship sailed from here and the captain supposedly charted out its course here while supping schooners.

The Angel *(101 Bermondsey Wall East SE16).* Somewhat closer to civilisation as we know it, the Angel is a riverside pub dating from the 15th century (though the present building is early 17th century). Captain Cook supposedly prepared for his trip to Australia from here and Samuel Pepys quenched his thirst after gorging on fruit in Cherry Gardens to the south-west. Just opposite in Cathay St are the remains of Edward III's Moated Manor House built in 1361.

Southwark These pubs are all on Map 8, except where indicated.

George Inn *(Talbot Yard, 77 Borough High St SE1;* ✪ *London Bridge or Borough).* The George is a rare bird indeed – a National Trust pub. It's London's last surviving galleried coaching inn, dates from 1676 and is mentioned in Charles Dickens' *Little Dorrit*. Here too is the site of the Tabard Inn (thus the Talbot Yard address), where the pilgrims gathered in Chaucer's *Canterbury Tales* before setting out.

The Royal Oak (*44 Tabard St SE1;* ✪ *Borough*). This authentic Victorian place owned by a small independent brewery is a short distance from the church of St George the Martyr where Little Dorrit (aka Amy) got married (see Literature in the Facts about London chapter). It's one of our favourite places in London so please don't tell your friends about it.

The Anchor (*34 Park St SE1;* ✪ *London Bridge*). This 18th-century place just east of the Globe Theatre has superb views across the Thames from its terrace and is the nicest (and perhaps the most popular) riverside pub in London.

Horniman at Hay's (*Hay's Galleria, Battle Bridge Lane SE1;* ✪ *London Bridge*). This *faux* – but less crowded – alternative to the Anchor is in a warehouse development where a fake Victorian iron-and-glass roof covers an atrium surrounded by offices, shops and cafés.

Doggetts Coat & Badge (*Map 6; Blackfriars Rd SE1;* ✪ *Blackfriars*). Just to the west of Blackfriars Bridge you'll find this pub, which has a certain history. Thomas Doggett was an 18th-century Irish comedian who set up what is believed to be the oldest rowing competition in the world in 1715. Ever since then six men have set out from London Bridge to race down river to Chelsea Bridge every July. The winner is rewarded with a red coat and a silver badge.

Waterloo & Lambeth Look for these pubs on Map 6.

The Fire Station (*150 Waterloo Rd SE1;* ✪ *Waterloo*). This immensely popular gastropub (from £7 to £10 for main courses, two course lunch or early dinner for £9.95) is in a part of town that was once a culinary desert but is always jammed. Jazz on Sunday afternoon.

The Wellington (*81-83 Waterloo Rd SE1;* ✪ *Waterloo*). An acceptable alternative if the Fire Station is full (as it will be), the Wellington is a veritable shrine to the eponymous duke and enough to make any French person arriving on Eurostar go apoplectic upon entry.

Wandsworth You will find this pub on Map 2.

The Ship (*41 Jew's Row SW18; Wandsworth Town station*). Though the Ship is right by the Thames, the views aren't spectacular (unless you're partial to cement works and workaday bridges). Still, the outside area is large and the summertime barbecues a real treat.

Chelsea, South Kensington & Earl's Court (Map 9)

Po Na Na Souk (*316 King's Rd SW3;* ✪ *Sloane Square*). This oddly named place is an African-style bar where you can drink in little tented alcoves, seated on leopard-skin sofas or chairs, and play backgammon.

Cooper's Arms (*87 Flood St SW3;* ✪ *Sloane Square*). This 'find', just off the King's Rd, has stuffed critters as 'decorative' items, newspapers to read and excellent food (starters £4.50, main courses from £7).

King's Head & Eight Bells (*50 Cheyne Walk;* ✪ *Sloane Square*). This attractive corner pub, pleasantly hung with flower baskets in summer, has a wide range of beers and was a favourite of the painter Whistler and the writer Carlyle, who lived at 24 Cheyne Row.

The Antelope (*22-24 Eaton Terrace SW1;* ✪ *Sloane Square*). This charming pub has been around longer than any of its neighbouring buildings, and it's music-free so a perfect place for a tête-à-tête.

Prince of Teck (*161 Earl's Court Rd SW5;* ✪ *Earl's Court*). This is a convivial pub with an Australian theme in the heart of Kangaroo Valley. But didn't they get that vowel wrong? Avoid it whenever Australia is playing anyone at anything.

Kensington, Knightsbridge & Holland Park (Map 5)

The Churchill Arms (*119 Kensington Church St W8;* ✪ *Notting Hill Gate*). This traditional English pub is renowned for its Winston memorabilia, chamber pots suspended from a great height and excellent-value Thai food (around £6) served in a lovely conservatory in the back.

Windsor Castle (*114 Campden Hill Rd W11;* ✪ *Notting Hill Gate*). The Windsor has one of the nicest walled gardens (with heaters in winter) of any pub in London.

Notting Hill & Bayswater (Map 5)

Beach Blanket Babylon (*45 Ledbury Rd W11;* ✪ *Notting Hill Gate*). This is one of our favourite 'crazies'; it boasts extraordinary Gothic décor and is a great place for observing Notting Hill trendies ('Oh, hi Hugh, hi Julia').

The Westbourne (*101 Westbourne Park Villas W2;* ✪ *Royal Oak or Westbourne Park*). The Westbourne is another place where the Notting Hill crowd congregates. The large forecourt is great in summer.

The Cow *(89 Westbourne Park Rd W2; ✪ West-bourne Park).* This Irish-themed pub owned by Tom Conran, son of restaurateur Sir Terence, is wildly popular, and fresh oysters with Guinness are a speciality.

The Market Bar *(240A Portobello Rd W11; ✪ Ladbroke Grove).* Convenient for the market, this place has an interesting, eclectic décor and an entertaining crowd but it can get mobbed later in the evening. There's jazz on Tuesday and Sunday and upstairs you'll find – here we go again – Thai food.

The Bridge House *(13 Westbourne Terrace Rd W2; ✪ Warwick Avenue).* This is in a lovely location just opposite the Grand Union Canal. The Canal St Theatre, with its popular satirical reviews, is upstairs.

Bar Oz *(51 Moscow Rd W2; ✪ Bayswater).* If you just can't stay away from your own, the Oz can oblige, with Aussie beers, tucker and Aussie Rules footie on video.

Maida Vale (Map 2)

The Warrington *(93 Warrington Crescent W9; ✪ Warwick Avenue).* This former hotel and brothel is now an ornate Art Nouveau pub with heaps of character and a very laid-back atmosphere. There's seating outside in the courtyard and – inevitably – a Thai restaurant upstairs.

Camden (Map 3)

Crown & Goose *(100 Arlington Rd NW1; ✪ Camden Town).* This is a new-style pub attracting a youngish crowd with decent, no-nonsense food.

The Engineer *(65 Gloucester Ave NW1; ✪ Chalk Farm).* A pretty Victorian place converted into a highly successful pub and gastropub restaurant, which upstairs attracts a groovy north London set.

Pembroke Castle *(150 Gloucester Ave NW1; ✪ Chalk Farm).* We love this light, airy retro place with lovely stained glass and a refined, sportsman's theme.

The Hogshead *(130 Albert St NW1; ✪ Camden Town).* This is a pleasant split-level pub with a good selection of beer, including German Weissbier.

Islington (Map 4)

Old Queen's Head *(44 Essex Rd N1; ✪ Angel).* Loud, popular and packed to the rafters with merrymakers, the Old Queen's Head was the first pub to introduce the stripped-down, open-plan look to Islington.

The Market Bar: well located for checking out the Notting Hill vibe.

Cuba Libre *(72 Upper St N1; ✪ Angel).* The lively bar at the back of the restaurant has cocktails (from £2.50 to £3.95) worth sampling and stays open late: Monday to Wednesday to 1 am, Thursday to Saturday to 2 am.

Bierodrome *(173-174 Upper St N1; ✪ Highbury & Islington).* The latest effort by the Belgo group (the people who introduced London to mussels and chips with mayonnaise) pays homage to beer: over 200 types are available.

Stoke Newington & Finsbury Park (Map 1)

Bar Lorca *(175 Stoke Newington High St N16; Stoke Newington station; bus No 73).* This lively tapas bar has good dance music and extended hours: weekdays to 1 am, on Friday and Saturday to 2 am.

The Old Dairy *(127 Hanley Rd N4; ✪ Finsbury Park).* The Dairy is a huge bar north-west of Finsbury Park station, with lots of cows (on the walls, not supping) and grog but no milk.

JULIET COOMBE

ENTERTAINMENT

Hampstead & Highgate (Map 11)

The Flask (14 Flask Walk NW3; ✺ Hampstead). The Flask is a friendly local handy for the tube, with high ceilings, real ale and good Asian-inspired food. It is not to be confused with its older sister pub across Hampstead Heath to the north-east, which is also called *The Flask (77 Highgate West Hill N6; bus No 214)* and is a maze of snugs.

The Holly Bush (22 Holly Mount NW3; ✺ Hampstead). Formerly stables, the Holly Bush is tucked away in a cul-de-sac above Heath St (reach it via Holly Bush Steps). It has a good selection of beers, and jazz on Sunday.

Spaniard's Inn (Spaniards Rd NW3; ✺ Golders Green, then bus No 210). This pub dates from 1585 and is associated with the outlaw Dick Turpin. Dickens, Shelley, Keats and Byron also bent their elbows here so you're in good company. In winter you can warm up around an open fire; in summer you'll enjoy the garden.

Jack Straw's Castle (North End Way NW3; ✺ Hampstead). This 'Gothic pub with Gothic food, Gothic hours and Gothic prices' (we don't get it either) is a favourite with ramblers around Hampstead Heath.

Old Bull & Bush (North End Way NW3; ✺ Golders Green). This is where Hogarth once spent his summers and no doubt mused on rakes and harlots (see the boxed text under Paintings & Sculpture in the Facts about London chapter).

East End & the Docklands (Maps 4 & 8)

Cantaloupe (Map 4; 35-43 Charlotte Rd EC2; ✺ Old Street or Liverpool Street). This was one of the first kids on the block when Hoxton and Shoreditch started to get trendy, and it still manages to feel arty enough without being overwhelming. There's a decent restaurant (tapas from £2.75, main courses from £7 to £14) at the back.

Bricklayers Arms (Map 4; 63 Charlotte Rd EC2; ✺ Old Street). Just up from Cantaloupe, this pub is also where the Shoreditch/Hoxton renaissance began and it continues to be something of a hang-out for the artists and artistes.

Home (Map 4; 100-106 Leonard St EC2; ✺ Old Street or Liverpool Street). This louche-feeling place with broken sofas, great cocktails and shots and a fine restaurant to the side is so laidback it's nearly comatose.

Shoreditch Electricity Showrooms (Map 4; 39A Hoxton Square N1; ✺ Old Street). The Showrooms is much edgier than Home and serves up everything with a side dish of attitude. It's the bar of the moment though.

Charlie Wright's International Bar (Map 4; 45 Pitfield St N1; ✺ Old Street). This is a useful address if you want to carry on after usual pub hours. It's open Monday to Wednesday to 1 am and the rest of the week to 2 am. The clientele is a mixed bag (as far as we can remember).

The Dickens Inn (Map 8; Marble Quay, St Katharine's Way E1; ✺ Tower Hill). Overlooking St Katharine's Dock near the Tower of London, this 18th-century wooden-framed brewery was uncovered when a warehouse was being demolished for new houses. The façade, bedecked with flower boxes, is a modern replica but the interior is still full of character.

Captain Kidd (Map 8; 108 Wapping High St E1; ✺ Wapping). The Kidd, with its large windows, fine beer-garden and mock scaffold recalling the hanging of the eponymous pirate in 1701, is our favourite riverside pub on the northern bank of the Thames.

Echoes of the buccaneering lifestyle at the Captain Kidd.

ELLIOT DANIEL

Prospect of Whitby (Map 8; 57 Wapping Wall E1; ⊖ Wapping). Farther afield than the Kidd, the Whitby dates from 1520 and is one of London's oldest surviving drinking houses, once known as the Devil's Tavern. It's firmly on the tourist trail, but there's a terrace overlooking the Thames, a decent restaurant upstairs and open fires in winter. Check out the pewter bar – Samuel Pepys once sidled up to it.

Greenwich (Map 13)

Trafalgar Tavern (Park Row SE10; DLR Cutty Sark). This cavernous pub with big windows looking onto the Thames and the Millennium Dome has a lot of history. It stands above the site of the old Placentia Palace where Henry VIII was born. Dickens knocked back a few here (the Trafalgar is mentioned in *Our Mutual Friend*) and prime ministers Gladstone and Disraeli used to dine on the pub's celebrated whitebait (£4.75) when the whitebait fishery at Greenwich was so famous that Parliament would suspend sitting for the day to feast on the little fish.

The Auctioneer (217-219 Greenwich High Rd SE10; DLR Greenwich; Greenwich station). The Auctioneer has none of the Trafalgar's history but is a pleasant, central place for a pint.

Hammersmith (Map 1)

Hammersmith is a fine place to go on a warm spring or summer day, where you can enjoy a pint – if you can manage to get to the bar – and watch Old Man River slowly roll along.

The Dove (19 Upper Mall W6; ⊖ Ravenscourt Park). The Dove, the oldest of the trio here, is a small 17th-century building close to the river and popular with rowers.

The Old Ship (25 Upper Mall W6; ⊖ Ravenscourt Park). The Ship is enviable for the large stretch of grass just outside for sitting, sipping, sunning and/or sleeping. The speciality here is flavoured vodkas.

The Blue Anchor (13 Lower Mall W6; ⊖ Hammersmith or Ravenscourt Park). This is a nautical-themed place where Gustav Holst supposedly wrote his *Hammersmith Suite*.

Fulham (Map 9)

Come the Revolution (541 King's Rd SW6; ⊖ Fulham Broadway). This 'designer dungeon bar' has an Italianate interior with murals and wrought-iron tables and chairs. Despite its size, it can get very crowded, although there's a large garden to escape to in summer. Thai food again.

Havana (490 Fulham Rd SW6; ⊖ Fulham Broadway). You could hardly miss this place even if you did blink: it's a neon-like blue-and-ochre-tiled bar/restaurant with zebra-striped and leopard-spotted seating. Rum cocktails start at £4.50 but during happy hour (from 6 to 8 pm daily) they drop to £3.

Chiswick & Kew (Map 1)

The Tabard (2 Bath Rd W4; ⊖ Turnham Green). This place was designed in 1880 by Norman Shaw as part of Bedford Park, London's first garden suburb. Despite restoration after a fire in 1971 it still boasts panels of William Morris wallpaper and tiles by William de Morgan and Walter Crane. There's a small theatre upstairs.

The City Barge (27 Strand on the Green W4; ⊖ Gunnersbury). The Barge was built in 1484 and perched dramatically close to the river's edge. A scene from the Beatles' film *Help!* was shot here.

The Bull's Head (15 Strand on the Green; ⊖ Gunnersbury). This is another good riverside choice, with an excellent Sunday lunch and a Cromwell connection.

Richmond & Isleworth

For the following pubs see the Richmond map in the Places to Eat chapter.

The White Cross (Water Lane, Richmond; ⊖ Richmond). The riverside location, good food and fine ales make the Cross a winner. When the river's at its highest tide, riverside Cholmondeley Walk floods and the pub is out of bounds to those not willing to paddle (wade).

The Bull & Bush (1 Kew Rd, Richmond; ⊖ Richmond). This pub just opposite the station has some enviable musical associations. As the Station Hotel, it was home to the Crawdaddy Club in the 1960s and hosted an amazing roll call of musicians – including the Yardbirds, Long John Baldy and the Hoochie Coochie Band, Elton John, and Rod Stewart with the Small Faces. The Rolling Stones got their first gig here in 1963 (they were paid £22) and in April of that year the Beatles came to hear them play. There's still music here Thursday to Saturday.

ENTERTAINMENT

The London Apprentice (*62 Church St, Isleworth; Isleworth station*). If you're really into sunning along the Thames, you may want to venture north-west of Richmond to this riverside pub dating from the 17th century, which boasts its own Hogarth drawings on the walls.

CLUBS

Though the majority of London's pubs still close at 11 pm, there are clubs where you can carry on partying, although you'll have to pay to get in and the drinks are always expensive.

Late-night venues often have a 'club' licence, which means you have to be a member to enter. In practice, they usually include the membership fee in the admission price. Many venues have clubs that only operate one night a week and cater for a specific crowd, such as techno-heads, gays or salsa aficionados.

Entry prices vary from £10 to £15 for most clubs, plus at least £3 per drink. The most happening clubs don't kick off until after midnight and stay open until 4 or 5 am; some are all-nighters. Dress can be smart (no suits) or casual; the more outrageous you look – within reason – the better the chance you have of getting in.

The Annexe (*Map 7;* ☎ *7287 9608, 1A Dean St W1;* ✪ *Tottenham Court Road*). A smallish venue that has the popular Metal Box clubnight on Saturday.

The Aquarium (*Map 4;* ☎ *7251 6136, 255-260 Old St EC1;* ✪ *Old Street*). Converted gym with its own cool pool, Jacuzzi and restaurant. Opens on Sunday too.

Bagley's Studios (*Map 4;* ☎ *7278 2777, King's Cross Freight Depot, York Way N1;* ✪ *King's Cross St Pancras*). A huge converted warehouse with five dance floors, four bars and an outside area in the summer.

Bar Latino (*Map 4;* ☎ *7704 6868, 145 Upper St N1;* ✪ *Angel*). The only dance bar open to 2 am in Upper St, with fusion on Friday, oldies on Saturday. Entry is free all week and before 10 pm at weekends.

Bar Rumba (*Map 7;* ☎ *7287 2715, 36 Shaftesbury Ave W1;* ✪ *Piccadilly Circus*). Small club (entry costs from £3 to £5) in the heart of Soho with a loyal following. Tuesday is a Rumba Pa'ti, Saturday is Garage City and there's Asian fusion one Friday a month.

Browns (*Map 7;* ☎ *7831 0802, 4 Great Queen St WC2;* ✪ *Holborn*). The stars' after-party piss-elegant hang-out – dress way, way up for this one.

Bug Bar (*Brixton map, page 287;* ☎ *7738 3184, Brixton Hill SW2;* ✪ *Brixton*). In the crypt of St Matthew's Methodist Church, with vaulted ceilings, pews and frescoes, this place is not for the superstitious. Bands play on Tuesday, DJs at weekends and there's a techno night on Thursday.

Café de Paris (*Map 7;* ☎ *7734 7700, 3 Coventry St W1;* ✪ *Piccadilly Circus*). A completely revamped 1920s ballroom, it's got a spectacular balcony for watching the action as well as a restaurant.

Camden Palace (*Map 3;* ☎ *7387 0428, 1A Camden High St NW1;* ✪ *Mornington Crescent*). A multilevel monster of a place thick with sweaty boppers and laser lights.

The Complex (*Map 4;* ☎ *7288 1986, 1-5 Parkfield St N1;* ✪ *Angel*). What was the Blue Note in Hoxton Square has moved to Islington and now has four floors of diverse sounds with the top one – the Love Lounge – reserved for chilling out (or whatever). Popstarz is a Friday gay night.

The Cross (*Map 4;* ☎ *7837 0828, King's Cross Freight Depot, N1;* ✪ *King's Cross St Pancras*). This is one of London's leading venues, hidden under the arches off York Way, completely renovated and with brilliant DJs. Friday night's Liquid (from 10.30 pm to 4.30 am) is aimed at 'the more sophisticated and educated clubbers' (the older crowd).

Cuba (*Map 5;* ☎ *7938 4137, 11-13 Kensington High St;* ✪ *High Street Kensington*). Downstairs bar with salsa lessons, a live band or a DJ every night, with dancing until 2 am and great mojito cocktails.

Dogstar (*Brixton map, page 287;* ☎ *7733 7515, 389 Coldharbour Lane SW9;* ✪ *Brixton*). As casual as you'd expect from a converted pub so dressing to kill is not imperative. Great Sunday tea dance from 2 pm to midnight.

Dust (*Map 6;* ☎ *7490 0537, 27 Clerkenwell Rd EC1;* ✪ *Farringdon*). A mixed-bag club/bar with everything from techno and house to Latin and French funk. Free entry all week.

Electric Ballroom (*Map 3;* ☎ *7485 9006, 184 Camden High St NW1;* ✪ *Camden Town*). Old dance hall ballroom that hosts a raucous studenty club on Friday and Saturday nights.

Emporium (*Map 7;* ☎ *7734 3190, 62 Kingly St W1;* ✪ *Oxford Circus*). Very popular with the beautiful set, Emporium is one of the trendiest clubs in town.

The End (Map 7; ☎ 7419 9199, 18 West Central St WC1; ✆ Holborn). Modern industrial décor with a free water-fountain. For serious clubbers who like their music underground.

Fabric (Map 6, ☎ 7490 0444, 77a Charterhouse St EC1; ✆ Farringdon). This latest feather in Clerkenwell's well plumed cap boasts three dance floors in a converted meat cold-store.

Fez Club (Map 9; ☎ 7352 5978, 222 Fulham Rd SW10; bus No 14). This cave-like club/bar is in the livelier part of Fulham Rd attracting a hip, playful crowd. Open Monday to Saturday to 2 am.

The Fridge (Brixton map, page 287; ☎ 7326 5100, 1 Town Hall Parade, Brixton Hill SW2; ✆ Brixton). The Fridge offers a wide variety of club nights in an excellent venue that is not too big, not too small. Saturday is gay night.

Hanover Grand (Map 7; ☎ 7499 7977, 6 Hanover St W1; ✆ Oxford Circus). Split-level venue, voted 'Best Club in London' two years running; worth queuing for. Saturday night is Future Perfect, with house, big beats and a strict dress-code.

Heaven (Map 7; ☎ 7930 2020, Under the Arches, Villiers St WC2; ✆ Charing Cross). Long-standing, popular gay nightclub with a new look.

Home (Map 7; ☎ 7287 6032, 1 Leicester Square WC2; ✆ Leicester Square). Massive new seven floor club attracting a motley though always glam crowd Thursday to Sunday.

HQ (Map 3; ☎ 7485 6044, West Yard, Camden Lock Place NW1; ✆ Camden Town). Predominantly a garage and house club; the cover charge is from £3 to £6, depending on the day of the week and what time you enter.

Iceni (Map 6; ☎ 7499 5333, 11 White Horse St W1; ✆ Green Park). Three floors (each with a dance floor) of contrasting music, six bars and a friendly atmosphere make this one of the more accessible clubs.

Ion (Map 5; ☎ 8960 1702, 165 Ladbroke Grove W11; ✆ Ladbroke Grove). Large new club with free admission seven nights a week.

The Junction (Brixton map, page 287; ☎ 7738 4000, 242 Coldharbour Lane SW9; ✆ Brixton). Up-and-coming venue that attracts an eclectic crowd with dance, dub and trance.

Leopard Lounge (Map 9; ☎ 7385 0834, Fulham Broadway SW6; ✆ Fulham Broadway). Large safari-theme club that attracts those who want to go wild. Open Thursday to Saturday to 3 am.

Ministry of Sound (Map 8; ☎ 7378 6528, 103 Gaunt St SE1; ✆ Elephant & Castle). This

ED HILLYER

Into the night life: London has one of the best club scenes in the world.

cavernous place, arguably London's most famous club (though well past its finest hour, they say), attracts hard-core clubbers as well as people who just want to chill out. It's open until 9 am.

Notting Hill Arts Club (Map 5; ☎ 7460 4459, 21 Notting Hill Gate W11; ✆ Notting Hill Gate). Cosy, groovy club whose jewel in the crown is Thursday's Future World Funk (from 8 pm to 2 am).

Propaganda (Map 4; ☎ 7613 3070, 89 Great Eastern St EC2; ✆ Old Street). Popular club in Hoxton open Tuesday to Sunday.

Salsa! (Map 7; ☎ 7379 3277, 96 Charing Cross Rd WC2; ✆ Leicester Square). A bar/club combo in the centre of everything with Latino music that will have you bopping upon entry.

Le Scandale (Map 7; ☎ 7437 6839, 54 Berwick St W1; ✆ Oxford Circus). Cheeky indie disco especially good on Saturday when it hosts Where It's At.

Smithfields (Map 6; ☎ 7236 4266, 341-343 Farringdon St EC4; ✆ Farringdon). Four room club with a different beat in each. Thursday night is Soirée, with French hip-hop and DJs fresh in from Paris.

Subterania (Map 5; ☎ 8960 4590, 12 Acklam Rd W10; ✆ Ladbroke Grove). Atmospheric place showcasing up-and-coming hip-hop acts.

Velvet Room (Map 7; ☎ 7439 4655, 143 Charing Cross Rd WC2; ✆ Tottenham Court Road). An intimate, friendly club swathed in red velvet.

ENTERTAINMENT

ELLIOT DANIEL

The old Truman Brewery, venue for the Vibe Bar.

The Verge (Map 3; ☎ 7485 2781, 147 Kentish Town Rd NW5; ⊖ Kentish Town). Neighbourhood club with a smallish dance floor and a good seating area. Party where the locals do.

Vibe Bar (Map 8; ☎ 7247 1231, Truman Brewery, 91 Brick Lane E1; ⊖ Shoreditch or Aldgate East). A watering hole in a former brewery in trendy Brick Lane with one-off club nights that attract students from the nearby Guildhall University. Friday is Bangla Town with Asian funk.

WKD Café (Map 3; ☎ 7267 1869, 18 Kentish Town Rd NW1; ⊖ Camden Town). Smallish club downstairs with varied live music – somewhere in that netherworld of jazz-rock the last time we visited. Upstairs, reserved for the glitterati, is too chichi for you and me, darling.

GAY & LESBIAN LONDON

The London gay scene has changed considerably over the past few years. From having just a couple of huge discos (eg Heaven) and pub once-a-weekers, London now boasts gay and (to a lesser extent) lesbian venues throughout the city.

The best starting point is to pick up the free *Pink Paper* (very serious, politically correct) or *Boyz* (more geared towards entertainment) available from most gay cafés, bars and clubs. Magazines like *Gay Times* (£2.50) and the lesbian *Diva* (£2) also have listings. The four-page gay section of *Time Out* is another excellent source of information. The Lesbian & Gay Switchboard (☎ 7837 7324) answers calls 24 hours a day. You might also try the LTB's Visitorcall service on ☎ 09068 141120 (50p per minute).

London's bars and clubs cater for every predilection, but there's a growing trend towards mixed gay and straight clubs. There are also men or women-only nights; check the press for details. A lot of the activity is centred in Soho but not all of it by any means; you'll find pubs, cafés and clubs in every direction.

Soho

In the 'gay village' of Soho (⊖ Tottenham Court Road or Piccadilly Circus) – particularly along Old Compton St – bars and cafés are thick on the ground. All the establishments in this section can be found on Map 7.

The *Old Compton Café* (☎ 7439 3309) at No 34 on this street is a friendly, sometimes frantic, 24-hour place while *Balans* (☎ 7437 5212), at No 60, is a popular, moderately priced, continental-style café. Around the corner you'll find the hyper-trendy *Freedom Café* (☎ 7734 0071, 60-66 Wardour St W1), serving food and drink to a mixed clientele. Piss-elegant *Rupert St* (50 Rupert St W1), London's trendiest gay bar, is on a corner and has large glass windows for looking, being looked at, looking at being looked at, and so on. Lots of looking, little cruising. The more relaxed *Yard* (57 Rupert St) has a pleasant courtyard where you can drink. Its nearby sister bar, *Village Soho* (81 Wardour St), is another good place for an early evening drink.

Near Tottenham Court Road tube station, the long-established, friendly *First Out* (☎ 7240 8042, 52 St Giles High St WC2) is a mixed lesbian-gay café that serves vegetarian food and has rotating exhibitions. Close by, the *Astoria* (☎ 7434 9592, 157-165 Charing Cross Rd WC2) is a dark, sweaty and atmospheric club, with good views of the stage and a huge dance floor. *LA2* (☎ 7434 6963) in the basement is a cheap gay night on Monday and Thursday. The Astoria is also the place to be on Friday and especially Saturday when Carwash lets loose 1970s disco

ENTERTAINMENT

and retro funk. **Substation Soho** (☎ 7287 9608, 1A Dean St W1) is a serious dance club with postmodern industrial décor.

West Central (30 Lisle St WC2; ✛ Leicester Square), in the heart of Chinatown, has a cruisy gay bar on the ground floor and a mixed club in the basement with alternating club nights. Towards Charing Cross, **Brief Encounter** (42 St Martin's Lane WC1; ✛ Charing Cross) is a cruisy pub with a ground floor bar and one in the basement. **Retro Bar** (☎ 7321 2811, 2 George Court WC2) is a friendly bar, tucked away down a small lane off the Strand, with a host of theme nights in the upstairs bar during the week. **Heaven** (see the previous Clubs section) is London's most famous gay club.

Candy Bar (☎ 7494 4041, 4 Carlisle St W1), the venue of choice among the London clitorati, has three floors and is always packed.

North

There are gay places around King's Cross and in Islington and Camden. The ever popular **Central Station** (Map 4; ☎ 7278 3294, 37 Wharfdale Rd N1; ✛ King's Cross St Pancras) has a bar with special one-nighters and the UK's only gay sports bar. In Islington, the **Angel Café Bar** (Map 4; ☎ 7608 2656, 65 Graham St N1; ✛ Angel) is a vegetarian café/bar open from noon with a DJ on Tuesday night and at weekends. The **Black Cap** (Map 3; ☎ 7428 2721, 171 Camden High St NW1; ✛ Camden Town) is a late-night bar famous for its drag shows.

South

Brixton and popular Vauxhall are south London's gay centres. The laid-back **Fridge Bar**, next to the huge Fridge club in Brixton (see the previous Clubs section), serves not-so-laid-back absinthe and other libations daily to 11 pm. **Substation South** (Brixton map, page 287; ☎ 7737 2095, 9 Brighton Terrace SW9; ✛ Brixton) is sleazier than its Soho sibling, with a healthy mix of cruising (Y-Front underwear party

on Monday, Massive on Tuesday) and dance nights (Queer Nation on Saturday).

The **Vauxhall Tavern** (Map 2; 372 Kennington Lane SE11; ✛ Vauxhall) is a long-running gay pub open late from Wednesday to Sunday.

East

Turnmills (Map 6; ☎ 7250 3409, 63B Clerkenwell Rd EC1; ✛ Farringdon) has three gay nights a week. From 4 am on Saturday it's Trade, London's first all-nighter and arguably *the* gay superclub, which goes until 1 pm on Sunday; breakfast is served at 6 am. On Sunday, at the same venue, Melt runs until 6 am on Monday with techno and trance. Monday brings in Club Epsilon from 10 pm to dawn.

If you're interested in barrow boys with buzz cuts (some real, lots *faux*), check out the **White Swan** (Map 8; ☎ 7780 9870, 556 Commercial Rd E14; ✛ Aldgate East), the East End's friendliest, cruisiest pub/club (especially BJ's on Saturday night to 3 am).

West

The west's gay area is centred around Earl's Court (Map 9; ✛ Earl's Court) and, despite being overshadowed by Soho, it still has a few places of interest. The **Coleherne** (261 Old Brompton Rd) is one of London's oldest pubs. **Brompton's** (294 Old Brompton Rd) is a popular bar/club open daily from 4 pm to 2 am (1 pm to midnight on Sunday). There's a branch of Balans, the popular, continental-style Soho café, called **Balans West** (☎ 7244 8838) at 239 Old Brompton Rd.

Saunas

London now has upwards of a dozen saunas where the action can get pretty steamy. Take the usual precautions. Entry costs £10 or £12 though there are student concessions at some, including Pacific 33.

Chariots Roman Spa (Map 4; ☎ 7247 5333, 201-207 Shoreditch High St E1; ✛ Liverpool Street or Old Street) is the largest gay sauna we've ever seen, with everything from steam rooms and saunas to a swimming pool. Serious OFB (out-for-business) types. A smaller branch of **Chariots** *(Map 6;* ☎ *7251 3113, Cowcross St EC1;* ✆ *Farringdon)* is quieter, friendlier and for the less buffed-up.

To the south, **Pleasuredrome Central** *(Map 6;* ☎ *7633 9194, 125 Alaska St SE1;* ✆ *Waterloo)* attracts a mixed-age crowd and is always busy. **Pacific 33** *(Map 2;* ☎ *7609 8133, 33 Hornsey Rd N7;* ✆ *Holloway Road)* is close to the University of North London so attracts students.

COMEDY
Central London plays host to a number of clubs whose *raison d'être* is comedy; there are even more venues – especially pubs – that set aside specific nights for stand-up comedy acts. The place to look for day-to-day details is *Time Out*, but the following are very popular venues:

Backyard Comedy Club *(Map 2;* ☎ *7739 3122, 231-237 Cambridge Heath Rd E2;* ✆ *Bethnal Green)*. Comic Lee Hurst's very own club in a converted textile factory.
Banana Cabaret *(*☎ *8673 8904, Bedford Arms, 77 Bedford Hill SW12;* ✆ *Balham)*. Touted as the finest comedy club in south London. Two acts run simultaneously on Saturday night.
Comedy Café *(Map 4;* ☎ *7739 5706, 66-68 Rivington St EC2;* ✆ *Old Street)*. There's something for everyone at this Hoxton club, just off Shoreditch High St. Wednesday is Try Out Night when you can give it a go.
Comedy Store *(Map 7;* ☎ *7344 4444, 1A Oxendon St SW1;* ✆ *Piccadilly Circus)*. Mostly big acts appear at London's longest-established comedy club, now in its third decade (from £12 to £13). Shows start Tuesday to Sunday at 8 pm with a midnight show on Friday and Saturday.
Improv Comedy Club *(Map 6;* ☎ *7387 2414, 161 Tottenham Court Rd W1;* ✆ *Warren Street)*. What was once the Cockney Cabaret has metamorphosed into a franchise of the American comedy chain. On Saturday at 10 pm there's the Rat Pack Club (£12.50), with 'Frank Sinatra', 'Sammy Davis Jr', 'Dean Martin' and 'Peter Lawford'.
Jongleurs *(*☎ *7564 2500)*. Popular comedy chain with venues in Battersea (Map 2), 49 Lavender Gardens SW11 (Clapham Junction station); Bow Wharf (Map 2), Bow Wharf, 221 Grove Rd E3 (✆ Mile End); and Camden Lock Place (Map 3), Dingwalls, 11 East Yard, Camden Lock NW1 (✆ Camden Town).
Top Dog Comedy & Cabaret *(Brixton map, page 287;* ☎ *7733 7515, Dogstar, 389 Coldharbour Lane SW9;* ✆ *Brixton)*. Themed nights, improv and name acts from Sunday to Thursday.

ROCK & POP
London boasts a wide range of rock and pop venues and you can hear everything from megastars at Wembley, Earl's Court and similar hangar-sized arenas to hot new bands at any number of more intimate places around town.

Ticketmaster has a 24-hour credit-card booking line (☎ 7413 1442, 0870 534 4444) as does Firstcall (☎ 7420 1000). You can also book on-line at www.ticketmaster.co .uk. Tickets are also available from HMV or Tower Records, from the Camden Ticket Shop (Map 3; ☎ 7344 0044) attached to the Jazz Café, 3 Parkway NW1 (✆ Camden Town), or from the London Tourist Board centres at Victoria and Liverpool Street train stations and in the Heathrow Terminals 1, 2, 3 Underground station concourse.

Here are some addresses you're likely to need:

Brixton Academy *(Brixton map, page 287;* ☎ *7924 9999, 211 Stockwell Rd SW9;* ✆ *Brixton)*. Enormous and very popular venue with a good atmosphere.
Earl's Court Exhibition Centre *(Map 9;* ☎ *7373 8141, Warwick Rd SW5;* ✆ *Earl's Court)*. Venue for blockbuster concerts – the type that sell out well in advance.
Forum *(Map 11;* ☎ *7344 0044, 9-17 Highgate Rd NW5;* ✆ *Kentish Town)*. Formerly the Town & Country Club and still an excellent roomy venue.
Garage *(Map 4;* ☎ *7607 1818, 20-22 Highbury Corner N5;* ✆ *Highbury & Islington)*. Good venue for rock, industrial and punk.
Hackney Empire *(Map 2;* ☎ *8985 2424, 291 Mare St E8; Hackney Central station)*. Superb Edwardian music hall; excellent venue for theatre, music, pantomime and comedy.
London Arena *(Map 12;* ☎ *7538 1212, Limeharbour, Isle of Dogs E14; DLR Crossharbour & London Arena)*. Renovated venue for huge capacity gigs.

Roundhouse *(Map 3; ☎ 7424 9991, 7420 0171, Chalk Farm Rd NW1; ⊖ Chalk Farm).* This famous 1960s music venue still holds a motley assortment of events – from rock concerts and exhibitions to circuses. It is to be converted into a theatre and concert hall seating 2400 people with TV and music studios below.

Royal Albert Hall *(Map 5; ☎ 7589 8212, Kensington Gore SW7; ⊖ South Kensington).* Huge, historic auditorium that attracts big-name performers (Eric Clapton is a regular) for one-off events.

Shepherd's Bush Empire *(☎ 8740 7474, 8771 2000, Shepherd's Bush Green W12; ⊖ Shepherd's Bush).* Once part of BBC Television and now one of the best venues in London.

Wembley Arena *(☎ 8902 0902, Empire Way, Wembley; ⊖ Wembley Park).* Huge venue with little to recommend it bar its high profile.

Smaller places that have a more club-like atmosphere and are worth checking for up-and-coming bands include:

Barfly *(Map 3; ☎ 7485 3834, 7328 1459, Camden Falcon, 234 Royal College St NW1; ⊖ Camden Town).* This small club, where Oasis played their first London gig (it was called Splash at the time), still gives a succession of small-time artists their big break.

Borderline *(Map 7; ☎ 7734 2095, Orange Yard W1; ⊖ Tottenham Court Road).* Small, relaxed venue with a reputation for big-name bands playing under pseudonyms.

Dingwalls *(Map 3; ☎ 7428 5929, 7267 3142, 11 East Yard, Camden Lock Place NW1; ⊖ Camden Town).* Indie acts from Sunday to Thursday and comedy acts at weekends (see Jongleurs Camden Lock in the previous Comedy section). Upstairs there's a terrace bar that looks onto Camden Lock.

Rock Garden *(Map 7; ☎ 7240 3961, Covent Garden WC2; ⊖ Covent Garden).* Small basement venue, often packed with tourists but also hosting good bands.

Underworld *(Map 3; ☎ 7482 1932, 174 Camden High St NW1; ⊖ Camden Town).* Beneath the huge World's End pub, a small venue featuring new bands.

JAZZ

London has always had a thriving jazz scene and, with its recent resurgence thanks to acid-jazz, hip-hop, funk and swing, it's stronger than ever.

Jazz Café *(Map 3; ☎ 7916 6060, 5 Parkway NW1; ⊖ Camden Town).* Very trendy restaurant venue; it's best to book a table. Acts cost from £8 to £15 at the door, cheaper in advance.

100 Club *(Map 7; ☎ 7636 0933, 100 Oxford St W1; ⊖ Oxford Circus).* Legendary London venue, once showcasing the Stones and at the centre of the punk revolution and now concentrating on jazz (tickets from £6 to £10). Once a month it hosts a Northern Soul all-nighter that is said to be the best dancing venue in London.

Pizza Express Jazz Club *(Map 7; ☎ 7439 8722, 10 Dean St W1; ⊖ Tottenham Court Road).* A small basement venue beneath the main restaurant.

Pizza on the Park *(Map 6; ☎ 7235 5273, 11-13 Knightsbridge SW5; ⊖ Hyde Park Corner).* Nightly jazz in the basement.

Ronnie Scott's *(Map 7; ☎ 7439 0747, 47 Frith St W1; ⊖ Leicester Square).* Operating since 1959; seedy and enjoyable but expensive if you're not a member (£50 a year): entry is from £5 to £9 for members, £9 for students (Monday to Wednesday only).

FOLK, TRADITIONAL & WORLD MUSIC

Places well worth checking out include:

Africa Centre *(Map 7; ☎ 7836 1973, 38 King St WC2; ⊖ Covent Garden).* African music concerts on Friday and other one-offs on other nights of the week.

Cecil Sharp House *(Map 3; ☎ 7485 2206, 2 Regent's Park Rd NW1; ⊖ Camden Town).* The headquarters of the English Folk Song & Dance Society, this is *the* venue for English folk music (an acquired taste, it must be said) – especially on Tuesday at 8 pm – as well as other such esoteric fare as barn and clog dancing, Cajun fiddling, Irish set-dancing and Balkan circle-dancing.

Mean Fiddler *(☎ 8961 5490, 22-24 High St NW10; ⊖ Willesden Junction).* Legendary venue for top-quality acoustic folk, Irish and country.

Swan *(Brixton map, page 287; ☎ 7978 9778, 215 Clapham Rd SW9; ⊖ Stockwell).* Traditional Irish music most nights.

CLASSICAL MUSIC

London is Europe's classical-music capital, with five symphony orchestras, various

ENTERTAINMENT

smaller outfits, brilliant venues, reasonable prices and high standards of performance.

There's so much on that you may have trouble deciding what to pick. On any night of the year the choice will range from traditional crowd-pleasers to new music and 'difficult' composers. Opera can be more problematic because it's costly to produce and consequently tickets are pricey.

South Bank

The *Royal Festival Hall*, *Queen Elizabeth Hall* and *Purcell Room* (*Map 6;* ☎ *7960 4242, 7921 0600;* ⊖ *Waterloo*) are three of London's premier venues for classical concerts – though the last two may disappear without a trace (see the South Bank section in the Things to See & Do chapter). Depending on who's performing and where you sit, prices vary from £5 to £50, but they are usually in the £12.50 to £30 range. The box office is open from 9 am to 9 pm daily (on Sunday from 9.30 am).

Wigmore Hall

The Art Nouveau *Wigmore Hall* (*Map 6;* ☎ *7935 2141, 36 Wigmore St W1;* ⊖ *Bond Street*), one of the best concert venues in London, offers a great variety of concerts and recitals. The Sunday recitals at 11.30 am (from £7) are particularly good. There are Monday lunch-time concerts (from £7 to £16) at 1 pm.

Barbican

The *Barbican* (*Map 8;* ☎ *7638 8891, Silk St EC2;* ⊖ *Barbican*) is home to the London Symphony Orchestra. Prices can go as high as £32 but stand-by tickets for £6.50 and £9 are sometimes available just before the performance to students and over-60s.

Royal Albert Hall

The *Royal Albert Hall* (*Map 5;* ☎ *7589 8212, Kensington Gore SW7;* ⊖ *South Kensington*) is a splendid-looking Victorian concert hall that hosts all kinds of performances, usually costing from £5 to £40.

Superb music by the bucketful with just a splash of flag-waving patriotism thrown in: the Proms at the Royal Albert Hall every summer.

From mid-July to mid-September it stages the Proms – one of the world's biggest and most democratic classical-music festivals. Seats cost from £5 to £32 depending on what's on, but the real Prom experience means queuing for one of the thousand or so standing (or 'promenading') tickets that go on sale one hour before the start of each concert for £3 each. You can choose to be in the gallery or the arena; there are two separate queues. The box office (door No 7; collect pre-paid tickets at door No 9) is open daily from 9 am to 9 pm.

Kenwood House

A highlight of a sunny summer is to go to an outdoor concert in the grounds of **Kenwood House** (Map 11; ☎ 7413 1443; ⊖ Archway or Golders Green, then bus No 210) on Hampstead Heath. People sit on the grass or on deck chairs, eat strawberries, drink chilled white wine and listen to classical music on a number of weekend evenings in July and August. Entry costs £11 to sit on the grass and £16 for a deck chair.

Churches

Many churches host evening concerts or lunch-time recitals. Sometimes they're free, with a suggested donation requested; at other times there's a charge. A few redundant churches now serve as concert halls.

All Hallows-by-the-Tower (Map 8; ☎ 7481 2928, Byward St EC3; ⊖ Tower Bridge). Organ recitals usually on Thursday at 1.15 pm; donation requested.

St George's Bloomsbury (Map 7; ☎ 7405 3044, Bloomsbury Way WC1; ⊖ Tottenham Court Road or Holborn). Tuesday lunch-time concerts usually at 1.10 pm; donation requested. Sunday evening concerts at 5.20 pm (£2).

St James's Piccadilly (Map 7; ☎ 7734 4511, 197 Piccadilly W1; ⊖ Piccadilly Circus). Daily lunch-time concerts at 1.10 pm; donation requested. Evening concerts at 7.30 pm cost from £7.50 to £15.

St John's, Smith Square (Map 2; ☎ 7222 1061, Smith Square SW1; ⊖ Westminster). Lunch-time concerts on Monday at 1 pm (£6). Evening concerts start at 7.30 pm; tickets cost from £6 to £18.

St Martin-in-the-Fields: 'royal parish church', popular café and music venue.

St Lawrence Jewry (Map 8; ☎ 7600 9478, 7344 9214, Gresham St EC2; ⊖ Bank). Piano recitals on Monday, organ recitals on Tuesday at 1 pm. Evening concerts at 7.30 pm; tickets £6.

St Martin-in-the-Fields (Map 7; ☎ 7930 0089, Trafalgar Square WC2; ⊖ Charing Cross). Lunch-time concerts on Monday, Tuesday and Friday at 1.05 pm; donations requested. Evening concerts (☎ 7839 8362) by candlelight Thursday to Saturday at 7.30 pm (tickets from £6 to £15).

St Paul's Cathedral (Map 8; ☎ 7236 4128; ⊖ St Paul's). Organ recitals on Sunday at 5 pm.

Southwark Cathedral (Map 8; ☎ 7407 3708, Montague Close SE1; ⊖ London Bridge). Lunch-time organ recitals take place on Monday at 1.10 pm; other music recitals on Tuesday at 1.10 pm.

Temple Church (Map 6; ☎ 7353 1736, 7353 8559, Inner Temple, King's Bench Walk EC4; ⊖ Temple, or Blackfriars on Sunday). Lunch-time concerts on Wednesday at 1.15 pm.

ENTERTAINMENT

JULIET COOMBE

From Leicester Square, for both home-grown
and Hollywood blockbusters ...

... to the Ritzy in Brixton, one of the most
popular of London's repertory cinemas.

CINEMAS

During the 1950s and 1960s many of London's great Art Deco cinemas shut down. The late 1980s saw the coming of the first multiplex cinemas and the revival continues to this day. Although these cinemas offer more choice of films at one site and much more comfortable seating arrangements, they also tend to be expensive and serve up primarily mainstream American fare. Although full-price tickets can cost from £8 to £10 for a first-run film, afternoon shows are usually cheaper on weekdays, and on Monday several places offer half-price tickets all day.

For less mainstream fare the following central London cinemas are the most promising:

Barbican (☎ 7382 7000, 7638 8891, Silk St EC2; ✪ Barbican)

Curzon Mayfair (☎ 7369 1720, 38 Curzon St W1; ✪ Hyde Park Corner)

Curzon Minema (☎ 7369 1723, 45 Knightsbridge SW1; ✪ Knightsbridge)

Curzon Soho (☎ 7734 2255, 93-107 Shaftesbury Ave W1; ✪ Leicester Square)

Everyman (☎ 0845 606 2345, Holly Bush Vale NW3; ✪ Hampstead)

Gate (☎ 7727 4043, Notting Hill Gate W1; ✪ Notting Hill Gate)

ICA (☎ 7930 3647, The Mall SW1; ✪ Charing Cross)

Lux (☎ 7684 0201, 2-4 Hoxton Square N1; ✪ Old Street)

National Film Theatre (☎ 7928 3232, 7633 0274 for a recording, South Bank; ✪ Embankment or Waterloo)

Renoir (☎ 7837 8402, Brunswick Square WC1; ✪ Russell Square)

Rio (☎ 7254 6677, 107 Kingsland High St E8; Dalston Kingsland station)

Ritzy (☎ 7737 2121, Brixton Oval, Coldharbour Lane SW2; ✪ Brixton)

Riverside Studios (☎ 7420 0100, 8237 1111 for a recording, Crisp Rd W6; ✪ Hammersmith)

Screen on Baker St (☎ 7935 2772, 96 Baker St NW1; ✪ Baker Street)

Screen on the Green (☎ 7226 3520, Islington Green N1; ✪ Angel)

Screen on the Hill (☎ 7435 3366, 203 Haverstock Hill NW3; ✪ Belsize Park)

The Prince Charles (Map 7; ☎ 0800 192192, 7437 8181 for a recording, Leicester Place WC2; ✪ Leicester Square) is central London's cheapest cinema, with tickets for new-release films for only £2 to £2.50. It shows several films each day so check the programme carefully; visit its Web site at www.cyborg.org/pcc for details. For French-language films, visit the ***Ciné Lumière*** at the French Institute (Map 9; ☎ 7838 2144, 17 Queensberry Place SW7; ✪ South Kensington).

An ambitious refurbishment of the Edwardian ***Electric Cinema*** (Map 5; 191 Portobello Rd W11), the oldest purpose-built cinema in the UK, began in early 1999 and it may now have reopened with a new three-storey annexe, 200 comfy seats, a bar and a bookshop.

Night fever: indulging in 70s kitsch in the West End.

From innovation to the classics: thespian excellence at the Royal National Theatre.

THEATRE

London is one of the world's great centres for theatre-lovers, and there's a lot more here than just *Cats*, *Rent* and *Phantom of the Opera*. With tickets so plentiful and reasonably priced, it would be a shame not to take in at least one or two of the best productions.

Booking Agencies

Most theatre box-offices are open Monday to Saturday from something like 10 am to 8 pm. If the production is sold out you may be able to buy a returned ticket on the day of the performance, although for something really popular you might need to start queuing before the returns actually go on sale.

On the day of performance you can buy half-price tickets for West End productions (for cash only) from the Leicester Square Half-Price Ticket Booth, on the south side of Leicester Square (Map 7; ✆ Leicester Square). It is the one with the clocktower – beware of imitations that may rip you off. It opens daily from noon to 6.30 pm and charges £2 commission per ticket. Note that you can't buy tickets for musicals like *Cats* and *Starlight Express* here nor for Agatha Christie's long-running *The Mousetrap*. Be particularly wary of commercial ticket agencies near Leicester Square that advertise half-price tickets without mentioning the commission added to the price.

Student stand-by tickets are sometimes available on production of identity cards one hour before the performance starts. Phone the Student Theatre Line on ✆ 7379 8900 for more details.

The Society of London Theatre (✆ 7836 0971) offers the following advice for people buying tickets from an agency:

- Find out the normal prices for the show first.
- Ask the agent what the ticket's face value is and how much commission is being added.
- Ask to be shown where you'll be sitting on a seat plan.
- Don't pay for the tickets until you've actually seen them and checked the face value.
- Don't agree to pick the tickets up later or have them sent to you.

Royal National Theatre

The nation's flagship theatre is the newly renovated *Royal National Theatre (Map 6; ✆ 7452 3000, South Bank; ✆ Waterloo)*, with three auditoriums: the Olivier, the Lyttleton and the Cottesloe. It showcases classics and contemporary plays, and hosts appearances by the world's best companies.

Tickets for evening performances at the Olivier and Lyttleton cost from £10 to £32.50. Visitors to the box office can sometimes buy one or two tickets for same-day performances for £10 or £12.50. Stand-by tickets are sometimes available two hours before the performance for £14; students with ID pay just £7.50 but must wait until

45 minutes before the curtain goes up. You can save money by going to a weekday matinee performance, when prices range from £9 to £18.50.

Under-18s pay from £8 to £10 for matinees and seniors from £11 to £12.50. Registered disabled visitors are eligible for discounts at all performances.

Most tickets at the smaller Cottesloe cost £20, although some seats with restricted views cost £12.

Barbican

The **Barbican** *(Map 8;* ☎ *7638 8891, Silk St EC2;* ❷ *Barbican)* is the London home of the Royal Shakespeare Company, with two auditoriums – the Barbican Theatre and the smaller Pit. Midweek matinee tickets are from £5 to £28 at the Barbican and £12 to £20 at the Pit. Tickets are half-price for anyone aged under 25 on the day of the performance. There are also price reductions for anyone aged over 60 at matinees and Wednesday evening performances.

Royal Court

The **Royal Court** *(Map 9;* ☎ *7565 5000;* ❷ *Sloane Square)* has returned to its home on the eastern side of Sloane Square

Spoilt for choice: as much theatre as you could wish for on Shaftesbury Avenue.

following a four-year, £25 million refurbishment, during which time the company operated out of the Duke of York's and Ambassadors theatres. It tends to favour the new and the anti-establishment – various *enfants terribles*, from John Osborne to Caryl Churchill, got their start here.

Globe Theatre

The **Globe Theatre** *(Map 8;* ☎ *7401 9919, 21 New Globe Walk SE1;* ❷ *London Bridge)*, a replica of Shakespeare's 'Wooden O' that opened in 1997, now dominates Bankside where several Elizabethan theatres once stood. Come here for a very different theatrical experience. Although there are wooden-bench seats in tiers around the stage, many people emulate the 17th-century 'groundlings' who stood in front of the stage, shouting, cajoling and moving around as the mood took them. The Globe makes few concessions to modern sensibilities. With no roof, it is open to the elements; you should wrap up warmly and bring a flask (thermos), although no umbrellas are allowed. Performances of plays by Shakespeare and his contemporaries are staged from May to September only. Two pillars holding up the stage canopy (the 'Heavens') obscure much of the view in section D; you'd almost do better to stand.

Tickets for seats cost from £10 to £25. The 500 standing spaces per performance cost £5 each and can be booked, although you may find a few unsold on the day. The box office is open Monday to Saturday from 10 am to 8 pm (to 6 pm when the theatre is closed). The theatre's Web site at www.shakespeares-globe.org is worth checking out.

West End Theatres

Every summer the dozens of West End theatres stage a new crop of plays, musicals and other performances. For full details, consult *Time Out*. Addresses and box office phone numbers of the West End theatres are given below; all are on Map 7:

Adelphi (☎ *7344 0055, Strand WC2;* ❷ *Charing Cross)*

Albery (☎ 7369 1740, St Martin's Lane WC2; ⊖ Leicester Square)

Aldwych (☎ 7416 6075, Aldwych WC2; ⊖ Holborn)

Ambassadors (☎ 7836 6111, West St WC2; ⊖ Leicester Square)

Apollo (☎ 7494 5070, Shaftesbury Ave W1; ⊖ Piccadilly Circus)

Cambridge (☎ 7494 5083, Earlham St WC2; ⊖ Covent Garden)

Comedy (☎ 7369 1741, Panton St SW1; ⊖ Piccadilly Circus)

Criterion (☎ 7369 1737, Piccadilly Circus W1; ⊖ Piccadilly Circus)

Dominion (☎ 7656 1857, Tottenham Court Rd W1; ⊖ Tottenham Court Road)

Drury Lane (☎ 7494 5000, Theatre Royal, Catherine St WC2; ⊖ Covent Garden)

Duchess (☎ 7494 5075, Catherine St WC2; ⊖ Covent Garden)

Duke of York's (☎ 7565 5000, St Martin's Lane WC2; ⊖ Leicester Square)

Fortune (☎ 7836 2238, Russell St WC2; ⊖ Covent Garden)

Garrick (☎ 7494 5085, Charing Cross Rd WC2; ⊖ Charing Cross)

Gielgud (☎ 7494 5065, Shaftesbury Ave W1; ⊖ Piccadilly Circus)

Haymarket (☎ 7930 8800, Haymarket SW1; ⊖ Piccadilly Circus)

Her Majesty's (☎ 7494 5400, Haymarket SW1; ⊖ Piccadilly Circus)

London Palladium (☎ 7494 5030, 1-4 Argyll St W1; ⊖ Oxford Circus)

Lyceum (☎ 7656 1800, Wellington St WC2; ⊖ Covent Garden)

Lyric (☎ 7494 5045, Shaftesbury Ave W1; ⊖ Piccadilly Circus)

New London (☎ 7405 0072, Drury Lane WC2; ⊖ Holborn)

Palace (☎ 7434 0909, Shaftesbury Ave W1; ⊖ Leicester Square)

Phoenix (☎ 7369 1733, Charing Cross Rd WC2; ⊖ Tottenham Court Road)

Piccadilly (☎ 7369 1734, Denman St W1; ⊖ Piccadilly Circus)

Prince Edward (☎ 7447 5400, Old Compton St W1; ⊖ Leicester Square)

Prince of Wales (☎ 7839 5987, Coventry St W1; ⊖ Piccadilly Circus)

Queen's (☎ 7494 5040, Shaftesbury Ave W1; ⊖ Piccadilly Circus)

St Martin's (☎ 7836 1443, West St WC2; ⊖ Leicester Square)

Shaftesbury (☎ 7379 5399, 210 Shaftesbury Ave WC2; ⊖ Tottenham Court Road or Holborn)

The Palace Theatre, home of Les Misérables.

Savoy (☎ 7836 8888, Strand WC2; ⊖ Charing Cross)

Strand (☎ 7930 8800, Aldwych WC2; ⊖ Covent Garden)

Vaudeville (☎ 7836 9987, Strand WC2; ⊖ Charing Cross)

Wyndham's (☎ 7369 1736, Charing Cross Rd WC2; ⊖ Leicester Square)

Other Theatres

On a sunny day it's fun to take in a Shakespearean play or musical at the *Open Air Theatre* (Map 3; ☎ 7486 2431; ⊖ Baker Street) in Regent's Park.

And as if all of that wasn't enough, at any time of the year London's many off-West End and fringe theatre productions offer a selection of the amazing, the boring, the life-enhancing and the downright ridiculous. Some of the better venues include:

Almeida (Map 4; ☎ 7359 4404, Almeida St N1; ⊖ Angel or Highbury & Islington)

CHARLOTTE HINDLE

A night at the opera: the Coliseum is just a short stroll up from Trafalgar Square.

Bridewell Theatre (Map 6; ☎ 7936 3456, Bride Lane, Fleet St EC4; ✚ Blackfriars)
Donmar Warehouse (Map 7; ☎ 7369 1732, Earlham St WC2; ✚ Covent Garden)
Hampstead Theatre (Map 2; ☎ 7722 9301, 98 Avenue Rd NW3; ✚ Swiss Cottage)
King's Head Islington (Map 4; ☎ 7226 1916, 115 Upper St N1; ✚ Highbury & Islington)
Old Vic (Map 6; ☎ 7494 5372, Waterloo Rd SE1; ✚ Waterloo)
Tricycle Theatre (Map 2; ☎ 7328 1000, 269 Kilburn High Rd NW6; ✚ Kilburn)
Young Vic (Map 6; ☎ 7369 1736, 66 The Cut SE1; ✚ Waterloo)

OPERA
Royal Opera House
Following a £213 million redevelopment, the *Royal Opera House (Map 7; ☎ 7304 4000, Covent Garden WC2; ✚ Covent Garden)* has reopened and has welcomed home the peripatetic Royal Opera and Royal Ballet. As a result of the makeover, it has become much more proletarian: the renovated Floral Hall is now open to the public during the day, with free lunch-time concerts, exhibitions and daily tours. For the best seats, you'll still need to consider a second mortgage (up to a staggering £150 for opera, £60 for ballet) although a not-so-good seat can be had for as little as £6. The cheapest seats with clear views of the stage range from about £7.50 to £29.

Coliseum
The home of the English National Opera, the *Coliseum (Map 7; ☎ 7632 8300, St Martin's Lane WC1; ✚ Leicester Square)* is a lot more reasonably priced than the Royal Opera House (from £5 to £55) and presents opera in English. From 10 am on the day of performance balcony seats with a restricted view go on sale for £2.50 (it's £27 in the dress circle); expect a long queue.

BALLET & DANCE
London is home to five major dance companies and a host of small and experimental ones. The Royal Ballet, the best classical-ballet company in the UK, led a nomadic existence for a few years during redevelopment of the Royal Opera House in Covent Garden but will have returned home by the time you read this.

Sadler's Wells (Map 4; ☎ 7863 8000, Rosebery Ave EC1; ✚ Angel), which reopened in 1998 after a total refurbishment, has been associated with dance ever since Thomas Sadler set up a 'musick house' next to his medicinal spa in 1683. Its new, ultramodern theatre attracts contemporary and classical-dance troupes from around the world. Its second venue, the *Peacock Theatre (Map 7; ☎ 7863 8222, Portugal St WC2; ✚ Holborn)*, will now host the London Contemporary Dance Theatre and London City Ballet.

Riverside Studios and the *ICA* (see the previous Cinemas section) are the most important venues for small experimental and avant-garde dance companies. Another important address is *The Place (☎ 7387 0031, 17 Duke's Rd WC1; ✚ Euston)*, home to the Richard Alston Dance Company.

The annual contemporary dance event in London is Dance Umbrella (see Special Events in the Facts for the Visitor chapter) in October and early November. For more information about dance in the capital visit the London Dance Network's Web site at www.london-dance.net.

ORGANISED ENTERTAINMENT
Inevitably there are a few places where you can do the full tourist thing over a themed dinner, with entertainment, food and drink all laid on for one all-inclusive price. Here are a few of the better ones:

London Entertains *(Map 6; ☎ 7387 2414, Embassy Rooms, 161 Tottenham Court Rd W1; ⊖ Warren Street).* Singing, dancing, comedy and music from the best of the West End shows on Wednesday and Saturday at 6.30 pm (£34.50).

Talk of London *(Map 7; ☎ 7405 0072, New London Theatre, Drury Lane WC2; ⊖ Holborn).* Dinner and cabaret Thursday to Saturday at 7.30 pm (£37.50).

Medieval Banquet *(Map 8; ☎ 7480 5353, Ivory House, St Katharine's Dock E1; ⊖ Tower Hill).* Five course medieval banquet, with jesters, fighting knights, minstrels and serving wenches. Doors open daily at 7.45 pm and the show (from £37.50 to £39.50 depending on the night and £22 for kids aged under 12) begins half an hour later.

It's also possible to go on a lunch or dinner cruise on the Thames, complete with dancing and live music. Bateaux London (☎ 7925 2215) offers lunch cruises on Friday and Saturday for £20, dinner-dance cruises daily for £56 and Sunday lunch cruises for £27.50. The lunch cruises board at 12.15 pm, the dinner cruises at 7.15 pm. Departures are from Embankment Pier.

Catamaran Cruises (☎ 7839 3572) does Captain's Table dinner cruises on Wednesday, Friday and Sunday (8 pm) from May to September. They cost £35 and depart from Embankment Pier. Four-hour weekend disco cruises kick off at 7 pm on Friday and Saturday and cost £12.50 a head.

City Cruises (☎ 7237 5134) offers a London Showboat dinner cruise for £42,

departing from Westminster Pier, early April to October, from Wednesday to Sunday at 7 pm and returning at 10.30 pm. From November to early April cruises leave on Friday and Saturday only. A four-hour evening disco cruise with Thames Cruises (☎ 7928 9009) from Westminster Pier goes weekdays at 7 pm and on Saturday at 8 pm. It costs £13/10 with/without food Monday to Thursday and £16.65/12 on Friday and Saturday.

SPECTATOR SPORTS
London plays host to an infinite number of sporting events year-round. As always *Time Out* is the best source of information on fixtures, times, venues and ticket prices.

Football
Wembley Stadium (☎ 8902 8833), where the English national side has traditionally played international matches and the FA Cup Final has taken place in mid-May, will close in August 2000 and the present building (1923) with its two landmark towers will be demolished. It will be replaced by a state-of-the-art, 80,000-seat national stadium designed by Norman Foster to be used for football, rugby league and athletics. The new £310 million stadium's coming-out will – hopefully – be the World Athletics Championships in 2003; the football World Cup may also be held here in 2006. In the meantime, for details of tours see Wembley Stadium in the Things to See & Do chapter.

There are a dozen league teams in London and usually around six enjoy the big time of the Premier League, meaning that on any weekend of the season, from August to mid-May, quality football is just a tube or train ride away.

These are the current Premier Leaguers in and around London (although tickets for Arsenal, Chelsea, Tottenham Hotspur and West Ham United are almost always sold out well in advance):

Arsenal *(Map 1; ☎ 7704 4040, Avenell Rd N5; ⊖ Arsenal).* Tickets cost from £15 to £34; for credit card bookings ring ☎ 7413 3366.

MARK HONAN

Cricket is played at all levels in London, from local fixtures on open spaces, such as Kew Green, to international test matches.

Chelsea (Map 9; ☎ *7385 5545, Stamford Bridge, Fulham Rd SW6;* ⊖ *Fulham Broadway).* Tickets cost from £10 to £28; for credit card bookings call ☎ 7386 7799. Ground tours take place daily at 11 am and 1 and 3 pm and cost £7/4.50 for adults/seniors & children.

Tottenham Hotspur (Map 1; ☎ *8365 5000, White Hart Lane N17; White Hart Lane station).* Tickets cost from £27 to £46; for credit card bookings call ☎ 0870 840 2468.

Watford (☎ *01923-496000, Vicarage Rd, Watford;* ⊖ *Watford).* Tickets cost £20; for credit card bookings ring ☎ 01923-496010.

West Ham United (Map 1; ☎ *8548 2748, Green St E13;* ⊖ *Upton Park).* Tickets cost from £22 to £35; for credit card bookings ring ☎ 8548 2700.

Wimbledon (☎ *8771 2233, Selhurst Park, Park Rd SE25; Norwood Junction or Selhurst station).* Tickets cost from £16 to £25; for credit card bookings call ☎ 8771 8841.

Cricket
Cricket continues to flourish, despite the dismal fortunes of the England team. Test matches take place at two cricket grounds: *Lord's (Map 3;* ☎ *7289 1300, St John's Wood Rd NW8;* ⊖ *St John's Wood)* and *The Oval (Map 2;* ☎ *7582 6660, Kennington Oval SE11;* ⊖ *Oval).* Tickets are expensive (from £15 to £45) and tend to go fast; you're better off looking out for a county fixture (from £8 to £10). Middlesex plays at Lord's, Surrey plays at The Oval.

For details of tours of Lord's, see Lord's Cricket Ground under St John's Wood & Maida Vale in the Things to See & Do chapter.

Rugby Union & League
For rugby union fans south-west London is the place to be, with a number of good-quality teams like Harlequins, Richmond and Wasps. Each year, starting in January, England, Scotland, Wales, Ireland, France and Italy compete in the Six Nations championship; this guarantees two or three big matches at *Twickenham Rugby Stadium (Map 1;* ☎ *8892 2000, Rugby Rd, Twickenham;* ⊖ *Hounslow East, then bus No 281; Twickenham station),* the shrine of English rugby union. For details of tours of the stadium and its museum, see the Richmond & Twickenham section in the Things to See & Do chapter.

The London Broncos (☎ 8410 5000), Stoop Memorial Ground, Craneford Way, Twickenham (Twickenham station), is the only rugby league side in southern England.

Tennis
Tennis and *Wimbledon (*☎ *8944 1066, 8946 2244 for a recording;* ⊖ *Southfields or Wimbledon Park)* are almost synonymous; the All-England Lawn Tennis Championships

have been taking place here every June since 1877. But the queues, exorbitant prices, limited ticket availability and cramped conditions may have you thinking Wimbledon is just a – well – racket. Although a limited number of seats for the Centre Court and Court Nos 1 and 2 go on sale on the day of play, the queues are painfully long. The nearer to the finals it is, the higher the prices; a Centre Court ticket that costs £25 a week before the final will cost twice that on the day. Prices for the outside courts cost less than £10 and are reduced (£5) after 5 pm. For the latest on the championships ring the LTB's Visitorcall on 09064 123417.

Between 1 September and 31 December each year there's a public ballot for tickets for the best seats at the following year's tournament. Between those dates you can send a stamped addressed envelope to the All England Lawn Tennis & Croquet Club, PO Box 98, Church Rd, Wimbledon SW19 5AE, to try your luck.

Athletics

Athletics and swimming meetings attracting major international and domestic stars take place regularly throughout the summer at the *Crystal Palace National Sports Centre (Map 1; ☎ 8778 0131, Ledrington Rd SE19; Crystal Palace station)*. Tickets start at £10.

Racing

If you're looking for a cheap and thrilling night out, consider sampling greyhound racing. Entry to 'the dogs' costs as little as £2 to £4.50 for a 12-race meeting. A few small bets will mean guaranteed excitement, and you'll rub shoulders with a London subculture that's gregarious and more than a little shady:

Catford Stadium (Map 1; ☎ 8690 2240, Adenmore Rd SE6; Catford Bridge station)
Walthamstow Stadium (Map 1; ☎ 7531 4255, Chingford Rd E4; Highams Park station)
Wimbledon Stadium (☎ 8946 8000, Plough Lane SE19; ⊖ Wimbledon Park)

Alternatively, there's horse racing with plenty of top-quality courses within striking distance of London. In June Ascot (☎ 01344-622211) in Berkshire can be nice if rather posh. On Derby Day in June Epsom (☎ 01372-470047) in Surrey can be a crushing experience in more ways than one. Sandown Park (☎ 01372-463072), also in Surrey, is another top racecourse. Windsor (☎ 01753-865234), by the castle and the Thames, is an idyllic spot for an afternoon of racing and a summer evening picnic, about 2.5km (1½ miles) west of the town centre. There are also plans to build a new £50 million racecourse to the north-east of London at Fairlop Waters.

Shopping

Napoleon described Britain as a nation of shopkeepers, but as standardised chain stores decimate the small shops along the high streets, it would be more accurate to say that it's now a nation of shoppers. Indeed, shopping is one of London's most popular recreational pastimes.

WHAT TO BUY

London is a mecca for shopaholics from around the UK and continental Europe, and if you can't find it here, it probably doesn't exist.

If you're looking for something with a British 'brand' on it, eschew the Union Jack-emblazoned kitsch of Carnaby and Oxford Sts and go for things that the Brits themselves know are of good quality, sometimes stylish and always solid: Dr Marten boots and shoes, Burberry raincoats and umbrellas, tailor-made shorts from Jermyn St and costume jewellery (be it for the finger, wrist, nose, eyebrow or navel). London's music stores and especially bookshops are celebrated on the street and in literature; many cater for the most obscure of tastes. And the word 'antique' does not always have to be prefaced by 'priceless'; you'll find any number of interesting and affordable curios and baubles at the Antiquarius Antiques Centre in Chelsea and Bermondsey Market.

In general, shops open Monday to Saturday from 9 or 10 am to about 6 or 6.30 pm, with the usual 'late night' (to 8 pm) on Thursday. A growing number of stores open on Sunday, most typically from noon to 6 pm but sometimes from 10 am to 4 pm. Shoppers who can't get enough should buy the annual *Time Out Shopping Guide* (£7), with details of virtually every shopping opportunity in the capital.

Antiques

Antique hunters may find something worthwhile at the Saturday antiques market along Portobello Rd, but better pickings are to be had at Camden Passage or Bermondsey Market (see the special section 'The Markets of London' after this chapter). For a truly specialist antique shop try Sean Arnold Sporting Antiques (Map 5; ☎ 7221 2267), 21-22 Chepstow Corner W2 (⊖ Bayswater), for pricey old toys for grown-up boys.

Antiquarius Antiques Centre Antiquarius (Map 9; ☎ 7969 1500), 131 King's Rd SW3 (⊖ Sloane Square), is packed with 120 stalls and dealers selling everything from top hats and corkscrews to old luggage and jewellery. It's definitely worth a look.

Chelsea Old Town Hall This solid pile (Map 9) built on King's Rd in 1886 is the venue for a popular antiques fair one Sunday a month from 11 am to 5.30 pm. For information and the exact date, ring ☎ 01225-723094.

London Architectural Salvage & Supply LASSCO (Map 4; ☎ 7739 0448), St Michael's Church, Mark St EC2 (⊖ Old

CHARLOTTE HINDLE

These boots were made for walking: foot fashion on Camden High St.

From bric-a-brac and knick-knacks
in Kensington ...

... to weighty tomes and ancient maps
in Greenwich.

Street), is a recycler's dream come true, with everything from slate tiles and oak floorboards to enormous marble fireplaces and garden follies. Its location, in an old church, is worth the trip alone.

London Silver Vaults The 72 subterranean shops in Chancery House, 53-63 Chancery Lane WC2, collectively known as the London Silver Vaults (Map 6; ☎ 7242 3844; ✆ Chancery Lane), form the largest collection of silver under one roof in the world. The shops sell anything and everything made from silver – from jewellery and picture frames to candelabra and tea services for a dozen people. Though everything is for sale, you might just want to ogle at some of the merchandise – much of it seriously over the top – and wonder which stately home it came from.

Books
General For those who read the book or saw the film *84 Charing Cross Road*, Charing Cross Rd (Map 7; ✆ Tottenham Court Road or Leicester Square) will need no introduction. This is where to go when you want reading material old or new.

Foyle's (☎ 7437 5660), 113-119 Charing Cross Rd WC2, is the biggest and by far the most confusing bookshop in London, but it often stocks titles you may not find elsewhere. Much better organised is Waterstone's (☎ 7434 4291), 121-129 Charing Cross Rd WC2, a chain that has transformed book buying for Londoners with its knowledgeable staff. Its new mega-branch (Map 7; ☎ 7851 2400), the biggest bookshop in Europe, is at 203-206 Piccadilly W1 (✆ Piccadilly Circus); there's also a branch in Bloomsbury (Map 6; ☎ 7636

1577) at 82 Gower St WC1 (⊖ Goodge Street). Blackwell's (☎ 7292 5100), 100 Charing Cross Rd WC2, has a lot of academic titles but stocks general books as well.

Close to Oxford Circus is Borders (Map 7; ☎ 7292 1600), 203 Oxford St W1 (⊖ Oxford Circus), the big American chain with three floors of books, magazines and newspapers from around the world and a coffee shop/bar in which to read them. There's a smaller branch at 120 Charing Cross Rd WC2 (☎ 7292 1600), with a great selection of general titles as well as academic ones.

One of the best places for half-price second-hand books is the book market on the South Bank under the arches of Waterloo Bridge (Map 6). It's open at weekends from 10 am to 5 pm, though a few stalls open throughout the week.

Specialist There are also plenty of specialist bookshops on or around Charing Cross Rd (Map 7), from the self-explanatory Sportspages (☎ 7240 9604) at Nos 94 to 96, and Murder One (☎ 7734 3485) at Nos 71 to 73 for crime fiction, to Silver Moon (☎ 7836 7906) at Nos 64 to 68 for anything by or about women and Zwemmer (☎ 7379 7886), 24 Litchfield St WC2, for all kinds of art book. Helter Skelter (☎ 7836 1151), 4 Denmark St WC2, specialises in popular music.

Charing Cross Rd's bookshops are always worth dipping into, whatever your interests.

Farther afield, Gay's the Word (Map 4; ☎ 7278 7654), 66 Marchmont St WC1 (⊖ Russell Square), stocks guides and literature for, by and about gay men and women. Compendium (Map 3; ☎ 7485 8944), 234 Camden High St NW1 (⊖ Camden Town), focuses on left-wing and alternative titles. Books for Cooks (Map 5; ☎ 7221 1992), 4 Blenheim Crescent W11 (⊖ Ladbroke Grove), has an enormous collection of cookery books; there's also a small café where you can sample some of the recipes. The train-spotter in you won't be able to resist Ian Allan (Map 6; ☎ 7401 2100), 45-46 Lower Marsh SE1 (⊖ Waterloo), which specialises in transport and defence: aircraft, motor vehicles and, of course, trains.

Positively the best foreign-language bookshop in London – for books in or about everything from Arabic to Zulu – is Grant & Cutler (Map 7; ☎ 7734 2012), 55-57 Great Marlborough St W1 (⊖ Oxford Circus). For books *en français* and about France, head for the French Bookshop (Map 9; ☎ 7584 2840), 28 Bute St SW7 (⊖ South Kensington). Al Saqi Books (Map 5; ☎ 7229 8543), 26 Westbourne Grove W2 (⊖ Bayswater), in a beautiful building topped with a dozen busts, specialises in second-hand books in English about the Middle East and Islam and new books in Arabic.

The major chains are adequate sources of guidebooks and maps, but there are also several specialist travel bookshops:

Beaumont Travel Books (Map 7; ☎ 7637 5862), 31 Museum St WC1 (⊖ Tottenham Court Road or Holborn). This is arguably the best place for antiquarian travel books.

Daunt Books (Map 6; ☎ 7224 2295), 83 Marylebone High St W1 (⊖ Baker Street). Daunt has a wide selection of travel guides and books on other subjects in a beautiful old sky-lit shop.

Stanford's (Map 7; ☎ 7836 1321), 12-14 Long Acre WC2 (⊖ Covent Garden). Stanford's has one of the largest selections of maps, guides and travel literature in the world. It has a smaller branch at British Airways (Map 7; ☎ 7434 4744), 156 Regent St W1 (⊖ Piccadilly Circus).

Travel Bookshop (Map 5; ☎ 7229 5260), 13 Blenheim Crescent W11 (☉ Ladbroke Grove). This is London's best 'boutique' travel bookshop and was apparently the inspiration for the shop in *Notting Hill*. It has all the new guides, plus out-of-print and antiquarian gems.

Camping & Backpacking Equipment

The YHA Adventure Shop (Map 7; ☎ 7836 8541), 14 Southampton St WC2 (☉ Covent Garden), is an excellent place to stock up on all sorts of camping and walking gear. There's a branch (Map 5; ☎ 7938 2948) at 174 Kensington High St W8 (☉ High Street Kensington).

The national Camping & Outdoor Centre chain has two branches in London, one in the City (Map 6; ☎ 7329 8757) at 41 Ludgate Hill EC4 (☉ Blackfriars) and another in Pimlico (☎ 7834 6007) at 27 Buckingham Palace Rd SW1 (Map 10; ☉ Victoria). Taunton Leisure (☎ 7924 3838), 557-561 Battersea Park Rd SW11 (Clapham Junction station), also has a good reputation. Nomad Traveller's Store & Medical Centre (☎ 8889 7014), 3-4 Wellington Terrace, Turnpike Lane N8 (☉ Turnpike Lane), stocks all the other bits and bobs (mosquito netting, moneybelts etc) that a traveller could possibly want.

Clothing

Designer Fashion Any international designer worth his or her threads has at least one outlet in London, usually in Sloane or Bond Sts or in Knightsbridge. But watch out for hip British designers like Alexander McQueen, Christian Lacroix, Tracey Mulligan, Antonio Beradi, Andrew Groves, Bruce Oldfield and Lisa Bruce, who mix formal design with hip streetwear.

The following designer shops are always windowshoppable even if you can't avoid their fripperies (which, we're not surprised to learn, comes from the Old French *frèpe* for 'rag'):

Agnès B (☎ 7379 1992), 35-36 Floral St WC2 (☉ Covent Garden)

DOUG McKINLAY

Top hats: sartorial sophistication in the West End.

Amanda Wakeley (☎ 7584 4009), 80 Fulham Rd SW3 (☉ South Kensington)

Betty Jackson (☎ 7589 7884), 311 Brompton Rd SW3 (☉ South Kensington)

Comme des Garçons (☎ 7493 1258), 59 Brook St W1 (☉ Bond Street)

DKNY/Donna Karan (☎ 7499 8089), 19 & 27 New Bond St W1 (☉ Bond Street)

Emporio Armani (☎ 8823 8818), 187-191 Brompton Rd SW3 (☉ Knightsbridge)

French Connection (☎ 7836 0522), 11 James St WC2 (☉ Covent Garden)

Jean-Paul Gaultier (☎ 7584 4648), 171-175 Draycott Ave SW3 (☉ South Kensington)

Katherine Hamnett (☎ 7823 1002), 20 Sloane St SW1 (☉ Knightsbridge)

Nicole Farhi (☎ 7499 8368), 158 New Bond St W1 (☉ Bond Street); 75-83 Fairfield Rd E3 (☎ 7399 7000; ☉ Bow Road) for samples, seconds and last season's designs

Paul Costelloe (☎ 7589 9480), 156 Brompton Rd SW3 (☉ Knightsbridge)

Paul Smith (☎ 7379 7133), 40-44 Floral St WC2 (☉ Covent Garden)

Prada (☎ 7647 5000), 16-18 Old Bond St W1 (☉ Piccadilly Circus or Green Park)

Red or Dead (☎ 7379 7571), 33 Neal St WC2 (☉ Covent Garden)

Tomasz Starewski (☎ 7235 4526), 177-178 Sloane St SW1 (☉ Knightsbridge)

Vivienne Westwood (☎ 7629 3757), 6 Davies St W1 (☉ Bond Street)

For that most London of articles of clothing – the raincoat – head for Burberry (Map 7; ☎ 7930 3343), 18-22 Haymarket SW1 (⊖ Piccadilly Circus), which also has a factory outlet in the East End at 29-53 Chatham Place E9 (☎ 8985 3344; Hackney Central station), or for Aquascutum (Map 7; ☎ 7734 6090), 100 Regent St W1 (⊖ Piccadilly Circus). No one, but no one, makes and stocks umbrellas (along with canes and walking sticks) like James Smith & Sons (Map 7; ☎ 7836 4731), 53 New Oxford St WC1 (⊖ Tottenham Court Road); the shop's exterior is a museum piece.

Street Fashion Carnaby St, south-east of Oxford Circus tube station, was the centre of the world in the swinging 1960s but no more. Nowadays you'd be better off checking out the shops on or around Kensington High St and the King's Rd.

Hype Designer Forum, or Hype DF (Map 5; ☎ 7938 3801), 46-52 Kensington High St W8 (⊖ High Street Kensington), and the CM Store (Map 9; ☎ 7351 9361), 121 King's Rd SW3 (⊖ Sloane Square), are large emporia crammed with street

Living in the past: hippy psychedelia and 60s nostalgia on Carnaby St.

fashion by struggling young designers who are more than a little keen to sell their imaginative glad rags. Two other good choices for such items as fetish gear, leather boots and lace-up tops are the Dispensary (☎ 7727 8797), 200 Kensington Park Rd W11 (Map 5; ⊖ Ladbroke Grove), and Ad Hoc (☎ 7938 1664), 28 Kensington Church St W8 (Map 5; ⊖ High Street Kensington).

Retro & Second-hand Three-storey Kensington Market (☎ 7938 4343), 49-53 Kensington High St W8 (Map 5; ⊖ High Street Kensington), is a bit of a dinosaur (and a hot, sticky shambles in summer), but it's still a lot of fun. It's more leather and patchouli oil than high fashion – more 1960s than 21st century – and the place to come for second-hand Levis, army jackets, chain-mail bikinis, handmade jewellery and anything with that Goth look to it. Be warned that at the time of writing the market's future was uncertain.

Among the better places for second-hand and retro gear (beaded flapper-dresses from the 1920s, 1950s prom-dresses, Nehru jackets from the 1960s etc) are the following:

Blackout II (☎ 7240 5006), 51 Endell St WC2 (⊖ Covent Garden)
Cornucopia (☎ 7828 5752), 12 Upper Tachbrook St SW1 (⊖ Victoria)
Delta of Venus (☎ 7387 3037), 151 Drummond St NW1 (⊖ Euston)
Steinberg & Tolkien (☎ 7376 3660), 193 King's Rd SW3 (⊖ Sloane Square)
Yesterday's Bread (☎ 7287 1929), 29-31 Foubert's Place W1 (⊖ Oxford Circus)

Underwear M&S – Marks & Spencer (see the Department Stores section in this chapter) – is celebrated from Hong Kong to Hammersmith for its high-quality yet affordable 'smalls', but for women's knickers to die for (or over, or in), check out Agent Provocateur (Map 7; ☎ 7439 0229), 6 Broadwick St W1 (⊖ Oxford Circus), with a branch at 16 Pont St SW1 (☎ 7235 0229; ⊖ Knightsbridge). As some of their placards read: 'More S&M, less M&S.' Both shops are decidedly windowshoppable.

Food & Drink

Run-of-the-mill food shops are 10-a-penny all over London, but the food halls at Harrods and Fortnum & Mason (see the Department Stores section later in this chapter) are attractions in their own right. It's also worth tracking down some of the more specialist stores, a selection of which follows.

Cheese Neal's Yard Dairy (Map 7; ☎ 7379 7646), 17 Shorts Gardens WC2 (✪ Covent Garden), is the place to go to sample some of Britain's more esoteric cheeses. London's oldest cheesemonger is Paxton & Whitfield (Map 7; ☎ 7930 0259), 93 Jermyn St SW1 (✪ Piccadilly Circus), which claims to stock 200 different varieties. Arguably the best French-style cheese shop in London is La Fromagerie (☎ 7359 7440), 30 Highbury Park N5 (✪ Arsenal or Highbury & Islington).

Meat Simply Sausages (Map 6; ☎ 7287 3482), 93 Berwick St W1 (✪ Oxford Circus), is a great place to stock up for a barbecue. Among the many sausages on sale are ones made with duck, black cherry and port, as well as Thai sausages and vegetarian mushroom and tarragon sausages. There's a branch (Map 6; ☎ 7329 3227) in Smithfield Market on the corner of Charterhouse and Farringdon Sts.

Sugar & Spice The Hive (☎ 7924 6233, 93 Northcote Rd SW11; ✪ Clapham South) boasts a choice of more than 40 different types of honey, plus a cutaway section through a hive so you can see the bees going about their business. It also carries royal jelly, beeswax candles and other apiarian products.

Chocoholics will have a field day in London with everything from British Cadbury's to Belgian Godiva and French Valrhona available. Among the best places are Rococo (☎ 7352 5857), 321 King's Rd SW3 (Map 9; ✪ Sloane Square), and Dugan's Chocolates (☎ 7354 4666), 149A Upper St N1 (Map 4; ✪ Angel).

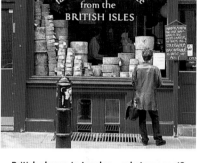

British cheese in London – whatever next? Dairy delicacies in Covent Garden.

CHRISTOPHER WOOD

Konditor & Cook (Map 6; ☎ 7261 0456), 22 Cornwall Rd SE1 (✪ Waterloo), is arguably the best 'bespoke bakery' in London. There's also a branch in Borough Market at 10 Stoney St SE1 (☎ 7407 5100; ✪ London Bridge).

Jane Asher, actress and cookery-book writer, has the cake-decorating market cornered in London. Check out and/or try her offerings at Jane Asher Party Cakes (Map 9; ☎ 7584 6177), 22-24 Cale St SW3 (✪ South Kensington or Sloane Street).

The Oil & Spice Shop (Map 8; ☎ 7403 4030), Butlers Wharf, Shad Thames SE1 (✪ Tower Bridge), has the delightful aroma of a Middle Eastern bazaar and a dazzling array of different oils in beautifully shaped bottles. It's open daily from noon to 6 pm. Another place to try is the Spice Shop (Map 5; ☎ 7221 4448), 1 Blenheim Crescent W11 (✪ Ladbroke Grove).

Coffee & Tea The Algerian Coffee Stores (Map 7; ☎ 7437 2480), 52 Old Compton St W1 (✪ Leicester Square), is *the* place to go to buy all sorts of tea and coffee, including Maragogype, the biggest coffee bean in the world. The nearby Angelucci (Map 7;

☎ 7437 5889), 23B Frith St W1, is friendlier, has almost as big a selection and its own blend – Mokita – is excellent.

The Tea House (Map 7; ☎ 7240 7539), 15 Neal St WC2 (⊖ Covent Garden), has a great range of teas plus pots to put them in.

Alcohol Gerry's (Map 7; ☎ 7734 4215), 74 Old Compton Rd W1 (⊖ Leicester Square), stocks a frightening array of alcohol garnered from far-flung parts. Come here if you just can't manage without a bottle of Cuban rum, Peruvian *pisco* or Polish *zubrówka*. Nearby, Milroy's of Soho (☎ 7437 9311), 3 Greek St W1, stocks over 500 whiskies, including 350 malts and 30 Irish whiskeys.

Furnishings & Household Goods

The Conran Shop (Map 9; ☎ 7589 7401), Michelin House, 81 Fulham Rd SW3 (⊖ South Kensington), is the brainchild of Terence Conran, who created Habitat (see below) and many classy London restaurants. Now his retro-style farmhouse interiors, furniture and kitchenware are available more exclusively, with more exclusive prices to match. The shop's great appeal lies partly in its setting (see Michelin House under Chelsea, South Kensington & Earl's Court in the Things to See & Do chapter).

Habitat (Map 6; ☎ 7631 3880), 196 Tottenham Court Rd W1 (⊖ Goodge Street), the chain that brought design into British homes, has furniture as well as great home accessories. There are Habitat branches throughout London, including a large one at 208 King's Rd SW3 (☎ 7351 1211).

Heal's (Map 6; ☎ 7636 1666), 196 Tottenham Court Rd (⊖ Goodge Street), a long-established furniture store with some very classy designs, has an excellent kitchenware section. There's a branch at 224 King's Rd SW3 (☎ 7349 8411).

For something really unusual, head for Kitschen Sync (☎ 7652 1070), 9 The Pavement, Clapham Common SW4 (⊖ Clapham Common), a shop with a cringey name but very groovy retro kitchenware like zigzag-shaped brooms, shocking-pink kettles and polka-dot plastic chairs.

Jewellery

If you're just after a pair of common-or-garden studs, you'll be able to pick them up at any of the markets or at stalls in the main-line stations. If it's classic (ie old-fashioned) settings and unmounted stones you want, stroll along Hatton Garden (Map 6; ⊖ Chancery Lane); it's chock-a-block with gold, diamond and jewellery shops, especially towards the southern end.

For the sort of trinkets you'll need to win the National Lottery to afford, the following are your best bets:

Asprey & Garrard (Map 7; ☎ 7734 7020), 165-169 New Bond St W1 (⊖ Green Park)
Cartier (Map 6; ☎ 7493 6962), 175 New Bond St W1 (⊖ Green Park)
Mappin & Webb (Map 7; ☎ 7734 3801), 170 Regent St W1 (⊖ Oxford Circus)
Tiffany (Map 7; ☎ 7409 2790), 25 Old Bond St W1 (⊖ Piccadilly Circus or Green Park)

For more up-to-date baubles, try Janet Fitch (☎ 01932-866449), a chain of shops that showcases the best of young British jewellery designers, with branches at 25A Old Compton St W1 (Map 7; ⊖ Tottenham Court Road); 37A Neal St WC2 (Map 7; ⊖ Covent Garden); 1 The Market, Covent Garden WC2 (Map 7; ⊖ Covent Garden); and 188a King's Rd W9 (Map 9; ⊖ Sloane Square). The Portobello Green arcade in Portobello Rd Market (see the special section 'The Markets of London' following this chapter) is home to some cutting-edge jewellery designers.

If you want to get some – any, really – part of your body pierced or tattooed, Into You (☎ 7253 5085), 144 St John St EC1 (Map 6; ⊖ Farringdon), will oblige and stocks lots of interesting body jewellery.

Music

For the largest collections of CDs and tapes in London check out any of the following three Goliath-sized music shops, all in the West End (Map 7):

HMV (☎ 7631 3423), 150 Oxford St W1 (⊖ Oxford Circus). Open weekdays from 9.30 am to

8pm, on Saturday from 9 am to 7.30 pm, and on Sunday from noon to 6 pm.

Tower Records (☎ 7439 2500), 1 Piccadilly Circus W1 (⊖ Piccadilly Circus). Open Monday to Saturday from 9 am to midnight, and on Sunday from noon to 6 pm.

Virgin Megastore (☎ 7631 1234), 14-30 Oxford St W1 (⊖ Tottenham Court Road). Open Monday to Saturday from 9 am to 9 pm, and on Sunday from noon to 6 pm.

London also has a wide range of excellent music-shops specialising in everything from jazz and big band to world music. Worth trying are:

Black Market (Map 7; ☎ 7437 0478), 25 D'Arblay St W1 (⊖ Oxford Circus)

Dub Vendor (☎ 7223 3757), 274 Lavender Hill SW11 (Clapham Junction station)

Honest Jon's (Map 5; ☎ 8969 9822), 278 Portobello Rd W10 (⊖ Ladbroke Grove)

Mole Jazz (Map 4; ☎ 7278 8623), 311 Gray's Inn Rd WC1 (⊖ King's Cross)

Ray's Jazz Shop (Map 7; ☎ 7240 3969), 180 Shaftesbury Ave WC2 (⊖ Tottenham Court Road)

Rough Trade (Map 5; ☎ 7229 8541), 130 Talbot Rd W11 (⊖ Ladbroke Grove or Notting Hill Gate)

Trax (Map 7; ☎ 7734 0795), 55 Greek St W1 (⊖ Tottenham Court Road)

For second-hand and rare vinyl try Kensington Market (see the Clothing section earlier in this chapter) or any of the following (all Map 7):

Division One (☎ 7637 7734), 36 Hanway St W1 (⊖ Tottenham Court Road)

On the Beat (☎ 7637 8934), 22 Hanway St W1 (⊖ Tottenham Court Road)

Reckless Records (☎ 7437 4271), 26 & 30 Berwick St W1 (⊖ Oxford Circus)

WHERE TO SHOP

Some of London's bigger stores are tourist attractions in their own right; very few visitors leave the city without having popped into Harrods and Fortnum & Mason, even if only to browse around. And the cult TV series *Absolutely Fabulous* has made Harvey Nichols (or 'Harvey Nicks') another must-see attraction.

London's Auction Houses

Fancy a spot of upmarket shopping without the hassle of fixed price tags? What better way than to pop into one of London's auction houses, those household-name powerhouses where Van Goghs routinely change hands for zillions of pounds but where sales of more affordable ephemera also take place. The following are the best known:

Christie's (Map 6; ☎ 7839 9060)
    8 King St SW1
    (⊖ Green Park or Piccadilly Circus)
Sotheby's (Map 6; ☎ 7493 8080)
    34-35 New Bond St W1
    (⊖ Bond Street)
Phillips (Map 6; ☎ 7629 6602)
    7 Blenheim St W1
    (⊖ Bond Street)
Bonhams (Map 5; ☎ 7393 3900)
    Montpelier St SW7
    (⊖ Knightsbridge)

Although most things can be bought throughout London, there are also streets known for their own specialities. Tottenham Court Rd, for example, is full of electronics and computer shops, while Charing Cross Road is still the place to go for books. Cecil Court has antiquarian bookshops while Denmark St has musical instruments, sheet music and books about music. Hanway St is great for used records. All these streets are on Map 7.

Some shopping streets rest on their laurels, their claim to fame having more to do with their past than what they have to offer today (eg Carnaby Street). Covent Garden (Map 7), the vegetable market of the West End for a century and a half, was redeveloped in the 1980s; the twee shops and stalls inside the old market building in the centre tend to be pricey and tourist-oriented, but the streets running off it remain a happy hunting-ground for shoppers, with Neal St and Neal's Yard in particular offering an interesting range.

Oxford St (Map 7) can be a great disappointment. Selfridges is up there with Harrods as a place to visit, John Lewis claims to be 'never knowingly undersold' and the flagship Marks & Spencer at the Marble Arch end has its fans. But the farther east you go, the tackier and less interesting it gets. Regent St, with Liberty and Hamleys, is much more upmarket. Kensington High St (Map 5) is a good alternative to Oxford St. In the City check out some of the lovely boutiques in Bow Lane (Map 8), which runs between Cheapside and Cannon St.

Many tourist attractions have shops selling good-quality souvenirs: war books and videos at the Imperial War Museum, designer fans at the Fan Museum, William Morris-designed rugs at the William Morris Gallery and so on. Buying from these shops also contributes towards the building's maintenance. For one-stop shopping check out the Museum Store (☎ 7240 5760), 37 The Market, Covent Garden WC2 (Map 7; ⊖ Covent Garden), which sells a wide variety of souvenirs from British and overseas museums.

Department Stores

The biannual sales at London's department stores, when every tourist, local and their grandmother seem to be queuing up outside Harrods, take place in January and late June/July.

Harrods This well known store (Map 5; ☎ 7730 1234), 87 Brompton Rd SW1 (⊖ Knightsbridge), even more famous since Diana, Princess of Wales, and the owner's son, Dodi Fayed, were killed in a car crash together in 1997, is truly unique: it can even lay claim to having installed the world's first escalator in 1898. There are the downsides – it's always crowded, there are more rules than at an army boot camp and it's hard to find what you're looking for. But the toilets are fab, the food halls will make you swoon, and if they haven't got what you want, it ain't worth having. It's open on Monday, Tuesday and Saturday from 10 am to 6 pm, Wednesday to Friday to 7 pm.

Harvey Nichols Harvey Nichols (Map 5; ☎ 7235 5000), 109-125 Knightsbridge SW1 (⊖ Knightsbridge), is the city's heart of high fashion. It has a great food hall on the

No, this isn't an old photograph that's been coloured up – Harrods really does still have a horse and carriage that can sometimes be seen trotting along Knightsbridge.

5th floor, an extravagant perfume department and jewellery worth saving up for. But with all the big names (from Miyake to Lauren and Hamnett to Calvin Klein) and a whole floor of up-to-the-minute menswear, it's fashion that Harvey Nichols really does better than the rest and the store's own clothing line is reasonable. It's open on Monday, Tuesday, Friday and Saturday from 10 am to 7 pm, on Wednesday and Thursday to 8 pm and on Sunday from noon to 6 pm.

Fortnum & Mason Fortnum & Mason (Map 7; ☎ 7734 8040), 181 Piccadilly W1 (✛ Piccadilly Circus), is noted for its exotic, old-world food hall on the ground floor, but it also carries plenty of fashion wear on the next four floors. All kinds of unusual foodstuffs can be purchased here along with the famous food-hampers. This is where Scott stocked up before heading off for the Antarctic. It's open Monday to Saturday from 9.30 am to 6 pm.

Liberty Almost as unique and with as much history as Harrods, Liberty (Map 7; ☎ 7734 1234), 214-220 Regent St W1 (✛ Oxford Circus), was born at the turn of the century out of the Arts & Crafts Movement and in Italy Art Nouveau is still called *Stile Liberty* after the store. Liberty has high fashion, great modern furniture, a wonderful luxury-fabrics department and those inimitable Liberty silk scarves. It's open Monday to Wednesday and on Friday and Saturday from 10 am to 6.30 pm, on Thursday to 7.30 pm and on Sunday from noon to 6 pm.

Marks & Spencer Marks & Spencer (Map 6; ☎ 7935 7954), 458 Oxford St W1 (✛ Bond Street or Marble Arch), is almost as British as fish and chips, beans on toast and warm beer. It carries the full range of fashion goods but most people shop here for underwear, well made affordable clothes like cashmere sweaters and ready-made meals. It's open weekdays from 9 am to 8 pm, on Saturday to 7 pm and on Sunday from noon to 6 pm.

Mock Tudor with an Art Nouveau pedigree: Liberty on Regent St.

GLENN BEANLAND

Peter Jones & John Lewis Peter Jones (Map 9; ☎ 7730 3434), Sloane Square SW1 (✛ Sloane Square), and John Lewis (Map 6; ☎ 7629 7711), 278-306 Oxford St W1 (✛ Oxford Circus), both part of the same group, are London institutions – the places to know about if you're planning the sort of extended stay that requires stocking up with household goods. Peter Jones, which caters for a more well heeled clientele due to its location, has been described as the 'best corner shop in Chelsea', but that would hardly start to describe the wide range of goods on sale at both stores: from electrical goods through china and glass to towels and bedding. Peter Jones is open on Monday and Tuesday and from Thursday to Saturday from 9.30 am to 6 pm, and on Wednesday to 7 pm. John Lewis' opening hours are Monday to Wednesday and on Friday from 9.30 am to 6 pm, on Thursday from 10 am to 8 pm and on Saturday from 9 am to 6 pm.

Selfridges Arguably the grandest shop on Oxford St and the one with the longest history, Selfridges (Map 6; ☎ 7629 1234), 400 Oxford St W1 (✛ Bond Street), has recently undergone a major renovation. Many people come here for the food halls (enter from Orchard St on the west side), which are much less confusing, cramped and crowded than the ones at Harrods and have a branch of Yo! Sushi (see the West End section in the Places to Eat chapter). Selfridges is open Monday to Wednesday from 10 am to 7 pm, on Thursday and Friday to 8 pm, on Saturday from 9.30 am to 7 pm and on Sunday from noon to 6 pm.

Speciality Stores

Hamleys (Map 7; ☎ 7734 3161), 188-196 Regent St W1 (⊖ Oxford Circus), is an Aladdin's cave of toys and games, but its prices can be high.

For cartoons and playing cards with everything imaginable on the reverse, try the London Cartoon Gallery in Gosh! (Map 7; ☎ 7636 1011), 39 Great Russell St WC1 (⊖ Tottenham Court Road).

Fancy taking home a model of a Victorian theatre? Then try Benjamin Pollock's Toy Shop (Map 7; ☎ 7379 7866), 44 The Market, Covent Garden WC2 (⊖ Covent Garden). The nearby Kite Store (☎ 7836 1666), 48 Neal St WC2, stocks at least one hundred different models.

Papier Marché (Map 4; ☎ 7251 6311), 53 Clerkenwell Close EC1 (⊖ Farringdon), is a lovely shop selling all manner of birds and animals made out of papier-mâché. This is also the place to come when you're in the market for a fur-lined mirror.

Compendia (☎ 8293 6616) at No 10 in Greenwich Market (Map 13; DLR Cutty Sark) is piled high with board and other games, including a good selection of travel-themed ones. Nearby, the Linen & Lace Company (☎ 8293 9407) at No 7 stocks just what you'd expect – beautiful things like bed and table linens, quilts and cushions.

If you know someone who'd like a ship's clock or a ship's bell or even a jigsaw of HMS *Victory*, head straight for Nauticalia (Map 8; ☎ 7480 6805), Ivory House, St Katharine's Dock E1 (⊖ Tower Hill).

For the well-groomed male in your life, check out Taylor of Old Bond St (Map 7; ☎ 7930 5321), 74 Jermyn St SW1 (⊖ Green Park), which has every sort of razor, shaving brush and flavour of shaving soap imaginable, from lavender to mint. DR Harris (Map 6; ☎ 7930 3915), 29 St James's St SW1 (⊖ Green Park), chemists and perfumers since 1790, stocks such esoteric goods as moustache wax, tiny beard-combs and DR Harris Crystal Eye Drops to combat the visual effects of late nights, early starts and jetlag. Best of all they've got their own hangover cure – a bitter herbal concoction called DR Harris Pick-Me-Up. If it works for us, it will work for you.

THE MARKETS OF

LONDON

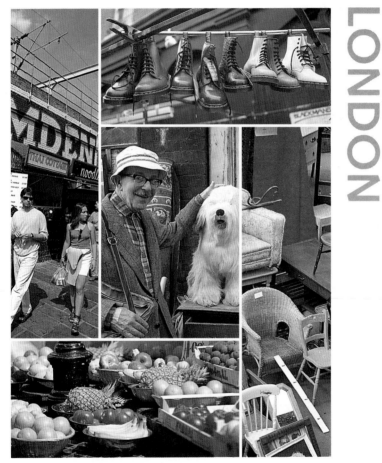

RICHARD I'ANSON

Believe it or not, London has more than 350 markets selling everything from antiques and curios to flowers and fish. For a more complete rundown, get hold of The London Market Guide (Metro Publications; £3.99) by Andrew Richard Kershman, which also gives details of smaller local markets and ones farther afield (eg Shepherd's Bush, Swiss Cottage, Walthamstow and Wembley markets). A prettier but less useful title is Antique and Flea Markets of London and Paris (£12.95) by Rupert Thomas & Eglé Salvy.

Bermondsey

Bermondsey Market (Map 8; ☎ 7351 5353), Bermondsey Square SE1 (✚ Borough), is the place to come if you're after old opera glasses, bowling balls, hatpins, costume jewellery, porcelain or any other 'antique'. The main market on Friday (from 4 am to 2 pm) takes place outdoors on the square although adjacent warehouses shelter the more vulnerable furnishings and bric-a-brac. Tower Bridge Rd is another good street to check out; the Old Cinema Antique Warehouse (☎ 7407 5371) at No 157 specialises in 19th-century items and Victoriana.

Berwick St

ELLIOT DANIEL

South of Oxford St and running parallel to Wardour and Poland Sts, Berwick St Market (Map 7; ✚ Oxford Circus) is a city fruit and vegetable market that has managed to hang onto its prime location since 1830; check out the lovely row of Georgian houses to the west at 46-58 Broadwick St. This is a great place to put together a picnic or shop for a prepared meal. It's open Monday to Saturday from 9 am to 5 pm.

Billingsgate

The wholesale Billingsgate Fish Market (Map 12), Trafalgar Way E14 (DLR West India Quay), is open to the public, and you'll hear a lot of colourful Cockney banter from the market porters, but you'll have to be up at the crack of dawn. People will tell you that you have to buy in bulk here, but most vendors are prepared to do a deal. It livens up at 5 am and is over by 8.30 am.

JULIET COOMBE

Top: Blue is the colour: groovy ceramics.

Middle: Fresh fruit and veg at Berwick St Market.

Bottom: A fishy for your dishy.

Title page: Collage of market images (centre photograph by Juliet Coombe).

JULIET COOMBE

Borough

There has been a fruit and vegetable market on the site of today's covered Borough Market (Map 8; ⊖ London Bridge) since at least the 13th century. Until recently it served only the wholesale trade, but now on the third Saturday of every month from 9 am to 5 pm retailers from around the country sell edibles ranging from English farm cheeses and specialist sausages to gourmet patisserie and fresh fish to the public.

Brick Lane

A few streets east of Petticoat Lane and Spitalfields markets, Brick Lane Market (Map 8), Brick Lane E1 (⊖ Shoreditch or Aldgate East), is more fun. Activity kicks off on Sunday at around 8 am and spreads out along Bethnal Green Rd to the north. By 2 pm it's all over. There's a mix of stalls selling clothes, fruit and vegetables, household goods, paintings and bric-a-brac.

Brixton

Brixton Market (see the Brixton map on page 287; ⊖ Brixton) is a cosmopolitan treat that mixes everything from the Body Shop and reggae to slick Muslim preachers, South American butcher shops and exotic fruits. On Electric Ave and in the covered Granville Arcade you can buy wigs, unusual foods like tilapia fish and Ghanaian eggs (really a type of veg), unusual spices and homeopathic root cures. The market is open Monday to Saturday from 8 am to 5.30 pm (on Wednesday to 1 pm only).

Camden

Camden Market (Map 3) stretches north from Camden Town tube station to Chalk Farm Rd. It's busiest at weekends between 10 am and 6 pm, although there'll be a few stalls up and running most days.

As you head north along Camden High St the Electric Market, in an old ballroom at No 184, is first on the right. There are sometimes record sales on Sunday, but 1960s clothes usually dominate. Opposite is a covered area with stalls selling a mishmash of leather and army-surplus goods. Next up on the right is Camden Market, which houses stalls for fashion, clothing and jewellery.

Farther north beyond the canal bridge is Camden Canal Market,

Top: Technicolour boots at Brick Lane Market.

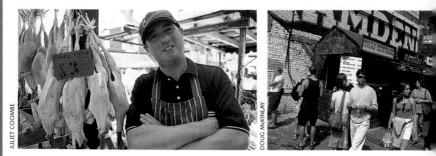

JULIET COOMBE

DOUG McKINLAY

with bric-a-brac from around the world. Inside on the left, and beyond the comparatively new indoor market, is the small section where the market originated. This area, right next to the canal lock, houses a diverse range of food, ceramics, furniture, oriental rugs, musical instruments, designer clothes and so on.

From here you can walk along the Railway Arches, which contain mostly second-hand furniture, to the Stables (☎ 7485 5511), the northernmost part of the market, where it's possible to snap up antiques, eastern artefacts, rugs and carpets, pine furniture, and 50s and 60s clothing. If you want to get straight to the Stables there's an entrance on Chalk Farm Rd opposite the start of Hartland Rd.

Camden Passage

At the junction of Upper St and Essex Rd, you'll find Camden Passage (Map 4; ☎ 7359 9969; ⊖ Angel), a cavern of almost three dozen antique shops and stalls that has nothing to do with Camden Market. The stalls sell pretty much everything to which the moniker 'antique' or 'curio' could reasonably be applied, and the stallholders know their stuff so real bargains are rare. Wednesday is the busiest day when the action kicks off at 7.30 am and is all over by 2 pm; on Saturday it's worth coming along until about 5 pm. There's a second-hand book market on Thursday from 7 am to 4 pm. (Camden Passage is also where to come to spot international film stars; Sophia Loren and Sylvester Stallone were recently seen haggling over gewgaws.)

Chapel Market

There's an all-day fruit and vegetable market in the Islington street called Chapel Market (Map 4; ⊖ Angel), just off Liverpool Rd, on Tuesday, Wednesday and Friday, and on Thursday and Saturday to 12.20 pm only.

Church St

The reason to come to Church St Market (Map 5), Church St NW8 (⊖ Edgware Road), is to visit Alfie's Antiques Market (☎ 7723 6066), home to some 200 dealers who specialise in decorative antiques, garden paraphernalia and 20th-century design.

Top left: Fresh chicken at Portobello Rd Market.

Top right: Taking in the atmosphere at Camden Market.

RICHARD I'ANSON

JULIET COOMBE

Columbia Rd

Although visitors may have little need of geraniums or pelargoniums, a stroll up to the flower market on Columbia Rd, between Gosset St and the Royal Oak pub (Map 4; ⊖ Bethnal Green; Cambridge Heath station; bus No 26, 48 or 55), is a fun way to spend a Sunday morning (from 8 am to 2 pm). Along with the flower and plant stalls, a couple of arty shops throw open their doors.

Covent Garden

While the shops in the Covent Garden piazza (Map 7; ⊖ Covent Garden) are open every day, several markets also take place here. The best is the Apple Market (☎ 7240 7405) in the North Hall with quality crafts available Tuesday to Sunday from 10.30 am to 7 pm; Monday is for antiques and collectibles. There's an antiques and bric-a-brac market on Monday in Jubilee Hall on the southern side of the piazza; the rest of the week it's full of tat.

Greenwich

Every Friday, Saturday and Sunday, from 9.30 am to 5 or 5.30 pm, Greenwich hosts a covered arts and crafts market (Map 13; DLR Cutty Sark) between King William Walk and Greenwich Church St; you can also enter from College Approach. It's an excellent place to look for decorated glass, rugs, prints, wooden toys and so on. On Thursday, there's also an antiques and curios market.

At the southern end of Greenwich Church St, opposite St Alfege Church, there's also the small Village Market Antiques Centre, with the usual mix of second-hand clothes, handmade jewellery, plants and household bric-a-brac.

Top left: Tired after all that walking around? Have a seat.

Top right: In bloom: fresh flowers at Columbia Rd Market.

Leadenhall

Leadenhall Market (Map 8), Whittington Ave off Gracechurch St EC1 (⊖ Bank), serves food and drink to busy City folk as well as fresh fish, meat and cheese. The selection is excellent for an urban market and Victorian glass-and-iron market hall, designed by Horace Jones in 1881, is an architectural delight. It's open weekdays from 7 am to 4 pm.

JULIET COOMBE

Leather Lane

South of Clerkenwell Rd and running parallel to Hatton Garden, Leather Lane Market (Map 6; ↔ Chancery Lane) attracts local office workers with its suspiciously cheap videos, tapes and CDs, household goods and clothing sold by archetypal Cockney stallholders. It's open weekdays from 10.30 am to 2 pm.

Petticoat Lane

Petticoat Lane (Map 8; ↔ Aldgate, Aldgate East or Liverpool Street) is east London's long-established Sunday market (from 8 am to 2 pm) on Middlesex St, on the border between the City and Whitechapel. These days, however, it's full of run-of-the-mill junk and tourists.

Portobello Rd

ANTHONY BATTLE

After Camden Market, Portobello Rd (Map 5; ☎ 7727 7684; ↔ Notting Hill Gate, Ladbroke Grove or Westbourne Park) is London's most famous (and crowded) weekend street market. Starting near the Sun in Splendour pub in Notting Hill, it wends its way northwards to just past the Westway flyover.

Antiques, handmade jewellery, paintings and ethnic stuff are concentrated at the Notting Hill Gate end of Portobello Rd (roughly from Chepstow Villas as far as Elgin Crescent to the west and Colville Terrace to the east). The stalls dip downmarket as you move north (fruit and veg, second-hand clothing, cheap household goods, bric-a-brac). Beneath the Westway a vast tent covers yet more stalls selling cheap clothes, shoes and CDs, while the Portobello Green arcade is home to some cutting-edge clothes and jewellery designers. On Friday and Saturday bric-a-brac goes on sale here too.

Fruit and vegetables are on sale all week at the Ladbroke Grove end, with an organic market operating on Thursday. The other stalls are rolled out for the weekend, with most of the antiques on sale on Saturday from 6 am to between 2 and 5 pm. There's a flea market on Portobello Green on Sunday morning.

Top: It's a doll's life: a pretty crowd at Petticoat Lane Market.

Middle: Sifting through antiques on Portobello Rd Market.

Ridley Rd

In some ways the Caribbean/African/Turkish/Jewish market along Ridley Rd (Map 2; Dalston Kingsland station or bus No 149, 242 or 243 from Liverpool St) is more colourful than the one in Brixton and it's certainly less tourristed. You'll find more types of Turkish delight and Caribbean tuber than you'll know what to do with. Fans of *East-Enders* should walk the short distance south-east to Fassett Square, the model of Albert Square in the long-running TV series.

Roman Rd

The market along Roman Rd (Map 2; ⊖ Bethnal Green or Mile End) is famous for discount fashion clothes. It's open Tuesday and Thursday morning but is at its best on Saturday from 8 am to 4 pm.

Smithfield

Smithfield Market (Map 6), West Smithfield EC1 (⊖ Farringdon), is central London's last surviving meat market and would be a vision of hell itself for vegetarians. Though the eastern end has been wonderfully restored to its 1868 original design (the man responsible was Horace Jones, who also designed Leadenhall Market and Tower Bridge), it remains to be seen whether the meat market can hang in here or whether it will be forced to follow the Billingsgate Fish Market and the New Covent Garden fruit and vegetable market and move out of central London. Smithfield is open weekdays from about 3 am to 10 am, but most everything is finished by 8 or 9 am.

Spitalfields

Not only is Spitalfields (Map 8; ☎ 7247 6590), the large market between Bishopsgate and Commercial St (⊖ Liverpool Street), in a huge covered Victorian warehouse, but there's a great mix of arts and crafts, organic fruit and veg, stylish and retro clothes, and second-hand books, with interesting ethnic shops ringing the central area and a football pitch and children's model railway to keep those not interested in shopping entertained. Most of the shops in the market are open weekdays from 10.30 am to 5 pm. The market itself takes place on Sunday from about 9.30 am to 5.30 pm.

Middle: Classic market grub: sausages and onions.

Bottom: Everyone drops in at Spitalfields.

Excursions

As Britain is relatively small and its transport systems generally fan out from London, almost nowhere is impossibly far away from the capital. However, there are several places within a 150km (93 miles) radius of London that can be visited on a day trip. These include destinations as diverse as Windsor Castle, the university town of Oxford and Stratford-upon-Avon, the birthplace of William Shakespeare, to the west and north-west; the cathedral city of St Albans and the University of Cambridge to the north; the medieval pilgrimage site of Canterbury to the east; and Brighton, a wonderful seaside town, to the south.

This chapter assumes you'll be returning to London the same day. There are plenty of other places within easy reach of London – from Bath and Stonehenge to Waltham Abbey and Whipsnade Wild Animal Park. For details of these places as well as where to spend the night if you miss your train or bus or if you just decide you like the place, consult Lonely Planet's *Britain* guide.

The number to ring for information about National Express bus services is ☎ 0870 580 8080. For train details, ring the 24-hour National Rail Enquiries line on ☎ 0845 748 4950. The Green Line group of companies, whose buses leave from and arrive at the Green Line bus station at Bulleid Way at the Victoria Place shopping centre (Map 10), just south of Victoria train station, can be reached on ☎ 8668 7261. See the Getting There & Away chapter for more on travel services.

If you're planning to do a lot of rail travel in south-east England, a Network Railcard is worth considering. It costs £20 and covers all the destinations in this chapter apart from Stratford-upon-Avon. Discounts of 34% apply to up to four adults travelling together provided one is a card-holder. Children pay a flat fare of £1. Travel is permitted only after 10 am on weekdays and at any time at weekends.

ORGANISED TOURS

If you're pressed for time, there are several companies that organise excursions outside London.

The Adventure Travel Centre (☎ 7370 4555), 131 Earls Court Rd SW5 (Map 9; ⊖ Earls Court), does Sunday day trips specifically aimed at the Australasian market. Each trip takes in two destinations (say Oxford and Blenheim Palace or Leeds Castle and Canterbury) and costs £12, or £10 to members of the Deckers London Club (see Australasian Clubs under Useful Organisations in the Facts for the Visitor chapter).

Another company worth trying is Astral Tours (☎ 0700 078 1016), whose so-called Magical Tours in mini-coaches cover one or several of the following: Bath, the Cotswolds, Oxford, Salisbury, Stonehenge, Avebury, Glastonbury and Brighton. A day trip costs from £30 to £48, including all entrance fees. There's also a half-day tour to Windsor, Runnymede, Eton and Henley-on-Thames for about £20. Students and YHA (HI) members are eligible for a 20% discount. For further details visit Astral Tours' Web site at www.astraltravels.co.uk.

Evan Evans Tours (☎ 7950 1777), a much more commercial outfit, offers both half-day and full-day excursions with pick-ups from more than 60 London hotels. A morning trip to Windsor and Runnymede costs £25/22.50 (including admission to Windsor Castle) for adults/ children aged three to 16 and leaves from the tourist information centre (TIC) at Victoria train station on Monday, Wednesday, Friday and Sunday at 8.25 am. An afternoon trip to Leeds Castle (£31.50/ 29) leaves the TIC on Tuesday, Thursday and Sunday at 12.45 pm. The Evan Evans Web site is at www.evanevans.co.uk. Golden Tours (☎ 7233 7030) offers similar tours; its Web site is at www.goldentours .co.uk.

EXCURSIONS

DOUG McKINLAY

Just a few of the dreaming spires of Oxford.

Historic & Seaside Towns

OXFORD
☎ 01865

The poet Matthew Arnold described Oxford, 92km (57 miles) north-west of London, as 'that sweet city with her dreaming spires'. These days the spires coexist with a flourishing commercial city that has some typical urban social problems. But for visitors the superb architecture and the unique atmosphere of the colleges, synonymous with academic excellence, and their courtyards and gardens remain major attractions.

Orientation & Information

The train station is to the west, with frequent buses to the centre, or you can walk (about 1km). The bus station is just off the green-less Gloucester Green, where you'll also find the TIC (☎ 726871). It is open Monday to Saturday from 9.30 am to 5 pm, and from April to September on Sunday from 10 am to 3.30 pm. Staff here can book accommodation for a £2.50 fee (plus 10% deposit) and sell the useful *Welcome to Oxford* booklet (£1). Two-hour guided walking tours of the colleges leave the TIC at 11 am and 1 and 2 pm, with an extra one at 10.30 am in summer; they cost £4.50/ 2.50 for adults/children.

Walking Tour

The colleges are scattered around the city, with the most important ones in the centre.

Carfax Tower, at the junction of Queen and Cornmarket Sts, makes a useful central landmark. There's a fine view from the top (open April to October from 10 am to 5.30 pm, to 3.30 pm the rest of the year; entry costs £1.20/60p for adults/children).

Starting at the tower, walk south along St Aldates to **Christ Church** (☎ 276150), the grandest of the colleges and founded in 1525. The main entrance is below Tom Tower, the top of which was designed by Sir Christopher Wren in 1682, but the visitors' entrance is farther down St Aldates via the wrought-iron gates of the Memorial Gardens and Broad Walk, which faces Christ Church Meadow. The college is open weekdays from 9 am to 5.30 pm (from 1 pm at weekends) and costs £3/2 for adults/children. The college chapel, **Christ Church Cathedral**, is the smallest cathedral in the country and is a wonderful example of late Norman architecture.

From Broad Walk continue east and turn left (north) up Merton Grove to Merton St. On your right is **Merton College** (☎ 276 310), which was founded in 1264. The 14th-century **Mob Quad** contains the oldest medieval library still in use in the UK. The college is open weekdays from 2 to 4 pm and at weekends from 10 am to 6 pm. **Corpus Christi College** is on the left.

Continue heading north, up Magpie Lane, to the High St. In front of you, on the corner of High and Catte Sts, is the **University Church of St Mary the Virgin**, with a 14th-century tower offering splendid views for £1.50/75p for adults/children. It's open daily from 9 am to 7 pm in July and August (to 5 pm the rest of the year).

From St Mary's, walk east along the High St, with its fascinating mix of architectural styles, to **Magdalen College** (☎ 276 000) on the River Cherwell. Magdalen (**Maud**-len) is one of the richest colleges in Oxford and has the most extensive grounds, including a deer park. It is open daily from noon to 6 pm mid-June to September and from 2 pm the rest of the year. There's an entry charge of £2.50/1.25 for adults/children (April to September only).

If you retrace your steps and walk north up Catte St, you'll come to the circular, Palladian-style **Radcliffe Camera** (1749), a reading room for the **Bodleian Library** just to the north across the courtyard. The Radcliffe Camera is closed to the public, but the library and the Divinity School, a masterpiece of 15th-century English Gothic architecture, can be visited on guided tours (☎ 277000) daily at 10.30 and 11.30 am, and 2 and 3 pm (mornings only on Saturday; £3.50).

Continue north along Catte St, passing the **Bridge of Sighs**, a 1914 copy of the famous one in Venice, that spans New College Lane. When you reach Broad St you have one of two options. Walking north along Parks Rd for some 500m will bring you to the **University Museum of Natural History** (☎ 272950), famous for its dinosaur and dodo skeletons, and the newly renovated **Pitt Rivers Museum** (☎ 270927), crammed to overflowing with everything from a sailing boat to a collection of shrunken heads from South America. The

Merton – one of the oldest of Oxford's colleges, in one of its loveliest corners.

EXCURSIONS

CHRIS MELLOR

museums are open Monday to Saturday – the former from noon to 5 pm, the latter from 1 to 4.30 pm. Admission is free.

If you go west along Broad St, you'll pass the **Sheldonian Theatre** (1667), Sir Christopher Wren's first major work, on your left. This is where all important Oxford ceremonies, including graduations, take place. On the right is **Trinity College**, founded in 1555, and next to it, at the corner with Magdalen St, is **Balliol College**. The wooden doors between the inner and outer quadrangles still bear scorch marks from when Protestant martyrs were burned at the stake in the mid-16th century.

A short distance north, along St Giles, is the **Ashmolean Museum** (☎ 278000), which you enter from Beaumont St. Opened to the public in 1683, the Ashmolean is the country's oldest museum and houses extensive displays of European art and Middle Eastern antiquities. It is open Tuesday to Saturday from 10 am to 5 pm, on Sunday from 2 pm, and admission is free.

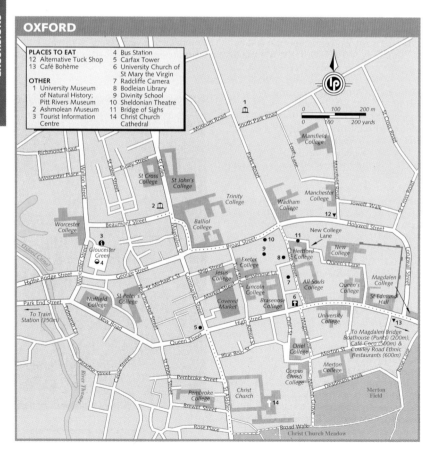

OXFORD

PLACES TO EAT
12 Alternative Tuck Shop
13 Café Bohème

OTHER
1 University Museum of Natural History; Pitt Rivers Museum
2 Ashmolean Museum
3 Tourist Information Centre
4 Bus Station
5 Carfax Tower
6 University Church of St Mary the Virgin
7 Radcliffe Camera
8 Bodleian Library
9 Divinity School
10 Sheldonian Theatre
11 Bridge of Sighs
14 Christ Church Cathedral

Punting

There's no better way to soak up Oxford's atmosphere than to take to the river in a punt. You can hire one at the Magdalen Bridge Boathouse (☎ 202643) for £9/10 per hour on weekdays/weekends (£25 deposit) from March to October. If you're not up to punting yourself, a chauffeured boat for four people with a bottle of wine thrown in costs £18/20.

Places to Eat

Self-caterers should visit the *Covered Market*, on the northern side of the High St near Carfax Tower. The *Alternative Tuck Shop* on Holywell St does excellent filled rolls and sandwiches at lunch time. There are lots of ethnic eateries – from Indian and Jamaican to Lebanese – along Cowley Rd, which leads off the High St south-east of Magdalen College; try *Café Coco* (☎ 200232, 23 Cowley Rd) for a pizza or a salad from £6.50. The *Café Bohème* (☎ 245858, 73 High St) does wonderful breakfasts (from £3.50 to £5.95) and up-market sandwiches and salads (from £4.75 to £5.95).

Getting There & Around

Oxford Tube buses (☎ 772250) go from Victoria Coach Station every 12 to 15 minutes round the clock via Marble Arch, Notting Hill Gate and Shepherd's Bush (1½ hours). A return ticket costs £7.50/6.50 for adults/seniors, students & children. Oxford Citylink (☎ 785400) has frequent bus departures to/from London for the same fares. The Oxford Tube's Web site is at www.stagecoach-oxford.co.uk and Oxford Citylink's at www.oxfordbus.co.uk. There are frequent trains from Paddington (one to 1½ hours, £14.20 return).

Guide Friday (☎ 790522) runs a hop-on, hop-off city bus-tour of Oxford every 15 minutes from 9.30 am to 6 pm in summer, less frequently in winter. Tickets cost £8/6.50/2.50 for adults/seniors & students/children under 12 (family £18). You can visit the Guide Friday Web site at www.guidefriday.com. Bikezone (☎ 728877), at

Going loco at the Café Coco in Oxford.

6 Lincoln House in Market St, rents out bicycles for £15 a day (£50 deposit).

STRATFORD-UPON-AVON
☎ 01789

Stratford-upon-Avon, 150km (93 miles) north-west of London and *just* about a comfortable day trip, is not only the birthplace of one William Shakespeare but also the last pure example of an Elizabethan town extant in the UK (there are plenty of Elizabethan villages). Needless to say, it is one of the busiest tourist attractions outside London and can only get more frenetic with the success of the Oscar-winning film *Shakespeare in Love* (see the boxed text 'William's the Bard, the Lad's Willy').

EXCURSIONS

JULIET COOMBE

Orientation & Information

Stratford is easy to explore on foot. The main street changes its name several times as it runs from the train station south-eastwards to the River Avon. The TIC (☎ 293127), close to the river on Bridge-foot, is open Monday to Saturday from 9 am to 6 pm and on Sunday from 11 am to 5 pm; from November to March it closes an hour earlier and all day on Sunday. For further details check out the TIC's Web site at www.shakespeare-country.co.uk.

The Shakespeare Houses

You can visit five properties associated with the Bard's life, all run by the Shakespeare Birthplace Trust (☎ 204016): Shakespeare's Birthplace, Nash's House & New Place and Hall's Croft in the centre and Anne Hathaway's Cottage and Mary Arden's House a

---

William's the Bard, the Lad's Willy

We've always loved William Shakespeare for his language, his consummate understanding of the human condition, his romance and his sheer unadulterated (or even adulterated) bawdiness. And now that we know he looked like Joseph Fiennes and was Willy the Lad, we like him even more (that skinny Gwyneth Paltrow ain't half bad either). But *was* the Bard a lad and did he ever suffer from writer's block as *Shakespeare in Love* suggests?

Not a tremendous amount is known about the young Willy Shakespeare but in 1582 at the age of 18 he married Anne Hathaway, eight years his senior and pregnant – he was a medieval toy-boy, if you like. She bore him three children in as many years, but then the trail goes cold. It is not known what he got up to for the nine years before 1594, when his name appears as a member of the Lord Chamberlain's company of players, but there are stories of his earning a living by poaching deer, minding the horses of theatre-goers in London to get work as an actor and enlisting as a soldier in the Low Countries. He stayed in London away from Anne for 18 years and famously bequeathed her his 'second-best bed' when he died in 1616 (who got the first-best one?).

Shakespeare in Love is full of funny, nudge-nudge anachronisms and familiar lines that flatter the audience's knowledge of Shakespeare's plays. It's Hollywood taking licence again, but why not? If it allows the audience to flesh out the passionate man that was William Shakespeare, we're all for it. Some points, however, cannot go unchallenged:

- Shakespeare's body of work includes some three dozen plays and hundreds of sonnets; he wrote *Othello*, *King Lear*, *Macbeth* and *Anthony and Cleopatra* in just two years (from 1604 to 1605). It is highly unlikely that the man was ever stuck for ideas as he is with *Romeo and Ethel, the Pirate's Daughter* in the film.
- In the film Shakespeare takes the heat off himself by hinting to Wessex, Viola's fiancé, that his fellow playwright, Christopher Marlowe, is fooling around with her. Of course, no one would have believed that, even a buffoon like Wessex; everyone in Elizabethan London knew Kit 'Those Who Don't Like Boys and Tobacco Are Fools' Marlowe was homosexual.
- At the end of the film Viola is seen surviving a shipwreck and walking the shores of Virginia, where Wessex supposedly had a tobacco plantation. What was Wessex doing in Virginia when Jamestown, the first settlement there, was not established until 1607 – a dozen years after the action in the film takes place?

But we still liked this entertaining, very enlightening film.

bit farther out of town. A £11/10/5.50 Passport ticket for adults/seniors & students/children aged five to 16 (family £26) lets you into all the houses, or you can pay £7.50/6.50/3.70 (£18) for just the three houses in the town. From late March to mid-October the properties are open Monday to Saturday from 9 or 9.30 am to 5 pm, and on Sunday from 9.30 or 10 am, and for the rest of the year Monday to Saturday from 9.30 or 10 am to 4 pm, and on Sunday from either 10 or 10.30 am. The trust has a Web site at www.shakespeare.org.uk.

Other Attractions

Getting to see a production at the Royal Shakespeare Theatre (☎ 403403) is a must. Tickets (from £8 to £37) are often available on the same day, but get there before the box office opens at 9.30 am. Stand-by tickets for around £12 are available to students, under-25s and over-60s on the day of the performance, and standing-room tickets may be available for £5.

If you want to pay your respects to the Bard's mortal remains, they lie at the foot of the altar in Holy Trinity Church, next to those of his wife Anne Hathaway; the church is on the river about 450m south of the Royal Shakespeare Theatre.

Getting There & Around

National Express buses link Stratford with London (three hours, £12 return) three times a day. The Shakespearean bus run by Oxford Tube (☎ 01865-772250) departs from Grosvenor Gardens opposite Victoria train station daily at 9 am, leaving Stratford at 6.20 pm (£10 return). There are several daily direct trains from Paddington (2½ hours, £18.50 return).

Guide Friday (☎ 294466) operates open-top buses that do circuits past the Shakespeare houses every 15 to 30 minutes for £8.50/7.50/4.20 for adults/seniors & students/children (family £21).

ST ALBANS
☎ 01727

Just 30km (19 miles) to the north of Lon-

EXCURSIONS

JULIET COOMBE

Waiting for the muse: Shakespeare looking over his home town.

don, the cathedral city of St Albans makes a pleasant day trip. To the Romans, this was Verulamium, and their theatre and parts of the ancient wall can still be seen to the south-west of the city.

The town centre is St Peter's St, a 10-minute walk west of the train station. The cathedral lies to the west, off High St, with the ruins of Verulamium even farther west.

The TIC (☎ 864511) in the grand town hall on Market Place stocks the useful (and free) guide *Discover St Albans*. Staff here can provide George Bernard Shaw fans with details of Shaw's Corner (☎ 01438-820307), one of the playwright's homes, which is 20km north-east of the town.

St Albans Cathedral

In 209, a Roman soldier named Alban was put to death for sheltering the priest who had converted him to Christianity and thus became England's first Christian martyr. In the 8th century King Offa of Mercia founded an abbey on the site where St Alban was beheaded. The Norman abbey church was built in 1077, incorporating parts of the Saxon building and many Roman bricks, most obviously in the central tower. After the monasteries were dissolved (1536-40) the abbey church became the parish church. Much restoration took place in 1877 when it was designated a cathedral.

The heart of the cathedral is St Alban's shrine immediately behind the presbytery and overlooked by a wooden watcher's loft, where monks stood guard to ensure pilgrims didn't pilfer relics. Look out for a particularly fine 14th-century mural of St Wilfrid on a nearby column. The Norman nave columns are painted with 13th and 14th-century crucifixion scenes.

Other Attractions

The **Verulamium Museum** (☎ 819339), Britain's best museum of everyday life in Roman times, is in St Michael's St and is open daily from 10 am to 5.30 pm (from 2 pm on Sunday); admission costs £3/1.70 for adults/seniors, students & children (family £7.50). In the surrounding streets and the adjacent Verulamium Park, you can also inspect the remains of a basilica, theatre and bathhouse.

The **Museum of St Albans** (☎ 819340) in Hatfield Rd gives a quick rundown of the city's history since Roman times. It's open Monday to Saturday from 10 am to 5 pm and on Sunday from 2 pm. Admission is free.

Getting There & Away

There are up to eight trains an hour from King's Cross to St Albans (25 minutes, £7.10 return) on Thameslink.

CAMBRIDGE
☎ 01223

The university at Cambridge, 87km (54 miles) north of London, was founded in the 13th century, several decades later than Oxford. There is a fierce rivalry between the two cities and their universities, and an ongoing debate over which is the best and most beautiful. If you have time, you should visit both. But if you only have time for one and – this is an important caveat – the colleges are open, choose Cambridge. Oxford draws far more tourists and often seems like a provincial city that happens to have a university. Cambridge, an architectural treasure-house, always feels like just what it is: an English university town.

Orientation & Information

The centre of Cambridge lies in a wide bend of the River Cam. The best-known section of river bank is the Backs, which combines lush scenery with superb views of half a dozen colleges. The other 25 colleges are scattered throughout the city.

The bus station is in the centre on Drummer St, but the train station is a 1.5km walk to the south-east. Sidney St is the main shopping street and changes its name many times.

The TIC (☎ 322640), on Wheeler St just south of Market Square, is open Monday to Saturday from 10 am to 6 pm (to 5 pm on Saturday) all year, and on Sunday from 11 am to 4 pm, April to September. It organises two-hour walking tours at 1.30 pm year-round, with more during the summer (£6.50/4 for adults/children under 12 including King's College, £6/4 including St John's College). TIC staff can also arrange accommodation in town for £3. The TIC's Web site is www.cambridge.gov.uk/leisure. Contact the TIC for up-to-date information on college opening times before you visit.

Walking Tour

Starting at Magdalene Great Bridge to the north, walk south-east along Bridge St until you reach the amazing **Round Church** (or Church of the Holy Sepulchre) built in 1130 to commemorate its namesake in Jerusalem. It's open daily in summer from 10 am to 5 pm, 1 to 4 pm in winter. Turn right down St John's St to **St John's College**. On the other side of the gatehouse (1510) are three beautiful courtyards, the second and third

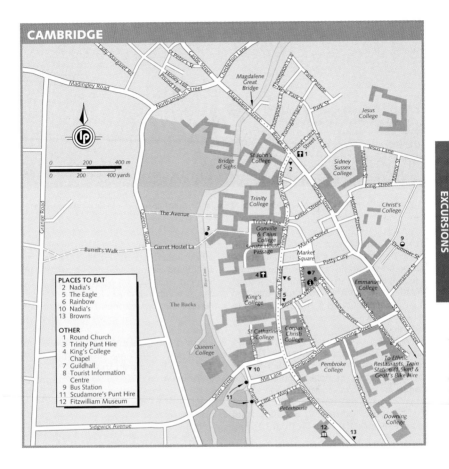

CAMBRIDGE

Lady Margaret Rd
Madingley Road
St Peter's St
Castle Street
Chesterton Lane
Honey Hill Street
Pound Hill Street
Northampton Street
Magdalene Street
Magdalene Great Bridge
Thompson's La
New Park St
Park Parade
Portugal Place
Park St
Jesus College
Round Church Street
Jesus Lane
Grange Road
Queen's Road
The Avenue
Burrell's Walk
Garret Hostel La
St John's College
Bridge of Sighs
Trinity College
Bridge Street
Sidney Street
Sidney Sussex College
King Street
Christ's College
Drummer St
Trinity Lane
Gonville & Caius College
Senate House Passage
Green Street
Market Street
Market Square
Petty Cury
Hobson Street
King's Parade
River Cam
The Backs
King's College
St Catharine's College
Queens' College
Bene't St
Trumpington Street
St Mary's
Corpus Christi College
Free School La
Corn Exchange Street
Emmanuel College
St Andrew's St
St Tibb's Row
Emmanuel Street
Downing Street
Downing Place
Pembroke Street
Pembroke College
Mill Lane
Silver Street
Granta Place
Little St Mary's La
Trumpington Street
Tennis Court Road
Peterhouse
Sidgwick Avenue
Downing College
To Ethnic Restaurants, Train Station (1.5km) & Geoff's Bike Hire

0   200   400 m
0   200   400 yards

PLACES TO EAT
2   Nadia's
5   The Eagle
6   Rainbow
10 Nadia's
13 Browns

OTHER
1   Round Church
3   Trinity Punt Hire
4   King's College Chapel
7   Guildhall
8   Tourist Information Centre
9   Bus Station
11 Scudamore's Punt Hire
12 Fitzwilliam Museum

EXCURSIONS

dating from the 17th century. From the third court, the picturesque **Bridge of Sighs**, a replica of the one in Venice, spans the Cam.

Just south of St John's, **Trinity College** is one of the largest and most attractive colleges. It was established in 1546 by Henry VIII, whose statue peers out from the top niche of the great gateway (he's holding a chair leg instead of the royal sceptre as students kept stealing it). The **Great Court**, the largest structure of its kind in the world, incorporates some fine 15th-century buildings. Beyond the Great Court are the cloisters of Nevile's Court and the dignified **Wren Library**, built by Sir Christopher in the 1680s. Admission to the college is £1.75/1 for adults/seniors, students & children aged 12 to 17.

Next comes Gonville and Caius (pronounced keys) College and **King's College** and its chapel (☎ 331100; £3/2 for adults/children), one of the most sublime buildings in Europe. The chapel was begun in 1446 by Henry VI and completed around 1516.

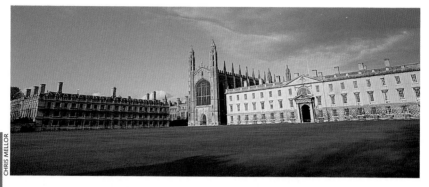

CHRIS MELLOR

EXCURSIONS

King's College and its chapel (centre), one of England's finest examples of Gothic architecture.

Henry VI's successors, notably Henry VIII, added the intricate fan vaulting and elaborate wood-and-stone carvings of the interior. The chapel comes alive when the choir sings and there are services during term-time and in July. Evensong is at 5.30 pm, Tuesday to Saturday (men's voices only on Wednesday), and at 3.30 pm on Sunday.

Continue south on what is now King's Parade to Trumpington St and the **Fitzwilliam Museum** (☎ 332923), which houses ancient Egyptian sarcophagi and Greek and Roman art in the lower galleries and a wide range of paintings upstairs. The museum (free) is open Tuesday to Saturday from 10 am to 5 pm and on Sunday from 2.15 pm.

Punting

Taking a punt along the Backs is great fun, but it can also be a wet and hectic experience, especially on a busy weekend. Cheapest boats are those at Trinity Punt Hire (☎ 338483), Garret Hostel Lane, for £7 per hour plus £25 deposit. Trinity also does chauffeured tours of the river from £6 per person. Down by Mill Lane, Scudamore's (☎ 359750) charges £10 per hour plus £50 deposit.

Places to Eat

The *market* in Market Square is open Monday to Saturday from 9 am to 5 pm. *Nadia's*

is a small chain of excellent-value takeaway bakeries with filled baguettes for £1.75 and cakes from 65p. There are convenient branches on St John's and Silver Sts. A number of cheap Indian and Chinese *restaurants* can be found where Lensfield Rd meets Regent St in the direction of the train station.

For a pub lunch, head for *The Eagle* (☎ 505020, Bene't St), just down from the TIC. Across the road from King's College is *Rainbow* (☎ 321551, 9a King's Parade), a good vegetarian restaurant with soups from £1.95 and main courses such as couscous for £6.25.

Browns (☎ 461655, 23 Trumpington St) is a lovely restaurant full of plants and light, with a £5 lunch weekdays from noon to 4.30 pm. Pastas are from £7 and excellent pies average £8.

Getting There & Around

National Express runs hourly shuttle buses from London to Cambridge (two hours, £8 return) between 7.30 am and 11.30 pm. There are trains every 30 minutes from both King's Cross and Liverpool Street stations (one hour, £13.50 return).

There's a free, gas-powered shuttle service making its way round Cambridge; bus No 1 links the train station with the town centre. Guide Friday (☎ 362444) runs hop-on, hop-off tour buses round the city that also call at the train station. Tours operate year-round; tickets cost £8/6.50/2.50 for adults/seniors & students/children aged five to 12 (family £18). Bicycles can be hired from Geoff's Bike Hire (☎ 365629), 65 Devonshire Rd, a few minutes' walk from the train station, for £6 a day.

AROUND CAMBRIDGE

This former RAF airfield at Duxford, 14km (9 miles) south of Cambridge next to Junction 10 of the M11, houses the award-winning **Duxford Imperial War & American Air Museum** (☎ 835000). It is home to Europe's biggest collection of historic aircraft, ranging from biplanes and Spitfires to jets, including Concorde. It is open daily from 10 am to 6 pm (4 pm in winter) and admission costs £7.20/5/3.50 for adults/seniors & students/children (family £20). A free bus leaves Cambridge for Duxford at 9.30 and 11 am and 12.30 and 1.45 pm from in front of the Holiday Inn on Downing St and, 15 minutes later, from the train station.

CANTERBURY
☎ 01227

Canterbury, in Kent, is 90km (56 miles) east of London and makes an easy day trip from the capital. Its greatest treasure is its magnificent cathedral, the successor to the church St Augustine built after he began converting the English to Christianity in 597. After the martyrdom of archbishop Thomas à Becket in 1170, the cathedral became the focus for one of Europe's most important medieval pilgrimages, immortalised by Geoffrey Chaucer in *The Canterbury Tales*.

Today Canterbury is one of Britain's most impressive and evocative cathedrals and a World Heritage Site. The bustling city centre is atmospheric and alive.

Orientation & Information

The centre is enclosed by a medieval city wall and a modern ring road. The TIC (☎ 766567), 34 St Margaret's St, is open daily from 9.30 am to 5 pm (6 pm in July and August). You can visit its Web site at www.canterbury.co.uk. Guided walks leave from the TIC daily at 2 pm from early April to October and also Monday to Saturday at 11.30 am in July and August. The tour costs £3.50/3 for adults/seniors, students & children (family £8.50) and lasts 1½ hours.

Canterbury Cathedral

Like most great cathedrals, Canterbury Cathedral (☎ 762862) evolved over the centuries and reflects several architectural styles. Since there are treasures tucked away in corners and a trove of associated stories, a tour is highly recommended. One-hour tours start at 10.30 am, noon and 2.30 pm and cost £3/2/1.20 for adults/seniors & students/children. If the crowd looks daunting, you can take a 30-minute audioguide tour that costs £2.95/1.95 for adults/children.

The traditional approach to the cathedral is along narrow Mercery Lane, which used to be lined with small shops selling souvenirs and votive offerings to pilgrims, to Christ Church Gate. Once inside the gate, turn right and walk east to get an overall picture.

St Augustine's original cathedral burned down in 1067. The first Norman archbishop

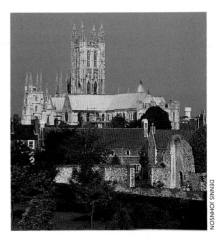

DENNIS JOHNSON

Canterbury Cathedral dominating the skyline.

EXCURSIONS

began construction of a new cathedral in 1070, but only fragments remain. In 1174 most of the eastern half of the building was again destroyed by fire, but the magnificent crypt beneath the choir survived.

The fire presented the opportunity to create something in keeping with the cathedral's new status as England's most important pilgrimage site. In response, William of Sens created the first major Gothic construction in England, a style now described as Early English. Most of the cathedral east of Bell Harry tower dates from this period.

In 1391 work began on the western half of the building, replacing the south-west and north-west transepts and nave. The new Perpendicular style was employed, and work continued for over a century, culminating in 1500 with the completion of Bell Harry.

The main entrance is through the **south-west porch**, built in 1415 to commemorate the English victory at Agincourt. From the centre of the nave there are impressive views east down the length of the church, with its ascending levels, and west to the **window** with glass dating from the 12th century.

From beneath **Bell Harry**, with its beautiful fan vaulting, more impressive stained glass that somehow survived the Puritans is visible. A 15th-century screen, featuring six kings, separates the nave from the choir.

Becket is believed to have been murdered in the north-west transept; a modern **altar and sculpture** mark the spot. The adjoining **Lady Chapel** has beautiful Perpendicular fan vaulting. Descend a flight of steps into the Romanesque crypt, the main survivor of the Norman cathedral.

The **Chapel of Our Lady** at the western end of the crypt has some of the finest Romanesque carving extant in England. St Thomas was entombed in the Early English eastern end until 1220. This is where Henry II allowed himself to be whipped in penance for having provoked Becket's murder with the infamous words 'who will rid me of this turbulent priest?', and is said to be

the site of many miracles. The **Chapel of St Gabriel** features 12th-century paintings, while the **Black Prince's Chantry** is a beautiful Perpendicular chapel, donated by the prince in 1363.

In the south-west transept the **Chapel of St Michael** includes a wealth of tombs, including that of archbishop Stephen Langton, who helped persuade King John to seal the Magna Carta in 1215. The superb **12th-century choir** rises in stages to the **High Altar** and Trinity Chapel. The screen around the choir stalls was erected in 1305 and evensong has been sung here every day for 800 years. **St Augustine's Chair**, dating from the 13th century, is used to enthrone archbishops.

The stained glass in **Trinity Chapel** is mostly 13th century and celebrates the life of St Thomas à Becket. On either side are the tombs of Henry IV, buried with his wife Joan of Navarre, and of the Black Prince, with its famous effigy along with the prince's shield, gauntlets and sword.

Opposite **St Anselm's Chapel** is the **tomb for Archbishop Sudbury** who, as Chancellor of the Exchequer, was held responsible for a hated poll-tax – he was beheaded by a mob during the Peasants' Revolt of 1381.

Go around the eastern end of the cathedral and turn right into Green Court, which is surrounded on the eastern (right) side by the Deanery and on the northern side (straight ahead) by the early-14th-century Brewhouse and Bakehouse. In the north-western corner (far left) is the celebrated Norman Staircase (1151).

The cathedral is open Monday to Saturday from 9 am to 7 pm from Easter to September, and from 9 am to 5 pm from October to Easter; on Sunday it is open from 12.30 to 2.30 pm and 4.30 to 5.30 pm year-round. Choral evensong is at 5.30 pm weekdays, and at 3.15 pm at weekends. Admission to the cathedral is £3/2.

Other Attractions
The Canterbury Tales (☎ 454888, 479227 for a recording), St Margaret's St, is an automated historical recreation of Chaucer's

famous stories. It's open from 9.30 am to 5 pm year-round and admission costs £5.25/4.50/4.25 for adults/seniors & students/children (family £16.50).

The only remaining city gate, the **West Gate**, dates from the 14th century and survived because it was used as a prison; it now houses a small museum (☎ 452747) with collections of arms and armour. It's open Monday to Saturday from 11 am to 12.30 pm and 1.30 to 3.30 pm; admission costs 90/45p.

The **Canterbury Heritage Museum** (☎ 452747), in a converted 14th-century building in Stour St, gives good, though rather dry, coverage of the city's history. The building, once the Poor Priests' Hospital, is worth visiting in its own right. It's open Monday to Saturday from 10.30 am to 5 pm year-round, but on Sunday from 1.30 to 5 pm June to October only. Admission costs £2.30/1.15 (family £5.15).

Places to Eat
The *Three Tuns Hotel* (☎ 767371, St Margaret's St) dates from the 16th century and serves good-value pub meals for under £5. *Il Vaticano* (☎ 765333, 33-35 St Margaret's St) has a wide range of pastas from £4.50. *Flap Jacques* (☎ 781000, 71 Castle St) is a small, inexpensive French bistro serving Breton-style pancakes.

Getting There & Away
National Express operates up to 16 shuttle buses (one hour 50 minutes, £9 return) a day between London and Canterbury. Canterbury has two train stations: Canterbury East is accessible from Victoria, and Canterbury West is for trains to/from Charing Cross and Waterloo. The journey takes about 1¾ hours and costs £14.80 return.

BRIGHTON
☎ 01273

Just 82km (51 miles) south of London, Brighton, with its heady mix of seediness and sophistication, is most Londoners' favourite seaside resort.

The town's character essentially dates from the 1780s when the dissolute, music-loving Prince Regent (later George IV)

EXCURSIONS

GUY MOBERLY

Go for a paddle on Brighton beach, just an hour's train ride from Victoria station.

began indulging in lavish parties by the sea. Brighton still has some of the hottest clubs and venues outside London, including the largest gay club on the southern coast, a vibrant student population, excellent shopping, a thriving arts scene, and countless restaurants, pubs and cafés.

Orientation & Information

The TIC (☎ 292599), a short distance west of the bus station at 10 Bartholomew Square, is open weekdays from 9 am to 5 pm, on Saturday from 10 am to 5 pm and on Sunday in summer only from 10 am to 4 pm.

Royal Pavilion

The Royal Pavilion (☎ 290900) is an extraordinary fantasy – all Indian palace on the outside and Chinese temple on the inside. It began with a seaside affair, when the Prince Regent came here to hang out with his wayward uncle, the Duke of Cumberland. He fell in love with both the seaside and a local resident, Maria Fitzherbert, and decided that this was the perfect place to party.

The first pavilion, built in 1787, was a classical villa. It wasn't until the early 19th century, when everything Asian became the rage, that the current creation began to take shape. The final Mogul-inspired design was produced by John Nash, architect of Regent's Park and its surrounding crescents, and was built between 1815 and 1822. George is said to have cried when he first saw the Music Room, with its nine lotus-shaped chandeliers and Chinese murals in vermilion and gold. It was badly damaged by fire in 1975 but has since been lovingly restored.

The entire over-the-top edifice, which Queen Victoria – who found Brighton 'far

Not an over-the-top Indian restaurant, but the wonderfully over-the-top Royal Pavilion.

too crowded' – sold to the town in 1850, is not to be missed, but have an especially good look at the Long Gallery, the Banqueting Room, the South Galleries and the superb Great Kitchen. Also keep an eye out for Rex Whistler's humorous painting *HRH The Prince Regent Awakening the Spirit of Brighton* (1944) in which the overweight (and naked) prince is rousing a nubile 'Brighton' with a lascivious look in his eye. It's in the North Gallery on the 1st floor.

The Royal Pavilion is open daily from 10 am to 6 pm (to 5 pm October to May) and costs £4.50/3.25/2.75 for adults/seniors & students/children (family £11.75).

Other Attractions

Originally designed as an indoor tennis court, the **Brighton Museum & Art Gallery** (☎ 290900) houses a quirky collection of Art Deco and Art Nouveau furniture, archaeological finds, surrealist paintings and costumes. The most famous exhibit, Salvador Dali's lips-shaped sofa, is often away on loan though. The museum is open Monday to Saturday (except Wednesday) from 10 am to 5 pm, on Sunday from 2 to 5 pm. Admission is free.

The **Palace Pier**, with its Palace of Fun, is the very essence of Brighton. This is the best spot to buy sticks of the famous sweet called Brighton Rock.

Places to Eat

Brighton is jam-packed with good-value eating places. Wander around the Lanes, a maze of alleyways crammed with shops and restaurants just north of the TIC, or head down to Preston St, which runs back from the seafront near West Pier, and you'll encounter all sorts of interesting, affordable possibilities. The *Dorset Street Bar* *(☎ 605423, 28 North Rd)* is a friendly pub with decent food in the heart of the buzzy North Lane area. *Food for Friends* *(☎ 736236, 18a Prince Albert St)* is the most enduring vegetarian haunt, with excellent platters for around £5. The *Yum Yum Noodle Bar (☎ 606777, 22-23 Sydney*

St) has good-value Chinese, Malay, Thai and vegetarian specials for lunch from £3.95.

Getting There & Away

National Express runs a shuttle service up to 15 times a day from London (one hour 50 minutes, £8 return). There are some 40 fast trains a day from Victoria train station (one hour, £13.80 return) and slower Thameslink trains (£14 return) from King's Cross, Blackfriars and London Bridge.

Castles & Palaces

WINDSOR
☎ 01753

Windsor Castle is one of the nation's premier tourist attractions and, since it is only 37km (23 miles) from central London and easily accessible by rail and road, it crawls with tourists. If possible, avoid visiting at weekends and during the peak months of July and August. Across the river from Windsor is Eton and its celebrated college.

Orientation & Information

Windsor Castle overlooks the River Thames and the town of Windsor spreading out to the west. Eton is essentially a small village linked to Windsor by a pedestrian bridge over the Thames.

Windsor & Eton Central train station is on Thames St, directly opposite the Windsor Castle entrance. Riverside train station is near the bridge over to Eton.

The TIC (☎ 743900), 24 High St, is open Monday to Saturday from 10 am to 5 pm, and on Sunday to 4.30 pm. In winter the daily hours are 10 am to 4 pm, and the centre stays open till 6.30 pm in July and August.

Windsor Castle

Standing on chalk bluffs overlooking the Thames, Windsor Castle (☎ 868286, 831118 for a recording) has been a home to British royalty for over 900 years and is one of the greatest surviving medieval castles in the world. It started out as a wooden motte-and-bailey castle in 1070, was rebuilt in stone in 1165 and successively extended and rebuilt right through to the 19th century.

Castle areas to which the public are admitted are generally open 10 am to 5.30 pm (last entry at 4 pm) March to October, closing an hour earlier the rest of the year. In May and June, weather (and other events) permitting, the changing of the guard takes place Monday to Saturday at 11 am. In July it takes place on even dates.

Entry to the castle is £10/7.50/5 for adults/seniors/children (family £22.50), except on Sunday when it costs £8.50/6.50/4 because St George's Chapel, a prime attraction, is closed for services. The royal Web site is at www.royal.gov.uk.

State Apartments & Other Areas The State Apartments are a combination of formal rooms and museum-style exhibits. In 1992 a fire badly damaged St George's Hall and the adjacent Grand Reception Room. Restoration work costing £37 million was completed in 1998.

Like other parts of the castle, the State Apartments have gone through successive reconstructions and expansions, most notably under Charles II who added lavishly painted ceilings by Antonio Verrio and delicate woodcarvings by Grinling Gibbons. Further extensive modifications were made under George IV and William IV in the 1820s and 1830s.

After the Waterloo Chamber, created to commemorate the Battle of Waterloo and still used for formal meals, and the Garter Throne Room, the **King's Rooms** begin with the King's Drawing Room, also known as the Rubens Room, after the three paintings hanging there. The King's State Bedchamber has paintings by Gainsborough and Canaletto, but Charles II actually slept in the King's Dressing Room next door. Some of Windsor's finest paintings hang here including works by Holbein, Rembrandt, Rubens and Dürer. The King's Closet was used by Charles II as a study and contains works by Canaletto, Reynolds and Hogarth.

From the King's Rooms you come to the **Queen's Rooms**. The Queen's Ballroom has a remarkable collection of Van Dycks. Only three of the 13 Verrio ceiling paintings from Charles II's time survive, one of them in the Queen's Audience Chamber. Gobelins tapestries and another Verrio ceiling can be found in the Queen's Presence Chamber.

Queen Mary's Doll's House was the work of architect Sir Edwin Lutyens and was built on a 1:12 scale in 1923. It's complete in every detail, right down to running water in the bathrooms.

St George's Chapel One of Britain's finest examples of late-Gothic architecture, the chapel was begun by Edward IV in 1475 but not completed until 1528.

The nave is a superb example of the Perpendicular style with beautiful fan vaulting arching out from the pillars. The chapel contains **royal tombs**, including those of George V and Queen Mary, George VI and Edward IV. The **wooden oriel window**, built for Catherine of Aragon by Henry VIII, is a fine example of the Tudor style. The **Garter Stalls** are the chapel's equivalent of choir stalls. Dating back to between 1478 and 1485, the banner, helm and crest above each stall indicates the current occupant. Plates carry the names of earlier knights who have occupied the stalls since the 14th century.

Between the Garter Stalls, the **Royal Vault** is the burial place of George III, George IV and William IV. Another vault between the stalls contains the remains of **Henry VIII**, his favourite wife Jane Seymour, and **Charles I**, reunited with his head, which had been removed after the Civil War.

From the chapel you enter the Dean's Cloister and the adjacent **Albert Memorial Chapel**. This originated in 1240 and became the first chapel of the Order of the Garter in 1350 but fell into disuse when St George's Chapel was built. It was completely restored after the death of Prince Albert in 1861.

Other Attractions

On High St beside Castle Hill, Windsor's fine **Guildhall** was built between 1686 and 1689, its construction completed under Sir Christopher Wren's supervision. The central columns in the open area don't actually support the 1st floor; the council insisted upon them despite Wren's conviction that they were unnecessary. Wren left a few centimetres of clear air (still visible) to prove his point.

Some of the oldest parts of Windsor lie along the cobbled streets behind the Guildhall, including Queen Charlotte St, the shortest road in Britain. The visibly leaning **Market Cross House** is right next to the Guildhall. Nell Gwyn, Charles II's favourite mistress, lived at 4 Church St (now a restaurant).

The 1940-hectare **Windsor Great Park**, where Elizabeth II's consort, the Byzantine Prince Philip, had an avenue of ancient trees beheaded because they got in the way of his horse and buggy (or because he was jealous of their crowns), extends from behind the castle almost as far as Ascot. It is open from 10 am to 6 pm March to October, closing at 4 pm the rest of the year.

Places to Eat

From the tiny, precarious-looking Market Cross House, the ***Crooked House*** turns out excellent but expensive sandwiches and French sticks. Peascod St and its extension St Leonard's Rd are good restaurant hunting grounds. ***Francesco's*** (☎ 863773, 53 Peascod St) is a very popular pizza, pasta and cappuccino specialist with meals for around £6. The ***Crosses Corner*** (☎ 862867, 73 Peascod St) also pulls in the crowds with its pub lunches.

Getting There & Around

Green Line's nonstop bus No 700/702 to Windsor (about one hour, £6.50/3.25 for adults/children) departs from Bulleid Way, Victoria, between eight and 16 times a day from 8 am (on Saturday from 8.30 am, on Sunday from 8.10 am) to 3.50 pm (on Saturday to 5 pm, on Sunday to 4.05 pm).

The last return bus leaves at around 8 pm. Trains run from Waterloo to Riverside station every 30 minutes (hourly on Sunday) and take 50 minutes. Services from Paddington to Windsor & Eton Central require a change at Slough, five minutes from Windsor, but only take about half an hour. The fare is £5.90 return on either route.

Guide Friday's (☎ 01789-294466) open-top double-decker bus tours of the town cost £6.50/5.50/2.50 for adults/seniors & students/children. French Brothers (☎ 851900) operates boat trips between Windsor and Runnymede. A 30-minute trip costs £4.80/6.40 single/return (half price for children).

AROUND WINDSOR
Eton College

Cross the River Thames by the pedestrian Windsor Bridge to reach another enduring symbol of Britain's class system: Eton College, a famous public (meaning private) school that has educated no fewer than 18 prime ministers and the princes William and Harry. Several buildings date from the mid-15th century when Henry VI founded the school.

The school (☎ 01753-671177) is open to visitors during term-time from 2 to 4.30 pm, and during the Easter and summer holidays from 10.30 am to 4.30 pm. Admission costs £2.60/2 for adults/children. Guided tours (daily at 2.15 and 3.15 pm) cost £3.80/3.

LEEDS CASTLE

Just to the east of Maidstone some 70km (43 miles) from London, Leeds Castle (☎ 01622-765400) is justly famous as one of the world's most beautiful palaces. Like something from a fairy tale, it stands on two small islands in a lake surrounded by rolling wooded hills. The building dates from the 9th century, but Henry VIII transformed it from a fortress into a palace. It's open from 10 am to 5 pm March to October (to 3 pm the rest of the year). Admission to the castle, park and gardens is £9.30/7.30/6 for adults/seniors & students/children aged five to 15 (family £25).

National Express has a daily direct service from Victoria Coach Station leaving at 9 am (one hour 20 minutes) and returning in the late afternoon; it must be prebooked and costs £12/9 for adults/children aged under 16. Green Line has a similar deal for £13/7.70, with bus No 980 departing weekdays at 9.35 am. The nearest train station is Bearsted; a combined rail-travel, coach-transfer and admission ticket from either Victoria or Charing Cross train station costs £18.50/9.25.

HEVER CASTLE

Idyllic Hever Castle (☎ 01732-861702, 865224 for a recording) near Edenbridge, about 56km (35 miles) from central London, was the childhood home of Anne Boleyn, mistress to Henry VIII and then his doomed queen. The moated castle was built in the 13th and 15th centuries and restored in the early 20th century by William Waldorf Astor. The exterior remains unchanged from Tudor times, but the interior now has superb Edwardian woodwork. The castle is surrounded by a garden, again the creation of the Astors, that incorporates a formal Italian garden with classical sculpture.

It's open daily from noon to 6 pm (the grounds from 11 am), March to November. Admission to the castle and gardens costs £7.30/6.20/4 for adults/seniors & students/children (family £18.60), or £5.80/4.90/3.80 (£15.40) to just the gardens. The closest train station is at Hever, about 1.5km from the castle (£6.90 return from Victoria via Oxsted).

Stately & Historic Homes

DOWN HOUSE

Charles Darwin, the great Victorian evolutionary theorist, lived at Down House (☎ 01689-859119), Luxted Rd, Downe, near Orpington, Kent, for over 40 years. The stunning Victorian interior of this fine Georgian house has been restored to show his study, where he wrote the seminal *On the Origin of Species* (1859), to best effect. Temporary exhibitions are housed upstairs, and you can also explore the garden.

Down House is open Wednesday to Sunday from 10 am to 6 pm, mid-April to September, to 5 pm in October, and to 4 pm during the rest of the year, except in February when it is closed. Admission costs £5.50/4.10/2.80 for adults/seniors & students/children under 15 (free to English Heritage members).

Though it has a Kent postal address, Down House is in south-east London. To get there take a train from Victoria to Bromley South and then catch bus No 146.

KNOLE HOUSE

For the most part dating from 1456, Knole (☎ 01732-462100, 450608 for a recording) is not as old as some of the great country houses that incorporate medieval fortresses but is more coherent in style. It seems as if nothing much has been changed since the early 17th century, something the Sackville family, who have owned it since 1566, can take credit for.

The writer Vita Sackville-West was born here in 1892, and her friend Virginia Woolf based her novel *Orlando* on the history of the house and family. It is a vast complex, with seven courtyards, 52 staircases and 365 rooms, so the excellent guidebook is recommended.

The house is open Wednesday to Saturday from noon to 4 pm, and on Sunday from 11 am to 5 pm, from late March to October. The surrounding park is open year-round. Admission to the house costs £5/2.50 for adults/children (free to National Trust members who also get to park for free; everyone else pays £2.50). A family ticket costs £12.50.

Knole is to the east of Sevenoaks, 39km (24 miles) south-east of London. Sevenoaks train station is a 2.5km walk from the house; there's a special connecting bus service (☎ 0845 748 4950 for details). A return from Charing Cross costs about £10.

CHARTWELL

Winston Churchill bought Chartwell (☎ 01732-868381, 866368 for a recording), a large country house just north of Edenbridge, 34km (21 miles) south-east of London, in 1922 and it remained the family home until his death. It is open Wednesday to Sunday from 11 am to 5 pm from late March to October; in July and August it also opens on Tuesday. Admission costs £5.50/2.75 for adults/children (free to National Trust members); a family ticket is £13.75. Entry to just the garden and studio is £2.75/1.35.

To get there take a train from Victoria to Bromley South and then bus No 246 to the house. From May to September there's a package costing £13/6.50 (£8.50 for NT members), which includes return train travel from Charing Cross to Sevenoaks, the Chartwell Explorer bus to the house and admission.

EXCURSIONS

LONELY PLANET

Guides by Region

Lonely Planet is known worldwide for publishing practical, reliable and no-nonsense travel information in our guides and on our Web site. The Lonely Planet list covers just about every accessible part of the world. Currently there are thirteen series: travel guides, shoestring guides, walking guides, city guides, phrasebooks, audio packs, city maps, travel atlases, diving and snorkeling guides, restaurant guides, first-time travel guides, healthy travel and travel literature.

AFRICA Africa – the South ● Africa on a shoestring ● Arabic (Egyptian) phrasebook ● Arabic (Moroccan) phrasebook ● Cairo ● Cape Town ● Cape Town city map● Central Africa ● East Africa ● Egypt ● Egypt travel atlas ● Ethiopian (Amharic) phrasebook ● The Gambia & Senegal ● Healthy Travel Africa ● Kenya ● Kenya travel atlas ● Malawi, Mozambique & Zambia ● Morocco ● North Africa ● South Africa, Lesotho & Swaziland ● South Africa, Lesotho & Swaziland travel atlas ● Swahili phrasebook ● Tanzania, Zanzibar & Pemba ● Trekking in East Africa ● Tunisia ● West Africa ● Zimbabwe, Botswana & Namibia ● Zimbabwe, Botswana & Namibia travel atlas
Travel Literature: The Rainbird: A Central African Journey ● Songs to an African Sunset: A Zimbabwean Story ● Mali Blues: Traveling to an African Beat

AUSTRALIA & THE PACIFIC Auckland ● Australia ● Australian phrasebook ● Bushwalking in Australia ● Bushwalking in Papua New Guinea ● Fiji ● Fijian phrasebook ● Islands of Australia's Great Barrier Reef ● Melbourne ● Melbourne city map ● Micronesia ● New Caledonia ● New South Wales & the ACT ● New Zealand ● Northern Territory ● Outback Australia ● Out To Eat – Melbourne ● Papua New Guinea ● Papua New Guinea (Pidgin) phrasebook ● Queensland ● Rarotonga & the Cook Islands ● Samoa ● Solomon Islands ● South Australia ● South Pacific Languages phrasebook ● Sydney ● Sydney city map ● Tahiti & French Polynesia ● Tasmania ● Tonga ● Tramping in New Zealand ● Vanuatu ● Victoria ● Western Australia
Travel Literature: Islands in the Clouds ● Kiwi Tracks ● Sean & David's Long Drive

CENTRAL AMERICA & THE CARIBBEAN Bahamas and Turks & Caicos ● Bermuda ● Central America on a shoestring ● Costa Rica ● Cuba ● Dominican Republic & Haiti ● Eastern Caribbean ● Guatemala, Belize & Yucatán: La Ruta Maya ● Jamaica ● Mexico ● Mexico City ● Panama ● Puerto Rico
Travel Literature: Green Dreams: Travels in Central America

EUROPE Amsterdam ● Amsterdam city map ● Andalucía ● Austria ● Baltic States phrasebook ● Barcelona ● Berlin ● Berlin city map ● Britain ● British phrasebook ● Brussels, Bruges & Antwerp ● Budapest city map ● Canary Islands ● Central Europe ● Central Europe phrasebook ● Corsica ● Croatia ● Czech & Slovak Republics ● Denmark ● Dublin ● Eastern Europe ● Eastern Europe phrasebook ● Edinburgh ● Estonia, Latvia & Lithuania ● Europe ● Finland ● France ● French phrasebook ● Germany ● German phrasebook ● Greece ● Greek phrasebook ● Hungary ● Iceland, Greenland & the Faroe Islands ● Ireland ● Italian phrasebook ● Italy ● Lisbon ● London ● London city map ● Mediterranean Europe ● Mediterranean Europe phrasebook ● Norway ● Paris ● Paris city map ● Poland ● Portugal ● Portugal travel atlas ● Prague ● Prague city map ● Provence & the Côte d'Azur ● Romania & Moldova ● Rome ● Russia, Ukraine & Belarus ● Russian phrasebook ● Scandinavian & Baltic Europe ● Scandinavian Europe phrasebook ● Scotland ● Slovenia ● Spain ● Spanish phrasebook ● St Petersburg ● Switzerland ● Trekking in Spain ● Ukrainian phrasebook ● Vienna ● Walking in Britain ● Walking in Ireland ● Walking in Italy ● Walking in Switzerland ● Western Europe ● Western Europe phrasebook
Travel Literature: The Olive Grove: Travels in Greece

INDIAN SUBCONTINENT Bangladesh ● Bengali phrasebook ● Bhutan ● Delhi ● Goa ● Hindi/Urdu phrasebook ● India ● India & Bangladesh travel atlas ● Indian Himalaya ● Karakoram Highway ● Kerala ● Mumbai ● Nepal ● Nepali phrasebook ● Pakistan ● Rajasthan ● Read This First: Asia & India ● South India ● Sri Lanka ● Sri Lanka phrasebook ● Trekking in the Indian Himalaya ● Trekking in the Karakoram & Hindukush ● Trekking in the Nepal Himalaya
Travel Literature: In Rajasthan ● Shopping for Buddhas

LONELY PLANET

Mail Order

Lonely Planet products are distributed worldwide. They are also available by mail order from Lonely Planet, so if you have difficulty finding a title please write to us. North and South American residents should write to 150 Linden St, Oakland, CA 94607, USA; European and African residents should write to 10a Spring Place, London NW5 3BH, UK; and residents of other countries to PO Box 617, Hawthorn, Victoria 3122, Australia.

ISLANDS OF THE INDIAN OCEAN Madagascar & Comoros • Maldives • Mauritius, Réunion & Seychelles

MIDDLE EAST & CENTRAL ASIA Arab Gulf States • Central Asia • Central Asia phrasebook • Hebrew phrasebook • Iran • Israel & the Palestinian Territories • Israel & the Palestinian Territories travel atlas • Istanbul • Istanbul to Cairo • Jerusalem • Jordan & Syria • Jordan, Syria & Lebanon travel atlas • Lebanon • Middle East on a shoestring • Syria • Turkey • Turkish phrasebook • Turkey travel atlas • Yemen
Travel Literature: The Gates of Damascus • Kingdom of the Film Stars: Journey into Jordan

NORTH AMERICA Alaska • Backpacking in Alaska • Baja California • California & Nevada • Canada • Chicago • Chicago city map • Deep South • Florida • Hawaii • Honolulu • Las Vegas • Los Angeles • Miami • New England • New Orleans • New York City • New York city map • New York, New Jersey & Pennsylvania • Pacific Northwest USA • Puerto Rico • Rocky Mountain States • San Francisco • San Francisco city map • Seattle • Southwest USA • Texas • USA • USA phrasebook • Vancouver • Washington, DC & the Capital Region • Washington DC city map
Travel Literature: Drive Thru America

NORTH-EAST ASIA Beijing • Cantonese phrasebook • China • Hong Kong • Hong Kong city map • Hong Kong, Macau & Guangzhou • Japan • Japanese phrasebook • Japanese audio pack • Korea • Korean phrasebook • Kyoto • Mandarin phrasebook • Mongolia • Mongolian phrasebook • North-East Asia on a shoestring • Seoul • South-West China • Taiwan • Tibet • Tibetan phrasebook • Tokyo
Travel Literature: Lost Japan

SOUTH AMERICA Argentina, Uruguay & Paraguay • Bolivia • Brazil • Brazilian phrasebook • Buenos Aires • Chile & Easter Island • Chile & Easter Island travel atlas • Colombia • Ecuador & the Galapagos Islands • Latin American Spanish phrasebook • Peru • Quechua phrasebook • Rio de Janeiro • Rio de Janeiro city map • South America on a shoestring • Trekking in the Patagonian Andes • Venezuela
Travel Literature: Full Circle: A South American Journey

SOUTH-EAST ASIA Bali & Lombok • Bangkok • Bangkok city map • Burmese phrasebook • Cambodia • Hanoi • Healthy Travel Asia & India • Hill Tribes phrasebook • Ho Chi Minh City • Indonesia • Indonesia's Eastern Islands • Indonesian phrasebook • Indonesian audio pack • Jakarta • Java • Laos • Lao phrasebook • Laos travel atlas • Malay phrasebook • Malaysia, Singapore & Brunei • Myanmar (Burma) • Philippines • Pilipino (Tagalog) phrasebook • Singapore • South-East Asia on a shoestring • South-East Asia phrasebook • Thailand • Thailand's Islands & Beaches • Thailand travel atlas • Thai phrasebook • Thai audio pack • Vietnam • Vietnamese phrasebook • Vietnam travel atlas

ALSO AVAILABLE: Antarctica • The Arctic • Brief Encounters: Stories of Love, Sex & Travel • Chasing Rickshaws • Lonely Planet Unpacked • Not the Only Planet: Travel Stories from Science Fiction • Sacred India • Travel with Children • Traveller's Tales

FREE Lonely Planet Newsletters

We love hearing from you and think you'd like to hear from us.

Planet Talk

Our FREE quarterly printed newsletter is full of tips from travellers and anecdotes from Lonely Planet guidebook authors. Every issue is packed with up-to-date travel news and advice, and includes:

- a postcard from Lonely Planet co-founder Tony Wheeler
- a swag of mail from travellers
- a look at life on the road through the eyes of a Lonely Planet author
- topical health advice
- prizes for the best travel yarn
- news about forthcoming Lonely Planet events
- a complete list of Lonely Planet books and other titles

To join our mailing list, residents of the UK, Europe and Africa can email us at go@lonelyplanet.co.uk; residents of North and South America can email us at info@lonelyplanet.com; the rest of the world can email us at talk2us@lonelyplanet.com.au, or contact any Lonely Planet office.

Spot the LP Taxi

To celebrate the launch of the first edition of Lonely Planet's *London* guide, we asked readers to send us photos featuring the Lonely Planet taxi.

The best entry we received was from Lyndsay Ammon of Diamond Barica, USA (pictured here in her prizewinning shot).

Thanks Lyndsay and all the other readers who sent in their contributions.

Index

Text

Bold indicates maps.

Boxed Text

MAP 2 – CENTRAL LONDON

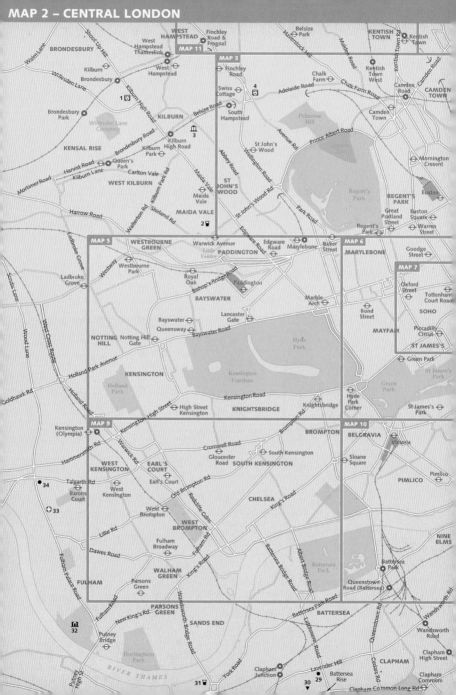

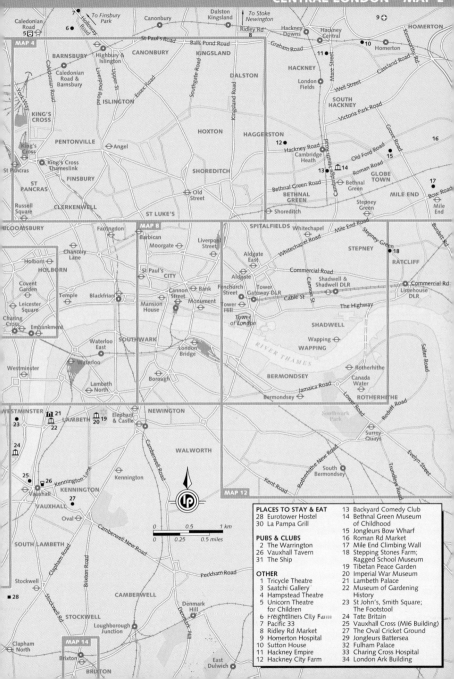

MAP 4

To Finsbury Park
Caledonian Road
Canonbury
Dalston Kingsland
To Stoke Newington
Holloway Road
St Paul's Road
Balls Pond Road
Ridley Rd
Hackney Downs
Hackney Central
HOMERTON
BARNSBURY
Highbury & Islington
CANONBURY
KINGSLAND
Graham Road
Homerton
Caledonian Road & Barnsbury
Liverpool Road
Upper St
Essex Road
Southgate Road
DALSTON
HACKNEY
Mare Street
Well Street
London Fields
Cassland Road
ISLINGTON
Kingsland Road
Victoria Park Road
SOUTH HACKNEY
Grove Road
KING'S CROSS
King's Cross
HOXTON
HAGGERSTON
Hackney Road
GLOBE TOWN
PENTONVILLE
Angel
Cambridge Heath
Old Ford Road
King's Cross Thameslink
Roman Road
MILE END
St Pancras
FINSBURY
SHOREDITCH
Bethnal Green Road
Cambridge Heath Road
Bethnal Green
Stepney Green
Mile End
Russell Square
Old Street
BETHNAL GREEN
Bow Road
ST PANCRAS
CLERKENWELL
ST LUKE'S
Shoreditch

BLOOMSBURY
Farringdon
MAP 8
Barbican
SPITALFIELDS
Whitechapel
Mile End Road
Stepney Green
Moorgate
Liverpool Street
Chancery Lane
Whitechapel Road
STEPNEY
Holborn
St Paul's
Aldgate East
RATCLIFF
HOLBORN
CITY
Commercial Road
Ratcliff
Covent Garden
Bank
Aldgate
Shadwell & Shadwell DLR
Commercial Rd
Leicester Square
Temple
Blackfriars
Cannon Street
Monument
Fenchurch Street
Cable St
Limehouse DLR
Charing Cross
Mansion House
Tower Gateway DLR
The Highway
Salter Road
Embankment
Tower Hill
SOUTHWARK
Tower of London
SHADWELL
Waterloo East
London Bridge
Wapping
Westminster
Waterloo
WAPPING
Rotherhithe
RIVER THAMES
Canada Water
Lambeth North
Borough
BERMONDSEY
ROTHERHITHE
Jamaica Road
Lower Road
Redriff Road
WESTMINSTER
LAMBETH
NEWINGTON
Bermondsey
Elephant & Castle
Southwark Park
WALWORTH
Surrey Quays
Kennington
Vauxhall
KENNINGTON
South Bermondsey
Rotherhithe New Road
Evelyn Street
Trundleys Road
Oval
VAUXHALL
MAP 12
Kent Road
SOUTH LAMBETH
Camberwell New Road
Stockwell
Peckham Road
Brixton Road
STOCKWELL
CAMBERWELL
Denmark Hill
Clapham North
28
MAP 14
Loughborough Junction
Brixton
BRIXTON
East Dulwich

Scale: 0.5 km / 1 km / 0.25 / 0.5 miles

MAP 3

PLACES TO STAY
51 St Pancras International
   YHA Hostel
54 Jenkins Hotel
55 Crescent Hotel;
   Euro Hotel
56 John Adams Hall
   Student Residence
57 Passfield Hall Student
   Residence
59 Hotels
61 Hotels
65 International Students
   House

PLACES TO EAT
2 Mulan Chinese Restaurant
3 Lemonia
4 Trojka Russian Tea Room/
   Primrose Brasserie
6 Marine Ices
8 Belgo Noord
9 Nando's
10 Cottons Rhum Shop,
   Bar & Restaurant
11 Silks & Spice
12 Thanh Binh
18 Sauce barorganicdiner
21 Mango Room
24 Pizza Express

26 Wazobia
27 Lemon Grass
28 Castle's
33 Bar Gansa
34 Curly Dog Café
38 China Blues
39 New Culture Revolution
43 Ruby in the Dust
45 Café Delancey
46 Taste of Siam
48 Asakusa
49 El Parador
62 Ravi Shankar
63 Diwana
64 Chutneys

PUBS & CLUBS
5 Pembroke Castle
14 HQ
15 Dingwalls; Jongleurs
   Camden Lock
22 WKD Café
23 The Verge
25 Camden Falcon; Barfly
30 World's End;
   Underground
31 Black Cap
32 Jazz Café; Camden
   Ticket Shop
35 The Engineer

36 Cecil Sharp House
40 The Hogshead
44 Crown & Goose
47 Camden Palace

OTHER
1 Freud Museum
7 Roundhouse
13 London Waterbus
   Company
16 Waterside Café;
   Jenny Wren Cruises
17 Compendium
19 Camden Market
20 Electric Market;
   Electric Ballroom
29 Sainsbury's Supermarket
37 Forco Laundrette
41 Jewish Museum
50 Camley St Natural Park
52 STA Travel
53 St Pancras New Church
58 Petrie Museum of
   Egyptian Archaeology
60 University College
   Hospital
66 Open Air Theatre
67 London Central Mosque
68 Abbey Rd Zebra Crossing

MAP 5

MAP 3

MAP 4

MAP 4

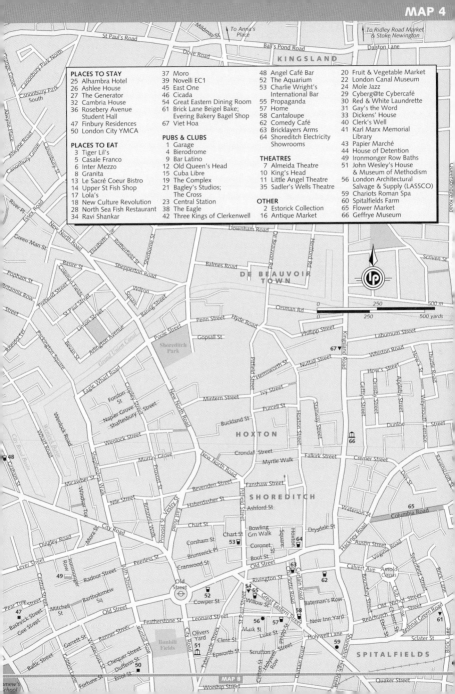

PLACES TO STAY
25 Alhambra Hotel
26 Ashlee House
27 The Generator
32 Cambria House
36 Rosebery Avenue
   Student Hall
47 Finbury Residences
50 London City YMCA

PLACES TO EAT
3 Tiger Lil's
4 Casale Franco
6 Inter Mezzo
8 Granita
13 Le Sacré Coeur Bistro
14 Upper St Fish Shop
17 Lola's
18 New Culture Revolution
28 North Sea Fish Restaurant
34 Ravi Shankar

37 Moro
39 Novelli EC1
45 East One
46 Cicada
54 Great Eastern Dining Room
61 Brick Lane Beigel Bake;
   Evering Bakery Bagel Shop
67 Viet Hoa

PUBS & CLUBS
1 Garage
4 Bierodrome
9 Bar Latino
12 Old Queen's Head
15 Cuba Libre
19 The Complex
21 Bagley's Studios;
   The Cross
23 Central Station
38 The Eagle
42 Three Kings of Clerkenwell

48 Angel Café Bar
52 The Aquarium
53 Charlie Wright's
   International Bar
57 Propaganda
57 Home
58 Cantaloupe
62 Comedy Café
63 Bricklayers Arms
64 Shoreditch Electricity
   Showrooms

THEATRES
7 Almeida Theatre
5 King's Head
11 Little Angel Theatre
35 Sadler's Wells Theatre

OTHER
2 Estorick Collection
16 Antique Market

20 Fruit & Vegetable Market
22 London Canal Museum
24 Mole Jazz
29 Cyberg@te Cybercafé
30 Red & White Laundrette
31 Gay's the Word
33 Dickens' House
40 Clerk's Well
41 Karl Marx Memorial
   Library
43 Papier Marché
44 House of Detention
49 Ironmonger Row Baths
51 John Wesley's House
   & Museum of Methodism
56 London Architectural
   Salvage & Supply (LASSCO)
59 Chariots Roman Spa
60 Spitalfields Farm
65 Flower Market
66 Geffrye Museum

MAP 5

To The
Warrington

Goldney Rd.

Harrow Road

Shirland Road

Clifton Gardens

Warwick
Avenue

Woodfield

Sutherland Avenue

Blomfield Road

Warwick Pl.

18

19

20

21

22

Elkstone Road

Grand Union Canal

Delamere Terrace

Bourne Terrace

Westbourne Terrace

Cotbrook Rd.

Warrington Road

St Ervan's Road

Bevington Road

Westway

Alfred Rd.

Harrow Road

Senior Street

Westbourne
Park

Great Western Road

Tavistock Crescent

Tavistock Road

Portobello Road

Acklam Rd.

1

2

3

14

13

15

16

17

Westbourne Park Villas

Lord Hills
Bridge

Royal
Oak

Randolph
Bridge

Cloucester Terrace

Orsett Terrace

Bishop's Bridge Road

Craven
Hill
Gdns

50

6

Lancaster Road

Westbourne Park Road

Westbourne Park Road

Talbot Road

Cropston Road

Kildare Terrace

Hereford Road

Newton

63

64

62

65

59 60 61

To Ladbroke
Grove Tube
Station

4

5

Westbourne Park Road

Blenheim Crescent

Elgin Crescent

7

8 9

11

10

12

Talbot Rd.

Colville Terrace

Artesian Road

Westbourne Grove

71

70

69

67 66

68 Leinster Sq.

58

57

55

Whiteley's
Shopping
Centre

Porchester Gardens

Queensway

Bayswater

56

Bayswater

NOTTING
HILL

74

Lonsdale Rd.

73

Westbourne Grove

72

Chepstow Villas

Pembridge Villas

Chepstow
Cres.

Dawson Place

Prince's

Square

Moscow Rd.

BAYSWATER

54

53 52 51

Arundel Gdns.

75

Stanley
Gdns.

76

Kensington Park Gdns.

Portobello Road

Pembridge Cres.

Pembridge
Square

Ledbury Road

77

Pembridge Gardens

Hereford Road

Ossington Street

Clanricarde Gardens

83

Queensway

Bayswater Road

North Walk

Ladbroke Crescent

Ladbroke Grove

Ladbroke Gardens

Kensington Park Road

78

79

80

81

82

84

85

Notting
Hill Gate

Notting Hill Gate

Pembridge Road

KENSINGTON
GARDENS

St John's Gdns.

Clarendon Road

Lansdowne Walk

Ladbroke Road

Ladbroke Square

Ladbroke
Square
Gardens

90

89

91

88 87

86

Uxbridge St.

Palace Gardens Terrace

Palace Gardens Mews

Kensington Palace Gardens

Portland Road

Holland
Park

92

Holland Park Avenue

Holland Park Avenue

Hillgate Road

Kensington Place

94

Peel Street

Camden Street

Bedford Gardens

Brunswick Gardens

Church Street

The
Round Pond

109

KENSINGTON

Aubrey Road

Aubrey Walk

93

Sheffield Terrace

Campden Hill

Hornton Street

Kensington Church Street

95

Kensington
Palace Green

Kensington
Palace

The Broad Walk

HOLLAND
PARK

HOLLAND
PARK

Holland Park Mews

Holland Park

Holland Park

Holland Walk

Campden Hill

Duchess of Bedford's Walk

Holland House

96

Phillimore Gardens

Campden Hill Road

Sheffield Terrace

Campden Gr.

Pitt Street

Holland Street

Hornton Street

Vicarage Gate

Palace Green

Palace Avenue

The Dutch Garden

Abbotsbury Road

Addison Road

Holland Walk

Phillimore Walk

Kensington High Street

Wright's Lane

Kensington Square

High Street
Kensington

106

105 107

108

104

103

St Alban's
Grove

Victoria Road

Palace Gate

Oakwood Ct.

Ilchester Place

Abbotsbury Close

Melbury Rd.

97

100

99 98

MAP 9

101

102

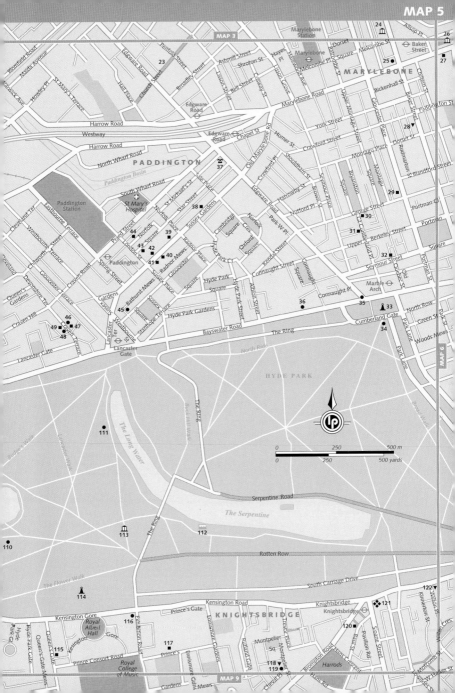

MAP 5

PLACES TO STAY
27 University of Westminster Student Hall
29 Wigmore Court Hotel
30 Bryanston Court Hotel
31 Glynne Court Hotel
32 Edward Lear Hotel
38 Pavilion Hotel
39 Gresham Hotel
40 Europa House Hotel
41 Balmoral House Branch
42 Balmoral House Hotel
43 Cardiff Hotel
44 Norfolk Court & St David's Hotel
47 Elysée Hotel
49 Oxford Hotel; Sass House Hotel
50 The Hempel; I-Thai Restaurant
51 Queen's Park Hotel
52 Hyde Park Hostel
53 Inverness Court Hotel
54 Quest Hotel; Royal Hotel
57 Garden Court Hotel
66 Leinster Inn
75 Portobello Gold Hotel; Buzz Bar Cybercafé
76 Portobello Hotel
77 Gate Hotel
79 Abbey Court Hotel
81 Hillgate Hotel
83 Manor Court Hotel
92 Kensington Guesthouse
95 Abbey House; Vicarage Hotel
96 Holland House YHA Hostel
115 The Gore
117 Imperial College Student Hall
120 Basil St Hotel

PLACES TO EAT
3 Sausage & Mash Café
5 Belgo Zuid
6 Café Grove
8 Osteria Basilico
14 Bali Sugar
15 Anonimato
19 Green Olive
28 Reubens
55 Kalamaras Micro
58 L'Accento
59 The Standard
60 Khan's
61 Tawana
64 Churrería Española
67 Inaho
68 Veronica's
69 Assagi; The Chepstow Pub
71 Mandola
78 Modhubon Tandoori
80 Manzara
85 Novelli W8
86 Kensington Place
87 Geales
88 Costas Fish Restaurant
90 Pharmacy
91 Nachos
100 Sticky Fingers
103 Wódka
105 Spago 2
107 Arcadia; Bellini's
109 The Orangery
118 Montpeliano
122 Vong

PUBS & CLUBS
1 Subterania
4 Ion
13 Market Bar
16 The Cow
17 The Westbourne
21 Bridge House; Canal St Theatre
56 Bar Oz
72 Beach Blanket Babylon
84 Notting Hill Arts Club
93 Windsor Castle
94 The Churchill Arms
108 Cuba

OTHER
2 Honest Jon's
7 Books for Cooks
9 Travel Bookshop
10 Electric Cinema
11 Spice Shop
12 Rough Trade
18 Jason's Canal Trips; Jason's Restaurant
20 British Waterways Office
22 London Waterbus Boats
23 Market
24 Sherlock Holmes Museum
25 LRT Lost Property Office
26 Madame Tussaud's; London Planetarium
33 Marble Arch
34 Speakers' Corner
35 Tyburn Tree Site
36 Tyburn Convent
37 CallShop
45 Hyde Park Stables (Horse Riding)
46 Sandwich Bar Laundrette
48 Drifters
62 Laundrette Centre
63 Porchester Spa
65 Al Saqi Books
70 Sean Arnold Sporting Antiques
73 Award-Winning Toilets
74 Portobello Rd Market
82 Notting Hill Laundrette
89 Airbus Stop
97 Linley Sambourne House
98 Usit Campus; YHA Adventure Shop
99 Trailfinders (Main Office)
101 Commonwealth Institute
102 Trailfinders (Branch)
104 Leith's School of Food & Wine
106 Hype DF
110 Bandstand
111 Peter Pan Statue
112 Serpentine Lido
113 Serpentine Gallery
114 Albert Memorial
116 Royal Geographical Society
119 Bonhams
121 Harvey Nichols; Fifth Floor Restaurant

MAP 6

PLACES TO STAY
2 Indian Student YMCA
4 Ramsay Hall
5 Carr Saunders Hall
9 Hotel Cavendish; Arran House Hotel
10 Jesmond Hotel; Ridgemount Hotel
20 Academy Hotel
21 St Margaret's Hotel
22 Repton Hotel
23 Ruskin Hotel
24 Museum Inn Hostel
25 Haddon Hall Hotel
37 The Rookery
78 City of London YHA Hostel
91 King's College Student Hall
107 Travel Inn Capital
138 The Halkin
142 Park Lane Hotel
143 The Metropolitan; Nobu Japanese Restaurant
144 Hilton Hotel
147 Chesterfield Hotel

MAP 6

MAP 6

MAP 6

MAP 7

MAP 7

MAP 7

MAP 7

On the up and up: revellers celebrate their sexuality at the London Mardi Gras in Soho.

MAP 8

MAP 4

Worship Street

Quaker Street

Fann St
1

City
University

Finsbury

Folgate Street
12

Chiswell Street

Earl St

Spital Sq
6

Hanbury Str
11

Beech Street

Barbican
Centre

Ropemaker St

Lackington
St

Sun St

Arnold St

Lamb St
7

Wilkes St
9
10

SPITALFIELDS
Spitalfields
Market

Fournier Str
8

Brushfield St

Moorgate

Fore Street

South Pl

Eldon Street

3

Liverpool
Street
Station

Artillery Lane

White's Row

Brune St

Aldgate
East

Finsbury
Circus

5

Liverpool Street
4
Liverpool
Street

New St

Middlesex St

Cobb St

Fashion St

Bartholomew's
Hospital

London Wall

London Wall

Wormwood St

Great
Winchester
Street

Petticoat
Lane
Market

36

Basinghall
Ave

Coleman

Old Broad St

Houndsditch

37

Guildhall

Angel St le Grand

35

CITY

33

Bishopsgate

Bevis Marks

St Botolph St

Aldgate

Newgate St

38

Lothbury

34

Stock
Exchange

Threadneedle Street

Leadenhall St

24
23

St Paul's

39

Cheapside

Poultry

Bank of
England
32

Royal Exchange

28
Cornhill

Bank

Lloyd's
of
London

Mitre St

Aldgate High St

St Paul's
Cathedral
41

Watling Street

40

Queen Victoria Street

50

31

30

27
26
25

29

Fenchurch Street

Haydon St

St Paul's
Churchyard

42
44

45

Cannon Street

51

52

Cannon
Street

53

Mark Lane

Fenchurch
Street Station

Portsoken St
Goodmans Yd

43
Castle
Baynard Street

46

Mansion
House

47

48

Hill

Monument

Eastcheap

57

58

Pepys St

61

Tower Hill

Shorter St

Upper Thames Street

Cannon
Street
Station

Cousin La

Monument

Pudding
Lane

55

56

Great Tower St

59
60

Tower Hill

Gloucester
Court

Swan
Lane Pier

London Bridge

Lower Thames Street

54

Old Billingsgate
Market

Custom
House

Lr Thames St

Tower
of
London

Bankside

100

Southwark Bridge

Swan Lane Pier

Bankside

98

Tower
Pier

Upper Pool

69

70

Tate
Modern

101

99

97

Park Street

96

Clink St

94

95

93

92

Tooley St

88

89

Southwark
Crown Court

86

Zoar St

Southwark Bridge Road

Duke
Hill

London
Bridge

91

Tooley Street

Abbots La

Vine Lane

Lavington St

102

103

Borough
Market

104

Rlwy App

90

London
Bridge
Station

Magdalen
St

87

81
80

82

SOUTHWARK

King's
Head Yd

105

106

107

Gt Maze Pond

Crucifix Lane

85

83

Copperfield St

108

Guy's
Hospital

Newcomen Street

Druid St

84

Mint St

109

Borough

110

BOROUGH

Long Lane

Leathermarket St

Tanner St

Abbey Street

BERMONDSEY

To Manze's
Pie Shop
(100m)

Bermondsey
Market

0   250   500 m

0   250   500 yards

111

To Elephant
& Castle

LP

MAP 8

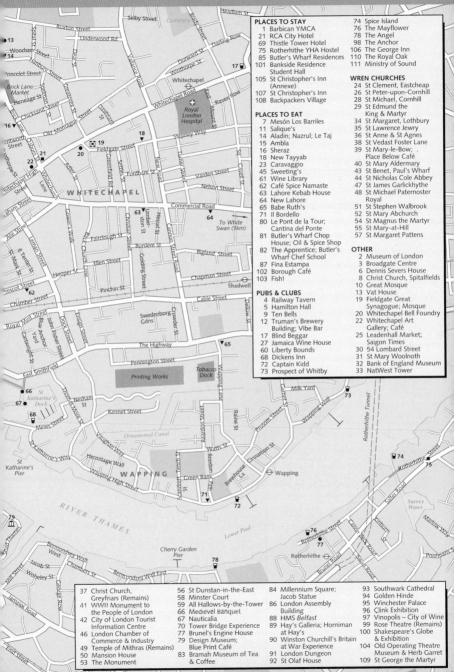

PLACES TO STAY
1 Barbican YMCA
21 RCA City Hotel
69 Thistle Tower Hotel
75 Rotherhithe YHA Hostel
85 Butler's Wharf Residences
101 Bankside Residence
    Student Hall
105 St Christopher's Inn
    (Annexe)
107 St Christopher's Inn
108 Backpackers Village

PLACES TO EAT
7 Mesón Los Barriles
11 Salique's
14 Aladin; Nazrul; Le Taj
15 Ambla
16 Sheraz
18 New Tayyab
23 Caravaggio
45 Sweeting's
61 Wine Library
62 Café Spice Namaste
63 Lahore Kebab House
64 New Lahore
66 Babe Ruth's
71 Il Bordello
80 Le Pont de la Tour;
    Cantina del Ponte
81 Butler's Wharf Chop
    House; Oil & Spice Shop
82 The Apprentice; Butler's
    Wharf Chef School
87 Fina Estampa
102 Borough Café
103 Fish!

PUBS & CLUBS
4 Railway Tavern
5 Hamilton Hall
10 Ten Bells
12 Truman's Brewery
    Building; Vibe Bar
27 Blind Beggar
27 Jamaica Wine House
60 Liberty Bounds
68 Dickens Inn
72 Captain Kidd
73 Prospect of Whitby

74 Spice Island
76 The Mayflower
78 The Angel
98 The Anchor
106 The George Inn
110 The Royal Oak
111 Ministry of Sound

WREN CHURCHES
24 St Clement, Eastcheap
26 St Peter-upon-Cornhill
28 St Michael, Cornhill
29 St Edmund the
    King & Martyr
34 St Margaret, Lothbury
35 St Lawrence Jewry
36 St Anne & St Agnes
38 St Vedast Foster Lane
39 St Mary-le-Bow;
    Place Below Café
40 St Mary Aldermary
43 St Benet, Paul's Wharf
44 St Nicholas Cole Abbey
47 St James Garlickhythe
48 St Michael Paternoster
    Royal
51 St Stephen Walbrook
52 St Mary Abchurch
54 St Magnus the Martyr
55 St Mary-at-Hill
57 St Margaret Pattens

OTHER
2 Museum of London
3 Broadgate Centre
6 Dennis Severs House
8 Christ Church, Spitalfields
10 Great Mosque
13 Vat House
19 Fieldgate Great
    Synagogue; Mosque
20 Whitechapel Bell Foundry
22 Whitechapel Art
    Gallery; Café
25 Leadenhall Market;
    Saigon Times
30 54 Lombard Street
31 St Mary Woolnoth
32 Bank of England Museum
33 NatWest Tower

37 Christ Church,
    Greyfriars (Remains)
41 WWII Monument to
    the People of London
42 City of London Tourist
    Information Centre
46 London Chamber of
    Commerce & Industry
49 Temple of Mithras (Remains)
50 Mansion House
53 The Monument

56 St Dunstan-in-the-East
58 Minster Court
59 All Hallows-by-the-Tower
    Medieval Banquet
67 Nauticalia
70 Tower Bridge Experience
77 Brunel's Engine House
79 Design Museum;
    Blue Print Café
83 Bramah Museum of Tea
    & Coffee

84 Millennium Square;
    Jacob Statue
86 London Assembly
    Building
88 HMS *Belfast*
89 Hay's Galleria; Horniman
    at Hay's
90 Winston Churchill's Britain
    at War Experience
91 London Dungeon
92 St Olaf House

93 Southwark Cathedral
94 Golden Hinde
95 Winchester Palace
96 Clink Exhibition
97 Vinopolis – City of Wine
99 Rose Theatre (Remains)
100 Shakespeare's Globe
    & Exhibition
104 Old Operating Theatre
    Museum & Herb Garret
109 St George the Martyr

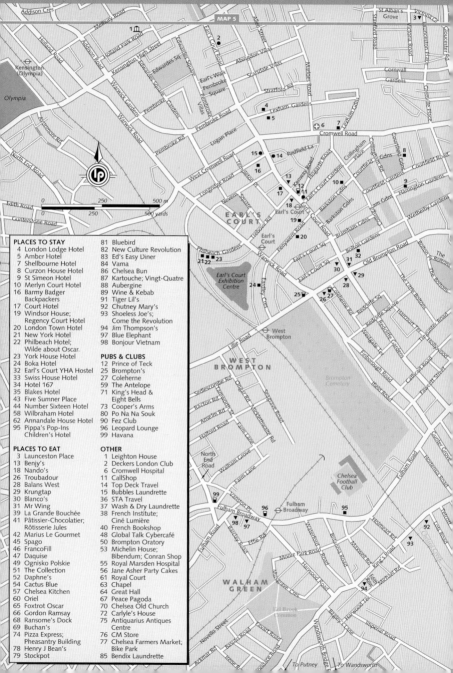

MAP 9

MAP 5

PLACES TO STAY
4 London Lodge Hotel
5 Amber Hotel
7 Shellbourne Hotel
8 Curzon House Hotel
9 St Simeon Hotel
10 Merlyn Court Hotel
16 Barmy Badger
   Backpackers
17 Court Hotel
19 Windsor House;
   Regency Court Hotel
20 London Town Hotel
21 New York Hotel
22 Philbeach Hotel;
   Wilde about Oscar.
23 York House Hotel
24 Boka Hotel
32 Earl's Court YHA Hostel
33 Swiss House Hotel
34 Hotel 167
35 Blakes Hotel
43 Five Sumner Place
44 Number Sixteen Hotel
58 Wilbraham Hotel
62 Annandale House Hotel
   Pippa's Pop-Ins
   Children's Hotel

PLACES TO EAT
3 Launceston Place
13 Benjy's
18 Nando's
26 Troubadour
28 Balans West
29 Krungtap
30 Blanco's
31 Mr Wing
39 La Grande Bouchée
41 Pâtissier-Chocolatier;
   Rôtisserie Jules
42 Marius Le Gourmet
45 Spago
46 FrancoFill
49 Ognisko Polskie
51 The Collection
52 Daphne's
54 Cactus Blue
57 Chelsea Kitchen
60 Oriel
65 Foxtrot Oscar
67 Gordon Ramsay
68 Ransome's Dock
69 Buchan's
74 Pizza Express;
   Pheasantry Building
78 Henry J Bean's
79 Stockpot

81 Bluebird
82 New Culture Revolution
83 Ed's Easy Diner
84 Vama
86 Chelsea Bun
87 Kartouche; Vingt-Quatre
88 Aubergine
89 Wine & Kebab
91 Tiger Lil's
92 Chutney Mary's
93 Shoeless Joe's;
   Come the Revolution
94 Jim Thompson's
97 Blue Elephant
98 Bonjour Vietnam

PUBS & CLUBS
12 Prince of Teck
25 Brompton's
27 Coleherne
59 The Antelope
71 King's Head &
   Eight Bells
73 Cooper's Arms
80 Po Na Na Souk
90 Fez Club
96 Leopard Lounge
99 Havana

OTHER
1 Leighton House
2 Deckers London Club
6 Cromwell Hospital
11 CallShop
14 Top Deck Travel
15 Bubbles Laundrette
36 STA Travel
37 Wash & Dry Laundrette
38 French Institute;
   Ciné Lumière
40 French Bookshop
48 Global Talk Cybercafé
50 Brompton Oratory
53 Michelin House;
   Bibendum; Conran Shop
55 Royal Marsden Hospital
56 Jane Asher Party Cakes
61 Royal Court
63 Chapel
64 Great Hall
66 Peace Pagoda
70 Chelsea Old Church
72 Carlyle's House
75 Antiquarius Antiques
   Centre
76 CM Store
77 Chelsea Farmers Market;
   Bike Park
85 Bendix Laundrette

MAP 9

MAP 10

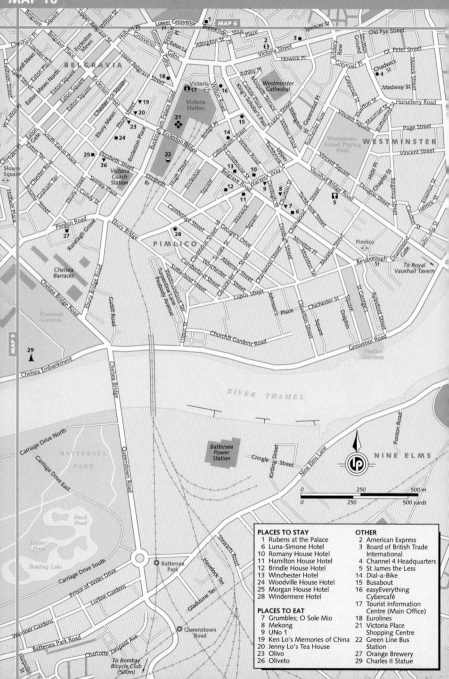

MAP 6

MAP 9

BELGRAVIA

WESTMINSTER

PIMLICO

Chelsea Barracks

Ranelagh Gardens

Chelsea Embankment

RIVER THAMES

NINE ELMS

BATTERSEA PARK

Duck Pond

Ladies' Pond

Boating Lake

Battersea Power Station

Battersea Park

To Bombay Bicycle Club (500m)

Victoria Station

Victoria Coach Station

Westminster Cathedral

Westminster School Playing Field

To Royal Vauxhall Tavern

Pimlico Gardens

| 0 | 250 | 500 m |
| 0 | 250 | 500 yards |

PLACES TO STAY
1 Rubens at the Palace
6 Luna-Simone Hotel
10 Romany House Hotel
11 Hamilton House Hotel
12 Brindle House Hotel
13 Winchester Hotel
24 Woodville House Hotel
25 Morgan House Hotel
28 Windermere Hotel

PLACES TO EAT
7 Grumbles; O Sole Mio
8 Mekong
9 UNo 1
19 Ken Lo's Memories of China
20 Jenny Lo's Tea House
23 Olivo
26 Oliveto

OTHER
2 American Express
3 Board of British Trade International
4 Channel 4 Headquarters
5 St James the Less
14 Dial-a-Bike
15 Busabout
16 easyEverything Cybercafé
17 Tourist Information Centre (Main Office)
18 Eurolines
21 Victoria Place Shopping Centre
22 Green Line Bus Station
27 Orange Brewery
29 Charles II Statue

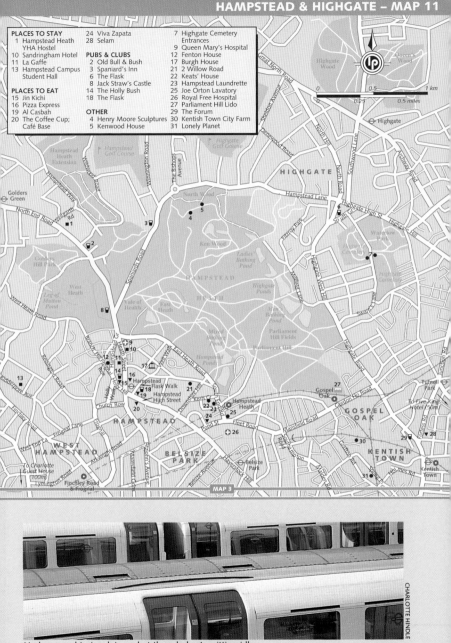

PLACES TO STAY
1 Hampstead Heath YHA Hostel
10 Sandringham Hotel
11 La Gaffe
13 Hampstead Campus Student Hall

PLACES TO EAT
15 Jin Kichi
16 Pizza Express
19 Al Casbah
20 The Coffee Cup; Café Base

24 Viva Zapata
28 Selam

PUBS & CLUBS
2 Old Bull & Bush
3 Spaniard's Inn
6 The Flask
8 Jack Straw's Castle
14 The Holly Bush
18 The Flask

OTHER
4 Henry Moore Sculptures
5 Kenwood House

7 Highgate Cemetery Entrances
9 Queen Mary's Hospital
12 Fenton House
17 Burgh House
21 2 Willow Road
22 Keats' House
23 Hampstead Laundrette
25 Joe Orton Lavatory
26 Royal Free Hospital
27 Parliament Hill Lido
29 The Forum
30 Kentish Town City Farm
31 Lonely Planet

Underground trains doing what they do best – sitting idle.

CHARLOTTE HINDLE

MAP 12 – DOCKLANDS

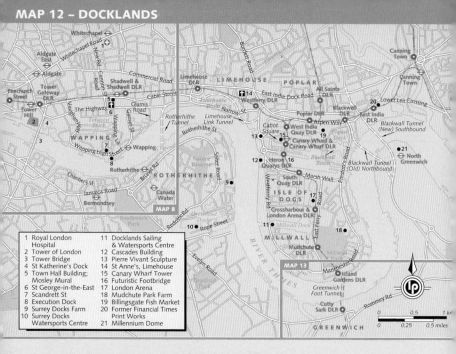

1	Royal London Hospital	11	Docklands Sailing & Watersports Centre
2	Tower of London	12	Cascades Building
3	Tower Bridge	13	Pierre Vivant Sculpture
4	St Katherine's Dock	14	St Anne's, Limehouse
5	Town Hall Building; Mosley Mural	15	Canary Wharf Tower
		16	Futuristic Footbridge
6	St George-in-the-East	17	London Arena
7	Scandrett St	18	Mudchute Park Farm
8	Execution Dock	19	Billingsgate Fish Market
9	Surrey Docks Farm	20	Former Financial Times Print Works
10	Surrey Docks Watersports Centre	21	Millennium Dome

MAP 13 – GREENWICH

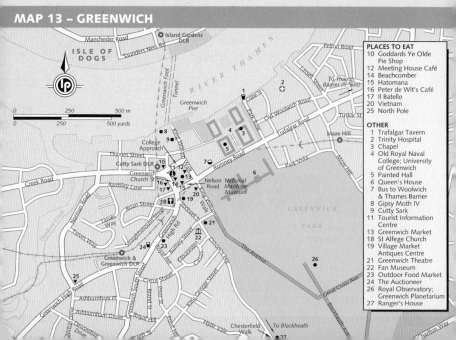

PLACES TO EAT
10 Goddards Ye Olde Pie Shop
12 Meeting House Café
14 Beachcomber
15 Hatomana
16 Peter de Wit's Café
17 Il Batello
20 Vietnam
25 North Pole

OTHER
1 Trafalgar Tavern
2 Trinity Hospital
3 Chapel
4 Old Royal Naval College; University of Greenwich
5 Painted Hall
6 Queen's House
7 Bus to Woolwich & Thames Barrier
8 Gipsy Moth IV
9 Cutty Sark
11 Tourist Information Centre
13 Greenwich Market
18 St Alfege Church
19 Village Market Antiques Centre
21 Greenwich Theatre
22 Fan Museum
23 Outdoor Food Market
24 The Auctioneer
26 Royal Observatory; Greenwich Planetarium
27 Ranger's House

LONDON UNDERGROUND – GEOGRAPHICAL

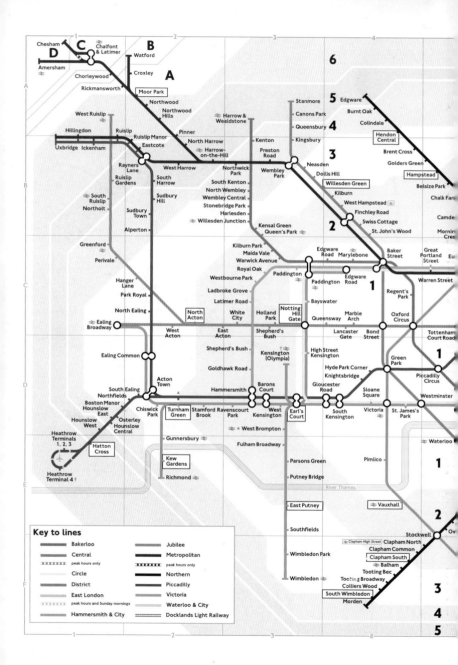

Key to lines

Bakerloo	Jubilee
Central	Metropolitan
peak hours only	peak hours only
Circle	Northern
District	Piccadilly
East London	Victoria
peak hours and Sunday mornings	Waterloo & City
Hammersmith & City	Docklands Light Railway